Bur

Ⓞ **Optional assignment**
In this case, the student may choose to work on a section of the assignment in line with his or her interests.

Ⓢ **Supplementary assignment**
These assignments consolidate existing knowledge and can be worked on additionally to the foregoing assignments.

key terms
→ **special key terms** with explanation

westermann GRUPPE

Druck A[1] / Jahr 2018
Alle Drucke der Serie A sind im Unterricht parallel verwendbar.

Redaktion: John Attfield, Buchholz; Steffen Stierhof
Umschlaggestaltung: JANSSEN KAHLERT Design & Kommunikation GmbH, Hannover
Layout: JANSSEN KAHLERT Design & Kommunikation GmbH, Hannover; Yvonne Behnke, Berlin
Druck und Bindung: westermann druck GmbH, Braunschweig

ISBN 978-3-14-**115235**-7

I Agricultural production 8

The field of tension between nutrition and food provision for a growing world population

II Economic regions in transition 40

Contributing factors and consequences

III Population development and migration 70

Causes of spatial problems

IV Global disparities 92

The challenge of unequal regional development

V Towns and cities as complex settlement areas 128

Between tradition and progress

VI Metropolisation and marginalisation 156

Unavoidable processes in the context of worldwide urbanisation?

VII The city, a good place for all to live in? 174

Problems and strategies for future-oriented urban development

VIII Goods and services – always available? 202

The importance of logistics and freight transport

Appendices 224

Models and theoretical approaches

Agricultural production

The field of tension between nutrition and food provision for a growing world population

Large monocultures and neighbouring small farming operations near Maputo, Mozambique

M1 Products containing palm oil

M3 Products containing rubber

Agriculture in the tropics – the basis for an adequate supply of food for a growing global population?

Life without agricultural products from the tropics would be virtually inconceivable for most people today. Products which, like pepper, were once worth their weight in gold or, like sugar, were sold in small quantities in shops specialised in "colonial goods", are taken more or less for granted today.

Tropical agricultural products have long since lost their aura of luxury and are now regarded as quite ordinary by modern consumers.

Under the influence of the growing world population and increasing prosperity in some parts of the world, the demand for agricultural raw materials is rising steadily.

Population growth is particularly strong in many countries in the Southern Hemisphere and in countries in or on the periphery of the tropics. Substantial segments of the population in these often largely agrarian economies depend on small-scale and subsistence farming for their basic food supply. Under the influence of rising local and global demand, competition between production for the world market and meeting the nutritional needs of the local population is growing progressively stronger. Will there be room enough for both in future?

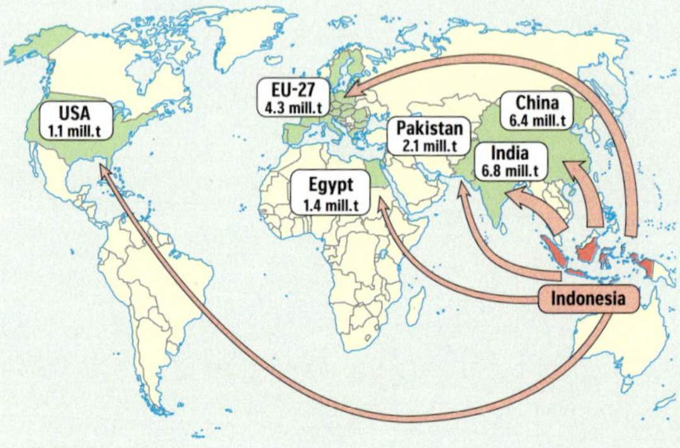

M4 Palm oil trade routes from Indonesia (2011)

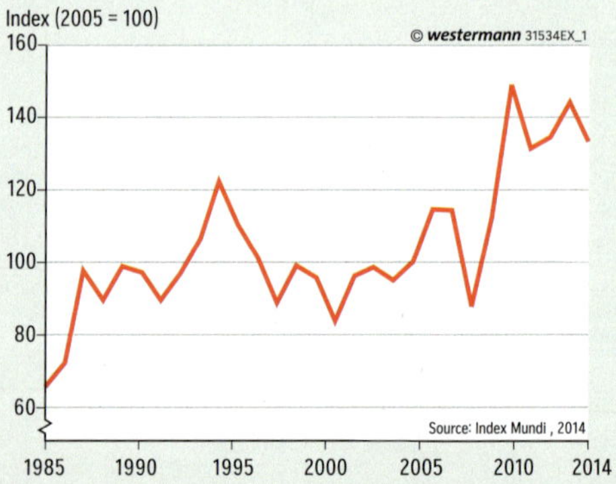

M5 Development of prices for agricultural raw materials

M2 Constantly expanding oil palm plantations

M6 Small farming operations

M7 Feed and food products

M10 Tropical fruits

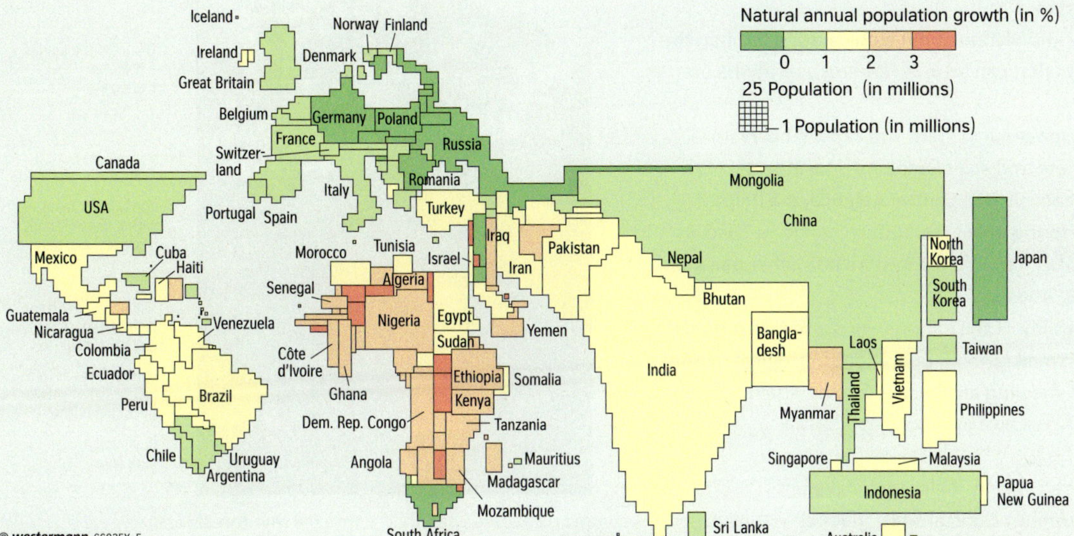

© westermann 6602EX_5
Source: Index Mundi, 2016

M8 Population growth (2014)

Maize	814
Wheat	645
Rice	452
Soybeans	256
Sugar	153
Rapeseed	58
Palm oil	48
Cotton	25
Rubber	10
Coffee	8

Source: destatista.com

M9 Global production of selected agricultural products, 2010/2011 (in million tonnes)

China	204
India	153
Indonesia	69
Vietnam	43
Thailand	37
Bangladesh	34
Myanmar	33
Philippines	18
Brazil	11
Japan	10

Source: destatista.com

M11 Top 10 rice-producing countries worldwide, 2012 (in million tonnes, raw rice)

1. Give examples of products you use every day that consist entirely or partially of raw materials produced in the tropics.
2. Give examples of tropical or subtropical countries that exhibit particularly strong natural population growth.
3. Consider the specific challenges faced by these countries.
4. Map M4 shows the countries of origin and destination for palm oil. List the potential land-use conflicts that may arise from the large-scale cultivation of agricultural products for exporthe specific challenges faced by these countries.

Subsistence farming in the tropics – a centuries-old tradition

The milpa-solar system in Yucatán, Mexico – a tradition with a promising future?

Subsistence and small-scale farming play a dominant role in the tropical regions of Latin America. In spite of the often highly inequitable distribution of property, farming on small plots of land is the basic source of food for millions of people. Is this type of farming obsolete or can sustainable small-scale agricultural operations make a significant contribution to ensuring an adequate food supply and slowing the exodus from rural areas?

1. Classify Yucatán topographically and describe its characteristic climate (M1, Atlas).
2. Name the favourable and unfavourable factors affecting farming in Yucatán.
3. Reactivate your knowledge about tropical soils. Explain the typical problems that can arise in farming operations on tropical soil.
4. Describe the milpa-solar system and explain how it is adapted to climate and soil conditions (M2, M3, M5, M7).
5. Once widely established in Central America, the milpa-solar system is found only in remote areas today. Discuss the possibility of expanding the system into other parts of Mexico (M6, M8, Atlas).

Ⓢ 6. Evaluate the viability of the milpa-solar system as a model for sustainable small farming operations in tropical regions. Prepare a table showing arguments for and against the system.

→ Cation exchange capacity, Milpa-solar system, Subsistence farming, Tropical soils, Viability

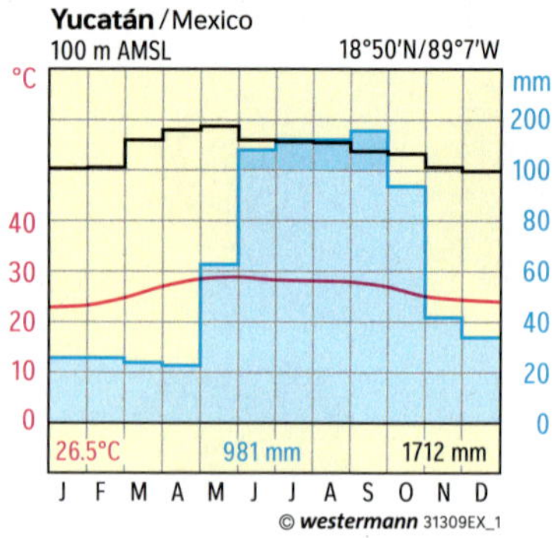

M1 Climate graph for Yucatán (Mexico)

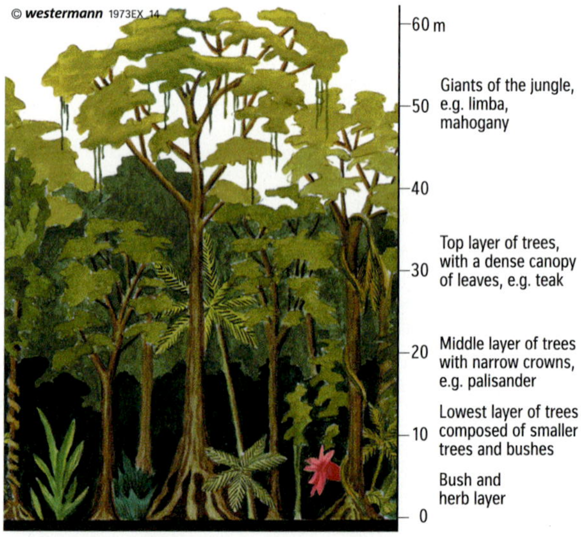

M2 Layered growth in a tropical rain forest

→ Tropical soils

Soil fertility is the capacity of a given soil to supply plants with sufficient nutrients. It is influenced above all by the weathering depth, the cation exchange capacity and the humus content of the soil. In deeply weathered tropical soil, the parent rock is inaccessible as a source of minerals for plants. The rapid decomposition of organic material and frequent heavy rains favour the accumulation of a thick layer of humus. The cation exchange capacity of tropical soil is very low due to the preponderance of two-sheet clay minerals. Therefore the permanently wet tropics are sometimes referred to as "tree-covered deserts".

The extremely high primary output of tropical rainforests is not the product of fertile soil but of a short nutrient cycle. Fallen leaves and other dead organic materials are mineralised immediately by destruents (decomposers), such as bacteria and fungi, and introduced to

the plants through a finely branched root system in a symbiotic relationship with mycorrhiza fungi before the nutrients can be washed out or superficially rinsed away.

The traditional Central American milpa-solar planting system is characterised by two different types of cultivated fields.

The first type is the "milpa", a field that is first fire-cleared and then planted with the three main crops: maize, beans and squash. These are complemented by other plants, which vary from one region to another and may include peppers, pepper plants or herbs.

Maize is a sensible choice, as the stalks serve as climbing support for the beans. Beans belong to the leguminosae family of plants with a nitrogen-fixing capacity and thus enrich the soil. The leaves of the squash provide ground cover and effective protection against erosion.

The second type of field – the "solar" – is a kind of large household garden in which a wide variety of plants are grown, including different types of maize, amaranth, quinoa, potatoes, peas, avocados, squash, coffee and vanilla, and near which farm animals such as cows, chickens, turkeys or pigs are kept. The animals are fed with weeds and the parts of harvested plants that are regarded as inedible by humans. Their dung is used as fertiliser. The yield from milpa and solar fields is ordinarily consumed by the farming families themselves. Meat, milk and other dairy products as well as selected fruits are sold.

M3 The milpa-solar planting system

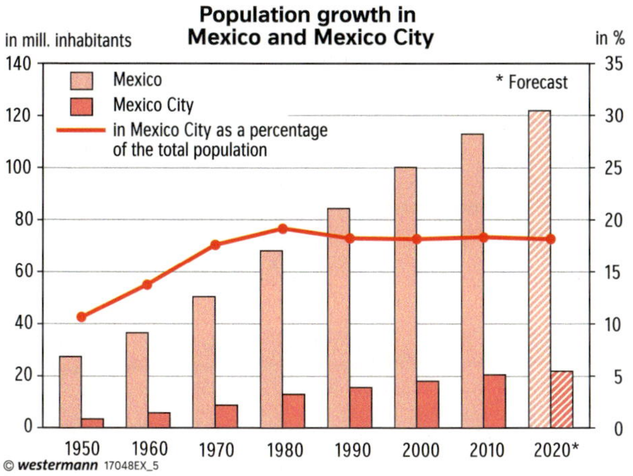

M4 Population growth in Mexico

M7 A milpa in Yucatán

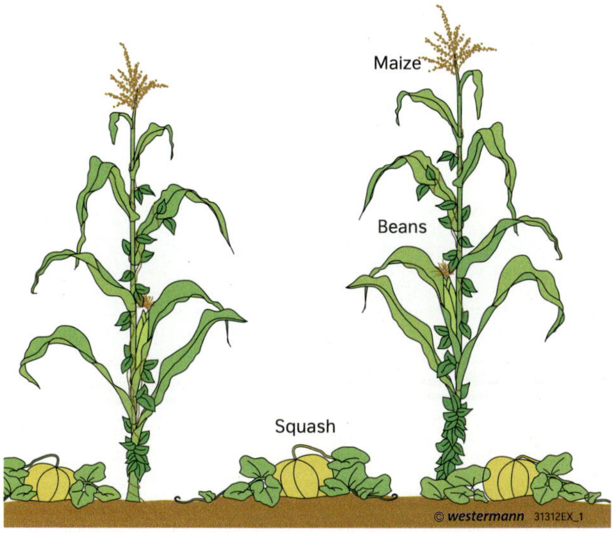

M5 The heart of the milpa-solar system: a combination of beans, maize and squash

Maize is the most important basic food crop in Mexico. With a total yield of 23.3 million tonnes, Mexico was the world's seventh-largest producer of maize in 2014. The government and leading agricultural firms exert strong pressure on farmers to grow maize or other products (e.g. sugar cane and tobacco) in monocultures in order to produce more efficiently on larger plots of land. The Mexican government, which subsidises these agricultural firms, expects this policy to produce higher yields with less labour input. The companies hope to attract new buyers of seeds, fertilisers and pesticides.

M8 Maize cultivation in Mexico

	Milpa-solar system	Maize cultivation in monoculture or cattle farming
Net primary production	consistently very high	high at first, then declining progressively
Labour intensity	very high	high, increasing due to rising demand for fertilisers and agricultural chemicals
Input (seeds, agricultural chemicals)	low (some of the harvested seeds can be replanted)	very high (hybrid varieties – no replanting; 2.5 – 3 tonnes of fertiliser per year / ha, pesticides, herbicides)
Crops	Polycultures (up to 244 different plants)	Monocultures (risks: high risk of rapidly spreading plant diseases, one-sided soil depletion)
Harvest yield (as compared to input)	200%	140% (initially, less later, as yields decline unless fertiliser and pesticide input is increased)
Risk of failed harvests	low due to polycultivation	high
Farming system	primarily subsistence farming; certain crops and surpluses are sold	commercial farming, substantial profits from good harvests at high global market prices
Farmers' income (money)	low	considerably higher
Support capacity	supports several large families on 4 ha (average size of a 'milpa')	one family per plantation (appox. 200 ha)
Space required for cattle grazing	1 cow / ha	1 cow / 20 ha on soil that is subject to rapid degradation

Source: A comparison between the milpa system and new forms of agriculture, in Nagle, Garret / Guinness, Paul, Cambridge International A and AS Level Geography, London 2011, p. 223

M6 Comparison of the milpa-solar system with monoculture or cattle farming

Plantation farming in the tropics – producing for the global market

Banana cultivation in Colombia – who profits?

A substantial portion of the agricultural products produced for export in the tropics are grown on plantations – e.g. coffee, cocoa, sugar, pineapples and palm oil. What are the characteristic features of plantation farming? What opportunities and risks does it pose for producers and consumers? Can organic farming be a solution for the problems associated with plantation farming? The most important structures and processes involved in plantation farming are described with reference to banana cultivation in Colombia.

1. Locate Colombia on the map and determine whether the climate conditions there are suitable for banana cultivation (M3, M4, Atlas).
2. Illustrate the global distribution of the leading banana producers and the most important banana-exporting countries. Consider the factors involved in determining banana prices (M2, M5).
3. List the characteristic features of plantation farming, and decide which of these features apply to banana cultivation in Colombia (M1, M2, M6, M8).
4. Discuss the environmental problems associated with monocultures with reference to the example of banana cultivation (M4, M7).
5. Research the question of whether and where organically-grown bananas are sold near your home. Discuss whether organic farming can reduce the negative environmental effects of monocultivation (M10).
6. Discuss the question of whether expanding organic banana cultivation leads to more sustainable production.
7. Conduct a survey of your fellow students/teachers/parents, etc., to learn whether they would be willing to pay more for organically-grown bananas. Discuss your findings.

→ Cation exchange capacity, Monoculture, Organic farming, Plantation, Sustainability

Plantation farming originated during the colonial period, primarily during the 17th and 18th centuries, when the colonial powers grew tobacco, sugar cane, coffee and other crops for the markets of Europe with the help of African slaves.
Several characteristic features of colonial plantation farming are still in evidence today. Farming operations are highly labour-intensive (much of the work is performed by poorly-paid plantation labourers), and plantations occupy extensive areas of land. Today as in the past, cash crops are not cultivated for the purpose of feeding the local population but rather to satisfy the needs of both national and global markets. As in the past, plantation farming competes for land with small, family-owned farms. Many plantations today are owned or managed by multinational corporate groups, only few of which are based in the producing countries. They provide machinery, high-yield seeds and agricultural chemicals. Tranportation and distribution operations are often controlled by a small number of large, multinational corporations as well. Consequently, a substantial portion of profits flows out of the producing country.

M1 Plantation farming

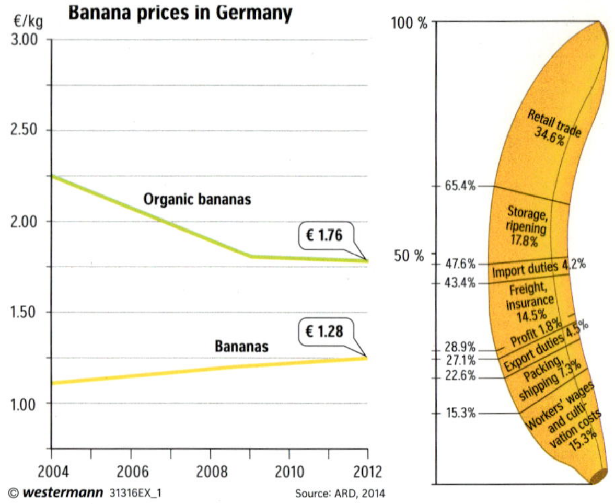

M2 Banana prices in Germany: trends and contributing factors

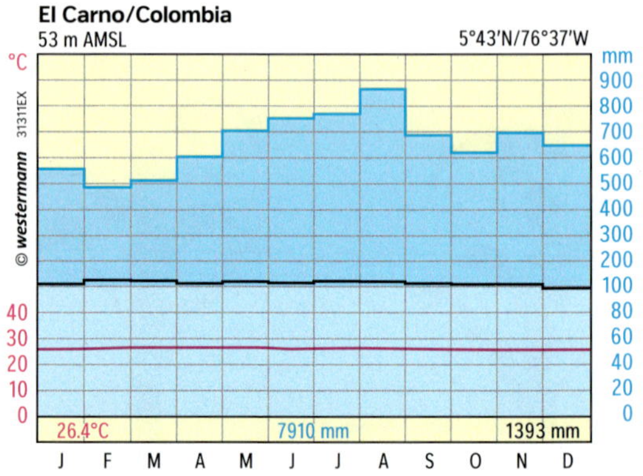

M3 Climate graph for El Carno (Colombia)

According to the United Nations Food and Agriculture Organization, bananas are one of the eight most important foodstuffs in the world. They are grown in 135 countries, primarily by small farmers who produce them for their own consumption and for sale in local markets. Bananas are also an important export product, however. The average German, for example, consumes 10.5 kg of bananas per year. For optimum growth, bananas need a warm, humid climate with temperatures above 20 °C and evenly-distributed precipitation amounting to no less than 100–200 mm per month. Bananas are capable of vegetative propagation, and are normally ready to harvest between seven and nine months after shoots are first planted.
Bananas can be harvested all year round in tropical regions. Banana crops are not harvested all at once; instead, each individual bunch of bananas must be carefully checked for ripeness. Following a harvest, the remaining banana stalks are cut down and used as fertiliser. A banana plantation will continue to produce for more than 20 years. Banana cultivation is highly labour-intensive. The shoots must be replanted and trimmed several times, and regular additions of fertiliser are very important. Banana plantations also require the extensive use of pesticides and herbicides.

M4 Bananas as a cash crop

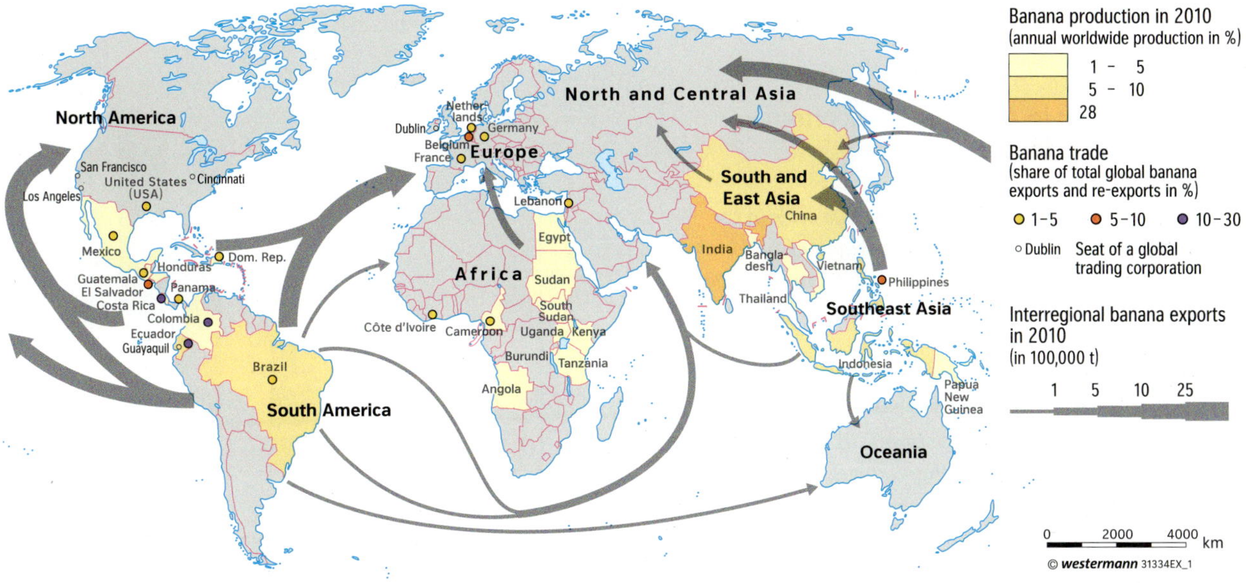

M5 Banana production and trade routes

In spite of significant improvements in efficiency, banana farming is highly labour-intensive. The physical work involved is extremely strenuous. Workers regularly come into contact with toxic and carcinogenic agricultural chemicals. Some employers have reacted to this lamentable situation and positive signs of improvement are evident. Some plantation owners provide protective clothing for their workers, for example, and ensure that crop-dusting aircraft fly only before or after normal working hours. National laws have put an end to child labour on plantations. In Colombia, where trade unions play an important role, most plantation workers are paid a minimum wage. Wages are often insufficient, however, and fail to provide a sustainable livelihood.

M6 Working conditions on banana plantations

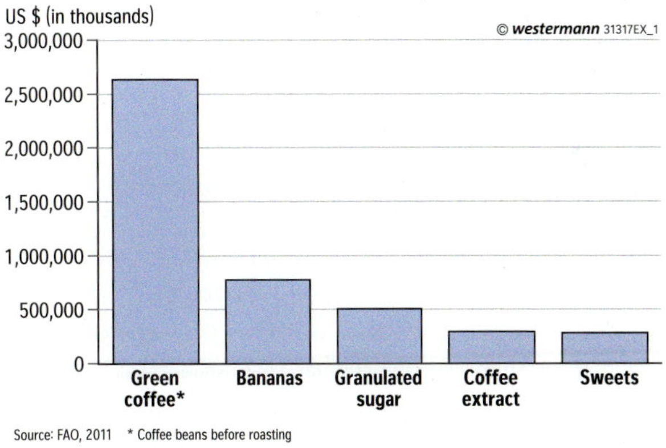

M8 Colombia's most important agricultural exports (2011)

Monocultivation is an important element of plantation farming. Coupled with industrialised cultivation methods, it can enhance productivity significantly. More bananas can be harvested per acre and per plantation worker.

Banana plantations are virtual paradises for pests that attack plants (insects, fungi and nematodes). Pests multiply easily where the same fruits are grown close together for years at a time. Massive quantities of agrochemicals (herbicides, insecticides, fungicides and nematicides) are needed to keep them under control. Crop protection measures account for roughly 30 percent of the price that producers receive for their bananas.

Pesticides pose an extremely severe health hazard for the workers who apply them. They can cause cancer, nervous disorders, sterility and deformities in newborn infants. Heavy rains quickly wash these toxins out, thus contaminating soil, groundwater and nearby streams. Where crop-dusting aircraft are used, a portion of these poisonous substances is carried away by the wind and distributed over nearby housing estates, gardens, forests and the people who live in those areas.

Bananas are fast-growing plants that absorb large quantities of nutrients from the soil. Consequently, and due as well to the high depletion rate and the low cation exchange capacity of tropical soils, large quantities of mineral fertilisers are required.

M7 Monocultures in banana cultivation

M9 Transporting bananas via cable car

- No use of pesticides
- Mixed cultivation with other plants
- Use of green fertiliser, no readily-soluble mineral fertilisers
- Exclusive use of mechanical weed-control methods
- Organic certification (results in higher prices)

M10 Prerequisites for organic banana cultivation

Conflicts resulting from the expansion of large-scale monocultures

Soybean cultivation in Argentina – economic success with side effects?

One example of a plant that is cultivated on a large scale in the tropics and subtropics is the soybean. The total area of land under cultivation nearly doubled, from 59 million hectares to 111 million hectares, between 1993 and 2013 (total area of Germany: 35.7 million hectares).
Because of their high protein content, the vast majority of soybean plants (80 percent) are exported and processed into feed for chickens, pigs and cattle raised on large farms.
The USA, Brazil and Argentina are the three largest soybean-producing countries and account for 79 percent of total world production (2013). Farmers in those countries grow soybeans with the aid of industrial methods on a large scale and on expansive areas of land. In this chapter you will examine the conditions under which soybeans are grown as well as the national and local effects of soybean cultivation with reference to Argentina.

1. Discuss the importance of soybean production for Argentina (M2, M3, M5).
2. Explain the changes that have taken place in agriculture in Argentina (M2, M4, M7).
3. Cite the specific aspects of soybean cultivation that characterise it as industrial farming (M1, M3, M6, M7).
4. Explain the land-use conflicts that arise from the expansion and intensification of soybean cultivation in Argentina (M1, M4, M6).
5. Discuss the changes that have taken place in agriculture in Argentina within the context of sustainability (M2 – M8).

→ Pesticides, Total herbicides

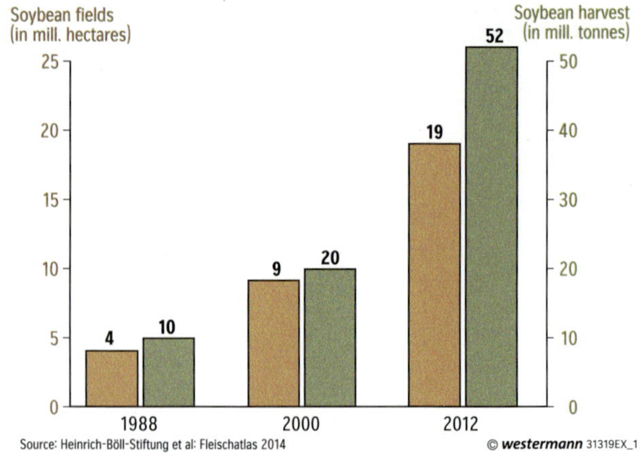

M2 Growth of cultivation areas for soybeans and soybean harvests in Argentina

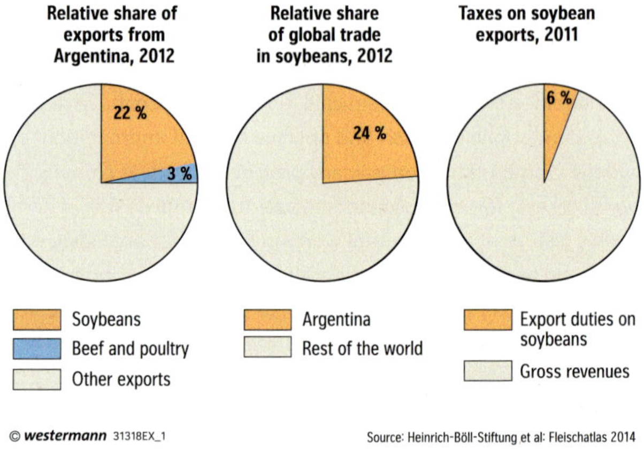

M3 The economic importance of soybeans for Argentina

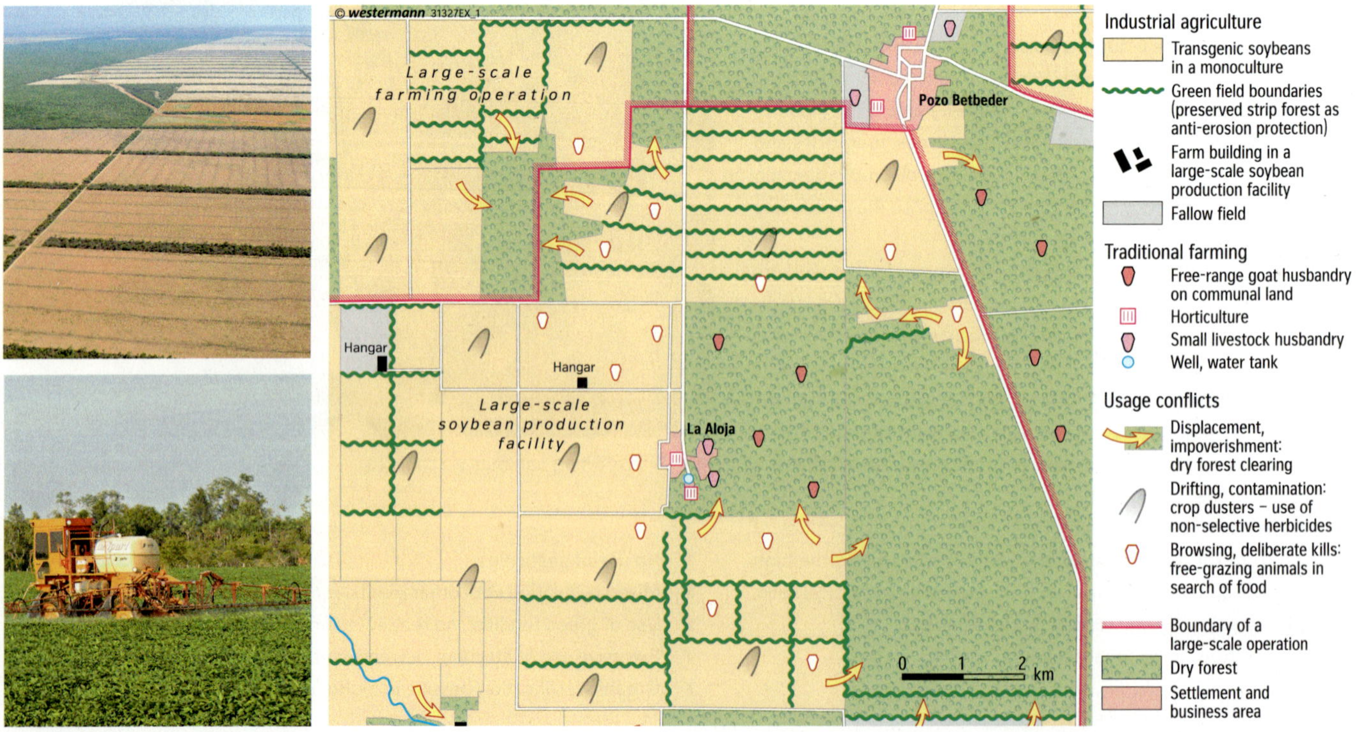

M1 Soybean cultivation in northern Argentina

Agriculture and forestry	Unit	1995	2000	2005	2010
Farmland	% of total land area	46.7	47.1	49.1	51.3 (2009)
Forested area	% of total land area	12.2	11.6	11.2	10.8 (2009)
People gainfully employed in the agricultural sector	1,000	1,462	1,458	1,442	1,405
Agricultural production index	2004 to 2006 = 100	74	86	103	115
Tree-felling: industrial round timber	million m³	6,916	9,005	9,846	9,841

Source: www.destatis.de/DE/Publikationen/Thematisch/Internationales/Laenderprofile/Argentinien2012.pdf?__blob=publicationFile/FAO

M4 Developments in agriculture in Argentina

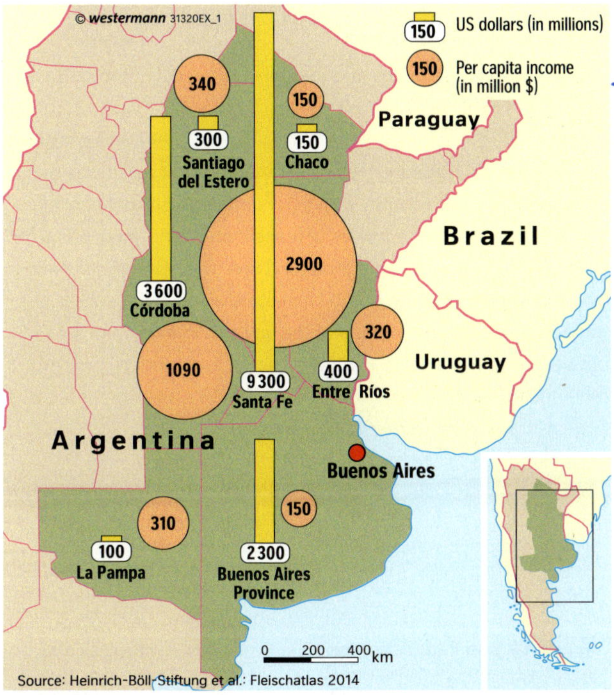

M5 Revenues from soybean exports in the provinces of Argentina (2010)

"Soybeans are one of the world's fastest growing cash crops [...]. Deforestation to make way for the expansion of soybean cultivation poses a significant threat to the environment in Argentina, Brazil, Bolivia and Paraguay. Areas under cultivation have expanded into areas formerly used for other agricultural purposes or as grazing land, while the additional transformation of natural vegetation plays and important role as well."

Source: www.weltagrarbericht.de/fileadmin/files/weltagrarbericht/IAASTD-Berichte/GlobalReport.pdf, September 2014

"Monocultures are displacing the jungle and its native populations. Indigenous inhabitants are actually hunted in some areas. Soils are being rapidly depleted. And as soybean cultivation continues to spread, and as weeds and insects become increasingly resistant to herbicides, pesticides and fungicides, more and more of these chemicals are sprayed in a series of new combinations. In 1990, 34 million litres of such chemicals were used in Argentina. By 2013, the figure had risen to 317 million litres. In addition to genetically modified soy, producers also grow genetically modified maize and rice."

Source: Burghardt, P.; Vernaschi, M., Der Tod kommt mit dem Wind, Süddeutsche Zeitung Magazin 47, 2014.

M6 Effects of the expansion of soybean cultivation

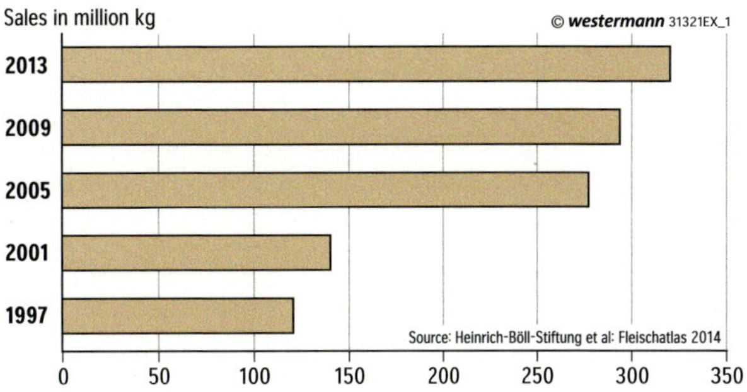

M7 The increasing use of pesticides in Argentina

Soy, soy and more soy ...

Nearly one hundred percent of the soybeans grown in Argentina are genetically modified varieties. The country is [...] the world's third-largest supplier of soy products. At the same time, reports about starving population groups have been circulated in the media. The GID (Genetic Information Service) had the opportunity to speak with the Argentinian molecular biologist Lilian Joensen about this problem. [...]

This market is controlled primarily by three firms, two of which have acquired the rights to Monsanto's Roundup technology. [Note: Roundup is a total herbicide that kills all plants with the exception of those that have been rendered resistant to the herbicide through genetic modification. If the herbicide works, only a single agent is needed.]

Fourteen different types of weeds are known to be resistant to Roundup today. Use of the herbicide has increased five-fold since it was first introduced in 1997.

Reducing the quantities of chemicals that must be sprayed has always been one of the most compelling arguments in favour of the use of genetically modified plants ...

... and our experience in Argentina proves that this argument is untenable. [...]

What was different before large-scale cultivation of soybeans was introduced in Argentina?

There was an extensive agricultural system in which animal husbandry alternated with crop-growing. This allowed soil to regenerate. [...]

Who are the farmers who grow soybeans for the global market?

They are not farmers in the European sense of the word. They are large business enterprises that lease land owned by impoverished members of the rural population. Many of the firms operating in Argentina are from other countries [...] They do not own the land, but they own the sales and distribution infrastructure; they bring in the genetically modified seed and chemicals, spray agents and fertilisers, and they own the machinery. [...]

Argentina is traditionally known in this part of the world as an exporter of beef, which is very popular in Europe.

Agriculture in Argentina has changed considerably in that regard. The fact is that we export primarily soy, soy and more soy. And [...] we are no longer capable of feeding our own population.

Source: Gen-ethischer Informationsdienst Nr. 164 (June 2004), pp. 21-23 (www.gen-ethisches-netzwerk.de)

M8 Interview with Lilian G. Joensen, a representative of the Grupo de Reflexion Rural, an NGO that is critical of genetic engineering, on soybean cultivation in Argentina

Farmland in the tropics – scarce and coveted

Land grabbing as a contribution to food security?

Acquisitions of large areas of farmland, especially in the tropics, have increased substantially in recent years. Experts at the World Bank estimate that six million hectares of farmland annually will be converted to new uses or newly developed by the year 2030 (for comparison: Germany currently has roughly 17 million hectares of farmland).
The motives behind these large-scale acquisitions of land are many – as are the players involved as well.
Where is land bought and sold on the largest scale? Who are the players involved in major land purchases? What are their underlying motives? What advantages do countries in such regions as sub-Saharan Africa hope to gain from these land sales? How do these sales impact on the local population?

1. Enter the names of the countries listed in M1 in a sketch map (M1, Atlas).
2. Describe the global distribution of land purchases (M1).
3. Define the term “land grabbing” in your own words. Give examples of cases in which similar processes have taken place in the past.
4. Identify the major players in land acquisitions and discuss the motives that underlie such purchases (M1 – M5).
5. With the aid of appropriate maps from the Atlas, research the food supply situation and determine the percentage of workers employed in agricultural operations in the countries with the largest land sales (M1, Atlas).
6. Land sales often trigger protests on the part of the local population. Draw a mindmap showing how land grabbing can lead to poverty and starvation within the local population (M2 – M7).
7. Formulate the prerequisites that must be met if large-scale land sales are to result in an improvement of living conditions – especially for the affected local populations (M7).
8. Ⓢ Research the circumstances and consequences of “land grabbing” with reference to a concrete example (M7, Internet).

→ Land acquisition, Land grabbing

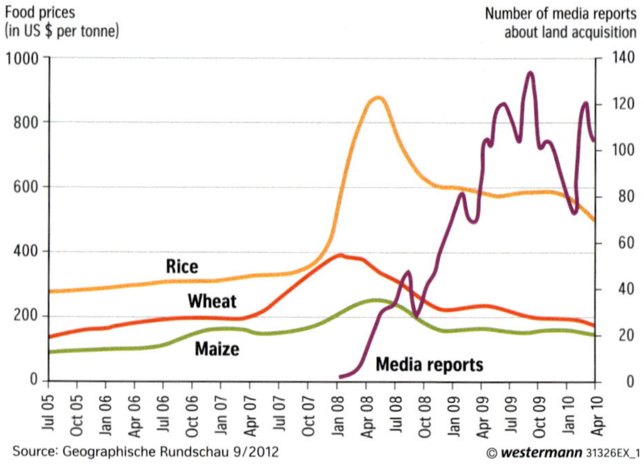

M2 Trends in food prices and frequency of media reports about land acquisition

→ Land grabbing

“The term ‘land grabbing’ refers to large-scale acquisitions by either private or government investors and agricultural enterprises that purchase farmland or lease it on a long-term basis for the purpose of producing agricultural raw materials under their own management. Both the [...] investors and the [...] sellers often operate within grey areas of the law and in a no-man’s-land between traditional land-utilisation rights and modern property relationships [...]”.
Source: www.weltagrarbericht.de/themen/

Player groups	Purpose
In industrialised nations (energy companies, investment funds, etc.)	Production of agricultural raw materials (feed, agricultural fuels); acquisition of land for the purpose of speculation
In heavily populated countries with high rates of population growth (India, China, United Arab Emirates, Egypt)	Production of foodstuffs, feed plants and agricultural raw materials to meet their own needs
In countries that have very limited land and water resources but substantial liquid capital (Kuwait, Qatar, Saudi Arabia)	Reduction of dependence on the world market for food
National organisations in the target countries (often in cooperation with foreign investors)	Profit maximisation

M3 Investors/groups of parties to land-grabbing contracts

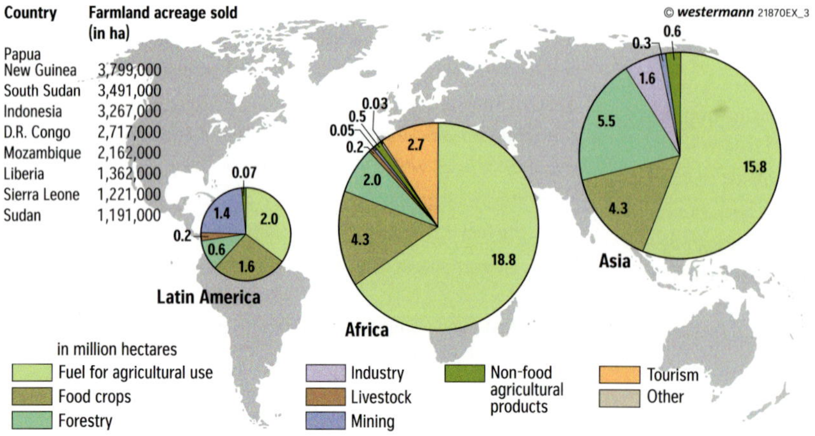

M1 Land purchases (2001 – 2011): investments in Africa, Latin America and Asia by type of usage

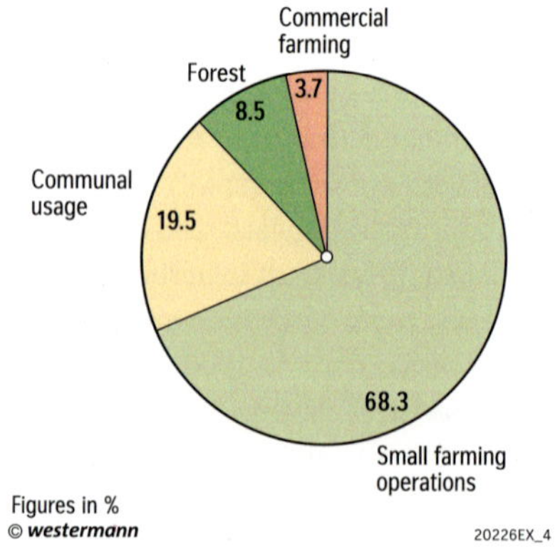

M4 Previous usage of acquired land

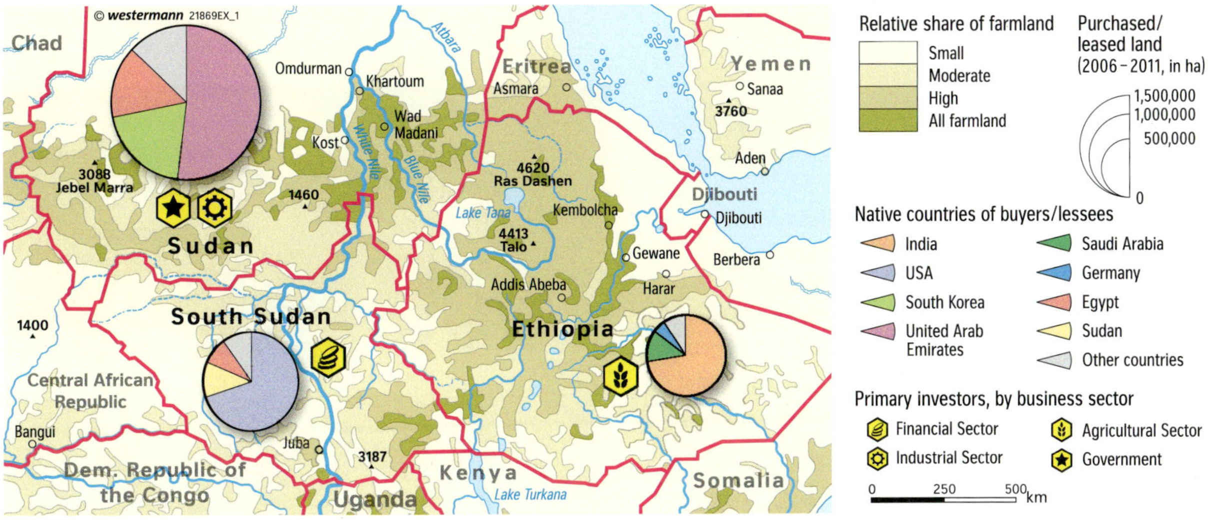

M5 Land grabbing in East Africa

M6 Cartoon in an Angolan newspaper

[...] In this regard, agricultural investments offer developing countries enormous opportunities, provided that fundamental human rights principles as well as social, economic and environmental principles are observed. Such investments can lead to the transfer of capital and technology, easier market access and improved infrastructure, increased productivity, income generation and, therefore, to better levels of food security.

Source: www.bmz.de/en/publications/archiv/type_of_publication/strategies/Strategiepapier321_02_2012.pdf

There are a growing number of reports that many of these large-scale land purchases and leases bring considerable disadvantages for the countries affected and the local populations. They can result in displacement, cause environmental problems and endanger local and national food security. [...] Due to the particular role assigned to the resource of water in this context, the term 'land and water grabbing' is also increasingly being used.

Source: www.bmz.de/en/publications/archiv/type_of_publication/strategies/Strategiepapier321_02_2012.pdf

M7 Statements on the issue of land grabbing

M8 Protests against land grabbing in Papua New Guinea

"No one informed us. No one said a single word. They just took the land by force. [...] The people from the neighbouring village demonstrated. They were told that the government had given the land to the Indians, and that they were not to demand anything back or protest. Several people went to prison for that. [...] I'm going to go away and leave [my family] behind."

Statement by a farmer from the Gambella region in Ethiopia affected by land grabbing. The land traditionally used by the indigenous Anuak people was sold, along with their access to water, to a major investor from India.
Source: www.planete-a-vendre.arte.tv/de/athiopien/

Land grabbing is primarily a problem in countries with poor government control, as the lax prevailing legal standards make it easy for investors to purchase or lease land. Oxfam analysed land transactions concluded in 56 countries between 2000 and 2011. Three-quarters of the countries in question were found to have deficits in terms of people's rights of expression, government accountability and corruption control.

Source: www.weltagrarbericht.de/fileadmin/files/weltagrarbericht/GlobalAgriculture/OxfamPoorGovernance.pdf

weblinks

- http://landmatrix.org/en/get-the-idea/dynamics-overview/
- http://landmatrix.org/en/get-the-detail/
- www.weltagrarbericht.de/themen-des-weltagrarberichts/landgrabbing.html
- http://land-grabbing.de/land-grabbing/
- www.oxfam.de/informieren/landgrabbing
- http://planete-a-vendre.arte.tv/de/athiopien/

The rise of genetic engineering

Increasing yields through genetic engineering – a reasonable and effective approach?

Following the introduction of a high-yield variety of rice within the context of the Green Revolution in the 1960s with the promise of ensuring an adequate supply of food, especially for the people of Asia, "green genetic engineering" has become the magic word in conventional farming in recent years. But to what extent has genetic engineering already taken control of farming operations? Where is it used most extensively, and for what types of plants? And how 'green' is genetic engineering after all?

1. Reactivate your knowledge about the Green Revolution. Discuss the cultivation methods used during the years of the Green Revolution.
2. Locate the countries in which genetically modified seed is used in agriculture (M2, M4).
3. Describe the growing use of farmland for the cultivation of genetically modified plants (M2, M3).
4. Name the types of plant for which genetically modified seed is used (M3).
5. Discuss the potential risks associated with genetically modified seed and its increasing use (M5).
6. The increasing use of farmland for the cultivation of genetically modified plants is accompanied by an increasingly critical attitude towards genetically manipulated plants (M1).
   a) Form two groups, representing the advocates and the critics of genetic engineering respectively. Research the benefits and risks of genetic engineering.
   b) Conduct a discussion in which you present the results of your research.
7. Compare and contrast the different approaches to the optimum use of land available for agricultural purposes.
   a) Describe the policies of the G8 countries (M6).
   b) Describe the ecological approach with reference to the example of sustainable rice cultivation in Vietnam (M8).
   c) Discuss the question of how far the two different approaches are environmentally, economically and socially sustainable in the light of population growth and the increasing demand for food (M2, M3, M5, M6, M8).

Ⓢ 8. Interpret the cartoon (M7).

→ Green genetic engineering, Green Revolution

→ Green genetic engineering

Genetic engineering methods in plant breeding: selected genes are sytematically introduced into plant genomes, thus making them resistant to certain diseases and other influences (e.g. weeds).

M1 Protest against genetic engineering during a meeting of EU Ministers of Agriculture in Brussels

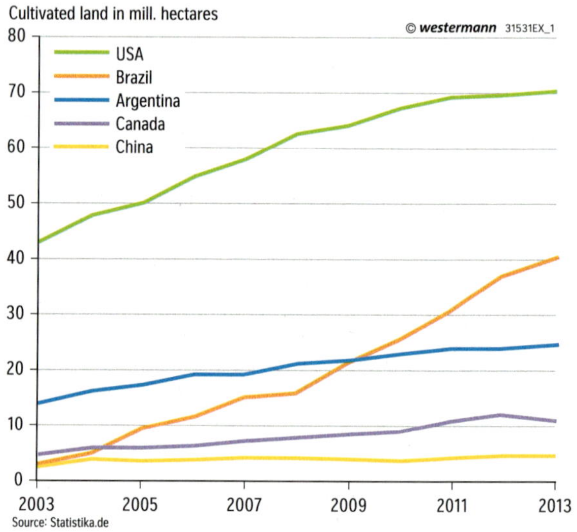

M2 Land used for the cultivation of genetically modified plants in selected countries

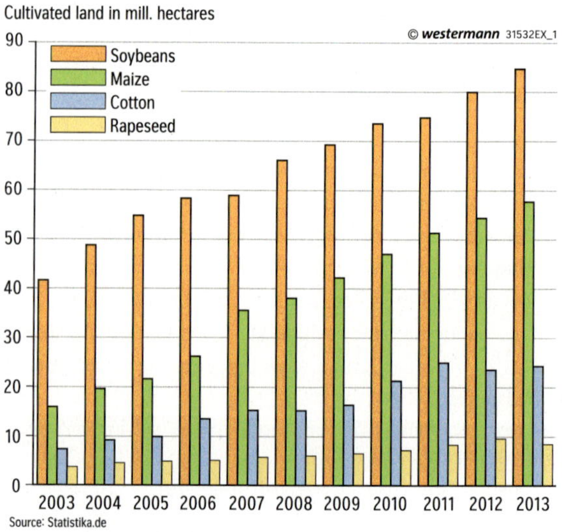

M3 Growing use of land for the cultivation of genetically modified plants (worldwide)

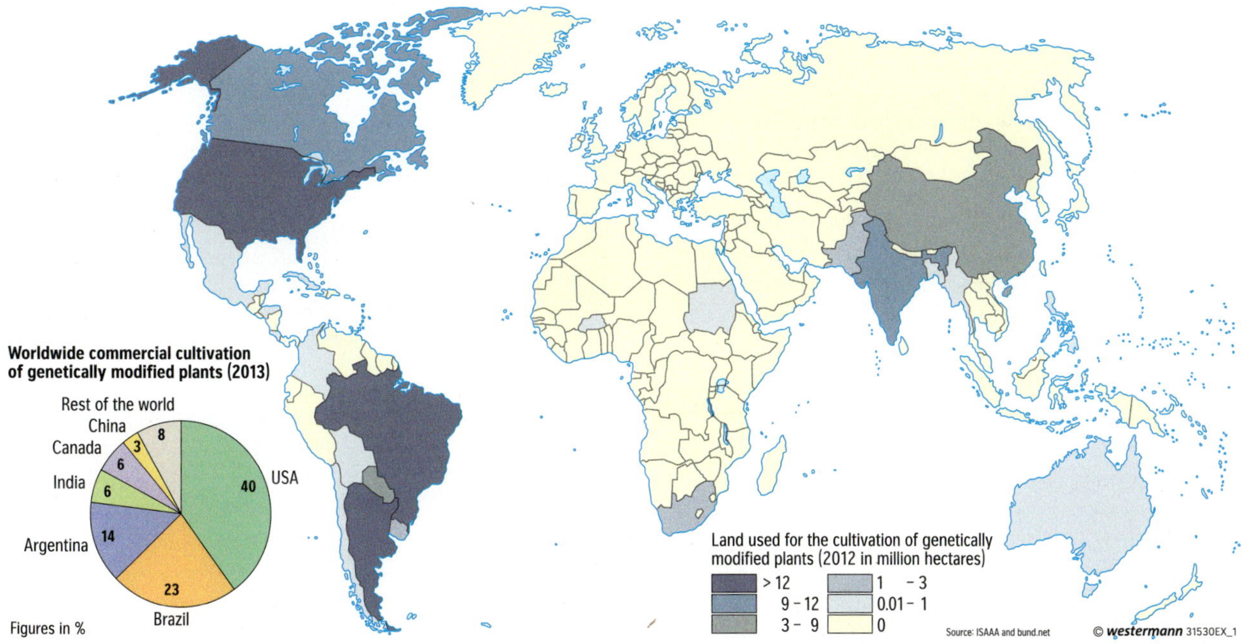

M4 The cultivation of genetically modified plants

Most of the genetically manipulated plants cultivated in the world today are resistant to herbicides. In other words, herbicides can be applied to these plants without damaging them or impairing their growth. All other plants located near them die, however. Ordinarily, both the genetically modified plant seeds and the corresponding herbicides are supplied by the same producer. Thus, for example, genetically modified Roundup Ready soybeans from Monsanto are resistant to glyphosate, the effective ingredient in Monsanto's broadband herbicide known as Roundup. Bayer also offers a similar total herbicide (glufosinate) and genetically modified glufosinate-resistant plants. Glufosinate might be banned in the EU in 2017, as the human health risks are regarded as too high. Total herbicides like glyphosate are not only problematic from an environmental point of view, they also pose serious health hazards for humans. According to BUND, glyphosate poses a threat to unborn children, increases the risk of cancer and may have a negative impact on the human hormone system.

Source: Oxfam Deutschland: Gefährliche Partnerschaft, 2014

M5 A dangerous mix: genetic engineering and total herbicides

M7 Cartoon

[...] The US and other major agricultural exporting countries have joined seed producers and members of the scientific community to declare the advent of a "new green revolution", which they even refer to proudly as "evergreen". In much the same way as in the 1960s, they are relying above all on the use of artificial fertilisers and high-yield seed to grow more plants as food and energy sources for the "bioeconomy" of the future. Genetic engineering is also expected to contribute to the development of new plants that are capable of thriving under depleted soil conditions and surviving droughts and floods. In the hope of conserving soil and water supplies, the advocates of this policy want to dispense with the use of ploughs and employ new, highly efficient irrigation methods. Activities in support of development policies are focused above all on regions of poor countries in which favourable climate conditions and fertile soils offer the prospect of rapidly rising production. [...] Increased technological inputs, coupled with high output, are expected to result in prosperity and progress.

Source: Le monde diplomatique: Atlas der Globalisierung, 2012

M6 The vision of governments and concerned business enterprises in the G8 nations

The System of Rice Intensification (SRI) is an agroecological rice cultivation method. The objective of SRI is to increase the productivity of rice cultivation by employing better planting methods rather than by increasing inputs in the conventional manner. SRI is flexible. It is tested by farmers and adapted and developed in accordance with local conditions and requirements. In most cases, rice seedlings are transplanted earlier than usual and individually, rather than in bundles. The seedlings are planted farther apart and in rows instead of random arrangements; and the fields are kept wet but not flooded. More than a million small farmers in Vietnam are now using this method, and the results are impressive. Studies show that SRI increases yields by an average of 47 percent, and requires 80 to 90 percent less seed, 20 to 50 percent less water and less nitrogen fertiliser. As a result, the average costs of cultivation are 23 percent lower and income is 68 percent higher on average.

Source: Oxfam Deutschland: Gefährliche Partnerschaft, 2014

M8 Sustainable rice cultivation with SRI in Vietnam

The changing structure of US agriculture

From family farm to large-scale agroindustrial operation

Many traditional family farms in the United States (farms operated by a farmer and his family) have given way to large, in some cases global, agroindustrial enterprises. What are the causes of this trend and what are the characteristic features of the agricultural landscape in the USA today?

1. Identify the changes that have taken place in US agriculture (M1 – M3).
2. Compare the average sizes of farms in the US to the sizes of farming operations in Germany and selected European countries (M3, Internet).
3. Describe the characteristic features of US agriculture today (M4, M5, M8)

ⓞ 4. Monfort of Colorado is one example of a large-scale cattle feedlot.
   - A Illustrate the developments that have taken place in the-field of livestock husbandry with reference to the example of the feedlot in Colorado (M6, M7).
   - B Discuss the concepts of "vertical and horizontal integration" as they apply to the Monfort of Colorado production group (M7).

Ⓢ 5. The changes in the structure US agriculture have been accompanied by numerous problems. Discuss.

→ Agribusiness, Feedlot, Integration (vertical and horizontal), Mechanisation, Structural change

The number of people depending either directly or indirectly on farming for a living declined within just two generations from over 30 million in the 1930s to roughly 4.6 million in the early 1990s. Only two percent of the working population were employed in the agricultural sector in 2010. In spite of this marked decline, production volumes rose steadily and substantially during the 20th century. This growth is attributable above all to progressive increases in productivity, rather than to farmland expansion.

The present dual structure of the agricultural sector is the product of efficiency-enhancing measures initiated by the US government since the 1950s. In nearly every region of the country, direct or indirect farm policies implemented since the 1930s have prompted many people to give up farming entirely. Most often affected by this trend since the expiration of subsidy programmes in the 1980s were farms operating with marginal economic efficiency. The death of these farms is not evidence of a weak agricultural sector, but indeed of a strong one, whose output continues to grow despite the dwindling number of farms and can be adapted to both modern patterns of consumption and the strategic geographic and economic needs of the United States.

The substantial increases in US agricultural productivity have resulted at times in huge surpluses of agricultural products and a corresponding decline in the prices of many farm products. Consequently, many farmers have been forced to give up their farms due to excessive indebtedness.

M1 Structural change in agriculture

M2 An American family farm in the 1950s

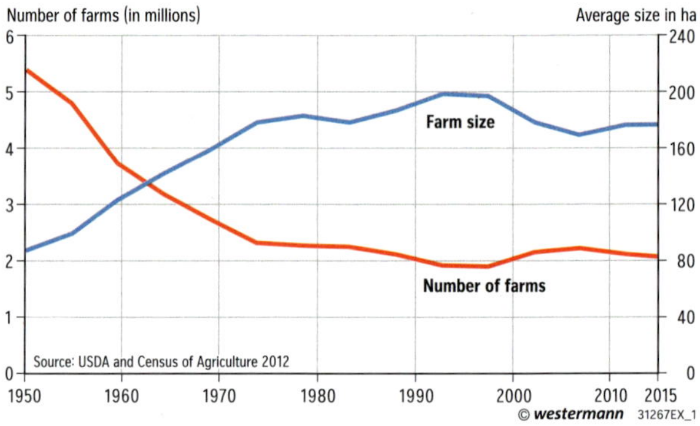

M3 Trends in the average size of US farms

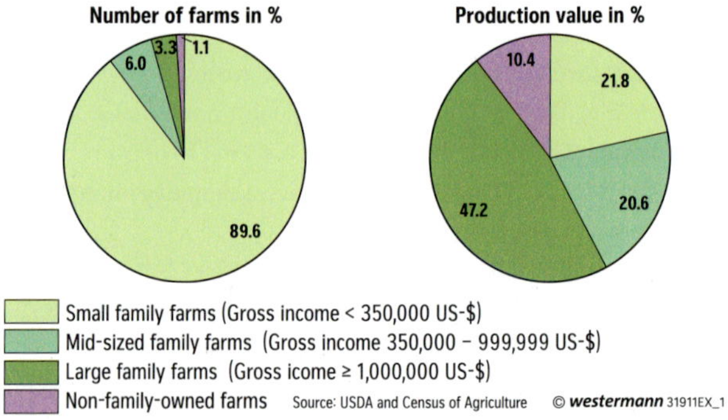

M4 The number of large farms relative to the total number of farms and the total value of production in the USA (2012)

Sales volume from ... to ... US-$	Percentage of farms	Percentage of sales proceeds
under 1,000	28.5	n.d.
1,000–4,999	17.9	0.3
5,000–24,999	21.8	1.4
25,000–99,999	13.3	3.6
100,000–999,999	14.7	28.3
1–4.99 million	3.4	34.7
5 million and more	0.4	31.7
	100	100

M5 Farm size distribution in the USA

M6 Up to 120,000 steers are fattened on the 200-hectare grounds of the Kuner Feedlot in Colorado every year

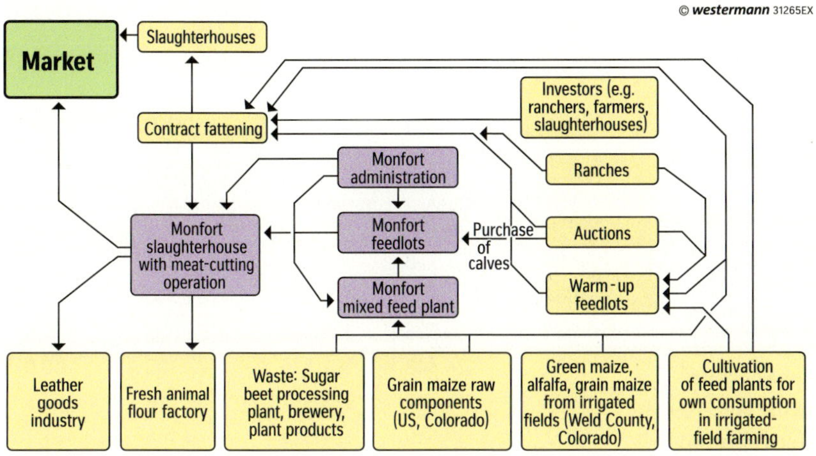

Progressive consolidation processes in the agricultural sector have given rise to large-scale agroindustrial operations. Their productive interrelationships reveal vertical and horizontal connections with a geographic focal point. One example of this system is Monfort of Colorado (see the diagram above), a large-scale feedlot and meat-producing operation in Weld County (Colorado), in which the production alliance can be broken down into individual elements. Distinguishing features of the vertical structure (including upstream and downstream production processes) are company-owned slaughterhouses and affiliated meat-cutting operations. Company-owned outdoor feedlots supply 38 percent of the animals destined for slaughter. One example is the Kuner Feedlot (Diercke Weltatlas 2008/ 2015, pp.204,2/ 220,2). Additional calves are purchased as needed and some are assigned to warm-up feedlots prior to slaughtering. The green corn and alfalfa needed to feed the animals come from contract farms. Additional beef cattle must often be purchased from family farms in order to ensure full capacity utilisation. These animals are purchased at fixed prices in advance of the fattening period and delivered by a fixed slaughtering date.

M7 Monfort of Colorado – production alliance in the beef-cattle production industry

Type of farm	Number	%	Average farm size (in ha)
Oilseed, grain	369,332	17.5	318
Vegetables, melons	43,021	2.0	77
Fruit, nuts	93,020	4.4	57
Horticultural products	52,777	2.5	34
Other plant products or mixed plant-growing operations	496,837	23.6	113
Cattle ranching	619,172	29.4	220
Cattle feedlots	13,734	0.6	350
Mixed livestock farming	46,005	2.2	164
Pig farming	21,687	1.0	97
Poultry farming, egg production	52,849	2.5	49
Sheep and/or goat farming	73,272	3.5	65
Aquacultures, other animal products or mixed livestock farming	227,597	10.8	124
All farms	*2,109,303*	*100.0*	*176*

M8 Farms in the USA by primary product group and average farm size (2012)

The changing structure of US agriculture

Irrigation farming as the trigger for far-reaching structural processes in agriculture – the Great Plains (USA)

Due to their location in the rain shadow of the Rocky Mountains, precipitation levels are low on the Great Plains. Yet the largest groundwater reserve in the United States, the Ogallala Aquifer, lies beneath the Great Plains. Intensive use of this source of water was not possible until the 1950s, when powerful pumps and cheap natural gas first became available.
How has agriculture on the Great Plains changed in the meantime? What are the economic and environmental effects of this changing agricultural structure?

1. Review the natural and geographical prerequisites for the agricultural use of land on the Great Plains (Atlas).
2. Describe the location and size of the Ogallala Aquifer (M1, M2, Atlas).
3. Ⓞ Outline the present structure of the agricultural landscape on the Great Plains (M5).
   A Write a short essay.
   B Draw a sketch showing the essential features of the agricultural landscape.
4. Investigate the development of agriculture with reference to two counties in Kansas.
   a) Compare your findings; explain the differences and similarities. Relate your findings to the overall pattern of development (M6).
   b) Show how agriculture has developed in Finney County (M3) and Haskell County (M4). Determine the output per unit area (t/ha). Identify the relationships involved (M2, M6).
5. Ⓢ Discuss the problems associated with groundwater usage and problem-solving approaches from different perspectives (M1, M2, M7).

→ Aquifer, Output per unit area

Year	Grain maize		Irrigated farmland (in ha)	Cattle stocks
	Cultivated land (ha)	Yield (t)		
1954	203	372	22,169	35,322
1964	2,000	12,861	41,987	55,478
1974	22,600	180,962	61,018	122,554
1982	26,787	282,325	83,891	148,106
1987	20,403	213,831	74,536	193,533
1992	28,121	380,110	90,955	204,369
1997	41,565	569,949	93,218	278,105
2002	31,433	402,356	80,344	300,121
2007	36,916	519,522	72,559	264,133
2012	37,448	410,824	75,566	212,712

Source: Klohn, W., Windhorst, H.W., Die Landwirtschaft der USA, VMG, H. 1, 2005/2011, USDA Census of Agriculture, 2012.

M3 Finney County, South-West Kansas: changing trends in farming

Year	Grain maize		Irrigated farmland (in ha)	Cattle stocks
	Cultivated land (in ha)	Yield (in t)		
1954	6	3	4,786	14,249
1964	875	5,533	32,256	27,552
1974	34,395	328,079	64,036	102,885
1982	24,448	267,536	73,106	160,068
1987	22,649	235,352	62,516	134,383
1992	39,629	597,332	78,168	161,280
1997	47,519	725,527	71,327	221,184
2002	41,067	564,522	65,456	281,883
2007	37,073	593,082	63,327	350,395
2012	24,439	308,263	47,243	400,552

Source: Klohn, W., Windhorst, H.W., Die Landwirtschaft der USA, VMG, H. 1, 2005/2011, USDA Census of Agriculture, 2012

M4 Haskell County, South-West Kansas: changing trends in farming

The Ogallala Aquifer is a water-saturated geological formation that originated during the late Tertiary Period (roughly 10 million years ago) and consists primarily of sand and gravel deposits lying close to the surface. These deposits are highly porous and contain large quantities of exploitable water. The water-storage capacity varies considerably, however, due to major differences in the composition of the formation. The thickness of the groundwater-conveying layers also varies significantly. According to estimates, the aquifer holds about four billion cubic metres of water. Because the aquifer is renewed only to a small extent by seepage from precipitation, the water it contains is often referred to as "fossil water".

Source: Klohn, W. and H. W. Windhorst, Die Landwirtschaft der USA, VMG, H. 1, 2005

M1 The Ogallala Aquifer

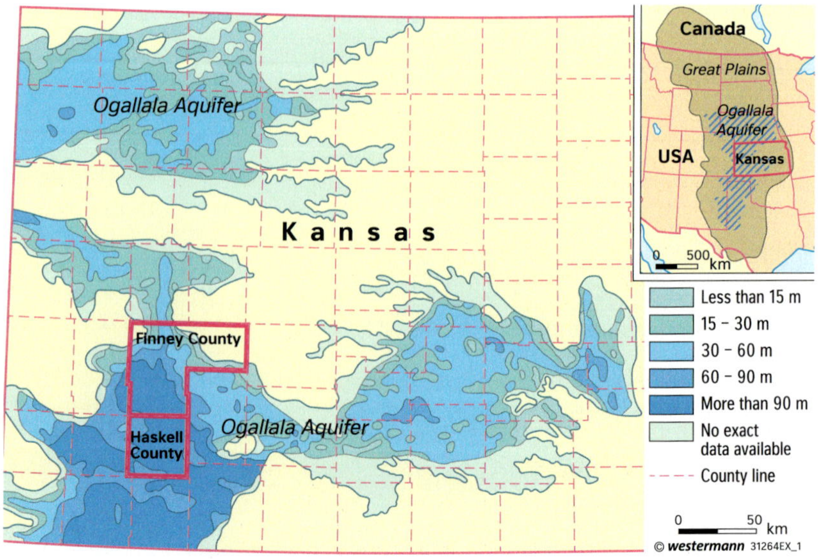

M2 The original thickness of the water-conveying layer in the central area of the Ogallala Aquifer in Kansas

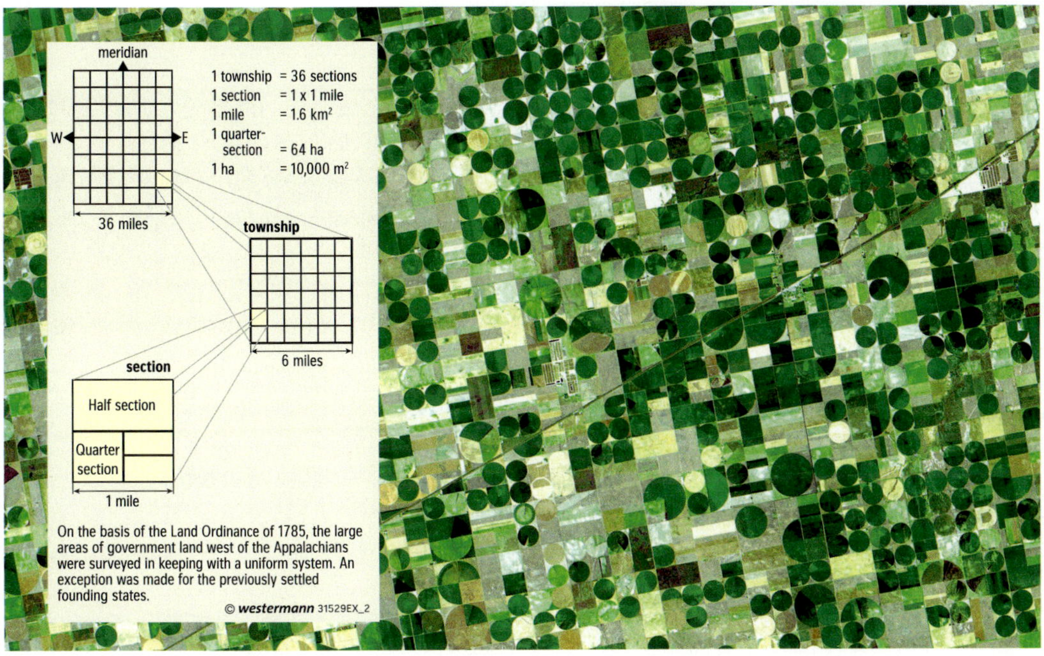

M5 Irrigation farming on the Great Plains

The green circles and squares represent areas of irrigated land. Superimposed over the underlying chessboard pattern of the quadratic land survey is the pattern created by the circle or central-pivot irrigation systems. The most common feature is the 400-metre span of the circulating irrigation pipe of this system. This structure makes it possible to irrigate roughly 53 ha of a 64-hectare quarter section. More than 200 ha can be irrigated with an 800-metre span.

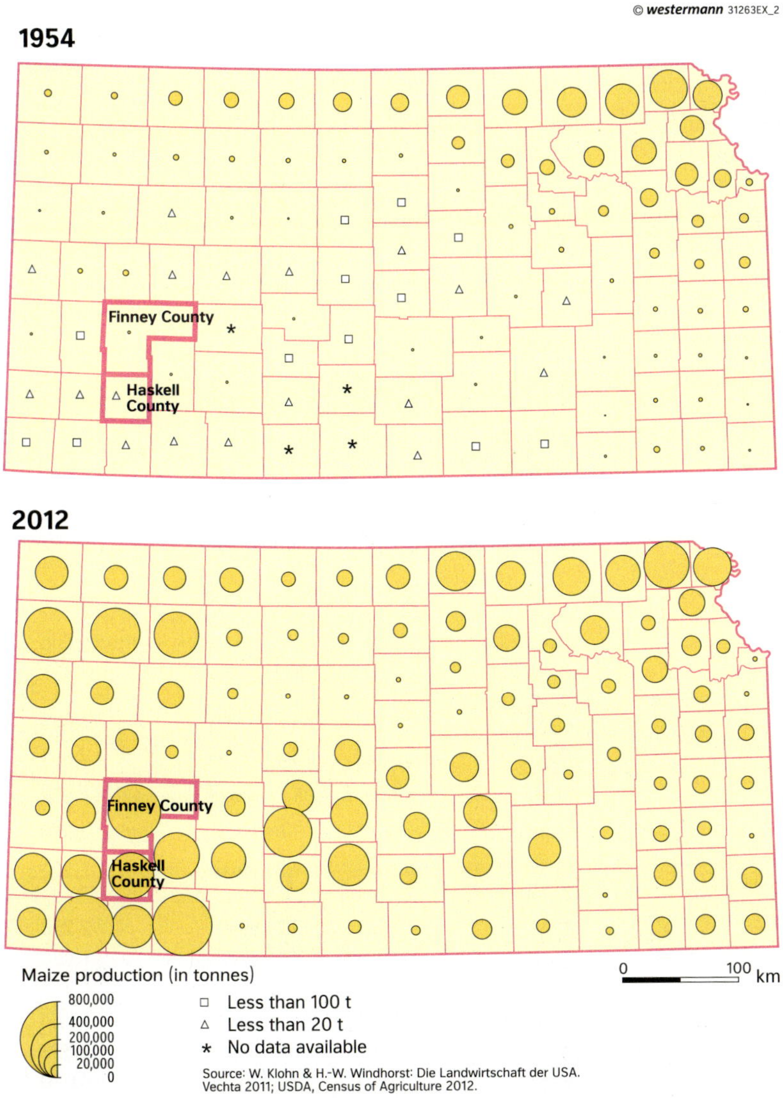

M6 Maize production in Kansas in 1954 and 2012. A total of 15.9 million tonnes of maize was harvested in Kansas in 2007. The figure fell to 10.7 million following the great drought of 2012. Harvest losses were reported in nearly every county.

The thickness of the water-saturated layer of the Ogallala Aquifer has diminished substantially in Kansas since the aquifer was first tapped. Yet the figures must be viewed in relation to the original thickness of the water-conveying layer. Where the original thickness was greatest, significant withdrawals could be made without negative consequences. In areas of low natural thickness however, even much lower withdrawals can cause severe impairments of irrigation capacity.

The lowering of the Ogallala Aquifer groundwater table confronts farmers with major problems. The water they need must be pumped from greater depths, and under the influence of rising energy prices, that is possible only at considerable expense. In some areas, the quantity of water conveyed is not sufficient to provide for adequate irrigation. A substantial reduction in the amount of water withdrawn would be necessary in order to ensure sustainable use of the aquifer. The extent of the reduction of water usage necessary to achieve that goal is particularly large in regions where water usage is very high and in areas with a high concentration of assigned water rights. In the central part of the irrigation region in western and southwestern Kansas, water is used at four times the rate at which it is renewed by natural means.

Source: Klohn, W. and H. W. Windhorst: Die Landwirtschaft der USA, VMG, H. 1, 2005/2011

M7 Over-utilisation of the Ogallala Aquifer

Increasing agricultural productivity by specialisation and intensification?

Industrial poultry production on the rise

Global meat production tripled from 100.7 million tonnes in 1970 to 308.2 million tonnes in 2013. The global demand for meat continues to rise as well. By the year 2022, poultry will account for nearly half of the increase in the quantity of meat consumed (Fleischatlas, 2014).
What are the causes of this trend? Are all regions of the world contributing equally to the growth of consumption and production?
What are the regional consequences of this trend? Given the importance of poultry production in future, developments in this sector should be examined more closely.

1. a) Outline the current trend in global meat production (M2, M3).
   b) Compare the relevance and validity of the statistics (M2) and the graphic (M3). Identify the advantages and disadvantages of each form of presentation.
2. Investigate and explain the global trend in chicken production (M1, M4, M5, M8).
3. Characterise the regional distribution and structure of poultry breeding and fattening operations in Germany. Identify the reasons for the specific regional concentration (M6, M7, M9).
4. The booming countries of Asia will account for roughly 80 percent of the growth in global meat production by 2022. Discuss the possible consequences affecting production.
5. Industrial poultry production in Europe impacts on poultry production in African countries. Explain this and study the current developments in the Internet (M10).
Ⓢ 6. Draw a mindmap (structural diagram) in which you depict the developments in poultry production at the global, national and regional levels as well as specific individual interrelationships.

→ Intensification, Specialisation

Product	1962	1990	2012	2021*
Beef	29,203	53,051	63,289	75,422
Pork	26,056	69,867	109,122	125,322
Poultry	9,206	41,426	105,636	126,502

Source: Windhorst, H.-W. (2014):
a) Aktuelle Trends in der Geflügelhaltung auf globaler Ebene und in der EU, lecture delivered in Jena on 07.03.2014
b) Zur Dynamik der globalisierten Geflügelwirtschaft, lecture delivered in Vechta on 05.06.2014
c) Forecast from: Windhorst, K.-H., Die Globalisierung der Fleischproduktion. Räumliche Verlagerungsprozesse und ihre Ursachen, in gh, Vol. 319, 2014, pp. 28 – 31; Materialheft, p. 23.
* Forecast

M2 Growth in global meat production (in 1,000 t)

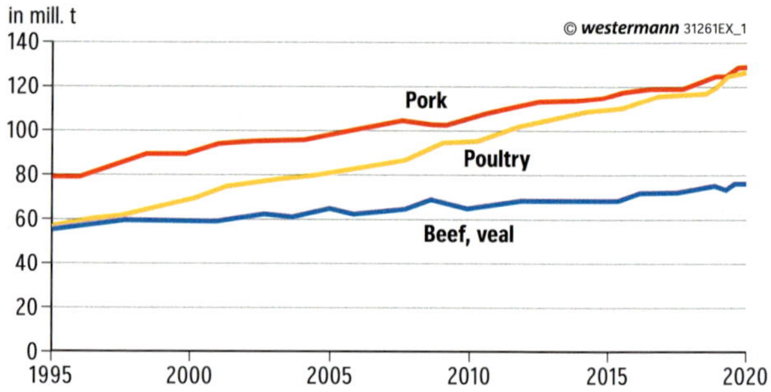

M3 Growth of meat production (in million tonnes)

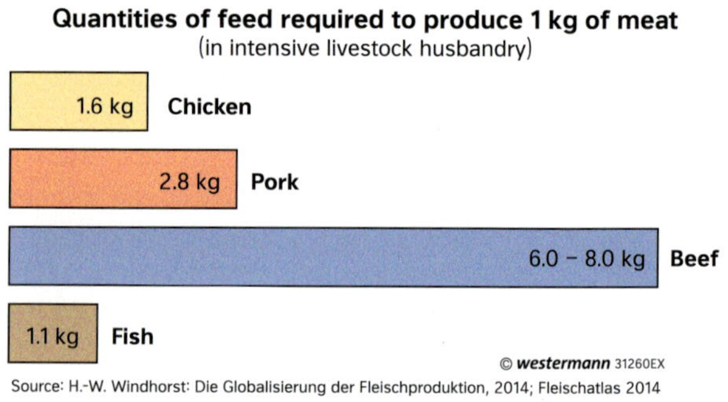

M4 Feed quantities in livestock husbandry

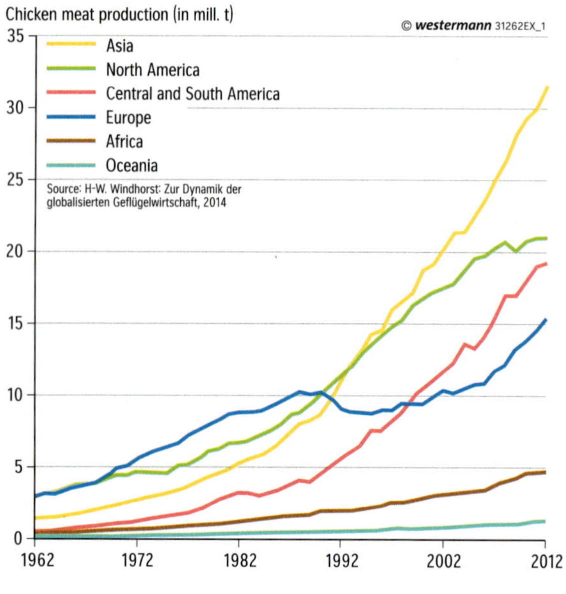

M1 Growth in global chicken production

	1962			2012	
Country	Production (1,000t)	Share of total (%)	Country	Production (1,000t)	Share of total (%)
USA	2,626	33.3	USA	17,035	18.4
USSR *)	822	10.4	China	12,661	13.6
China	460	5.8	Brazil	11,553	12.4
France	458	5.8	Russia	3,299	3.6
Great Britain	307	3.9	Mexico	2,792	3.0
Italy	293	3.7	India	2,219	2.4
Canada	187	2.4	Iran	1,950	2.1
Japan	155	2.0	Indonesia	1,752	1.9
Germany	150	1.9	Turkey	1,724	1.9
Brazil	130	1.6	Argentina	1,665	1.8
10 Countries	5,588	70.9	10 countries	56,630	61

*) Union of Soviet Socialist Republics, dissolved in 1991
Source: Windhorst, H.-W., Zur Dynamik der globalisierten Geflügelwirtschaft, lecture delivered on 05.06.2014 in Vechta

M5 Leading chicken-producing countries

M6 Young broiler chickens

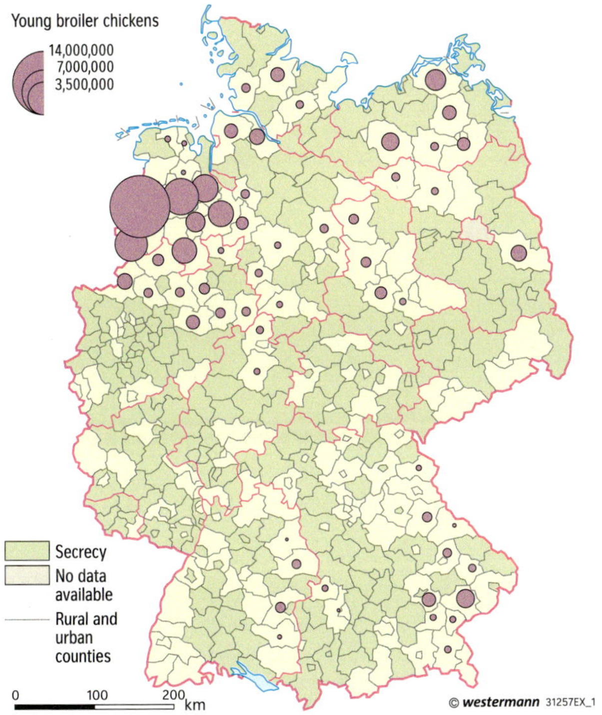

M7 Young broiler chicken farms in Germany, 2010

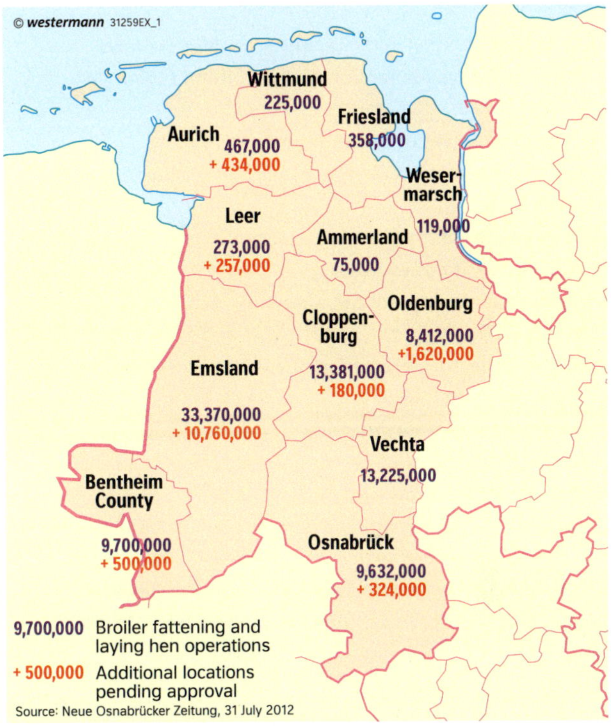

M9 The chicken heartland of Lower Saxony

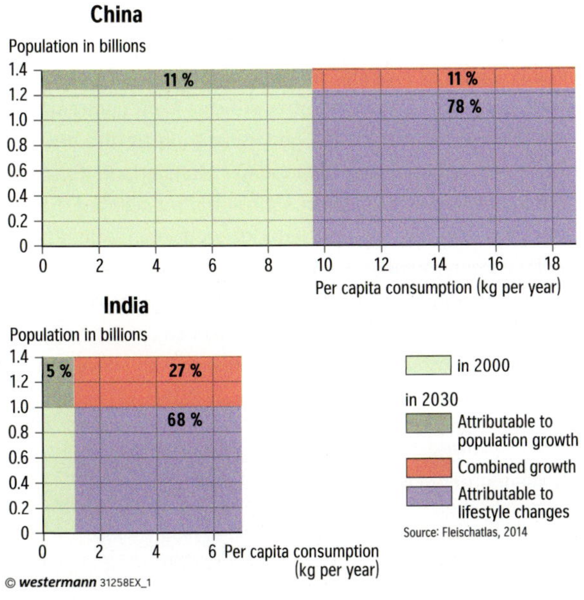

M8 Demand for poultry meat in India and China (in percent)

[Angola], Benin, the Democratic Republic of the Congo, Ghana and South Africa are the leading import countries for European poultry meat in Africa. Exports were triggered by the outbreak of mad cow disease. The use of meat- and bone-meal as feed was restricted progressively in the EU in response to the BSE epidemic from 1996 onward and eventually prohibited entirely. That set the boom in motion. Highly profitable sales of chicken breast fillets financed the production of other parts, including legs and wings. Producers regard everything other than breast fillet as waste. And those parts were sold to the feed industry for many years. Once it became illegal to feed animals with animal by-products, producers were left with no buyers. [...] Exporters then began buying up these chicken parts, which are perfectly suitable for human consumption, for next to nothing. The prices of these products (including shipping costs) upon arrival in West Africa are two-thirds lower than the average local prices for chicken [...] . The poultry sector had been a stable source of additional income for many small farmers in Africa. Today, however, poultry farming has virtually disappeared in Ghana and Benin.

Source: Heinrich-Böll-Stiftung et al., Fleischatlas, 2013

M10 Crises in West Africa due to imports of leftover chicken parts

Increasing agricultural productivity by specialisation and intensification?

The agricultural industry alters regions – the Oldenburger Münsterland

In 2010, every third pig, every seventh laying hen and every tenth broiler chicken in Germany was raised in the Oldenburger Münsterland, a region with poor soil that accounts for only 0.6 percent of the total area of Germany.
What factors led to the development of an agricultural region with such a massive concentration of livestock farms?
How have these changes affected the region?

1. Describe the situation in the Oldenburger Münsterland and the early development of the agricultural region (M1, Atlas).
2. Discusss the growth of livestock farming (M3).
3. An agroindustrial cluster has emerged in the Oldenburger Münsterland.
   a) Identify the essential characteristics of this cluster and explain how it has evolved.
   b) Depict the structure of the cluster in a schematic diagram (M4, M5, M7).
4. Describe the vertical integration of a poultry breeding operation (M5).
5. Ⓢ Research the corporate structures of the PHW Group in Visbek-Rechterfeld (producers of the Wiesenhof brand) and the EW Group (Internet).
6. The processes of concentration, specialisation and intensification have certain consequences. Show their impact from different perspectives and discuss the sustainability and future viability of the local agrarian economy (M5, M6, M8, Atlas).

→ Cluster, Processing industry, Regional concentration

Until 1865, agricultural production in the Oldenburger Münsterland was limited entirely to subsistence farming. The situation circa 1880 was characterised by low crop yields due to inferior sandy soil, low stocking density figures attributable to the insufficient feed supply and poor connections to transport routes.
Following the arrival of the first railway lines in 1895, feed and mineral fertilisers could be shipped to the region and livestock could be transported to slaughterhouses in the heavily industrialised areas along the rivers Rhine and Ruhr.
A second intensification phase began in the 1950s, triggered by increasing prosperity, growing demand for meat and poultry products, practically unlimited possibilities for the importation of animal feed, innovations in farming technology and production (such as computer-controlled feeding systems and the introduction of hybrid animals) and further development of the infrastructure.
Source: Klohn, W. and A. Voth, Das Oldenburger Münsterland. Entwicklung und Strukturen einer Agrar-Komp,etenzregion. Vechtaer Materialien zum Geographieunterricht (VMG), Vol. 2, 2008, 4. Neu bearbeitete Auflage, p. 16

M1 Development of the agrarian economy in the Oldenburger Münsterland

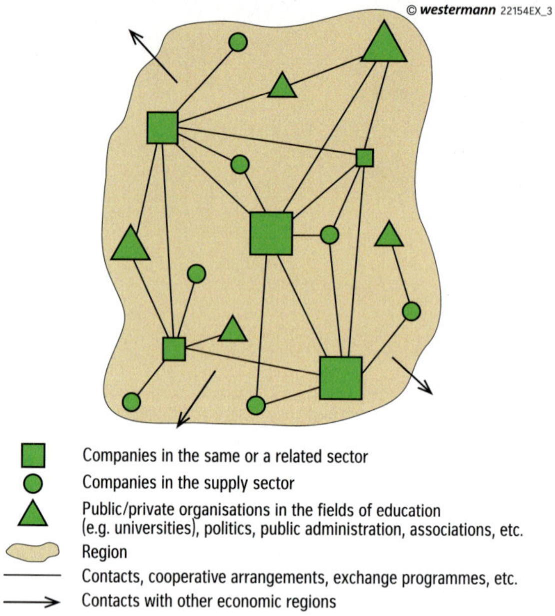

M2 Cluster model

Year	Pigs		Broiler chickens *)	
	Number of farms	Number of animals	Number of farms	Number of animals
1960	14,655	470,090	6,244	9,578
1980	7,835	1,356,794	89	2,948,976
2001	2,706	1,834,705	62	2,558,798
2010	1,904	2,300,850	33	1,451,180
			Cloppenburg **) 100	Cloppenburg **) 4,833,969

*) Figures for Vechta County only **) Cloppenburg County

Sources: Klohn, W. and A. Voth, Das Oldenburger Münsterland. VMG Vol. 2, Bäurle, H., Tamásy, Chr.: Regionale Konzentrationen der Nutztierhaltung in Deutschland. Mitteilungen ISPA, Vol. 79, 2012, statements by Mr Klohn, Vechta (22.08. 2014)

M3 Livestock husbandry in the Oldenburger Münsterland (Vechta and Cloppenburg Counties)

Ordinarily, areas of regional concentration are employment and innovation drivers. A large number of firms from upstream and downstream industries specialised in catering for the needs of farmers have settled in the Oldenburger Münsterland. Examples include companies in the fields of agricultural engineering and stall equipment, seeds, fertiliser and herbicide production, animal health and animal safety, hygiene and pest control, feed and feed-additive production, slaughtering, meat cutting and meat processing as well as sales and logistics. In addition, government and private providers offer services in such areas as financing, research and development, marketing and consulting.
Source: Bäurle, H. and Chr. Tamásy, Regionale Konzentrationen der Nutztierhaltung in Deutschland, Mitteilungen ISPA, Vol. 79, 2012, p. 85

M4 Oldenburger Münsterland as a region of agricultural specialisation

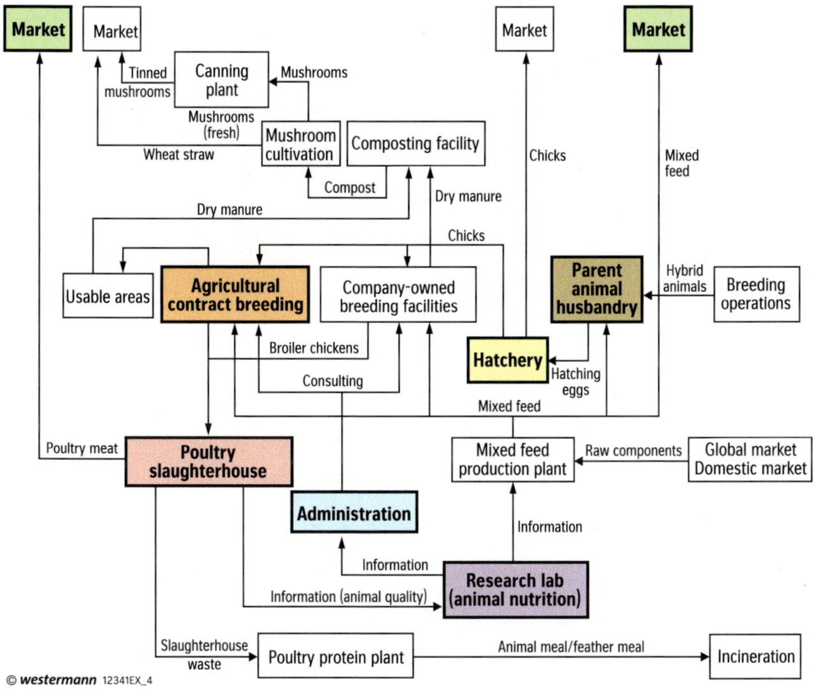

M5 Production alliance in a vertically integrated firm specialising in poultry meat production in South Oldenburg

The growth of pig and/or poultry stocks in such areas of intense agricultural concentration as the Oldenburger Münsterland in particular, has led to an increase in the volume of farmyard or green manure. For some years now, it has been impossible to recycle all of the green manure produced, a portion of which must be shipped out to other regions. [...] Today, "the increasing quantity of green manure deposited on fields in Lower Saxony is responsible for the fact that the groundwater on roughly 27% of the land in the state can be regarded as polluted with nitrates and/or pesticides" (agrarheute.com 2012, revised). The situation is exacerbated in some counties, at least at the local community level, by another problem as well: due to the large number of farm enlargements and new stall construction projects, the ability of building authorities to manage the allocation of land (e.g. for residential or commercial zones) within the framework of an orderly urban development scheme is already severely limited. And last but not least, popular resistance to the unpleasant odours and possible health hazards (e.g. from bio-aerosols) attributable to emissions from livestock breeding operations is growing increasingly strong. [...]
Problems affecting the acceptance of intensive livestock husbandry (e.g. increased risk of epidemics and aspects of animal welfare) have also become the focus of numerous discussions.

Source: Bäurle, H. and Chr. Tamásy, Regionale Konzentrationen der Nutztierhaltung in Deutschland. Mitteilungen ISPA, Vol. 79, 2012, pp. 5, 83–84

M6 Problems in areas of intensive agricultural concentration

Businesses in clusters benefit in three different ways.

1. Through informal contacts. An informal exchange of information takes place within the regional milieu in which the players are embedded. This knowledge, which is not generally accessible, is passed on through personal channels and contributes to the creation of a know-how and information edge over companies outside of the cluster.
2. Through competition: The regional concentration and geographic proximity of companies offering identical or similar products and services leads to increased competition among the companies in question, as they are always well informed about the activities of their competitors and undertake increased efforts to improve their own competitive strength.
3. Through cooperation: Close cooperation among businesses within a regionally concentrated value chain encourages the development of innovative networks, which in turn promote innovation.

Source: Pantazis, N. and E. Schricke, Clusterentwicklung und Unternehmensgründungen am Beispiel der Optischen Technologien in Südostniedersachsen, in Kiese, M. and L. Schätzl (eds.): Cluster und Regionalentwicklung. Theorie, Beratung und praktische Umsetzung. Dortmund, 2008, p. 71.

M7 Competitive advantages offered by business clusters

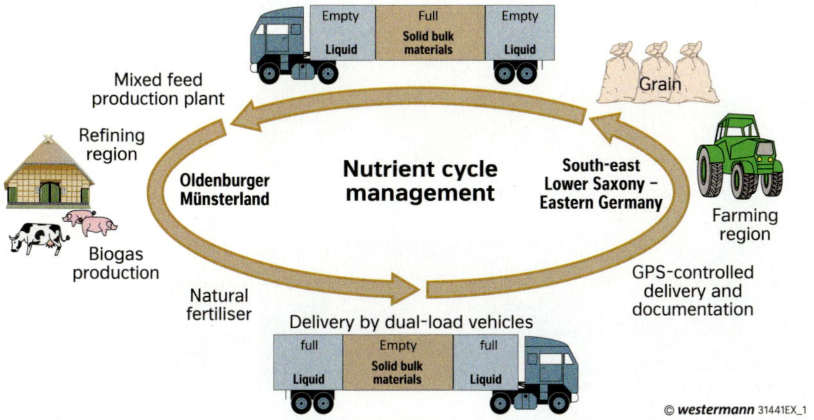

Farmers in Vechta and Cloppenburg Counties need roughly 15,000 tonnes of grain per day to feed their livestock. Most deliveries are effected by lorries, which often return empty to the grain-growing regions of south-eastern Lower Saxony and eastern Germany. With the aid of newly developed combi-lorries, liquid natural fertilisers can be delivered on the return journey to the growing regions. This eliminates unnecessary dead freights.

◁ **M8** Grain and natural fertiliser transport

Increasing agricultural productivity by specialisation and intensification?

Greenhouse cultivation in the Netherlands

The Netherlands holds a leading position in the EU in terms of the intensity and productivity of agricutural operations. The country is also the leading exporter of agricultural products in the EU.
54.6percent of all land in the Netherlands is used for agricultural purposes. That amounts to 1.9 million ha. Although only roughly 0.6 percent (72,300 farms) of all farming operations in the EU are located in the Netherlands, these farms account for 6.5 percent of the EU's gross agricultural production value (2011). The Netherlands exported agricultural products valued at a record 79.2 billion euros in 2013. In addition to dairy products, pigs and pork, exports include above all horticultural products such as vegetables, cut flowers and potted plants.
But what enables Dutch greenhouse farmers to operate so productively?

1. Illustrate the spread of greenhouse cultivation in the Netherlands (M1, M9, Atlas).
2. Greenhouse cultivation is characterised as a soil-independent, specialised horticultural operation. Discuss this characterisation (M2, M3, M4, M7).
3. Illustrate the development of greenhouse cultivation with reference to the growth of productivity (M8).
4. Describe the cluster structure of Dutch greenhouse horticulture with reference to the example of the Naaldwijk region (M1, M6).
5. Show how the establishment of greenports contributes to promoting the growth of horticultural regions (M5, M9).
6. ⓞ Is Dutch greenhouse cultivation viable in the long term?
   A List the advantages and disadvantages of greenhouse farming in a table.
   B Can Dutch horticultural operations compete with farms in regions with more favourable climates (in Spain, for example)?

→ Greenhouse cultivation, Horticulture

M2 Greenhouse complexes in the Netherlands

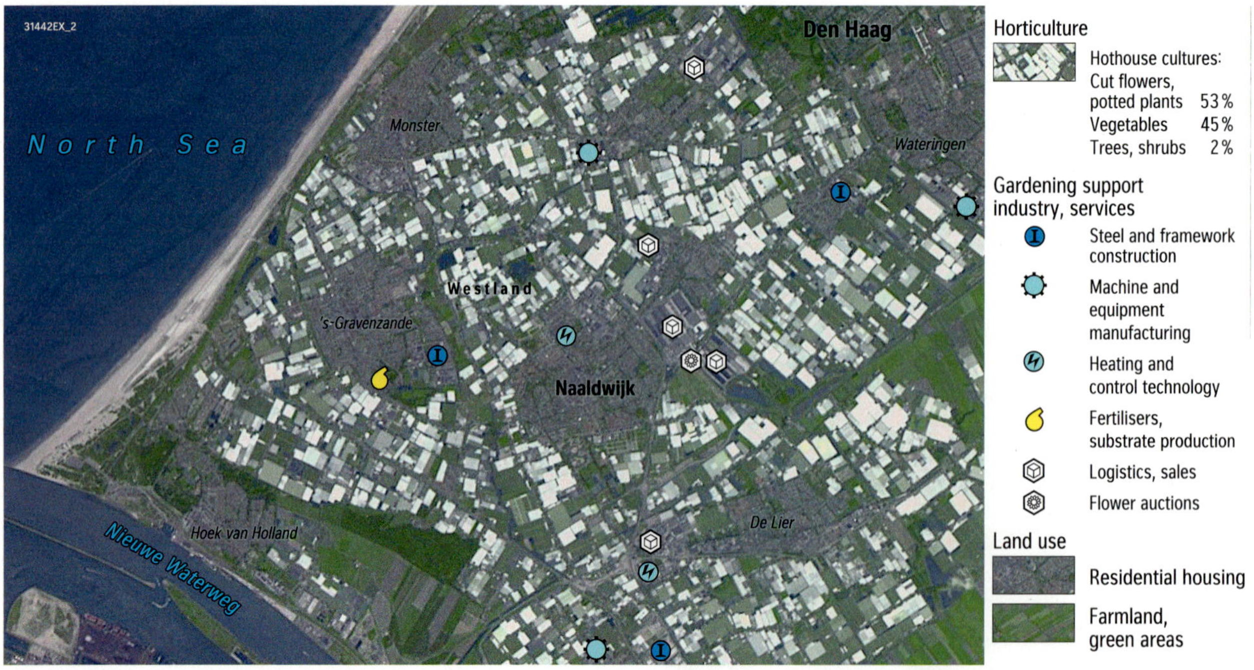

M1 Soil-dependent greenhouse cultivation in the Netherlands (Naaldwijk)

M3 Tomato cultivation on rock wool

M7 Greenhouse cultivation: flowers

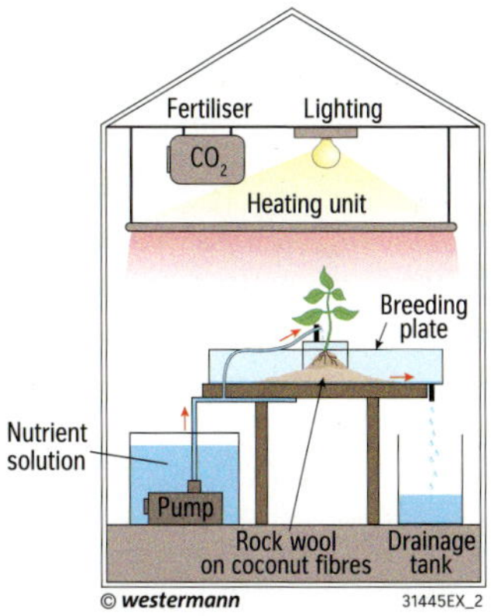

M4 Substrate-based horticulture under glass

	Total greenhouse operations		of which: operations with vegetable cultivation	
	2000	2013	2000	2013
Number of greenhouse operations	8,182	3,600	2,558	1,100
Area under glass (in ha)	17,333	13,000	6,163	5,300
Average size of operations (ha/operation)	0.34	0.36	0.41	0.38
Average income (in €/ per operation)	102,000	129,000	96,000	119,000

Source: CBS (Centraal Bureau voor de Statistiek), www.cbs.nl, article dated 30.01.2014

M8 Trends in greenhouse operations

The Netherlands has designated six "greenports", in which horticultural agribusiness complexes of significant importance to Dutch foreign trade enjoy priority support from the Dutch government and to a certain extent from the EU as well, most notably through expansion of the business-related infrastructure. A greenport is defined as "a large horticultural cluster in which plants, trees, flower bulbs, flowers and various types of vegetables are produced and marketed. This includes both production under glass (in greenhouses) and field cultivation (primarily flower bulbs and nurseries for decorative plants). The concept also encompasses an entire chain of activities in addition to production and trade, such as greenhouse construction, technology, transportation, training and education, research, and finishing."

Source: Wieger, A. and L. Wieger-Schlungs, Höchste Effizienz auf engem Raum. I: PG, H. 4, 2013, Förderung regionaler Cluster in den Niederlanden: die Greenports, pp. 33–39

M5 Greenports – promoting regional clusters

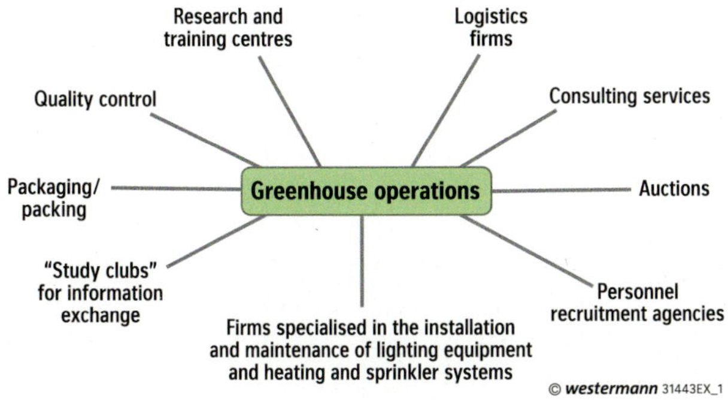

M6 Clusters in Dutch greenhouse cultivation

M9 Greenhouse cultivation and greenports in the Netherlands

Intensification in the oceans as well?

Can aquacultures contribute to food security? The example of salmon breeding in Norway

Fish has already become the most important source of protein for human nutrition, ranking ahead of both poultry and pork. Roughly 17 percent of the human population satisfy their protein requirements primarily by consuming fish. Demand will continue to rise as the global population increases – yet most of our oceans are already overfished. So why not simply breed fish? Could we both protect our oceans and feed the growing world population with the aid of aquaculture? Freshwater fish breeding in ponds is an ancient technique practised above all by small farmers in Asia. Saltwater fish were first bred on a large scale in the late 20th century. Today, fish (especially salmon) are bred in offshore farms in coastal waters. Norway is one of the leading producers.

1. Trace the global development of fishing and aquaculture (M3).
2. Name the world's largest aquaculture producers and examine the respective production methods. Discuss Norway's importance as an aquaculture producer on a global scale (M1).
3. Explain the growth of salmon breeding and its geographical distribution in Norway (M4, M5, M7).
4. Explain the process of salmon breeding in fish farms (M2, M6).
5. High-tech fish breeding in industrial fish farms – not without problems! Discuss (M8, Internet).
6. Ⓢ Discuss the question of whether sustainable fish breeding is possible. Research this issue (M8, Internet).
7. Can the "blue revolution" contribute to solving the problems involved in ensuring an adequate food supply? Collect arguments for a discussion of the pros and cons.
8. Ⓢ Investigate the development, type and importance of aquaculture for another country (one of the 10 leading aquaculture producers, cf. M1) (M1, Atlas, Internet).

→ Aquaculture

M2 Aquaculture operation in northern Norway (Lofoten)

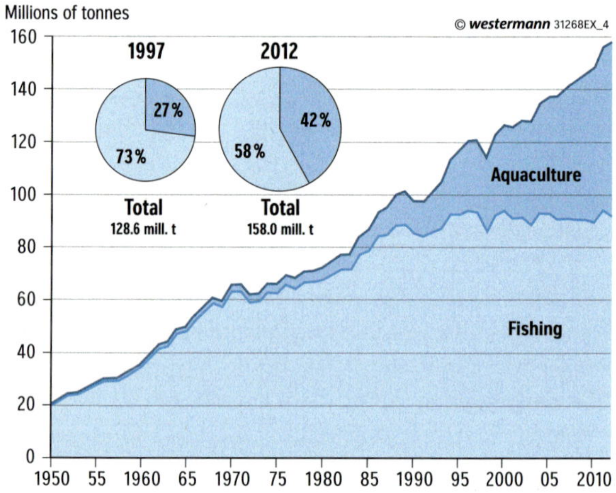

Source: FAO: The State of World. Fisheries and Aquaculture. Updated in 2014

M3 Growth of fishing and aquaculture production

Producer	Fish		Crustaceans (e.g. shrimp, crabs, lobsters)	Molluscs (e.g. oysters, mussels)	Other types	Total	Percentage share of global production
	Inland breeding	Breeding in coastal waters					
China	23,341,134	1,028,399	3,592,588	12,343,169	803,016	41,108,306	61.7
India	3,812,420	84,164	299,926	12,905	–	4,209,415	6.3
Vietnam	2,091,200	51,000	513,100	400,000	30,020	3,085,500	4.6
Indonesia	2,097,407	582,077	387,698	–	477	3,067,660	4.6
Bangladesh	1,525,672	63,220	137,174	–	–	1,726,066	2.6
Norway	85	1,319,033	–	2,001	–	1,321,119	2.0
Thailand	380,986	19,994	623,660	205,192	4,045	1,233,877	1.9
Chile	59,527	758,587	–	253,307	–	1,071,421	1.6
Egypt	1,016,629	–	1,109	–	--	1,017,738	1.5
Myanmar	822,589	1,868	58,981	–	1,731	885,169	1.3
10 leading nations	35,147,649	3,908,342	5,614,236	13,216,574	839,289	58,762,271	88.1
Other nations	3,451,871	1,643,563	832,582	1,954,164	25,253	7,870,987	11.9
World	38,599,520	5,551,905	6,446,818	15,170,738	864,542	66,633,253	100

Source: FAO (ed.) (2014), The State of World Fisheries and Aquaculture. Opportunities and challenges, Rome, p. 3.

M1 The world's aquacultures: fish, crustaceans and molluscs, in tonnes (2012)

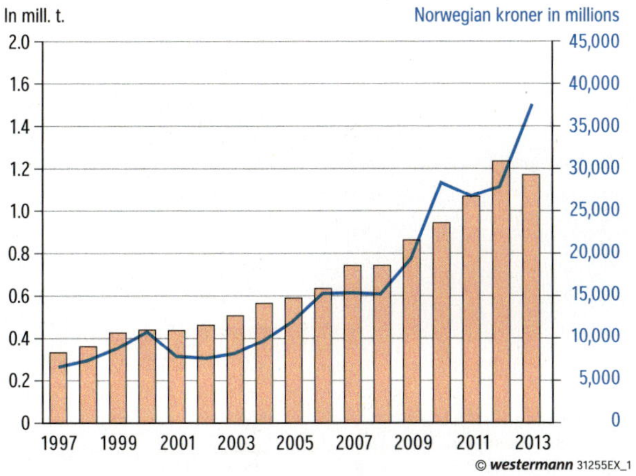

M4 Growing sales volumes and proceeds from sales of salmon from aquacultures in Norway (1 euro ≙ 8.4 NOK (Norwegian kroner))

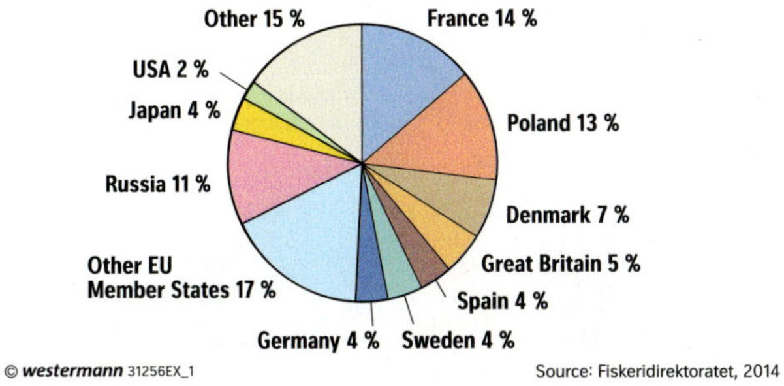

M5 Leading importing countries for Norwegian salmon (2014)

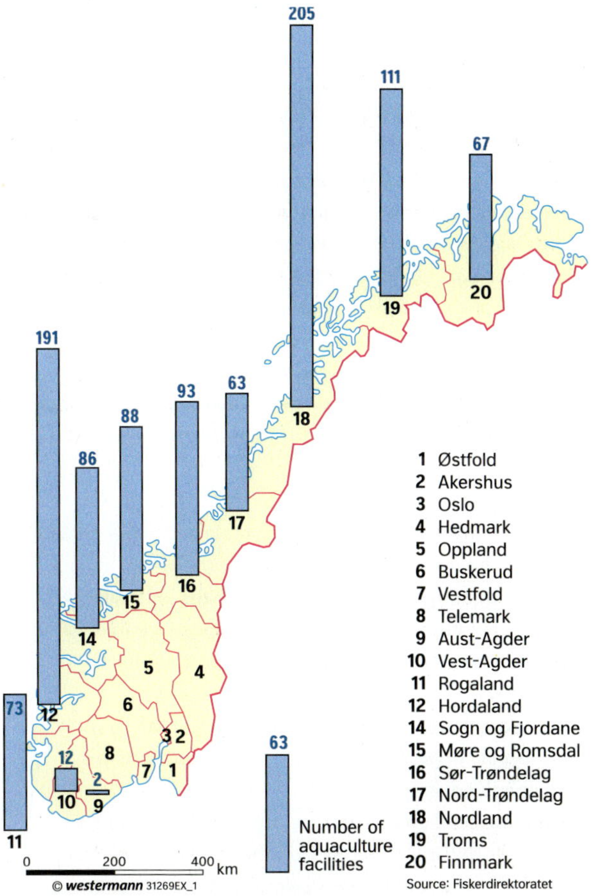

M7 Aquaculture operations (salmon and rainbow trout) in Norway (distribution by province) (2013)

Wild salmon: Salmon are anadromous fish. They spend most of their life in the sea. When the reproduction period begins, they swim upstream in rivers to spawn. Young salmon (parr) spend one to two years in fresh water before returning to the ocean as full-grown smolts.

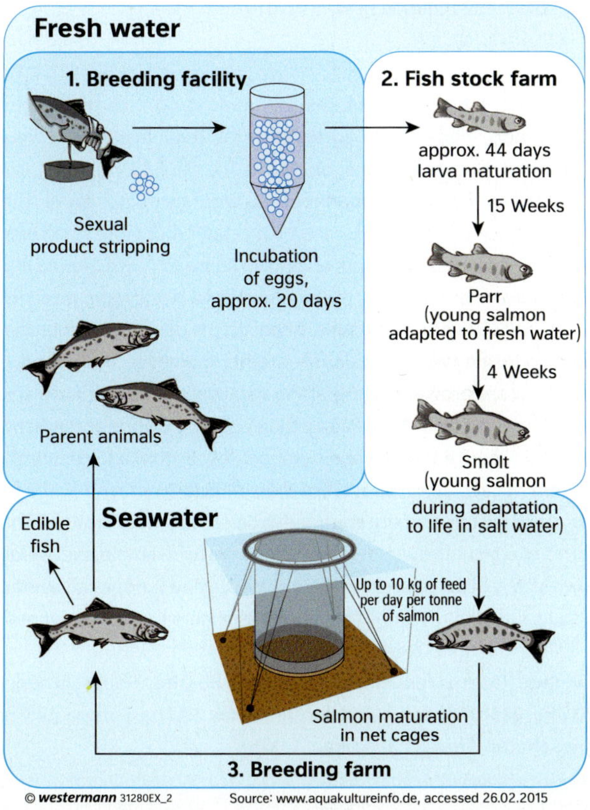

M6 Salmon breeding

Most of the salmon sold on the market today probably come from breeding farms in Norway or Chile. At first, those involved in production and marketing hoped that aquaculture would not only bring business success but would also benefit the environment. The idea was that demand would be met, while depleted fish populations would gradually recover. In other words, sustainable fishing seemed a real possibility.

Yet every type of large-scale animal husbandry has its downside as well. Livestock raised in a confined space are susceptible to parasites and disease. Breeders are compelled to use pesticides and antibiotics. And the excrements left behind by salmon have a negative impact on the marine ecosystem.

Farm-raised salmon often escape confinement and reproduce with their wild relatives, thereby endangering the wild salmon population, as farm-raised salmon are bred to put on weight rapidly.

Norway has been pursuing efforts to solve the problems facing aquaculture for many years. It is hoped that, supported by intensive research and strict regulations, salmon breeding will become a poster child for healthy nutrition and environmental safety. After all, fish are Norway's third-largest export commodity.

Norwegian salmon farmers have since achieved some early successes. Instead of antibiotics, fish are given timely vaccinations. And the number of fish per cage is limited by law (approximately 25 kilograms of salmon per cubic metre of water are permitted).

The underwater cages are moved regularly, thus allowing the ocean floor and its inhabitants to recover from the influence of salmon excrements.

Source: Bredlow, S., Lachs aus dem Käfig. www.mdr.de/lexi-tv/Lachs104.htmln, accessed 26.02.2015

M8 Salmon from cages

Agribusiness or small-scale farming operations?

Who ensures food security for humanity?

The question is sometimes asked whether agribusiness can solve the problem of feeding the world's population. You have been introduced to a series of differing examples of agroindustrial operations and of regions marked by the agricultural industry. These make clear that it is possible to achieve major increases in productivity in farming, but that this development is also associated with ecological and socio-economic problems. Is it possible for the market- and export-oriented agroindustrial operations – despite such problems – to ensure the future nutrition of humanity, or will small-scale farming operations also have to make a contribution?

1. Investigate the distribution of large-scale and small-scale farms (by area) worldwide (M3, M4).
2. Outline the connections between farm sizes and numbers of people employed in agriculture. Also give examples of the connection between farm size and productivity (M1, M4, M7).
3. Ⓢ Using examples from the preceding pages (p. 22–33) compile a list of problems that are associated with the agricultural industry.
4. Present the key findings of the current IAASTD report on small-scale and industrial agriculture (M1, M6).
5. Illustrate the concept of agroecology and the development concept for sustainable systems in agriculture (M7, M8).
6. Comment on the question at the top of this page: "Market- and export-oriented agribusiness or small-scale farming operations: Who ensures food security for humanity?" (M1–M8).

→ Agroecological concept

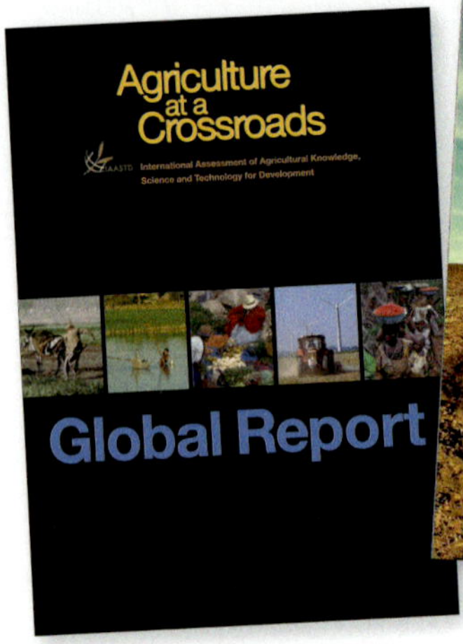

M2 IAASTD report 2009

M5 UNCTAD report 2013

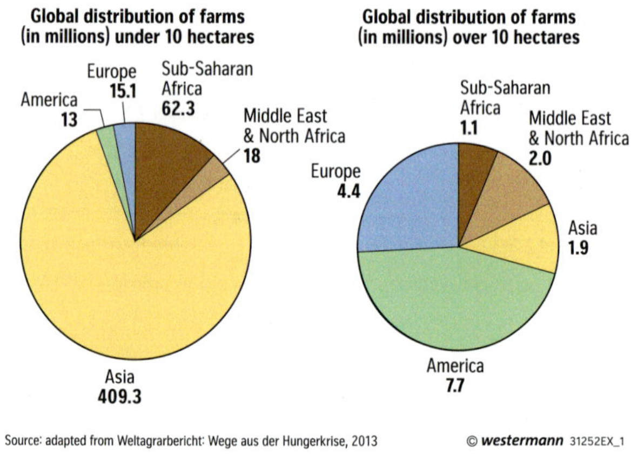

M3 Global distribution of farms (2010)

In general, the large-scale industrialisation of agriculture in North and South America, Australia and Europe and the smaller-scale "Green Revolution" in Asia have led to impressive successes in increasing productivity and rationalisation over the past fifty years. The increase in global agricultural production has outstripped population growth. [...] However, industrialised agriculture focusing on raising productivity exploits the available natural resources to an unsustainable extent. The basic strategy to replace human labour with farm machinery, agrochemicals and fossil energy is proving to be a dead end in times of climate change, dwindling oil reserves and overexploited natural resources.

The IAASTD report thoroughly and honestly counters the myth that industrial agriculture is superior in economic, social and ecological terms. Instead the report formulates a new paradigm for agriculture in the 21st century: Small-scale, labour-intensive structures that focus on diversity are the bearers of hope and the guarantee of a form of food supply that is socially, economically and environmentally sustainable and that is based on resilient cultivation and distribution systems.

Source: Foundation on Future Farming (publ.), Wege aus der Hungerkrise, 2013, www.weltagrarbericht.de, accessed 10.10.2014 (adapted)

M1 Small-scale and industrialised farming

Approximately 2.6 billion people, almost 40% of the world's population, depend on agriculture for their livelihood. Nearly half of humanity lives on the land. Of 537 million farms worldwide, 83% are smallholders who farm no more than 2 hectares, and 97% have less than 10 hectares. But these small farms produce the largest amounts of food (in Asia and Africa around 80%) and cultivate around 60% of the arable land worldwide, often less fertile and poorly irrigated soils. Although the percentage of farmers relative to the world population is getting smaller, their absolute numbers are growing, especially in Asia where average farm sizes are decreasing while farms are getting bigger in Europe and America. In Latin America the average numbers result from a large number of small-scale farmers with less than 2 hectares of land and a few huge operations that are engaged in one of the most industrialised forms of agriculture worldwide. In Argentina for example, the average farm size is 582 hectares. In North America and Europe the average also includes many small farms whose owners can no longer make a living from agriculture.

Average farm sizes: North America: 186.0 ha, South America: 50.7 ha, Central America and the Caribbean: 22.2 ha, Europe: 14.7 ha, Subsaharan Africa: 1.3 ha, Asia: 1.06 ha

Source: Foundation on Future Farming (publ.), Wege aus der Hungerkrise, 2013, p.22. www.weltagrarbericht.de, accessed 10.10.2014 (adapted)

M4 Average farm size in hectares

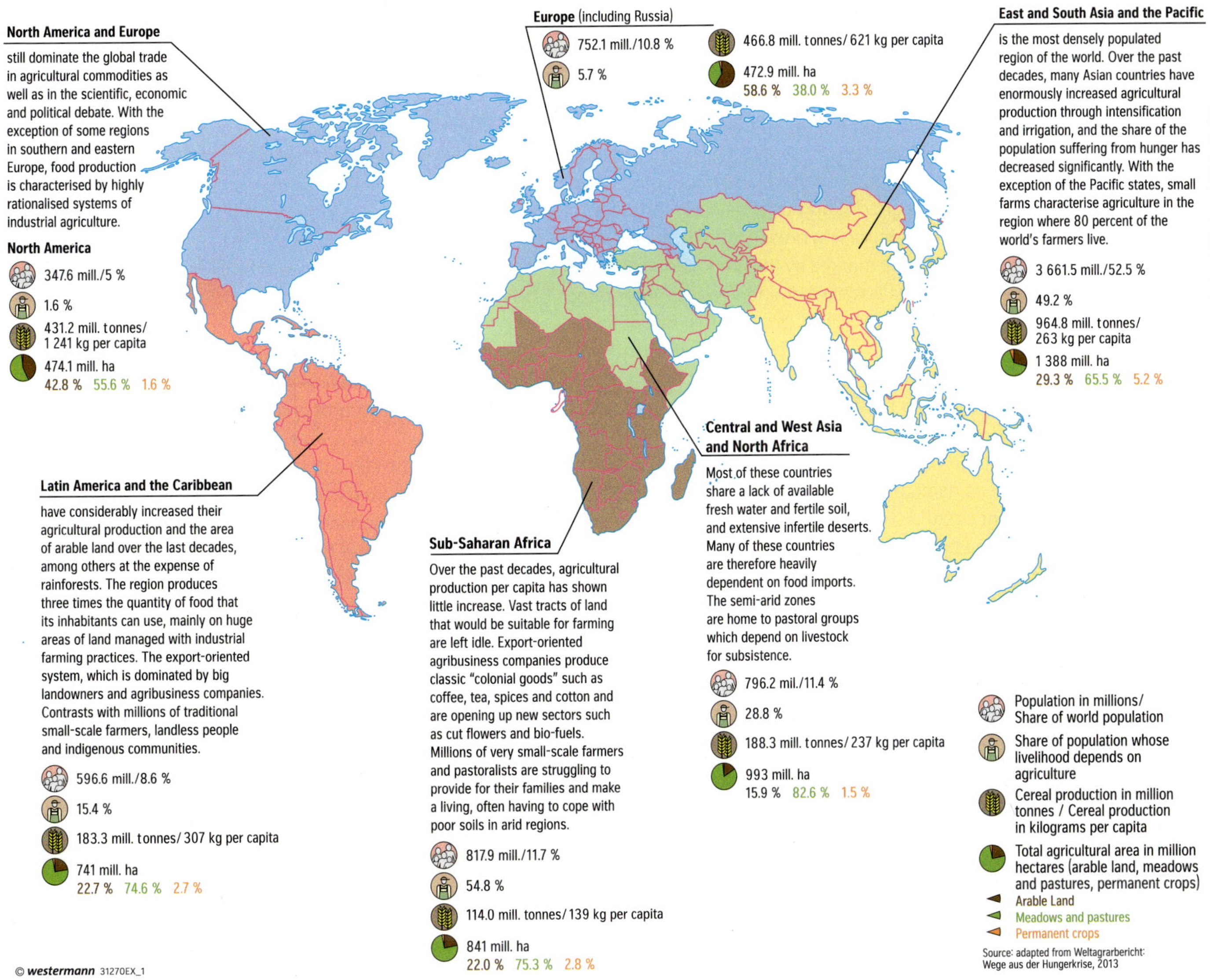

M6 Regions in the IAASTD report

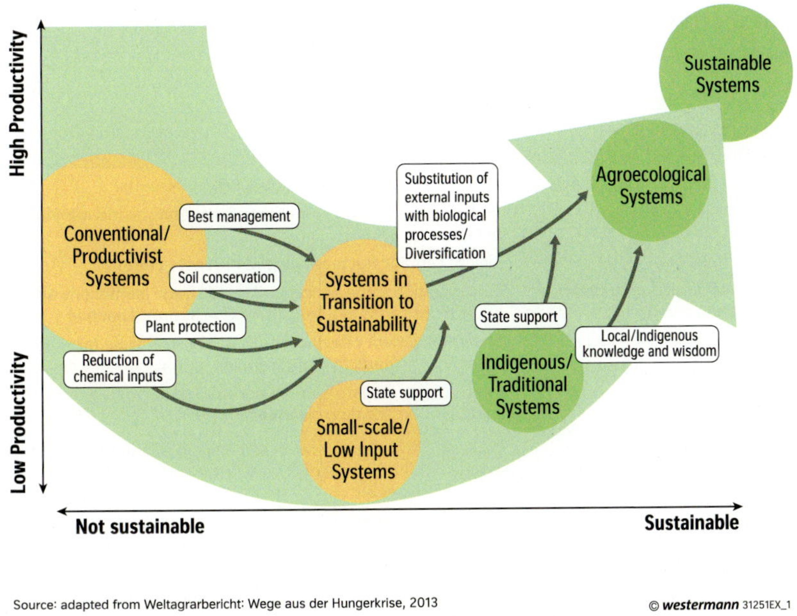

Source: adapted from Weltagrarbericht: Wege aus der Hungerkrise, 2013

M7 Agriculture at a crossroads: transition to sustainable systems

Agroecological concepts are based on traditional and local knowledge and its corresponding cultures, and combines this knowledge with the findings and methods of modern science. Its strength lies in the combination of ecological, biological and agricultural sciences, along with medicine, nutritional and social sciences. Agroecology incorporates the knowledge of all the parties involved. Their practical contribution to solving complex problems with the help of locally available resources is decisive. Apart from sun, water and soil, other resources that are particularly important are the natural and cultivated diversity of plant species and varieties, along with the people's knowledge of how they interact.

Source: adapted from Foundation on Future Farming (publ.), Wege aus der Hungerkrise. Die Erkenntnisse und Folgen des Weltagrarberichts, 2013; www.weltagrarbericht.de, accessed 10.10.2014

M8 Agroecological concepts

The essentials in brief

Products from the tropics have become an everyday component of our lives. At the same time, many tropical countries are recording high birth rates. Both aspects – rising global demand for agricultural raw materials (also) from the tropics as well as population growth and thus rising local demand in the tropics – lead to increasing pressure on the land. Many countries of the South are marked by the predominance of the agricultural sector. Small-scale farming is a very important employment factor and also plays an essential role in feeding the local population. Against this, tropical agricultural products are grown for the world market on plantations which are associated with a multiplicity of ecological and social problems.

The great demand for foodstuffs and agricultural raw materials, as well as rising prices in this sector against the background of anticipated shortages of food and drinking water, have made investments in the field of agriculture increasingly attractive. Moreover, land acquisitions are attractive for states which can transfer parts of their agricultural production to other regions.

Here too, land-use conflicts are on the agenda between industrialised agriculture oriented to the world market and traditional farming and grazing. Land acquisitions can only foster development for the local population when the contracts are transparent, the local people have a say, and the interests of local population groups as well as traditional usage rights are respected.

In view of the worsening conflicts in the above-mentioned areas, the urgent question arises of what the future of farming in the tropics will look like, and – even more importantly – what it should look like.

Since the 1950s, a decisive structural change has also taken place in farming in industrialised countries. Modern and rational methods of cultivation, especially through the greater use of chemicals and machinery, have made it possible to boost productivity many times over. The large-scale industrialisation of agriculture in North and South America, Australia and Europe, and the smaller-scale "Green Revolution" in Asia, have led to impressive successes in increasing productivity and rationalisation over the past fifty years. The examples from the USA (the Great Plains), the Netherlands and the Oldenburger Münsterland show how extremely productively farming operations can work with the aid of specialisation and intensification.

But meanwhile the complex problems associated with the growth of agribusiness have become apparent. With increasing resource prices and worsening environmental problems, the principle of industrialised farm production is reaching its limits. At the same time, economic problems also sometimes arise from integration in the global world market (e.g. dependence on bought-in animal feed, dependence on global customers). The decline in species diversity represents a further problem. Vast quantities of agricultural raw materials are produced in monocultures with a small number of high-yield crops. In animal farming too, breeding has produced high-performance animals that can deliver large volumes of e.g. meat, milk or eggs in a short space of time. The problems that are faced today by agricultural regions with intensive farming are shown by the examples from the Great Plains and the Oldenburger Münsterland. Often, state subsidies have driven forward agro-industrial developments in these regions and ultimately made the farming operations dependent on the subsidies.

For over 50 years, the principle of "grow or die" led to a high rate of farm deaths in the USA, but also to the abandonment of many smaller farming operations in Europe. Meanwhile, not only the IAASTD report and current studies by UNCTAD but also many academic and political experts see small-scale, ecologically-oriented farming as a solution leading to greater food security while at the same time protecting the environment and bringing socio-economic benefits. Sustainable agriculture and the promotion of ecologically-oriented small-scale farms, both in the tropics and in temperate zones, are expected to play a key role in future solutions to the problem of feeding the world.

	+	–
Economic	– Efficient production and processing thanks to specialisation and economies of scale. – Centralised, professional management. – Uniform quality standards. – Good marketing possibilities (among other things due to greater market strength and a stronger negotiating position). – Large production volumes ensure reliable supply of customers. – High export incomes with rising world market prices for foods and agricultural raw materials.	– Very unbalanced seasonal labour requirements. – High dependence on sometimes fluctuating world market prices. – Risk of climatic fluctuations and harvest failures. – Concentration in the agricultural sector: large plantations are often in the hands of a few; increase in social disparities. – The employment effect is less than in small-scale farming; unemployment leads to flight from the land. – International investors in the agricultural sector – a high proportion of profits flow overseas.
Social	– Despite increasing mechanisation, the production of many plantation products is still labour-intensive – local workers are required. – Some companies have enshrined social standards in their guidelines and also give support to e.g. education projects.	– Work on plantations is often seasonal, badly paid, physically exhausting and – especially with intensive use of pesticides – damaging to health. – The spread of cultivation in areas that were traditionally used for subsistence or small-scale farming destroys the basis for the livelihood of the local population.
Ecological	– High output per unit area can lead to a reduction in overall land use. – There are efforts to integrate principles of ecological farming into plantation agriculture.	– Monocultures leach out the soil in a one-sided way and favour the massive proliferation of pests – they require large-scale, intensive use of fertilisers and pesticides. – Monocultures reduce species diversity.

M1 Plantation agriculture against the background of sustainability

Skill check

All the skills that you were able to acquire in this chapter are listed here.
You can judge for yourself if you have mastered each skill: ***securely***, ***moderately*** or ***barely***.

Explanatory skills

Can I ...		Unsure? Look it up on these pages
1.	compare plantation farming and subsistence farming with respect to their operating structures and market orientation as well as their impact on employment and their economic significance?	12–16
2.	identify instances of increasing competition for use in view of the limited amount of available farmland and the increasing demand for agricultural products?	12–34
3.	describe reciprocal effects of local and regional agricultural production and the global agricultural market?	14–17
4.	outline threats to the tropical rainforest posed by human interventions in nutrient and water cycles and the resulting changes?	12–15
5.	clarify the characteristics of structural changes in agriculture, such a mechanisation, intensification and specialisation?	22–33
6.	explain structural change in agriculture as a result of changing economic and technical conditions?	22–33
7.	establish correlations between consumption patterns and changes in agriculture?	22–33
8.	present irrigation farming as a method used for the purpose of overcoming the climatic drought limit and the cause of deep-seated processes in agricultural structure?	24/25

Methodological skills

Can I ...		
9.	develop questions regarding land-use conflicts involving competition between subsistence farming/ small-scale farming and large-scale farming oriented towards the global market?	12–33
10.	identify problematic geographic circumstances with reference to the phenomenon of land grabbing and independently develop appropriate questions and hypotheses by employing the problem-oriented, analytical approach to the acquisition of knowledge?	18/19, 22–31
11.	analyse various (simple and complex) tools and means of presentation, such as statistics, graphics and texts as a basis for developing statements regarding developments in agriculture, particularly in the tropics?	10–35
12.	search independently for information in libraries and the Internet and analyse my findings with reference to specific questions?	18, 20

Evaluation skills

Can I ...		
13.	discuss the field of tension between the intensification of agricultural production and the need to ensure an adequate food supply?	12/13
14.	evaluate the effects of structural changes in farming methods, focusing on their impact on employment and corresponding changes in cultivated and natural landscapes?	12/13, 22–31
15.	discuss the conflict of goals between the increasing demand for agricultural goods by a growing world population and the requirements of sustainable production?	14–35
16.	undertake a self-critical evaluation of my role as a consumer with respect to the environmental, economic and social consequences of my own consumption patterns?	14/15, 26–33

Activity skills

Can I ...		
17.	present the results of various different forms of cultivation and farming (especially in the tropics) within the context of the growing local and global demand, objectively and using appropriate technical terminology?	12–33
18.	defend different perspectives and positions regarding land-use conflicts such as those between small-scale and agroindustrial farming operations and substantiate them with factual arguments?	12/13, 18/19, 22–33

Examination training

Is agribusiness economically and ecologically sustainable? The example of tomato cultivation in California

1. Locate California and describe the climatic conditions required for tomato cultivation and the spread of tomato farming in California.
2. Illustrate the development of tomato cultivation.
3. Assess the future prospects for agroindustrial tomato farming in California from both an economic and an environmental perspective.

These additional materials are required to complete the assignments:

M1 Atlas maps of your choice
M2 Kalifornien – Landwirtschaft, Diercke Weltatlas (2015), p. 221,5
M3 Kalifornien – Wasserwirtschaft, Diercke Weltatlas (2015), p. 221,6

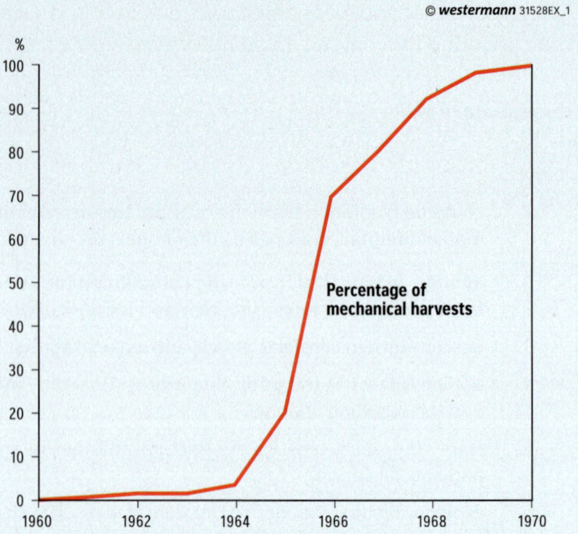

M5 Adaptation to mechanical tomato harvesting in California

Tomato harvester

Time period	Growing use of tomato harvesters
World War II	Labour shortage raises the question of the feasibility of mechanising the process of tomato harvesting.
1942	A tomato farmer suggests the possibility of breeding a tomato that can be harvested by machine to Prof. Hanna (University of California at Davis).
1949	Prof. Hanna presents the results of his breeding experiments. Work begins on the development of a tomato harvester.
1959	The University of California at Davis builds a prototype of the harvester.
1961	The harvester is used by farmers for the first time.
1964	The Bracero Program comes to an end. (It was based on a treaty between the US and Mexico regulating the supply of cheap Mexican labour to farmers.)
1966	A minimum wage is set for farm workers as well.
1970	The process of converting to mechanical harvesters for industrial tomato harvesting is completed.
1976	Deployment of the electronic sorter; 20% of the mechanical harvesters are fitted with it.

M4 The growing use of tomato harvesters

Year	Harvesting costs in US-$/acre		Percentage of machines in use
	Manual labour	Harvesters	
1960	467.1	–	0.0
1962	530.4	407.5	1.3
1964	573.7	458.6	3.5
1966	626.9	509.6	70.0
1968	680.9	560.6	92.0
1970	–	611.7	100.0

Source: Klohn, W., Windhorst, H.-W., Die Landwirtschaft der USA. VMG 1. Vechta, 2005

M6 Development of harvesting costs for industrially produced tomatoes and the percentage of mechanical harvesters in use

Year	Cultivated area (%)
1952–1956	33.4
1962–1966	52.1
1972–1976	74.2
1982–1986	81.1
1994	87.6
2002	93.3
2007	93.1
2012*	92,3

Sources: Klohn, W., Windhorst, H.-W., Die Landwirtschaft der USA. VMG 1. Vechta, 2005, S. 75, * USDA, Census of Agriculture, 2012.

M7 California's share of total farmland used in the industrial cultivation of tomatoes in the USA

Year	Number of farms	Cultivated area (ha)	Average size (ha)
1954	2,896	37,595	13.0
1964	1,883	64,421	34.2
1974	1,493	104,942	70.3
1982	1,558	102,159	65.6
1992	1,441	102,857	71,4
2002	1,769	134,780	76.2
2007	1,782	135,628	76.1
2012*	3,176	119,483	37.6

Sources: Klohn, W., Windhorst, H.-W.: Die Landwirtschaft der USA. VMG 1. Vechta, 2005, S. 773. *USDA, Census of Agiculture, 2012

Note: Figures in M8, M9 and M10 should be analysed in relation to one another, especially for 2012. Small farms are mostly food tomato operations (fresh market); the variability from year to year can be very great, e.g. due to market prices or overproduction and due to the allocation of water utilisation rights, which also leads to farms splitting up.

M8 The changing structure of tomato farming in California (industrial and food tomatoes)

Year	Number of farms	Average area under cultivation (in ha)
1956	not reported	34.6
1964	1072	52.8
1975	845	144.8
1987	445	188.8
2002	596	197,5
2007	490	245.6
2012*	631	164.2

Sources: Klohn, W., Windhorst, H.-W.: Die Landwirtschaft der USA. VMG 1. Vechta, 2005, p. 77. *USDA, Census of Agriculture, 2012.

M9 Changes in the number of farms engaged in industrial tomator production and average farm sizes in Califormina

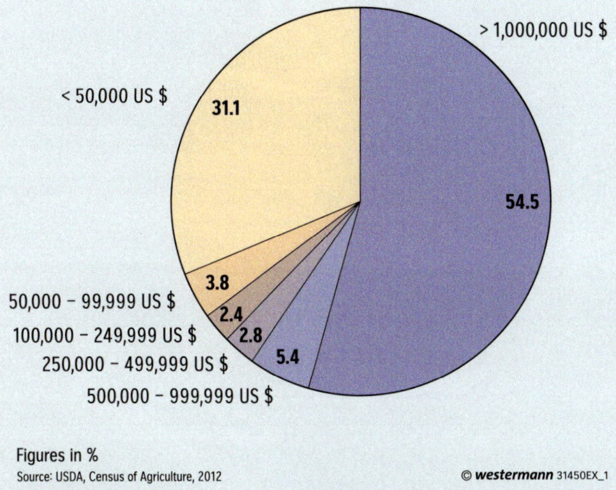

M10 Size distribution of farms engaged in industrial tomato production (in total sales value) (2012)

Drought of the century in the south-western United States *By Markus Becker*

The entire south-western United States is suffering from what appears to be a drought of record proportions. Fields are dried out, reservoirs are depleted and a state of emergency has been declared in California and other states. All of this could be a taste of what the future holds for this huge region.

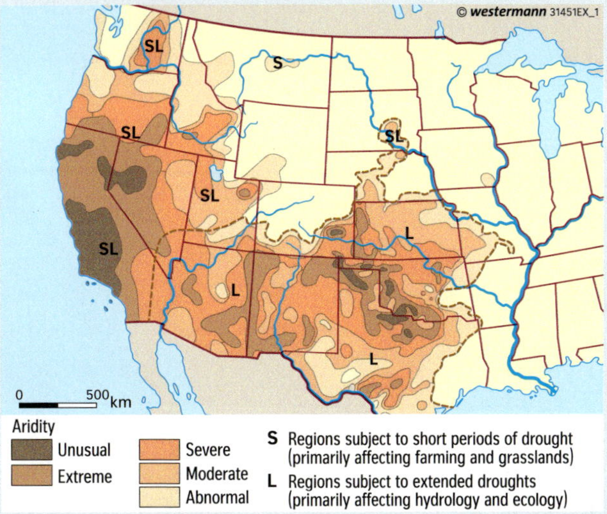

The plight is clearly visible from space. In January 2013, the Sierra Nevada range was covered with a thick layer of snow, as were the Cascades and the Coast Range in California. Now, just a year later, scarcely a spot of white can be seen on the satellite photo released by NASA, the US Aeronautics and Space Administration. In areas ordinarily covered by snow one now sees nothing but dry, barren ground. Governor Jerry Brown declared a state of emergency in California on January 17. Citizens and communities were called upon to conserve water wherever possible. Brown said that water consumption would have to be reduced by at least 20 percent. And the situation could worsen in the months to come. According to NASA, California meets one-third of its demand for water with melt water from the mountains, but the snow cover has now fallen to between 10 and 30 percent of its normal volume.

Temperatures have also reached record highs, rising to 22°C in San Francisco and 28°C in Oakland last week. Never before have Californians experienced such warm weather in January. The satellite photo shows a similarly dismal picture of the vegetation in California's Central Valley. The 600-km-long valley that looked bright green in January 2013 has since turned almost completely brownish. Many people living in the region now fear that the current situation may be only a hint of what is yet to come. The hope that things will return to normal may well be misleading. "Normal" doesn't necessarily mean wetter. Recent studies show that the 20th century was one of the wettest in the past 1,300 years. If so, the southern and western US could be facing major water supply problems, especially in view of the rapid population growth in the region.

Experts are uncertain about whether global warming will exacerbate the situation in the region in the months and years to come. Climate simulations indicate the likelihood that aridity will increase in the region. Eighteen models suggest that the south-western US will grow much dryer over the course of this century and only one predicts a moister climate for the region, as reported in an article published in Science magazine in 2007. According to the authors, the trend is already in progress.

Source: www.spiegel.de/wissenschaft/natur/notstand-in-kalifornien-rekord-duerre-trifft-suedwesten-der-usa-a-945235.html, accessed 19.01.2015

M11 State of emergency in California

Moß
Abbruch
Erdbau
Recycling

II Economic regions in transition

Contributing factors and consequences

Former cokery Kaiserstuhl: Demolition of the coal tower

M1 The textile industry was a major employer during the post-war years

M3 The textile industry in Asia: China? Much too costly!

The changing economy

From an agrarian to a service society

Sustainable economic success requires constant change. This simple rule applies at every level – to nations, regions, economic sectors and individual companies.In recent years, entire industries and economic regions have changed in keeping with this principle. Wholly new sectors – such as the high-tech industry – have emerged in some cases. This trend is attributable to progressive changes in the conditions of production, to technical and social change and to the impact of changing political influences. There are many examples of upward-striving, stagnating and shrinking industries in Germany and other countries. Whereas business enterprises in the textile coal and steel industries still played a significant role in the German economy 50 years ago, they are much less important today. At the same time, the importance of the impact on the labour market of young, modern start-up firms in the high-tech industry is clearly increasing. VW (Volkswagen) once produced almost exclusively in Germany, but now has facilities all over the world. The business strategy pursued by VW has been adopted by many other international corporations today.

Thus economic change affects not only individual corporate strategies but entire economic regions as well. The issue of "evolving economic regions" raises a number of interesting questions:

Which industries and sectors have been affected by change in recent years?
What factors have contributed to this process of economic change?
How do changes in economic regions relate to changes in the globalised world economy?
What problems do changes in the global economy pose for specific economic regions?
What are the consequences of change for specific economic regions?
What strategies are business enterprises pursuing in order to enhance their competitive strength?
How important is Germany as a business location?
How does government influence business decisions?

"Oberhausen has gained considerably in quality of life due to structural change"
(12.09.2014, WAZ)

"Losses in the millions: Russian investors avoid Germany as a business location"
(27.08.2014, Deutsche Wirtschafts Nachrichten)

"Daimler builds first car plant in Mexico"
(22.06.2014, Stuttgarter-Zeitung)

"Volkswagen Group produces its 700,000th vehicle in Kaluga"
(26.11. 2013, Volkswagen AG)

"Something is going on"
(11.09.2014, SEAT head of production Andreas Tostmann)

"Daimler invests millions in German Mercedes plants"
(10.09.2014, Reuters)

"Many company founders in Berlin and Silicon Valley are looking for the next big software idea"
(15.09.2014, Manager Magazin)

"Apple invites to the show"
(28.09.2014, Neue Zürcher Zeitung)

M2 The changing economy in headlines

M4 PHOENIX – a centre of iron and steel production in Dortmund for more than a century

M7 TechnologieZentrumDortmund – Europe's top address for researchers and entrepreneurs (2013)

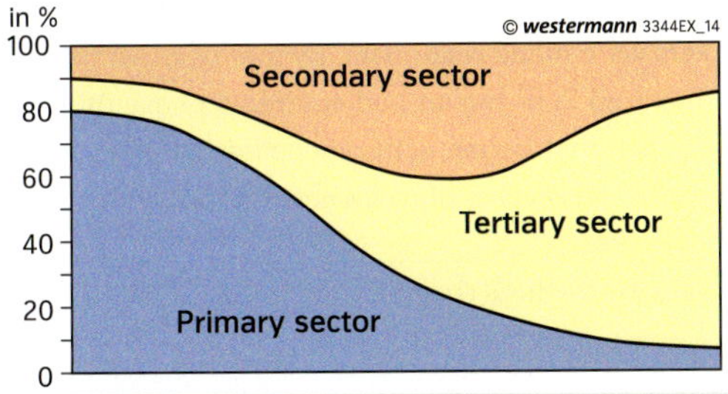

M5 Employment by economic sector according to the model developed by Fourastié

Primary sector (raw-material production)
Farming, forestry and fishing
Secondary sector (production of goods)
Processing industries/production of goods
Mining
Energy and water supply; sewage and waste disposal, remediation of environmental pollution
Construction industry / building
Tertiary sector (services)
Motor vehicle sales, maintenance and repair
Hospitality industry
Transportation and logistics
Information and communication
Financial and insurance services
Real estate and housing
Freelance, scientific/scholarly and technical services
Other business services
Public administration, defence, social security
Education
Health and social welfare
Art, entertainment and recreation
Miscellaneous services
Private housholds with domestic employees

Source: © Statistisches Bundesamt (Destatis) – own translation into English

M6 The system of economic sectors

The structure of an economy – that is, the roles and relative importance of the various economic sectors in the economy at large – changes significantly over the course of history. It can be measured in terms of the relative numbers of workers employed in the different sectors and the relative contributions of the respective sectors to total economic output. Jean Fourastié first described and explained fundamental, long-term changes in the economy and in society in his Sector Theory in 1954. According to his theory, the focal points of economic activity in all societies tend to shift from the primary to the secondary sector and eventually from the secondary to the tertiary sector.

Source: Schöpke, H., Wirtschaftsräume in Deutschland. Braunschweig, 2008, p. 8

M8 Sectoral subdivision of the economy

→ Structural change

The term structual change refers to the long-term and often inevitable changes in the structure of a socio-economic region.

Structural change can be broken down into the following elements:

Sectoral structural change comprises changes in the relative importance of the major economic sectors, i.e. the transition from an agrarian to an industrial society and from an industrial to a service society. In view of the increasing importance of information technology, we often speak of structural change involving a transition to the information society.

Intrasectoral change involves shifts in the organisational structures of business enterprises both between sectors and within individual sectors.

Finally, economic structures also change within regional economic sectors. This **regional structural change** is often a by-product of sectoral structural change, especially when a given region is home to an unusually large number of stagnating or shrinking indusries.

→ Agricultural society, Economic sector (primary, secondary, tertiary), Industrial society, Information-based society, Service-based society, Structural change (sectoral, intrasectoral, regional)

1. **Evaluate the headlines and photographs (M1 – M4, M7) in the context of "the changing economy".**
2. **Formulate hypotheses and questions on the subject of "evolving economic regions" (M1 – M4, M7).**
3. **Describe Fourastié's model (M5, M6, M8).**
4. **Cite examples of industrial sectors that have been affected by structural change (M6, technical terms).**

Spatial and structural change in old industrial regions

The Ruhr region – a coal and steel district in transition

"In the far west, where the sun is shrouded in dust, things are better, much better, than people think! In the far west. You're no beauty; your labour has turned you grey! You love yourself as you are. You're an honest soul; totally overbuilt, but that's what makes you what you are! You've got a pulse of steel. It's loudest at night. You're just too modest! The gold from your mines has brought us back up again, you flower of the district. Bochum, I come from you! Bochum, I'll cling to you always! Ah, good luck to you."

This song text by Herbert Grönemeyer was written in 1984 and evokes associations with the Ruhr Region for many people. But are those associations still current today? What do you associate with the Ruhr region today? How has the Ruhr region changed since the song was written?

1. Discuss the associations you have with the Ruhr region and compare them with those listed in M1.
2. (O) A Describe the economic development of the Ruhr region (M2 – M4, Atlas).
   B Illustrate the economic development of the Ruhr region with the aid of a mindmap (M2 – M4, Atlas).
3. The most recent structural change affecting the Ruhr region was triggered by the coal and steel crisis. Describe the causes and countermeasures in a diagram showing interactive effects. Use keywords such as "monostructure", "deindustrialisation", "reindustrialisation" and "tertiarisation" (M2 – M9).
4. Explain why the diversification of industrial and corporate structures serves as an important basis for structural change (M2, M3, M6 – M9).
5. (S) Discuss the phrase "symbol of structural change" as it applies to the Zollverein colliery.

→ Coal and steel industry, Deindustrialisation, Diversification, Economic sector (primary, secondary, tertiary), Industrialisation, Monostructure, Old industrial region, Re-industrialisation, Structural change (sectoral), Tertiarisation

M1 Typical associations with the Ruhr region

Industrialisation and deindustrialisation in the Ruhr region

The economic importance of the Ruhr region is largely attributable to its extensive hard-coal deposits. The region experienced an economic boom during the Age of Industrialisation around the turn of the 18th to the 19th century. During the era of reconstruction following the Second World War, the old economic structure was retained and the coal and steel industry continued to hold a dominant position. Under the influence of the liberalisation of the coal markets and slumping sales of expensive Ruhr coal, the Ruhr region suffered a "coal crisis". The number of mines and miners dwindled by half within a single decade. The steel industry also experienced a "steel crisis" in the 1970s due to the increasing use of plastic as a substitute for steel and to growing competition from suppliers of cheaper goods in the global market. Steel mills were forced to close and thousands of steelworkers were made redundant. By that point, at the latest, the monostructured Ruhr region had entered a phase of massive deindustrialisation that began with rationalisation measures and corporate mergers and eventually culminated in the demise of entire steel-producing sites.

M2 From boom to structural crisis

The reindustrialisation of the Ruhr region

The crisis that gripped the Ruhr region in spite of its favourable local conditions is attributable to the monostructural focus on the coal and steel industry and the global crisis affecting that economic sector, coupled with the high costs of production in the region. [...] There was virtually no mid-sized sector characterised by flexibility and the willingness to accept business risks. Nor was the region blessed with many educational institutions capable of training innovation-minded young people. [...] The region's poor image and the often less than cooperative behaviour of its municipalities made it less attractive for new business enterprises. [...] Thus the Ruhr region failed to catch on to the intraindustrial modernisation trend that was typical of the period. Instead, coal and steel were kept alive for many years by government subsidies [...] . The remaining large corporations, such as ThyssenKrupp, have since reacted and bid farewell to the mass production of cheap steel, opting instead to specialise in the production of high-quality steel and derivative products. [...] A new structural policy had set the stage [beginning in the late 1980s] for promising new approaches to reindustrialisation and the implementation of programmes designed to prevent full-scale deindustrialisation. The most noteworthy contributors were the new colleges, universities and research institutes that gave birth to numerous small, innovative companies. That led in turn to the emergence [...] of the first high-tech clusters [in which] the focus shifted to technologies of the future, such as logistics, microsystem engineering, information technology and biomedicine. Thus a number of mid-sized enterprises established themselves in the Ruhr Region, although large corporations [in the energy and chemicals sectors] continued to play a dominant role. [...] Yet in spite of these positive developments, the new industries have failed to stem the rising tide of unemployment in the industrial sector.

Source: Hoppe, W. et al, Das Ruhrgebiet im Strukturwandel, Braunschweig, 2010, pp. 30f

M3 The changing face of industry

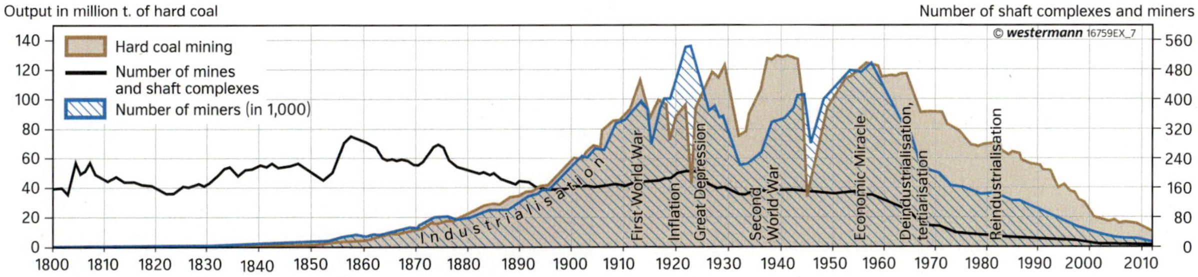

M4 Hard coal mining in the Ruhr region

- Monostructure with integrated economy
- Large-scale operations with thousands of workers
- Shortage of mid-sized businesses with flexible policies and willingness to accept risks
- High levels of pollution from industrial operations/towns and cities/traffic
- Heavy concentration of industrial facilities and towns/cities subject to agglomeration costs resulting from competition for land and deficiencies in infrastructure
- Few educational and cultural institutions
- Lack of growth industries / advanced technologies
- Massive government subsidies

Source: Schöpke, H., Wirtschaftsräume in Deutschland. Braunschweig, 2008, p. 74

M5 Characteristic features of old industrial regions

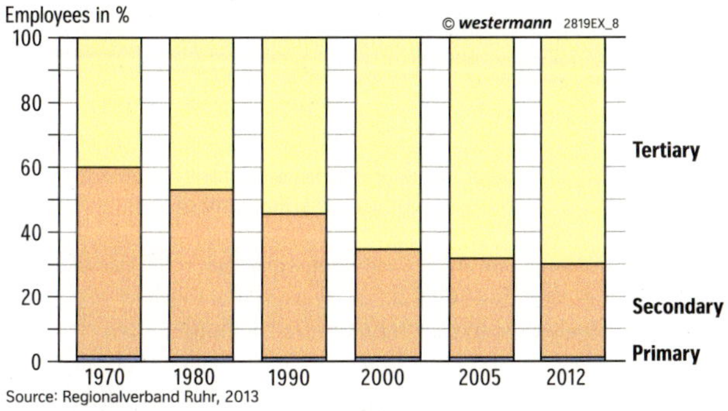

M6 Workers by economic sector in the Ruhr region

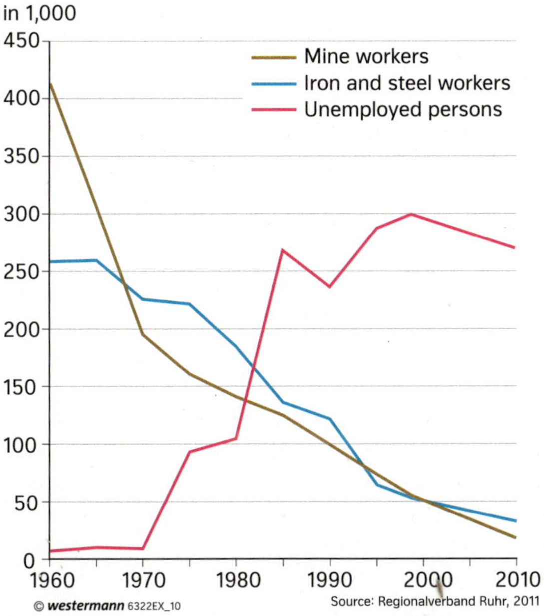

M7 Employment in coal and steel in the Ruhr region

Tertiarisation in the Ruhr region

Local communities have invested considerable effort in campaigns devoted to promoting diversification in monostructured areas. New branches of industry have emerged and new sources of income have been created in sectors outside of the coal and steel industry. Communities have attracted service enterprises, research and development institutes and business estates with highly diversified branch structures, and promoted the establishment of shopping centres and leisure and sport facilities. [The Ruhr region is now among the regions with the largest number of colleges and universities in Europe.] [...] Shopping centres that now attract customers from Belgium and the Netherlands (e.g. CentrO in Oberhausen) have also helped offset the deficit caused by the loss of mining operations. In an effort to enhance the environmental quality of the core zone, the former Ruhr Region Community Alliance developed and implemented a concept for the creation and preservation of regional green areas. During the "Internationale Bauausstellung Emscher Park (International Building Exhibition Emscher Park" (IBA)), the local public transport system was upgarded and a dense autobahn network was created. [...] Old buildings and the grounds of former industrial firms have been renovated, redesigned and preserved for future generations, from the disused smelting works in Duisburg ("Landschaftspark Nord") to the Zollverein colliery in Essen, which was named as UNESCO World Cultural Heritage Site in 2001, to the Gasometer in Oberhausen which has been refurbished as a concert and exhibition venue. No longer needed harbour facilities have been converted into restaurants, museums, office buildings and flats [...] .

Source: Schöpke, H., Wirtschaftsräume in Deutschland, Braunschweig, 2008, p. 75

M8 The Ruhr region as a service location

M9 The Zollverein colliery in Essen was an active coal mine from 1847 until 1986. Today, the buildings and grounds are protected as a UNESCO World Cultural Heritage Site.

Spatial and structural change in old industrial regions

CentrO in Oberhausen – an example of successful structural change?

The path from a community based around coal and steel to a service and industrial location has been rocky and the journey is still in progress. Virtually no other industrial region in western Germany has experienced structural change comparable to that which has taken place in the Ruhr region in recent decades. The CentrO leisure and shopping park in Oberhausen serves as an example of how such a process can take place, how complex and profound the changes have been since the "coal and steel" era and how quickly they have been effected.

ⓞ 1. Outline the process of structural change with reference to CentrO in Oberhausen (M1 – M4, M7, M8) by:
   A describing the changes that have taken place since 1965 in a text.
   B listing the changes that have taken place since 1965 in a table.
2. Characterise the structure and the dimensions of CentrO in Oberhausen (M3 – M6, M8).
3. Summarise the opinions expressed regarding CentrO and your critical responses to them (M5).
4. Answer the headline question – "CentrO in Oberhausen – an example of successful structural change?" – with reference to the materials in M1 – M8.

ⓞ 5. Conduct a search for other projects that represent structural change in the Ruhr Region, such as
   A PHOENIX Lake in Dortmund.
   B the Emscher landscape park.

ⓢ 6. You are a journalist writing for an interregional daily newspaper. Write an objective article about CentrO in Oberhausen.

→ Coal and steel industry, Economic sector (primary, secondary, tertiary), Service-based society, Structural change (sectoral, intrasectoral, regional)

CentrO under construction

1929	Amalagamation of the towns of Sterkrade, Osterfeld and Oberhausen to form the city of Oberhausen. Located in the centre of the three city districts were the grounds of Gutehoffnungshütte (founded in 1873).
1968	Acquisition of Gutehoffnungshütte (iron and steel production plant) in Oberhausen by Thyssen AG
Beginning in the mid-1980s	Declining production volume at Gutehoffnungshütte resulting in limited use of the grounds for industrial operations
1988	The gasometer is shut down.
1991	A British investment group purchases the grounds of the former Gutehoffnungshütte.
24.09.1992	Demolition of old plant facilities begins on 83 hectares of the former Gutehoffnungshütte
24.09.1994	Laying of the foundation stone for CentrO
12.09.1996	Opening of the CentrO shopping centre
27.09.2012	Opening of the extension wing in CentrO (approx. 17,000 m² of sales space)

(Source: CentrO Management GmbH, Oberhausen – eine Stadt im Strukturwandel, www.centro.de, accessed 13.02.2015)

M2 From steelworks to the "New Centre" in Oberhausen

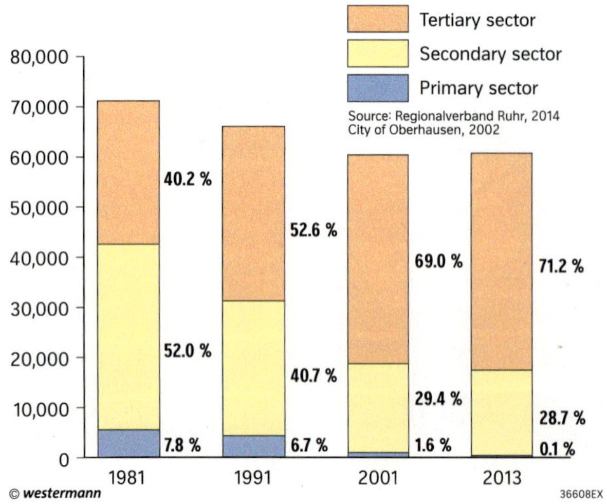

M1 Employment figures by economic sector in Oberhausen

CentrO is one of the most ambitious structural-change projects in the Ruhr region. It encompasses a number of different subprojects – the shopping centre, the Coca-Cola Oasis, the Promenade, the leisure park and the business park. CentrO is the heart and centrepiece of the "Neue Mitte", in which you will also find the Gasometer, the [...] ARENA (with seating for 12,000 people), the CineStar multiplex cinema, the Adventury Park, Oberhausen SEA LIFE, the LEGOLAND Discovery Centre, the Marina, a smart centre and the Metronom Theatre. More than 250 retail stores are distributed over two levels comprising 116,000 square metres of sales space. Covering a total of 83 hectares, CentrO is the largest shopping and leisure centre in Europe. It attracts millions of visitors every year. [...] Free parking is available for 14,000 cars. A road built by the city guarantees fast and comforable travel to and from CentrO by bus or rail. [...]
Designed in a Mediterranean style, the Coca-Cola Oasis is directly adjacent to the shopping centre. More than 20 different gastronomy stands offer a diverse range of food and beverages. Seating is available for 1,100 guests in the Oasis. [...]

Source: CentrO Mangement GmbH, CentrO – Daten & Fakten, 11/2014, www.centro.de, accessed 13.02.2015

M3 An overview of CentrO

Total investment volume	
Private and public funding	**Over 1.15 bill. €**
Shopping centre	460 million
Arena Oberhausen	51 million
Leisure park	36 million
Business park	153 million
OTHC sports centre	10 million
Promenade with multiplex cinema	51 million
Interior finishing by tenants and partners	163 million
Infrastructure (internal)	64 million
Local public transport line	141 million
Enlargement of the "Neue Mitte" interchange	22.5 million
Optimisation of traffic conditions on Essener Straße and creation of 2,000 additional parking spaces in P9/P10	11 million

Source: CentrO Management GmbH, CentrO – Daten & Fakten. 11/2014, www.centro.de, accessed 13.02.2015)

M4 CentrO – investments since groundbreaking

"Oberhausen in three days" is a package deal recently offered by local tourist agencies. Apart from a tour on the Rhine-Herne Canal, visitors who wish to experience "Oberhausen in three days" apparently needn't leave the Neue Mitte district at all. [...]
More than 15 years after its opening, CentrO has long since become much more than a shopping centre. It is the heart of what experts call an "urban entertainment centre", while critics view it as a soulless consumer landscape. It is an agglomeration of stores, pubs and restaurants, and entertainment offerings. [...]
Representatives of the city of Oberhausen regard CentrO as a showcase structural-change project. Today, industry has largely disappeared from Oberhausen, the "cradle of Ruhr industry". People are thankful for CentrO as a job and tourist engine, despite its negative effects – one of which is the demise of the "old centre", for which CentrO is at least partly responsible. And the temple of consumption has also failed to live up to expectations regarding employment. CentrO now claims to have created 4,000 jobs. Yet including suppliers and other service providers, the total comes closer to the figure of 10,000 with which the project was originally advertised. Critics, on the other hand, speak of a mere redistribution process and complain about the quality of the jobs in question. [...]
According to its management, some 23 milllion visitors come to CentrO every year. The city's tourist experts rave about a "magnetic attraction". The significant increase in bookings for overnight accommodation is attributed at least in part to the "Neue Mitte". Some residents of Oberhausen still express dissatisfaction with the "city within the city", however. And CentrO doesn't make it easy for even long-time residents to love it. When the local anti-nuclear-power initiative requested permission to hold its regular vigil outside the gates of the shopping centre following the Fukushima disaster, arguing that the nearby "Platz der guten Hoffnung" had become the most heavily frequented spot in Oberhausen, they were brusquely turned away. "Private property", they were told.

Source: Sibum, H., Das Centro ist das ungeliebte Vorzeigeprojekt Oberhausens, 12.05.2012, www.derwesten.de., accessed 09.11.2014

M5 CentrO is Oberhausen's unloved showcase project

Traffic connections
- Direct access to Autobahns A2, A3, A42, A40 and A516
- A new tram and bus line with a separate CentrO stop
- Travel time to Düsseldorf International Airport: 30 min.
- 14,000 free parking places

Catchment area
- 3 million people can travel to CentrO in 30 minutes.
- 12 million people can travel to CentrO in 60 minutes.
- 30 million people can travel to CentrO in 2 hours.
- 60 million people live within 250 km of CentrO.

Source: Knetsch, J., CentrO Management GmbH, CentrO – Daten & Fakten, 11/2014, www.centro.de, accessed 13.02.2015

M6 CentrO – traffic connections and catchment area

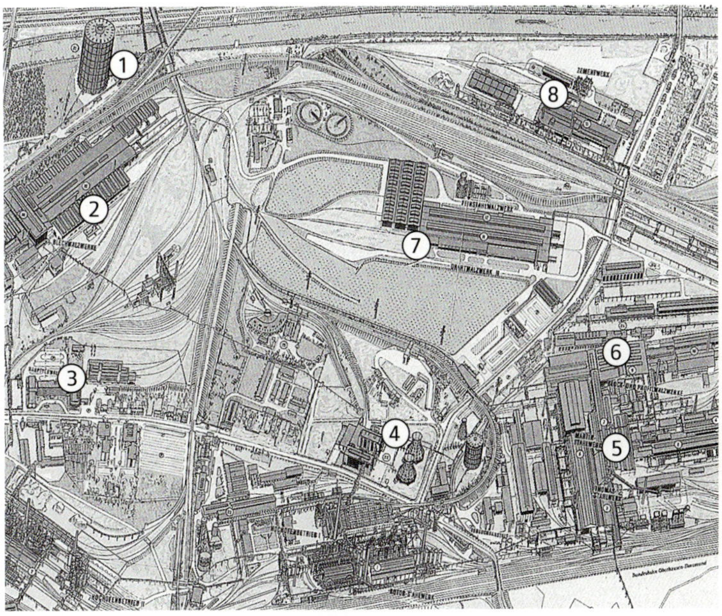

1 Gas tank, 2 rolling mills, 3 main admin building, 4 steam plant, 5 steel mills, 6 beam and section mills, 7 rod and finishing mills, 8 cement plant

M7 Oberhausen – smelting works, 1965

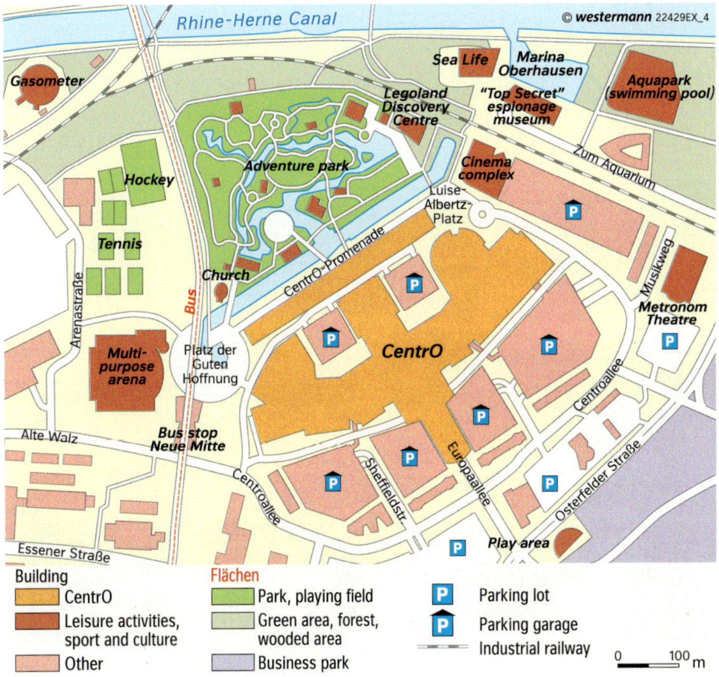

M8 Oberhausen – the CentrO shopping and leisure park, 2014

Location factors and decisions regarding location

Agonising choices

Would you open a rainwear shop in the Sahara?
Where should a baker set up shop? Where would you locate as the owner of a sporting goods shop?
The right choice of location can determine the success or failure of a business. An entrepreneur will establish a plant only at a location where he can produce economically and profitably. He must weigh the advantages and disadvantages of a potential future location very carefully.
The reasons for selecting the location for a business are generally referred to as "location factors". What location factors are relevant for businesses in different sectors? Do they differ from one region to the next or are they much the same eveywhere?
Do certain location factors become less important over time?

1. With reference to the newly established Star Park Halle A14 industrial estate, work out a set of reasons why a high-tech industrial firm might choose to locate there (M1 – M5, Atlas).
2. Show why several different location factors play crucial roles in the selection of the right location for a given business (M3 – M6).
3. List the basic concepts of Weber's location theory with reference to a concrete example and discuss the extent to which they are still valid today (M7 – M8).
4. Ⓞ With the aid of the materials in M3 – M5, make a justified recommendation for a choice of location for:
   A a newsstand in your school district.
   B a furniture store in your school district.
5. Ⓢ Design a brochure advertising for the location of an industrial firm in your school district.

→ Globalisation, Industrial location theory (A. Weber), Location factor (soft, hard), Sales market

M1 The Star Park Halle A 14 industrial estate – Halle (Saale)

Star Park Halle A 14 industrial estate – expansive, ideally located, fully developed

230 ha from a single source +++ Top location and top infrastructure +++ maximum building freedom +++ legal and planning security +++ building permits issued on short notice +++ available immediately +++ especially well suited for large-scale industrial settlements +++ priority funding

Perfect conditions for your production site:
An expansive estate in the Halle business area in the heart of central Germany. Perfectly located with direct access to the A14, in the immediate vicinity of the Leipzig-Halle Intercontinental Airport and other important industrial firms, the Star Park has ideal logistical and travel connections. The estate offers excellent conditions for building and development as well as fully developed utility services [...].

Your benefits in terms of labour productivity:
The region is home to a strong pool of experienced industrial workers and well-trained college and university graduates. Here, know-how is coupled with moderate wage and salary costs in combination with flexible 24/7 work schedules – ideal preconditions for efficient production. [...]

Home to internationally successful industrial firms
IT Solar of Norway and GA Pack of China have established production centres in the Star Park estate. They are regarded as stars of their industry and benefit from the top location along Orionstraße and Polarisstraße. The "Walk of Fame" in the Star Park is occupied by Enka Tecnica, a company that manufactures spinnerets for the production of plastic fibres, and a logistics centre established by eBay as a provider of e-commerce solutions in the fulfilment business, thus enhancing the radiance of this premium location in the heart of Europe.

Source: EVGmbH – Entwicklungs- und Verwaltungsgesellschaft Halle-Saalkreis mbH, Industriegebiet Star Park Halle A 14. www.starpark-halle.de, accessed 17.11.2014

M2 Advertisement by the city of Halle (Saale) for the Star Park Halle A 14 industrial estate

Before a firm moves to a given location, its managers take a close look at the local conditions under which it will be operating. The location must meet two basic requirements, [...]. First of all, it must have a positive impact on operating costs. In other words, it must either be possible to produce more cheaply there than elsewhere, or the location must offer advantages in terms of time. Secondly, each location must offer distinctive characteristics. It must distinguish itself clearly from other locations in terms of size, price and quality. Location factors are divided into two groups: hard and soft factors. Hard location factors are more or less calculable and impact directly on a company's balance sheet. [...] Soft location factors are difficult to quantify and have only an indirect impact on operations. They reflect subjective preferences and are not subject to direct cost-benefit analysis.

Source: Schöpke, H., Wirtschaftsräume in Deutschland, Braunschweig, 2008, pp. 12f

M3 Is every location right for every company?

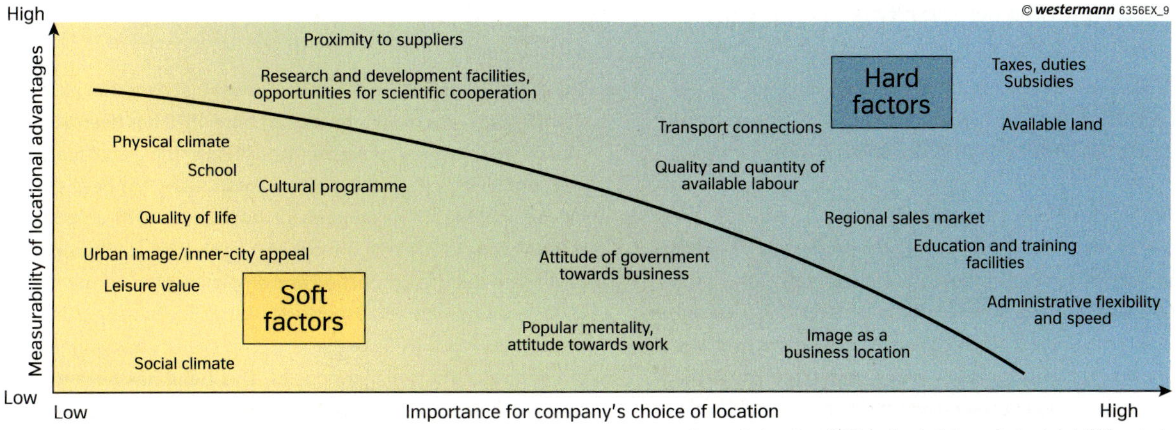

Source: Grabow, B. et al: Weiche Standortfaktoren. Stuttgart et al, 1995, revised

M4 The importance of location factors in the high-tech industry

Hard location factors	Soft location factors
– Raw material supply – Supply and disposal – Saleable land and buildings – Traffic infrastructure – Proximity to research facilities – Energy costs – Labour supply (quantity, quality, wage level) – Land prices/real estate prices – Market volume – Buying power – Available services – Environmental regulations – Persistence – Taxes/duties – State/local benefits – Agglomeration advantages/ benefits of proximity – Political, economic and social stability – Climate	– **Personal** • Residential quality (rents, transportation connections • Leisure and local recreational opportunities • Education and training opportunities • Cultural programme • Medical care • Shopping facilities • Environmental quality (landscape appeal, ecological situation) • Mentality of the local population (social acceptance, hospitality, etc.) – **Business-related** • Location image • Business climate and attitude towards business © westermann 31521EX_1

M5 Hard and soft location factors

One of the earliest location theories developed from the perspective of an individual business operation was published by Alfred Weber in 1909. Weber's theory [...] focused on the goal of minimising transport costs.
According to his theory, an industrial firm locates at the point between its source of raw materials and its sales market at which it can produce at the most favourable cost. If material costs resulting from major losses in quantity, weight and value are the decisive location factor, production facilities will be located as close as possible to the sources of raw materials. If, on the other hand, transport costs are low, the sales aspect becomes the determining factor and the location shifts closer to the sales market.
It may well have been just that simple during the early years of the Age of Industrialisation. But the economic landscape has changed over the course of the last century, and these changes have impacted on both location theories and approaches to the choice of location.

Source: Schöpke, H., Wirtschaftsräume in Deutschland, Braunschweig, 2008, pp. 10f

M7 Alfred Weber's industrial location theory

Many traditional principles governing the choice of location are no longer applicable today. New developments in communication, travel and transportation (e.g. the increasing importance of the internet and the growth of world trade), technical progress in the fields of production and organisation (e.g. global production concepts and networks) and changes in global political constellations (e.g. economic alliances) have led to a reassessment of business and industrial locations. Under the influence of globalisation, business enterprises often move to locations abroad and/or produce at multiple locations. In many cases, several firms produce a single product within the context of an international division of labour.

M6 Location factors in the context of globalisation

→ Globalisation

Globalisation is a dynamic process involving the worldwide integration of business relationships. The process has been triggered by changes in basic political, institutional, technological and economic conditions. Globalisation can be measured by comparing the growth rates of foreign and domestic activities. The declining importance of political boundaries leads to an intensification of global competition for location.

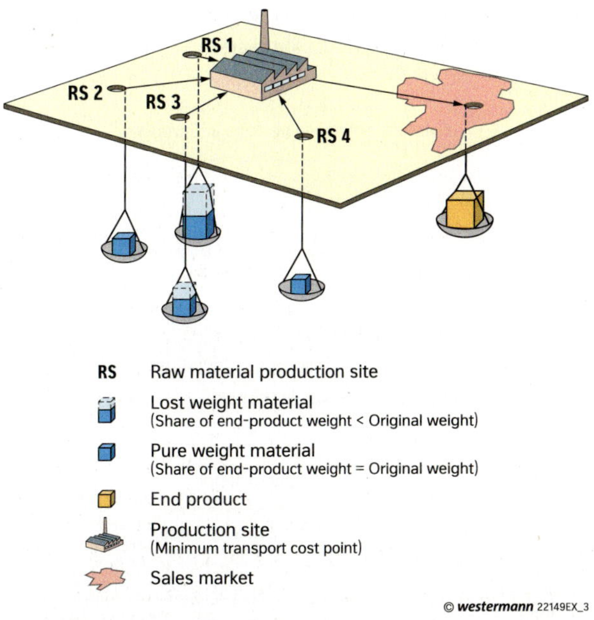

M8 Minimum transport cost point (A. Weber)

The secondary sector – innovative and global

The German textile industry – ensuring viability through innovation

Where do the clothes in your closet come from?
In which countries were your T-shirt and your jeans produced? They most probably came from East Asian or Southeast Asian countries.
Although Germany ranked among the world's most important textile-producing countries (with production sites in Baden-Württemberg and eastern Westphalia, among other regions) for many years, many German firms have disappeared from the market today. The EU alone imported clothing and accessories worth more than 45 billion euros from Asia in 2012. Forty-two percent of all imported clothing comes from China, and 12 percent from Bangladesh.
What role does Germany play in the highly competitive global textile market? What types of textiles are still produced in Germany?

1. Describe the changing trends in the German textile industry over the past seveal decades (M1–M5).
2. "Developments in the German textile industry are driven by location factors." Offer a critical assessment of this statement (M1–M5).
3. Explain Kondratiev's theory of long waves (M7).
4. Evaluate the assertion that the sixth Kondratiev wave has already begun (M7).
5. (O) Analyse the phases of the product life cycle (M6, M8) with reference to a product from:
   A the textile industry,
   B the automotive industry,
   C the electronics industry.
6. Cite an example illustrating how a product life cycle can be extended (M8).
7. (S) Classify the Kondratiev cycles and their corresponding basic innovations by major economic regions.

→ Basic innovation, Kondratiev's theory of long waves, Low-wage country, Product life cycle

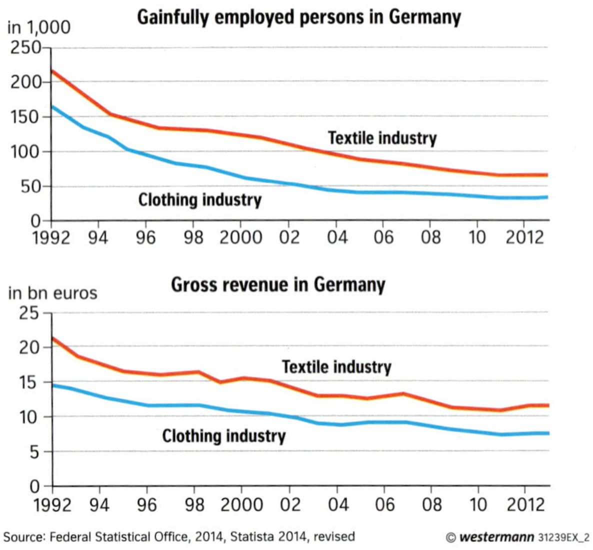

M1 Workers and revenues in the textile and clothing industry

The sustained process of structural change that has taken place in the German textile and clothing industry since 1970 has been accompanied by a relative worsening of its position in the global market [...]. The number of firms and workers in the industry has been declining for years. Of the 7,704 companies in business in 1970, only 545 were still operating in 2013 – a cutback of roughly 93%. [...] The persistent downward trend in production and employment in Germany, which impacts on imports and exports as well, is attributable to improvements in productivity as well as the progressive internationalisation of the textile and clothing industry. This trend has been driven by cost pressure generated by international competition, which the clothing industry is trying to counteract by shifting production to low-wage countries (especially in Central and Eastern Europe). [...] The German textile and clothing industry will be compelled to concentrate on its particular strengths. [...] Strong, innovative brands and designs marketed by German textile and clothing firms are in demand all over the world, and serve as guarantors for success in international trade [...]. Producers are also investing in research and development. Thanks to its flexibility and innovative power, the textile industry has managed to improve its market position in promising business segments (e.g. technical textiles), and gain a larger share of the export market.

Source: Federal Ministry for Economic Affairs and Energy, Textil und Bekleidung, www.bmwi.de/Redaktion/DE/Artikel/Branchenfokus/Industrie/branchenfokus-textil.html, accessed 25.09.2014

M2 Structural change in the textile and clothing industry

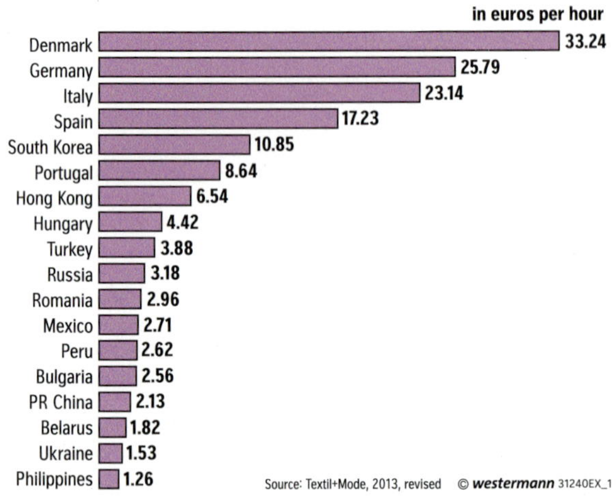

M3 Labour costs in the textile industry (2011)

M4 Technical textiles defy the trend

German textile and clothing industry experts realised early on that innovation can contribute significantly to efforts to tap new growth potential, reduce cost pressure in the industry and promote the successful and sustainable operation of production sites in Germany as well. [...] Particularly important in this context are technical textiles. According to the trade association, they account for over 50% of total revenue in the German textile industry. [...]
The production of technical textiles in Germany benefits from the fact that many customer firms produce locally, and German industry is quite capable of integrating different industrial sectors in the process of developing complex product solutions. This intersectoral production alliance gives Germany a strategic advantage over other national locations. [...]
The spectrum of potential applications for technical textiles is extensive and growing steadily. [...] Technical textiles are well suited for use in the clothing industry. Articles of clothing based on technical textiles protect wearers against external influences [...] or help regulate bodily functions (e.g. safety and work clothing or sportswear). [...] Automobile manufacturers use technical textiles to enhance passenger comfort or reduce vehicle energy consumption. Familiar examples of technical textiles employed in the automotive industry include airbags, safety belts and seat covers [...].
Source: Deutsche Bank Research, Textil und Bekleidungsindustrie, 2011, pp. 4ff

M5 Technical textiles as growth drivers

One dynamic, cyclical location theory originated in the 1960s. According to Vernon's **product life cycle theory,** the dynamic factor of time also impacts on the process of location development. A given product passes through various ageing processes in which the producing firm poses different location requirements and may change locations accordingly. When a new product is to be introduced, for example, appropriately qualified personnel and suppliers play important roles, which means that a location in the home country is probably most appropriate. During the growth phase, the firm may consider foreign locations. Cheap labour and relatively inexpensive production conditions become increasingly important and moving to a location abroad becomes a conceivable option.

M6 Product life cycle

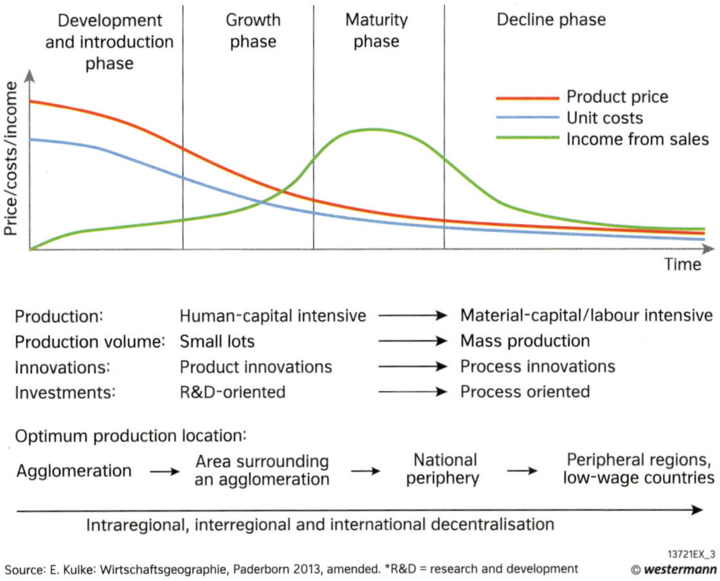

Source: E. Kulke: Wirtschaftsgeographie, Paderborn 2013, amended. *R&D = research and development

M8 Phases of a product life cycle

→ Kondratiev's theory of long waves

In the past, inventions and the basic innovations they generate have repeatedly triggered economic upswings, as in the case of the spinning machine in the textile industry in the 19th century. Technical innovations gave rise to new branches of industry, such as the plastics and microelectronics industries. Upswings often lead to downturns in other sectors and even to economic decline in entire regions. The Russian economist Nikolai Dmitriyevich Kondratiev (1882 – 1938) recognised that these innovation processes trigger wavelike phases of economic growth and decline. Kondratiev waves can extend over several decades. The interval between the emergence of basic innovations is also referred to as the Kondratiev cycle. This interval appears to have diminished in recent years under the influence of the increasingly rapid succession of basic innovations.
Geographic shifts in location also occur over the course of these Kondratiev cycles. New economic regions take shape in response to basic innovations, while the importance of certain old centres diminishes. Thus like a product, a region may also experience a life cycle during which income, employment and prosperity initially increase, only to decline again later on.

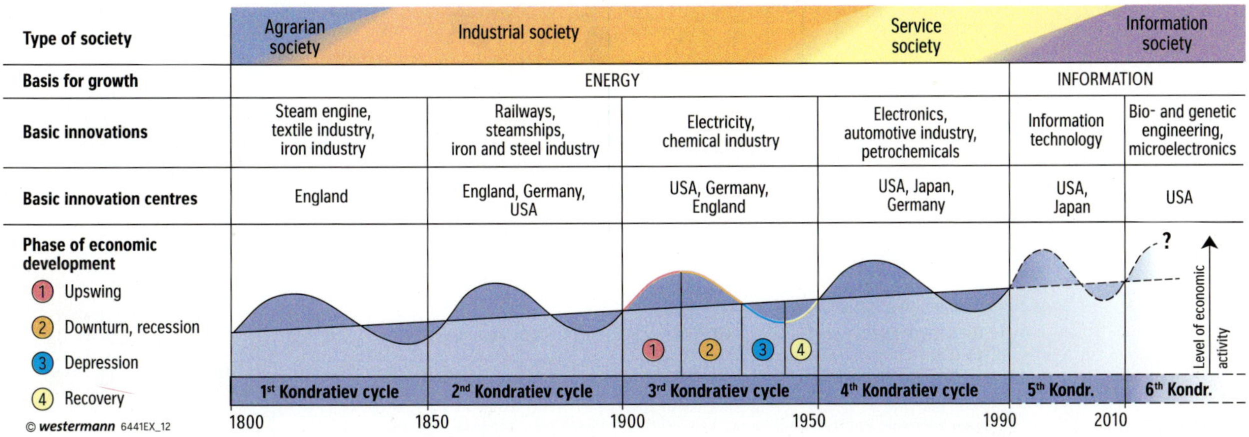

M7 Basic innovations provide the impulse for industrialisation cycles (Kondratiev's theory of long waves)

The secondary sector – innovative and global

Volkswagen, a global player – building a future with new production sites?

"Ever larger, faster and more effective" is a slogan often heard in the global market. Large global corporations have grown strong on the basis of that spirit. According to a survey conducted by the German Chamber of Commerce and Industry (DIHK, 2013), nearly one out of every two German industrial firms plans to invest abroad. Foreign production by German automobile manufacturers rose to a new record level in 2012. A total of 7.8 million German passenger cars were produced abroad. These firms have production plants and subsidiaries all over the world, and are capable of amassing considerable economic power by virtue of their size and capital resources. In certain circumstances they may even exert influence on political decisions.

1. Using Volkswagen as an example, outline the strategies and structures of a global player (M1, M2, Atlas).
2. Discuss the motives that prompted Volkswagen to establish a production site in Kaluga, Russia (M1 – M7, Atlas).
3. (O) Discuss the advantages and disadvantages of the new Volkswagen production site in Kaluga (M3 – M7) from the point of view of:
   A the plant manager in Kaluga,
   B a worker at the Kaluga plant,
   C a politician in Kaluga.
4. Express an opinion on the headline question, "Volkswagen, a global player – building a future with new production sites?" (M1 – M7).
5. (S) Develop a questionnaire you could use for an operational investigation into the subject of "expansion abroad".

→ Direct foreign investments, Global player, Multinational corporation

→ Multinational corporation

Multinational corporations, also known as global players, are business enterprises that operate worldwide through subsidiaries, branches and/or production facilities. Multinationals seeking to establish subsidiaries abroad must invest directly in the respective countries. They take advantage of favourable production conditions, such as low wages, liberal environmental regulations and low energy costs, while profiting from close proximity to markets and customers, lower transport costs and fewer import duties.

1937	The "Gesellschaft zur Vorbereitung des Deutschen Volkswagens mbH" is founded.
1947	Export operations begin: five limousines are delivered to the Netherlands.
1952	The Volkswagen Canada Ltd. sales company is founded.
1953	The Volkswagen do Brasil Ltda. sales company is founded.
1955	The Volkswagen of America Inc. sales company is established.
1964	Volkswagen de Mexico, S.A. de C.V. is founded.
1985	The Shanghai-Volkswagen Automotive Company is founded and production is launched.
1991	The FAW-Volkswagen joint venture is founded in Changchun (PR China).
2007	The production facillity in Kaluga, Russia, is commissioned.
2009	A new Volkswagen plant is opened in Pune, India.
2011	A new Volkswagen plant is opened in Chattanooga,Tennessee (USA)
2014 – 2018	VW plans to invest another 1.2 million euros in Russia.

Source: Volkswagen AG, www.volkswagen.de, accessed 17.11.2014

M2 Volkswagen – milestones on the way to becoming a global corporation

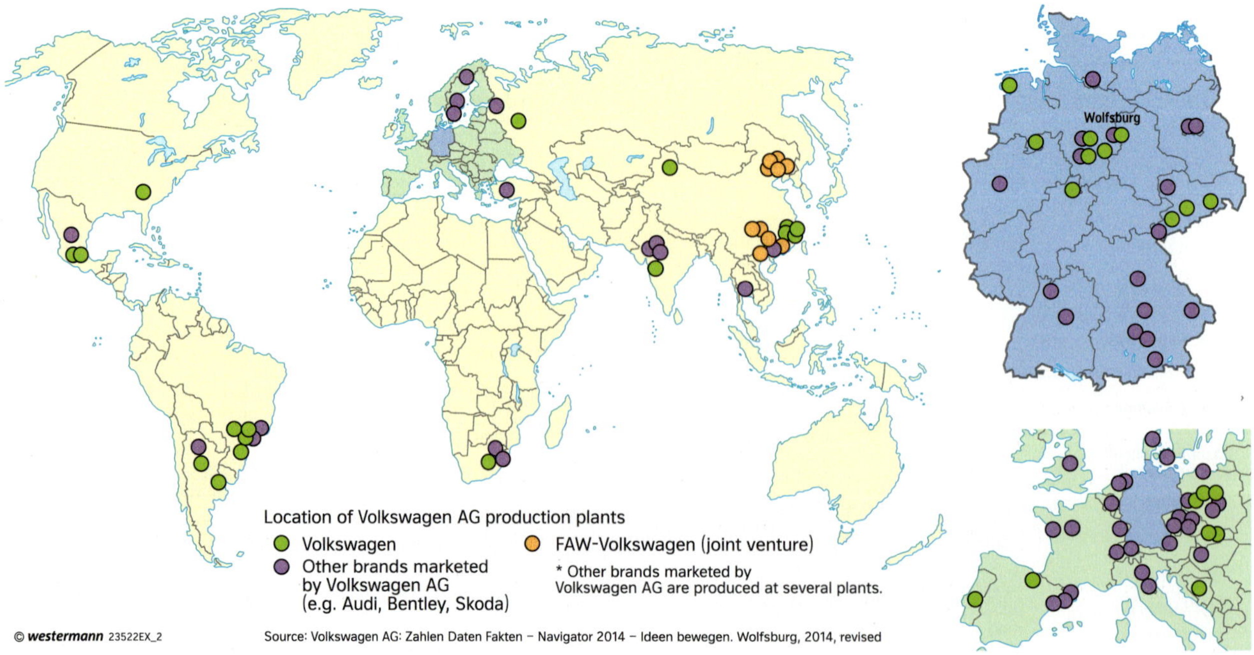

Source: Volkswagen AG: Zahlen Daten Fakten – Navigator 2014 – Ideen bewegen. Wolfsburg, 2014, revised

M1 Locations of Volkswagen AG production plants (2013)

M3 Assembly line at the Kaluga plant

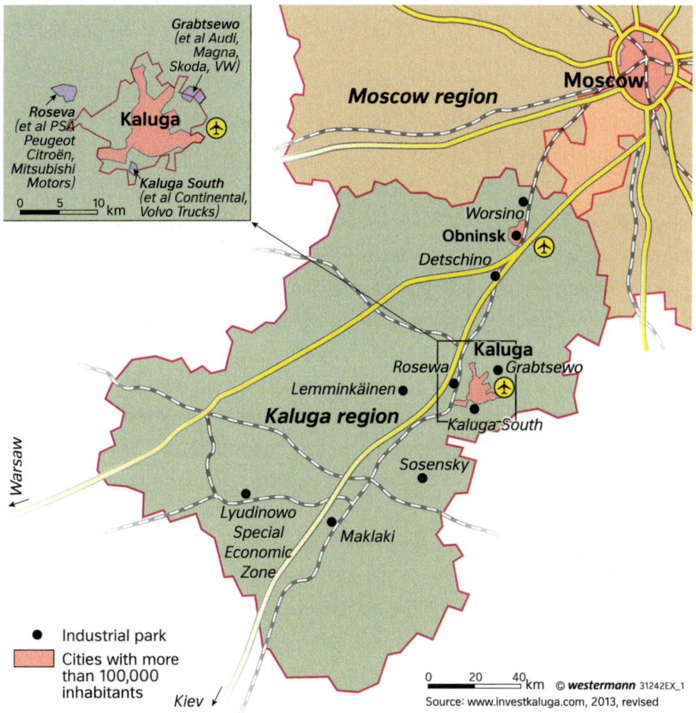

M5 The Kaluga economic region

The Volkswagen Group

is one of the largest foreign investors in the Russian automotive industry. Roughly 1.3 billion euros were invested in local production facilities and new models for the Russian market between 2006 and 2013. The Volkswagen Group will have invested another 1.2 billion euros in the Kaluga plant alone by the year 2017.

Volkswagen in Kaluga

"With 5,500 direct jobs and its strong commitment to the training and qualification of its employees, Volkswagen is an important destination on our business delegation's tour and an impressive example of Lower Saxony's successful engagement in Russia", noted Prime Minister and Supervisory Board member Stephan Weil on the occasion of his visit [Nov. 2013]. [...]

Since November 2007

Volkswagen has been producing vehicles for the Russian market in order to save the high import duties (25% at the time) by producing locally. The plant, which is situated in the Grabzevo technology park, occupies an area of 400 hectares. Three Volkswagen models are currently produced there: the VW Tiguan and Polo and the ŠKODA Fabia. The group also launched contract production at the facility of its partner GAZ in Nizhny Novgorod in 2012. Local component production was launched at a new engine plant in 2015. The group also plans to build a logistics centre near Moscow.

The Volkswagen Group Rus

unites the activities in support of the seven Group brands, Volkswagen passenger vehicles, Audi, ŠKODA, SEAT, Volkswagen utility vehicles, Bentley and Lamborghini, in the Russian market. Overall sales in Russia rose to 316,000 vehicles in 2012, an increase of 38 percent over the preceding year. Of that total, roughly 175,000 vehicles were produced in Kaluga.

Source: Volkswagen AG, Volkswagen Konzern produziert 700 000stes Fahrzeug in Kaluga, press release 26.11.2013, www.volkswagen-media-services.com, accessed 24.02.2015

M4 The Volkswagen Group produces in Kaluga

According a report in the industry and business journal *Automobilwoche*, Volkswagen cut back production in Russia in response to the weak rouble and the effects of the Ukraine crisis. Only 120,000 vehicles were to roll off the assembly line in 2014, instead of the 150,000 that were originally planned. [...]
Volume sales by Volkswagen in Russia fell by 10 percent by the end of July and deliveries by all German manufacturers were down by 14 percent after the first seven months of 2014. A VW spokesman refused to comment on the report, although he pointed out that production would be discontinued at the Kaluga plant for a period of ten days.

Source: Industriemagazin, VW fährt Produktion in Russland zurück, 08.09.2014, www.industriemagazin.at, accessed 19.09.2014

M6 VW cuts production in Russia

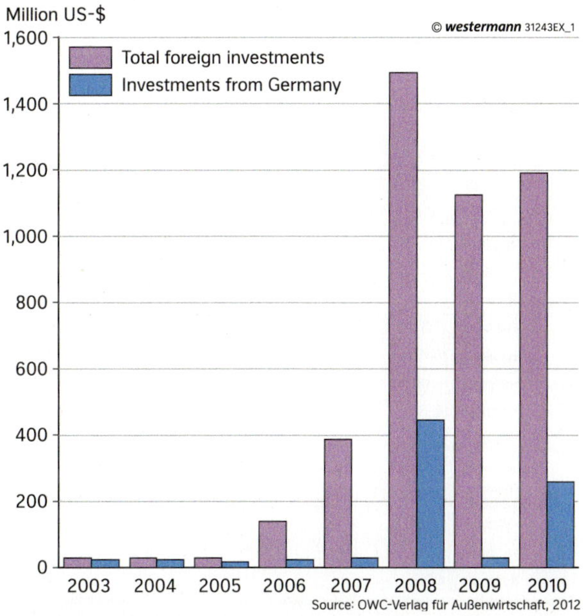

M7 Investments from Germany and other countries in the Kaluga region

Clusters – hotspots of innovation

Silicon Valley – a high-tech location with a bright future?

Silicon Valley, which takes its name from the element used in the production of semiconductors, is located southwest of San Francisco in the southern San Francisco Bay area and its extension in the broad Santa Clara Valley between two chains of California's Coast Ranges.
Because of its historical origin and development, Silicon Valley is regarded as the world's most prominent showcase cluster. The cooperation area has become a globally recognised model cluster by virtue of the many interfaces between the scientific and business communities. The extent of the local diversity of networked fields of science and technology is extraordinary.
Where do the strengths of this region lie? Does this kind of economic development have a downside? What does this concentration of high-tech firms mean for the people who live in the area?

1. Describe the industrial structure of Silicon Valley (M1–M4, Atlas).
2. Name the location factors for high-tech industry in Silicon Valley (M1–M8, Atlas).
3. Analyse the development and significance of Silicon Valley as a high-tech location (M1–M8).
4. ⓞ A Examine the strengths and weaknesses of Silicon Valley in view of the heavy concentration of high-tech firms (M1–M11, Internet).
   B Perform a SWOT analysis of the Silicon Valley high-tech location (M1–M11, Internet).
5. Discuss the headline question "Silicon Valley – a high-tech location with a bright future?" (M1–M11, Internet).
6. ⓢ Classify Silicon Valley in accordance with Kondratiev's theory of long waves and explain your reasoning.

→ Advantages/ disadvantages of agglomeration, Cluster, High-tech industry, High-tech region, Value chain

Business enterprises	Annual revenue in 2013 (in milllion US-$)	Changes in revenue from the preceding year (in %)	Profit for the year 2013 (in million US-$)
Apple	173,992	+ 6 %	37,031
Hewlett-Packard	112,093	– 6 %	5,306
Google	59,825	+ 16 %	12,920
Intel	52,708	– 1 %	9,620
Cisco Systems	47,873	+ 1 %	8,173
Oracle	37,901	+ 2 %	11,116
eBay	16,047	+ 14 %	2,856
Gilead Sciences	11,202	+ 15 %	3,075
Synnex	10,845	+ 5 %	152
Applied Materials	8,126	0 %	475
Facebook	7,872	+ 55 %	1,490
Symantec	6,799	+ 1 %	869
Agilent Technologies	6,781	+ 2 %	740
NetApp	6,393	+ 1 %	614
SanDisk	6,170	+ 22 %	1,043
Sanmina-SCI	5,870	+ 4 %	102
Advanced Micro Devices	5,299	+ 2 %	83
VMware	5,207	+ 13 %	1,014
Yahoo	4,680	+ 6 %	1,366
Juniper Networks	4,669	+ 7 %	440

Source: Bloomberg Financial Markets 2014, revised © westermann 31580EX_1

M1 The twenty largest computer firms in Silicon Valley (by annual revenue)

M2 High-tech industry in Silicon Valley

The Silicon Valley story began with two graduates from the prestigious Stanford University in Palo Alto, who developed a precursor of the first PC in a garage. Somewhat later, the two young men, William Hewlett and David Packard, founded the Hewlett-Packard company, which now employs some 321,000 people in 170 different countries, at the same location. Nourished by the research-intensive milieu of the nearby universities, numerous software development firms settled there, took advantage of the agglomeration benefits offered by the high-tech cluster and pursued research and development in a climate of close cooperation.

Source: Waldeck, W., Angloamerika, Braunschweig, 2011, pp. 74f

M3 Silicon Valley's high-tech industry: a driver of economic growth

Occupational group	Employees, 2013	Percentage of all employees working in Silicon Valley	Changes in percentages of employees 2007 – 2013	2012 – 2013
Internet & information services	35,356	2.5%	72.7%	19.1%
Software	27,333	1.9%	33.3%	5.8%
Technical & management consulting cervices	25,101	1.8%	31.4%	9.9%
Technical research & development (includes life sciences)	32,621	2.3%	22.8%	5.0%
Personal services	14,760	1.0%	22.3%	3.4%
Computer hardware design & manufacturing	128,155	9.0%	17.8%	3.8%
Healthcare & social services	132,797	9.3%	15.8%	42%

Source: www.siliconvalleyindex.org, accessed 20.11.2014

M4 The fastest-growing occupational groups, from 2007 to 2013

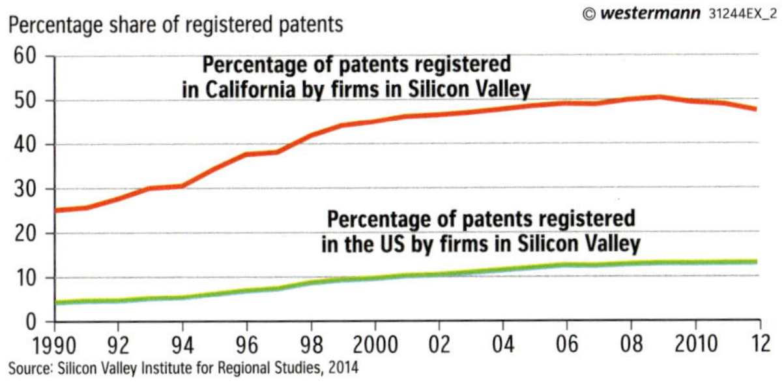

M5 Patents registered by firms in silicon valley relative to total patent registrations in California (red) and the US (green)

Sun Microsystems, Inc.	International Business Machines Corp.	Agilent Technologies, Inc.	Marvell International LTD.
Applied Materials, Inc.	Hewlett-Packard Development Co., L.P.	Broadcom Corporation	Genentech, Inc.
Advanced Micro Devices, Inc.	Apple, Inc.	National Semiconductor Corp.	Micron Technology, Inc.
Cisco Technology, Inc.	University of California	Xilinx, Inc.	Stanford University
Intel Corp.	Hitachi Global Storage Technologies Netherlands B.V.	Altera Corporation	LSI Logic Corporation

31588EX_1 © westermann

Source: Silicon Valley Institute für Regional Studies, 2014

M6 Companies in Silicon Valley that registered the most patents (2001 – 2011)

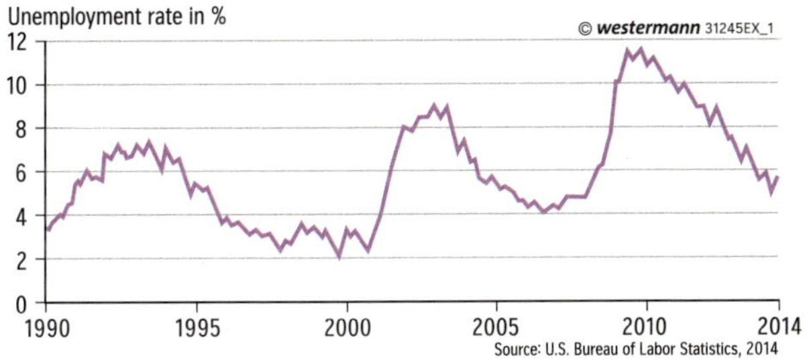

M7 Changing unemployment rates in Santa Clara County, California (1990 – 2014)

One of the fundamental problems facing high-tech regions is the pressure to promote a high level of flexibility and consistent innovative drive when it comes to the development of new products in order to maintain a sustainable leading position in the business world. Thus Silicon Valley is subject to a constant process of change. While microchip and computer manufacturing played a major role in the early years, the production of fully mature products in large series later shifted to low-wage regions of the US or to countries abroad under the pressure of high production costs. Following the early period, in which all phases of the value chain were represented, the large firms gradually began splitting off certain segments, although the most know-how-intensive and customer-specific tasks remained in Silicon Valley. In the more recent past, the trend has been dominated by the rise of such Internet service providers as Google, eBay and Yahoo. Silicon Valley has experienced its share of crisis-related phenomena, however. By 2004, the crisis that struck the "New Economy" at the dawn of the new millennium resulted in a huge loss of jobs and a significant increase in unemployment in the field of information technology.

Source: Laux, H. D., Thieme, G., Diercke Handbuch. Braunschweig, 2008, p. 357

M8 Change in Silicon Valley

The boom in the San Francisco Bay Area also came with negative agglomeration effects. Due to strong demand and the influx of new residents, the real estate market in San Francisco is now one of the most expensive in the entire United States. Rents have tripled within a very short period of time. Many areas of the city in which people in the middle and lower income classes once settled because of the relatively low rents are now being upgraded through the creation of modern residential and office complexes, and many residents have been forced to move away.

Source: Waldeck, W. Angloamerika. Braunschweig, 2011, pp. 74f

M9 The less positive side of Silicon Valley

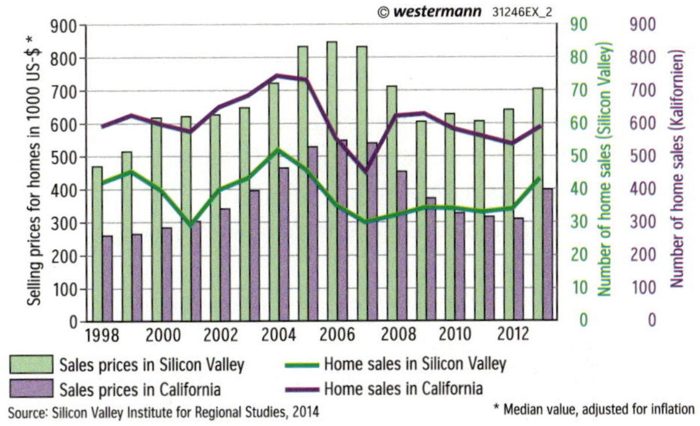

M10 House prices and home sales (absolute) in Silicon Valley

Wherever young Google or Apple employees move, rents soar rapidly to new heights. This has led to social conflict in the greater San Francisco area. Angry residents even went so far as to attack a Google bus. The anger that had built up over the years finally came to a head on December 20, 2013. At a stop in Oakland, protesters surrounded an air-conditioned luxury bus that carries employees of Google, the Internet giant, to corporate headquarters in Silicon Valley free of charge every morning. Stones were thrown, a window was broken, demonstrators gained entry to the bus and the situation threatened to escalate beyond control.

At about the same time, a bus carrying Apple employees was held up in San Francisco's Mission District. These ordinarily unmarked buses with dark-tinted windows have become a symbol of the unjust distribution of income and assets in the United States. And except for New York, the phenomenon is hardly as drastically pronounced anywhere as it is in Silicon Valley and San Francisco. And now in Oakland, a poor city only ten minutes from San Francisco, to which everyone who has been forced to leave their San Francisco apartments has fled. But now, the young tech workers have caught up with them and displaced them there as well.

Google has now decided to take its employees out of the line of fire. Starting Monday, two ferries will travel the short distance from the San Francisco harbour to Redwood City. From there, passengers will travel in unmarked buses to Google headquarters in Mountain View. [...] From Monday, firms will also have to pay to have their luxury buses pick up passengers at public bus stops. That is more than a minor problem: a total of 30 bus companies carry their people to work at the California think tank.

Source: Postinett, A., Der Sozialneid erfasst das Silicon Valley, 09.01.2014, www.handelsblatt.com, accessed 28.09.2014

M11 Social conflict in Silicon Valley

Tertiarisation of the economy

The Frankfurt am Main region – a centre of the service sector

Major cities like Frankfurt am Main offer a diverse range of consumer and business services. Home to a high concentration of firms in the financial sector, Frankfurt am Main is now the leading financial centre in Germany and one of the most important in the world. The city's outstanding status is attributable above all to its strong banking sector (the largest German stock and securities exchange), its international orientation and its role as host to European supervisory authorities. However, this preponderance of financial institutions has had a significant impact on the periphal communities in the greater Frankfurt metropolitan area.

1. Describe the characteristics that distinguish Frankfurt am Main as a financial centre (M1–M3).
2. Characterise the cluster comprising the financial centre of Frankfurt am Main (M1–M3).
3. (O) Illustrate some of the potential effects of Frankfurt as a financial cluster by:
   A writing an article for the Frankfurter Allgemeine Zeitung (M1 – M5, Internet).
   B compiling a causal network (M1–M5, Internet).
4. Discuss the the factors involved in the decision to locate a service company in Eschborn (M4, M5, Atlas, Internet).
5. Discuss: "Eschborn – a location for business-oriented services with good prospects" (M4–M8).
6. (S) Draft a profile of the financial and service centre of Frankfurt am Main (M1–M8).

→ Cluster, Services (business-related), Tertiarisation

Along with London and New York, Frankfurt am Main is one of the world's most important financial centres. From an international perspective, the economic significance of the Frankfurt-Rhine-Main region is closely linked to the global importance of the financial sector. The presence of the headquarters of the European Central Bank (ECB) also gives Frankfurt the status of a European capital. The region is also home to the Bundesbank, the German Stock Exchange and the German Federal Financial Supervisory Authority (BaFin). The Frankfurt-Rhine-Main region also boasts the highest concentration of people employed in the financial sector of any metropolitan area in Germany [...]. The more than 4,600 business entities (most of which are corporate headquarters) employ a total of some 138,000 people, Only in the more densely populated Rhine-Ruhr region are more people employed in the financial sector. [...]
A closer look at the inter-regional agglomerations within the cluster reveals that Frankfurt's inner city has the highest employment density. This is a function of the logic of the financial centre, which is expressed above all in the spatial concentration of banks in Frankfurt. Specialised firms within the financial cluster are concentrated in Frankfurt am Main and the neighbouring districts of Main-Taunus- and Hochtaunus. The regional focus of the financial cluster is underscored above all by the relocation of Deutsche Börse AG from Frankfurt am Main to Eschborn. [...]
The business enterprises in the Frankfurt-Rhine-Main financial cluster have access to an abundant array of public and private support services. Offering a diverse range of educational programmes in the field of finance, the regional landscape of colleges and universities serves as an important basis for the recruitment of skilled personnel.

Source: Ebner, A., Raschke, W., Clusterstudie FrankfurtRheinMain, Frankfurt am Main, 2013, pp. 51ff

M3 The financial centre of Frankfurt am Main

M1 Frankfurt am Main - a major centre of the service industry

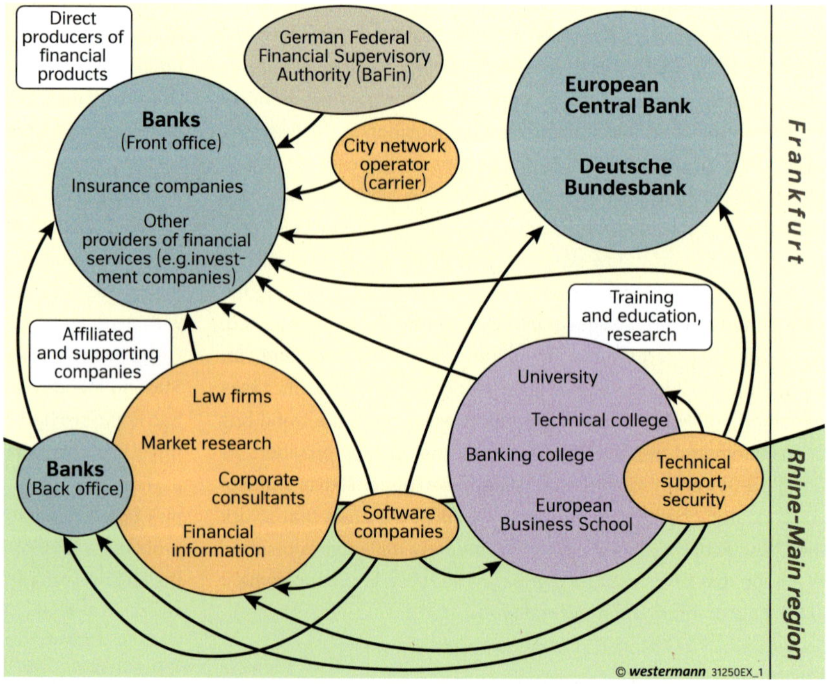

M2 Clusters within the financial centre of Frankfurt am Main

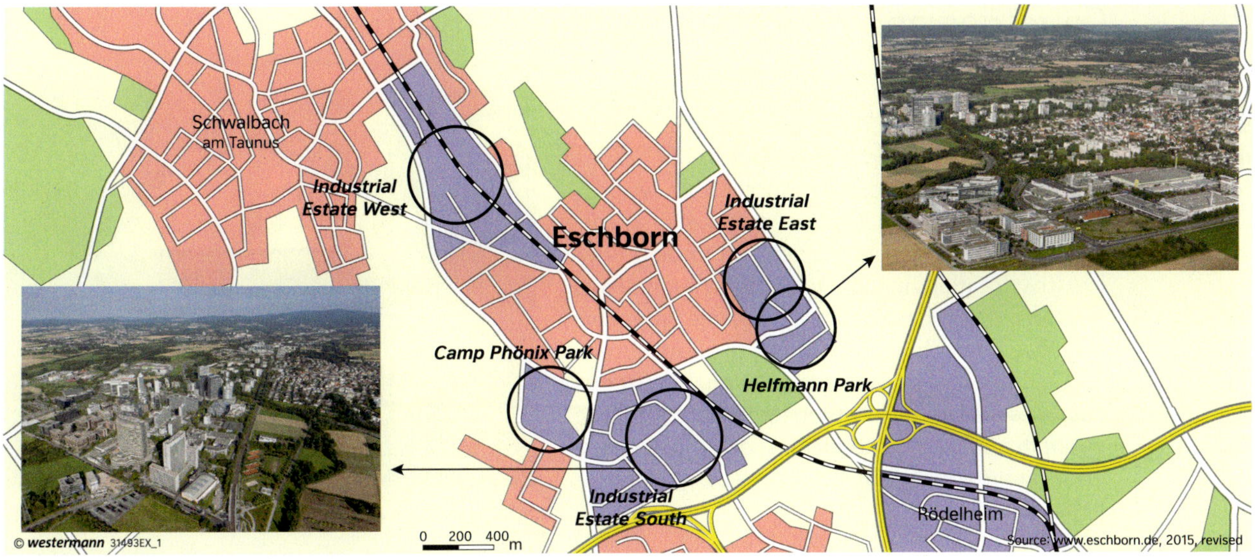

M4 Business locations for the service industry in Eschborn

Eschborn is located on the eastern fringe of Main-Taunus County in the immediate vicinity of the city of Frankfurt am Main. A modern office and commercial centre with the highest number of employees in the county, Eschborn is also a city with rural charm and appealing residential quality.
Rapid economic growth in the Rhine-Main region, the decreasing availability of building sites in Frankfurt and the city's extraordinarily favourable geographic position have attracted numerous firms to Eschborn since the early 1960s. The relatively low trade tax multiplier of 280 percent has also had a favourable impact on business growth and attracted a number of international corporations. The importance of business for the city is reflected in the fact that trade taxes account for a large share of total tax revenues.
The distance from Eschborn to the nearest autobahns (A66, A5) is about 1.5 km, to downtown Frankfurt roughly 10 km and to Frankfurt Airport approximately 15 km. Two public S-Bahn (suburban rail) lines offer direct connections to Darmstadt.
Along with the growth of commerce, the population has also increased at a rapid pace. New residential estates, schools, sport facilities, kindergartens, playgrounds and green areas as well as various cultural institutions have been established in Eschborn over the years.
Source: Stadt Eschborn, www.eschborn.de, accessed 02.10.2014

M5 The city of Eschborn – a centre of the service sector

Area within city limits	12.14 km²
Residents 2012	20,486
Employed persons, 2012	30,828
Number of business enterprises	4,265
Percentage of businesses in the service sector	97.8 %
Per capita buying power in € (2012)	27,543
Buying power index, 2012 (Germany = 100 %)	137.6
Tax revenues in million € (2012)	121.9
Percentage contributed by trade taxes	83 %
Rental price for office space in €/m²	5.50 – 14.50
Purchase price for commercial property in €/m²	270 – 630

Source: Stadt Eschborn, www.eschborn.de, 02.10.2014

M6 An overview of structural data for Eschborn

- **Industrial Estate South:** The Industrial Estate South occupies 50 hectares of land and borders on the A66 and the railway line. Most of the 19,000 jobs are offered by such corporations as Vodafone, Deutsche Bank AG, BAFA, British Telecom, Deutsche Börse AG, Ernst & Young, Deutsche Telekom, Samsung, Huawei, Infosys, Rödl und Partner [...].
- **Industrial Estate East:** A substantial part of the 10 hectares of Industrial Estate East is occupied by major supermarkets and wholesalers, including SELGROS, Real, [...] Möbel Boss, Reddy Küchen, Aldi and Lidl, the Central Laboratory for German Pharmacists and the National Federation of German Pharmacists' Associations.
- **Camp Phönix Park:** This industrial estate comprises 24 hectares along the A66. It is home to XXXL Mann Mobilia, NSK-Europe, Autohaus Nix, Sanitär Richter & Frenzel, Rewe, dm-Drogerie, KFC, Aldi, Fressnapf, Vino, denn's Biomarkt and Burger King among other firms.
- **Industrial Estate West:** This industrial estate occupies 40 hectares and borders on state road L3006 and the S-Bahn line (with two stops). IBM, Cisco Systems, VR LEASING, Deutsche Telekom, techem, Yaskawa, Monster.de, Swatch Group Deutschland and the Gesellschaft für Internationale Zusammenarbeit (GIZ) have established facilities here.
- **Helfmann Park:** This small (7.7 ha) but modern estate is home to Hypothekenbank Frankfurt AG, Compass Group, Accovion, Randstad, St. Jude Medical, Waters, ConCardis and two Mercure Hotels.

Source: Stadt Eschborn, www.eschborn.de, accessed 02.10.2014

M7 The structure of the service industry in Eschborn

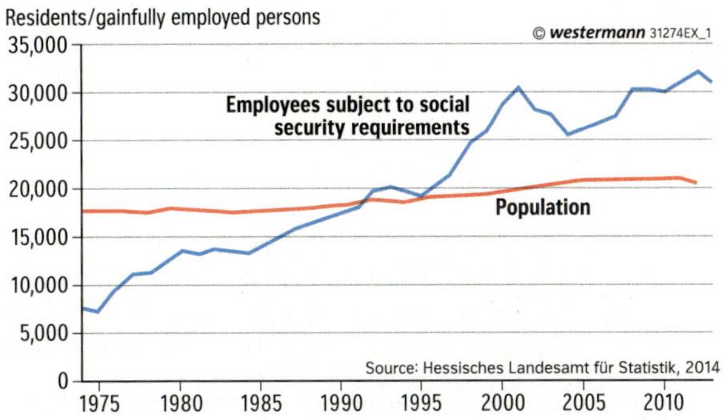

M8 Residents and employed persons in Eschborn (1974 – 2013)

Countries and regions in global competition

→ Free-trade agreement, Regional integration, Special economic zones

The economic regions of the world are engaged in increasingly intense competition for investments and capital. Competition for locations puts nations and regions under pressure to succeed. As key drivers of economic globalisation, multinational corporations are particularly intent on finding new, low-cost locations in order to develop new markets and cut costs. When conditions become untenable for these firms, they simply move to another location in the next most favourable region. The various countries differ significantly in terms of competitive strength and location conditions, and these differences impact on their ability to take part in the globalisation process.

Governments carry out various measures designed to promote economic growth in order to make their own locations more appealing and attract capital. Some countries establish special economic zones for the purpose of encouraging direct investments from abroad. The first such special economic zone was created in Shannon, Ireland, in 1959. The concept has since been applied in countries all over the world. Many nations also pursue an active foreign trade policy devoted to strengthening regional integration. In other words, they conclude free trade agreements or form economic alliances in order to facilitate and thus promote trade and the flow of capital. Others isolate themselves by enacting restrictive customs regulations as a means of protecting their own industries from foreign competition.

Have these strategies been successful? What advantages and disadvantages do they bring for the countries involved? We address these questions in this chapter.

M2 Production in a special economic zones in southern China

- Special Economic Zone (SEZ)
- Free Production Zone (FPZ)
- Export Production Zone (EPZ)
- Free Trade Zone (FTZ)
- IT Zone
- Industrial Zone
- Financial Services Zone

M3 Special economic zones – many designations, similar meanings

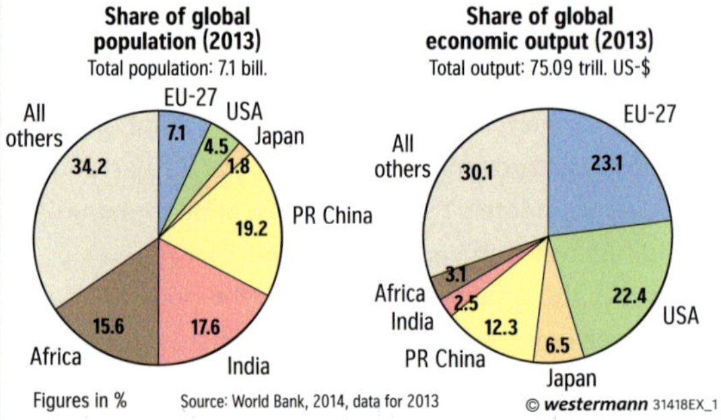

M4 Relative shares of global population and global economic output

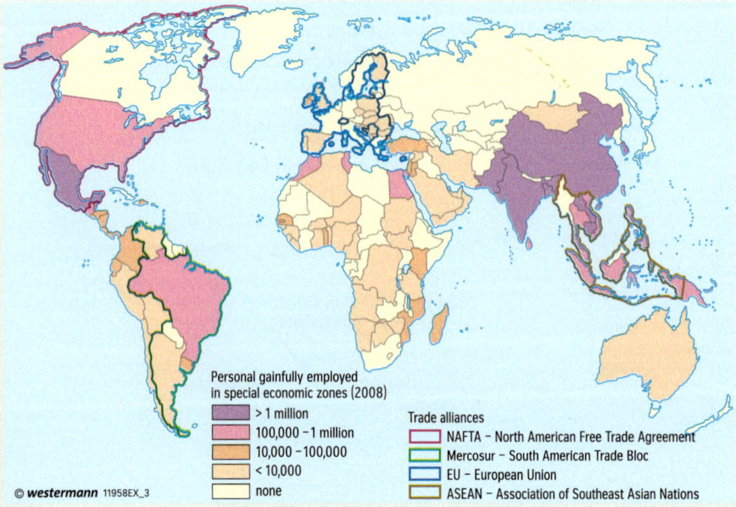

M1 World map of economic zones and numbers employed in zones

Rank 2013/2014	Country	Rank 2012/2013
1	Switzerland	1
2	Singapore	2
3	Finland	3
4	Germany	6
5	USA	7
6	Sweden	4
7	Hong Kong	9
8	Netherlands	5
9	Japan	10
10	Great Britain	8
29	People's Republic of China	29
60	India	59

(FAZ-Institut für Management-, Markt- und Medieninformationen GmbH, Außenwirtschaft, Jahrbuch 2014. Frankfurt am Main, p. 77),

M5 Global competive strength rankings

Special economic zones do not share a uniform structure. They exhibit major differences in terms of manifest form and the incentive programmes they offer to business enterprises. Thus it is difficult to make generally applicable statements about these zones. The word "special" clearly indicates that these areas differ from other economic regions in a given country. [...]

Governments all over the world have established special economic zones (SEZ) for the purpose of attracting foreign investment capital. The International Labour Organisation (ILO) estimates that there are now over 3,800 such zones in 130 countries. These zones are settled – more or less systematically – by transnational corporations that ordinarily produce for export. National governments expect them to have a positive effect on employment and to provide growth impulses for the national economy as well as access to advanced technologies. Firms that locate in these zones are offered a wide range of "investment incentives", including free access to infrastructure, exemption from customs duties on imports and exports, limited trade union rights, low environmental and social standards as well as various different tax benefits. In most cases, governments guarantee investors total exemption from taxes (tax holidays) for at least five to ten years. And even afterwards, they are often taxed at lower rates than domestic firms that cater for demand in their own countries.

Also problematic from the standpoint of development policy is the fact that capital and profits from special economic zones ordinarily flow out of the country unhindered. When the caravans of investors move on to invest their capital in other countries at more favourable conditions, the economic bottom line for the original country may actually be negative.

Source: DGB Bildungswerk BUND et al, Sonderwirtschaftszonen: Entwicklungsmotoren oder teure Aufmodelle der Globalisierung? 2010, pp. 4f

M6 Special economic zones

- External infrastructure costs covered by the government.
- Consulting and administrative costs.
- Social opportunity costs for land and infrastructures.
- Value of revenue from taxes and customs duties lost due to the establishment of special economic zones:
  1. Limited to shifts of location by existing firms without operational expansion.
  2. Dead-weight effect: the extent to which a new investor would have initiated his activities without an economic zone project.

M7 Costs of developing national economic zones

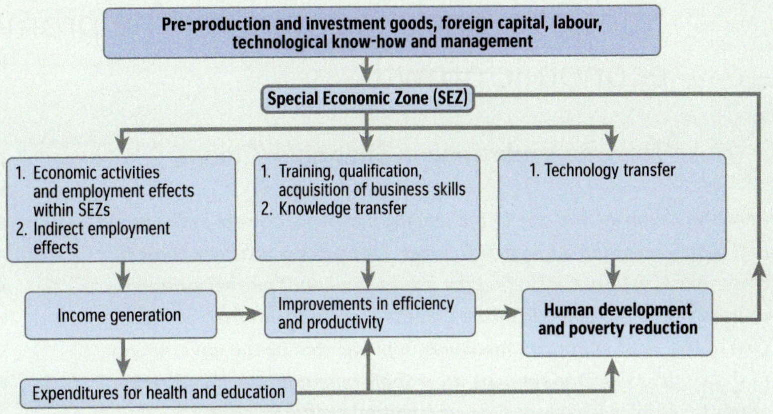

Source: Aggarwal, A.: Impact of Special Economic Zones on Employment, Poverty and Human Development. ICRIER Working Paper No. 194, 2007

31417EX_1 © westermann

M8 Effective relationships between eonomic zones and socio-economic development

- ***Free trade agreement***: step-by-step reduction of customs duties and contingents in trade between the partner countries. They differ from ***customs unions*** in that parties to the agreement remain autonomous with respect to their trade policies vis-à-vis third countries.
- ***Customs union***: additional common customs policy vis-à-vis third countries.
- ***Common market:*** free trade and unlimited mobility of production factors (labour, land and capital).
- ***Economic community (or economic union):*** goes beyond the common market; members coordinate their national economic policies.

M9 Stages of regional integration

Special economic zones in many countries are focused on labour-intensive production segments and the production of standardised products for export. International firms shift particularly labour-intensive production segments or entire production processes to locations with low wage costs, but also with poor working conditions and low environmental, safety and social standards, as in Bangladesh, for example. This applies above all to the clothing, textile and leather industry. Electronic equipment or components, including computers, are produced in nearly one-third of these zones. The agricultural and food-processing sector plays an equally large role, followed by trade and financial services, automotive supply, chemicals and pharmaceuticals. However, these zones have evolved into service and logistics centres or IT parks in many countries.

M10 Industry structures in special economic zones

1. **Explain the pressure to succeed with which countries and regions are forced to cope (M4, M5).**
2. **Name possible reasons for the global competitive strength rankings and illustrate the resulting consequences for the attractiveness of certain locations (M5).**
3. **Develop an overview of the 10 most important countries with special economic zones (M1).**
4. **Prepare a table listing the countries that are members of different economic alliances at the same time (M1, Atlas).**
5. **Illustrate the stages of regional economic integration. Identify differences between them (M9).**

Special economic zones for the promotion of economic growth

The free trade zone in Shanghai (China)

China has evolved into one of the leading industrial powers in the world and is now recording high growth rates. This success is attributable to a number of reforms, including the establishment of market-oriented principles and the opening of the Chinese market to international firms. One of the most important measures implemented by the government in this context was and remains the establishment of special economic zones for foreign investors. One such special economic zone was created in Shanghai's Pudong district in the mid-1990s. It has been complemented by a free trade zone since 2013. Shanghai is expected to serve as a model for all of China. How has Pudong progressed in the meantime? What benefits does such a special economic zone offer investors and how does it impact on the region and the nation at large?

1. Locate Pudong and describe the special economic zone and the free trade zone (M9, Atlas).

Ⓞ **2. A** Illustrate the structure and development of the special economic zone in Pudong (M1 – M3, Atlas).

B Evaluate the importance of Pudong for China's economic development.

3. From the perspective of international investors, outline the location factors:

a) for China as a macro-location (M5 – M8).

b) for Pudong as a micro-location (M2, M3, M9, M11).

4. Identify the goals national governments hope to achieve by establishing special economic zones (M4).

5. Discuss the function of joint ventures from the perspectives of China and foreign business enterprises (M7).

6. Explain the preconditions for foreign investments from the perspective of China and discuss them from the investors' perspective (M7).

7. Numerous additional special economic zones have now been established along the Chinese coast. Research the effects of these zones on the coastal region and report on your findings (Atlas, Internet).

Ⓢ **8.** "The establishment of special economic zones heightens the appeal [of a region] in the eyes of international investors and improves its prospects for economic development." Assess this statement and take a position.

→ Joint venture, Location factor, Special economic one

In 1990, the Chinese government declared the Pudong district, a former vegetable-farming area east of Huangpu Province, a special economic zone, thereby initiating the rise of the Shanghai economic region to the status of China's leading business and financial centre. A commercial centre, the Zhangjiang high-tech park, universities and research institutes, recreational facilities and housing units were build on the 520-km^2 estate. International firms were also attracted by the well-developed infrastructure. The zone was initially occupied primarily by logistics firms, before it began to attract industrial enterprises and other service providers as well. Pudong's gross domestic product rose from six million yuan in 1990 to 645 billion yuan in 2013, and is still growing today. With a per-capita GDP of 89,444 yuan, Shanghai is one of the richest cities in China.

M1 Pudong – special economic zone and boomtown

- Above-average economic growth
- A commercial, financial and service centre
- China's largest container harbour
- Two airports
- Transrapid railway line
- 50 universities
- 4,000 research institutes
- Technical and management experts
- Home to 15,000 industrial firms
- Residence of 20% of Shanghai's population
- Accounts for 25% of Shanghai's gross annual income
- Destination of one-third of all foreign and domestic investments flowing into Shanghai
- Accounts for 50% of Shanghai's foreign trade

(Source: Tichauer, P., Shanghais Drachenkopf: Pudong, 9/2014, www.owc.de, accessed 19.11.2014)

M2 Pudong: fact sheet (2013)

The new Free Trade Zone in Shanghai, 2013

- GDP growth in 2012: 8.75%
- Industrial production value: 149.3 billion US-$
- Value of services by the service sector: 67.9 billion US-$
- Growth in the service sector in 2012: 16.18%
- Realised direct investments 77.69 billion US-$
- Growth in 2012: 10.51%
- Value of foreign trade: 249.61 billion US-$

Source: Tichauer, P., Shanghais Drachenkopf: Pudong, 9/2014, www.owc.de, accessed 19.11.2014)

M3 Pudong: economic data, 2013

1. Direct foreign investments; stimulus for domestic investments
2. Job creation
3. Economic growth, diversification
4. Support for economic reforms / "test lab" for new economic policy tools
5. Technological development and know-how
6. Promotion of exports and the competitive strength of domestic firms
7. Increase in tax revenues and other income
8. Promotion of new growth centres / regions
9. Capital commitment (infrastructure, companies)

M4 Special economic zones – benefits for China

Population (in millions)	1,361
Employable persons (people older than 15 and younger than 15 years of age) in millions	1,004
Gainfully employed persons (in millions)	770
Unemployment rate, official (in %)*	4.1
Persons with university degrees (in millions)	6.7

* Statistics reflect only urban unemployment.
Source: National Bureau of Statistics of China, 2013

M5 Labour market figures for China, 2012

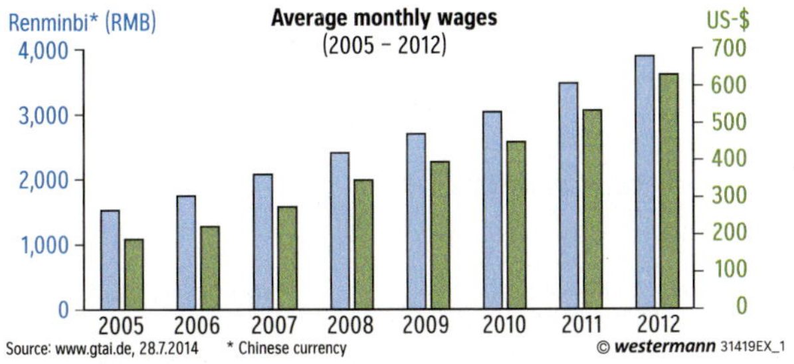

M6 Growth in average gross monthly wages

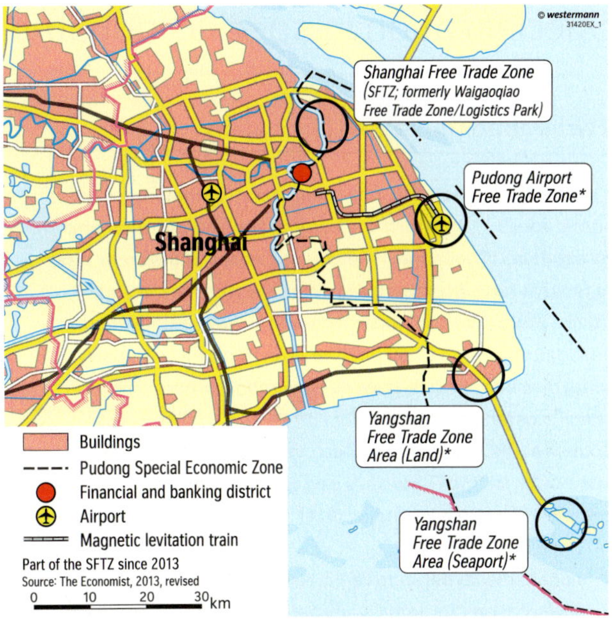

M9 Map of Shanghai-Pudong and the new free trade zone

Those who wish to invest in China must be willing to accept clearly-defined conditions. In several key sectors of the Chinese economy, such as the automotive industry, foreign firms are permitted to operate in the market only as partners in joint ventures. Several industries are actually closed to foreign investors. This is specified by an investment steering catalogue with which the government seeks to limit the extent of foreign influence on the Chinese economy. In a joint venture, foreign enterprises establish companies with Chinese partners in which they may not hold a more than 50 percent interest. The Chinese government pursues the policy in order to promote the transfer of technology and strengthen the domestic industry. Benefits of joint ventures include resource and network sharing. Disputes often arise between joint venture partners regarding the level of participating interest, the scope of influence of the respective partners and conflicting interests. Foreign investors frequently feel disadvantaged. Other problems associated with joint ventures include the costs of bureaucratic measures, uncertain legal relationships, the obligation to share information and technology and, last but not least, product piracy.

M7 Joint ventures as a precondition for foreign investment

M8 Sino-German joint venture in the automotive industry

China faces a number of major challenges. Its capacity to compete at the international level is threatened by rising wages, an increasingly strong currency and structural imbalances. [...] Consequently, China's leaders are intent on raising the nation's value-creation power to a new level by enacting market reforms. The Shanghai Free Trade Zone plays an important pilot role in the process of testing reforms that could eventually be applied to the entire country. Far-reaching reforms were promised when the China (Shanghai) Pilot Free Trade Zone (SFTZ) was announced in September 2013. Not all expectations have been met to date. Improvements in registration and administrative processes for business enterprises, more liberal financial market regulations and new freedoms for foreign firms (especially in the service sector) are currently being implemented step by step. [...] A second major reform package is devoted to reducing bureaucratic obstacles. [...] The third focus of reform efforts is the goal of facilitating cross-border investments in China and abroad. [...] Up till now, individual branches of the service sector have been opened to a certain extent.

Source: Haug, A., Testlauf für Reformen in Shanghais neuer Freihandelszone. 17.04.2013, www.gtai.de, accessed 28.07.2014

M10 Initial reforms in the Shanghai Free Trade Zone

Deutsche Bank [...] was the first European banking house to open a branch in the Shanghai Free Trade Zone. The bank and its customers could well benefit [...] in future from the more liberal regulations regarding financial transactions [...].
[This opening is also an important] step forward in support of internationalisation and full convertibility of the Chinese renminbi (yuan). Until now, the central bank in Beijing has controlled the exchange rate and capital transactions have been subject to strict controls. [...] In Shanghai, Deutsche Bank identifies strong demand for services permitted in the Free Trade Zone under the new regulations. Many international corporations are now represented or are planning to establish branches there [...].
The quintessential purpose of the reforms is to make it easier for foreign firms to finance commercial transactions and investments in China.

Source: Geinitz, C., Deutsche Bank zieht es nach Shanghai, 08.05.2014, www.faz.net, accessed 28.07.2014. © All rights reserved. Frankfurter Allgemeine Zeitung GmbH, Frankfurt

M11 Deutsche Bank opens a branch in the new Shanghai Free Trade Zone

Specialisation in specific industries

Hyderabad (India): an IT location

To a greater extent than practically any other country, India relies on special economic zones in its efforts to promote the liberalisation and opening of its economy. Thousands of economic zones of different sizes and business focuses have been established, in most cases through private initiatives. Many international corporations have established branches, most notably in the IT sector. The growth of the IT industry began in a small number of cities, such as Hyderabad, where India's second-largest IT cluster and a facility for call centres and business process outsourcing (BPO) was established. What location conditions does Hyderabad offer for the IT industry and what do the local structures look like? How is Hyderabad evolving as an IT location?

1. Locate the Hyderabad region (Atlas).
2. Give reasons for India's specialisation in the IT industry (M4 – M9).
3. Characterise the Hyderabad IT cluster (M3, M5).
4. (O) Evaluate the importance and impact of growth regions in India by
   A listing positive and negative effects in a table (M10);
   B writing a Wikipedia entry (M8 – M10).
5. (O) A Illustrate the concept and the advantages of the extended workbench (outsourcing) with reference to the IT industry (M9).
   B Discuss the consequences for the global location structure of the IT industry (M2, M8, M9).
6. (S) Draft a location brochure for the Hyderabad region.

→ Business Process Outsourcing (BPO), Cluster, Extended workbench, Special economic zone

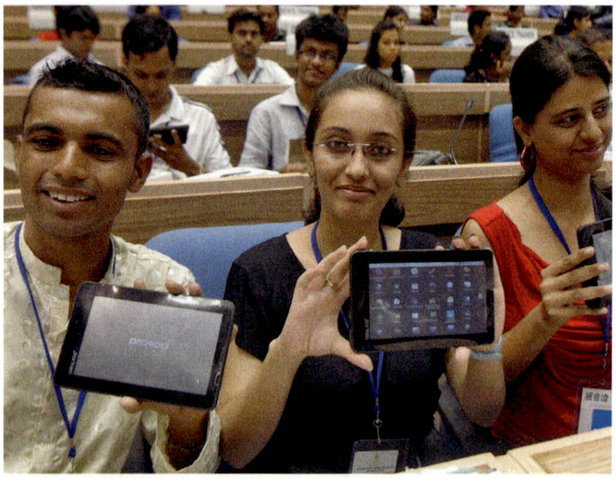

M1 IT students in India

IT position	2013 (in euros)
IT support staff member (desktop engineer)	180 – 233
IT engineer	203 – 296
SAP developer	253 – 412
System administrator	288 – 345

Source: www.gtai.de, 28.07.2014

M2 Average gross monthly wages in the Indian IT industry

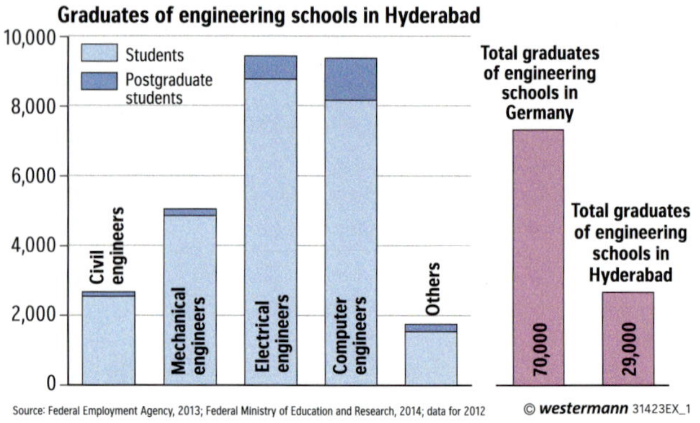

M3 Graduates in different academic disciplines in Hyderabad

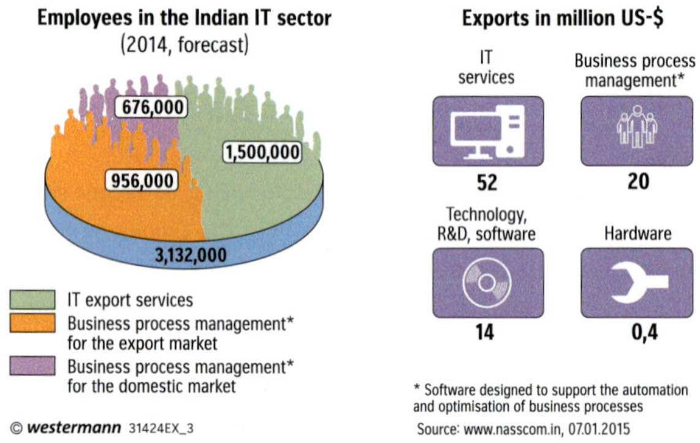

M4 Personnel and exports in the Indian IT Industry

With a population of 6.8 million, Hyderabad is the sixth-largest city in India. It is also the capital of the newly founded states of Telangana and Andhra Pradesh. The city has the largest number of special economic zones in India and the cluster is a global centre for the IT industry. Hyderabad last reported GDP of 74 billion US-$. In the years 2012 to 2013 alone, the city attracted direct foreign investments amounting to roughly 1.16 billion US-$. From 2007 to 2012, Hyderabad accounted for 6.8 percent of all Indian FDI* projects. Direct investments have led to the creation of 70,000 new jobs. Andhra Pradesh ranks sixth nationwide in terms of foreign investment volume. Numerous software and IT firms have located in Hyderabad under the influence of the Internet boom since the 1990s. Some 500,000 people are currently employed in more than 1,000 IT firms in Hyderabad. The ample supply of skilled personnel and the low local wage rates prompted multinational corporations such as Google, Microsoft (which operates one of its four international development centres in Hyderabad) and Amazon to consider locating in the city. The location conditions are good for foreign firms. A "Doing Business in India" study released by the World Bank identifies Hyderabad as the city with the second-best economic standards in India. In 2013, over 12 percent of all Indian IT exports originated in Hyderabad. The heart of the IT Industry is a "HITEC City" with an area of 61 hectares, which is home to IT parks and zones like the "Mindspace Cyberabad SEZ". The government decided to establish a large "Investment Region Hyderabad" in 2013. More research centres, special economic zones and IT parks are to be created there. Investments in the "e-City Manufacturing Cluster" and other such zones are being encouraged in order to attract more firms in the hardware industry.

*FDI = Foreign Direct Investment

M5 Hyderabad: a major IT centre

The IT services industry is one of India's booming economic sectors. It offers firms from English-speaking countries programming, call-centre and accounting services. The value of exported services of this kind has risen from two billion to over 60 billion US-$ since the late 1990s. Of these services, which are in demand all over the world, 44 percent are rendered in India. The number of IT jobs surpassed the 11 million mark in 2011. 2.23 million people are directly dependent on IT and another 9 million are indirectly dependent on the sector. The basis for the boom is a supply of well trained, favourably priced workers who are recruited by foreign firms. Thousands of young people complete a course of training in IT every year. Other advantages of the location are the high level of English-language skills in the population and "follow the sun" principle – the exploitation of time-zone differences. Global corporations are able to operate multiple facilities in different time zones and thus offer 24-hour service. Customer enquiries can be processed in real time (e.g. calls placed in the US at three o'clock in the morning are answered at three in the afternoon in India). Firms can extend the work day by operating a branch in India. Negative aspects of the location include bureaucracy, corruption and an inadequate infrastructure. The role of the IT sector is also problematic in a social sense, as it offers jobs primarily to the well-educated urban population.

M6 Location factors in the Indian IT sector

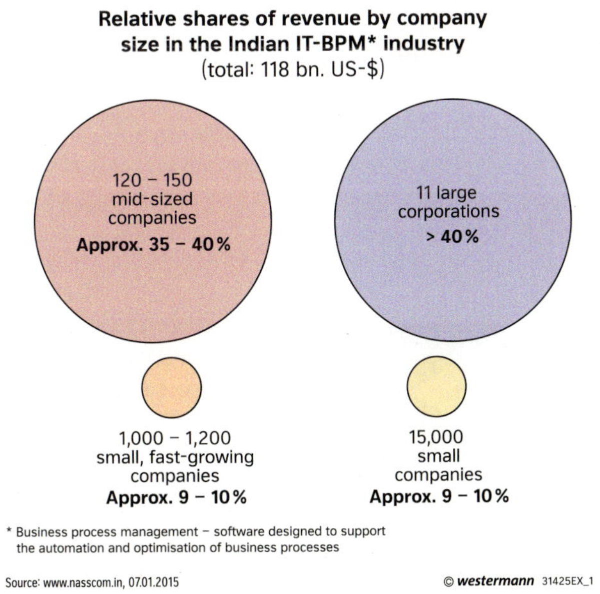

M7 Revenue shares of Indian IT companies by size category

- IT sector revenue: over 100 billion US-$
- 5.5 percent of India's GDP
- Growth rate: 16 percent
- Turnover up by a factor of one thousand in the last 20 years
- Turnover target for 2020: 225 billion US-$
- Labour shortages compel firms from Europe to rely on outsourcing in India.

(Source: Mauer, S., Indiens IT-Branche erlebt einen Boom, 05.08.2012, www.handelsblatt.de, accessed 28.07.2014)

M8 Development of the IT sector in India

To an increasing extent, European and American firms are shifting business processes to Asian countries such as India and China. IBM, SAP, Capgemini and Microsoft now employ thousands of specialists in modern computer centres. Some 300,000 engineers graduate from universities in India every year [...]. Despite their initial resistance, American and European IT firms have come to rely on the Asian workbench. [During the economic crisis,] companies everywhere were compelled to cut costs and carry out their business processes with less-expensive personnel. India's trump cards include tax exemptions, investment subsidies, low hourly wage rates for Asian computer specialists [...]. "A computer specialist fresh from school can expect to earn about 200 euros a month", notes Salil Parekh of Capgemini in Mumbai. "That more than makes up for the roughly 5% additional costs of outsourcing to India." Matthias Hartmann, General Manager of IBM Germany, explains the current reasoning: "We have to work with global capacities in Germany in order to be competitive at the international level." That is especially convenient in the case of standardised processes, such as call-centre operations, operating, research, documentation and software development.

Source: Demmer, C., Indien als verlängerte Werkbank, 26.10.2007, www.ingenieur.de, accesssed 29.08.2014

M9 India, the extended workbench

While the urban middle class supports India's participation in the global market, economic zones are viewed as a threat by villagers in rural areas and members of the working class. Special economic zones in India are regarded as foreign territory in which special rules apply. Bureaucratic processes are simplified. Raw materials can be imported into a zone duty-free and firms have access to the labour market. Wage rates differ. People with no qualifications work in many firms for low wages, well-paid specialists in others. India has a substantial competitive edge when it comes to software. Even highly qualified people demand relatively low wages. What is more, labour laws apply only on paper in these zones. Special economic zones are meant to open the domestic economy to the global market. Unemployment, it is said, can only be eliminated through industrialisation. It is not clear how many new jobs have been created by the zones. Residents of the village of Nandigram were notified that their property would be expropriated to accommodate a zone. They responded by cordoning off the area, because expropriation robbed them of the basis for their existence.

M10 Negative effects of economic zones in India

Strategies employed to influence trade

Free trade and protectionism

Different countries employ different economic policy strategies and design their trade relationships accordingly. Individual countries and alliances seek to steer foreign trade policy in ways that will promote the growth of their own economies. In economic alliances, two or more nations cooperate by reducing trade restrictions in order to boost trade with each other and improve their prospects for economic growth. By doing so, they open their markets. In other cases, however, strategies are employed for the purpose of sealing off domestic markets and shielding them from foreign competition through protectionist measures. What economic policy strategies can be employed to control foreign trade, facilitate exports and increase production?

1. Citing a concrete example, describe the objectives of trade barriers and show how they work (M1 – M4).
2. a) Compare the economic policy concepts of free trade and protectionism.
   b) Discuss the advantages and disadvantages of free trade and protectionism.
3. (O) A Compare and contrast the goals of import substitution and policies designed to promote exports.
   B Compare the advantages of the two concepts.
4. "Trade barriers are disadvantageous for German firms and their ability to compete." Explain.
5. Search the Internet for recent cases involving protectionism and trade conflicts (e.g. China, Russia, the US and the EU with regard to the automotive and solar-energy industries or rare earth trade).
6. (S) Discuss how nations can protect themselves against protectionism.

→ Free trade, Import substitution, Protectionism

The European Union has sealed off its market to a number of products, such as sugar, bioethanol, coffee and rice. The countries affected by this policy are now fighting back and German firms that export to those countries are paying the price. CPH Chemicals Trade and Services is engaged all over the world wherever labels are affixed to PET or glass bottles. They mix a special glue for Malaysia, which does not accept standard goods from Germany. Customs regulations have forced CPH to modify its formula. The authorities insist upon this, and have threatened to close off the market otherwise. The problem in Malaysia is a customs law which specifies that glue used for food products must contain less than 49 percent rice starch. Glues with higher rice starch content are subject to customs duties of 25%; others can be imported duty-free. The standard glue contains 51 percent rice starch, which means that more work is required for an order for glue from Malaysia. Suppliers must pay duties in the three-digit range for rice from Malaysia, where rules are quite strict. The country wants to protect its agricultural sector. So CPH employees mix glue destined for Malaysia only with a protein harvested from milk. There are no dairy farmers in Malaysia and thus no measures to protect them. Trade barriers have been erected in recent years by fast-developing countries seeking to protect their own markets.

Source: Litz, Protectionism, 20.10.2010, www.impulse, accessed 23.07.2014

M1 Protectionism – threshold countries defend themselves

India

31426EX_5

India imposes customs duties of 75 percent on imported luxury cars. Entire industries in India are closed to foreign investors. The government has blocked access to the retail sector by refusing to issue licences to foreigners in order to protect local street merchants. Indian authorities also dictate prices for some medications, thus scaring off pharmaceuticals producers like Bayer.

Europe

31426EX_4

The EU pays subsidies to farmers in the double-digit billion range every year and offers a protected market. Raw cocoa can be imported to the EU duty-free. Cocoa butter is subject to a 7.7 customs duty and a certain amount of chocolate can be imported at 43 percent, after which the rate increases.

China

31426EX_1

The public contracts awarded by Beijing every year are valued at a total of 83 billion euros but only domestic firms qualify for them. Investors from abroad are systematically disadvanatged and forced to build their factories in cooperation with local partners and contribute their patents. NInety percent of the special raw materials that are so important to high-tech industry come from China. Rare earth exports are limited by quotas.

Brazil

31426EX_2

Customs duties average 13.7 percent, which ranks Brazil among the countries with the highest import duties in the world. With this policy, the government seeks to force business enterprises to locate inside the country and to exert downward pressure on the exchange rate. The strength of the Brazilian real is the result of high raw material exports and spoils export opportunities for Brazilan industry.

Argentina

31426EX_3

Argentina levies customs duties on German cars at a rate of 35 percent. Yet all automobile manufacturers accept the obligation to balance their trade accounts. Firms that import vehicles from plants abroad must export Argentinian products in return, such as wine, rice or leather.

M2 Protectionism, a global phenomenon

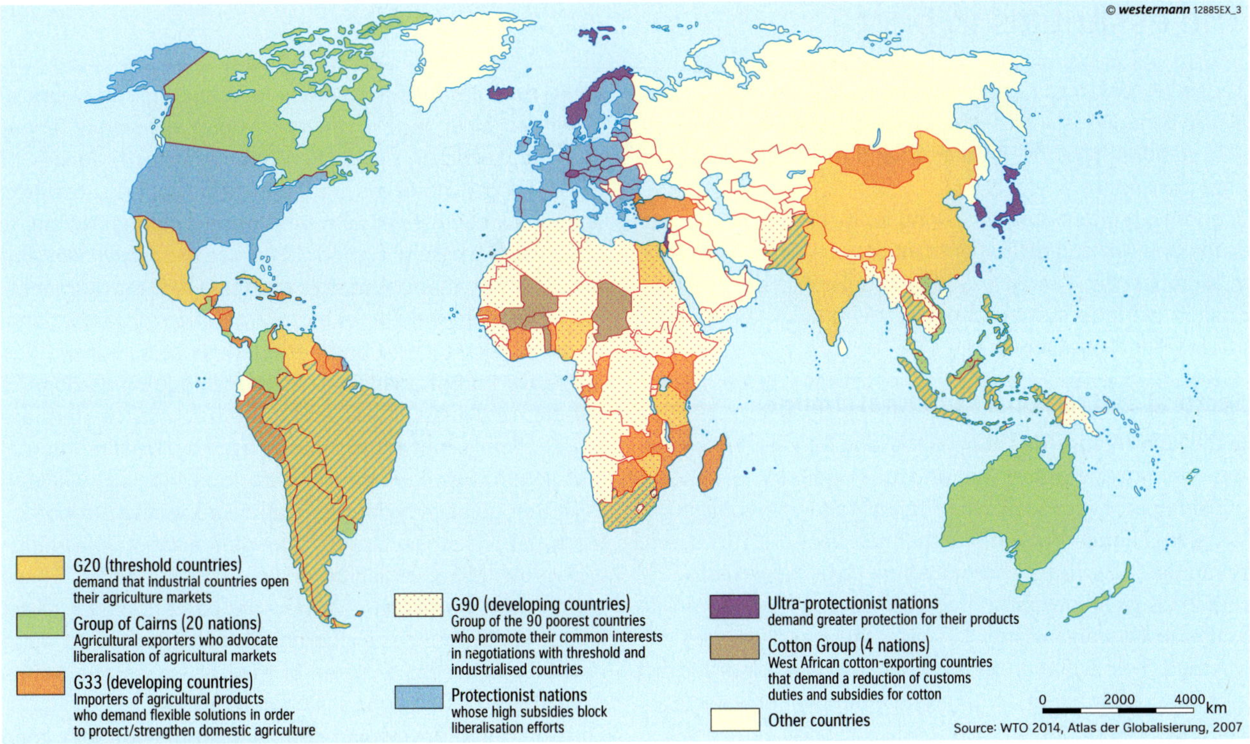

M3 WTO interest groups

1. ***Avoiding unilateral production structures***
   Income from export transactions would be endangered if unilateral specialisation were to result in strong dependence on fluctuating world-market prices.
2. ***Ensuring an adequate supply of essential goods***
   If a country ceases to produce essential goods, an adequate supply of such goods may no longer be ensured. Independence from imports is a desirable goal.
3. ***Securing jobs***
   Free trade may endanger jobs in industries that offer relatively high prices to customers. In these cases, customs duties or subsidies are used to secure jobs in those industries.
4. ***Consumer and environmental-protection factors***
   Health and environmental protection regulations are applied in such a way that foreign suppliers are subject to more demanding requirements.

M4 Benefits of protectionism

Import substitution is the practice of replacing imports with domestically produced products. Export promotion is precisely the opposite. In import substitution, industries that can be expected to have a sustained, positive effect on economic development are subsidised for limited periods of time. Support is provided for young industries that are initially unable to compete with foreign firms but can be expected to become fully competitive in the long term. Such policies are intended to reduce expenditures for foreign currency and stimulate growth. Related measures include import restrictions on foreign goods, customs duties and subsidies for production and investment as well as tax benefits. One disadvantage is the emergence of an isolated economy that produces inefficiently at excessively high cost. The goal of export promotion is to make exports "artificially" cheaper in order to stimulate foreign trade. Export subsidies make sense only when they are temporary and benefit young industries. Related measures include favourable credit terms for export transactions, currency devaluation, advertising abroad and export bonuses.

M6 Import substitution and promotion of exports as national economic policy measures

Import restrictions protect the domestic economy – according to advocates of protectionism. Actually however, consumers pay more for inferior goods [...]. [Protectionist policy] encourages governments to require citizens to buy domestically produced goods – or to impose customs duties to make foreign goods so expensive that the same effect is achieved. [...] Ultimately, it is not the free movement of goods that costs jobs, but protectionism itself. ... Allegedly, it is merely a matter of a bit more protection against foreign competition – when jobs are at stake. But that would be a dangerous game. Soon, all industries would demand the same protection against foreign competition. [...] In the end, no one would benefit from such a trade war. In fact, all countries would lose in terms of both jobs and prosperity. [...] And what remains of protectionist arguments? The advocates of such policies are rarely interested in the common good, although they usually claim otherwise. In truth, they are almost always motivated by the desire to protect themselves from competition – at the expense of others. In doing so, they twist not only the facts, but words as well. They are in favour of competition, of course, but it must be "fair". The protection against bothersome competition they seek is described as an "international competitive order" and less expensive competitors are defamed as "dirty competition" and "cheap suppliers". And then they denounce social injustices in competing countries, although such matters contribute only marginally to price differences.

Source: Van Suntum, U., Warum schadet Protektionismus? 08.01.2007, www.faz.net, accessed 24.07.2014.

M5 Protectionism and free trade – different perspectives

The essentials in brief

Those who wish to remain economically successful must evolve continuously. This simple maxim applies at all levels – to nations, regions, industries and individual business enterprises alike.
Economic regions progress along long-term development paths and are subject to constant change. Their economic significance, function and demographic dimensions change with the system of economic regions, as do their internal functional structures.

Sectoral and regional structural change

In the Ruhr region, for example, the long transition from the total dominance of the coal and steel industry to a modern service location is still in progress today. Not only have large, traditional corporations changed since the 1970s, but numerous new firms and industries have moved into the region as well, including high-tech companies and firms in the health-care, energy, leisure, culture and logistics industries. The evolution of the Ruhr region is regarded as a shining example of simultaneous regional and sectoral structural evolution.
Economic output has shifted progressively in Germany and other industrialised countries from the primary through the secondary to the tertiary sectors. This process is referred to as tertiarisation. The service sector has become increasingly important under the influence of rapid technological progress and the use of state-of-the-art equipment. As incomes and living standards have risen, people have also grown lazier and taken advantage of more and more personal services. Both the relative number of employees in the service sector and its contribution to gross national product are rising constantly.

Intrasectoral structural change

Many branches of the economy have also undergone intrasectoral structural change in recent years. In other words, changes have also taken place within individual sectors. Due largely to increasing globalisation, many of the old ideas about business locations no longer apply today. Innovations in communication and transport, technical progress in production and organisation (e.g. global production concepts and networks) and changes in the global political environment (e.g. economic alliances) have led to a reassessment of locations. Firms have moved their facilities to locations abroad under the influence of globalisation, and some now produce at multiple locations. In many cases, several firms engage in an international division of labour to produce certain products. Within specific branches of the economy, however, an increasing tendency towards spatial concentrations of related firms and institutions is observable. These so-called clusters (e.g. Silicon Valley and the Frankfurt financial centre) are home to firms representing networked industries as well as other organisational units of relevance to competitiveness (e.g. universities and government agencies). As spatial agglomerations of people, resources, ideas and infrastructure, clusters are highly complex networks characterised by dynamic internal interaction. Business enterprises hope that this will lead to further gains in productivity and competitive strength.
Many nations strive to profit from globalisation and worldwide growth by establishing special economic zones. These zones offer particularly favourable conditions for direct investments, and thus encourage foreign investors to found new firms or relocate some of their business operations from abroad to the special economic zones.
Threshold and developing companies are especially keen to position themselves as locations for investment, and have established more and more special economic zones at preferred locations with convenient transport connections and in structurally weak regions. In Asia, China above all has created numerous special economic zones and established them as models for success. Foreign firms in some industries are required to enter into joint ventures with domestic companies. In India, special economic zones have been developed in connection with sectoral clusters. Particularly important in this context is the IT sector. Thanks to the favourable location factors in India, numerous leading international firms are now using the country as an extended workbench.
International competition also influences trade policies. Many national governments are engaged in efforts to strengthen regional integration and establish common economic regions. These efforts often lead to the formation of economic alliances and the creation of free trade zones. Aside from the trend in favour of free trade, there is also a tendency on the part of countries all over the world to seal off their domestic markets, primarily by erecting trade barriers. This kind of protectionism is intended to protect national industries against international competition and promote the growth of import-substitution industries.

Skill Check

All the skills that you were able to acquire in this chapter are listed here.
You can judge for yourself if you have mastered each skill: ***securely***, ***moderately*** or ***barely***.

Explanatory skills

Can I ...		Unsure? Look it up on these pages
1.	explain structural change in predominantly industrial regions as the result of changing location factors?	44 – 47
2.	describe reindustrialisation, diversification and tertiarisation as strategies for overcoming structural crises?	44 – 47

3.	explain the progressive process of tertiarisation with reference to socio-economic and technical developments?	44–47
4.	cite examples of hard and soft location factors and explain changes in location factors resulting from technical progress, changing patterns of demand and political requirements?	48–51
5.	analyse growth regions on the basis of economic indicators?	52–55
6.	characterise the tertiary sector and its interaction with the secondary sector with reference to the example of consumer and business-related services?	56/57
7.	illustrate changes that have taken place in regional location structures as a result of the establishment of special economic zones, using concrete examples?	60–63
8.	explain the functions and goals of joint ventures from multiple perspectives?	60/61
9.	characterise the diversity of the tertiary sector and its interaction with the secondary sector with reference to trade, transport and business-related services?	62/63
10.	illustrate changes in global location structures resulting from the establishment of special economic zones, using concrete examples?	64/65

Methodological skills

Can I ...		
11.	orient myself with the aid of physical and topical maps as well as digital map services?	52/53
12.	identify problematic geographic issues and develop corresponding questions on the subject of "evolving economic regions"?	42–65
13.	analyse various presentation and research materials, such as maps, statistical summaries, graphs and texts?	42–65
14.	derive models of general geographic statements and compare them with concrete examples of geographic situations?	49/51/56
15.	present geographic information in graphic form (e.g. in the form of an interactive structure)?	44/45, 56/57
16.	find information independently using suitable search strategies in libraries, the Internet and Internet-based geographic information services and evaluate it with reference to specific questions?	46/47, 54/55, 58–65
17.	describe changes in local and global location structures resulting from the establishment of special economic zones orally, in writing and in an objective, logically structured and differentiated manner using appropriate technical terminology?	60–63

Evaluation skills

Can I ...		
18.	evaluate the changing importance of hard and soft location factors for the economic development of a region?	44–51
19.	evaluate the usefulness of models (e.g. the theory of long waves, the product life-cycle model, Weber's location theory) as they relate to the explanation of structural economic change?	48–51
20.	evaluate the significance of growth areas for the development of a region from economic, technological and social perspectives?	52–55
21.	discuss the importance of the education system for the social and economic development of a region?	54–57
22.	evaluate the functions and goals of joint ventures from different perspectives?	60/61
23.	evaluate the significance of growth regions for the development of a country from economic, technological and societal perspectives with reference to India and China?	60–63
24.	discuss concrete measures in support strategies for the development of economic regions with reference to concrete examples?	60–63
25.	assess the importance of a powerful and efficient infrastructure for the development of a synergetically networked economy?	60–63
26.	discuss the chances and risks in economic, ecological and social terms that arise from the establishment of special economic, free trade and economic integration zones?	60–65

Activity skills

Can I ...		
27.	present the results of research on the subject of "evolving economic regions" objectively using appropriate technical terminology?	46/47
28.	actively participate in discussions and make soundly reasoned contributions?	52–55
29.	plan and organise topical elements of instructional units?	52/53

Examination training

The changing automotive industry – the example of the USA

1. **Locate the automobile production locations in the US and charcterise their origins and development.**
2. **Illustrate the progressive development of the automotive industry in the US.**
3. **Discuss the future perspectives for the automobile production locations in the US.**

You will need these additional materials to complete the assignments:
M1 Atlas maps of your choice
M2 USA – Entwicklung der Automobilindustrie, Diercke Weltatlas (2015), p. 217

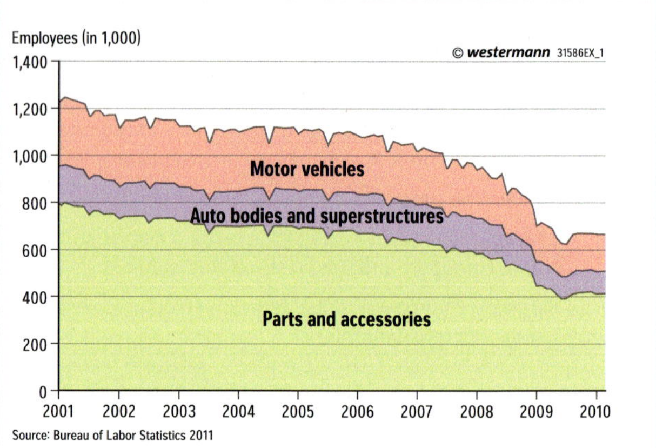

M5 Employment in the US automotive industry

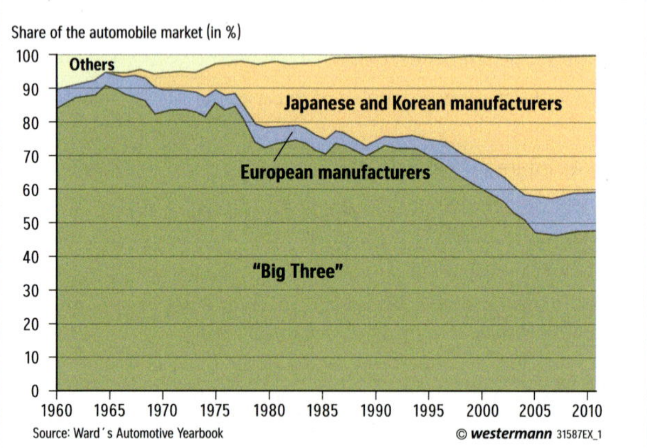

M3 Shares of the market for motor vehicles in the USA (the Big Three – General Motors, Ford, Chrysler)

State	Unemployment rate in %	Unionised employees in %	Weekly wages of industrial workers in US-$
North Carolina	10.6	3,2	642
Florida	11.5	5.6	755
South Carolina	11.2	4.6	689
Pennsylvania	9.7	4.7	619
Tennessee	8.7	14.7	672
Illinois	10.3	15.5	672
Indiana	10.2	10.9	776
Michigan	12.5	16.5	958
Ohio	10.1	13.7	752

M6 Structural data for selected US states

A number of factors make the southwestern United States attractive for German and other firms in the automotive industry. The states in this region pursue ambitious business settlement policies and offer attractive investment incentives, especially for firms that offer large numbers of jobs for local residents. These incentives include tax benefits, favourably priced sites and special training programmes. Firms are also attracted by the rather moderate wage costs (as compared to those in other regions of the US). Yet another factor is the presence of existing industry networks which offer a diverse range of opportunities for local producers and supplier firms. [...] In addition to its proximity to the traditional centres of the US automotive industry, the region is within easy reach of Mexico, which offers additional options for the outsourcing of costly, labour-intensive processes. [...] Thus the localisation economies are substantial and the preconditions for just-in-time production are [...] favourable, due in part to the good transport connections. [...] Yet the region has its problems as well. As Stefanie Jehlitschka, Deputy Managing Director of AHK USA-Süd, points out, the shortage of qualified professionals poses a challenge, as is does in other parts of the US as well.

Source: Germany Trade & Invest, Automobilindustrie im Südosten der USA setzt Expansionskurs fort, 05.03.2013, www.gtai.de, accessed 01.02.2015

M4 The southeastern USA as a location for the automotive industry

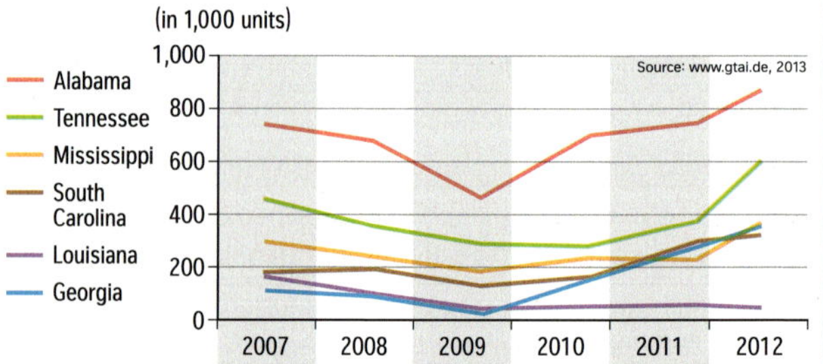

	2007	2008	2009	2010	2011	2012
Total	1,933.9	1,623.6	1,113.8	1,576.1	1,971.9	2,541.4
Change in production output as compared to the preceding year	-15.8 %	-16.0 %	-31.4 %	41.5 %	25.1 %	28.9 %
US total	10,584.9	8,520.9	5,611.8	7,636.2	8,470.9	10,140.8
Relative contribution of the six states to total US lightweight vehicle production	18.3 %	19.1 %	19.8 %	20.6 %	23.3 %	25.1 %

* Cars and light trucks (SUVs, pick-ups) up to 6.35 t

© westermann 31585EX_1

M7 Lightweight vehicle* production in the southeastern US (in 1000 units; changes and relative contributions in %)

In the face of harsh public criticism, BMW boss Norbert Reithofer has appealed to EU politicians to pass the free trade agreement between the US and Europe. "Trade barriers generate high costs", as the Chairman pointed out at the Annual General Membership Meeting in the Olympia Halle in Munich. "They have no place in the 21st century. And they have no place at all in the real world of US and European automobile markets." [...]
The automotive industry would profit significantly from the free trade agreement. Manufacturers like BMW produce for a global market. The Munich firm is currently producing all of its sport utility vehicles at the US plant in Spartanburg. If these vehicles are exported to Europe, they will be subject to customs duties amounting to ten percent. That would make a huge difference for BMW, as sport utility vehicles are becoming increasingly popular.

Source: Tauber, A., BMW pocht auf Freihandelsabkommen mit den USA, 15.05.2014, www.welt.de, accessed 01.02.2015

M8 BMW appeals for a free trade agreement with the USA

M12 Spartanburg overtakes Dingolfing: South Carolina will soon be home to the largest BMW factory. The Bavarian auto manufacturer plans to invest up to a billion dollars in the expansion of its US facilities by the year 2016.

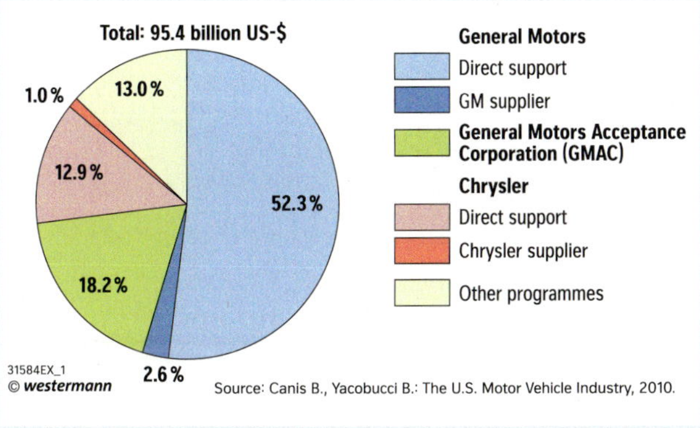

M9 US government subsidy programmes for the automotive industry, 2008 – 2009 (in billion US-$)

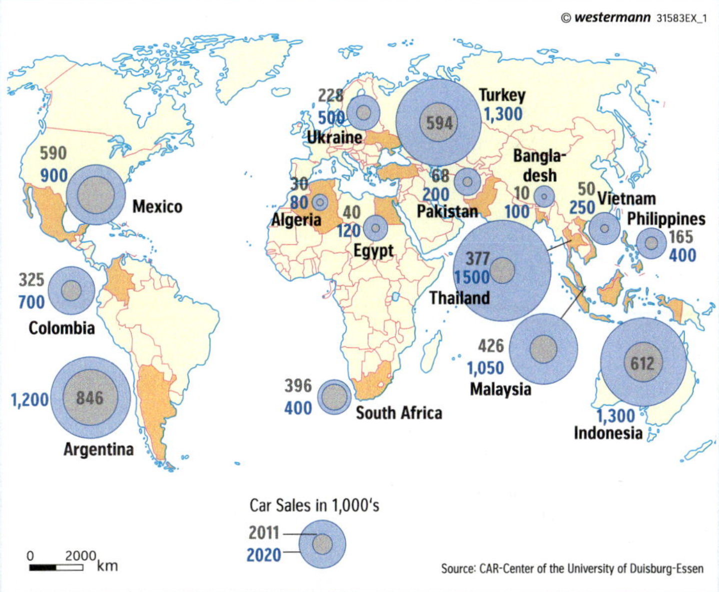

M13 The automobile markets of the future

Engine type	2011	2012	Jan – May 2013	Change Jan – May 2013 (compared to Jan – May 2012 in %)
Hybrid	269.2	434.5	212.7	16.1 %
Clean diesel	101.6	125.5	48.1	-5.0 %
Plug-in light vehicles*	17.8	53.2	32.7	129.9 %

*Plug-in hybrids and straight electric cars

M10 Sales of lightweight vehicles with alternative drive technologies (in 1000 units)

Producer	Volume of investment	Project status	Remarks
General Motors	1.3	Announced in December 2013	Expansion and modernisation of five US plants. Nearly 500 million US-$ of the total are to go for equipment systems for the production of a new 10-gear automatic transmission in Romulus (Michigan). 322 million US-$ to be invested in the development of fuel-conserving engines.
Ford	1.1	Announced in mid-2013	Expansion and modernisation of a plant in Kansas City (Missouri)
Fuji Heavy Industries (Subaru brand)	0.4	Investment presented at mid-year, 2013	Expansion of capacities in Lafayette (Indiana)
Toyota	0.36	Plans published in the spring of 2013	Assembly line for the production of "Lexus ES" luxury limousines in Georgetown (Kentucky)

Source: www.gtai.de

M11 Key investment projects in the US automotive industry (in billion US-$)

III Population development and migration

Causes of spatial problems

Refugees arriving on the coast of Sicily. Other refugees have lost their lives during the hazardous crossing. From 2000 to 2004, 23,258 people died off the coasts of Europe.

Migration on a global scale

→ Flight, Migration

As always throughout the course of human history, migratory movements across borders are a characteristic feature of human life today. People often resort to emigration on the one hand, or immigration on the other, in response to unjust policies and national or regional disparities.

Such disparities include significant differences in population growth between countries and regions in different stages of development. The resulting demographic divide is examined in greater detail in this chapter.

Many people see leaving their homeland or their home city as the best way to improve their living circumstances and chances for a better life. When such movements take them across national boundaries, we speak of international migration. Actually, two different processes are involved here: emigration and immigration. The term "flight" refers to migratory movements made necessary by war, persecution or environmental disasters, etc. The distinction between forced and voluntary migration is not entirely clear however, especially in cases in which migration becomes a survival strategy for people living in poverty with no prospects for a better life.

The first part of this chapter addresses the reasons that prompt people to migrate, the causes of migratory movements and the impact of migration on migrants' home and host countries. International migration is the focus of attention in this context.

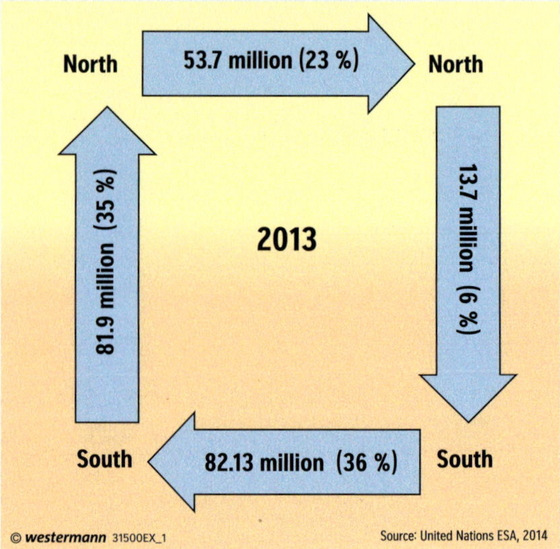

Facts about migration

The number of international migrants – people living in a different country than the one in which they were born – is estimated at over 230 million. That figure has risen in recent decades. Yet the percentage of migrants relative to the total world population has remained nearly constant from 1990 (2.9%) to 2013 (3.2%).

M2 Facts about global migration

M1 On the beach at Djibouti, a hub for migrants from Somalia, Ethiopia and Eritrea. They are holding up their mobile phones in the hope of receiving a strong signal from neighbouring Somalia and contacting their families. They are about to embark on what they hope is a journey to a better life.

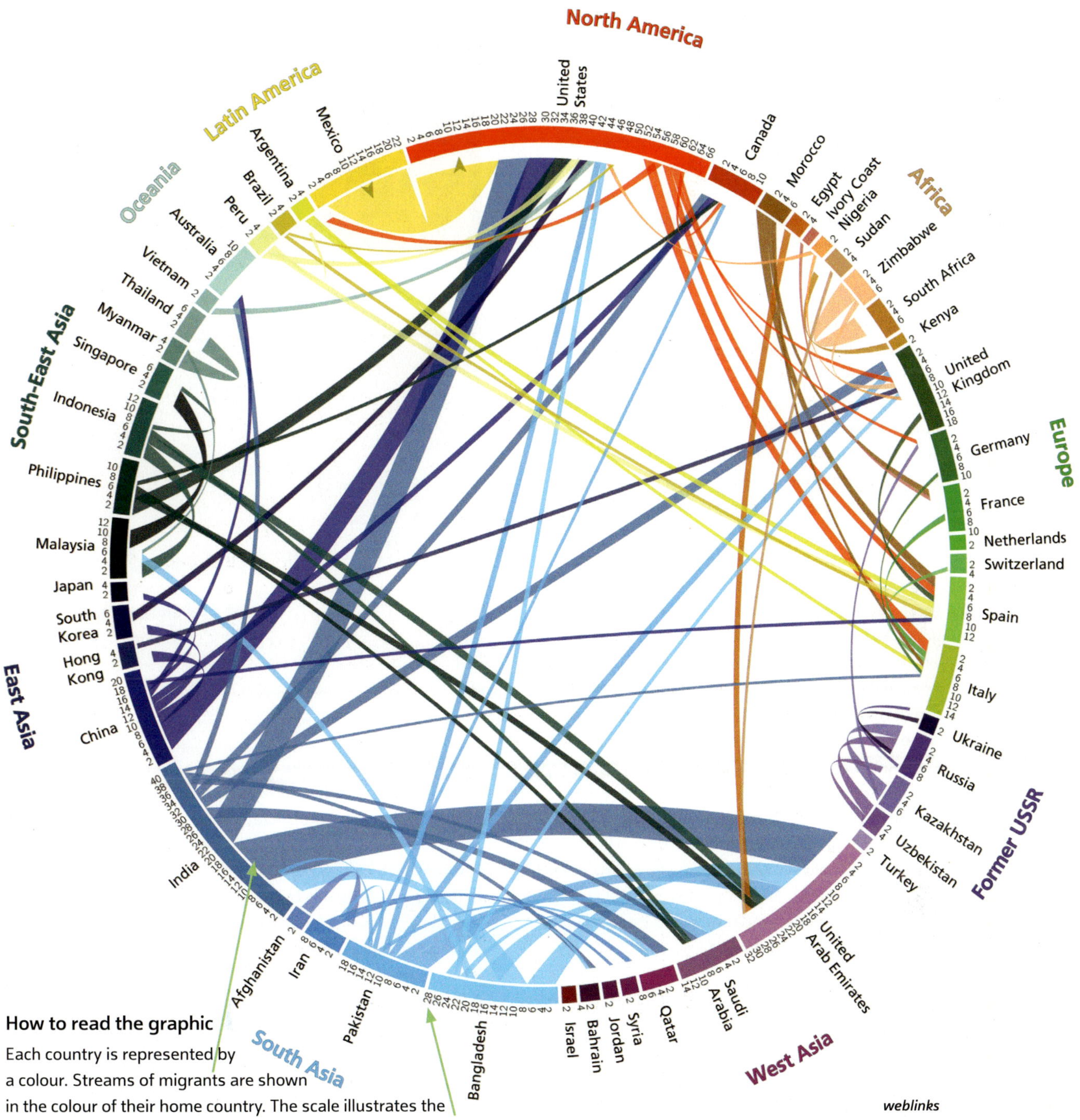

How to read the graphic

Each country is represented by a colour. Streams of migrants are shown in the colour of their home country. The scale illustrates the magnitude of all migration (immigration and emigration, in 100,000 persons). Included are migration streams of 70,000 persons and above.

(Source: Abel, G. J., Sander, N., Quantifying Global International Migration Flows. In: Science, Vol. 343, no. 6178, 03/2014, pp. 1520ff.)

weblinks

The global flow of people

- www.global-migration.info
- www.circular-world.com

M3 The top 50 countries of origin and destination for migrants (2005 – 2010)

1. Evaluate graphic M3:
   a) Describe the migration streams in the world.
   b) Make a general statement identifying the major regions of the world that have been most affected by migration.
   c) Choose a migration stream, research its causes and characteristics and prepare a brief presentation.
   d) Using the Atlas, compare the graphic representation in M3 with that of the map labelled "Earth – Migration".
2. Look ahead to the future: You are most likely to change your place of residence at some point – after graduating from high school, to take an attractive job ...
   a) Note at least five location factors your future place of residence should offer.
   b) Name at least three economic regions that conform to your location standards, and choose one. Explain your choice.

Crossing borders – international migration

The causes of migration

Migration is the product of the interplay of many different factors. The most important of these include living conditions that prompt people to relocate.
This chapter is devoted to identifying the causes of migration and migratory movements as well as the routes and goals pursued by migrants in the process. To that end, we shall take a closer look at the example of migratory movements on the Arabian peninsula.

1. a) List the push and pull factors that played key roles in Gopal's decision to emigrate in a table (M3).
b) Describe the migratory movements in the countries on the Arabian peninsula with reference to M3 on p. 73.
2. a) Illustrate the model (M6) and apply it to Gopal.
b) Does the phrase "individualistic interpretation of the push-and-pull paradigm" apply in this case? Explain your reasoning.
3. Roughly twenty percent of the German population have what is called a "migration background", which means that these people, their parents or their grandparents once immigrated to Germany. However, nearly every family in Germany has changed its place of residence at least once.
a) Discuss the push and pull factors that were instrumental in the decision by your family, friends or relatives to change their place of residence.
b) Identify other regions in which these factors have played a significant role.
Ⓞ **4. A** Evaluate M4 and M5. To what extent do agencies and migration policies influence migration?
B Migration nearly always follows paths forged by others. Explain.
Ⓢ **5.** Illustrate the possible push and pull factors involved in the migration stream cited in 1 c) on p. 73.

→ Migration, Push and pull factors

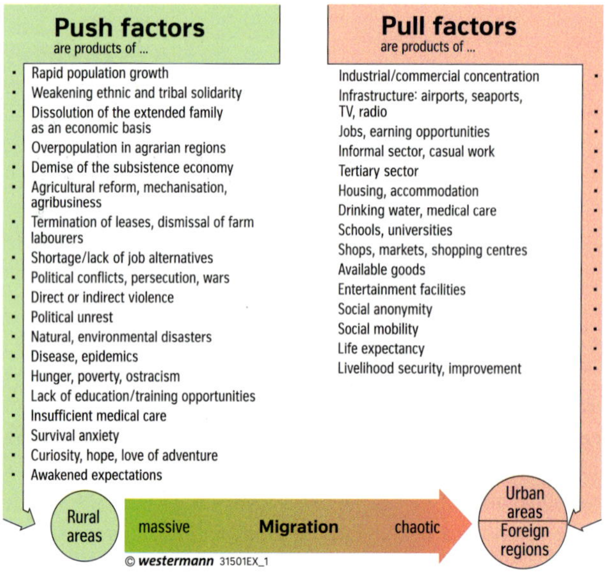

M1 Push and pull factors affecting migration

M2 The village of Ithampadal in Tamil Nadu

The city of his dreams

When Gopal arrived, he saw high-rise buildings and sparkling sand from the window of the aircraft. There are large buildings in the southern Indian city of Chennai as well – the only metropolis Gopal had ever seen before. His home village lies a thousand kilometres to the south. The buildings are higher in Dubai. They shimmer like jewels, as if they had been built only for their beauty. Gopal gazed from the aeroplane window and thought about the money – the 80,000 rupees (the equivalent of 1,600 euros) he had paid the agent in India for arranging for his visa, his ticket and his new job. He had no idea how much he would be earning, but he hoped to be able to pay off his debts in a couple of years. He didn't know that the poor received only very little of the wealth they generated. [...]
He comes from the village of Ithampadal in Tamil Nadu in southern India, his past the colour of dust. [...] A single paved road, a well, a pond full of muddy water and women doing laundry on its banks. Three thousand people live there from rice farming. Their poverty is a whim of nature, just like Dubai's wealth. Many villages in India are even poorer, and many families are poorer than the Gopals. Everyone in his village belongs to the caste of cattle and sheep breeders. "I'm destined for the lower class", says Gopal, and laughs – a strange, proud laugh. Every human being must submit to his destiny and Gopal doesn't think the idea is demeaning at all. His destiny is a place in which he feels secure. He carries it with him at all times. Gopal cleans hotel rooms in Dubai. He has work, while his people at home have nothing to do but wait for rain all summer. [...] He prays to Vakayadi, the god of his village, three times a day. [...] He prays for the future he saw from the aeroplane: a well-paid job, a house, a wife (his parents will choose the right one for him), five children, or perhaps only two. He wants them to become engineers or doctors.
Source: Burger, J., Tod eines Sklaven. In: Die ZEIT, 09/2008

M3 From an article about Guna Gopal in Dubai

Targeted emigration policy in the Philippines

The Philippines is one of the few countries that have been managing emigration systematically for decades. The temporary migration of workers has been promoted and regulated under the Overseas Employment Program since 1974. Initially, numerous contract workers were posted to the Middle East during the oil boom as a means of reducing unemployment and increasing the flow of foreign currency into the country. The primary objectives of the current programme are to combat unregulated migration and prostitution and improve working condition in the host countries. According to the government, more than 7.3 million Filipinos were living abroad in 2004. That figure equates to 8% of the national population. [...]
Saudi Arabia and Kuwait are still the most important countries of destination. However, private and government agencies post emigrant workers to other countries as well. In response to public pressure from both within and outside of the country, the government has been pursuing efforts to strengthen the rights and the social support system for Philippine labourers abroad since the 1990s. Additional preparatory courses have been introduced for the purpose of familiarising emigrant workers with the working conditions and the legal situation in the respective host countries in order to protect them against exploitation. A special ID with a bank account and integrated Visa card enables workers to send money home for a reasonable fee. [...]

Source: HWWI, Rückückberweisungen – Brückenschlag zwischen Migration und Entwicklung? In: focus MIGRATION, Kurzdossier Nr. 5, 2006, www.focus-migration.de, accessed 26.02.2015

M4 Emigration policy

Placement agencies

The ITUC (International Trade Union Confederation) has identified numerous workers who have come to Qatar from abroad. Each of them had to pay a placement fee amounting to an average of 1,000 US-$, and to several times that amount in extreme cases. These fees are paid to unscrupulous, often unlicenced agencies that promise high wages and good working conditions in the Gulf region. These promises are seldom kept, of course. Workers often have to borrow large sums of money at high interest rates to pay their placement fees. Their outstanding debts often force them to tolerate abusive conditions – a fact of which employers are only too well aware and which they use to their advantage. In many cases, workers put up their families' homes or assets borrowed from friends and relatives as security. The governments of their home countries bear a substantial share of the responsibility for such practices.

Source: IGB, Die Akte Katar. IGB-Sonderbericht 3/2014. www.dgb.de, accessed 26.02.2015

M5 Pathbreakers

The push-pull model of migration

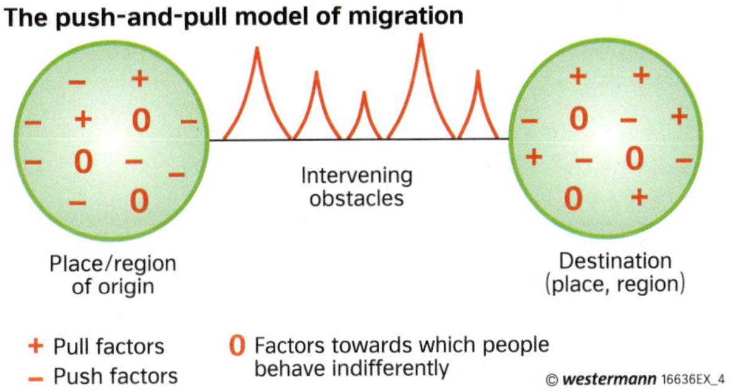

A plus sign in the diagram identifies the pull factors in the regions of origin or destination that attract people to the region in question or encourage them to stay. These factors include, for example, good jobs and earning opportunities as well as favourable climatic conditions. On the other side are the push factors identified by a minus sign, which prompt people to leave their regions of origin or to stay away from a given region of destination. Among these factors are high unemployment rates in the home countries and restrictive immigration policies in potential host countries. [...]
These factors and conditions differ in importance from one individual (one migrant) [...] to the next; for both the structural conditions in the potential host region and the additional, apparent intervening influences are perceived, evaluated and processed in psycho-social terms differently by different individuals. Thus they may also lead to different decisions. Therefore, the model also takes so-called personal factors into account, which, in addition to personality traits in the strictest sense, also include such aspects as the availability of certain socio-economic resources, a person's age, a person's current personal living situation, information, [...] as well as emotional ties to other people, the place of origin and the place of destination.

Source: de Lange, N. et al, Bevölkerungsgeographie. Paderborn, 2014. pp. 148f

M6 Factors influencing decisions about migration, the push-pull model

Crossing borders – international migration

Immigration – always in search of work

Foreign workers in Qatar are busy building the infrastructure for the 2022 FIFA World Cup at huge construction sites in Qatar. The award of the World Cup has made all of the Gulf States a focus of interest as destinations for migrant workers. Just as in Qatar, migrants are also at work building the new Dubai, for instance. Migrant workers are treated much the same in all of these countries. This chapter is devoted to an assessment of immigration to the Gulf States and related factors.

1. Characterise the working conditions for migrants (M2, M3, M6).
2. Illustrate the age structure of the population of Qatar. Distinguish between native citizens and migrants (M5).
3. Discuss the role played by the rentier economy in the Gulf States with respect to immigration (M8).
4. a) Until the mid-1980s, most migrant workers in the Gulf States came from non-oil-producing Arab countries. Describe the regions of origin of migrants today.
   b) Aside from economic reasons – Arab labourers were expensive – political factors are also regarded as responsible for this change. Discuss the possible reasons for this, e.g. in light of the Arab Spring.
5. (O) "The Gulf States and the corresponding regional migration patterns can be regarded as typical."
   A Take a position on this statement and explain your reasons.
   B Write a commentary on this statement.
6. (S) Express your opinion: Should a major international event like the FIFA World Cup take place in a country like Qatar?

→ Immigration

The FIFA World Cup in Qatar

Qater is currently carving a new city out of the desert ten kilometres from Doha. The future glamorous metropolis of Lusail City is planned as the hub for the 2022 FIFA World Cup competition – the first global football spectacle ever organised on Arabian soil. The huge arena for the final match – a stadium seating 90,000 spectators – will be built here, along with most of the 29 new hotels that will accommodate visiting football fans. The family of the Emir of Qatar plans to modernise the entire infrastructure of the tiny, super-rich nation at the same time. Over one hundred kilometres of Metro track will be laid; a highway bridge to Bahrain is planned, along with a completely new railway network […]. Last year, some 200 labourers from Nepal died in Qatar, many having suffered cardiac arrest following extremely long shifts in the blazing heat or fatal accidents at work. The figures are similarly high for labourers from India, Bangladesh and Sri Lanka, of whom more than 1,000 were injured at construction sites.

Source: Gehlen, M., Ist das Sklaverei? 06.10.2013, www.tagesspiegel.de, accessed 26.02.2915

M2 Migrants building the new Qatar

Female domestic workers

Because they are often beaten, emotionally terrorised or sexually abused, countries such as the Philippines, Nepal and Indonesia issued orders forbidding the recruitment of their female citizens by Arab states about two years ago. "All I ever got to eat was what my employers left on their plates", explained one Filipina who sought refuge in her country's embassy in Kuwait City. She had decided to flee when the family demanded that she wash the windows of their house at three o'clock in the morning. According to a report issued by the US State Department, abusive treatment of domestic help is so widespread in Kuwait that it effectively amounts to the crime of human trafficking.

Source: Gehlen, M., Zwangsarbeit für die Superreichen. In: Die ZEIT, Oct. 2013

M3 Domestic workers

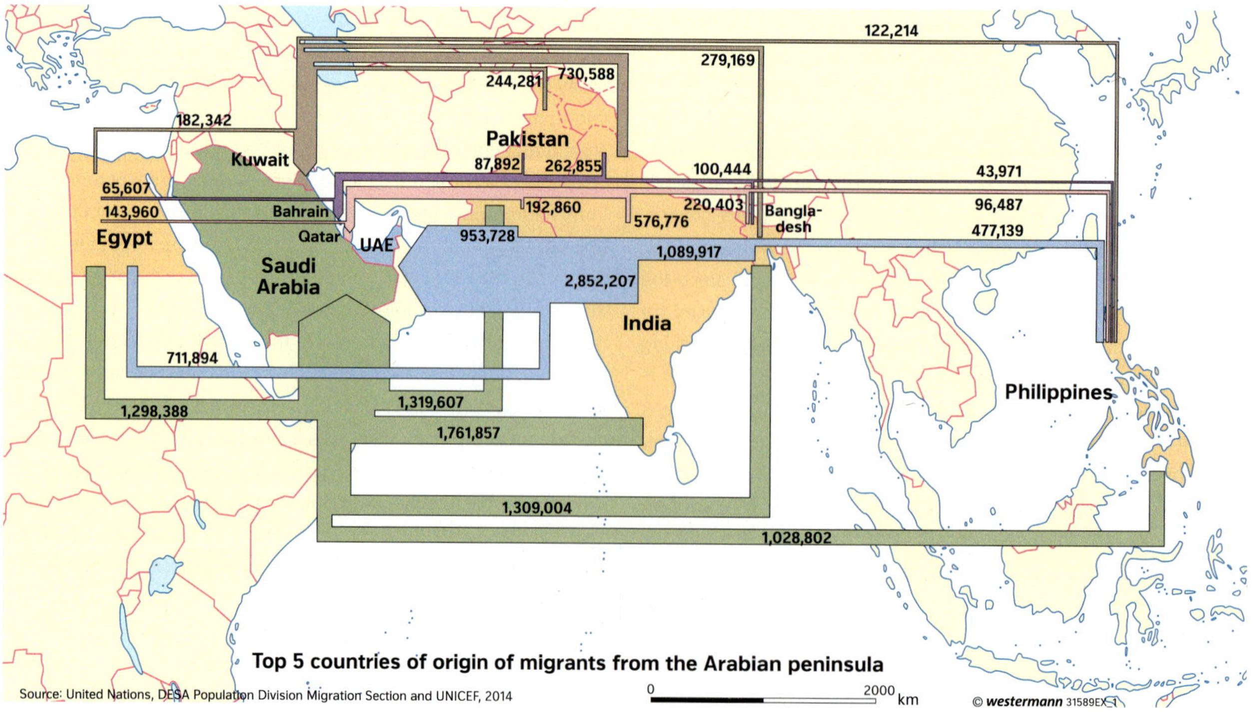

M1 Leading countries of origin of migrants working on the Arabian Peninsula (2010)

M4 Labourers in Dubai: city of luxury and the super-rich

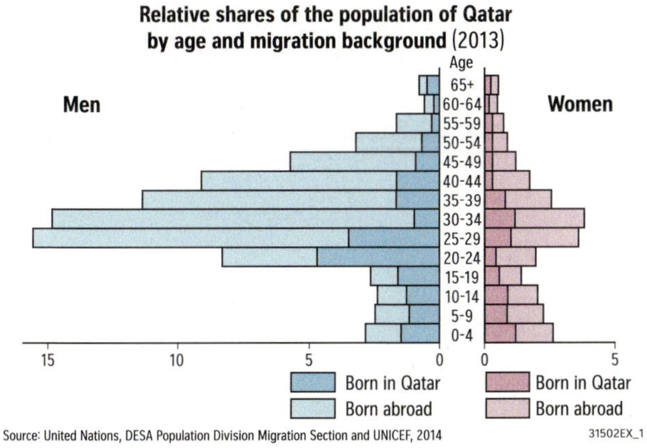

M5 The age structure in Qatar (figures in percent)

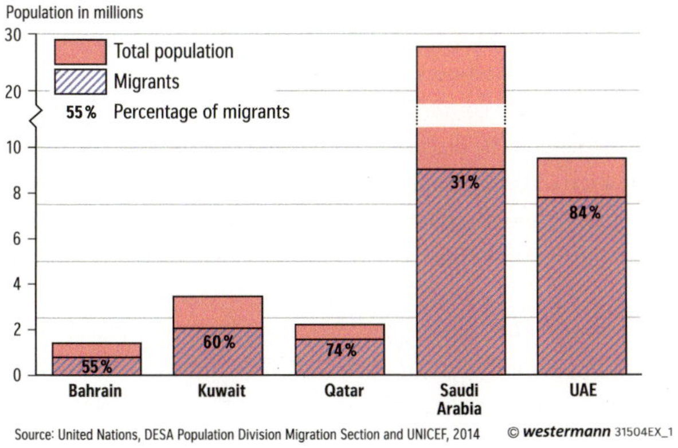

M6 Percentage of migrants in the total population (2013)

The kafala system

In order to obtain a work visa, every newly arriving migrant needs a local sponsor, to whom he ordinarily surrenders his passport. Under the terms of the kafala system, employers exercise full control of their workers and are free to decide whether they remain in Qatar, move to a different workplace or are permitted to leave the country. Workers subject to such strict control often hesitate to report abuses or assert their rights for fear of retribution.

M7 Working conditions

The "rentier" economy and "rentier" mentality

The term "rentier" refers to "income as a gift of nature". [...] The Gulf States [differ from most other countries] by virtue of the fact that at least 80 percent of direct state revenues come from rentier income – primarily from the sale of petroleum. Essential to the concept is the fact that rentier income comes from outside the country, which means that the national economy does not rely on a productive domestic sector. [... the government] provides for the most politically advantageous distribution of rentier income among its citizens. Consequently, a "rentier" mentality has emerged in the Gulf States, according to which the government is not viewed as a representative organ of the people, but rather as a provider of aid, subsidies and various services that are made available to citizens free of charge. In return, citizens waive their rights of participation in the political decision-making process. [...]
One of the most important tools used to distribute wealth generated by rentier income within the native population of a country is the practice of hiring citizens to high-paying jobs in the public sector under luxurious working conditions without requiring them to perform in return.

Source: Winckler, O., Das Aufkommen struktureller Arbeitslosigkeit und darauf folgende Politiken. 30.11.2012, www.bpb.de, accessed 26.02.2015

M8 Oil-producing countries

Crossing borders – international migration

Emigration – migration as an opportunity for development?

Within the context of the debate on migration and development in recent years, increasing emphasis has been placed on the potential power of emigration to stimulate economic development in the countries of origin. Particular attention has been focused on the role of remittances and the return of migrants to their home regions. Yet people sometimes fail to realise that emigration can also have a negative impact on economic development, as in the case of the emigration of trained, skilled personnel. What are the effects of emigration? Is it even appropriate to view emigration as an opportunity for development for the countries of origin?

Ⓞ **1. A** Illustrate the effects of brain-drain on a country's prospects for development with reference to several different occupations.
B Develop a schematic diagram illustrating the effects of the loss of physicians and nurses as well as people in other occupations.
2. Describe the importance of remittances from migrants (M1, M2, M4, M6).
3. Illustrate the potential impact of remittances from migrants and return or circular migration.
4. "Communities in the diaspora can play a bridging role in the development of trade relations, capital transfer processes and technological advancement". Explain (M3, M5).
5. Compare the different positions regarding the impact of emigration on the countries of origin.

Ⓢ 6. Emigration as the "expression of underdevelopment and as an individual solution for structural problems" or emigration as "structural solution for all individual problems". Illustrate the perspectives that ae reflected in these definitions.

→ Brain-drain, Brain-gain, Emigration, Reverse transfers (remittances)

→ Reverse transfers (remittances)
are payments made to families or others in the home country – probaly small amounts in most cases, but amounting to huge sums in total.

→ Brain-drain
"Brain-drain", the emigration of well-educated, qualified young people, is also deliberately encouraged in the countries of the North. This applies especially to IT specialists, physicians and nurses – and even to members of the clergy. [...]
Qualified migrants are trained at considerable expense to societies in their home countries. When they emigrate, these investments in people are lost to the countries of origin.
Not only is value transferred from the South to the North, but the migrant population generally includes all of the (academically) educated people who are needed to promote the development and proper functioning of the countries of origin. This results in concrete supply shortages.
Source: Scholz, F., Entwicklungsländer. Braunschweig 2012, pp. 46f

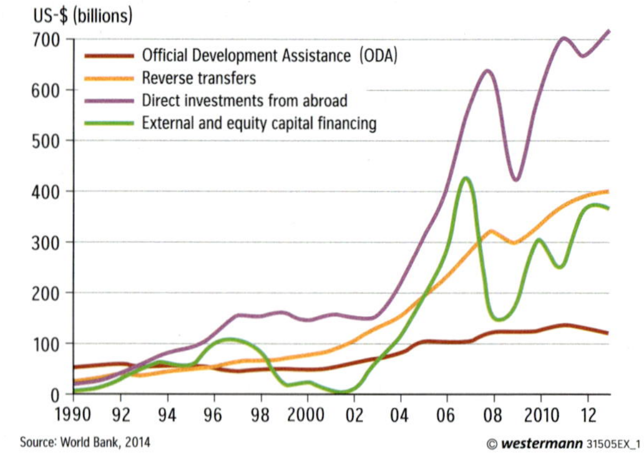

M1 Reverse transfers in comparison (1990 – 2013)

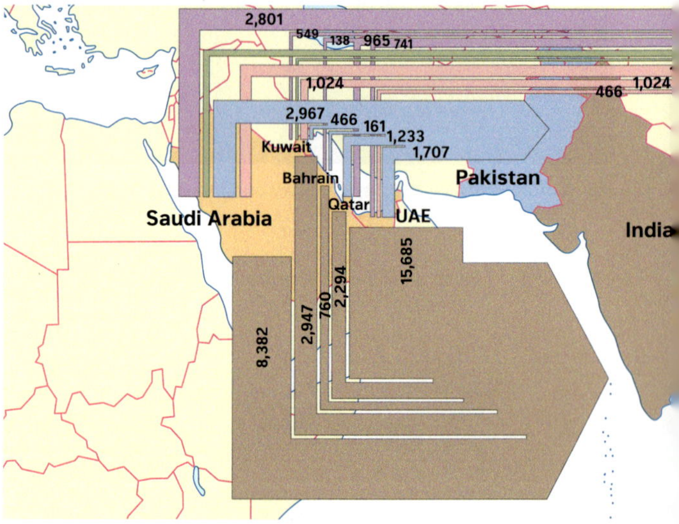

M2 Reverse transfers from the Arabian peninsula (2012)

The international migration of highly qualified people – advantage or disadvantage?

Politicians express concern about the huge numbers of well trained workers who leave Sub-Saharan Africa and the Caribbean ("brain-drain"). Expressed as a percentage of all well qualified people, the number of educated emigrants seems quite high. Yet on the whole, most of the qualified workers who emigrate to high-income regions come from larger countries with moderate income levels, such as Brazil and India. The prospect of migration gives rise to a greater accumulation of human capital [...]. Grounds for concern are the weak prospects for development in several African countries south of the Sahara, in Central America and in the Caribbean, where emigration is taking place on a much larger scale. [...] Critics of the debate over "brain-drain" and "brain-gain" point out that the real patterns of international migration are given too little serious consideration. Trained workers do not simply disappear; they "circulate" instead among the countries that participate in the global economy. [...] Aside from the fact that they account for substantial money-transfer streams, many trained migrants work very hard to be able to return to their home countries with better prospects as entrepreneurs and supplied with capital as well as new skills and ideas.
Source: World Bank, Weltentwicklungsbericht 2009. Wirtschaftsgeographie neu gestalten, 2009. p. 203

M3 Assessment of the migration of highly qualified people

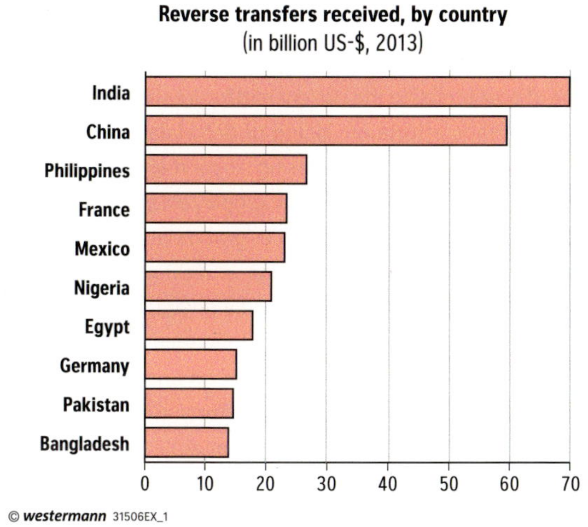

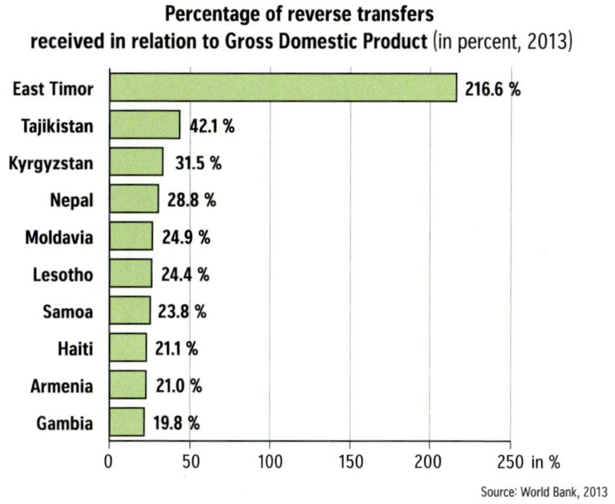

M4 Top 10 recipients of reverse transfers

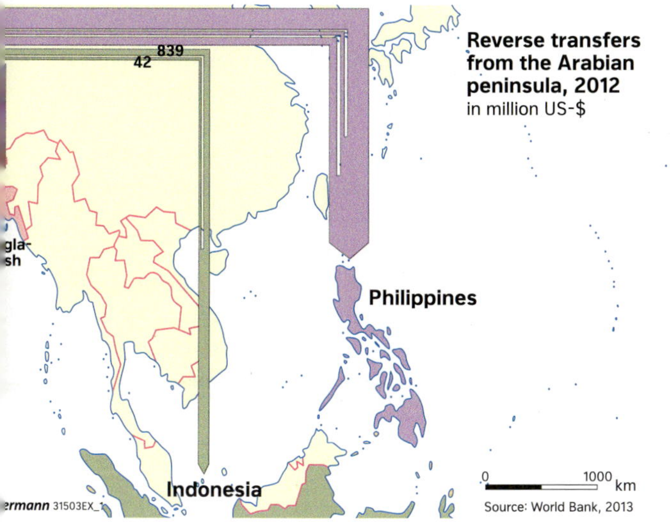

The substantial amounts of money remitted by migrants to their home countries do not compensate for [brain-drain], especially in view of the fact that the recipients of such payments tend to grow accustomed to having others assume responsibility for their existential risks. [...] For the most part, [remittances] are used to pay for consumer goods, education and health care. They secure the existence of families and increase their purchasing power, thus raising their living standards, yet they also contribute to a general increase in local prices and rising costs of living. Those who do not receive payments from abroad suffer as a result. Because such reverse-transfers are rarely invested in measures that generate income, the families in question remain dependent on their labour migrants and are compelled to send more and more of their members away to work abroad.

Source: Scholz, F., Entwicklungsländer, Braunschweig 2012, p. 47

M6 Reverse transfers

Migration as a development factor

People who leave their homes to seek their fortune in another part of their own country or continent, or who set their sights on an industrialised country, do not generally sever all ties with their own country. Quite the reverse is the case in fact. Once they have established a new home in a destination country, many of them regularly send money to their families and friends. [...] Many family members use the money to set up small businesses in the migrant's country of origin. They send their children to school and are able to pay for health care.

Associations and networks set up by migrants from the same source country, sometimes known as diaspora communities, often initiate non-profit or private-sector activities in their new homes which target their countries of origin. In this way they strengthen the local infrastructure and the economy in general. Capital and expertise acquired abroad are ploughed back into their home countries.

Frequently, migration means not only going away. It also means coming back. Migration is not generally intended to be a permanent state. [...] Those already in work return once they have saved up enough to allow them to establish a livelihood in their own country, or when circumstances in their country of origin have changed such that they can again see genuine prospects of a future there.

Source: www.bmz.de/en/publications/archiv/topics/social_security/BMZ_Information_Brochure_01_2010.pdf, p. 6-7

M5 Migration as opportunity

Effects of migration

Literature on the subject reveals an increasingly strong consensus in support of the idea that the [relationship] between migration and development must be viewed within the context of the specific situation in each country of origin, the characteristics of migrants themselves and the opportunities available to migrants in the host countries. Advocates of this view [...] argue that the probability that migration has primarily negative effects on development, or at least that it has no noteworthy positive effects, is highest in developing countries in which the conditions for development are generally unfavourable and in which social security systems and public services are inadequate or lacking entirely, markets are dysfunctional, massive inequality is prevalent and the political system is authoritarian or plagued by the progressive deterioration of governmental authority and access to non-exploitative forms of labour migration is either difficult or impossible. In contrast, the positive effects of migration on development are greatest in countries in which inequality is less pronounced and citizens have access to public services and social security systems.

Source: Kraler, A, in Atac, I. et al (eds.), Migration und Entwicklung, Vienna 2014. pp. 13f

M7 Academic findings

Crossing borders – international migration

The borders of Europe

The European Union is a popular destination for migrants. There is a huge prosperity and development gap between the EU and its neighbouring regions. Moreover, frequent wars and crises have unleashed major migratory movements as well.
The principle of freedom of movement is firmly established within the European Union. This means that individuals are permitted to move wherever they wish without regard for internal borders. Consequently, Germany has become the leading destination for migrants in Europe. Established on the basis of the Schengen Treaty, this zone is protected by strict border controls and secured against the influx of migrants and refugees. At the same time, however, the countries of the EU open their doors to "preferred" immigrants from third countries.

1. Describe and interpret the scene shown in the photograph (M4).
2. Ⓞ A Explain the relationship between the absence of rights and low pay (M3).
   B With reference to M5, take a position regarding the concept of "undesirable immigration" as it applies to irregular or illegal migrants.
3. Develop an overview of recent migratory activity within and into Europe on the basis of an Internet search (M3, M5).
4. Describe measures adopted by the EU and evaluate the extent to which undesirable inward migration can be limited through border controls (M1, M3).
5. Describe and characterise two of the subsystems of the European migration system (M6).
6. Ⓢ Working with the map entitled "Ceuta – a Spanish Exclave" in the Atlas, analyse the map with reference to Assignment 1 above. Prepare a brief presentation.

→ Irregular inward migration

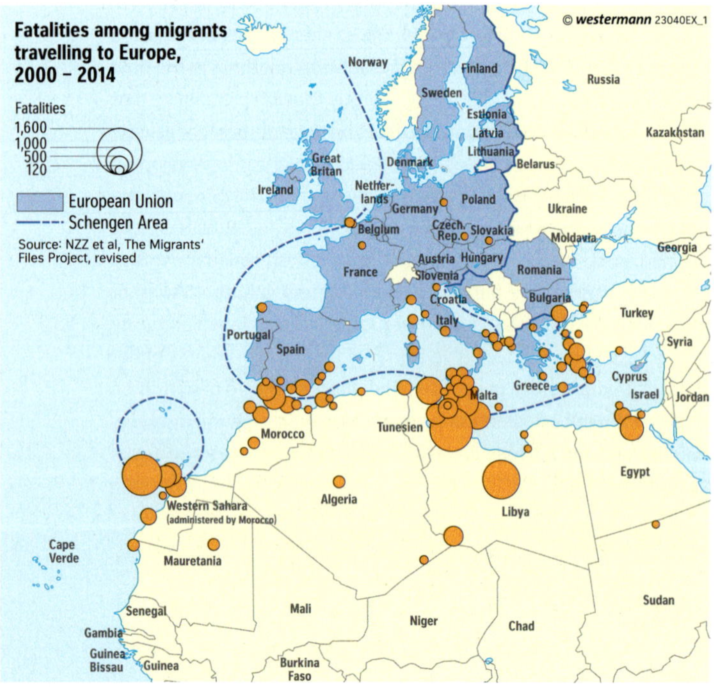

M1 Fatalities among migrants travelling to Europe

In the hope of counteracting the current and future shortage of skilled workers, systematic efforts are being undertaken in Germany to exploit the existing potential by increasing labour market participation and improving the qualifications of the employable segment of the population, while encouraging inward migration at the same time. Yet as the low rates of inward migration in 2008 and 2009 clearly indicate, a sufficient influx of migrants is by no means guaranteed. This is also underscored by the fact that Germany is only one of the countries which, under the influence of an ageing population, is seeking to attract migrants. Therefore, efforts are being made to enhance Germany's appeal to skilled personnel.
Thus, in addition to implementing EU regulations regarding foreign nationals with specific occupational qualifications (such as the Directive on the Recognition of Professional Qualifications and the introduction of the "Blue Card"), the Employment Directive has also been revised. In force since July 2013, the Directive entitles (non-academic) skilled personnel from third countries with professional qualifications to enter the country. The prerequisite for inward migration is a certificate of training attesting to qualifications equivalent to those required for a comparable profession in Germany. In addition, the need for additional skilled personnel in the respective field must be recognised. Such needs analyses are performed by the Federal Labour Agency and the results are recorded in a list of occupations, sectors and regions. The Blue Card entitles highly qualified individuals from non-EU states to enter Germany without going through complicated procedures. Prerequisites are a college degree and a minimum annual salary of roughly 45,000 euros.

Source: Carrel, N., Anmerkungen zur Willkommenskultur. In: APuZ, 47/2013, p.32

M2 Inward migration of qualified personnel

What does the label "illegal alien" really mean?

Their "illegal" status makes these mobile citizens of the world vulnerable to extortion and exploitation. They have no rights whatsoever. Yet their jobs and the services they provide serve a necessary function – necessary by all means for their own survival and that of their families beyond the borders of their host countries, but above all in the interest of wealthy Western societies and emerging, developing countries striving to attain that status. One can only react with moral outrage to the desperate situation in which these people find themselves – people who want nothing more than to do good work in order to feed their families, and are usually compelled to live in a state of extreme submission in European countries for decades at a time because they must be very careful to avoid attracting attention. But that is not the point. The point is that the demonstrative humanity of the West basically presupposes the inhumane treatment of "illegal aliens"! Without their active presence, without their low wages, which are closely related to their lack of rights, without their selfless contributions in the fields of geriatric nursing and child care in households struggling to achieve gender equality, these societies would collapse. Illegal aliens are simply "essential to the system", like the major banks and the courts that condemn them.

Source: Beck, U., Das Ohn-Machtspiel der Rechtlosen. In: Frankfurter Rundschau, www.fr-online.de, 04.01.2015, accessed 26.02.2015

M3 "Illegal aliens"

M4 Golfers in Melilla – Melilla and Ceuta are Spanish exclaves in northern Morocco. The fence marks the official boundary between Europe and Africa, at which thousands of people wait for an opportunity to enter the EU. Melilla is secured against the influx of illegal immigrants by three-to-six-metre-high fences and barbed wire, motion detectors and night-vision devices.

Inevitably irregular

A substantial percentage of migrants from Africa and the Near East are irregular. Many migrants travel without valid documentation. They cross national borders illegally. Many are victims of human trafficking and/or are forced to rely on criminal human smugglers. Thus the official immigration statistics provide only an incomplete picture. [...] Different channels exist for irregular migrations, most of which are only temporary. They are almost always located at the weakest points on the border to the EU or the Schengen Zone, which are always made more effectively secure once they have been identified. Thus the rate of irregular migration across the border between Turkey and Greece was high for many years. Once border controls were stepped up by the European border management agency Frontex, migration activity shifted in part to the border between Turkey and Bulgaria – until Frontex strengthened border controls there as well.

Source: Klingholz, R., Sievert, S., Krise an Europas Südgrenze. Berlin 2014, pp. 12f

M5 Irregular migrants

M6 European migration systems

Global population growth

More and more people every day

More than seven billion people now live on our Earth, and the world's population continues to grow. Two to three new earthlings are born every second and the annual total approaches 82 million.
The rates of population growth differ significantly however, especially between countries and regions in different phases of development. We shall take a closer look at this demographic divide in this chapter.
The first step will be to examine global trends in population growth and the possibilities for predicting future population trends. The impact of population growth on economic development will then be analysed.

1. **Describe the growth of the world's population, its global distribution and future development (M2, M6, M7).**
2. **Illustrate the concept of the demographic divide with the aid of M3.**
3. **Calculate the population of Ethiopia in 2030 at growth rates of 2% and 3% respectively (M1).**
4. **Describe the trend in fertility rates (M3).**
5. **Produce a graph illustrating the impact of persistent population growth on economic development (M4, M8–M10).**

→ Birth rate, Fertility, Growth rate, Mortality rate

Population growth and decline, 2015 to 2065 in selected countries
(in million inhabitants; middle variant)

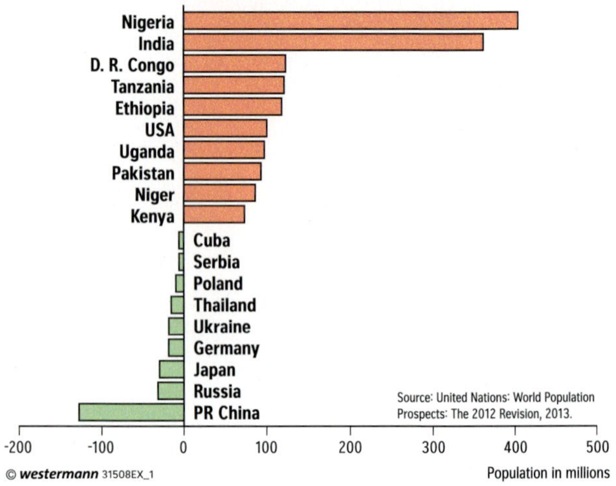

M2 The biggest "winners" and "losers" from 2015 to 2065 in comparison (in millions)

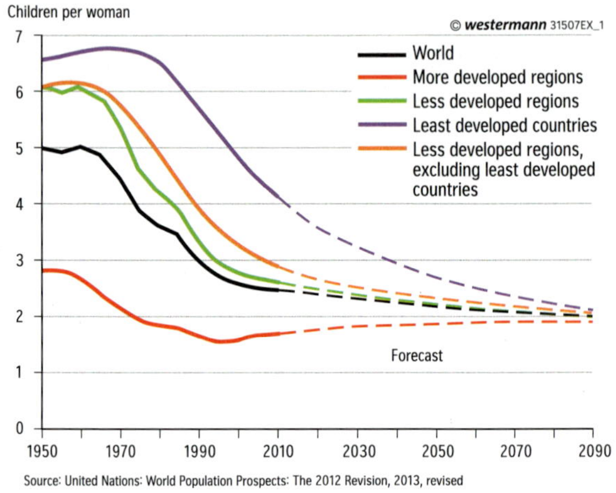

M3 Declining fertility rates, 1950 – 2090

→ Fertility
The number of children per woman in a given country or region.

→ Birth rate
The number of births per 1,000 inhabitants in a given year.

→ Mortality rate
The number of deaths per 1,000 inhabitants in a given year.

→ Growth rate
Birth rate minus mortality rate.

weblinks
Weltbevölkerungsuhr
www.weltbevoelkerung.de/meta/whats-your-number.html

	Ethiopia	Germany	South Korea
Population (in millions)	92.2	80.4	50.0
Birth rate (‰)	28	8	9
Mortality rate (‰)	8	11	5
Population in 2050 (in millions – mean projection	187.6	76.2	51.0

Source: United Nations, World Bank 2013

M1 Population growth data for selected countries, 2012

How population growth slows economic development

High fertility rates, the correspondingly high rate of population growth and the disproportionately high percentage of young people pose a number of different risks and obstacles to economic development.

Schools and health-care facilities are often in particularly short supply in rural regions. Rapid population growth exacerbates this problem, as the need for teachers, physicians and other service providers is greater in more densely populated areas. The lack of positive prospects for residents of rural regions leads to increasing migration to urban areas, which often evolve into megacities. These megacities are hardly capable of keeping up with the resulting population growth, since they also suffer from an infrastructural shortage of housing, running water and regular jobs. Thus most migrants end up at least temporarily in slums.

M4 Infrastructure

Three different variants have been calculated for the birth-rate scenarios projected by the United Nations. The UN generally assumes that fertility rates will continue to decline in countries in which people tend to have many children, as this corresponds to the prevailing trend in other countries.
Minor differences in the average numbers of children per woman have a significant impact on population development. The middle variant is based on the assumption that the global average of 2.5 children per woman will decline to two children per woman by the year 2100. The lower variant is calculated at one-half a child less. The "constant variant" (which reflects a constant fertility rate) represents a value that matches the current level.

M5 Population projections

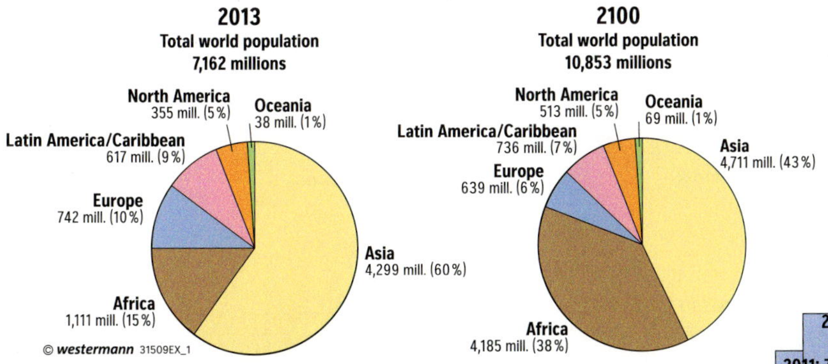

M6 Regional distribution of the world's population, 2010 and 2100

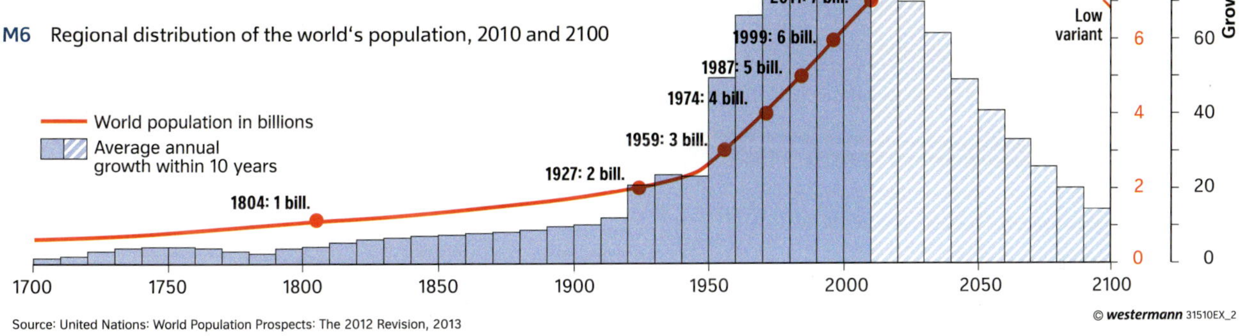

M7 Growth of global population and projections for the year 2100

Although a sufficient quantity of food is produced worldwide, it is not always available where it is needed. Higher yields resulting from the use of modern farming methods are rarely achieved in countries where population growth is the strongest. According to estimates, between 90 and 125 million more people could be suffering from hunger by the year 2080. And climate change contributes to a worsening of these food shortages. Developing countries are hardest hit by climate change, especially in the region south of the Sahara, and these countries are the least likely to be able to adjust accordingly. [...]
According to projections, between 350 and 600 million people in Africa alone will be forced to live with a shortage of water by the year 2050.

M8 Food and water supply

Harvest yields are also diminishing in some regions because fertile soil is being eroded due to improper farming methods or because irrigation is causing the groundwater table to sink and soil to turn salty. This in turn creates the need for more land in order to feed the growing population. Because population growth is strongest in tropical countries, species-rich rainforests are disappearing as well. [...] And to cite yet another example, 80 percent of the world's fish stocks, which provide food for more than 2.9 billion people, are overfished today. Furthermore, environmentally sound sewage treatment is lacking in many areas – and natural regional habitats are being destroyed above all by industrial waste water.

M9 The environment

Shortages of essential resources, such as drinking water and fertile soil, harbour a huge potential for conflict and may trigger migratory movements across national borders. Refugees and migrants can pose security risks when neighbouring countries are unable to accommodate them properly. Studies have also shown that countries with disproportionately high percentages of young people are more susceptible to political unrest and armed conflict. Young adults, and especially young men, tend to respond with violence when they are deprived of prospects for training, education and jobs. The most seriously endangered countries are located in Africa and the Hindu Kush – that is, in the regions with the highest rates of population growth.

Source M4, M8–M10: Sippel, L. et al, Afrikas demographische Herausforderung, Berlin 2011.

M10 National security

Global population growth

A model of population development

The 19th century witnessed the onset of rapid population growth in Europe and in many of today's industrialised countries. This trend reflected changes in birth and mortality rates resulting from modernisation. In comparison it is evident that, although these developments took place at different times in the various countries, they progressed in much the same ways and led to very similar results. These similarities were summarised in the Demographic Transition Model.
This section is concerned with the ways in which birth and mortality rates change, the underlying causes of those changes, the interpretation of that process in the model, critical responses to the model and the specific characteristics of the process as it unfolded in Germany.

1. a) Describe the model depicted graphically in M3. How do birth, mortality and population growth rates change? What are the characteristic features of each phase? How does the size of the population change?
   b) Summarise: In what sense does the model describe a "transition"?
2. a) Describe the development of birth and mortality rates in Germany and distinguish between the individual phases identified in the model. Complete the population growth curve (M5).
   b) Does the history of population development in Germany correspond to the model? Provide evidence in support of your opinion (M3, M5).
   c) Cite background developments and causes that could be used to explain each phase of development (M5).
   d) Illustrate how specific aspects impact on birth and mortality rates.
3. Discuss the change in age structure that is ilustrated in the age pyramids and interpret the cartoon accordingly.

→ Age pyramid, Age structure, Demographic transition

M2 Cartoon

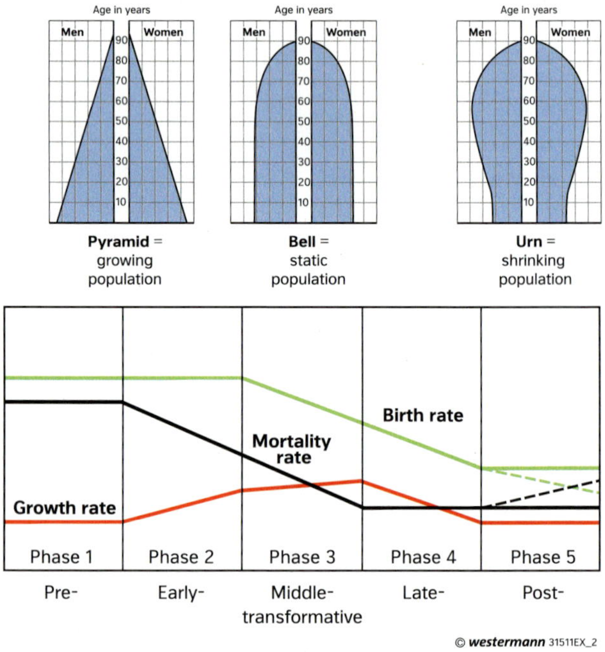

M3 The Demographic Transition Model and basic shapes of age pyramids

→ Age pyramid (also known as population pyramid)
Graphic representation of the age structure in a diagram.

Applications and limitations of the model

The Demographic Transition Model can be applied in at least four different ways. It can be used for the purposes of describing, classifying, explaining and predicting developments in the population of a given country. The first two of the aforementioned functions are undisputed. The model can provide a description of typical changes in fertility and mortality rates in Western industrialised nations over time. It also makes it possible to classify different countries according to their respective demographic status. Yet the model is of questionable value when it comes to explaining changes and predicting future population trends. Criticism of this application revolves around the argument that the model abtracts observed characteristics of European population movements and offers only a summary interpretation of development trends. The historical process of demographic change is represented in a highly simplified manner, even for the countries of Europe.
The low predictive value of the model is also attributable to the fact that the duration of individual process phases cannot be precisely determined [...].

Source: de Lange, N. u.a., Bevölkerungsgeographie. Paderborn, 2014.

M1 Assessment of the model

M4 Families, circa 1900 and in 2014

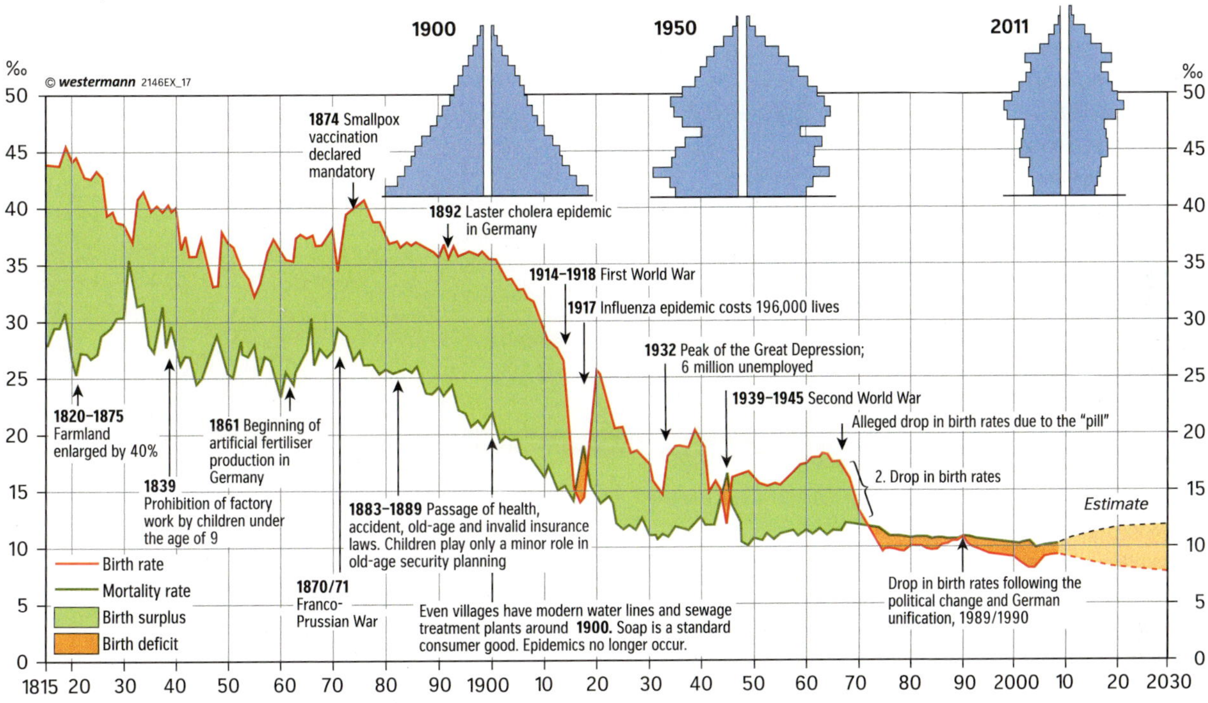

M5 Natural population development in Germany

Despite the fact that the model cannot be generalised, [...] it exerted a strong appeal in its graphic form [...]. The apparent plausibility of the graphic representation constantly tempts people to overlook two fundamental flaws. The mere juxtaposition of fertility and mortality rates has no explanatory value per se – thus it is absurd to speak of a "theory" of demographic transition – and no forecasts can be derived from it. Consequently, there is no justification for suggesting that the transition progresses automatically to Phase V in developing countries (at which point it would be completed) or that the matter of the eventual settling of mortality and birth rates at a low level is causally related to the modernisation of a country in the manner in which Western societies developed during the phase of industrialisation. There is no evidence for either claim, and both are radically oversimplified.

Source: Wehrhahn, R.V., Sandner Le Gall, V., Bevölkerungsgeographie. WBG, Darmstadt 2011.

M6 Criticism of the model

Factors that influenced developments in birth and mortality rates in European countries during the 19th and 20th centuries:

- Improvements in the food supply: modernisation and intensification in the agriculautral sector and expanding world trade combined to ensure a reliable supply of food.
- The initial lack of drinking water and sewage systems as well as inadequate hygiene in dairy operations in the major cities.
- Progress in the field of medicine; progressive development of healthcare services, improvements in hygiene.
- Urbanisation and transition from an agrarian to an industrial income structure: rising living standards, statutory changes (e.g. compulsory education), social policy measures [e.g. pension, accident, unemployment and health insurance], early efforts in support of women's emancipation.
- Children were gradually relieved of the obligation to serve as cheap labour and providers of social security.
- Upward social mobility grew increasingly dependent upon individual performance and thus on an individual's training.

M7 Factors influencing population developments

Global population growth

Ageing and shrinking populations – demographic change in industrialised countries

The term "demographic change" describes the recent population trend in industrialised countries. It is one of the changes that have taken place in these societies since the 1960s. "Germany is dying" and "the Methuselah problem" are scenarios that are frequently associated with demographic change. The idea of a shrinking population as an opportunity ("less is more") is heard less often.

1. Evaluate these materials (M2–M6, p. 85 M5): Describe the how the process of demographic change takes place, and list the reasons for this change.
2. Explain why the rate of 2.1 births per woman must be maintained in order to ensure population stability through natural growth alone.
3. Working with the Atlas (map, Population structure and dynamics in Germany) –
   a) illustrate the regional differences in ageing and population shrinkage in Germany;
   b) assess the statement that population shrinkage ordinarily leads to structural ageing.
4. a) Compare the present and future age structures of Germany and France and the respective patterns of change (M1, M2, M4).
   b) Interpret the cartoon in this context (M1, M2, M4).
5. Draw a mind map showing the causes of demographic change. Explain three of these aspects in greater detail.
6. ⓞ Choose three of the effects of demographic change cited in M9 and
   A explain why each of these effects poses a challenge to society;
   B describe these effects in concrete terms and prepare a brief presentation on one of them.

→ Demographic change, Population conservation level

A look across the border

The population of France is growing steadily. This growth is not attributable solely to the influx of migrants, but to a high fertility rate as well. The average number of children born to each woman in France is higher than in Germany. In 2010, for example, Germany reported a birth rate of 1.39 children per woman, as compared to 2.01 births per woman in France. [...] One reason for the difference is the French family welfare policy. The French government adopted extensive measures designed to provide support for families as early as 1939. The double-income family model has been promoted since the 1970s. A good child-care system has been established in support of the reconciliation of work and family life. Flexible employment models are also explicitly promoted by the government. Similar measures were not introduced in Germany until much later.

Source: de Lange, N. u.a., Bevölkerungsgeographie, Paderborn, 2014.

M1 Population growth in France

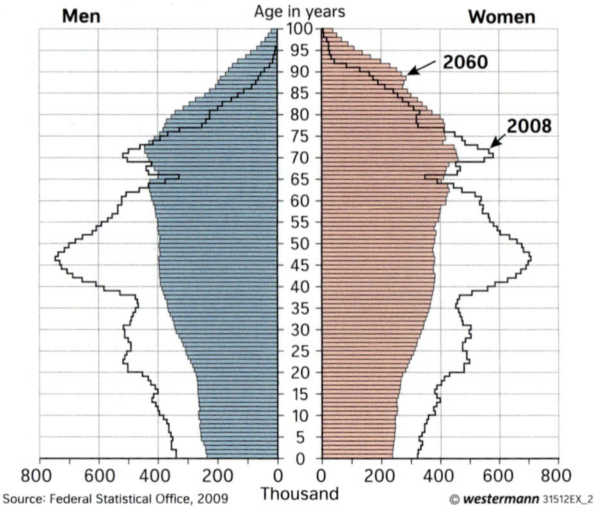

M2 Germany – age structure in 2008 and 2060

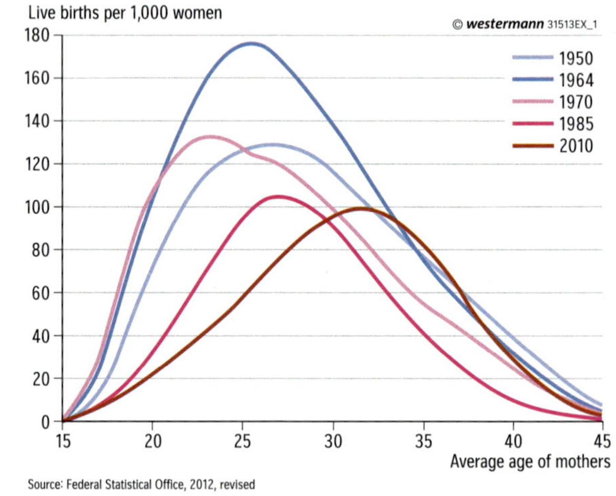

M3 Age-specific fertility in Germany

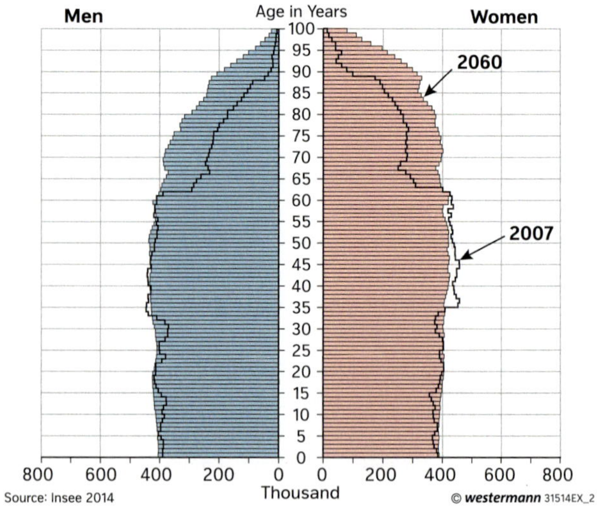

M4 France – age structure, 2007 and 2060

→ Population conservation level

This corresponds to a fertility rate of 2.1 children per woman – at which each generation completely replaces its predecessor.

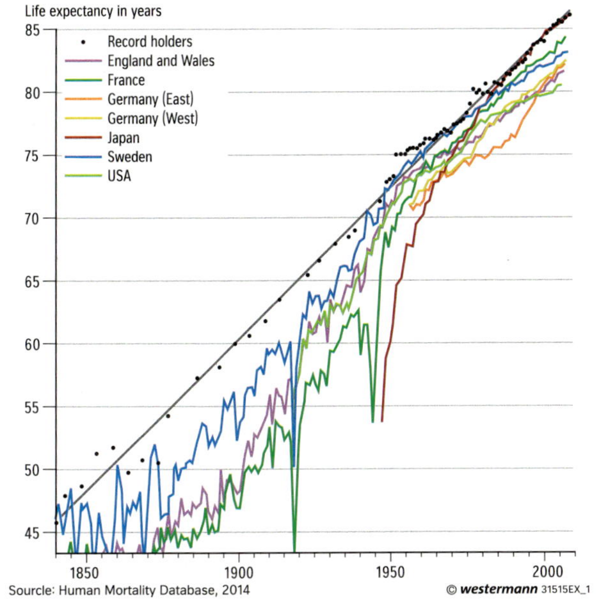

M5 Life expectancy at birth

A WONDERFUL VIEW

M8 Cartoon: "A wonderful view"

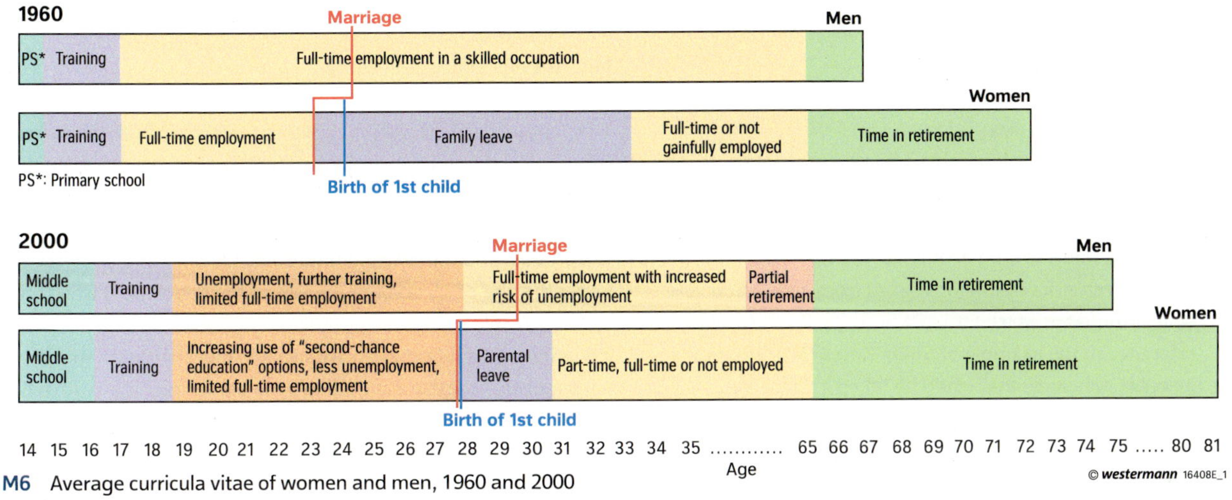

M6 Average curricula vitae of women and men, 1960 and 2000

Explanatory approaches

Prerequisites: Woman or couples enjoy freedom of choice when it comes to having children. The "fewer or no children" option is considered advantageous and people are aware of contraceptive methods and know how to use them effectively.

Contributing factors:

- Secularisation in combination with personal self-determination.
- Emancipation and enhanced women's rights, especially in matters relating to their own bodies.
- Cultural contexts that influence values and changes in values.
- Education, (paid) job opportunities.
- Social change, e.g. changes in lifestyle and family structures.
- Positive or negative economic circumstances and personal financial capital, which together offer longer-lasting economic security.
- Public support for the reconciliation of work and family life.

M7 Possible causes of declining birth rates

Effects

- Economic consequences in the form of general and regionally differentiated changes in demand and supply structures.
- Changes in labour market conditions (quantity, qualifications).
- Public and insurance-related budgets are uniquely affected.
- Technical and social infrastructures must be adapted to changing needs.
- Training and educational infrastructures need to be re-designed.
- Family living situations change.
- Household structures change.
- Changes in mobility patterns and transportation infrastructures must be taken into account.
- Recreational and tourist programmes must be adapted to changing patterns of demand.
- Health care, prevention and follow-up-care practices change.
- New forms of settlement structures, housing and urban architecture must be designed.

M9 Effects of demographic change

Global population growth

Growth – demographic changes in developing countries

In contrast to many industrialised countries, in which natural demographic change is characterised by shrinking populations, population growth rates in many less developed countries are still very high. That is the case in many African countries south of the Sahara. This section is devoted to identifying and explaining the causes of persistent population growth in less developed countries and the changes that lead to declining populations.

1. a) Describe the demographic situation of Ethiopia and compare it to the situation in Germany (M2, M3).
   b) Classify Ethiopia within the framework of the Demographic Transition Model and explain your reasoning.
   c) With reference to p. 82 M1/M2, M4, M8 – M10, discuss the challenges Ethiopia faces due to its demographic situation.
2. a) Illustrate the influence of education on demographic development (M6, M9).
   b) Prepare a graphic on the subject of "What factors lead to smaller families?" (M4).
3. a) Investigate the development of South Korea (M7). Illustrate the age structure that makes a demographic dividend possible. Why has the young population in Korea become a driving economic force?
   b) South Korea's development started from a situation very similar to that in which Ethiopia finds itself today. With reference to the example of South Korea (M7), discuss possible measures that could be taken in Ethiopia. Consider M4 as well.
4. Prepare an overview of the causes of population growth. Consider the information on p. 84 as well.

Ⓢ 5. Compare the age pyramids of Ethiopia and Germany. Summarise the causes of the differences between the two and note the challenges the two countries face in view of their age structures in an overview.

→ Age-structure effect, Demographic dividend

→ Age-structure effect
When women from baby-boom years become old enough to reproduce, birth rates remain high in spite of diminishing fertility rates.

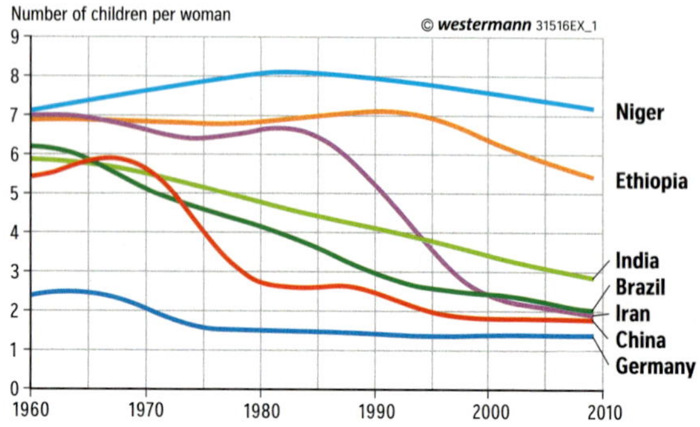

Source: R. Klingholz and K. Töpfer, Das Trilemma des Wachstums, Berlin, Institute for Population and Development (Discussion Paper, 8), 2012, p. 7

M1 Fertility rates in selected countries

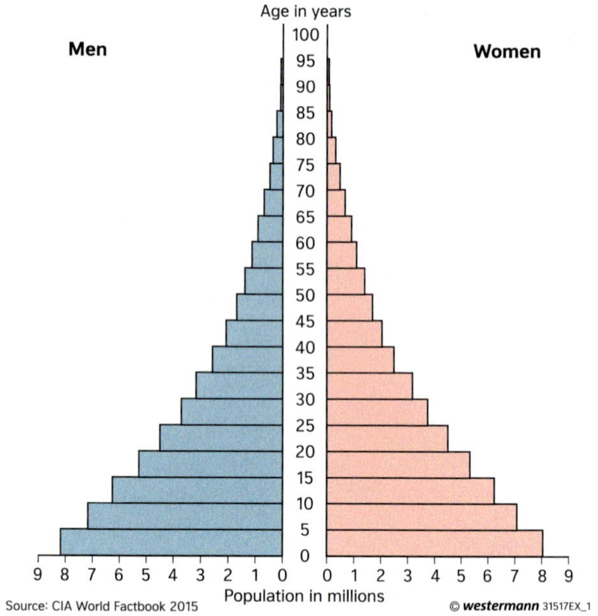

M2 The age structure in Ethiopia

The population of Ethiopia is expected to increase from the current 87 million to roughly 145 million by 2050. That equates to an annual growth rate of 2.1%. Since 1960, the fertility rate has declined from 6.9 to 3.9 children per woman. The population conservation level will probably not be reached until 2040. Children and adolescents under the age of 15 account for 41% of the population, while only 3% are over 65.
These indicators reflect explosive social changes in view of the growing population pressure and rising potential for migration within the country. With a per capita GNI of 1,040 US-$ (2010), Ethiopia faces major challenges in the years to come

Source: Schmidt, S., Bevölkerungsentwicklung in Deutschland und weltweit. In: APuZ, 4-5/2013, pp. 51f

M3 The example of Ethiopia

Factors that lead to smaller families

Birth rates are known to decline:

- when women have a greater voice in the affairs of their families and society at large and have access to alternatives to an exclusive role as mothers;
- when young girls and women have unhampered access to sex education, family planning and contraceptives;
- when young girls and women have better educational opportunities; women who attend secondary schools are likely to have children later in life and play a more active role in family planning;
- when new prospects for a better life emerge, through a move from the country to the city, better earning opportunities or new images of family life conveyed by the media;
- when infant mortality declines, because couples are willing to have fewer children only if every child has a better chance of survival.

Source: Sippel, L. et al, Afrikas demographische Herausforderung. Berlin, 2011.

M4 Reasons for declining birth rates

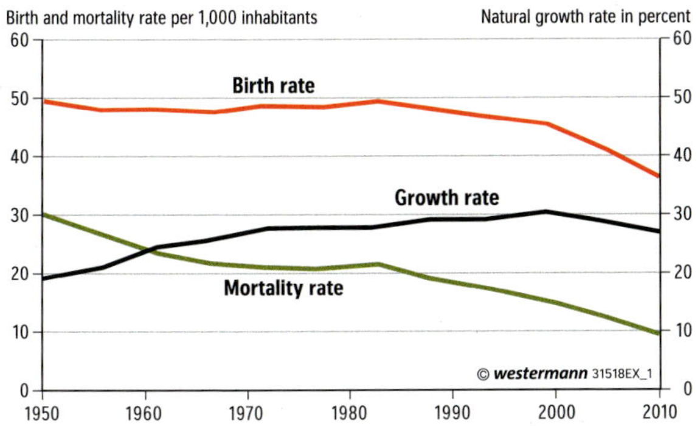

M5 Ethiopia: Birth and mortality rates

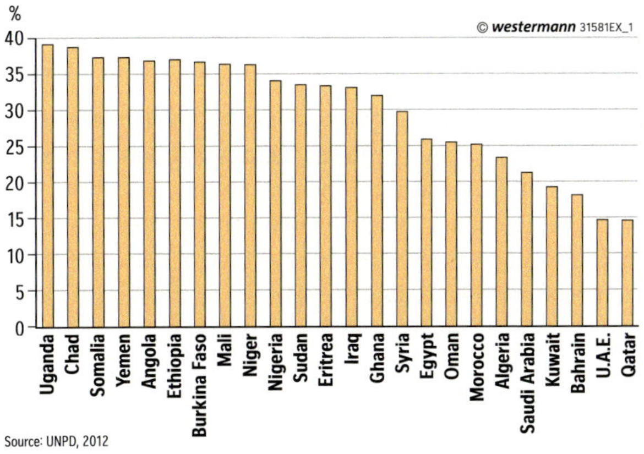

Source: UNPD, 2012

M8 Share of people aged 15 – 24 in the total adult population (all individuals over the age of 15) in 2015

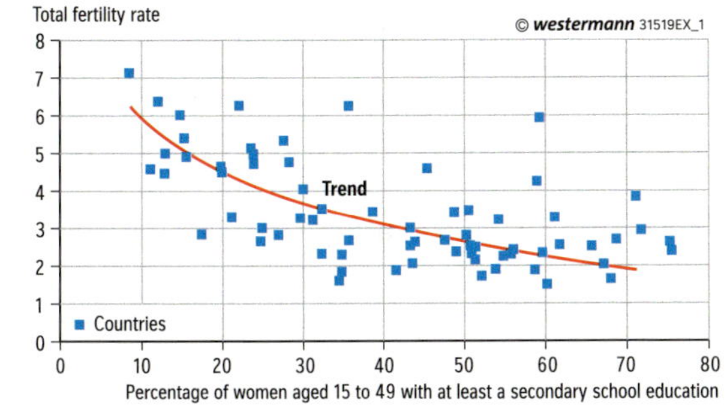

Source: R. Klingholz and K. Töpfer, Das Trilemma des Wachstums, Berlin, Institute for Population and Development (Discussion Paper, 8), 2012, p. 7

M6 Mothers: birth frequency and education level

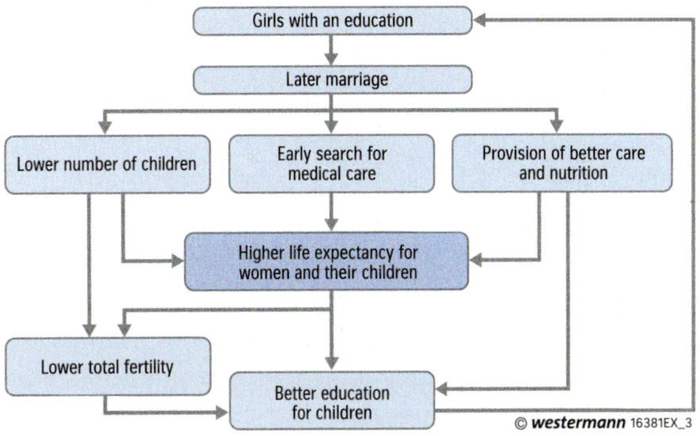

M9 The influence of education of demographic development

The example of South Korea

Fifty years ago, few development experts would have imagined that the war-torn, primarily agrarian nation of South Korea would eventually become the ninth-largest exporting country and one of the world's 20 richest nations (as measured by GNI). This success story began with massive investments in public education and an effective family-planning policy that included the distribution of contraceptives as well as improvements in health care for mothers and children. These policies led to a dramatic decline in birth rates. The average South Korean born in the 1960s had about five siblings. Twenty-five years later, he was the father of no more than two children, and has only one grandchild from each of his children today. Thus the employable population in South Korea (people between the ages of 15 and 64) has doubled to 35 million, while the number of people in the younger age group has diminished. South Korea reaped the benefits of this demographic bonus because it began educating its people – including women – early on and integrating them successfully into the labour market. Following the decline in birth rates by some years, South Korea's economy began to grow, thus making more and more capital available for investment in the further upgrading of the education and health-care systems, the national infrastructure and the development of more remote regions. South Korea also became increasingly attractive for private and foreign investors thanks to its better trained and educated population. During the past thirty years, the South Korean economy has grown by an average of 6.3 percent per year, in spite of the Asian crisis of 1997/98 and the financial crisis of 2008.

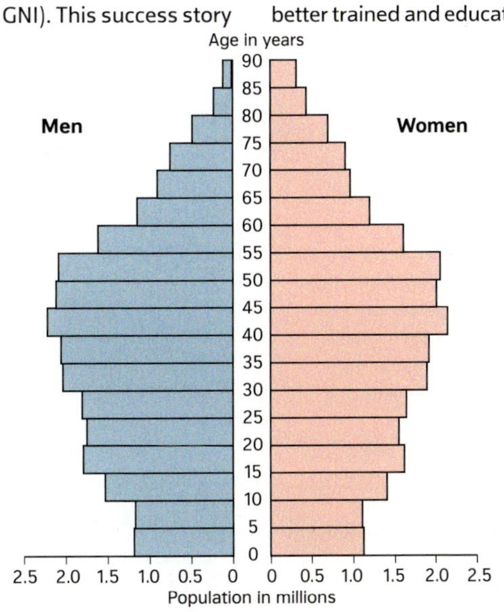

Source: Korean Statistical Information Service, 2012 © westermann 31520EX_1

The price for this demographic bonus is an ageing population. Because the fertility rate declined so rapidly in South Korea in the 1960s and 1970s, and is now one of the lowest in the world at 1.2 children per woman, the population is currently ageing faster than in any other country. Although only eleven percent of all South Koreans are now older than 64, forecasts indicate that this figure will rise to 34 percent by 2050. A steadily growing number of young people will have to support these older citizens. The government will have to make preparations to meet this need by making timely investments in social security systems, for example, and in measures designed to ensure that people can remain healthy, qualified and productive longer in life.

Source: Sippel, L. et al, Afrikas demographische Herausforderung. Berlin, 2011.

M7 The demographic dividend: declining birth rates and rapid economic growth

The essentials in brief

Migration

The causes of migration can be described with reference to push and pull factors. These are factors that prompt people to leave their homeland on the one hand, and others that attract them to a given place or region on the other. Generally speaking, migrants hope to improve their quality of life after reaching their destination. "Helpers", such as traffickers, placement agencies or social networks of relatives abroad, play an important role.
The example of the Gulf States, which boast the largest share of migrants and pursue active recruitment policies, illustrates the nature of the role migrants can play for their host countries or regions. The economies and societies in the rich oil-producing countries are dependent on foreign labour. The successful development of the oil-producing countries would have been inconceivable without the millions of labour migrants. Yet many of these immigrants live and work under exploitative, inhuman conditions in these countries.
An increasing number of people seek refuge in Europe, where they are confronted with reinforced border fortifications. They are often forced to take considerable risks. Major prosperity, security and development gaps often exist betweeen European and neighbouring countries. Immigration is likely to pose a huge challenge for Europe in future as well.

Demographic transition	Demographic change
Characteristics relating to marriage	
Rising marriage rates, declining age at first marriage	Declining marriage rates, rising age at first marriage
Relatively few non-marital domestic partnerships	Increasing number of non-marital domestic partnerships preceding and following marriages
Low divorce rates	Rising divorce rates; divorces shortly after marriage
High remarriage rates	Declining remarriage rates both following divorces and after the death of a spouse
Characteristics relating to fertility	
Declining fertility rates associated with fewer births at advanced age, falling average age of first-time parents	Persistently declining fertility rates due to postponement of births until later in life
Lack of reliable contraceptives	Efficient contraceptives
Decline in the number of illegitimate births	Rising numbers of illegitimate births to couples in non-marital domestic partnerships
Negligible numbers of married couples without children	Significant increase in the number of couples without children
Characteristic features of society	
Norms favouring material values (e.g. income, living conditions, health)	Values favouring self-realisation and autonomy
Intensive social cohesion, membership in parties and social networks	Individualism, withdrawal from social networks
Clear distribution of roles and social and family life	Withdrawal of government from everyday life; second wave of secularisation; sexual revolution, emancipation
Commitment to a specific lifestyle through marriage	Less early commmitment to a specific lifestyle; retention of options for action

M1 Demographic transition and demographic change in comparison

M2 Cartoon

The question of how the impact of migration on the regions and countries of origin is a focus of controversy. Migration can be regarded as an obstacle to development, as it is most often the young, well-trained people who leave their homelands. They are missed in their home regions, where so much has been invested in their training and education. This brain-drain may be compensated by return flows, not only of capital in the form of remittances to the families of migrants, but also in the form of ideas and know-how brought back by returning migrants. Thus it is evident that the impact of migration on development must be regarded from a number of different perspectives. Positive effects are recognised above all where the preconditions for development are already good.

Population growth

The world's population has grown substantially over the course of the past century. The seven-billion mark was surpassed in 2011. And population is still growing, most notably in the developing countries, where population growth has the power to slow progress in the development of infrastructures, food supplies, environmental protection and national security.
The Demographic Transition Model offers a tool for use in describing typical developments in the populations of premodern and postmodern societies on the basis of experience gained in Europe. Mortality and birth rates decline after a certain amount of time from high to low levels. This pattern is associated with strong population growth, as the gap between birth and mortality rates grows wider for a limited period of time.
The pattern that is now observable in many industrialised countries is described as "demographic change". It is characterised by ageing and shrinking populations, the progressive individualisation of society and great diversity resulting from immigration. In contrast, many countries of the South are still distinguished by strong population growth. The key to declining birth rates lies in training and education for women, although emancipation and enhanced women's rights are also important factors. Countries that succeed in lowering birth rates have the chance to benefit from a "demographic dividend". Larger numbers of employable people from strong birth years are faced by smaller numbers of children and seniors for whom care must be provided.

Skill Check

All the skills that you were able to acquire in this chapter are listed here.
You can judge for yourself if you have mastered each skill: ***securely***, ***moderately*** or ***barely***.

Explanatory skills

Can I ...		Unsure? Look it up on these pages
1.	illustrate the causes as well as the socio-economic and regional impact of migration and distinguish between its effects on regions of origin and destination?	74–79
2.	illustrate historical and current population trends in industrialised and developing countries and compare them with reference to the Demographic Transition Model?	84–89
3.	explain the factors that influence demographic change and the consequences of the respective changes?	82–89

Methodological skills

Can I ...		
4.	analyse complex presentation and research tools, such as maps, photographs, statistical information, graphs and texts for the purpose of responding to questions relating to the causes and consequences of migration and population growth?	72/73, 76–83, 86/87
5.	describe the Demographic Transition Model and assess its core statements as they apply to different examples?	84–89
6.	present geographic information in graphic form, e.g. in a schematic cause-and-effect diagram?	78/79, 82/83, 86–89

Evaluation skills

Can I ...		
7.	evaluate the expressive potential and limitations of models such as the Demographic Transition Model and the model of push and pull factors as they apply to migration?	74/75, 84–89
8.	evaluate the development opportunities and risks associated with migration?	76–81

Activity skills

Can I ...		
9.	develop differentiated approaches to the solution of complex problems, e.g. measures designed for the purpose of enabling a country to achieve a demographic dividend?	88/89

IV Global disparities

The challenge of unequal regional development

Summer Olympics in Beijing in 2008: a screen fence hides a slum directly adjacent to the sport facility from the eyes of passers-by.

Global development – global disparities

M1 People in Africa and Asia

→ Disparities
Within the context of geography, disparities are defined as inequalities in living conditions within a precisely specified area or between two or more regions. Such disparities relate to characteristics of significance to the societies in question. We speak of global, national and regional disparities. Eliminating regional disparities is the task of regional policy.

The concept of "one world" is an illusion.

Upon closer examination, the concept of "one world" that is often cited in demands voiced by politicians concerned with development issues turns out to be an illusion, as becomes apparent when we look at specific countries, regions and cities. Particularly dramatic are the differences in technical-economic development and living standards. According to recent estimates released by the World Bank, one out of every five people on earth is forced to live on less than 1.25 dollars a day.
Due to regional disparities within individual countries, country-to-country comparisons are often imprecise. Regional differences between the wealthy classes and those living in poverty are too large. Thus classification based on distinctions between underdeveloped, threshold and industrialised countries does not accurately reflect the actual situations in the countries in question. Yet such classifications do help us acquire an initial overview of global disparities. In any event, cities, countries and the global community are faced with the huge challenge of eliminating existing global disparities and promoting the development of regions and countries.

What is development?

Generally speaking, the word "development" is understood to mean "change or progress from an original status or condition after a certain period of time". The concept of development is often reduced to purely economic terms in discussion. Social indicators, such as health and education, are often neglected. In this context it is always interesting to ask who determines such classifications. The key aspects that define quality of life will always be different from one region, culture or religion to another.
It is important to ask in any case how so-called underdevelopment came about in different areas in cities, regions, countries or entire groups of nationss, and why such great differences continue to exist. After all, effective measures in support of positive development can only be adopted on the basis of investigation into the underlying causes. Such investigations are more difficult today, due to the progressive globalisation of the past two decades and the far-reaching interconnections in all areas of the economy and society. Thus the following questions are particularly relevant to the discussion of global disparities: What global and regional disparities exist today? How can we differentiate accurately between various stages of development? What internal, external and natural influences impact on development processes in specific regions and countries? How can positive and negative developments be explained?

The subject of basic human needs is a focus of discussion in various academic disciplines. From the perspective of development policy, material needs must be met above all in oder to ensure that people can survive over time, e.g. food, housing and clothing, drinking water, sanitary facilities, means of transportation, health-care and educational institutions. The minimum requirements for existence are met by ensuring that these basic human needs are satisfied. However, certain immaterial basic needs also play a crucial role in determining quality of life, such as participation in society, a sense of security and recognition.

M2 Basic human needs

The field of "happiness research" has become a focus of increasing attention in recent years. Extensive, serious comparative studies have been devoted to many regions and countries. Although these studies show that satisfaction with life rises under the influence of a certain level of prosperity, the increase is not proportional. According to the UN World Happiness Report, the happiest people live in Denmark, Norway and Switzerland. Germany ranks 26th behind such countries as Panama (15th) and Mexico (16th), but far ahead of other nations, including Japan (43rd) and Portugal (85th).

M4 Development doesn't necesssarily bring happiness.

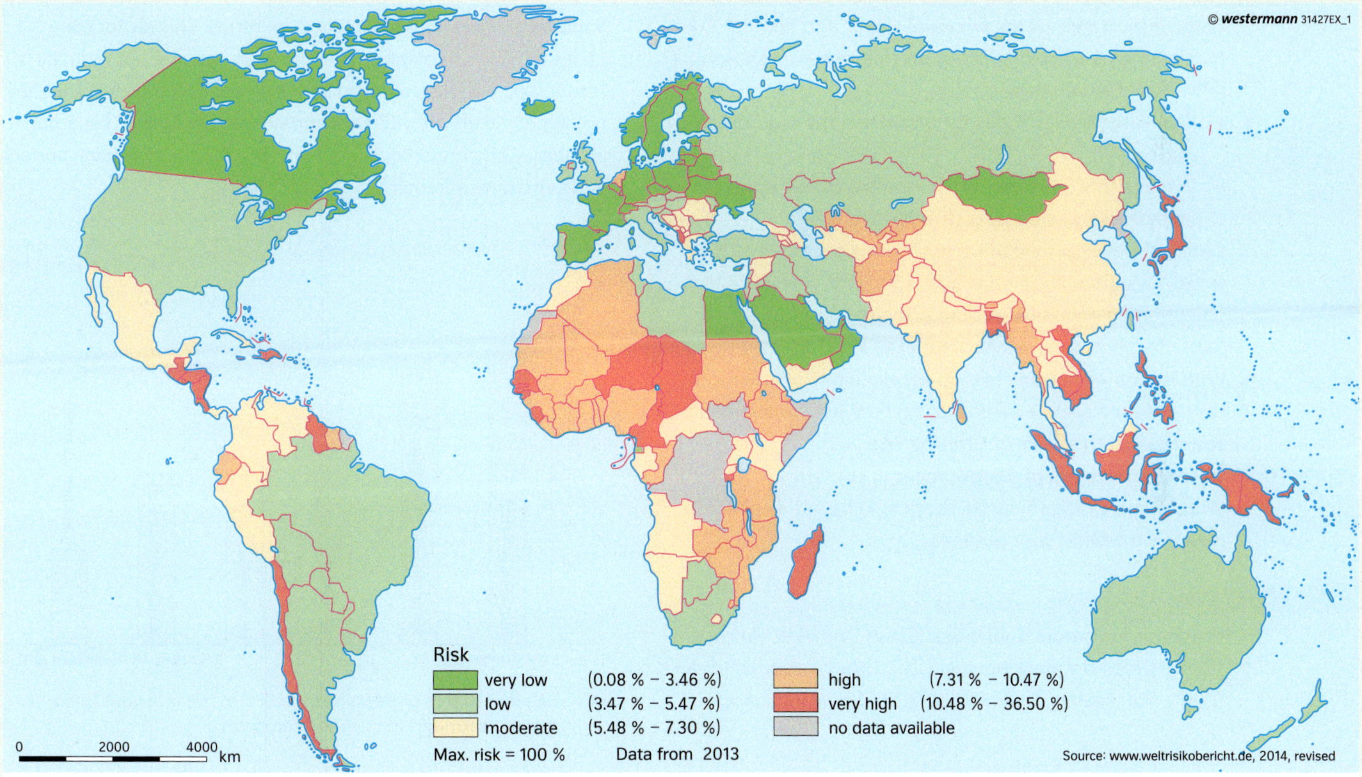

Note: The World Risk Index seeks to illustrate the risk of negative developments and the vulnerability of individual countries with reference to a combination of different aspects. The risk potential comprises four different indicators:

- Vulnerability to natural disasters (e.g. earthquakes, hurricanes, etc.)
- Susceptibility to risks associated with infrastructure, nutrition, housing and general economic conditions
- Coping capacities in terms of government management, preventive measures and early warning systems and medical care as well social and material security provisions
- Ability to adapt in response to natural events and climate change

M3 Global overview of the risk of negative development: the World Risk Index

1. List the possible characteristics of unequal living conditions for people in your city.
2. Describe the photographs in terms of basic human needs (M1, M2).
3. Illustrate the concept of disparities by discussing characteristics you consider socially significant.
4. The World Risk Index divides the nations of the world into classes. Explain the procedure involved in the classification process for the Index (M3)
5. Classify the countries cited in M4 within the framework of the World Risk Index. What do you recognise (M3, M4)?
6. A high level of development does not equate to happiness. State your position on this statement.

Comparing levels of development

Economic indicators

The levels of development in countries and regions are often compared with reference to certain economic indicators. What conclusions regarding the level of development can be drawn on the basis of economic indicators? How reliable are these indicators?

Ⓞ 1. Compare the status of economic development in specific countries and groups of countries in terms of Gross National Income (M1) by:
   A drawing a map entitled "Rich world – poor world";
   B writing a report for a news magazine.
2. Draw a map (as up to date as possible) showing the economic strength of the nations of the world. Divide the nations into two classes and then into six classes.
3. The value of GNI as a meaningful measure is in dispute due to the importance of the informal sector and the fact that purchasing power parity is not taken into consideration (M2 – M4). Explain this.
4. a) Illustrate the Gini Index by evaluating the reading guide (M3).
   b) Discuss this question: What would a curve representing an extremely unequal distribution look like?
5. Levels of development differ among the countries of the world. Describe the photographs (M5) with reference to basic human needs (p. 95 M2). In which countries do you think the photos were taken? Refer to M6.
6. With reference to three examples, explain why other indicators should also be taken into account when classifying countries on the basis of GNI (M2, M4).

Ⓢ 7. Describe the levels of development of countries X, Y and Z (M4), guess which countries they could be and explain the reasoning behind your guesses.

→ Economic indicators, Gini Index, Gross Domestic Product (GDP), Gross National Income (GNI), Gross National Product (GNP), Purchasing Power Parity (PPP), Social indicators

→ Gross Domestic Product (GDP)

Gross Domestic Product (GDP) represents the total value of all goods and services produced within the boundaries of a national economy in a given year after deduction of all advance payments. Based on the GDP, the Gross National Product (GNP) or Gross National Income (GNI) can be calculated by deducting income that is transferred abroad and adding the income that flows into the country from abroad.

→ Gross National Income (GNI)

Gross National Income is the value of all goods and services produced or rendered by residents of a country (both at home and abroad) in a given year. Since 1999, GNI has replaced the term Gross National Product (GNP). However, it is important to realise that economic indicators reflect only formal employment or occupational relationships and the corresponding proceeds. They do not account for the informal sector – which plays an especially important role in underdeveloped countries. This sector comprises all forms of employment and work that are not formally recognised. People employed in this sector have no insurance, do not appear in official statistics and do not pay taxes. This group includes such occupations as street sellers, shoe polishers, porters and subsistence farmers.

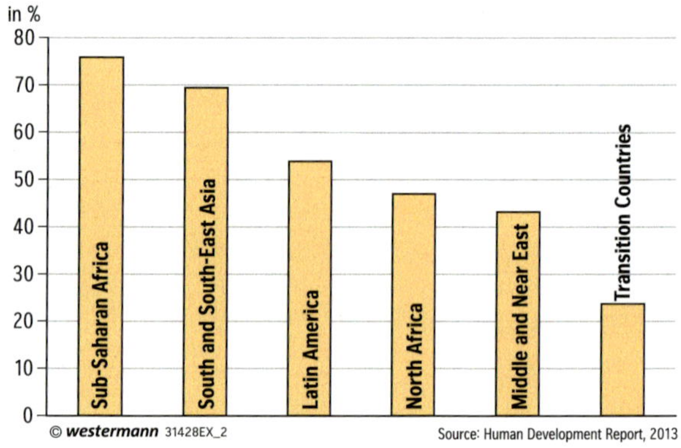

M2 Relative shares of people employed in the informal sector (excluding farming) in selected regions

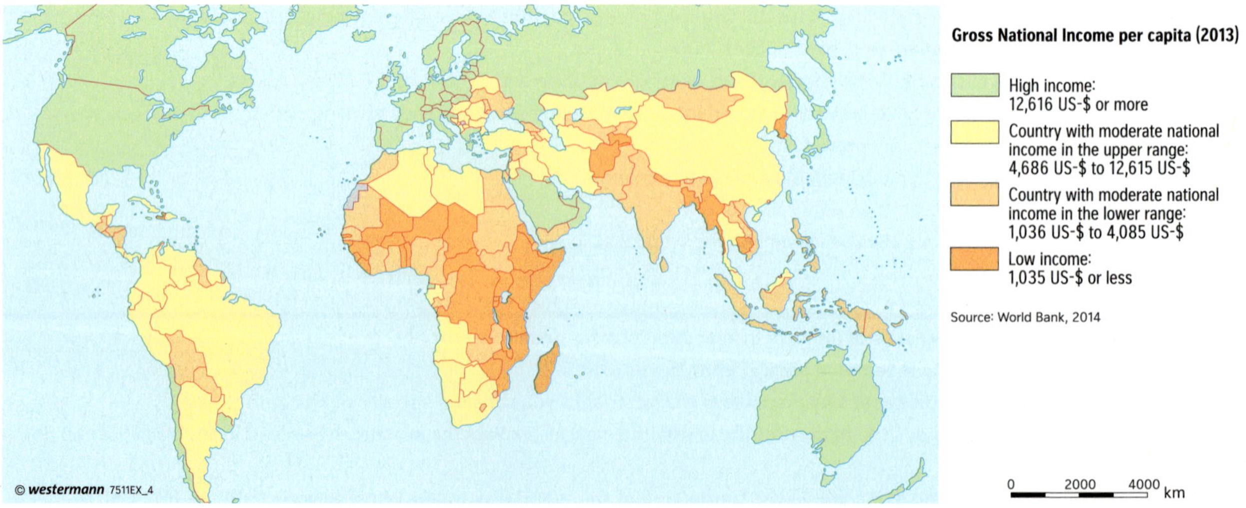

M1 Gross National Income per capita (World Bank Classification)

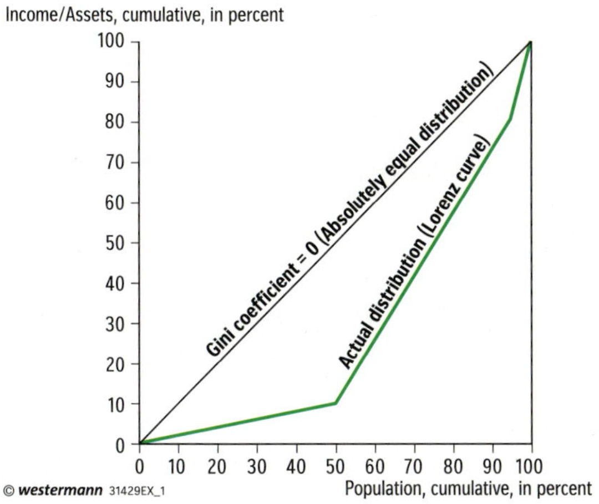

© westermann 31429EX_1

The graph shows the curve for absolute equal distribution, which means that wealth is distributed equally among all members of the population (Gini Index/Coefficient = 0). The curve representing "actual distribution" (green) indicates that 50 percent of the population possess only a very small share of the national wealth. In contrast, a very small portion of the population possesses 20 percent of the total wealth. The remaining 45 percent share 70 percent of total national wealth. Norway has an impressive Gini Coefficient of less than 0.30. Experts point out that values of more then 0.40 are regarded as extreme and indicative of a significant risk of social tensions.

M3 The Gini Index – example and reading guide

→ Gini Index

The Gini Index (or Gini Coefficient), named for the Italian statistician Corrado Gini, is a statistical unit of measure used to calculate unequal distribution. The population is entered on the X axis, the income or wealth on the Y axis. The representation of these values in such a Lorenz curve shows how much of the population (in percent) earns how much of the national income (in percent). In the case of absolutely equal distribution, the variance / Gini Coeffieicnt is 0. The Gini Coefficient in the case of maximum inequality of distribution is 1. In terms of income, the Gini Coefficient is 0.28 for Germany, 0.41 for the USA and 0.60 for South Africa..

M5 Different countries – different levels of development

Remarks on the photographs: **Huge differences in development are reflected in the two photographs. Judging on the basis of Gross National Income alone, the people in the upper photo should be nearly 40,000 US-$ richer than the woman in the lower photo. That is the difference in per capita GNI between the United States (upper photo = a slum in Louisiana, USA) and Brazil (lower photo = a boutique in Rio de Janeiro, Brazil).**

M6 GNI – an inexact measure of actual economic development (see remarks on the photos in M5)

Country	Per capita GNI (in US-$)	Per capita GNI as PPP* (in US-$)	Gini Index (income-based)	Life expectancy in years	Average years of school attendance	Number of doctors per 1,000 inhabitants
Argentina	9,740	18,745	0.445	76.1	9.3	3.2
Australia	59,570	43,170	0.352	82.0	12.0	3.0
Brazil	11,630	11,720	0.547	73.8	7.2	1.7
China	21,080	9,210	0.474	73.7	7.5	1.4
Egypt	3,000	6,640	0.344	73.5	6.4	2.8
Ethiopia	410	1,140	0.298	59.7	2.2	0.0
France	41,750	36,460	0.327	81.7	10.6	3.5
Germany	44,010	41,370	0.284	80.6	12.2	3.5
India	1,530	3,840	0.334	65.8	4.4	0.6
Kenya	840	1,670	0.425	57.7	7.0	0.1
Mexico	9,740	16,630	0.483	77.1	8.5	2.9
Mozambique	510	1,020	0.456	50.7	1.2	0.0
Russia	12,700	22,760	0.401	69.1	11.7	4.3
X	51,120	50,610	0.408	78.7	13.3	2.7
Y	47,210	61,100	0.425	81.2	10.1	1.8
Z	8,420	16,300	0.300	74.2	10.4	1.9

*Purchasing Power Parity represents the real value of money in a region, and thus adjusts for the price differences reflected in GNI. Thus amount x in Germany is worth less than in many developing countries. Source: Fischer Weltalmanach 2014; UNDP 2013

M4 Data for selected countries

Comparing levels of development

Social and multi-dimensional indicators

Economic indicators are of limited value when it comes to comparing levels of development. Which indicators can be helpful in developing a differentiated view of levels of development?

1. Illustrate the Big Mac Index (M1) with reference to what you have learned thus far about levels of development.
2. ⓞ A Discover as much as you can about meanings of the terms hunger, malnutrition and undernourishment and compare and contrast them.
   B Formulate possible reasons for nutritional problems on the basis of what you have learned thus far (M2, Internet).
3. Compare the Human Development Index (HDI) with the Multidimensional Poverty Index (MPI) (M3, M4).
4. Describe the global status of living conditions and its development with the aid of the HDI (M3, M5–M7).
5. a) Draw a world HDI map that is as up to date as possible with the aid of the DierckeWebGis.
   b) Print out your map and identify the ten countries with the highest and lowest GNI, respectively, with hatchings.
   c) Deviate from the specified classification in favour of a more detailed classification and print out a corresponding map.
6. Ⓢ Compare the account of an average German (M8) with your own experience and write a similar report for a young person in an underdeveloped country.

→ Human Development Index (HDI), Multidimensional Poverty Index (MPI)

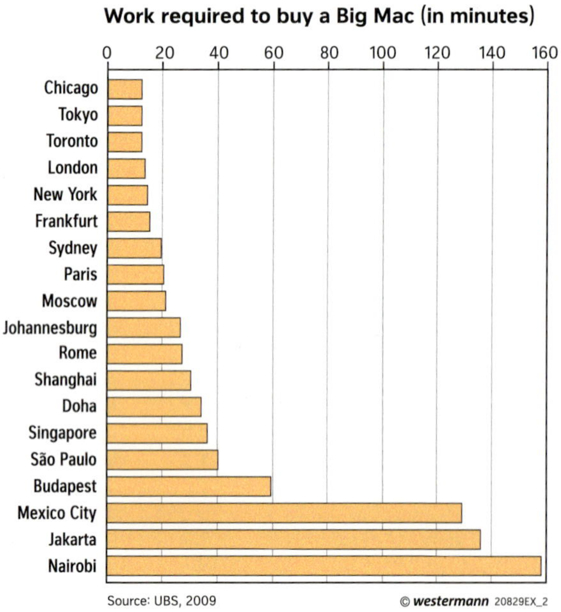

M1 The Big Mac Index 2009

M2 Food – a basic human need

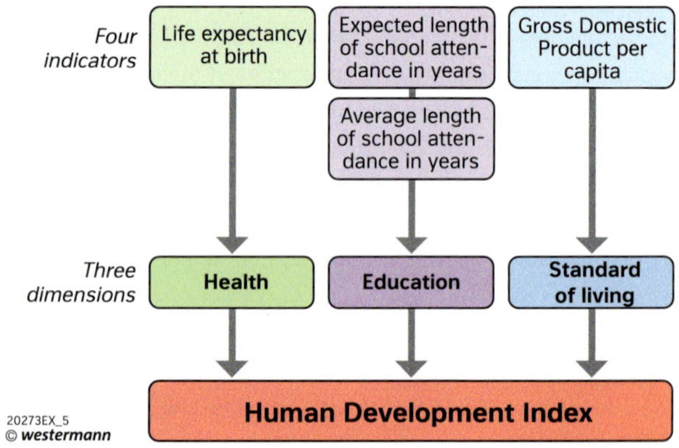

M3 The Human Development Index (HDI)

→ Human Development Index (HDI)

The Human Development Index (HDI) is a generalised value used to calculate living conditions. It has been set by the UN annually since 1990. The HDI ranges from 0 (totally undeveloped) to 1 (very highly developed).
The scale distinguishes between four different stages of development (low, medium, high and very high).

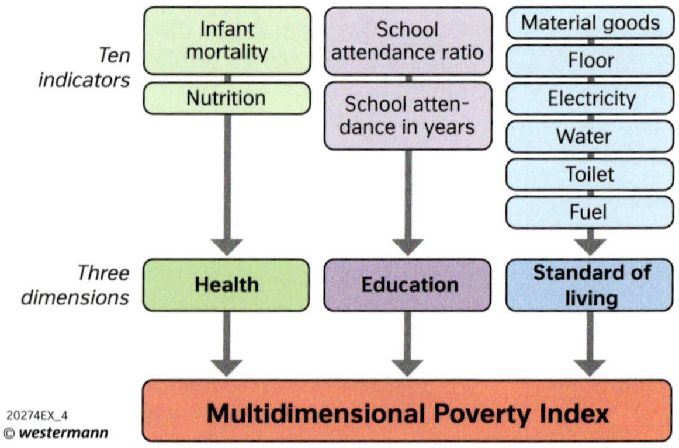

M4 The Multidimensional Poverty Index (MPI)

→ Mulitdimensional Poverty Index (MPI)

The Multidimensional Poverty Index classifies poverty levels in selected underdeveloped countries. It was developed at Oxford University for the United Nations Development Programme (UNDP) in 2010 and can be regarded as a supplement to the HDI. The first five places are occupied by Niger, Guinea, Ethiopia, Mali and Burkina Faso (UN, 2014).

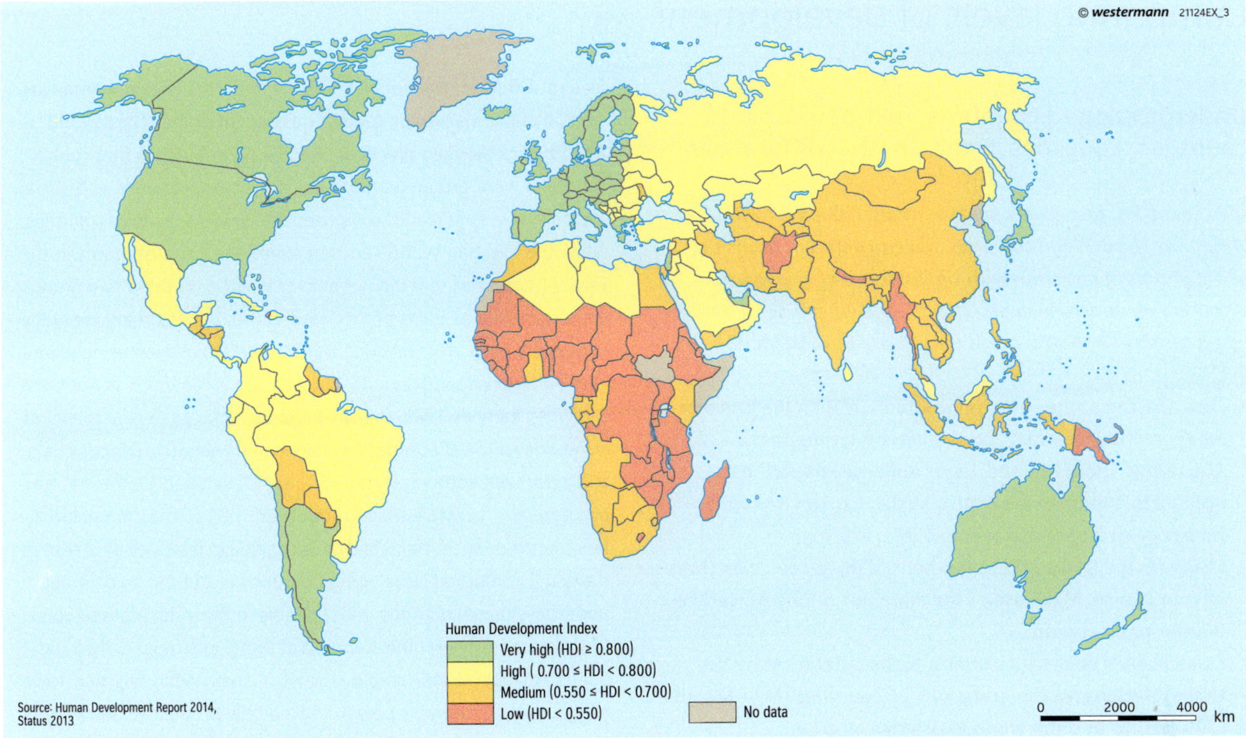

M5 The Human Development Index 2013 (HDI)

Regions	HDI	Life expectancy at birth (in years)	Average years of school attendance	Per capita GNI in PPP
Arab countries	0.652	71.0	6.0	8,317
East Asia and the Pacific region	0.683	72.7	7.2	6,874
Europe and Central Asia	0.771	71.5	10.4	12,243
Latin America and the Caribbean	0.741	74.7	7.8	10,300
South Asia	0.558	66.2	4.7	3,343
Sub-Saharan Africa	0.475	54.9	4.7	2,010

Source: UN HDR

M6 HDI and component indicators by region, 2012

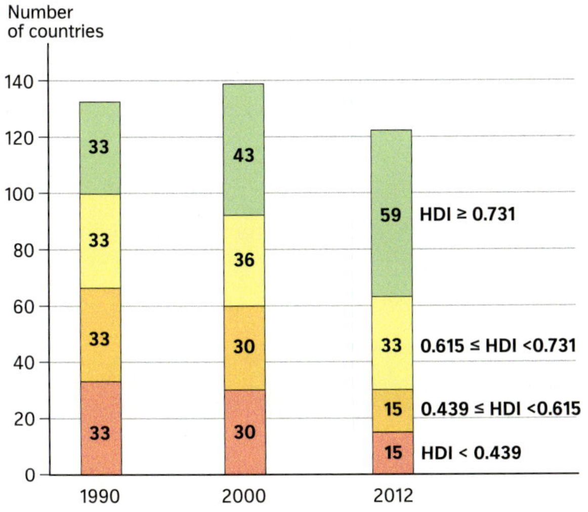

Sample reading: The number of countries with low HDI (base: 1990*) declined from 33 to 15 between 1990 and 2012.

* The threshold values are based on the 25th/50th/75th percentiles of the HDI values for 132 countries in 1990.

Source: Human Development Report, 2013, revised

© westermann 31430EX_1

M7 Changes in national HDI

I am the average German. I am 1.71 metres tall and weigh 74 kilogrammes. I start kindergarten at the age of three and primary school when I reach the age of six. I then move on to a secondary school before leaving school at the age of 16.8. About 35 percent of students from each graduating class enrol at a college or university. I spend 39 euros a month for clothes and have 0.69 children. Over the course of my life I read 9,304 newspapers. I use 3,651 rolls of toilet paper and smoke 107,000 cigarettes. I live for 79.36 years and consume 45.5 pigs and 926 chickens during my lifetime. I have 3,496 kcal per day at my disposal. I use 126 litres of water a day, and produce 173.4 kilogrammes of household waste per year. I travel 819,214 kilometres by car during my lifetime and spend 6.2 years watching television. I spend 732 euros a year for holiday trips, and get married at the age of 30.2. I live with 1.11 other people in 89 m^2 of space. Eighty-eight percent of my fellow citizens live in cities. My net monthly earnings amount to 1 ,452 euros, and every individual earns about 24,000 euros per year. Over the course of my lifetime I use 25 mobile phones, seven television sets and twelve computers. Fourteen percent of my fellow citizens are under the age of 14 and another 20 percent are older than 65.

Source: Landesakademie für Fortbildung und Personalentwicklung an Schulen, Fachportal Geographie, accessed: 12.03.2014

M8 The average German

Comparing levels of development

Underdeveloped countries, fast-developing countries, countries of the South – differences

Underdeveloped countries, fast-developing countries, industrialised countries and First- or Third-World countries. Several different terms are used to designate groups of countries with similar levels of development. But when is a country an underdeveloped country and when does it become a fast-developing country? And who needs these classifications at all?

1. Describe the scene in the photograph (M1) on the basis of what you have learned about levels of development.
2. The terms "industrialised" and "underdeveloped" as applied to countries are controversial. Explain this with reference to a concrete example (M2, M3, M5).
3. Compare the levels of development of three countries (M3) of your choice. Make use of the materials on the preceding double-page spread.
4. Classify each country according to the criteria set by the United Nations for the group of LDC countries (M3 – M5, the GNI on p. 96 and the World Risk Index on p. 95).
5. ⓞ Illustrate the concept of a fast-developing country by
   - A examining the situation in four exemplary countries;
   - B determining whether the BRICS nations should be regarded as fast-developing countries;
   - C determining whether the Tiger states should be called fast-developing countries.
6. Ⓢ Prepare a brief presentation on the subject of "Levels of development - very different worldwide" using all of the technical terms that appear on these two pages.

→ BRICS countries, Developing country, Fast-developing country, Industrialised country, Informal sector, Landlocked Developing Countries (LLDC), Least Developed Countries (LDC), Newly Industrialised Countries (NIC), Tiger states

Several different descriptive terms for underdeveloped regions are used in public discussion today. The concept of the "Third World" is a product of the Cold War years beginning in 1945. In that context, countries were grouped on the basis of their economic and social systems. The "First World" comprised the Western capitalist countries, while the "Second World" encompassed the socialist states in the East. All countries that did not belong to either of these two groups were classified as parts of the Third World. In customary everyday usage, the term "Third World" was equated to an increasing extent with underdeveloped regions. The concept is regarded as outdated today. As early as 1949, the UN began to refer to these nations as "Underdeveloped Countries". Because of its negative connotations, this term was soon replaced by "Less Developed Countries" and eventually by "Least Developed Countries" (LDCs). The UN also identifies countries that suffer disadvantages due to their lack of access to the sea (Landlocked Developing Countries or LLDCs). In contrast to underdeveloped countries, most people in the industrialised countries have a relatively high standard of living, and most of their basic needs are met (as indicated by the HDI). These countries also have a high level of economic power and a highly productive economy in which the tertiary sector usually plays a dominant role. Analogous to the English terms, the countries of the "Third World" are frequently described as "developing countries" in German. In recent years, the term "underdeveloped country" has been the focus of increasing criticism, as it is regarded as an expression of a Eurocentric point of view. Thus scholars in the field of geographic development research have now replaced it with the more neutral phrase "countries of the Global South" – which is naturally also not unproblematic when it comes to defining meaningful distinctions.

*Note: In the following pages the term "Developing Countries" is mostly used, because it comes closest to the terms "Underdeveloped Countries", "Less" and 'Least Developed Countries" that are used in English-language publications.

M2 From the "Third World" to "countries of the South"

M1 The Kibera slum in Nairobi

Country	Share of population below the poverty line (%)	Mortality rate for children aged 0–5 years (per 1,000 live births)	Foreign trade balance (in bill. US-$)
Australia	0.0	5	19
Brazil	6.1	19	2
China	13.1	18	260
Ethiopia	39.0	106	-9
Germany	0.0	4	198
India	32.7	63	-129
Kenya	43.4	85	-10
Mexico	1.2	17	-1
Mozambique	59.6	135	-3
Russia	0.0	12	208
South Africa	13.8	57	-9

Source: HDR, 2013; Fischer Weltalmanach, 2014, 2015

M3 Data for selected countries, 2012

According to the criteria set by the UN, a country should be classified as an LDC if:

1. Its average per capita Gross National Income over a three-year period is less than 905 US-$. In order to rise to the next level, a country must show evidence of average gross national per capita income in excess of 1,086 US-$.
2. A large percentage of the population is undernourished, and the country has a high infant mortality rate, a low percentage of first-year school pupils and a high illiteracy rate.
3. It has an unstable agriculture and a low level of industrial production, and if natural disasters followed by waves of refugees occur frequently.
   Exports are hardly possible in these countries, and farming and fishing account for the largest share of GDP, placing them in a state of economic dependence.

M4 UN criteria für Least Developing Countries (LDC), 2011*

*The values are adjusted annually by the UN.

M6 Meeting of BRICS heads of state in Fortaleza (Brazil) in 2014

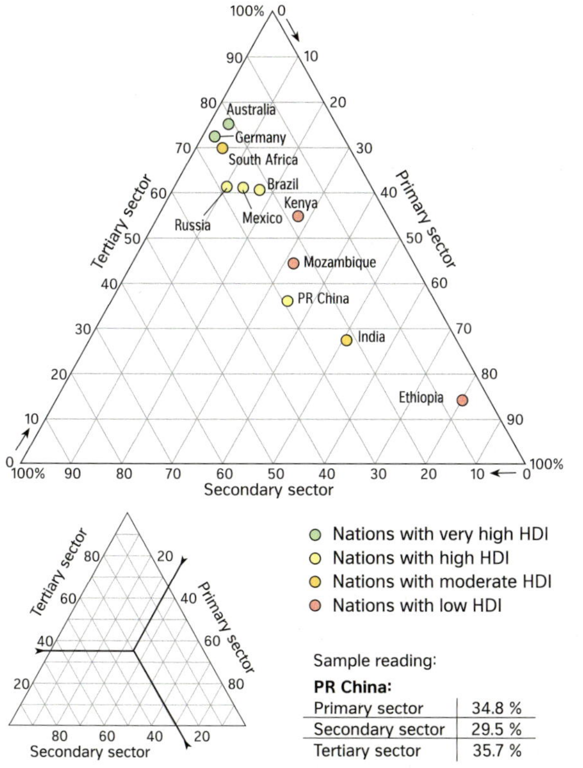

Source: Human Development Report, 2014; Fischer Weltalmanach, 2014 © westermann 7539EX_8

M5 Economic structures of selected countries, 2012

Absolute poverty

According to the World Bank, absolute or extreme poverty exists when average per capita income is less than one dollar (recently raised to 1.25 US-$) per day. Roughly 1.2 billion people fall into this category worldwide.

Relative poverty

We speak of relative poverty with reference to affluent societies in which absolute poverty is practically nonexistent, but the "lowest class" (more recently referred to as the "precariat") lives in a state of poverty. People whose income is less than half the average per capita income are classified as relatively poor.

Perceived poverty

Perceived or socio-cultural poverty cannot be identified on the basis of specific income levels. This type of poverty is more a state of mind. It affects those who view themselves as "poor" due to a general condition of social isolation or discrimination or live in fear of a worsening economic situation or in constant fear of succumbing to poverty.

Source: World Vision Institut für Forschung und Innovation. www.armut.de, accessed 03.12.2014

M7 Three types of poverty

→ Fast-developing country

A fast-developing country is generally understood as a country that is relatively far advanced in its development. Since 1970 the English term "Newly Industrialised Country" (NIC) has become established, which was originally applied mainly to the so-called Tiger States in Asia (South Korea, Taiwan, Hong Kong, Singapore). A fast-developing country undergoes an industrialisation process in which the agrarian economy becomes increasingly less and less significant. Frequently, such countries function as "extended workbenches" of the "North". The economic advance can be determined by various indicators. Characteristics that point to a fast-developing country are for example above-average growth rates, high labour productivity with at the same time low levels of wages or investments in infrastructure and education. There are no uniform criteria for determining which states belong to the fast-developing countries. The emergent states of the G20 are usually included, and the so-called BRICS states are often mentioned (Brazil, Russia, India, China, South Africa). The negative side of a fast-developing country is when its social development does not keep pace with its economic development. This leads to extreme disparities (see Gini Index), resulting in increasing vulnerability to political unrest.

Different countries – different preconditions for development

A Sahel nation with a colonial heritage – Mali

The development status of each individual state depends on a bundle of factors.
For example the development and development perspectives of Mali are marked by its natural spatial situation in the Sahel, the structure and development of the population and its colonial past.

1. Characterise the position of Mali in terms of the natural spatial potential for agriculture (M1, M2, Atlas), by:
   A producing a sketch map.
   B writing a text.
2. Describe Mali's colonial history (M3, Internet).
3. Outline Mali's current development situation (M4). Also use the preceding double-pages.
4. Illustrate which effects of the colonial history in Mali are still apparent today (M3 – M5, M7, M8).
5. a) Describe the demographic development in Mali (M4, M7).
   b) "Mali under population pressure?" Discuss how far the population development could represent a problem, taking into consideration the natural spatial potential and current population density (M2, M4, M5, M6, Atlas).
6. "Mali's future looks bleak, not least on account of its colonial history." Evaluate this thesis (M1 – M8).
7. Analyse barriers to a positive development of the country of Mali by producing a mindmap or a concept map.

→ Colonialism, Natural spatial potential, Population pressure

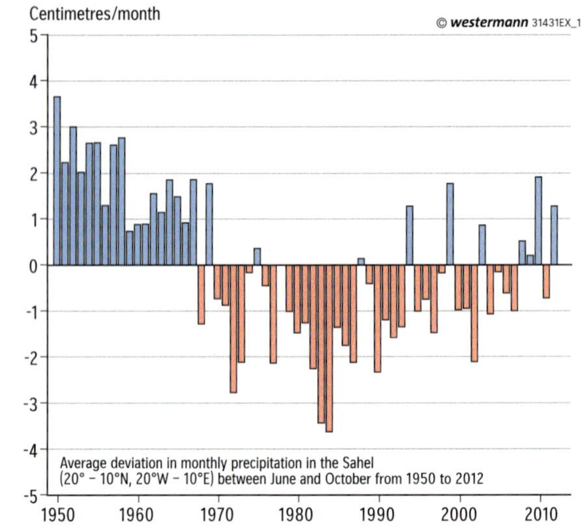

Source: JISAO, 2013; NOAA, 2013

M2 Precipitation variability in the Sahel Zone

Like many African states, Mali came into being in its present form as a result of borders drawn in colonial times. In 1883, French colonial troops invaded the territory of today's Mali and occupied Bamako. In 1904, after the colonial wars, France appended the territory to the colony of French Sudan. This was a part of French West Africa. The colonial rulers forced the inhabitants to cultivate agricultural products for export such as peanuts or cotton, which still represent important agricultural products today.
In 1960, Mali became independent in a federation with Senegal. Shortly afterwards the federation broke up with the departure of Senegal, so that the present-day territory of Mali has existed since the autumn of 1960. The drawing of borders was not oriented to traditions, ethnicities or languages, but was determined by the French colonial power. Even to this day, this has again and again led to conflicts. The first decades after independence were marked by political unrest, a military dictatorship and attempted coups. It was only since the 1990s that a slow process of democratisation set in. In January 2012, Tuareg tribesmen in the north of the country, the Azawad Region (Timbuktu, Gao and Kidal), launched a rebellion against the Malian government. The goal of the Tuareg was the establishment of their own state in the north of Mali. In the course of this development, other groupings also advanced claims, among others the AQMI (Al-Qaida in Islamic Maghreb). The rebels could only be pushed back with the aid of French troops. But the African country is still not at peace. At the beginning of 2015, Tuareg rebels in the north again recorded territorial gains and captured the towns of Kidal and Ménaka, killing at least 20 soldiers of the UN peace mission for Mali. The ceasefire that has been negotiated between the Malian government and the rebels remains fragile.

M3 Mali's colonial history

M1 Malian woman harvesting cotton

GNI per inhabitant (2000/2013)	374/670 US-$
Population density*	12 inhab./km^2
Population growth	3.0%
Life expectancy (2000/2013)	46.66/54.61
Proportion of the population with adequate access to drinking water supply	67.2%
Illiteracy rate	33.57%
Share of the primary sector in GDP	42%
Share of workers in the primary sector, a large part of which consists of small-scale activities in the subsistence economy	70%
Principal export products	Gold, cotton
HDI (ranking)	0.344 (rank 182)

*Average value – large parts of the north of Mali are practically empty of people; source: BMZ

M4 Key statistics for Mali, 2013

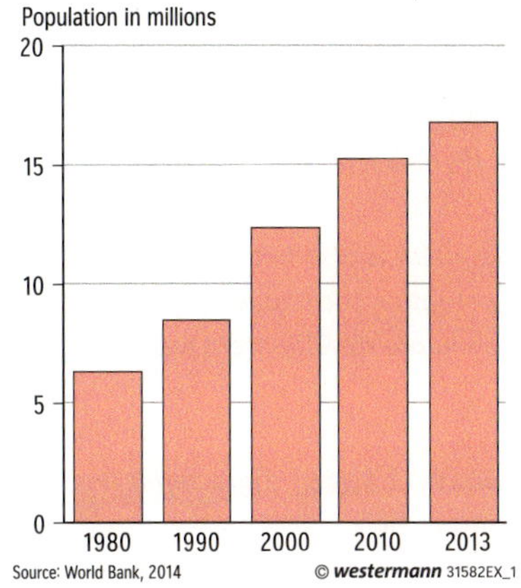

M6 Population growth in Mali

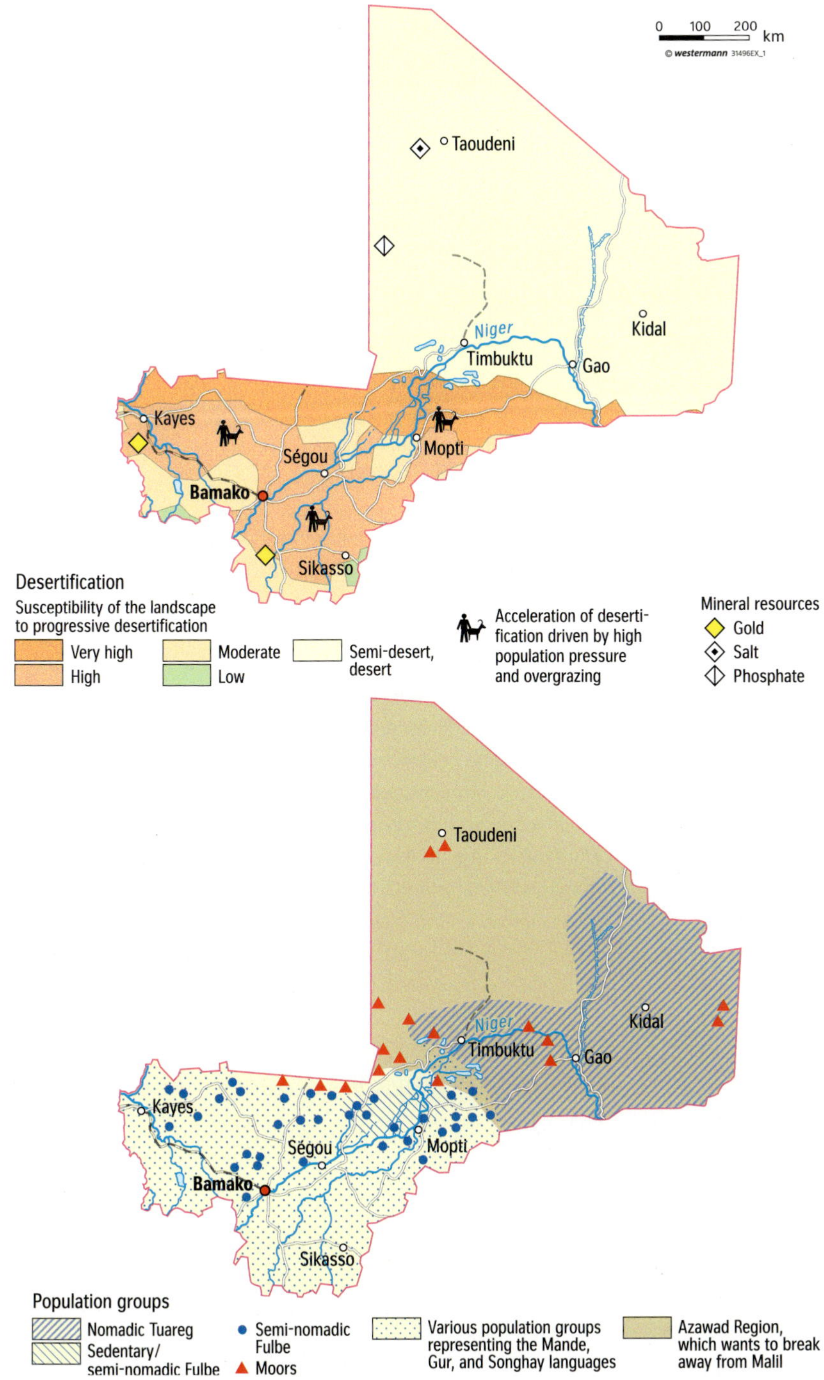

M5 Mali: potential natural-regional and social conflicts

M7 Burdensome legacy of a colonial power? A French soldier at the central market in the city of Timbuktu.

A United Nations soldier from Chad has been killed in a mine explosion in the north of Mali. Four further soldiers were injured in the incident in the conflict region of Kidal, a spokesman for the UN Mission in Mali reported. [...] Just at the beginning of the month, four UN soldiers were killed and a further 14 injured in a mine explosion in Kidal. In the past, numerous similar attacks have been associated with Islamic extremists [...]. [...] The UN peace mission is attempting to stabilise the north of Mali. In 2013, France launched a military offensive there against Al-Qaida fighters and other Jihadists who had seized power following a military coup in 2012. [...]. But extremists remain active in the north of the country.

(Source: www.nzz.ch, Blauhelmsoldat bei Minenexplosion getötet. 15.09.2014, accessed 16.09.2014)

M8 UN mission in Mali

Different countries – different preconditions for development

Mineral resources as a potential stimulus for development – Chile

Economic development is also heavily dependent on another aspect of natural spatial potential: the availability of raw materials. Minerals in particular can stimulate development processes, as the example of Chile shows.

1. Locate Chile and characterise its mining extraction areas (Atlas), by:
   A producing a sketch map.
   B writing a schoolbook text for Class 5.
2. Evaluate Chile's economic structure (M1, M3 – M6, Atlas).
3. Evaluate the economic development and the current status of development in Chile (M1 – M5).
4. Evaluate the importance of minerals for Chile's economic development with special reference to the raw material copper (M3 – M8).
5. Explain the terms of trade with reference to the importance of copper exports for Chile (M9 – M12).
6. "A heavily monostructural, export-oriented economic development like that of Chile cannot be the right path towards long-term development." Comment on this statement (M4 – M6, M9 – M12).
7. Illustrate why it is a problem for developing countries when a high share of their exports consists of agricultural products and raw materials (M11).
8. In a mindmap, outline the importance of the natural spatial potential for the development of a country.

→ Export-orientation, Monostructure, Natural spatial potential, Terms of trade

Share of sectors in GDP (in %)	
I	3
II	32
III	65
GNI per inhabitant. (2000/2013)	4,983/15,230 US-$
Unemployment rate (2000/2012)	9.0%/5.9%
HDI (ranking)	0.82 (rank 40)
Gini Index (2011)	0.50

Source: Fischer Weltalmanach 2015, CIA Factbook, 2013

M1 Economic data for Chile, 2013

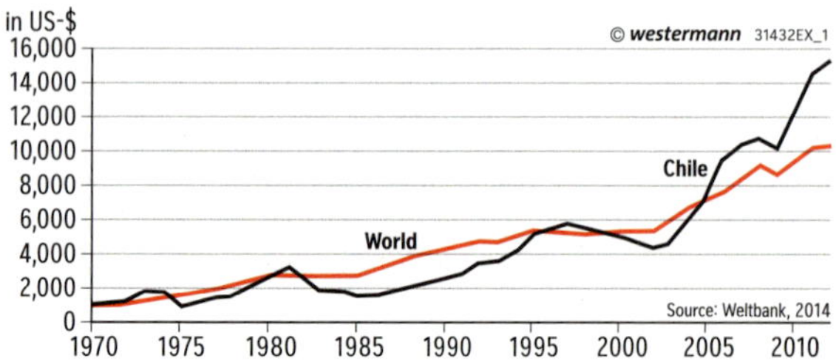

Source: Fischer Weltalmanach, different years

M2 Comparative development of per capita GDP in Chile and the world, 1970 – 2012

M3 Chuquicamata in Chile – the world's largest copper mine

	2010	2011	2012
Imports (in billion US-$)	59.4	74.9	79.5
Principal import products: petroleum (18.4%), vehicles and parts (11.6%), machinery (11.0%), chemical products (10.0%)			
Exports (in billion US-$)	70.9	81.4	78.3
Principal export products: copper* (35%), other raw materials (32.8%), foodstuffs (15.7%)			

* Copper is a so-called non-ferrous metal. Other non-ferrous metals are aluminium or zinc. In German, the term "Buntmetall" (literally "coloured metal") is sometimes used.

M4 Chile's foreign trade

Chile's copper production currently accounts for 34 percent of world production. Further important raw materials are molybdenum, rhenium, gold and lithium. Although the government is making efforts to diversify the economy, mining remains of predominant importance for exports. [...] Forestry, agriculture and fishing also remain important economic sectors. Chile possesses one of the largest fishing fleets in Latin America. Aquaculture, especially the factory farming of salmon, also plays an important role.

Source: Straßner, V., Chile – Das Wirtschaftssystem und seine Sektoren. GIZ, 12/2014, www.giz.de, accessed 15.12.2015

M5 Chile*s economy: no diversification, just exports

	Production in mill. t	Reserves in mill. t
Chile	5,623	160
PR China	1,299	30
Peru	1,235	63
USA	1,110	35

Source: Fischer Weltalmanach, 2014

M6 Ranking list of the most important copper producing countries and their reserves in million tonnes (2011)

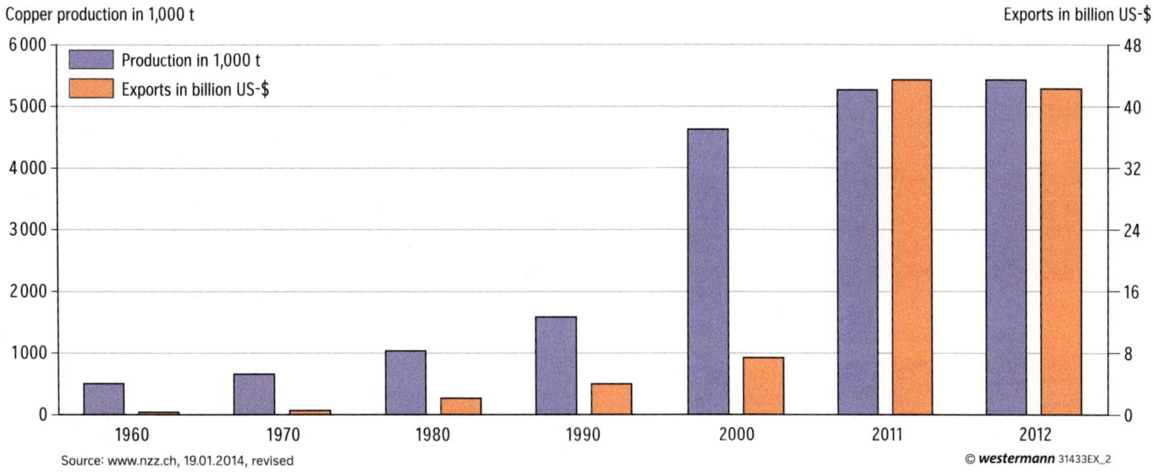

M7 Chile's copper production and exports

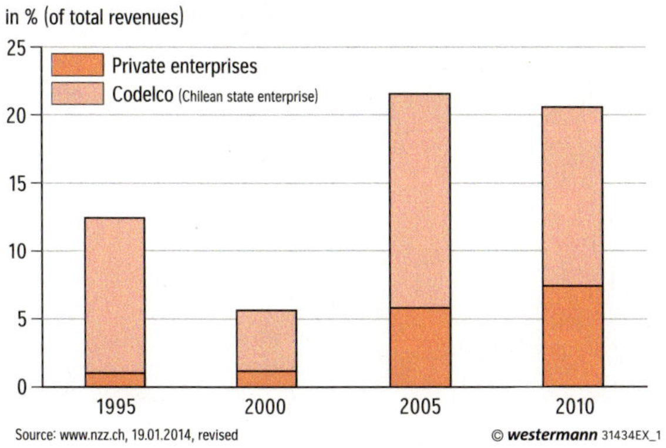

M8 Tax revenues from the copper business in Chile

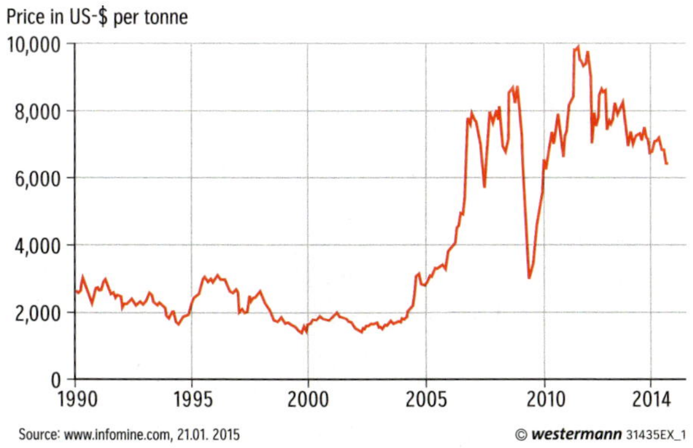

M9 Changing copper prices, 1990–2014

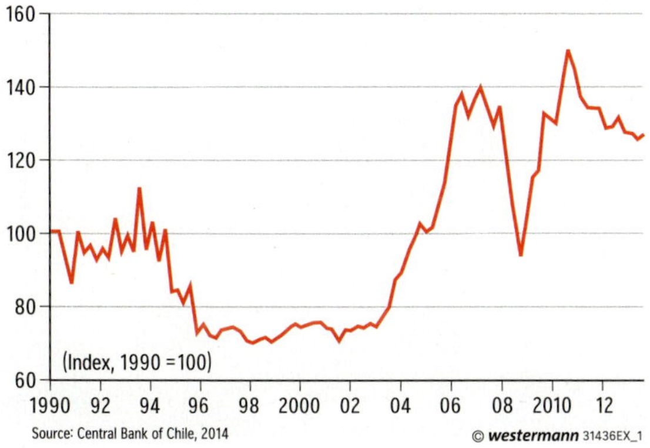

M10 Terms of trade: Chile

→ Terms of trade (TOT)

In simplified terms, the expression "terms of trade" (TOT) refers to the international exchange relationship between a country's exported and imported goods. If the value of an exported product increases, e.g. due to higher prices on account of greater demand or changes in currency values, the country's TOT improves. It is a problem especially for developing countries that a high proportion of their exports is made up of raw materials.

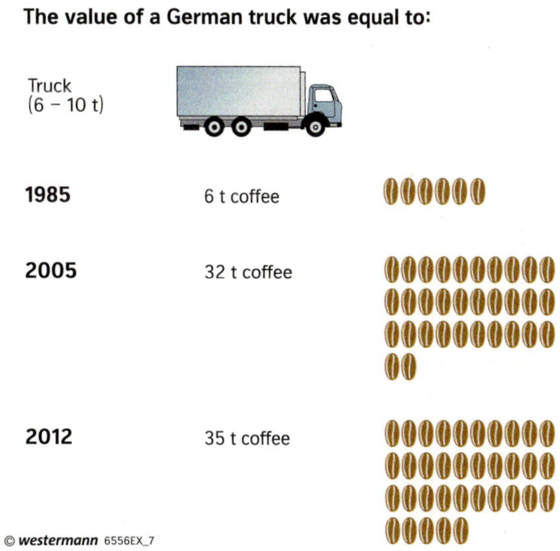

M11 The measure of export success: terms of trade

A bad omen: precisely at the moment when Michelle Bachelet took up office as the President of Chile, the price of copper – the country's most important export – has collapsed. In February alone, the red metal lost 4.5% and was thus traded at its lowest level for seven months. Further price falls are highly probable, because world production is increasing and demand especially from China is falling. The copper price is an essential factor in Chile's economy [...]. The mining industry and its suppliers are the most important investors in the country. No other country in Latin America is so heavily dependent on one raw material [...] as this Andean nation.

Source: Busch, A., Das Wirtschaftsmodell Chile auf dem Prüfstand. 12.03.2013, www.nzz.ch, accessed 26.02.2015

M12 Dependence on copper

Extreme disparities within national borders

Fragmentation in India

India has developed rapidly in recent years. However, the differences within this vast country are extreme.

1. Describe India's economy with its regional differences (M1, M4, Atlas).
2. Explain the model of global and local fragmentation according to F. Scholz (M5, M6).
3. Describe the pictures in M2 and M3 with the aid of the fragmentation model.
4. Characterise the situation of Bangalore and Chennai (M4).
5. ⓞ Illustrate the three case studies from Bangalore (M6, Atlas), by:
   A producing a concept map.
   B writing an essay.
   C preparing a short lecture.
6. Classify the case studies in terms of Scholz's fragmentation model (M5–M7, Atlas).
7. "The consideration of global and local disparities is impossible without taking the fragmentation approach into account." Evaluate this thesis.
8. Ⓢ Test whether India is a fast-developing country (M1 and p. 107).

→ Fragmentation (local and global), IT industry

M3 Slum in Calcutta

Share of sectors in GDP (share of employment) in %	
I	18 (47)
II	25 (25)
III	57 (28)
GNI per inhabitant (2000/2013)	449 US-$ 1,530 US-$
Unemployment rate	4.7% (official)
Growth of GDP 2000–2014	c. 500%
HDI (ranking)	0.586 (rank 135)
Development of exports since 2000	Growth of c. 600%
Internet users per 100 inhabitants	12.58
Illiteracy rate	70.4%

Source: Fischer Weltalmanach, 2015

M1 Key economic indicators for India, 2013

M2 Fragments of unequal development in Calcutta: The slum (M3) and the luxury apartments under construction are only 300 metres apart.

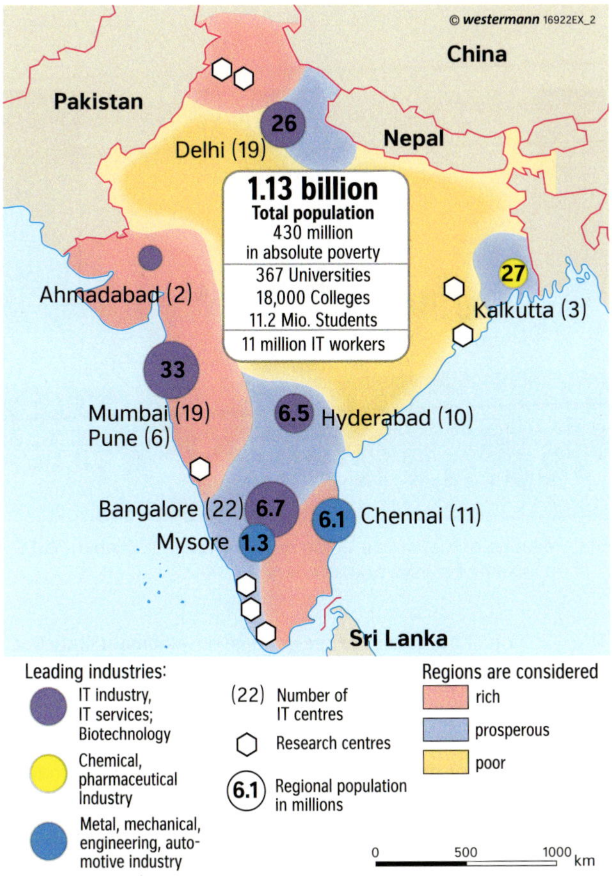

M4 Leading industries and regional disparities

In the year 2000, the geographer Fred Scholz in Berlin published work that led to a new view of underdevelopment. In his "model of global and local fragmentation" he explains his main argument that development takes place in a fragmented way and only certain places or sections of the population benefit from positive developments. Scholz sees the main reason for this statement as increasing globalisation. This, according to Scholz, is marked by excessive competition in a global division of labour. Processes of liberalisation, deregulation and privatisation accelerate this process. Moreover – especially in less developed countries – the model sees a local fragmentation in the larger and supposedly booming cities. In such cities, only a small part of the population participates in the effects of development. Extreme poverty exists in close proximity to prosperity.

M5 Global and local fragmentation according to Scholz

Case study 1: Mrs Gubta

At half-past-four in the morning, in the centre of Bangalore, Asha Gubta wakes up in complete darkness. There are no street lights to be seen anywhere, because there are no streets in the slum. And no light bulbs are alight in any of the shacks. All the slum dwellers save electricity during the night. On the threshold there are five pairs of flip-flops in five different colours. They belong to her husband Devi, their three children, and her. Through a slit in the slanting wall, the four of them can be seen lying on a simply-made bed. Even at first sight, the poverty in which Asha lives is overwhelming: one bed shared by five people, a hut as big as a horse box, no running water, no toilet. But Asha is happy that for the past three months she has had a job as a housemaid in the nearby villa district. For the moment, the family doesn't have to go hungry.

Case study 2: Mr Sen

Bageshri Sen has arrived. For three years he has been working for the global player Hewlett Packard in the heart of Bangalore. For the past year he has lived with his family in a smart owner-occupied apartment in Koramangala, one of the city's best districts, with a security service included. After completing his studies, financed by his family, he immediately succeeded in finding the job and he quickly rose up the career ladder. Every morning he drives proudly through the streets of his home city in his new Audi. Next year his daughter Maheri will begin her studies in Switzerland.

Case study 3: Romata

Romata's clothes are lying on a heap of red sandstones: a black shirt, a green bonnet and underwear. These are all the clothes that the little twelve-month-old girl possessed. Now they adorn her grave. Romata's father stands over it and sobs. A few hours before he had held his still-living daughter in his arms. "I had no idea that she was going to die," says Chunbad Dabi. They left their village two years ago, full of hope, to find their fortune in Bangalore. But it was no better. The hygienic conditions in the slum are catastrophic. Mr Dabi earns his money by cleaning car windows at the major intersections in the city. But this is rarely sufficient to feed his family. A visit to a doctor is out of the question. Otherwise, perhaps Romata's life could have been saved.

M7 Three lives and three worlds in Bangalore

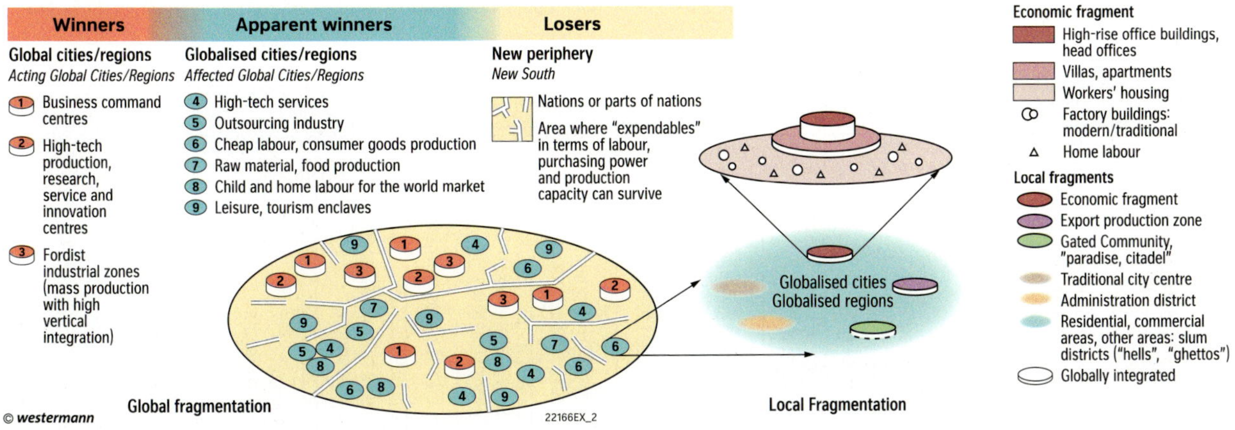

M6 Model of global and local fragmentation according to F. Scholz

Causes of underdevelopment

Different theories – different answers

Spain must pay back 211.2 billion dollars to Bolivia. At least, this is what Dante Gumiel of the University of La Paz claims. For him the case is clear: in the colonial era the colonies were exploited. This is the reason why they are underdeveloped countries today. But opinions about the causes of underdevelopment are widely divergent.

1. Outline the different theories of underdevelopment (M1, M4).
2. Compare the theoretical approaches to the possible causes of underdevelopment and substantiate them by means of spatial examples taken from this chapter (M1 – M4).
3. ⓞ Illustrate Rostow's model of the stages of economic growth (M5) by:
   A reconstructing the development of selected spatial examples from this chapter on the basis of the model.
   B categorising the development status of selected countries in terms of the model.
4. Substantiate the causes of underdevelopment that are presented in M2. Test which of the causes apply to the spatial examples from this chapter.
5. Describe the different perspectives of slum dwellers with regard to modernisation and dependence theories (M1, M4, M6).
6. Classify selected spatial examples from this chapter according to the model of global fragmentation (M7).
7. Ⓢ Write an article for a school magazine on the subject of "Rich North, Poor South".

→ Dependence theories, Fragmenting development, Modernisation theories, Triads, Vulnerability

M3 Meeting of the African Union in Addis Ababa (Ethiopia), 2015 – in search of causes and answers

The question of the causes of the unequal development status between the North and South has concerned scholars for a long time. For many years, the academic debate was dominated by two camps, modernisation theories and dependence theories.

Modernisation or growth theorists make the assumption that all countries gradually develop from an agrarian to an industrialised society. According to this theoretical model, the process passes through various stages of development. Modernisation theorists believe that underdevelopment is caused by problems in the respective countries (endogenous causes).

Dependence theories see the causes in a misguided development from outside the country (exogenous causes). Supporters of these theories point to colonial or post-colonial exploitation and resulting external control and dependence of individual countries, which sometimes continues to this day.

For a long time, both of these theoretical orientations have been criticised as too one-sided. Meanwhile an important role is played by approaches that place the focus on particular events (e.g. natural disasters, wars) and which can be summarised by the term "vulnerability research". Most recently the development theorist Fred Scholz has drawn attention to the influences of globalisation with his "theory of fragmenting development". According to this theory, in no way do whole countries profit from possible development stimuli, but only fragments of the country. Hoped-for improvements for the population at large (trickle-down effects) rarely take place. It is not states but transnational companies that are the main actors in the global economy.

M4 Causes of underdevelopment – different theories, different answers

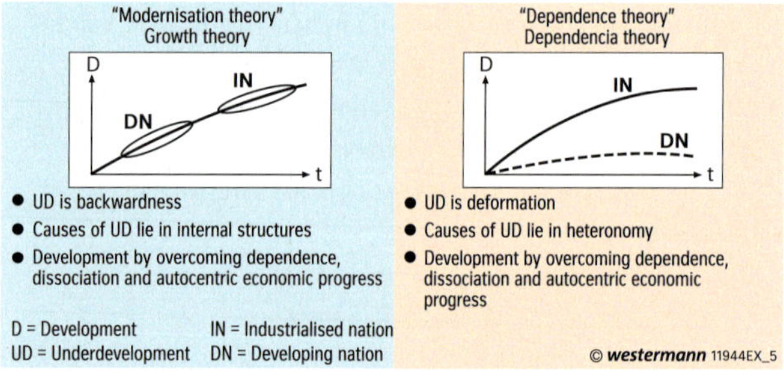

M1 Modernisation versus dependence theories

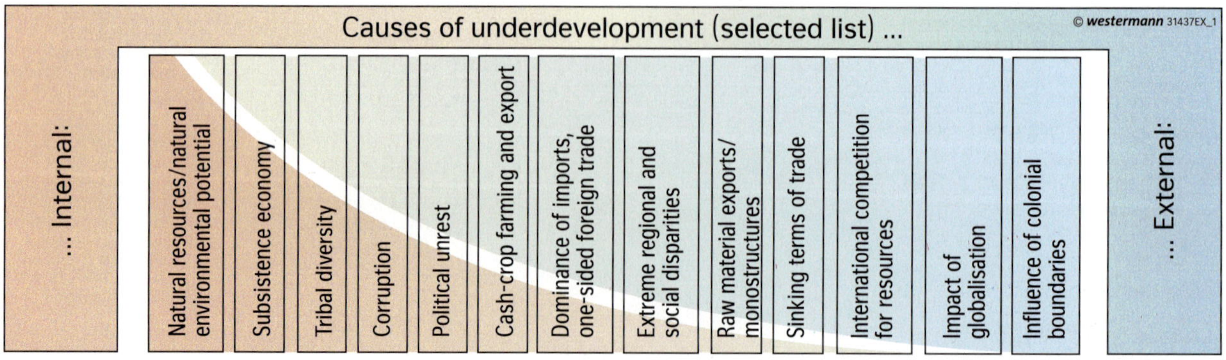

M2 Selected causes of underdevelopment

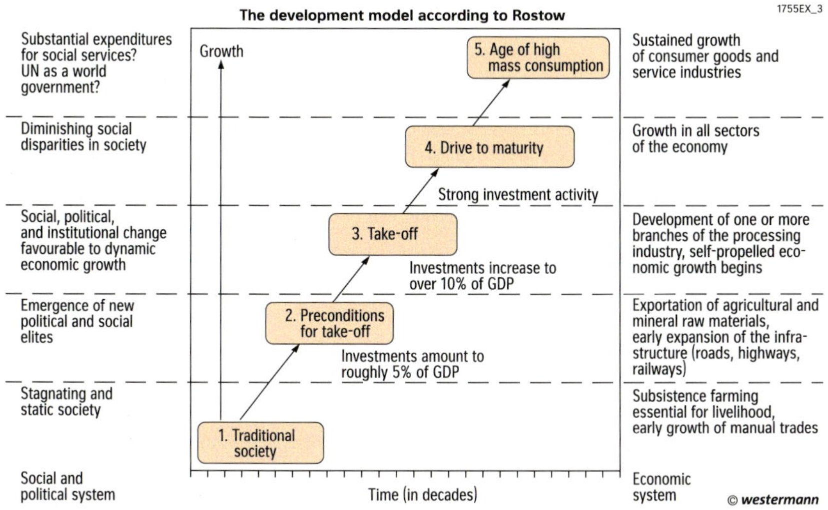

M5 Stages of economic growth according to Rostow (economic stages model)

The economic stages model originates from the US economist Walt W. Rostow (1916 – 2003) and consists of five stages. According to Rostow, the continuous development of a country can only come about with economic growth. The growth model is a classic among modernisation theorists. But critics point to its excessive orientation towards western societies. It is also doubtful whether a course of development such as this model presents is realistic in the modern world.

M6 Slum in Mumbai: differing perspectives

M7 Global fragmentation

Balancing global disparities

Strategies and ideas for development cooperation

What can be done against poverty, underdevelopment and global disparities? For decades, this question has concerned experts as much as politicians. How can poorer regions or countries be most effectively helped? And who should take the measures?

1. Locate the individual examples and illustrate the measures described against the background of development status (M2, Atlas).
2. Using the examples, explain the terms "development cooperation" and "development policy" (M2, M3).
3. Find information about organisations for development cooperation and summarise the contributions that the different organisations can make to development in individual countries (M1, Internet).
4. Outline the changes in development strategies since the 1950s (M4).
5. ⓞ Analyse in what way the individual examples (M2) can be classified in terms of specific development strategies (M4), by:
   A writing an article for a specialist magazine.
   B preparing a lecture.
6. Ⓢ "There is not one single development strategy, what matters is connecting them is a meaningful way." Comment on this statement.

→ Development aid, Development policy, Development cooperation, Non-Governmental Organisation (NGO), Official development assistance (ODA)

- Food and Agricultural Organization (**FAO**)
- International Labour Organization (**ILO**)
- International Monetary Fund (**IMF**): A special UN organisation, among other things to oversee the international currency system.
- **World Bank**: A supporting organ of the IMF. Its former goal was the reconstruction of countries that had suffered destruction in the Second World War. Today its main purpose is to reduce the gap between North and South.
- World Health Organization (**WHO**)
- World Trade Organization (**WTO**): Trade organisation with 160 member states. The principal goals are trade liberalisation and the removal of trade barriers.
- United Nations Development Programme (**UNDP**)
- United Nations International Children's Emergency Fund (**UNICEF**)

M1 Selected international organisations involved in development policy matters

Example 1: An international team of experts together with their local colleagues is analysing the technical feasibility, costs and economic and social benefits of asphalting a gravel road in Zambia to connect a rural region with the urban centres.
Example 2: A Nepalese non-governmental organisation (NGO) together with local experts is supporting the inhabitants of mountain villages in the development of village organisations. The aims, among other things, are to improve the water supply and to give a more effective voice to the interests of the population when dealing with merchants and the local administration.
Example 3: In negotiations within the World Trade Organisation (WTO), four West African cotton exporting countries are calling on the USA and EU to reduce the subsidies for their national cotton producers, because the surpluses they produce result in a drastic fall in the world market price.
Example 4: In 2004, Germany provided c. 670 million euros in immediate aid for the victims of the tsunami in the Indian Ocean. Indonesia received a large proportion of this.

M2 Development policy and development cooperation in actual practice

→ Development cooperation (formerly "development aid")

This covers all measures for the fostering of economic growth and social development. This may refer to cooperation between two countries or partners (bilateral), groups of countries (multilateral) or through international organisations. In many publications, the terms "development aid" or "development assistance" are still frequently used.

→ ODA (Official development assistance)

This refers to assistance provided by public donors which may be granted to developing countries in order to foster economic and social development.

→ Development policy

Development policy here means the forming of global, national or regional framework conditions, mainly developed by globally-active institutions (global governance), e.g. free trade agreements.

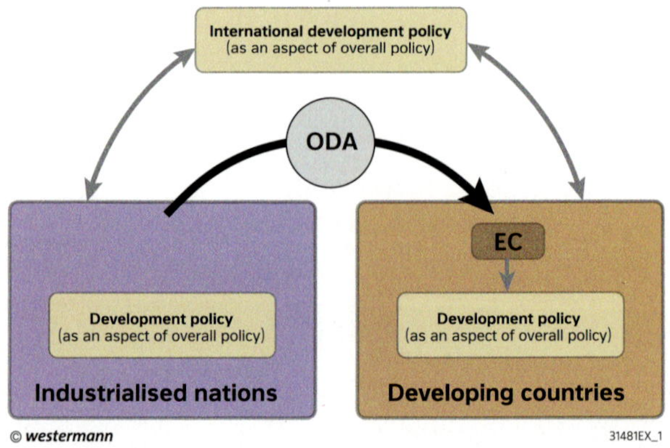

M3 Development policy and development cooperation

PHASE

c. 1950

Growth policy phase

Goal and characteristics:
After the independence of many former colonies, development was perceived as a catching-up process. Development of agriculture and industry was aimed for. The goals were full employment and mass purchasing power.

The green revolution in South Asia. A farmer with a rice sowing machine in Bangladesh

c. 1970

Phase of orientation to basic needs and poverty

Aid goods in Burkina Faso (Upper Volta)

Goal and characteristics:
The principal goal of this phase was growth for the poor (e.g. assistance for basic security, slum rehabilitation or literacy campaigns). Participation and sustainability became important guiding principles.

c. 1980

Phase of neo-liberal structural adjustment policy

Goal and characteristics:
The principal strategic goals were a market economy and the opening of markets. Debt relief by the World Bank and IMF were made possible, but linked to conditions (e.g. privatisation, reductions in government spending).

c. 1990

Grassroots participation phase

Goal and characteristics:
Local communities were to be placed in a position to recognise their potential and take the initiative (e.g. through workshops and counselling).

A development aid worker advising villagers in Afghanistan

Strengthening the role of women

Goal and characteristics:
The goal was to integrate women into all aspects of market economy processes with equal rights (e.g. loans to women's groups for village mills).

The struggle for sustainability

Solar cooker in Tanzania

Goal and characteristics:
The term sustainability became a watchword for development cooperation. Projects should be ecologically and socially acceptable and have a permanent basis.

The institutionalisation phase

Goal and characteristics:
The goal of this strategy is among other things to strengthen the performance of government institutions.
Development programmes are often linked to democratic structures (= good governance).

c. 2000

Rediscovery of poverty reduction (Millennium Goals)

Goal and characteristics:
Due to a lack of radical success in the fight against poverty, the focus of development policy shifted at the start of the 2000s. A working group of representatives from the UNO, World Bank, OECD and certain NGOs devised a list of eight goals (the Millennium Development Goals: MDG).

M4 Changes in development strategies according to T. Rauch

"Development from below"

Microcredits for the rural poor – Bangladesh

The economist Muhammad Yunus was awarded the Nobel Peace Prize in 2006 for his contribution to economic and social development. His concept of microcredits is now regarded by experts all over the world as an effective approach to the goal of balancing disparities and promoting sustainable development.
Support for individuals and families is particularly important in a nation like Bangladesh, one of the world's poorest and most densely populated countries, and a land that has been plagued by frequent natural disasters. What does the concept comprise?

1. Discuss the economic situation of Bangladesh (M2, Atlas).
2. Outline the concept of the Grameen Bank (M1, M3–M5).
3. Illustrate the potential advantages of the concept of microcredits (M4–M6).
4. (O) Evaluate the concept of the Grameen Bank in terms of its contribution to sustainable development in Bangladesh (M6–M8) by:
   A listing the advantages and disadvantages in a table;
   B writing an article from the perspective of an advocate of the concept;
   C writing an article from the perspective of an opponent of the concept.
5. "This development concept may be regarded as a contribution to sustainable development from below." Discuss this statement (M9).
6. Research the current situation of the Grameen Bank in the internet and write a brief commentary on your findings (M8, Internet).
7. (S) Women are the most important target group for microcredits. Explain.

→ Development from below, Help for self-help, Microcredits, Sustainable development

Per capita GNI (1980/ 2013)	220 US-$/ 900 US-$
HDI	0.52 (rank: 146)
Gini Index (2010)	34.5
Life expectancy (2000/ 2013)	60.16 years/ 70.29 years
Physicians per 1,000 persons	0.3
Illiteracy rate (2011)	Total population: 52.1% Women: 41.4%
Percentage of the population below the absolute poverty line (2010)	31.5%
Exports (of which 80% are textiles)	23.0 billion US-$
Imports (primarily food)	36.4 billion US-$

Source: CIA Factbook, Fischer Weltalmanach, 2015

M2 Basic data for Bangladesh, 2013

Chittagong, Bangladesh, 1976. The country remains in the grip of the recent floods and the impoverished population is suffering. Economics professor Muhammad Yunus is no longer willing to tolerate this situation, which is virtually hopeless for many people. Yunus sees the autonomous use of the country's existing resources as the key to solving the problem. The rural population is especially hard-hit by the lack of access to seed, fertilisers and equipment. Credit is seldom approved for farming families due to the lack of security. This is where the professor's idea takes hold and he founds the Grameen Bank (which means "village bank"). The bank grants microcredits to families (primarily to women thus far) that have less than 0.2 hectares of arable land. The average loan amount is 50 euros. Credit is granted on condition that the borrower can credibly affirm in the presence of all group members that the money will be used for an income-generating measure that will contribute to sustainable economic development for the family. An important aspect of this concept is support for borrowers at the village level. Today, the Grameen Bank operates over 2,000 centres in it own buildings all over the country. The bank has a total of 200,000 employees and is an influential business enterprise. Bank officials cite a repayment rate of over 90 percent.

M3 The concept of microcredits and the founding of a development bank

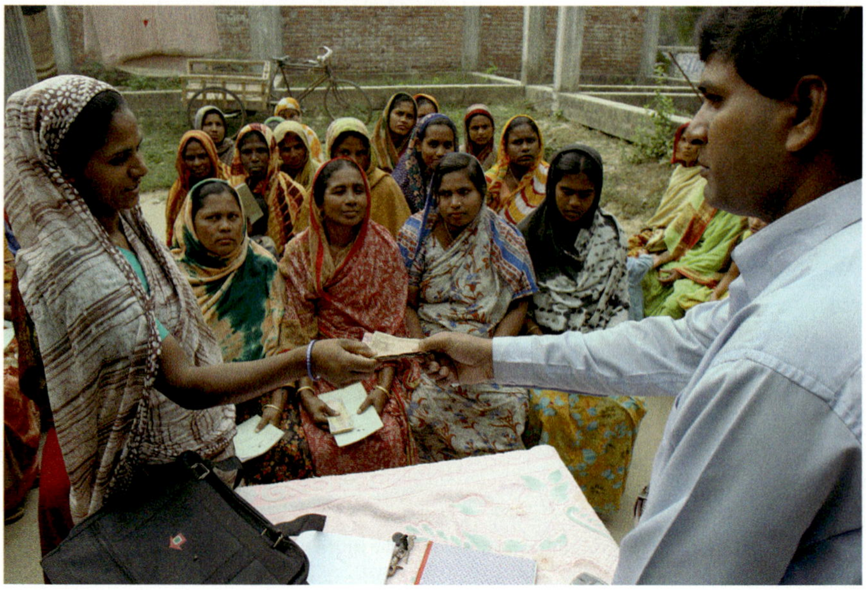

M1 A bank worker paying out microcredits

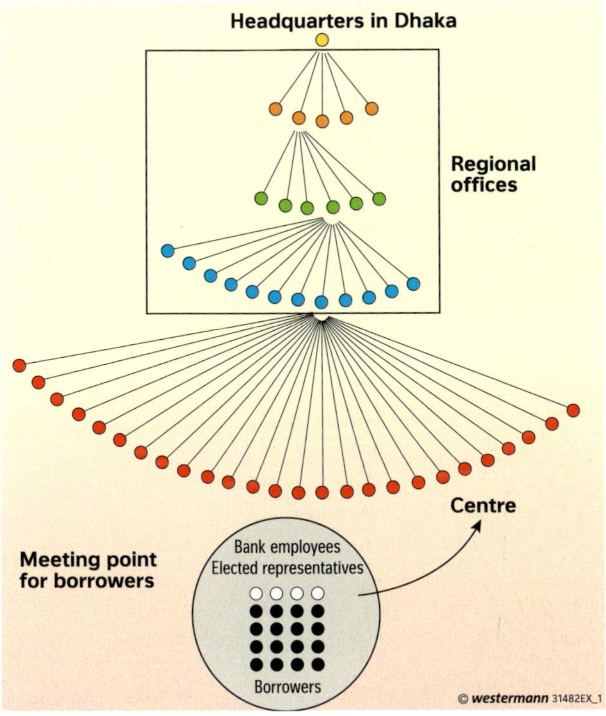

M4 The Grameen Bank concept

The banking centre is the most important pillar of the concept. Borrowers meet regularly in small, democratic groups at these centres. Elected representatives explain such matters as repayment methods, self-initiative and proper savings behaviour. The representatives are supported by employees of the Grameen Bank. These bank workers are trained at interregional offices. Centre representatives are often offered employment opportunities as bank workers.

M5 The centre as a fundamental element of the concept

Patma lives in a village roughly 150 km west of Dhaka. When she heard about the Grameen Bank in 1993, she attended a group meeting in her village. At first she couldn't believe that anyone would take her seriously as a "businesswoman". But she had a good idea and hoped to start a chicken- and duck-breeding operation. She presented her idea and received a loan equivalent to about 40 euros. Today, Patma is debt-free and earns enough money from the sale of her poultry to satisfy her family's basic needs without additional support.

M6 Effective help for self-help

Although the microcredit concept is generally highly regarded all over the world, some experts have expressed criticism as well. The focus of criticism is the fact that new loans are often used to repay old debts and that the high repayment rate is the result of that practice.
Microcredits are also used to an increasing extent for purposes that do not represent new sources of income, such as house construction, dowries or to cover wedding expenses.
Source: Scholz, F.: Entwicklungsländer. Braunschweig, 2012, p. 133.

M7 Criticism of the Grameen Bank

Bank fires Nobel Peace Prize winner Yunus

Following a lengthy dispute with Prime Minister Sheikh Hasina of Bangladesh, the country's national bank has dismissed Nobel Peace Prize winner Muhammad Yunus from his position as Director of the microcredit bank he founded years ago. [...] His supporters cite a series of political attacks staged since 2007, when Yunus clashed with Prime Minister Sheikh Hasina. Yunus had stated in an interview that politics in Bangladesh were essentially a matter of "[acquiring] power in order to make money". He was then sued for libel. Sheikh Hasina repeatedly accused the economist of exploiting the poor with exorbitant interest rates for loans from the Grameen Bank. [...] In 1983, the government of Bangladesh had passed a law declaring Yunus's lending company an independent bank. [...] The concept has now been adopted in over 40 countries; yet microcredits drew criticism last year after women in India doused themselves with petrol and set themselves on fire because they were no longer able to repay their loans.

Source: ZEIT Online, Bank entlässt Friedensnobelpreisträger Yunus. 02.03.2011, www.zeit.de, 02.03.2011, accessed 28.02.2015

M8 Criticism of Muhammad Yunus

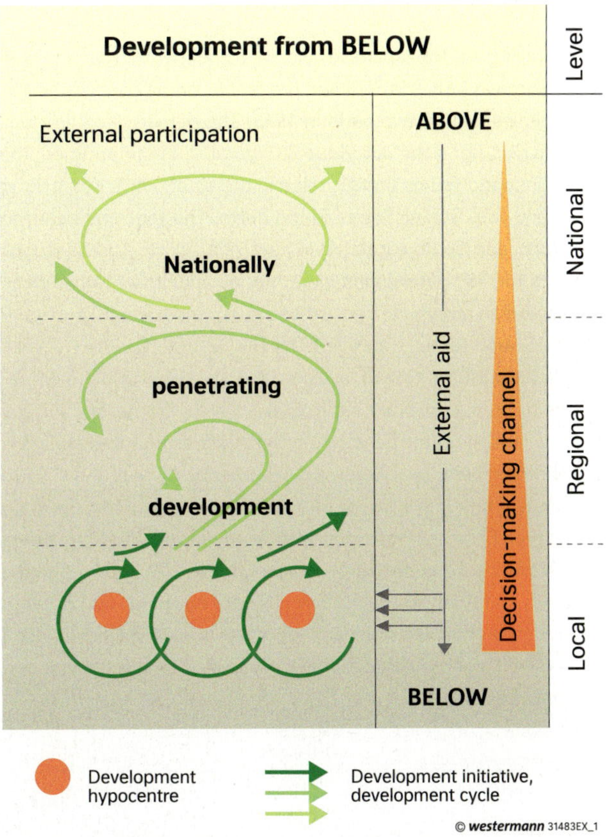

M9 The model of "development from below"

Development through industrialisation

Expanding the secondary sector – South Korea

South Korea was still a developing country in the 1960s. Per capita GNI, at 239 US-$, was as high as that of Ghana. Today, that indicator is nearly 15 times higher than that of the West African country. How did South Korea's positive economic growth come about?

1. Locate South Korea and outline the key events in the country's recent history (M1, Atlas, Internet).
2. Describe South Korea's economic development and its current economic situation (M2 – M6).
3. Discuss the reasons for South Korea's positive industrial development. Point out individual location factors that contributed to the growth of industry (M5, M8 – M10).
4. (O) Characterise the situation of economic centres in South Korea and illustrate the significance of global players for the national economy (M7, Atlas) by:
   A drawing a sketch map;
   B outlining the importance of an exemplary global player.
5. (O) A Illustrate the prevailing development strategy in South Korea.
   B Discuss whether and to what extent South Korea and Brazil exemplify "top-down development".
6. (S) Classify the development of South Korea's economy within the framework of Rostow's model (M5 on p. 109).

→ Development from above, Direct foreign investments, Export diversification, Export orientation, Import substitution, Research and development (R&D)

After driving out the Japanese colonial power [which had annexed all of Korea in 1910], the US and the Soviet Union divided the Korean peninsula into two parts in 1945. The demarcation line was established along the notorious 38th parallel. Singman Rhee, the dictator supported by the US, ruled in the south while Kim Il Sung governed with Stalinist force in the north. The tensions between the North and South escalated in June 1950. North Korean troops crossed the 38th parallel and were met by an initially rather weak South Korean army […].
The tide soon turned, however. The UN Security Council […] condemned the North Korean invasion and appealed to UN member states to provide military aid to South Korea. Troops from many nations landed on the peninsula and the US contributed substantial reinforcements. […] Assessing the possible defeat of his North Korean ally Kim Il Sung as a threat to his country, Mao Tse-tung dispatched Chinese troops to attack the advancing Western allies in late October […]. For the next two years, North and South engaged in largely stationary trench warfare. The war ended in July 1953 with an armistice and the establishment of the so-called Demilitarised Zone (DMZ) along the 38th parallel – precisely where the war had originally begun.

Source: Kister, K., Am Morgen flog alles in die Luft. 31.10.2010, www.sueddeutsche.de, accessed 20.01.2015

M1 Korea's turbulent history

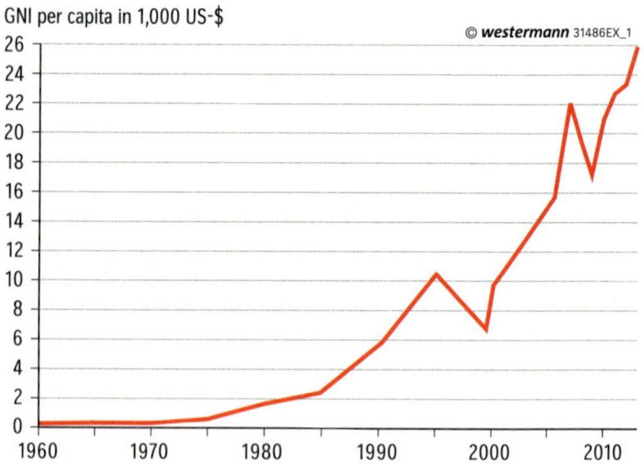

M2 Per capita GNI in South Korea

Population	48.4 million
Population density	503 inhabitants per km² (Germany has 229 inhabitants per km²)
Life expectancy	80.6 years
Infant mortality	0.4%
Illiteracy rate	2.1%
Urbanisation rate	83.3%
Per capita GNI	22,670 US-$
Relative share of GDP of the sectors (in %)	
I	3
II	39
III	58
Imports	520 billion US-$
Exports	548 billion US-$, including electrical equipment (16%) and auto parts (13%)
Unemployment rate (1960/1980/2013)	11.8%/5.1%/3.3%
HDI (ranking)	0.91 (rank 12)
Gini Index	31.0

Source: Fischer Weltalmanach. different years

M3 Basic data for South Korea, 2013

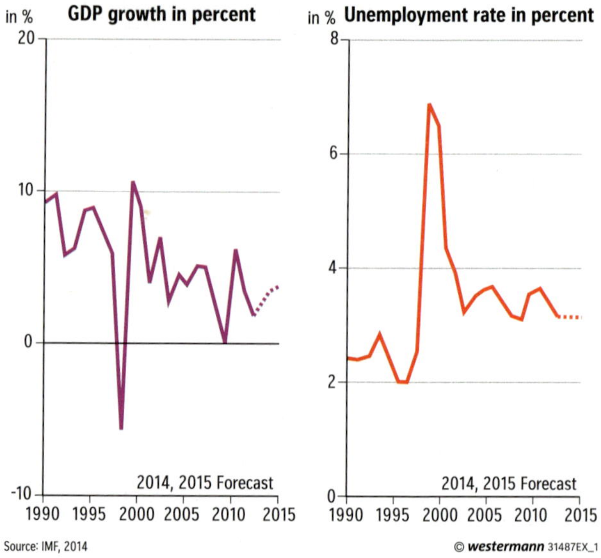

M4 GDP growth and unemployment in South Korea

Once the wheels get rolling

The Republic of Korea has advanced from a dirt-poor agricultural country to the eighth leading trading nation in the world within just two generations. The country has repeatedly reinvented itself on its way to the modern era. Its education system is one of the most efficient in the world in both scope and performance. Know-how is the nation's most important raw material [...]. Originally dominated by heavy industry and now by IT, the economy of the future is likely to be focused above all on environmental, bio- and nanotechnology. [...] Korean products have become part of globalised everyday life. While major electronics firms such as Samsung and LG have caused a stir with advanced technology and sometimes become global market leaders, the automotive industry, represented by Hyundai and Kia, has risen to the "top of the heap" – where ship-building and the construction industry have been positioned for some time – in terms of quality and design. [...] Politically, since overcoming the military dictatorship and adopting a policy of liberalisation and opening in the 1980s, South Korea has established itself as a stable democracy in the military alliance with the USA [...].

Source: Breitenstein, A., Wenn die Welle rollt. 10.05.2013, www.nzz.ch, accessed 26.02.2015.

M5 The rise of South Korea

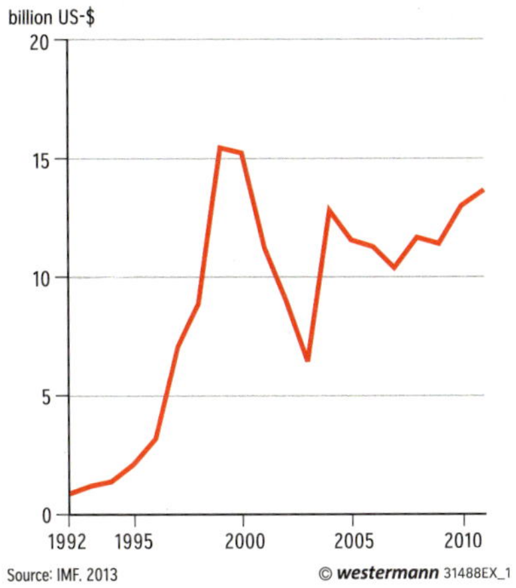

M9 Direct foreign investments in South Korea (in billion US-$)

	Expenditures for R&D* 2005-10 (in % of GDP)	High-tech exports in million US-$	High-tech exports in % of total value of exported goods	Registered patents	Scientists (per 1 million inhabitants)	Persons with academic degrees (25–34, in %)	Public expenditures for education (in % of GNI)
Brazil	1.16	8,415	9.7	2,705	3,092	no data	no data
Germany	2.80	183,371	15.0	46,986	68,961	26.1	4.55
Japan	3.26	126,478	17.5	287,570	107,898	56.7	3.80
South Korea	3.74	122,021	25.7	138,034	133,645	65.0	5.00

* R&D = research and development

M6 Research, education and development as location factors, 2012

Firm	Turnover in billion US-$	Global ranking*
Samsung Electronics (Electronics)	208.9	22
Hyundai Motors (Automobiles)	79.8	87
POSCO (Steel)	56.5	236
Shinhan Financial (Finance)	19.6	249
Kia Motors (Automobiles)	43.5	258

Source: Forbes Global 2000, 2014 * Ranking based on turnover and other indicators

M7 South Korean global players, 2013

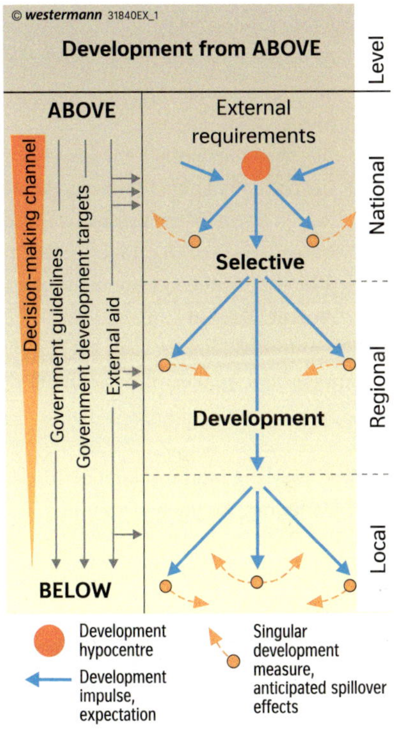

M10 Model of development from above

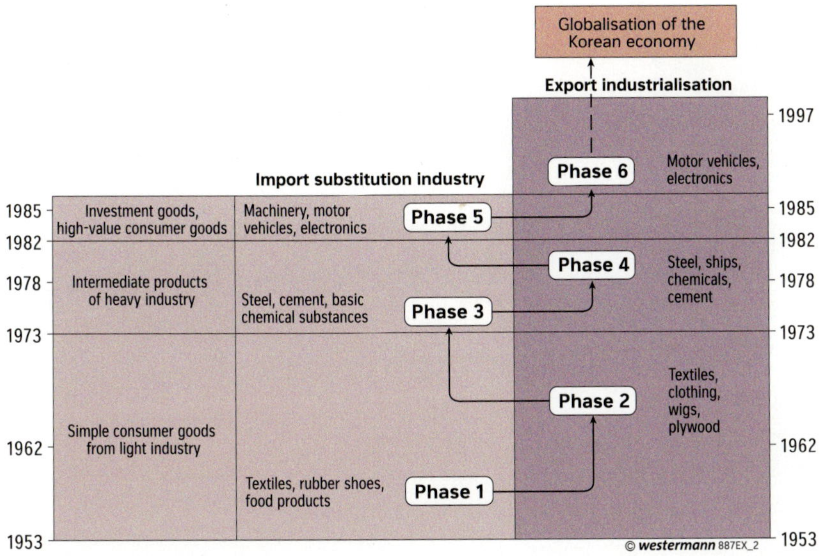

M8 Stages of economic development in South Korea

→ Import substituting industry or Import substitution

is an industrialisation strategy devoted to replacing imports with domestic industrial products.

→ Export-based industrialisation or Export orientation

is devoted to the goal of building industries whose products are sold primarily or solely abroad. This helps diversify the export sector, which is monostructural in many developing countries (export diversification).

Tourism as a development driver in a developing country

An island becomes a tourist destination – Phuket (Thailand)

International tourism in Thailand experienced a breakthrough in the 1960s, when easily affordable recreational opportunities were created for US soldiers under special rest and recreation (R&R) programmes. This sector has since grown rapidly and now represents a significant segment of the Thai economy. Tourism has become an important branch of the economy in many parts of the country – including Phuket, for example.
What prerequisites does Phuket meet for the development of tourism, and how has the island changed under the influence of tourism?

1. Characterise Phuket's potential as a tourist destination (M1–M3, M5, M7, Atlas).
2. Ⓞ Compare the numbers of tourists arriving from different regions of origin (M4).
   A Draw a map in which you show the numbers of tourists and the distances between the regions of origin and the tourist destinations.
   B Describe these relationships in a text.
3. a) Describe the spatial-chronological development of the tourist trade on the basis of Vorlaufer's model (M6).
   b) Assess the growth phases according to Vorlaufer with reference to the development of tourism on the island of Phuket (M2, M6).
4. Ⓢ "Uncontrolled tourism saws off the very branch it sits on." Express your opinion of this statement (M5, M7).

→ Mass tourism, Model of spatial-chronological development (K. Vorlaufer), Regional disparities, Trickle-down effect

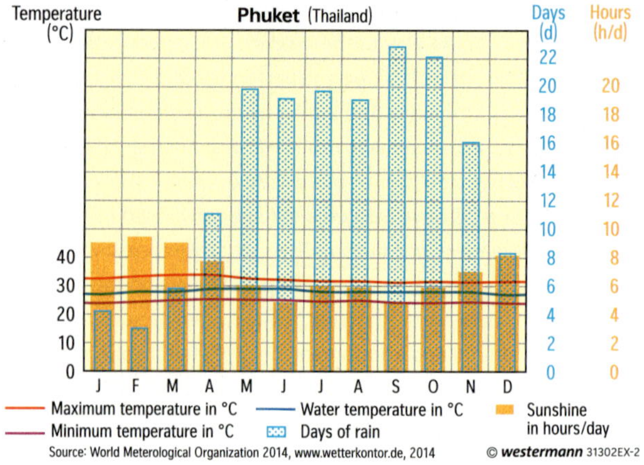

M3 Climate data for Phuket

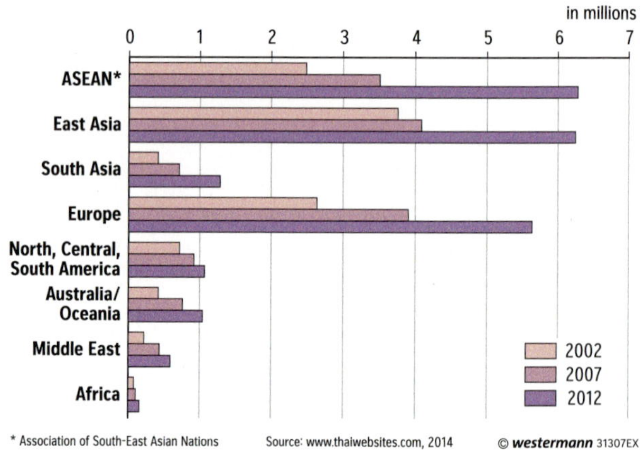

M4 Number of arriving tourists by region of origin

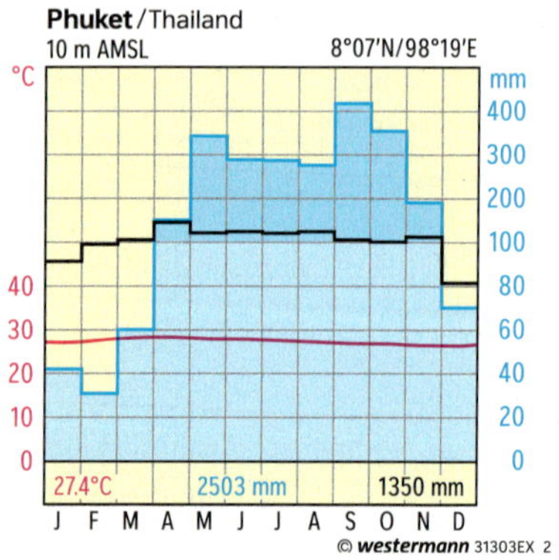

M1 Climate diagram for Phuket

→ Trickle-down effect
The term "trickle-down effect" refers to the slow downward movement of capital from the wealthy to the poorer social classes, which thus also benefit from ecnomic growth as a result. These benefits come in the form of wages and orders for goods and/or services.

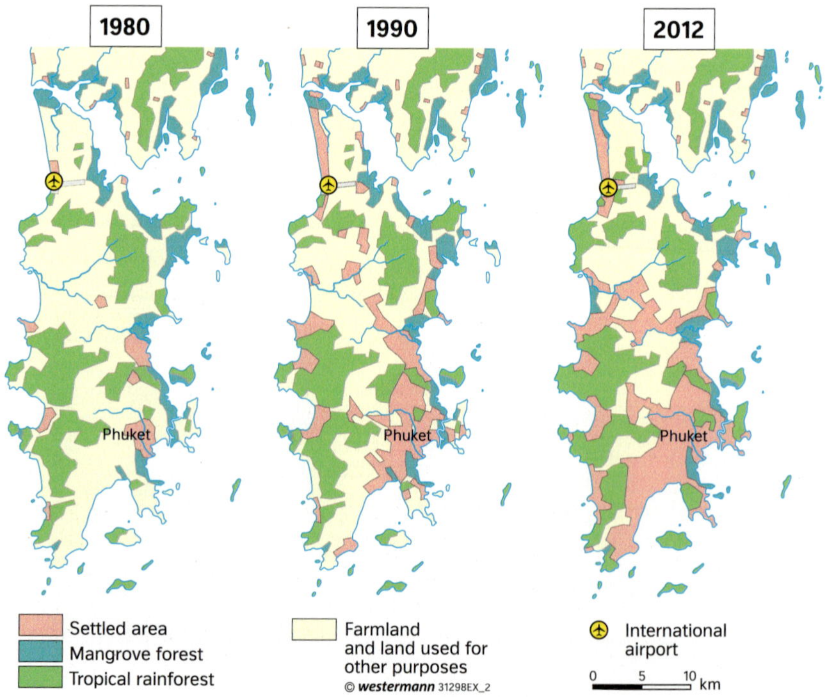

M2 Spatial development of tourism on the island of Phuket

M5 Unspoiled nature on the island of Phuket

M7 Mass tourism on the island of Phuket

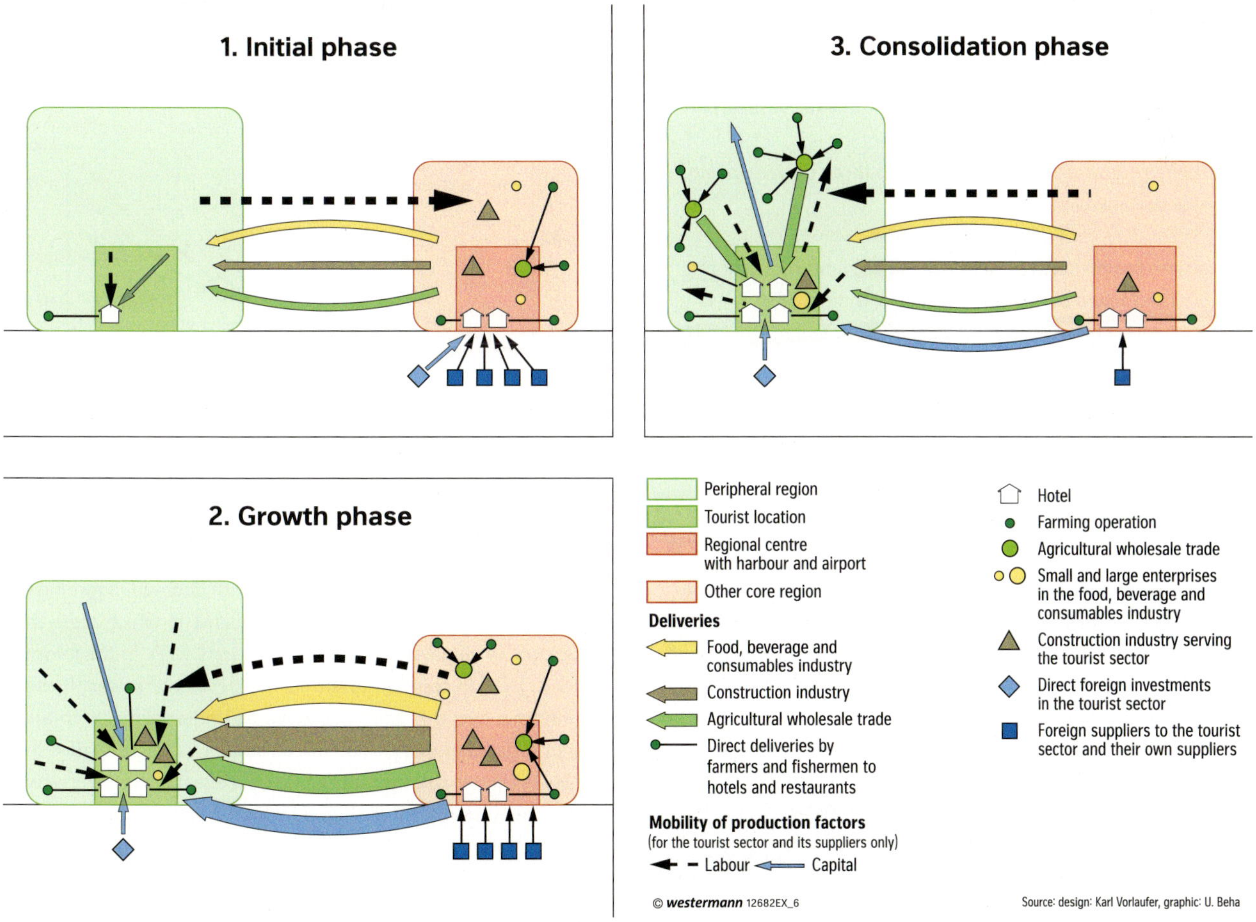

Nearly all developing countries exhibit extreme regional disparities. [Densely populated areas have more fully developed infrastructures than peripheral regions. This leads to migration from rural to urban areas, which reinforces the existing regional disparities.] Developing countries view tourism as an effective tool for reducing such disparities. Many types of tourism (including bathing, adventure, hiking, deserts, hunting, animal-watching, ethnological and ecological tourism) often take place only in unpopulated or thinly populated peripheral areas that offer favourable conditions ("unspoiled" nature, "exotic" peoples, etc.) that would represent location disadvantages for other branches of the economy. Even those locations that are relatively or totally unsuitable for subsistence farming (sandy beaches, coral reefs, upper reaches of mountain ranges or extremely arid regions) may still be used as tourist locations and thus contribute to economic growth. The development of peripheral regions in support of tourism is intended to reduce disparities while boosting economic growth by mobilising resources that are otherwise resistant to exploitation. In many peripheral areas, tourism initially results in intraregional polarisation, in a concentration of growth in a single centre, which assumes the role of counterweight to the core region, however [...]. Given the availability of corresponding resources, the economy of such peripheral regions can adjust to the demands of tourism.

Source: Vorlaufer, K., Tourismus in Entwicklungsländern. In: Geographische Rundschau 3/2003, p. 9

M6 The three-phase model of spatial-chronological development according to K. Vorlaufer

Tourism as a development driver in a developing country

The conflict between mass tourism and sustainable tourism

Tourism has had a significant economic, environmental and social impact on the island of Phuket. But is that impact sustainable? Analysis suggests that the triad of factors can serve as a foundation for sustainability, but the political consequences represent a fourth dimension that must be considered as well.

1. Explain the history of tourist arrivals on Phuket (M1, M2, M5).
2. a) Draw a mindmap illustrating possible services provided by the informal sector on Phuket (M4, M7, M8).
   b) Characterise the importance of the informal sector on Phuket (M4).
3. Evaluate the economic significance of tourism under the influence of the leakage rate (M5).
4. ⓞ Assess the sustainability of tourism on the island of Phuket. Consider the vulnerability of the region in your assessment (M1–M3, M6, M7, M9, M10).
   A List arguments for and against the three dimensions of sustainability in a table.
   B Formulate your arguments in a text.
5. Evaluate the predictive potential and the limitations of the model proposed by Vorlaufer (M7, M8, p. 117, M6).
6. ⓢ "Tourism is a fire you can use to cook your soup or burn your house down." Express an opinion on this Asian proverb.

→ Informal sector, Leakage rate, Sustainable tourism

M2 Phuket after the tsunami of 26.12.2004

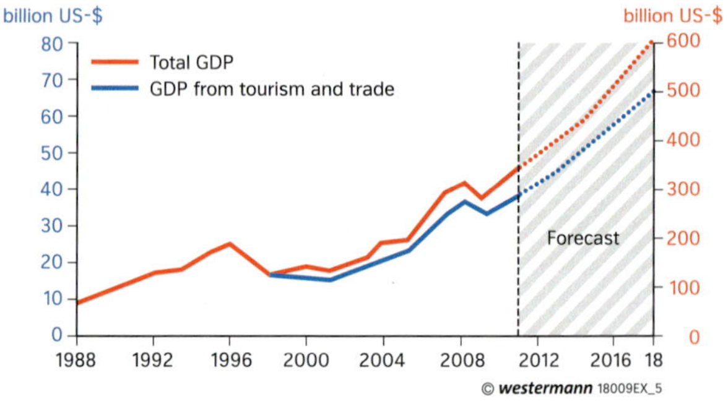

M3 GDP growth in Thailand

→ Leakage rate

The leakage rate is a measure of capital that is lost in a tourist region. Leakage occurs, for example, when food that cannot be produced locally has to be purchased or imported. According to UNCTAD (United Nations Conference on Trade and Development), the leakage rate in developing countries ranges between 40 and 50 percent.

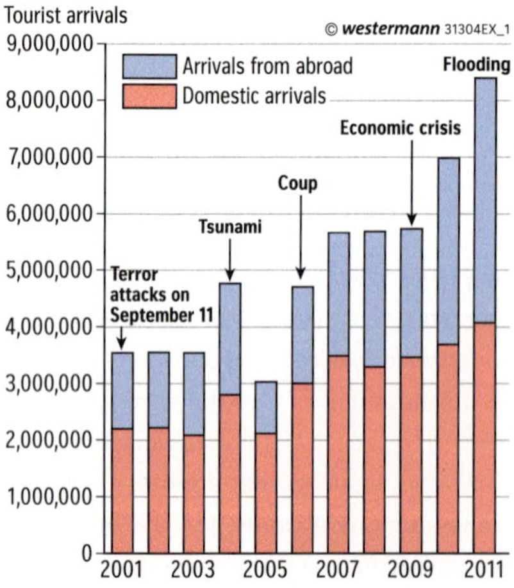

Source: www.phuketgazette.net, March 2013, revised

M1 Tourist arrivals on the island of Phuket

A substantial percentage of jobs in the tourist industry are found in the informal sector today. This accords with findings regarding the overall structure of the economy in Thailand, in which more than 50 percent of all gainfully employed persons work in the informal sector [...]. [...] In contrast to formal business enterprises, those in the informal sector [...] are described as undertakings with a low level of organisation that operate as small businesses, offer their employees no reliable income and do not have them registered with a government-administered social security system [...]. Because they are not registered with government authorities, the true magnitude of the informal sector, i.e. the number of informal enterprises and their employees, can only be roughly estimated. [...]

Because neither formal training nor official work permits are required in order to work in the informal sector, this sector offers people for whom the formal labour market offers few opportunities (e.g. women, disabled persons and refugees) a chance to earn a living. [...] Furthermore, the informal sector offers individuals who are otherwise engaged full-time (e.g. farmers and students) an opportunity to supplement their income and helps reduce seasonal unemployment in primarily agrarian regions [...].

Source: Gantner, B.: Schattenwirtschaft unter Palmen. In: ASEAS – Österreichische Zeitschrift für Südostasienwissenschaften 1/2011, pp. 56–58

M4 The informal tourist sector

	Share of total expenditures (in %)	Percentage of that share that remains in Europe
Bookings and travel agencies	20%	100%
Flights (with European airlines)	40%	90%
Hotels, meals	24%	20%
Excursions, souvenirs	16%	70%

M5 Breakdown of costs for a package tour (leakage rates)

- Coastal changes resulting from the construction of buildings, roads and seawalls.
- Damage to national parks caused by excessive tourist use.
- Loss of coastal mangrove forests (more than half in the past 30 years).
- Damage to forests caused by access-road construction and logging operations.
- Damage to coral reefs resulting from scuba-diving excursions and marina construction.
- Increased rubbish accumulation; rubbish disposal problems (incineration, landfill leakage).
- Problems associated with inadequate sewage processing, channeling of sewage into the sea.
- Noise and air pollution.

Source: Reuber, P., Probleme des Tourismus in Thailand. In: Geographische Rundschau, 3/2003, p. 16

M6 Environmental problems

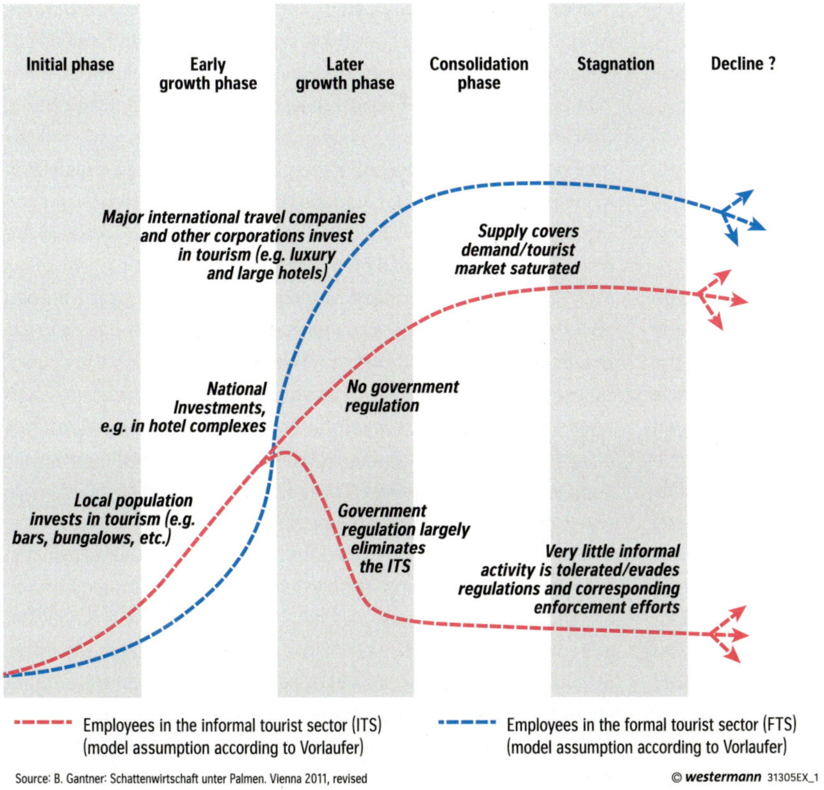

M7 Simplified ITS and FTS phase model according to Vorlaufer

During the initial growth phase of the tourist trade, the programme of tourist services in Patong [was] organised by local providers, most of whom represented the informal tourist sector [...]. With respect to accommodation, it was determined that small bungalows were operated by their owners or close relatives without hotel licences. In some cases, family members or friends were employed and compensated with low wages or board and lodging. [...] The roads on which tuk-tuk drivers provided informal transportation services for tourists were unpaved. As tourist activity increased (during the early growth phase), actors from outside of Patong recognised the economic potential offered by the tourist trade. As time passed, it was not the local population that profited most from the growth of tourism, but rather people from outside of Patong [...] who owned the larger tourist accommodation facilities. They usually hired people from their own cities, rather than local citizens, to run these operations. These business people eventually paved the way for lucrative investments through their [...] contacts in Bangkok and other countries. Local citizens who still owned land near the shore sold it at high prices. And later on, as more and more international investors began to take an interest in Phuket, the price of land rose substantially [...]. [Most local citizens migrated to the city after selling their land.] Even during the early growth phase of the tourist trade, the village community earned very little from the provision of services to tourists, as restaurants and hotels made most of their purchases in the urban markets of Phuket Town [...].

Source: Gantner, B., Schattenwirtschaft unter Palmen. In: ASEAS – Österreichische Zeitschrift für Südostasienwissenschaften 1/2011, pp. 64–66

M8 Development of the informal tourist sector in Patong/Phuket

Following the military coup in May 2014, the security situation in Thailand stabilised for the most part [...]. Martial law still applies in all parts of the country, and freedom of the press and freedom of assembly were severely restricted. Tourists are [...] advised to avoid demonstrations and gatherings of people in Bangkok and Thailand as a whole.
(Source: www.auswaertiges-amt.de, 2015)

M9 Political problems

The numbers of German tourists visiting Phuket has been declining for years [...]. In 2007, 250,000 Germans spent their holidays on the island in the Andaman Sea. That figure is down to 170,000 today, and could easily fall to 120,000 within the next two or three years. The unfavourable baht exchange rate and water pollution are cited as reasons for the diminished appeal of Phuket. [...] The environmental problems [...] are becoming increasingly obvious. Forests and coastlines are being sacrificed to the unchecked construction boom despite the surplus of hotel beds.

Source: Lenz, M., Tuk-Tuk-Mafia hat Phuket fest im Griff. www.stern.de, accessed 01.12.2014

M10 Results of a survey

Balancing regional disparities

Driving growth by promoting regional economic development – China

The first special economic zones in China were established on the east coast. The speed of the subsequent wave of economic development in the region is unparalleled in the history of the world (see pp. 60/61, 184/185). How has development on China's east coast affected the rest of the country?

1. Locate the focal points of economic development in China and the country's special economic zones (Atlas, M3).

Ⓞ 2. Compare the economic location factors and the living conditions of the population (M1 – M3):
   A in the coastal and inland regions of China;
   B in the urban and rural regions of China.

Ⓞ 3. A Characterise the migration patterns in China (M3);
   B Cite reasons for the specific characteristics and direction of labour-force migration (M1 – M3).

Ⓞ 4. A Describe the projected development of the Chengdu Tianfu special economic zone (M4).
   B Explain why the Chinese government is establishing an increasing number of special economic zones in the interior (M4). Refer to the example of the Chengdu Tianfu special economic zone.

5. "Special economic zones – a model for success for all regions of China." State your position.

Ⓢ 6. Plan a new special economic zone in the Chinese interior in addition to the ones shown on the map in M3. Justify your choice of location.

→ Direct foreign investments, Growth pole, Migrant workers, Migration, Special economic zone

→ Growth pole

A geographic unit based on the positive effects of its economic growth on outlying areas.

Traditional farming in a rural region

Main shopping street in Chengdu

Because of its better accessibility and its early opening to foreign trade, eastern China is much further developed than central and western China. Roughly 85 percent of direct foreign investments are concentrated in the coastal provinces. Costs are increasing in those areas, however, especially in the major cities. Provincial capitals and regional urban centres that have been systematically developed in recent years are now becoming increasingly interesting for investors. Within the context of regional programmes, such as the "Go West" campaign, the government is striving to accelerate economic development in the interior through infrastructure enhancement measures as well as tax and investment incentives. [...] Plans call for the construction of new highways, high-speed railway lines and airports in the next several years. [...] The goal is to promote more balanced social progress and improve the general standard of living.

Source: German Centre for Industry and Trade Beijing: In China leben und arbeiten – 100 Fragen & 100 Antworten. Beijing, 2012.

M1 Regional development and disparities in China

Although poverty has been reduced under the influence of economic growth and transformation, income differences, social problems and disparities between the coastal regions and the nation's under-developed interior have become increasingly severe in recent years. The boom has been driven primarily by the coastal regions, in which the demand for labourers is particularly high. The level of income and prosperity in rural western and central China is comparable to that of a developing country. A shortage of jobs and a deficient infrastructure are obstacles to growth. The official unemployment rate in China is about four percent, but it is significantly higher in the rural regions and the consequence is a rural exodus, especially by younger members of the population. Under the Chinese registration system however, migrant workers do not enjoy the same rights as urban residents and are paid lower wages. Average incomes in the cities are three times as high as in rural areas.

Migration to the cities impacts on incomes but also imposes a burden on infrastructure and leads to a worsening of living conditions in the overpopulated cities. China is promoting investment in the interior by establishing new zones, developing rural infrastructures and sponsoring regional development programmes. The advantages of locations in rural regions include lower costs and a sufficient supply of labour and land. China is also planning to build more new towns for the rural population. The objective is to encourage 250 million people to move to cities. In Anhui and other provinces, farming villages are being forcibly depopulated and farming families are being resettled in high-rise estates. In view of the fear that the already overpopulated cities will be unable to cope with the influx of migrants, increasing attention is being focused on developing smaller cities, such as Wuhan and Shenyang. Workers now tend to seek employment near their home towns instead of migrating to the coast.

M2 Urban-rural gap and migration in China

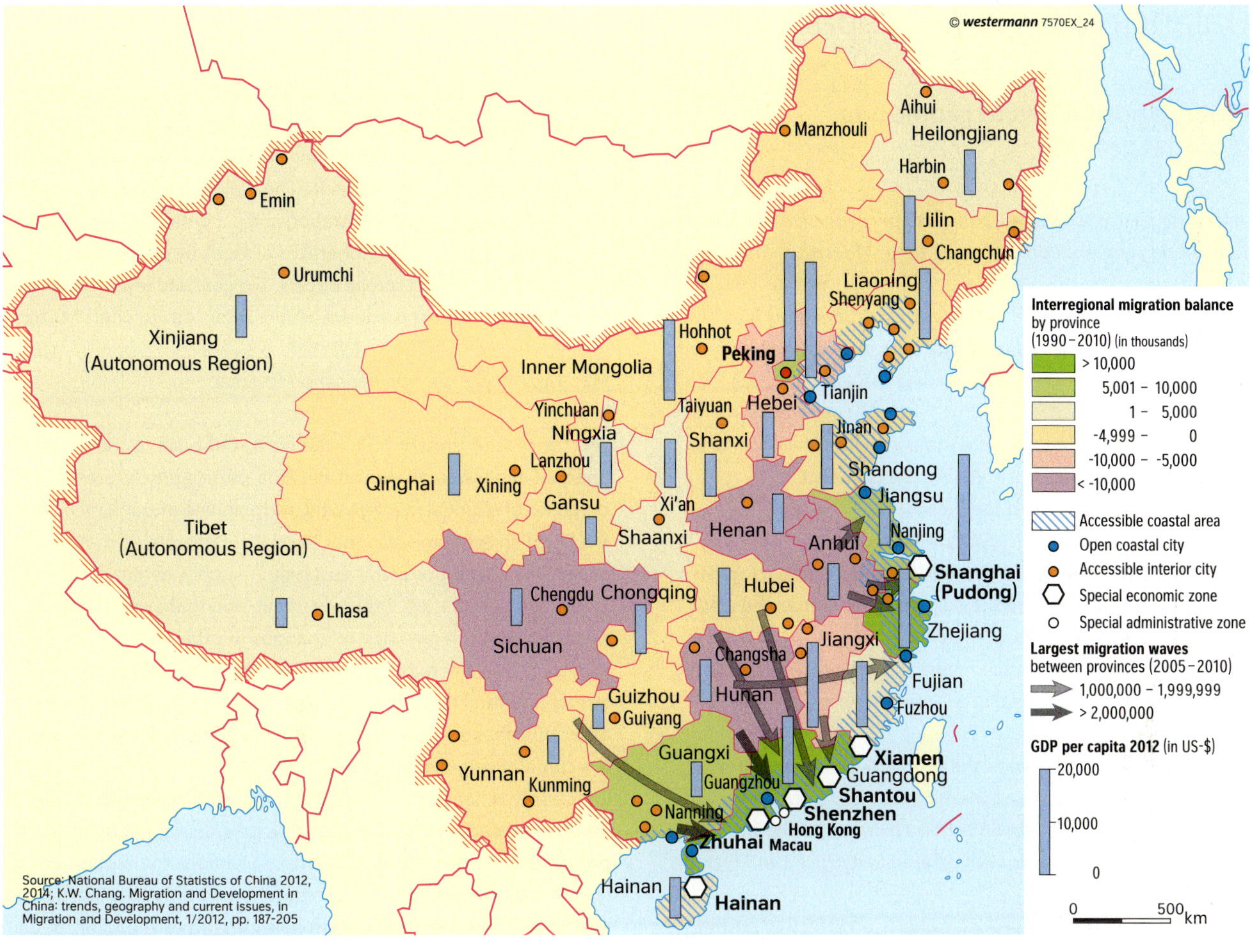

M3 Migration in China

An engine for economic development in western China

The Sichuan Provincial Government approved the construction of Chengdu Tianfu New Area [...]. The new area aims to develop into a national economic development zone following four other state-level development zones, including the Shanghai Pudong economic and development zone [...]. Meng also said the Chengdu Tianfu New Area is an ideal platform for the company to open up the south-western Chinese market. [...] Chengdu provides an optimised transportation and logistics system which can be compared to those in the coastal and riverbank cities in China [...]. With the rapid economic development of the Sichuan province together with its provincial capital Chengdu, the Southwest Chinese food and raw material market is facing an increasing larger gap between the production and consumer needs. [...] The Chengdu International Automobile Town is one of the key elements for development of the vehicle manufacturing industry of the Chengdu Tianfu New Area. The automobile town is planned to develop a vehicle cluster of tens of billion yuan by the end of 2020, attracting reputed companies like Sichuan Faw Toyota Motor Co Ltd, Faw Volkswagen Automobile Co Ltd, and the Volvo Group. The automobile town is located in the region of Chengdu's Economic and Development Zone that has attracted 38 World Top 500 companies and about 38 billion yuan in foreign directed investments (FDIs) in the recent five years. [...]

The Sichuan Toyota hopes to make good use of Chengdu's unique geographical location and enter the large market in Southwest China. [...] Enjoying favourable government policies, the company will also help boost economic and social developments in the Longquan area. In 2011, the company contributed 2.6 billion yuan in taxes, ranking the third among all companies in the Sichuan province. [...] The company also hosted many social and charity activities including donating a hope school to Xinjin county and funding a class of excellent students from deprived families together with the Chengdu Charity Union. [...] Chengdu is predicting that it will see a stronger development incentive to become one of the most important economic hubs in Southwest China.

Source: Zhilin, C., Engine for the West China economic development. 21.01.2012, www.chinadaily.com.cn, accessed 19.01.2015.

M4 The Special Economic Zone near Chengdu – a growth pole and development driver

Economic growth has its price. [...] Environmental pollution has assumed dramatic proportions.

Air

The People's Republic emits the highest quantities of CO_2 in the world, due above all to coal-fired power plants and vehicle exhausts. People in northern China tend to die younger from the effects of smog.

Water

Half of China's major lakes are polluted and groundwater quality is even worse. According to Greenpeace, half of the rural population has no access to drinking water that meets international standards.

Soil

China has lost one-fifth of its farmland to erosion and urban development. Most of the land is regarded as contaminated. An area the size of Belgium is so polluted that crops can no longer be cultivated there.

Source: Die WELT, China erklärt Umweltverschmutzung den Krieg. 07.03.2014, www.welt.de, accessed 03.12.2014.

M5 Environmental impact

Balancing regional disparities

Model approaches to promoting regional growth

The establishment of special economic zones is now regarded worldwide as the key to promoting regional growth – in China, Mauritius, India, Ireland and elsewhere.
What common concept underlies this view? What strategy does it reflect? Are there conceptual models that relate to the anticipated economic and regional consequences?

ⓞ 1. Explain the strategy of growth poles with reference to a concrete example (M1, M3). Choose between:
A the Shanghai region (pp. 60/61).
B the Chengdu region (pp. 120/121).
2. Discuss the significance of spread effects and backwash effects as they relate to the east coast of China (see also the polarisation model, pp. 162/163).
3. Illustrate how polarisation reversal theory is reflected in the settlement of special economic zones in China (M4, M5, p. 121 M3).
4. Myrdal called attention to the problematic aspects of the growth pole concept and the Polarisation Reversal Theory. His criticism has also been echoed by recent scholars. Describe these aspects with reference to the Pearl River region (Atlas, M6).
5. The establishment of growth poles is an effective strategy for the reduction of regional disparities. Express your opinion on this statement.
Ⓢ 6. The principle of growth poles is applied, for example, in the process of planning new commercial estates and innovation parks. Illustrate this on the basis of an example from your home region.

→ Backwash effect, Fragmenting development, Growth pole, Polarisation Reversal Theory, Special economic zone, Spread effect

Viewed from the perspective of development policy, the development of peripheral regions is one of the most important tasks facing regional planners in developing countries. Polarisation reversal theory offers a useful concept. Regional planners hope to initiate a turnabout in regional concentration and [...] promote the establishment of new centres in peripheral rural areas by promoting growth poles and the resulting spread effects. The goal is to reverse the trend toward polarisation and achieve a more balanced regional structure.
Source: Latz, W. (ed.), Diercke Geographie,. 2011, p. 380.

M2 Growth poles and polarisation reversal

The concept of growth poles can be traced back to the theory of unequal economic growth. It became particularly interesting for purposes of regional management and planning through the work of the Swedish economist Gunnar Myrdal. He postulated that specific aspects of a given regional economy – supply, demand, jobs and investments, etc. – are interdependent, and that a positive change in one aspect will give rise to changes in others. This means, for example, that the establishment of a business operation with a strong potential for growth can induce further economic growth in other business segments and in the whole region. What emerges is a cumulative growth process.
Conversely, a negative change in one aspect has a negative impact on other aspects. Thus the growth pole concept is based on the principle of a concentrated effort to promote the settlement of growth industries at a few selected locations. The hope is that spread effects emanate from the growth pole into the surrounding areas. Myrdal pointed out however, that in addition to positive spread effects, backwash effects can also impact on neighbouring regions. These effects, which are negative for the surrounding areas, can nevertheless have a strengthening influence on the growth pole. Backwash effects include migration of productive workers or the flow of capital from other regions into the prospering economic centre.
Source: Latz, W. (Hg.), Diercke Geographie. 2011, p. 328

M3 The concept of growth poles

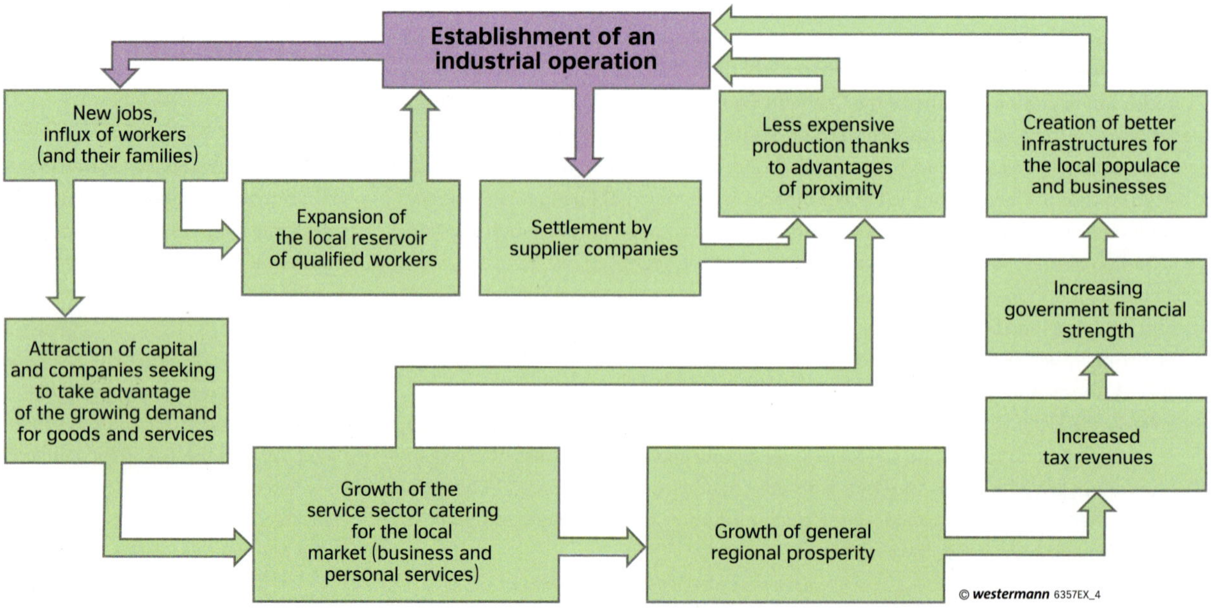

M1 Cumulative effects of the establishment of an industrial operation in a growth pole

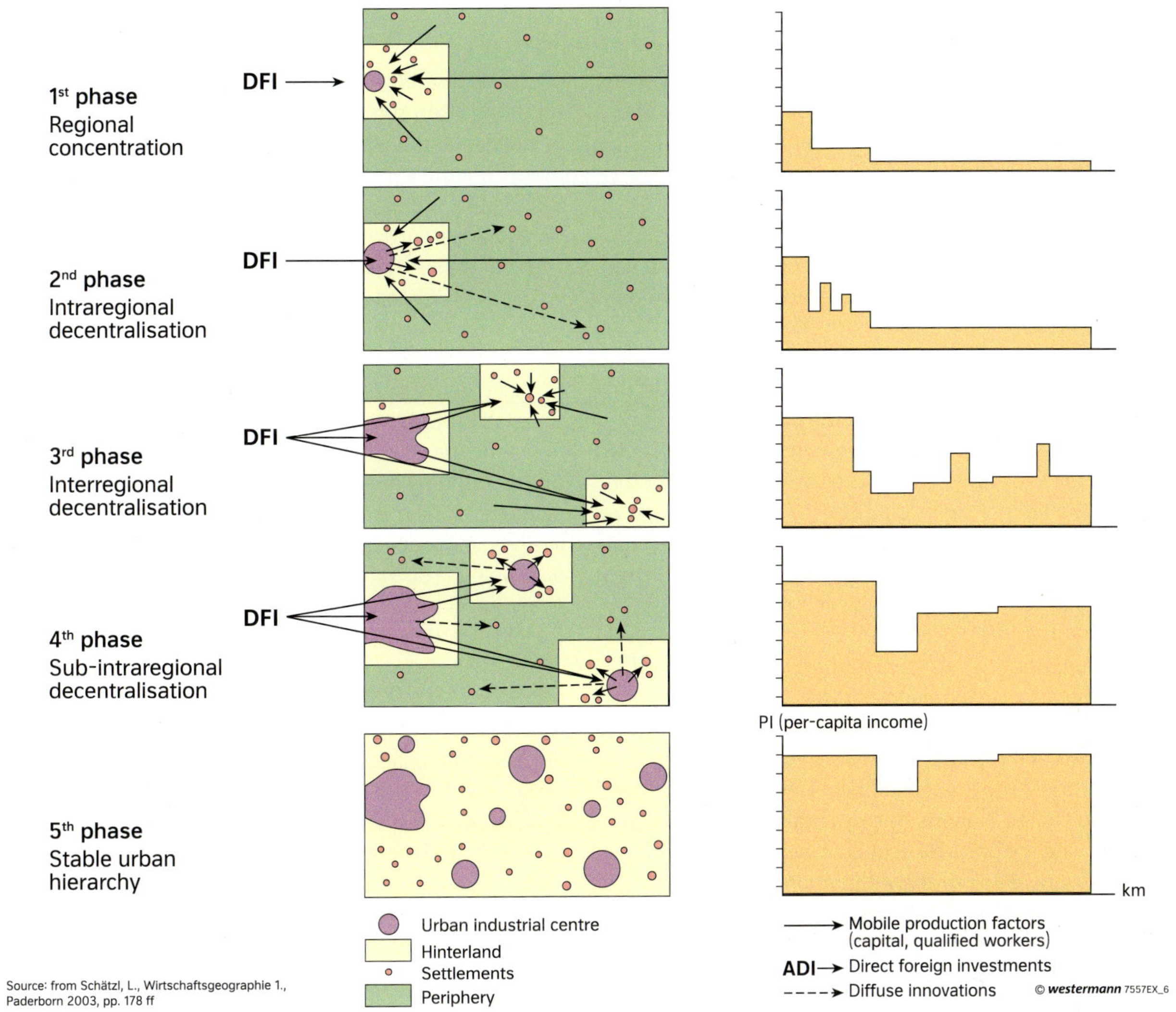

M4 Model of changing regional structure and per capita income according to H.W. Richardson's Polarisation Reversal Theory

1. Under the influence of a shortage of investment capital, the urban-industrial process of national economic development begins at a particularly favourable location which also attracts foreign investments. This sets cumulative growth and polarisation processes in motion.
2. The high growth rates and the influx of migrants into the central region lead to agglomeration problems (slums, environmental problems, etc.). This heightens the appeal of locations in the surrounding areas.
3. Subcentres in selected peripheral locations generate a dynamic growth trend accompanied by agglomeration benefits as well as backwash and spread effects.
4. This trend attracts initial direct foreign investments, encourages businesses to move into the area and triggers migratory movements from the central region into the subcentres.
5. The subcentres then serve as growth poles in their own right and more small subcentres emerge in the surrounding areas.
6. Over time, these mechanisms counteract the polarisation process and regional disparities are gradually reduced.

M5 Regional development according to the Polarisation Reversal Theory

Economists regard the [...] Pearl River region as a new form of spatial organisation known as a fragment. It is not a source of diverse economic impulses for the surrounding area,as would normally be expected of a growth centre. Instead, interrelated economic, infrastructural and communications operations are concentrated in previously existing and newly urbanised districts and industrial complexes. Interspersed among them are rural communities, farmlands and undeveloped areas, and even randomly distributed factory complexes. Thus the Pearl River Delta is characterised by a fragmentary accumulation of spatial units with widely differing functions and levels of development as well as weak links to the interior and an extremely strong reliance on overseas ties.

Source: Scholz, F., Globalisierung. Braunschweig, 2010, p. 87

M6 Fragmented development in the Pearl River region around Hong Kong

The essentials in brief

Global disparities have intensified dramatically in recent decades. The unequal development status of countries, regions or even individual localities represents a massive challenge for humanity.

Indicators to compare development status

A differentiated comparison of development status can only succeed with the aid of suitable indicators. Obviously there are firstly the economic indicators such as Gross Domestic Product or the Gini Index, which indicates the differences in wealth distribution within a country. At the same time, to be able to evaluate the development status of a spatial area and of the people living within it, it is essential to take social indicators into consideration. For this purpose, multidimensional indicators are available such as the Human Development Index (HDI) or the Multidimensional Poverty Index (MPI). Alongside these very comprehensive bundles of indicators, which can determine the development status of a country or region very precisely, numerous categories or designations are also used to roughly characterise development status. The most important category is certainly that of the developing countries or "countries of the South". For the particularly underdeveloped countries, the so-called Least Developed Countries (LDC), the United Nations has developed precise criteria which provide the basis for economic support, for example from the World Bank or the International Monetary Fund (IMF). As well as the LDCs there are also other groupings, such as countries with no access to the sea (Landlocked Developing Countries = LLDC) or particularly small islands that are often affected by climate change (Small Islands Developing Countries = SIDC).

Strong industrialised countries and emerging fast-developing countries

On the other hand there are many countries, often geographically located in the northern hemisphere, that have been economically very strong for a long time or have caught up in recent years. As a consequence of their economic situation, the social indicators in many of these countries also show a positive trend. The emerging countries are often referred to as fast-developing countries or newly industrialised countries (NIC). The Asian "Tiger States" (South Korea, Taiwan, Hong Kong, Singapore) or the BRICS states (Brazil, Russia, India, China, South Africa) are particularly frequently mentioned in this context. However, some of these states would see themselves as industrialised countries rather than as fast-developing countries.

Different development conditions

In the industrialised countries, GDP per capita is well above the global average. Most people have a good standard of living and the economy is productive. The dominant sectors of the economy are the industrial and service sectors.

In the developing countries, large sections of the population live below the poverty line, the basic needs of the majority of people are not satisfied, and many parts of the economy are unproductive. Large sections of the population earn their livelihood in the informal sector.

Causes of differences in development

Not infrequently, a country's exports display a monostructure with a predominance of raw materials – with negative consequences for the economy in the event of price fluctuations and deteriorating terms of trade. Not infrequently, spatial, economic and social structures have their roots in the colonial era.

Experts have long debated whether the causes of a lack of development are rather to be sought within the affected countries themselves (i.e. endogenous) or externally (i.e. exogenous). The endogenous approaches are referred to as modernisation theories, the exogenous approaches as dependence theories.

New theoretical approaches, such as that of local and global fragmentation, integrate the effects of globalisation into the pattern of explanation and speak of a fragmenting development. According to this, consideration of the situation in a whole country is not very meaningful because positive developments often only benefit a small section of society and are concentrated on fragments of the spatial area.

Skill Check

All the skills that you were able to acquire in this chapter are listed here.
You can judge for yourself if you have mastered each skill: ***securely***, ***moderately*** or ***barely***.

Explanatory skills

Can I ...		Unsure? Look it up on these pages
1.	define the terms GNI and GDP and illustrate global differences in GNI with reference to specific examples?	96/97
2.	identify economic disparities in selected countries on the basis of the Gini Index?	96/97
3.	distinguish between social and economic indicators and compare levels of development in different regions with the aid of these indicators?	96–99
4.	explain the meaning of the Human Development Index (HDI) and the Multidimensional Poverty Index (MPI) and analyse the level of development in specific countries and groups of countries?	98/99
5.	classify countries in the group of LDCs on the basis of the criteria set by the United Nations?	100/101
6.	characterise rapidly developing regions of the world on the basis of relevant indicators?	100/101

7.	analyse the importance of resources, available natural spaces and demographic factors to the economic development of individual regions?	102–105
8.	illustrate the model of local and global fragmentation?	106/107
9.	classify regional phenomena within the framework of the fragmentation model?	106–109
10.	illustrate possible causes of underdevelopment in individual countries?	108/109
11.	explain the terms "development cooperation" and "development policy"?	110/111
12.	trace the evolution of development strategies since 1950 and describe the concept of sustainability?	110/111
13.	compare development "from above" and development "from below" on the basis of regional examples?	112–115, 120/121
14.	illustrate the location factors required to support positive industrial development?	114/115
15.	describe the natural and infrastructural characteristics of a tourist region?	116–119
16.	show how a region changes in response to the rising demand for tourist services?	116/117
17.	explain both positive and negative effects of regional development influenced by tourism?	116–119
18.	classify different forms of tourism according to differen concepts of sustainability?	118/119
19.	illustrate how special economic zones contribute to reducing disparities in China?	120/121
20.	describe the most important principles of regional development models as proposed by Myrdal, Richardson and others?	122/123

Methodological skills

Can I ...		
21.	use topical and digital maps for the purposes of orientation and the representation of complex geographic phenomena?	96–99, 102–105, 120/121
22.	present complex geographic phenomena logically using appropriate technical terminology by explaining various technical terms used to define the levels of development in different countries or possible strategies for development cooperation with reference to appropriate regional examples?	100/101, 110/111
23.	support my statements with specific and detailed material references by describing developments and levels of development in individual countries, such as Chile or India, for example?	104/105, 106/107
24.	support written and oral statements with correct and appropriate material references and citations by analysing levels of development in specific countries on the basis of certain criteria?	100/101
25.	derive basic geographic principles from models and compare them with specific regional examples?	112–115, 122/123
26.	explain the temporal and spatial growth of tourism with the aid of Vorlaufer's model?	116/117
27.	evaluate the possible predictive potential and limitations of model-based descriptions of touristic development?	116–119

Evaluation skills

Can I ...		
28.	describe problems that result from underdevelopment in a given country or region on the basis of an assessment of such sources as the World Risk Report?	94/95
29.	assess the problems a colonial past could pose for the development of a given country?	102/103
30.	discuss the risks posed by monostructural economic development in a given country?	104/105
31.	explain the development concept underlying the idea of microcredits?	112/113
32.	discuss the positive and negative effects of regional development influenced by tourism?	116–119
33.	discuss the dilemma posed by the desire to satisfy individual recreational needs and the goal of sustainable development in tourist regions?	118/119
34.	evaluate the advantages and disadvantages of special economic zones for regional development?	120/121

Activity skills

Can I ...		
35.	present my findings regarding issues relating to regional disparities in a problem-oriented manner, giving due consideration to my specific audience and using appropriate technical language?	96–101
36.	assume and defend different positions in land-use conflicts relating, for example, to issues involving the exploitation of mineral reources in Chile?	104/105
37.	develop possible solutions for regional problems by illustrating possible obstacles to positive regional development in Mali or China?	102/103, 120/121
38.	present my findings regarding tourism as an impulse for development in peripheral and underdeveloped regions using appropriate technical language?	116–119

Examination training

Causes of underdevelopment – the example of Niger

1. Locate the state of Niger and illustrate the natural spatial preconditions for the country's economic development.
2. Explain the economic development and the development status of the country.
3. Evaluate the country's future development possibilities.

These additional materials are required to complete the assignments:

M1 Afrika – Klima, Diercke Weltatlas (2015), p. 148

M2 Afrika – Landwirtschaft, Diercke Weltatlas (2015), p. 149

M3 Afrika nördlicher Teil – Wirtschaft, Diercke Weltatlas (2015), p. 158/159

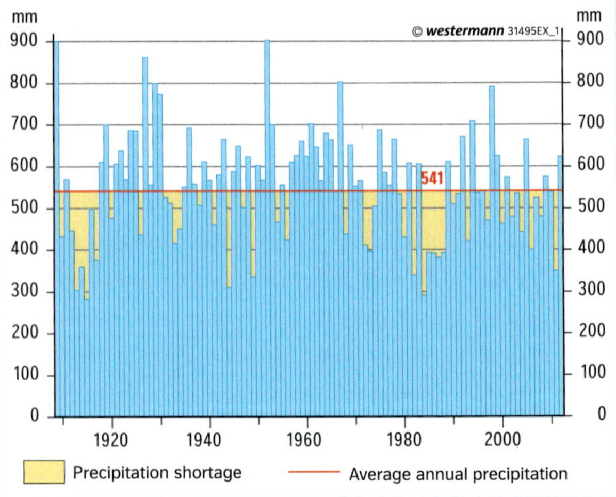

M5 Variable precipitation in Niamey

M4 Niger: resources and economic exploitation

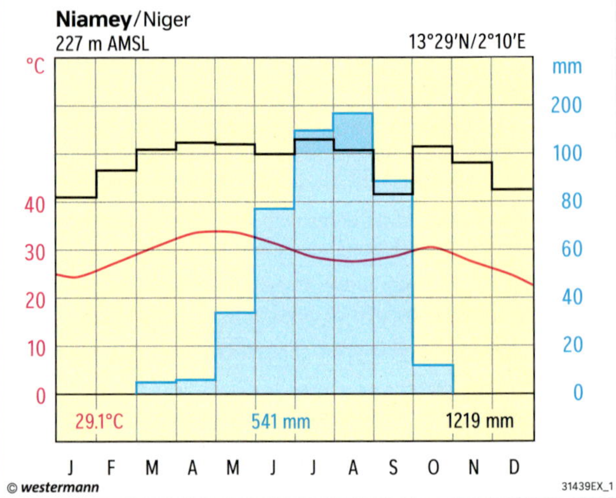

M6 Climate diagram for Niamey

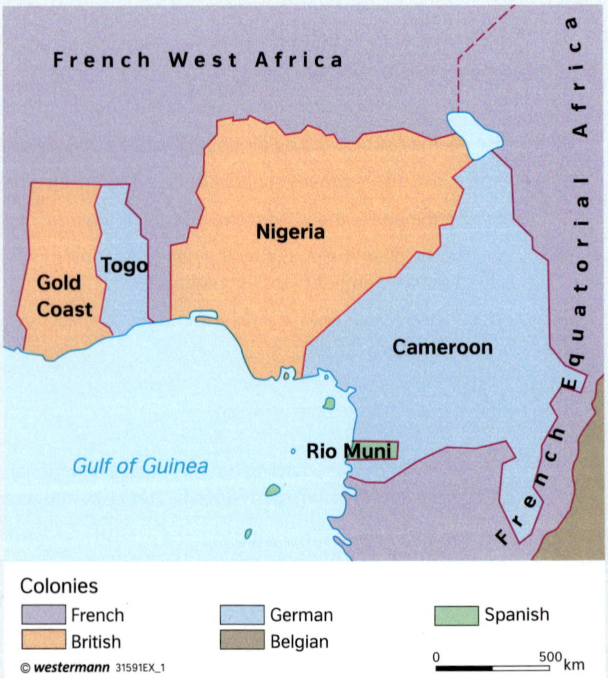

M7 The colonial situation in 1914

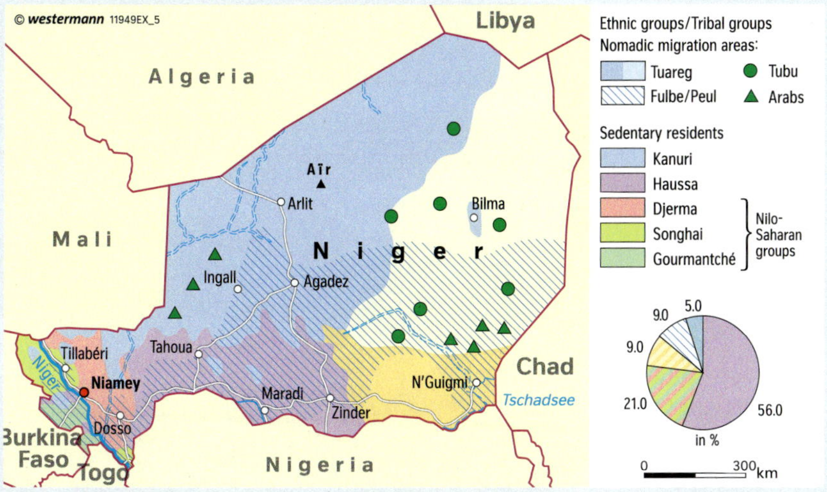

M8 Distribution of tribal and ethnic groups in Niger

1960	Independence from France. Even today, Paris has a major influence, not least through French companies in uranium extraction.
1970s and 1980s	Repeated military coups and violent unrest, countless conflicts around a democratic multi-party system.
1990s and 2000s	Conflicts between rival tribal groups, especially between nomads (Tuareg) and settled groups. Niger has a total of seven different large tribal groups.
2001	Start of the "Pan-Sahel Initiative", in which the USA enters into a cooperation with Sahel states. The goal is the containment of terrorism.
2010	Overthrow of President Tandja; installation of a military council to restore democracy.
2011	Free elections at local, regional and national levels. Mahamadou Issoufo becomes President.
2012	The democratisation process is carried forward. The new government earns international recognition for the work of its administration.
2013	Again and again, Niger is rocked by terror attacks by Islamist extremists, especially by Al-Qaida in the Islamic Maghreb (AQIM).

M9 The political situation in Niger since independence

Share of GDP in the sectors (numbers employed in brackets) (2013) (in %)	
I	38 (39.0)
II	20 (14.2)
III	42 (46.8)
HDI	0.304 (rank 186)
Population	17,157,042 (2012)
Population density	14 inhabitants per km^2
Birth rate (in ‰)	46.12
Growth rate	3.28
GNI (per capita)	410 US-$
Imports	2.9 billion US-$
Exports	1.5 billion US-$ (of which c. 48% uranium and c. 10% agricultural products)
Share of the population below the absolute poverty line	43.62% (2008)
Share of the population with a connection to the drinking water supply	52.33% (2012)

Source: CIA Factbook

M11 Basic data for Niger

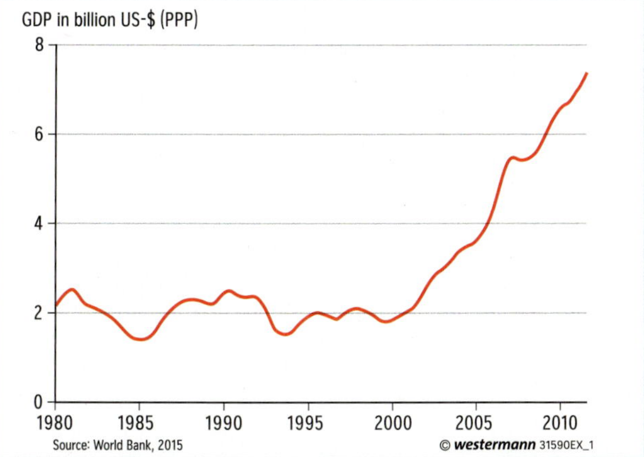

M10 Development of Niger's Gross Domestic Product, 1980 – 2010

Location of mining areas	Two mines in the north of the country near the city of Arlit. The opening of a third mine, 80 km south of Arlit, is planned for 2015.
Annual volume of production	About 5,000 tonnes (= fourth largest uranium mining country)
Problems	Threats to the health of mine workers and environmental pollution due to a lack of safety standards. Little benefit for Niger, because the foreign companies take out the capital. Especially the French company Areva mines uranium in large volumes. Threats from Islamic terror groups, the most recent bomb attack on the mine was on 23.5.2013.
Future scenarios	Following massive protests by the population in the capital of Niamey, the government of Niger started negotiations with Areva. It is no longer acceptable that c. 30 million euros per year is lost and too little is done for the environment.

Summarised from: Fischer Weltalmanach, www.theglobaleconomy.com, www.dw.de

M12 Information box on uranium mining in Niger

V Towns and cities as complex settlement areas

Between tradition and progress

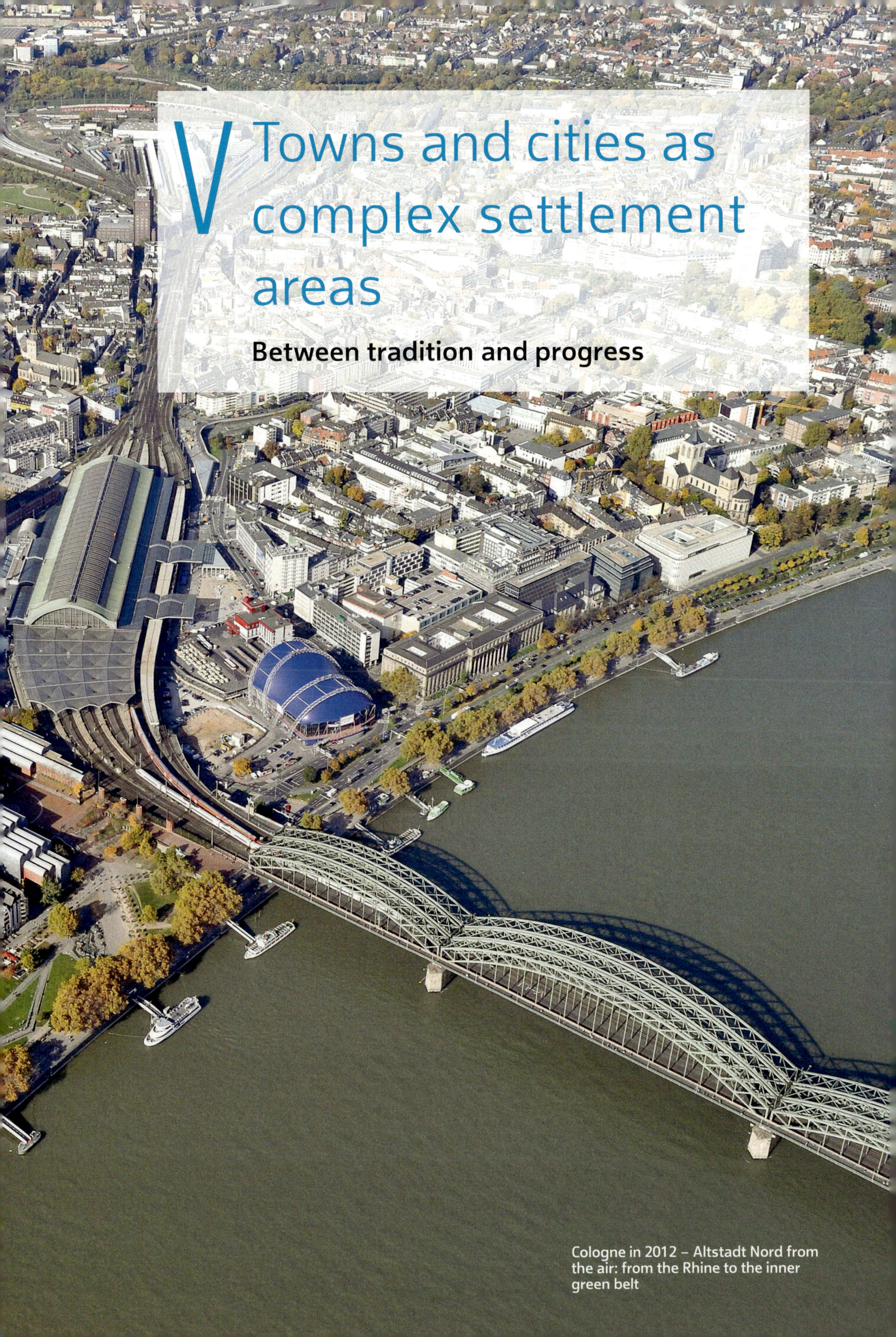

Cologne in 2012 – Altstadt Nord from the air: from the Rhine to the inner green belt

Towns and cities – historical legacy and present-day living space

Towns and cities have always acted as a driving force for the economic, political, social and cultural development of entire epochs. Thus, towns and cities have always been a magnet, drawing countless people towards them. In the present day, more than half of the global population already live in urban agglomerations – and the trend continues to increase. Due to these developments, towns and cities are subject to constant changes in their function and appearance. Management of the many-sided processes taking place in the urban living space represents a major challenge for urban and spatial planning, in which citizens also play an increasingly active part. Urban geography examines the urban living space on the basis of its size, form, function and history. Because all of these factors are interlinked, it makes sense to investigate them with the aid of a single spatial example.

The historical aspect is studied in terms of historical-genetic structure. When, where and why were towns established? And in what ways are historical epochs and building architectures from earlier centuries reflected in the towns and cities that we find today? Cologne is particularly suitable as an example of the historical-genetic structure of urban development in Central Europe, because this city is very old and was already established at the time of the Roman Empire.

Today it is important to conserve the historical elements of the different epochs of urban building as a cultural heritage. However it is often not easy to reconcile conservation with the demands of a modern town or city.

How can the historical, functional and social processes be understood in their complexity?

Subjective perception of a town or city

Every person has an image of the town or city as a living space, and at the same time perceives "my town" in a very individual way. [...] Everyone can capture their own view of their town in a mental map, in which they sketch their personal perception on a sheet of paper. These differ from person to person and are not "true to life" but they indicate the common features of the town or city that is illustrated.

(Claaßen, K., Die Stadt, p.6, Braunschweig 2013)

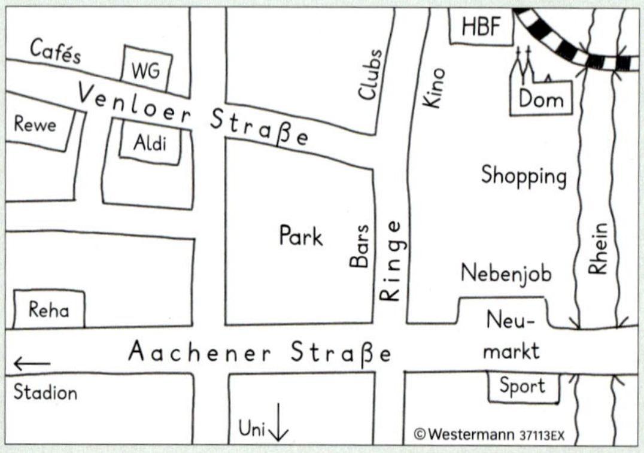

M1 A Cologne student's mental map of her urban environment

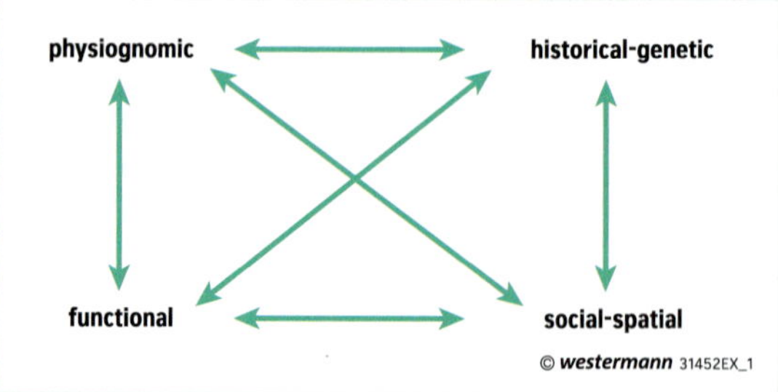

M3 Structural criteria for towns in urban geography

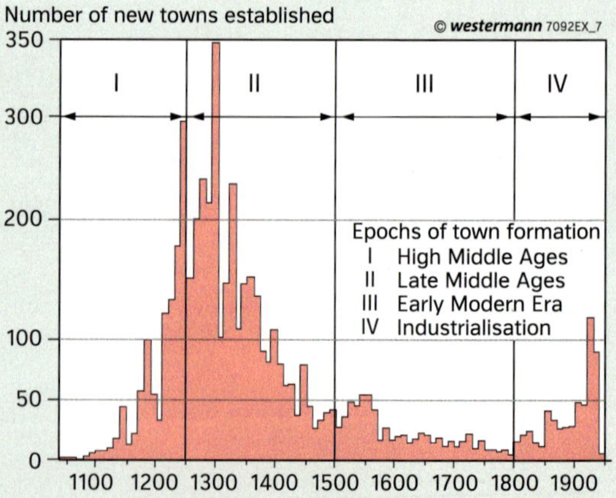

M4 Central Europe: epochs of town formation and growth

- Large and built-up settlement with high construction density and multistorey buildings
- Internal functional division (residential, commercial, leisure areas, ...)
- Differentiated socio-spatial structure
- High residential and workplace density
- Population growth and surplus of commuters
- Urban lifestyle, cultural and economic forms
- High traffic efficiency and density
- Largely artificially-shaped environment

M2 Aspects of the geographical concept of the town

The majority of Central European towns and cities emerged as new formations during the Middle Ages at places that offered particular locational advantages (e.g. river ford, bay, raw materials) and/or functional advantages (e.g. intersection of trade routes, ease of defence) for permanent settlement. Germs of urban development were royal courts along military and trade routes and fortified churches or monasteries [...].

Source: Claaßen, K.: Siedlungsräume, Braunschweig 2011, p. 26

M5 Locational and functional advantages of town formations in the Middle Ages

Towns and cities

The German language only has one word for an urban settlement: "Stadt". English has two words – "town" and "city" – whereby the distinction between them is a matter of debate. It may be a question of size: a city is usually larger than a town. Or it may be a question of function: in England a town with a cathedral is defined as a city, even when its population is small. The capital of a nation is normally a "city", not a "town". Or it may be a question of legal status: a town may become a city by obtaining a royal charter. In the USA, the definition of "city" is a matter of state law and varies widely from state to state.

In this chapter, the word "town" may be used in the context of historical town development and to distinguish urban settlements from "villages". The word "city" is mainly used for the discussion of particular large cities like Munich (p. 138) or Chicago (p. 148), or in the context of modern global urbanisation trends and the growth of megacities.

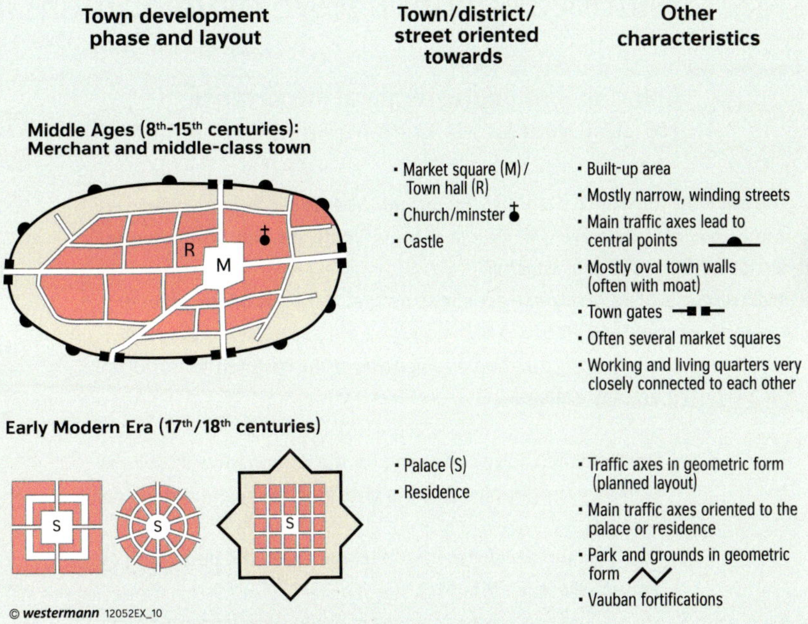

M6 Characteristic structural and building features of different town development phases

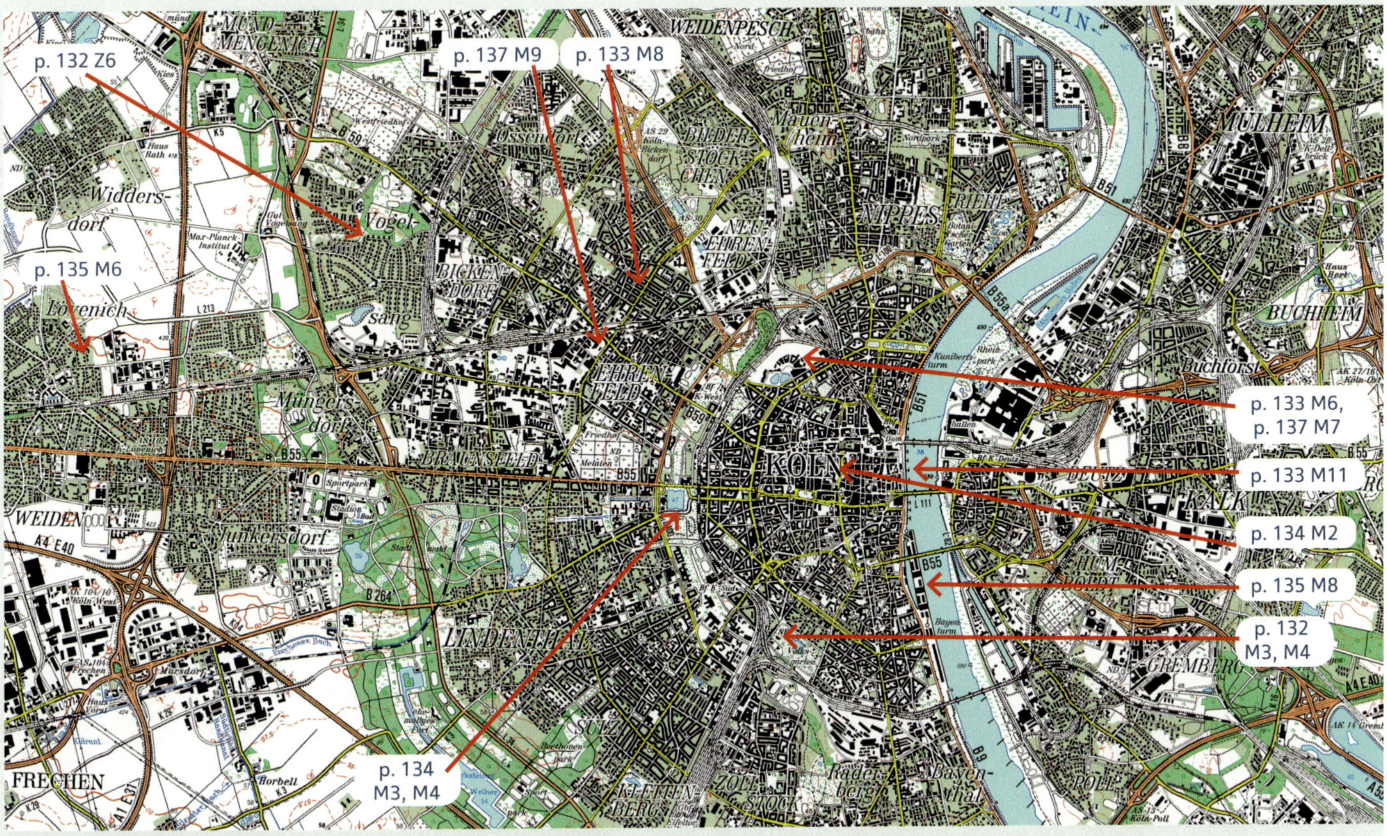

M7 Topographic map of Cologne (1:50000)

1. Illustrate the features of the geographical concept of the town using the example of your town or city, or the nearest town to where you live.

Ⓞ 2. Research some places where:
   - **A** the place name gives an indication of why the location was chosen.
   - **B** it can be explained, using the Atlas or Google Earth, which favourable locational factors may have been decisive for the choice of the location.

3. Describe the structural elements of the different phases of town formation in Germany.

Ⓢ 4. Draw a mental map of your living environment in the place where you live.

Historical-genetic town development in Europe

Cologne – of supra-regional importance for 2000 years

The building substance of today's towns and cities is extremely varied and came into being over the course of many centuries. But how can one recognise the individual epochs?
In an analysis of its historical-genetic structure, the parts of the town or city that came into existence in the successive phases of urban development are examined and classified on the basis of the building features of the period when they emerged.

1. Describe the choice of location for the Roman town of Colonia Claudia Ara Agrippinensium and its function in a geographical context.
2. Describe the development of Cologne up to the beginning of industrialisation (M1–M4).
3. Locate and explain the changes in urban development during industrialisation in the north-west of the city of Cologne (M3, M5, M6).
4. Produce a presentation on Vauban fortifications or on buildings from the Wilhelminian period.
5. Ⓞ Illustrate the structural and building features of the different phases of development of the city of Cologne that are visible in the maps and illustrations on this page using:
   A texts M5 and M10.
   B M6 on the previous page.
6. Ⓢ Locate Cologne Vogelsang in M7 on the previous page and compare the recognisable planning ideas with those of Howard's garden city (M7, p. 131 M7).

→ Athens Charter, Functional separation, Garden city model, Historical-genetic town structure, Industrialisation, Urban development principles

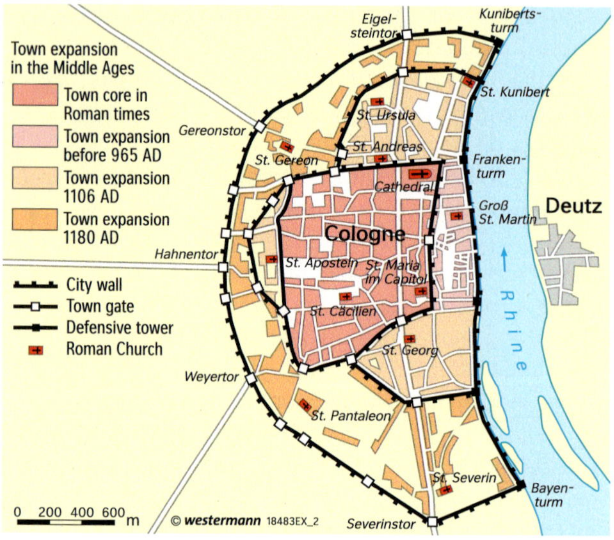

M2 The mediaeval town: Colonia Agrippina (Latin) or Coellen (German) 12th century.

M3 The fortified city of Cologne, 1850

M1 Model of the Roman town of Colonia Claudia Ara Agrippinensium in the Romano-Germanic Museum, Cologne

M4 Contemporary fortifications: Fort IV today

50 BC	Roman period M1, M2	c. 1100 to c. 1850 Middle Ages and early modern era M2–M4

Industrialisation was associated with mass migration into the towns, which subsequently led to the greatest socio-political problem of the industrial age: the need for housing for industrial workers and their families. The [...] growth of towns was accompanied and fostered by infrastructural development. Railway building was [...] oriented to the largest cities. [...] In many cases, ring roads were built where fortifications had previously existed. [...] A key feature of the reconstruction of the industrialised town was the development of housing for the rapidly-growing number of workers [...] through the erection of Wilhelminian tenement blocks [mostly in perimeter block building]. [...] Factories were only rarely integrated into the existing built-up area; instead they usually settled on the edge of the town. [...] Industry represented the motor of economic development; it provided for the growth and prosperity of the 19th and 20th century states.

Source: Fassmann, H., Stadtgeographie I, p. 96ff., Braunschweig 2009

M5 Urban development during the industrialisation phase

M9 Cologne in 1945

M6 North-western Cologne in 1895 (section of map M3)

The garden city model of Ebenezer Howard (1898) was developed in a phase of uncontrolled urban growth which was accompanied by poor social and hygienic living conditions. It was the first planning model designed to improve the conditions of life in towns and cities. [...] Howard foresaw the building of smaller and largely autonomous towns [...] around major cities at a distance of some 6.5 km. These individual "garden cities" were to be separated from the central city by a [...] green belt. To connect the cities, a transport network [...] was planned. Each garden city was to generate the necessary jobs for the population and have central facilities for the provision of public services. [...] [In Germany, all that remained] from the original concept was usually only a more spacious construction layout with green spaces which was implemented in estates of small houses and villas on the urban fringes.

Source: Claaßen, K., Siedlungsräume, Braunschweig 2011, p.32.

M7 The garden city model

Until today, the sharpest and most momentous break in the history of German towns and cities was the destruction of the Second World War. [...] The problem of wartime destruction, especially of housing, was exacerbated in western Germany by the problem of accommodating the population of displaced persons [...]. Up to the year 1956, central, regional and local government planned to create two million units of social housing. [...] [After 1956] special priority [...] was given to building houses for owner-occupiers. [...] A model for urban development was the concept of the "structured and spacious city" [which was influenced by the Athens Charter and foresaw a high degree of functional separation]. In the framework of conceptual discussions, a fundamental controversy arose on the question of "new build or reconstruction". [...] In many (larger) towns and cities [...], historical town cores were substantially reshaped, especially in order to cater for modern city traffic.

Source: Heineberg, H., Grundriß Allgemeine Geographie: Stadtgeographie, Paderborn 2000, p. 222f.

M10 Urban development in the early post-war years

M8 Perimeter block building

The Athens Charter

The model of the garden city [...] refers to a concept that since the publication of the Athens Charter (1941) has become known as functionalism in urban development. Its core demand was for the spatial separation of the four functions of housing, leisure, work and transport.

Source: Heineberg, H., Stadtgeographie, Paderborn 2006, p. 128 f.

M11 Partial view of Cologne's old town today

c. 1800 to 1941
Industrialisation, Wilhelminian period M5, M6, M8/ Garden city M7/ Athens Charter

1945 to 1950s
Model: structured and spacious city M10

Historical-genetic town development in Europe

Cologne – rising from the ruins

Today, German towns and cities are often marked by the building activities that took place after the Second World War. While in the first decades the focus of planning was on technology, in the course of time ecological ideas increasingly came to influence urban planning.

1. Using the example of Cologne, analyse the changes in priorities in urban planning after the Second World War as reflected in the differing planning principles (M1 – M9, Internet).
2. M3 shows a sketch of the area around Aachener Weiher at the time of the "car-friendly city" with plans for a city motorway that were never realised. M4 shows Aachener Weiher and its surroundings today. Evaluate the changes in the planning approach.
3. Illustrate the impact of individual motorisation of the population in the 20th century on the urban development of Col-ogne (M1 – M3, M5 – M7, Internet).
4. Discuss in what form the principle of the "sustainable city" has been implemented in the revitalisation of Rheinauhafen (M8, M9, Internet).
5. Ⓢ Examine how far the principle of "sustainable urban development" has been implemented in your own town or city, and what impact this has had on your personal environment.

→ Revitalisation, Suburbanisation, Sustainability, Urban development principles

From the 1960s, the car became the key medium in the structured urban landscape, and urban planning became primarily a question of traffic planning. [In the principle of] the "car-friendly city", all planning measures were subordinated to the unhindered flow of road traffic. The planning objective was to create settlements in which the traffic infrastructure, road building and ground plan were optimally oriented to the private individual motorist.
But at the same time, many urban planners were also inspired by the principle of "urbanity through density", in the course of which large housing estates were built in the city's outskirts, often supplemented by recreational facilities and public services. The intention of these forms of high-density development was to recreate the lost urbanity of the inner city. [...] The development of large high-rise housing estates was facilitated by industrialisation in the building industry, with its use of prefabricated concrete components. This enabled individual buildings to be constructed more cheaply than with the traditional brick-upon-brick building method. [...] But the accommodation and lifestyle offered by these oversized residential complexes and their traffic connections rarely corresponded to their residents' expectations, and already in the 1980s they descended into a state of crisis (vacant properties, fluctuation of tenants, development of slums) and required costly remediation.

Source: Claaßen, K., Die Stadt, Braunschweig 2013, p.35f.

M1 Principles of urban development in the 1960s

M2 Useful artery or architectural blunder?
The north-south highway slices through Cologne's old town

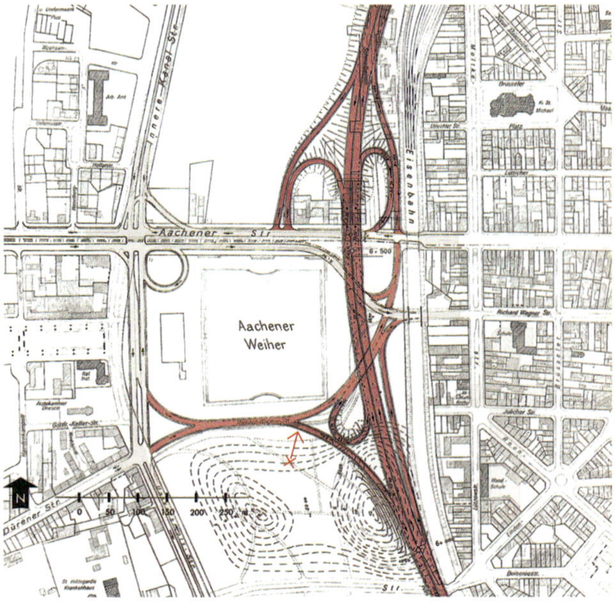

M3 Marked in red: the planned course of an inner-city motorway through Cologne's "inner green belt" recreation area in the Aachener Weiher area in the 1960s

M4 The "inner green belt" today as an inner-city recreation area with the Aachener Weiher. The photographer's location and direction of view is shown by the arrow in M3.

1960s
The car-friendly city M1, M2, M3/ Urbanity through density M1

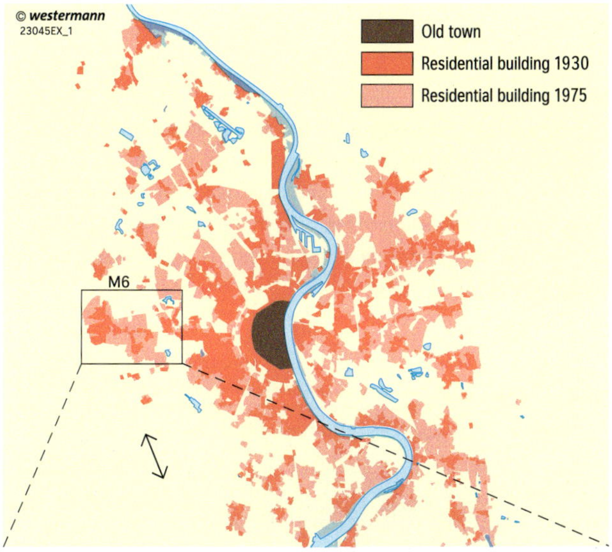

M5 Suburbanisation of Cologne (process of deconcentration and spatial urban growth beyond the city's borders caused by the movement of population and businesses to the city outskirts) 1930 – 1975

M6 Section of western Cologne in 1862/63 and 2000 (see M5)

"At the end of the 20th century, urban planners responded to problems such as the destruction of the landscape due to suburbanisation, the increase in individualised transport, the monotonous architecture of large housing estates, the large-scale redevelopment of inner cities and the increasing flight from the city, with new ideas. Thus, in the 1970s the principle of "conservational urban rebuilding" [or retentive urban renewal] focused on the restoration of the historic building fabric [...]."

"The resulting retention of large parts of the older or historic building fabric contributed to an improvement in the quality of life in the inner-city cores [...]. Through conservational urban renewal, not only historic old town cores but also older residential areas, e.g. from the Wilhelminian period, have gained in the quality of their urban environment.

In the 1980s [...] many municipalities started to try to organise urban development in a more ecologically-sustainable way [...]. Urban ecology found its place in planning in the form of improvements in living environments and traffic calming as well as urban greening, and could thus merge with conservational urban renewal into the principle of "ecological urban renewal".

Sources: Claaßen, K., Die Stadt, Braunschweig 2013, p.38 / Heineberg, H., Stadtgeographie p.134 f., Paderborn 2006. ***Note: For a more detailed discussion of suburbanisation based on the example of Chicago, see pages 148 – 149***

M7 Principles of urban development in the 1970s

M8 Rheinauhafen in the early 1970s and in 2014

As organising principles for sustainable urban development, three points were discussed among others:

1. **Density in urban development,** i.e. the creation of more compact but nevertheless high-quality building structures designed to hinder the uncontrolled spatial spread of settlements [...], through the better exploitation and extension of usage potential in already-existing inner-city built up areas. In land use, commercial and housing policy, sustainable urban development is thus based on the development of the existing stock: "the renovation, restoration and conversion of existing buildings as well as land recycling and consolidation [...]."
2. **Usage mix,** i.e. the objective [...] is among other things the creation of a functional mix within urban neighbourhoods through the integration of housing and work, but also of public services and recreation [...]. Also of importance is the fostering of a social mix [...]. The "compact city" or "city of short distances" [...] can also [contribute] to reducing individualised motor traffic.
3. **Decentralised concentration:** through this approach, the ongoing settlement pressure in the city's environs could be focused on selected settlement centres and could also result in greater efficiency for local public transport. [...]
These strategies [...] require the participation of actors from politics, administration, business and the population, such as is fostered by the Local Agendas 21.

Sourse: Heineberg, H., Stadtgeographie, Paderborn 2006, p.129 ff.

M9 The principles of sustainable urban development, formulated on the basis of the decisions of the United Nations Conference on Environment and Development in Rio de Janeiro in 1992

1970s and 1980s	1990s to the present
Conservational urban rebuilding M7/ Ecological urban renewal	Sustainable urban development M9

Functional structure of towns and cities in Central Europe

Cologne – one city, many functions

In the towns and cities of the Middle Ages, the functions of living and working were mixed together in a small area. In the last two centuries, the interplay of these functions has been subject to frequent spatial change. To what extent was urban planning involved in this change, and why did this change take place?

1. **With reference to urban development principles, show the spatial changes that have affected work and housing since the start of industrialisation.**
2. **Illustrate the changes in the function of work in the north-western part of Cologne's inner city (M7, M8, p. 133 M6).**
3. **Illustrate the regional, national and international transport function of the city of Cologne (M8, Atlas).**
4. ⓞ **Characterise Cologne and its functions in the form of:**
   A an article in a business newspaper, including a headline and introductory teaser text (M3–M8).
   B an advertising text for a travel magazine (M8, Internet).
5. **Explain the current principle of usage mix in the context of the principle of the "sustainable city" (M7, M9, p. 135 M9, Internet).**
6. **Research the current state of urban development with reference to the Helios site and explain the relationships between usage mix and participation in terms of the principle of the "sustainable city" (M9, p. 135 M9, Internet).**
7. Ⓢ **In a sketch, point out areas with a functional mix and those with functional separation in a section of your home town.**

→ Basic functions of existence, Functional change, Functional separation, Participation, Usage mix

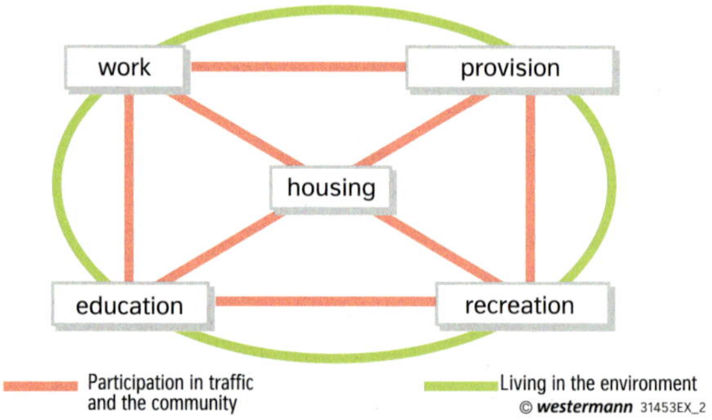

M1 Basic functions of existence

In the context of the rapid growth of our cities and city regions, uncontrolled processes of separation have developed. This refers to the increasing disintegration of the formerly closely interlinked functional areas of housing, work, provision and leisure. Particular examples of this are districts of detached housing without any public service and work function, as well as shopping centres on green-field sites, the deconcentration of office locations [...] and commercial sports venues that users can generally only reach by car.

Source: Heineberg, H., Stadtgeographie, Paderborn 2006, p. 52f

M2 The legacy of functionalism in urban development

Large areas of Cologne (with 1.017 million inhabitants) – in the old town, the Wilhelminian era districts, and also those districts that grew up with suburbanisation – are principally marked by the function of housing. In the downtown district and other mainly retailing areas, housing is only found in the upper storeys.

M3 The housing function in Cologne

Ford factory in the north of Cologne (production started in May 1931). In the background, the Bayer site in Leverkusen

Of a current total of some 145,000 member companies of the Chamber of Industry and Trade, whose catchment area reaches beyond the limits of the city of Cologne, around 118,000 are small businesses with up to nine employees. The mid-sized companies with up to 250 employees (2.8 percent) and the large companies with more than 250 employees (0.7 percent) together account for only 3.5 percent of all companies. Public sector employers such as the city, the army, the university or WDR [public broadcaster] are not included in these figures. According to experts, Cologne enjoys an outstanding reputation both nationally and internationally as a media centre, distinguished by its great creativity and variety.

M4 Facets of the work function in Cologne

With more than 300 schools and 13 colleges and universities, Cologne is ideally placed as an educational location. From the first school year until the final academic degree, Cologne's educational facilities offer a multiplicity of possibilities to prepare for a future career. Especially for the universities and technical colleges, close connections to business are very much in demand.

Source: City of Cologne, The Mayor, Office of Economic Development

M5 Cologne as an educational location

Retailing and shopping centres concept

- Securing and strengthening the shopping centres in their function of providing for the population
- Retention of the developed polycentric system of centres
- Securing and expansion of provision near to residential areas
- Fostering the attractiveness of Cologne as a retail location and as the main centre for the region
- Steering the establishment of retail businesses
- Taking account of special developments in retailing as well as the consequences of demographic change

M6 The function of provision in Cologne

M7 Functional change – Gereon goods station in 1927 (p. 133 M6) and Mediapark today

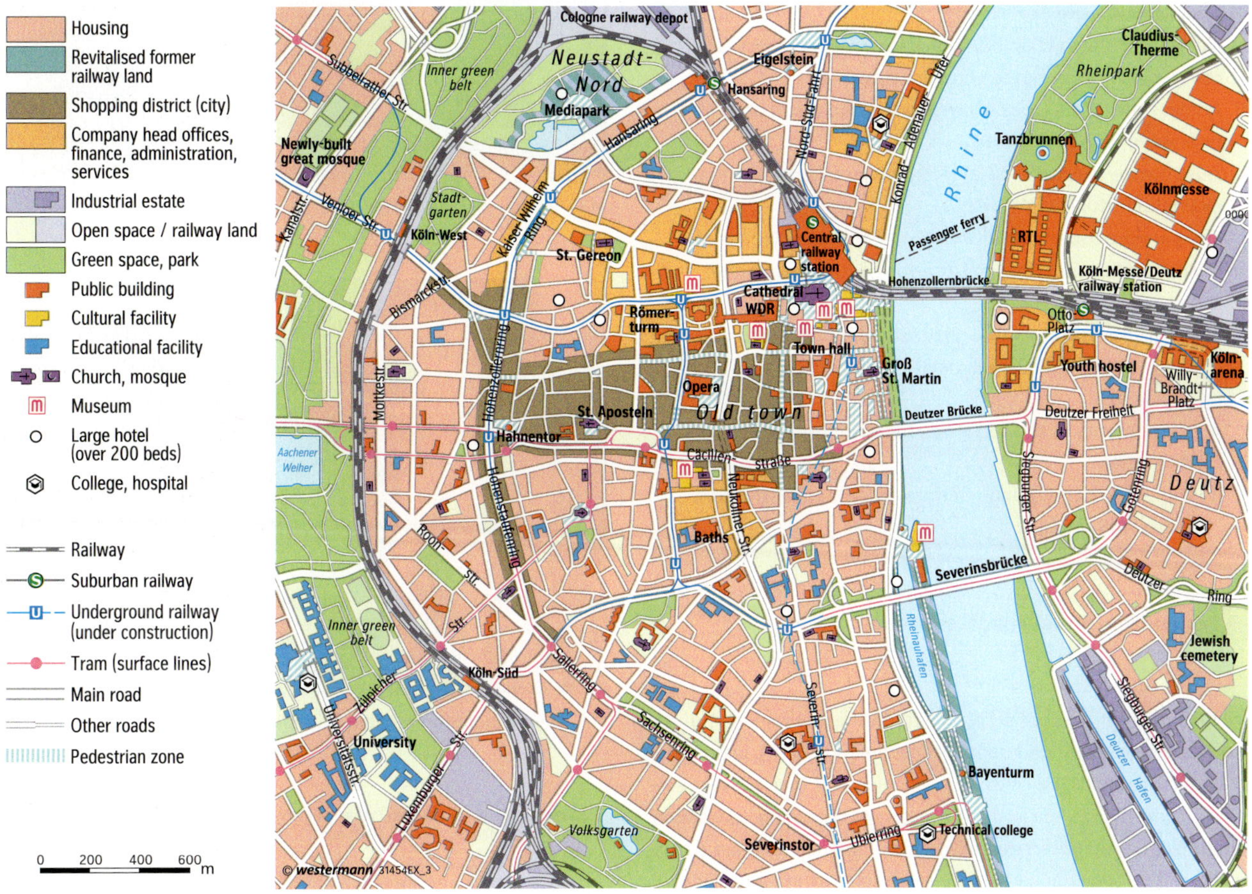

M8 Functions in Cologne's inner city

2008: [The Cologne company] Bauwens purchases [with a partner] the 40,000 m² Helios site [...]. After a time it becomes known that the owners are planning to build a large shopping centre. This gives rise to concerns and objections from the public and from Cologne's local politicians.

May 2010: The action group "Bürgerinitiative Helios" (BI Helios) is founded to organise resistance to the site owners' plans.

September 2010: At a public meeting of the action group, its objectives are clearly defined: "No shopping mall! Public participation now! Development appropriate to the structure of the district – for an Ehrenfeld worth living in!"

November 2010: The urban development committee resolves to conduct a public survey in order to develop planning objectives for the Helios site.

December 2010: The University of Cologne puts forward the idea of building an "inclusive university school" on the site. [...] This concept finds approval both among the public and from many local politicians in Cologne.

February 2012: The results of the public survey are announced. The citizens want the area to contain a mix of culture (24%), green space (22%), creative (13%), leisure (13%), housing (12%), school (8%), commerce (4%), shopping (4%).

November 2012: Bauwens announces that it has bought back the shares in the Helios site from its business partners. It stated in a press release: "[...] This substantial economic commitment has been made in reliance on the promised speedy handling of the pending topics on the part of the politicians and administration – and above all a clear positioning with regard to the school question". Thus the plans for a shopping centre are finally laid to rest.

January 2013: Bauwens [...] has applied for permission to demolish some of the buildings in Heliosstraße. This is said to be necessary because the soil is partly [...] contaminated, and this pollution must be removed.

Source: www.koelner.de/blog/2013/03/27/quo-vadis-helios-6425/, accessed 07.10.2014

M9 Usage mix and participation in planning? – the Helios site in Ehrenfeld, Cologne

Social-spatial structure of towns and cities in Central Europe

Boomtown Munich

Munich is growing. Between 2006 and 2012 alone, the number of inhabitants in Bavaria's capital city increased by 100,000 persons. But there is more to this bare figure than meets the eye: it is the result of a larger number of people moving into Munich than those moving out of Munich. But what are the reasons for this mobility in contrary directions?

1. Explain the factors that can play a role in the social-spatial structure of a city.
2. Illustrate the attraction of Munich for its inhabitants and for companies in selected business sectors (Atlas).
3. Analyse the social-spatial structure of the residential population of Munich (M6).
4. Illustrate the processes of segregation by reference to the example of Munich (M1 – M8).
5. Compare the social-spatial structure of selected districts of Munich that are as different from one another as possible (Internet).
6. Ⓢ Ⓞ Compare the social-spatial structure of Munich with that of Cologne and explain their similarities and differences with reference to:
   A the contents of the social-spatial structure maps (M6, Atlas).
   B the explanatory power of the social-spatial structure maps (M6, Atlas).

→ Segregation, Social-spatial structure

M3 Luxury property in Munich

M4 Needy people queueing for food at a food bank in Munich

In 2013, Munich [took...] second place in the city rankings of the Hamburg Institute of International Economics (HWWI), just behind Frankfurt am Main. The cities were examined for their present economic performance, the locational factors of education, innovation, internationalism and accessibility, as well as their forecast demographic development. [...] Munich's strengths lay in particular in its population development as well as in the proportion of its workforce employed in knowledge-intensive branches of the economy.

Source: www.muenchen.de, accessed 01.10.2014

M1 City rankings of the Hamburg Institute of International Economics (HWWI) 2013

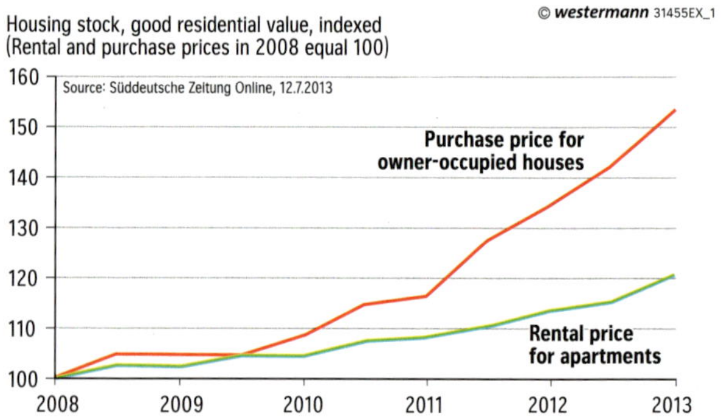

M5 Movement of house prices in Munich

A gross rent of 1,000 euros – that is all that many families can afford. But for that price there are hardly any three- or four-room apartments to be found in Munich. Even people on average incomes have to struggle. [...] According to the rent index, Bavaria's capital is the most expensive municipality in Germany, and prices in the affluent suburbs are being dragged upwards with it. Sites for building are scarce. In some places along the commuter railway axes one must pay – as in Munich itself – a net rent of 13.50 euros per square metre for good-quality and 11.60 euros for average-quality properties. Increasingly, high earners are moving out into the rural districts around the city. But for the middle classes, [...] the obligatory payment to the landlord eats a hole in their tight budget every month.

Source: www.sueddeutsche.de/muenchen/lebenshaltungskosten-die-miete-frisst-das-leben-auf-1.1373108, 05.06.2012, accessed 01.10.2014

M2 Rental prices in Munich

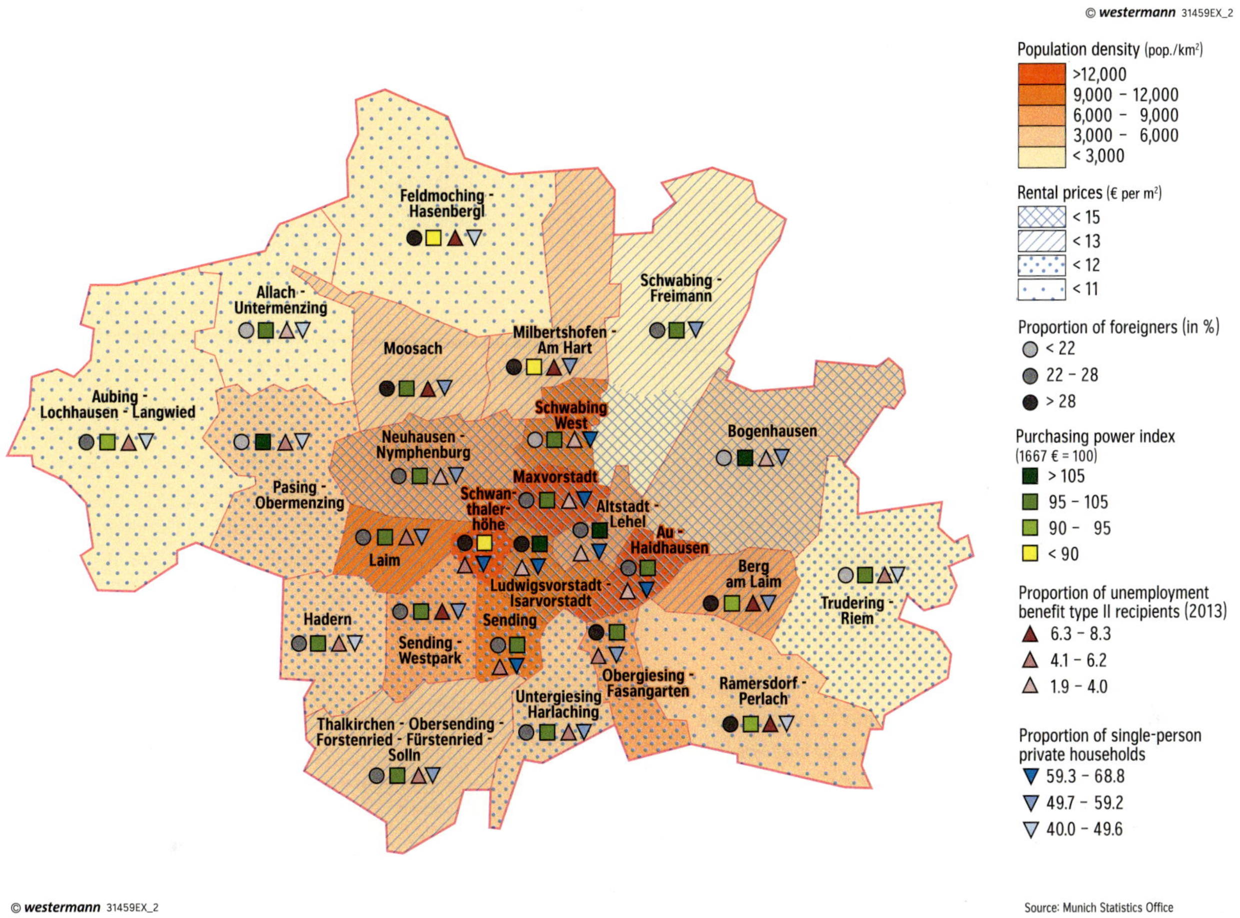

M6 Social-spatial structure of the City of Munich (2013)

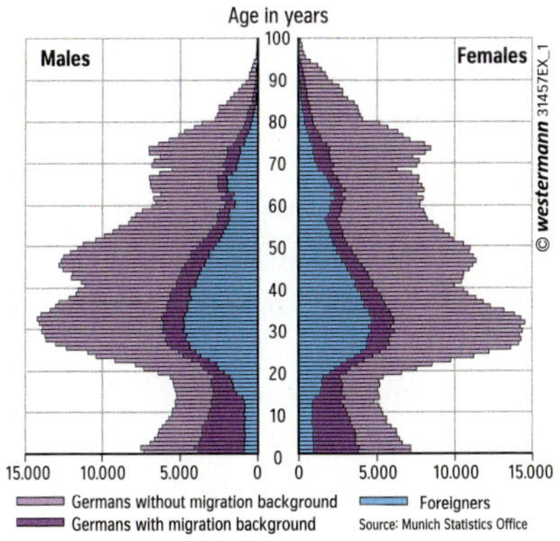

M7 The age distribution of the population in Munich (2013)

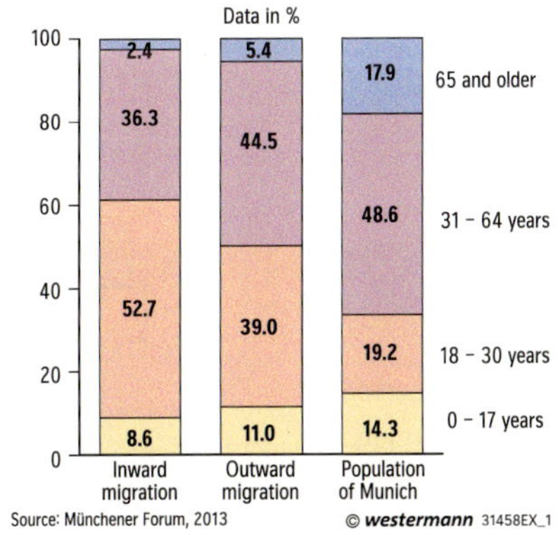

M9 Population movements to and from Munich (2013)

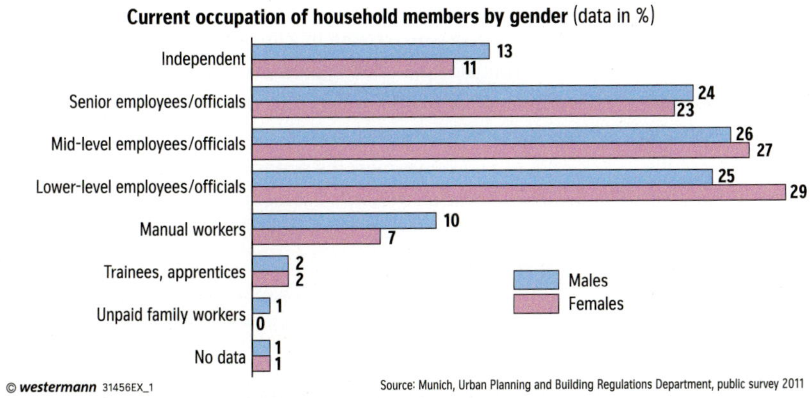

M8 Occupations of household members in Munich (2010)

→ Segregation

The term "segregation" means separation and division, and represents both a process and a condition. [...]
The population separates [...] according to social, demographic and ethnic criteria. [...] Social differentiation is "translated" into spatial separation on the one hand and concentration on the other hand.
[...] The affluent population which "takes possession" of certain residential districts may also profit from their very good transport links, locations, facilities [...] as well as from their pleasant and healthy environment.
The poorer population that is [...] forced out must accept the additional deficiencies of the spatial context. [...] The segregation of the residential population [...] is a consequence of selection mechanisms on the property market and the economic capacity of households.
[...] But segregation not only has structural causes (forced segregation), but also has the character of a voluntarily-chosen way of life. [...]

Source: Fassmann, H.: Stadtgeographie, Braunschweig 2009

Models of urban development in Germany

Urban models of the Chicago School – are they applicable to Germany?

Models have long been employed in urban geography. They have taken into account the criteria of the physiognomic, genetic, functional and social-spatial structure of a town or city with differing levels of explanatory power and varying degrees of abstraction. But why should one apply the models of the Chicago School to German towns and cities? Are the classic models of urban geography that are presented here transferable to the city of Cologne and other German towns and cities?

1. Describe the functional structure models and discuss whether US models can be applied to German towns and cities.
2. Using model M4, analyse the connections between the different structural criteria of a town or city.
3. (◎) Analyse:
   A the models in M2 using the example of Cologne,
   B model M3 using the example of Cologne,
   and give your opinion on the transferability of the models.
4. Test the transferability of models M3 and M4 to the town or city that is nearest to the place where you live. For this exercise, you can draw your own sketch or use a screenshot in Google Earth.
5. (S) Illustrate in what ways the contents of the models could be modified in order to further improve their relationship to reality.

→ Chicago School, Multiple nuclei model, Ring model, Sector model

After the First World War, the Chicago School of sociology developed a closed and theoretically-oriented construct of ideas regarding the fundamental context of social and spatial structure. This construct of ideas was referred to by the authors themselves as social ecology, thus expressing its central research subject, namely society and its habitat. [...] The Chicago School sees the town or city as a conglomeration of social-spatial units. In these social-spatial units, particular population groups or types of use have found "their" home. Just as a biotope possesses a very specific biotope population (=biocoenosis), parts of a town or city are characterised by selected types of use or population groups. These types of use or population groups are appropriate to the location. When external conditions alter the nature of the location, the appropriate composition of the population or types of use must also change. Every such change in the quality of the location has an impact which takes the form of processes of exchange, displacement and succession of types of use and user groups. Social ecology perceives the urban structure as the result of such [...] processes.

Source: Fassmann, H., Stadtgeographie I, Braunschweig 2009

M1 The urban structure model of social ecology (Chicago School)

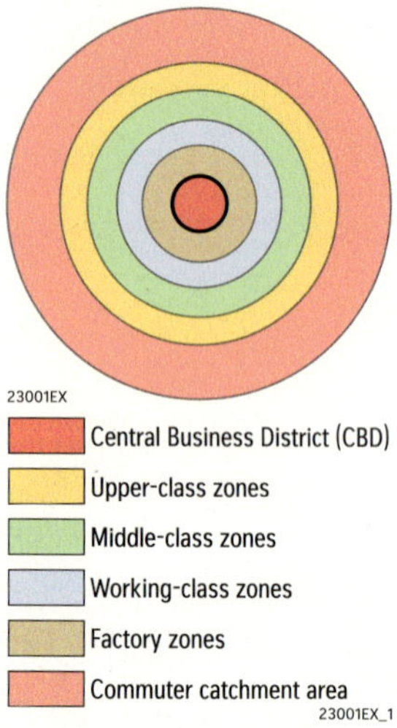

The ring model

The ring model, first published in 1925 by the Canadian sociologist Ernest Burgess, was developed on the basis of empirical research in Chicago and portrays the relationships in US cities in the inter-war years in ideal-typical form. It is based on the assumption that cities constantly change under the influence of competition for locational advantages. The city expands in concentric rings but its structure remains the same. [...] As a regularity, the model describes a division of the city into homogeneous rings around the CBD [Central Business District].

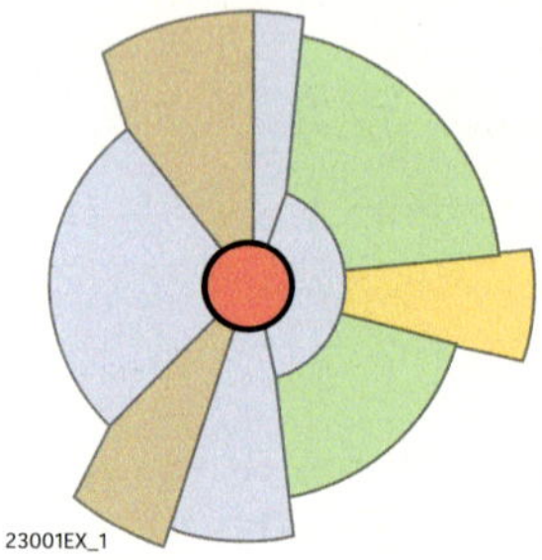

The sector model

The sector model, published in 1939 by Homer Hoyt, a student of Burgess, was based on empirical research into the cost of rents in thirty US cities. It is based on the assumption that urban development is determined by the impact of the major traffic axes [...] as well as by the choice of residential location by the higher-status population. The city is divided into homogeneous bands or sectors along the traffic axes and transport routes. [...]

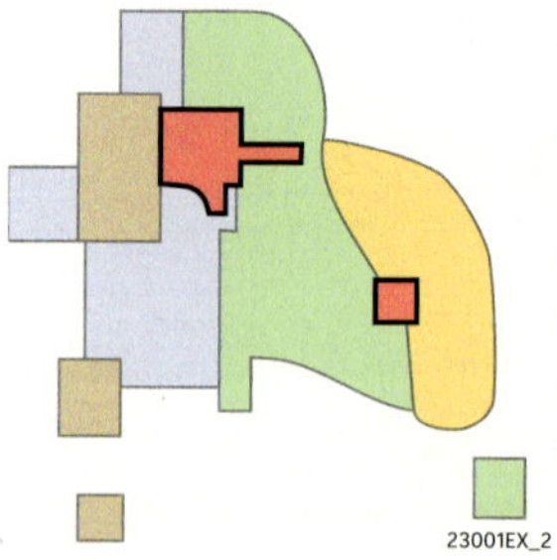

The multiple nuclei model

The multiple nuclei model, published in 1945 by Chauncy D. Harris and Edward L. Ullman, assumes that the structure of the city is determined by the configuration of workplaces. Working-class residential districts are connected with the city's industrial centres, just as the residential districts of middle and higher white-collar employees are connected with the distribution of workplaces in the service sector. It thus introduced the principle of work-related functional division as a new criterion alongside the existing principle of social differentiation of residential areas. The city is thus characterised by a series of constantly changing and growing nuclei. The traditional city centre can no longer meet the needs of businesses. Subsidiary centres emerge on the city's outskirts with offices and businesses as well as functional clusters of different and mutually interconnected types of use. [...]

Source: de Lange, E., Weiss, S., Die Stadtmodelle der Chicagoer Schule, in Praxis Geographie extra, Modelle in der Geographie, Braunschweig 2014, p.18ff

M2 The urban models of the Chicago School

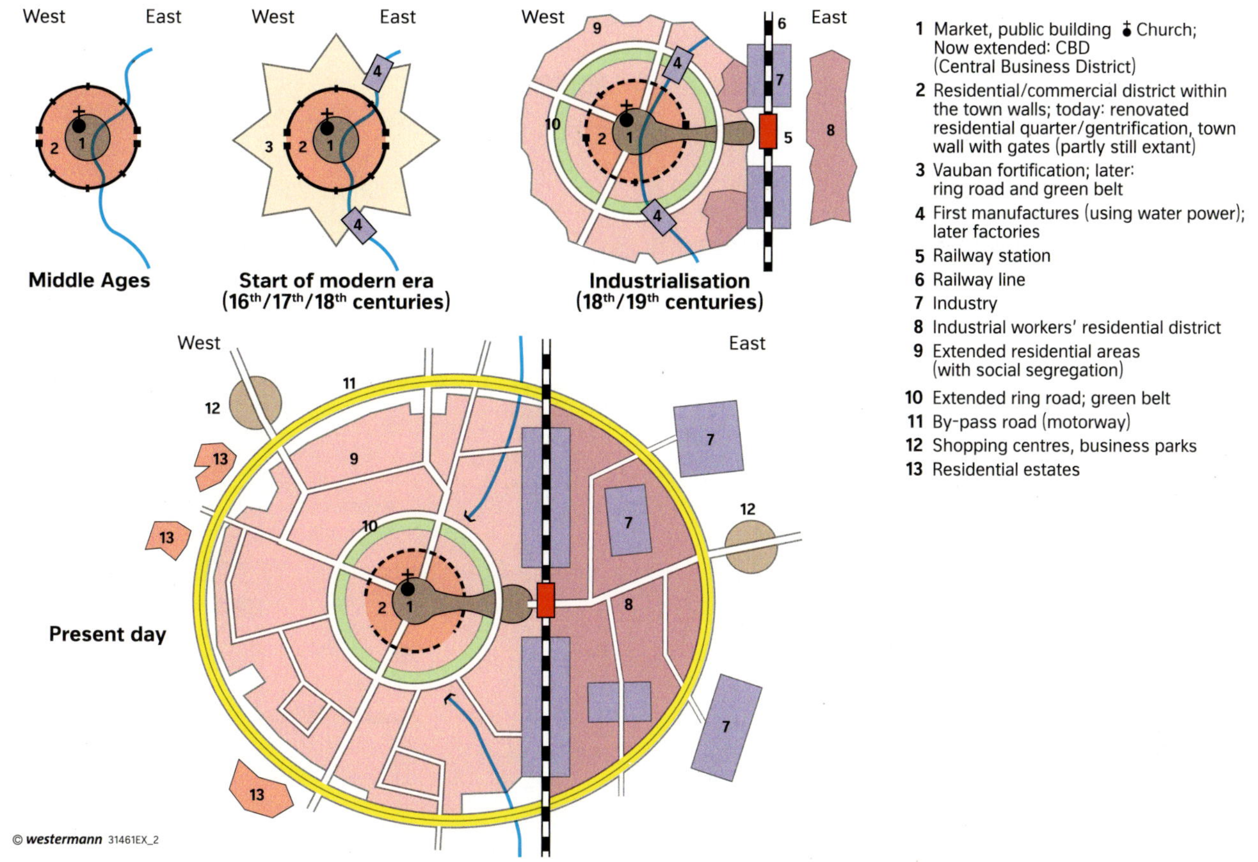

M3 Model of the emergence and structure of a German town

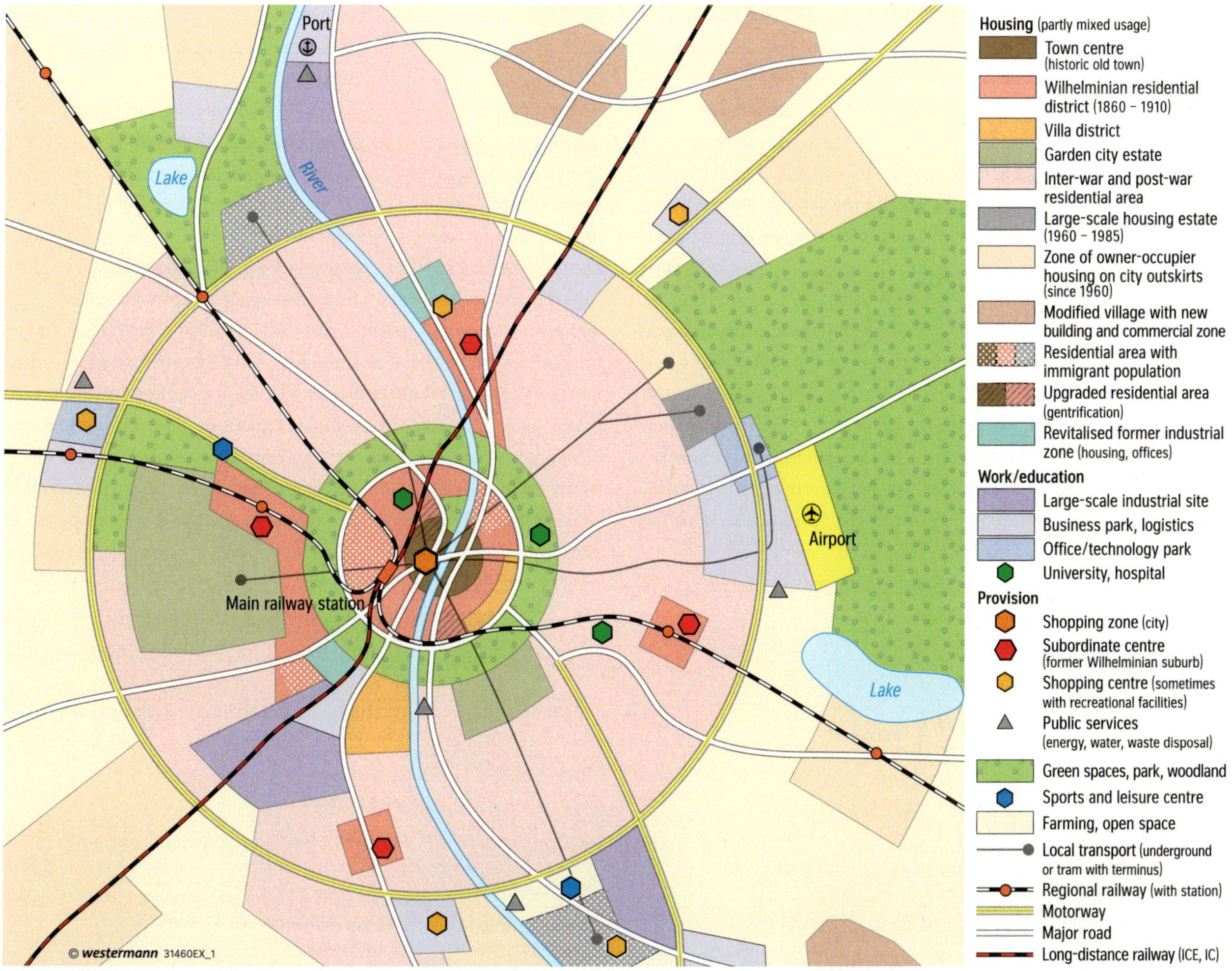

M4 Town model for Germany

The central business district as a focal point for services

In Bremen's inner city

The recognisable physiognomic and functional features of cities in Central Europe are the result of a historical process that is referred to as "city building". How are today's cities structured, and what future perspectives exist, e.g. for Bremen's central business district (CBD)?

1. Describe the features of a central business district (CBD) (M1 – M2, M4, M8).
2. Explain how far the requirements of business-oriented and consumer-oriented companies for a potential location can diverge from each other (M1 – M9).
3. Describe the geographical location of Bremen's CBD (M3).
4. ⓞ Illustrate the locational factors of Bremen's CBD:
   A for retailing (M2 – M5, M7 – M9).
   B for business-oriented services (M1 – M4, M6).
5. Research information on Bremen's Überseestadt and evaluate its chances as an area for the expansion of Bremen's CBD (Internet).
6. ⓢ Explain the negative consequences of the process of city building (M1, M2, M4, M8).

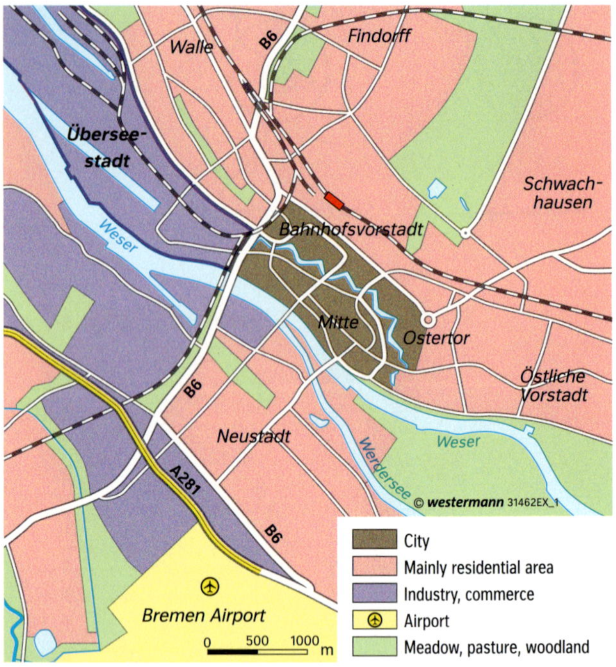

M3 Bremen's inner city

→ Business-oriented services, Central business district (CBD), Chain store development, City, Consumer-oriented services

The central business district (CBD) [the "city" in German usage] refers to the urban area with the greatest building density as well as the highest concentration of tertiary [...] occupations. It is also [...] mostly located in the central zone of the town or city. Other terms, which are not strictly synonymous but nevertheless go in the same direction, are the city core, the inner city, and – when the urban centre is really identical with the historic core – the old town or old city. [...]
As a rule, the functions concentrated into the "city" zone are those that yield a relative maximum of sales turnover per unit of area, have a special public significance, or are representative of the specific prestige of the city. The "city" contains not only public facilities [...], but also cultural facilities. [...] The physiognomic and functional features that we see today are the result of a historical process that has already taken place in Europe and which is called "city building". This is understood as a characteristic functional change in the inner city that leads to the displacement of the residential population and of economically weaker retailing and commercial activities. The areas thus released [...] are filled by the "production sites" of the tertiary [...] sector.

Source: Fassmann, H., Stadtgeographie I, Braunschweig 2009, p. 166ff

M1 City building and features of the "city"

The location of a property within a town or city determines its purchase and rental price through the differential site rent. Not all potential users are able or willing to pay the purchase and rental price. Thus the purchase and rental price acts like a natural selection of usage types and user groups. [...]
Some types of usage require a property location in the town or city centre and are willing to pay a higher site rent, while by contrast other user groups may prefer the outskirts. [...] Retailing and the specialised service sector need many customers and must therefore choose sites that are easily accessible. Suitable locations are in the town or city centre or at selected hubs with good accessibility. Many potential customers can easily reach the centre or the hub and can thus provide the business with a high income. In addition there are stores, institutions and businesses that prefer a location in the city centre for prestige reasons (e.g. banks and insurance companies, ministries, parliament and the seat of government). [...] Stores that sell luxury goods or those with very special offerings are more often likely to require locations with good accessibility than stores selling a normal range of goods. For economic reasons, large stores require more customers and are therefore compelled to attach greater importance to good accessibility than smaller stores. [...]

Source: Fassmann, H., Stadtgeographie I, Braunschweig 2009, p. 149

M4 Property prices and usage selection

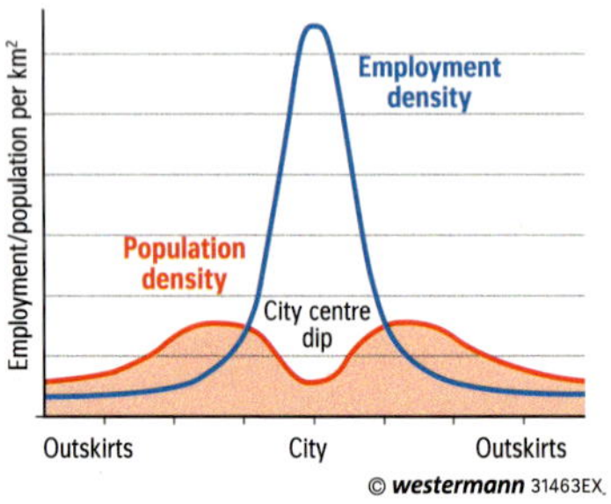

M2 Idealised model of the occupational and population density of a large city

Main centre	historic urban centre as shopping city or dominant local centre
Sub-centre	Local centre or neighbourhood centre in the suburbs
Shopping centre integrated into urban development	With the function of a local centre
"Green-field" centre	Focus on provision and shopping experience

M5 Retail locations

"Bremen is a small state. And that is its advantage. Because putting so many different decision-makers from business, science and politics together in an area of only 327 km² can only result in an extremely fruitful brain pool. And they benefit from the short ways to decision-making in a small federal state. It means that decisions are faster, ideas are easier to implement, and cooperation is less complicated. To sum up: goals are easier to reach. Closeness pays off."

M6 Short-Way City – from an image campaign by Wirtschaftsförderung Bremen GmbH

Retailing in the inner city	Business area		Sales area	
	m²	%	m²	%
Books/stationery/printing	13,718	6.4	10,700	6.7
Wellness/cosmetic/hairdresser	12,886	6.0	9,664	6.0
Food	11,386	5.3	7,970	5.0
Chemist/drug store/optician	6,679	3.1	5,009	3.1
Flowers/souvenirs/tobacco	1,959	0.9	1,469	0.9
Short-term needs	46,628	21.7	34,812	21.7
Clothing	72,350	33.7	56,433	35.1
Footwear	14,535	6.8	11,047	6.9
Sports goods/toys	7,710	3.6	6,014	3.7
Medium-term needs	94,595	44.1	73,494	45.7
Furnishing/household	32,388	15.1	23,319	14.5
Electrical/hifi/photo	18,535	8.6	12,604	7.8
Jewellery/umbrellas/bags	6,545	3.0	4,189	2.6
Travel	4,814	2.2	3,755	2.3
Long-term needs	62,282	28.9	43,867	27.2
Empty	11,441	5.3	8,580	5.4
Total retailing	214,946	100.0	160,753	100.0

Source: Bremen City Report 09/10, accessed 09.10.2014

M7 Bremen City – retailing in the inner city (2010)

Distribution of rented space by sector	m²	%
Retailing	214,946	17.0
Services	179,309	14.1
Residential	185,567	14.7
Public administration/ facilities	133,196	10.5
Banks/finance	121,703	9.6
Parking	121,037	9.6
Insurance/auditing firms/accountants/consultants	89,424	7.1
Logistics/shipping	68,906	5.4
Catering/hotels	67,337	5.3
Lawyers/notaries	38,050	3.0
Architects/building/real estate	21,641	1.7
Doctors/medicine	13,207	1.0
Others	12,683	1.0
Total	1,267,306	100.0

Source: Bremen City Report 09/10, accessed 09.10.2014

M9 Bremen City – distribution of rental space by sector (2010)

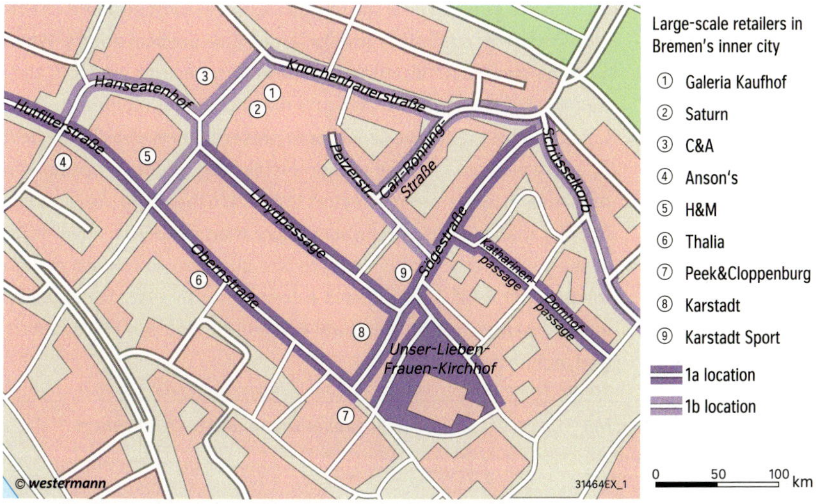

M8 Large-scale retail outlets in Bremen's inner city (2013)

→ Chain store development

The large retail chains are coming to dominate more and more shopping centres in German cities. [...] With 74.6%, Dortmund continues to have the highest proportion of chain store branches [in Germany], followed by Bremen (72%) and Nuremberg (70.3%). Berlin is now in fourth place. [...] "The spread of chain store branches in the inner cities is a sign of our times and is a reflection of consumer behaviour. [...] In some inner cities a certain monotony in retailing is therefore not to be overlooked," admits [...] a retail expert.

Source: Schwaldt, N., Die Welt, www.welt.de/finanzen/article13368161/Ladenketten-erobern-Einkaufsmeilen-der-Staedte.html, 12.05.2011

Urban tourism as an economic factor

Hamburg as a travel destination

In 2013, 5.9 million guests spent 11.6 million nights in Hamburg's 334 commercial accommodation facilities – making the city one of the most attractive tourist destinations in Germany. The average length of stay was two days. Tourism accounts for 6.1 percent of the budget of the City of Hamburg and is thus one of the city's most important and dynamic sources of wealth.

1. Outline Hamburg's tourism potential (M1– M5, Atlas).
2. Describe possible direct and indirect effects for Hamburg that could be generated by urban tourism as an economic factor.
3. ⓞ Characterise:
   A Hamburg as a city of culture
   B Hamburg as a city of sport
   and assess the value of culture or sport for the city (M6 – M7, Internet).
4. Put together the programme for a trip to Hamburg for a selected customer segment (M1, M2, M5, M8, Internet).
5. ⓞ Illustrate the unique tourism features of Hamburg in comparison to:
   A other cities in Germany
   B other cities in Europe
6. Ⓢ Comment critically on the increasing public presentation and festivalisation of cities (M4, M7 – M9, Internet).

→ Urban tourism

M2 Ten million visitors have seen the musical "The Lion King" since its premiere in 2001

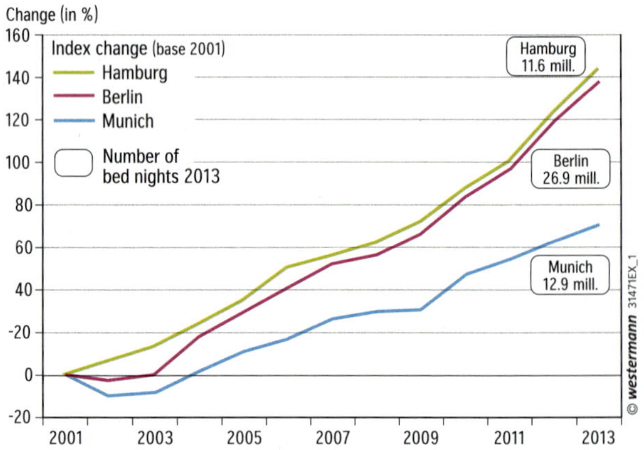

M3 Overnight stays in Hamburg (in comparison to Berlin and Munich)

"About 13,000 ships from all over the world call at Europe's second largest port. From the cruise ship terminal to the historic 'Speicherstadt' warehouse district and the landing bridges to the modern container port - aromas here redolent of freedom and far-away lands. [...] Visitors can experience first hand why Hamburg is also called the 'Gateway to the World'."
(Hamburg Tourismus online, 29.11.2014)

"Hamburg will gain a new cultural and urban landmark with the Elbphilharmonie in HafenCity. Classical music culture, music of the 21st century and sophisticated light music will have a spectacular venue here."
(Hamburg Tourismus online, 29.11.2014)

"Hamburg has many large churches - but only one "Michel": On its platform 106 metres high, there is a fabulous (and breezy) view of Hamburg, the port and the surrounding countryside – one that should not be missed!"
(Hamburg Tourismus online, 29.11.2014)

"On the Reeperbahn at half past midnight ...". Almost everyone in Germany knows the song by Hans Albers and can draw a conclusion about the variety of pleasures on Hamburg's "sexy mile" (Udo Lindenberg).
(Hamburg Tourismus online, 29.11.2014)

M1 The City of Hamburg promotes itself

[...] All large cities have made moves to market the quality of their location in the same way as e.g. an automobile company advertises its products. Large-scale events are particularly suitable for this. Large events serve to put the city in the limelight and show it in a positive light. [...] But since big city locations have grown increasingly similar, and the so-called "hard" locational factors are to be found in a satisfactory manner in very many cities, marketing depends heavily on the public presentation and festivalisation of the city, ultimately in order to please potential investors, tourists or the world at large. Many cities strive to host the Olympic Games, football world championships, world fairs, festivals or large-scale political events. When a city is successful in attracting these large events to itself, they function like a locomotive that pulls many carriages along with it. [...] Cities market themselves in order to present themselves in the best possible way as a unique and unmistakeable product, not only to purchasers, tourists and investors but also to their own populations. But city marketing is significantly more than simply an advertising strategy, because it also involves the question of how to design the product itself. This requires a comprehensive locational policy, which includes not only cultural events but also the city's history and architecture.
Source: Fassmann, H.: Stadtgeographie I, Braunschweig 2009, p. 163f.

M4 City marketing: public presentation and festivalisation

M5 Queen Mary 2 – a regular guest in Hamburg's port

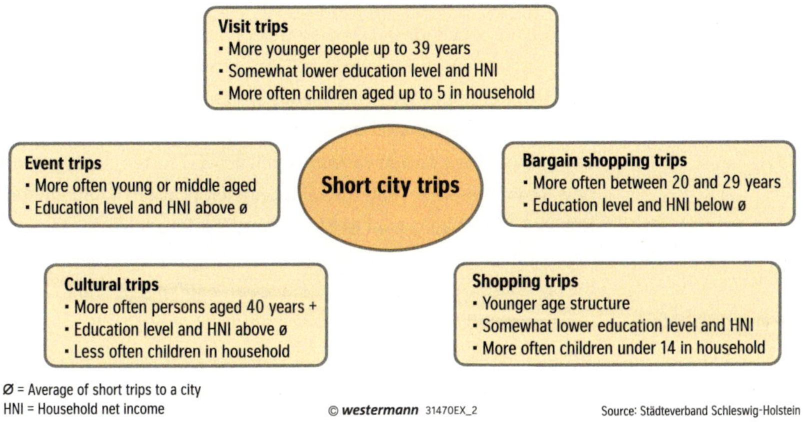

M6 Customer structure of private city trips in Germany

M8 The Elbphilharmonie – an unprecedented cultural project

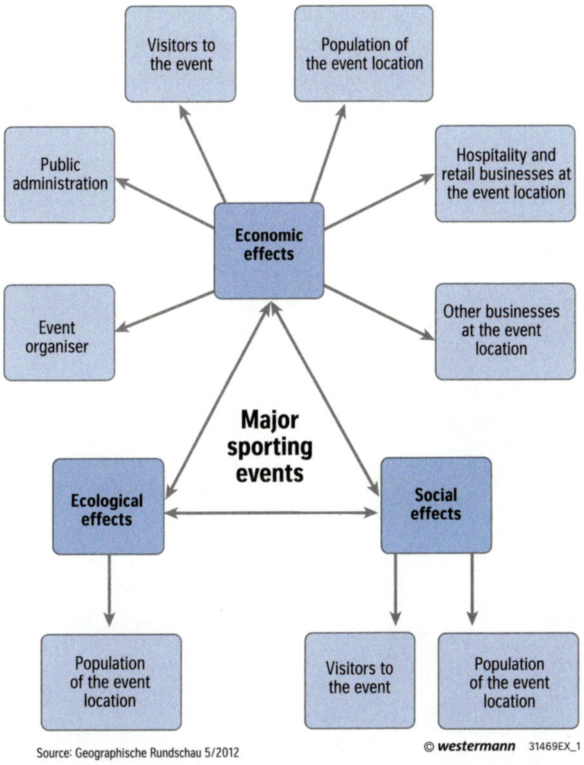

M7 Classification of the impact of large-scale sporting events

The provision of high-quality venues for active sportsmen and sportswomen, and the organisation of large-scale sporting events, require substantial private and public investments. This financial engagement by both public authorities and businesses comes about because of the positive effects that sporting events are expected to generate in various sectors of society. An attractive sports offering enhances the region's "soft" locational factors. These take on considerable importance in the context of international competition between cities and regions to attract businesses, high-spending consumers as well as tourists. [...] In terms of sustainability, the possible positive (benefits) and negative (costs) effects that can arise from large-scale sporting events can be seen in both economic, ecological and social dimensions.

Source: Horn, M. & Gans, P., in Geographische Rundschau 5/2012.

M9 The impact of large-scale sporting events

Urban development in North America

The history of settlement in North America

The historical-genetic development of North American cities followed a completely different course from that of cities in Central Europe. The different physiognomy of many American cities is a result of the history of settlement. What was the process of settlement in North America?

1. Describe immigration into and the opening-up and settlement of the USA (M1–M3).
2. Illustrate the role of the railway in the settlement of the USA and compare the chronological sequence of settlement with parallel events in urban development in Central Europe (M2–M4).
3. Illustrate the locational factors that led to the development of the Manufacturing Belt (M3, M4, Atlas).
4. ⓞ A Locate today's urban agglomerations in the USA (M6).
   B Compare the distribution of cities with the locations of industry and the positions of regions dominated by agriculture (M6, Atlas).
5. ⓢ Even today, the Land Ordinance of 1785 has a formative influence on the USA. Assess this theory (M5, M7).

→ Colonialism, Immigration, Manufacturing Belt

The number of Indians in the area of today's Canada and USA before the arrival of the Europeans is estimated at between 1 and 2 million people. Culturally, this Indian population was thoroughly diversified [...]. Its highest density was to be found in the wooded regions of the east. [...] With the constantly advancing settlement [by the European colonists...] the Indian population was increasingly robbed of its original habitats and destroyed. Numerous tribes were even driven out again from the settlement areas and reserves to which they had been allocated. Furthermore, countless Indians [...] fell victim to the "Indian Wars" waged by the American army with great harshness after 1860. [...] It was not until 1924 that the Indians obtained full American citizenship.

Source: Laux, H. D. and G. Thieme at www.diercke.de

M1 Destruction of the native American peoples

North America was marked by differing European colonial influences [...]. Spanish influences [were] [...] to be found exclusively in the south and west, French on the Gulf Coast and in Canada, and Dutch and British on the east coast as well as in Canada. The origins of this pattern of occupation go back to the early 17th century, when [...] European powers set out to establish overseas colonies of settlers on the one hand and traders on the other hand. Of necessity, this initially involved the identification of suitable harbours along the coasts or larger rivers, where settlement activity then took place. [...] Until the beginning of the 19th century, towns were isolated from one another and existed mainly as centres for the transshipment of agricultural goods and raw materials for export abroad. [...] Initially the only locations suitable for urban development were those where (sailing) ship transport was possible. This pattern changed dramatically with the development of the steam engine and the opening of the interior of the country by the railway. The advantages of sites along the railway lines and at railway junctions led to the emergence of new settlements. In 1850 the railway network was 14,480 km long, but by 1870 it had grown to 85,277 km. The larger towns and cities developed into centres for trade, industrial production and finance, and profited from the influx of European capital and cheap labour, which arrived from Europe in hundreds of thousands in various waves from different countries of origin. [...]
The intercontinental railway connections resulted in the growth of urban settlements in the west. But alongside technical innovations, this development also profited from the fact that – following its independence – the USA constantly expanded its territory and thus provided legal security. The Civil War gave a massive boost to industrialisation in the towns and cities in the north-east [where the Manufacturing Belt evolved into the largest industrial region in the world], and the "Gold Rush" on the Pacific Coast brought substantial investments with it.

Source: Bähr, J. and U. Jürgens, Stadtgeographie II, Braunschweig 2009, p. 168ff.

M3 The history of settlement in North America

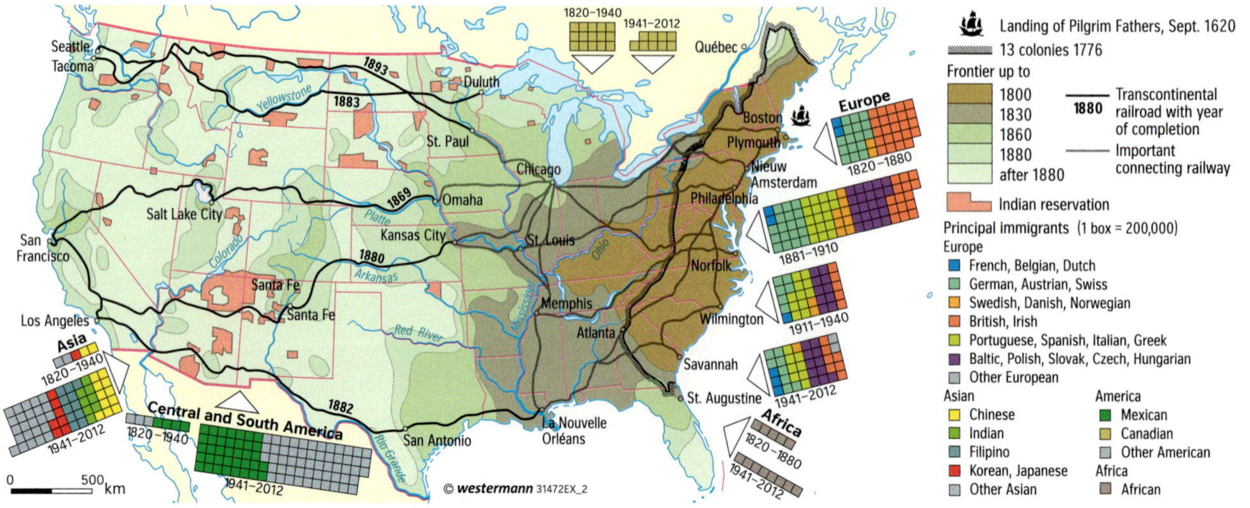

M2 Immigration to the USA and the settlement of the country

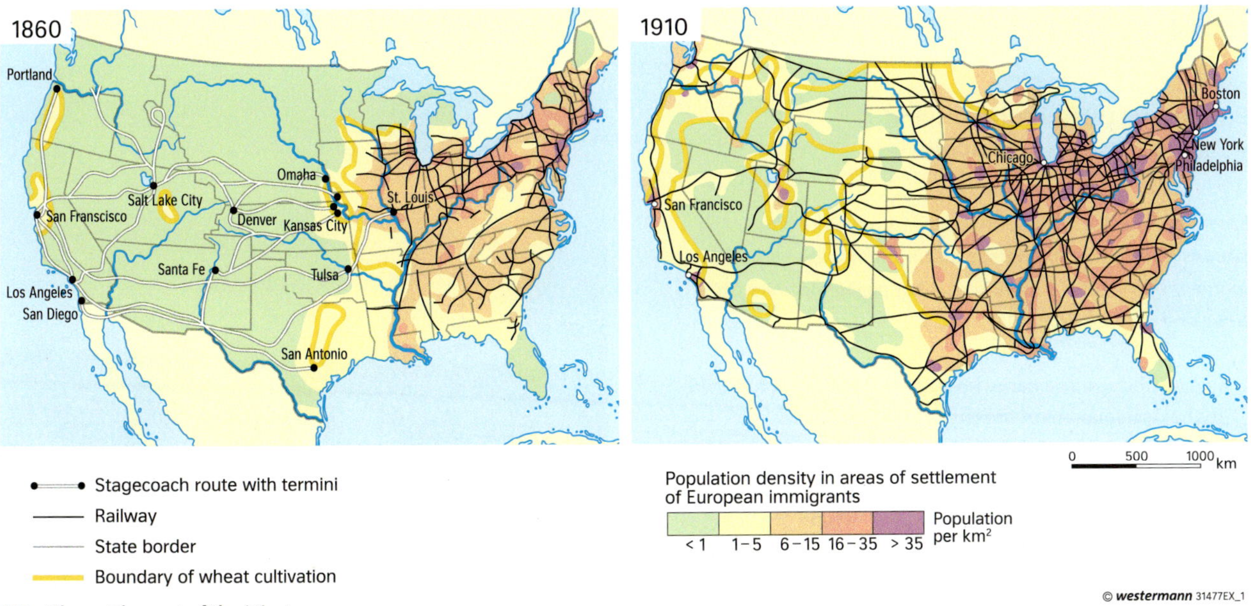

M4 The settlement of the West

The upward expansion of buildings in the vertical direction, reflecting the spirit of the age by seeking to express the technically possible in architectural terms (objective shortages of sites for housing or commercial building were clearly of lesser importance) gave the North American city an entirely new silhouette that was hitherto unknown in other types of cities elsewhere. [...]
The buildings were fitted into a street layout that is typical of US cities, in the form of a gridiron pattern oriented to the points of the compass. In the framework of the so-called Township and Range System in 1785, this system divided the whole of the federal lands west of the Appalachians into settlement parcels [see page 25 M5]. Typically, the cities are divided into blocks of 100 m x 100 m, which gives them on the one hand a certain monotony, but on the other hand a high degree of clarity for traffic flows. [...] Also in a state like New York, which lay outside of the Land Ordinance, a grid plan retrospectively agreed upon in 1811 provided for regulated expansion along narrowly-spaced "streets" running east-west and more generously spaced "avenues" running north-south.

Source: Bähr, J. and U. Jürgens, Stadtgeographie II, Braunschweig 2009, p. 171f.

M5 Causes of the physiognomy of North American cities

M7 West-to-east view of Denver, Colorado

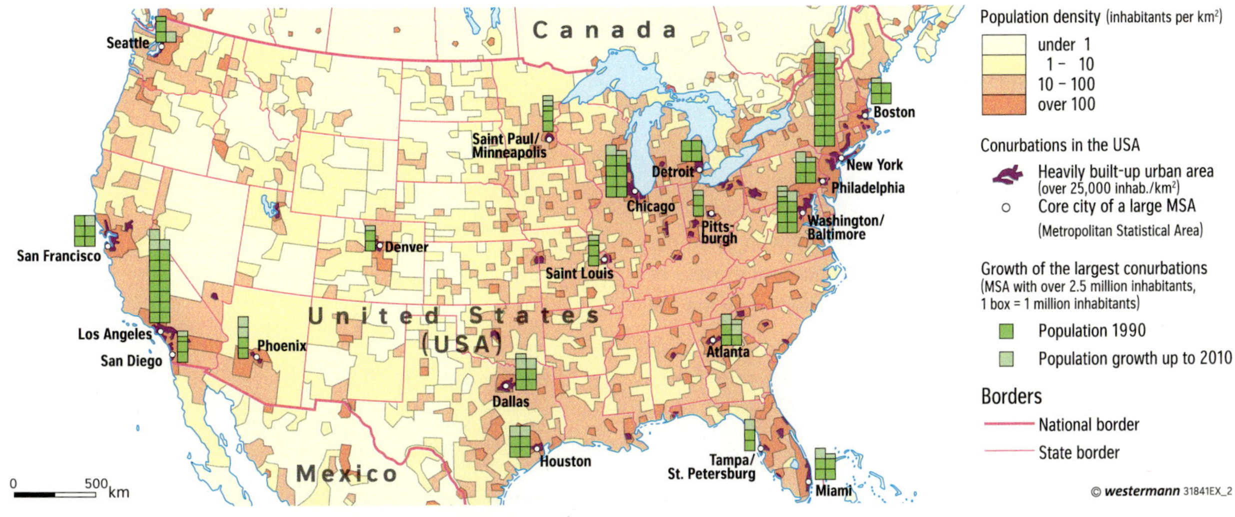

M6 Population density and urban regions in the USA today

Urban development in North America

Functional differentiation and suburbanisation – Chicago

The United States of America is often described as a land of cities. The large conurbations (metropolitan areas) contain 241 million inhabitants, i.e. some 83 percent of the total population. What problems arise from this for the cities and their environs?

1. Locate Chicago and name favourable factors that have led to the development of the city (p. 146 M3, Atlas).
2. Describe the physiognomic features of the city of Chicago (M2, M4, p. 147 M5).
3. Illustrate the extent and features of urban sprawl in the Chicago Metropolitan Area (M3).
4. Ⓞ Analyse the model of the North American city, by:
   - A explaining the processes that it describes (M5).
   - B comparing it with the Chicago School's models of functional division (M5, p. 140 M2).
   - C comparing it with the models of German cities (M5, p. 141 M3, M4).
5. Explain why the USA is often described as a land of cities.
6. Ⓢ In M7, various negative aspects of urban sprawl are listed. Explain the negative effects of these.

→ Central business district (CBD), City, Downtown, Edge cities, Functional differentiation, Suburbanisation, Urban sprawl, Zones in transition

M2 View from Willis Tower, the tallest building in Chicago, looking north …

→ City, Central business district

The "city" in German language usage corresponds to the downtown or CBD (central business district) in American usage. The CBD is the functional core area and the main business centre of the large North American city. While originally this only referred to the area in the city centre where retailing was concentrated, today the CBD is understood as the multifunctional provision and services zone, especially in the high-grade [tertiary] sector.

Synonymous for the flourishing and decline [of North American cities] are on the one hand the skyscrapers in the cities, where business life is concentrated in a vertical direction, and on the other hand ghettos of decline and the suburban periphery of owner-occupied homes, where the social contrasts of the city are manifested. Simply the sheer size of the country has led to spatial developments that are characterised as urban sprawl, i.e. the expansion of urban building into the surrounding countryside. [...] Emotional ties to city cores, which as a rule only have a very short historical architectural heritage [...], are of relatively little significance.
Because the population [in the 20th century] became more spatially mobile, aided by an extensive network of state-financed highways, more and more capital interests (shopping centres, recreational facilities) moved out to the periphery [and thus followed the population that had moved into the suburban areas]. The trend toward suburbanisation of residential space was thus intensified. [...] Higher earners and thus potential taxpayers moved to the suburbs and made room in the city cores for the less well-off who could not afford to pay for any alternative housing. A long-term process of social degradation and urban blight set in, culminating [in the 20th century] over a period of many decades.

Source: Bähr, J. and U. Jürgens, Stadtgeographie II, p. 166 ff.

M1 Flourishing and decline of North American cities

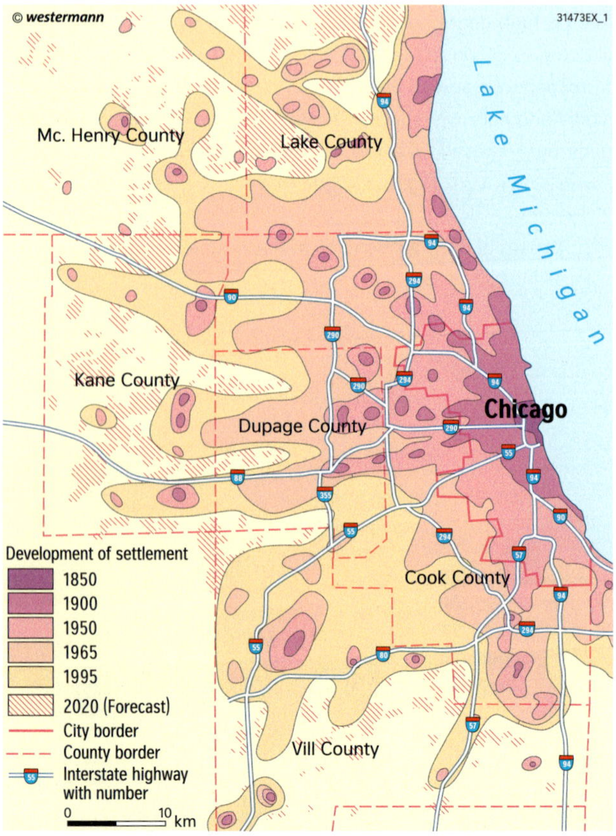

M3 Urban sprawl in the Chicago Metropolitan Area

M4 ... and south

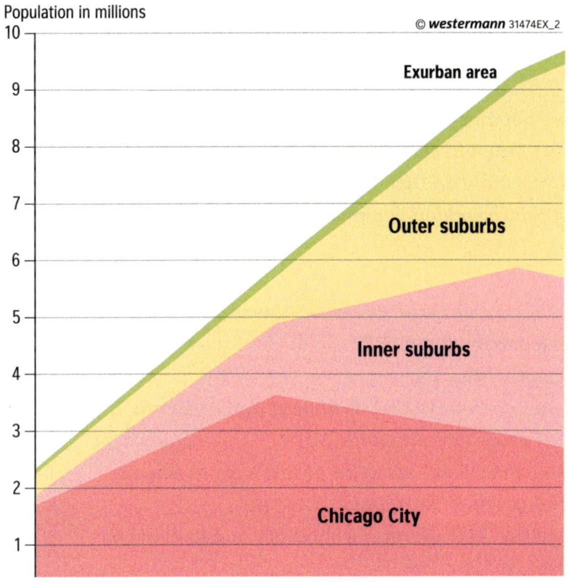

M6 Distribution of population in the Chicago Metropolitan Area

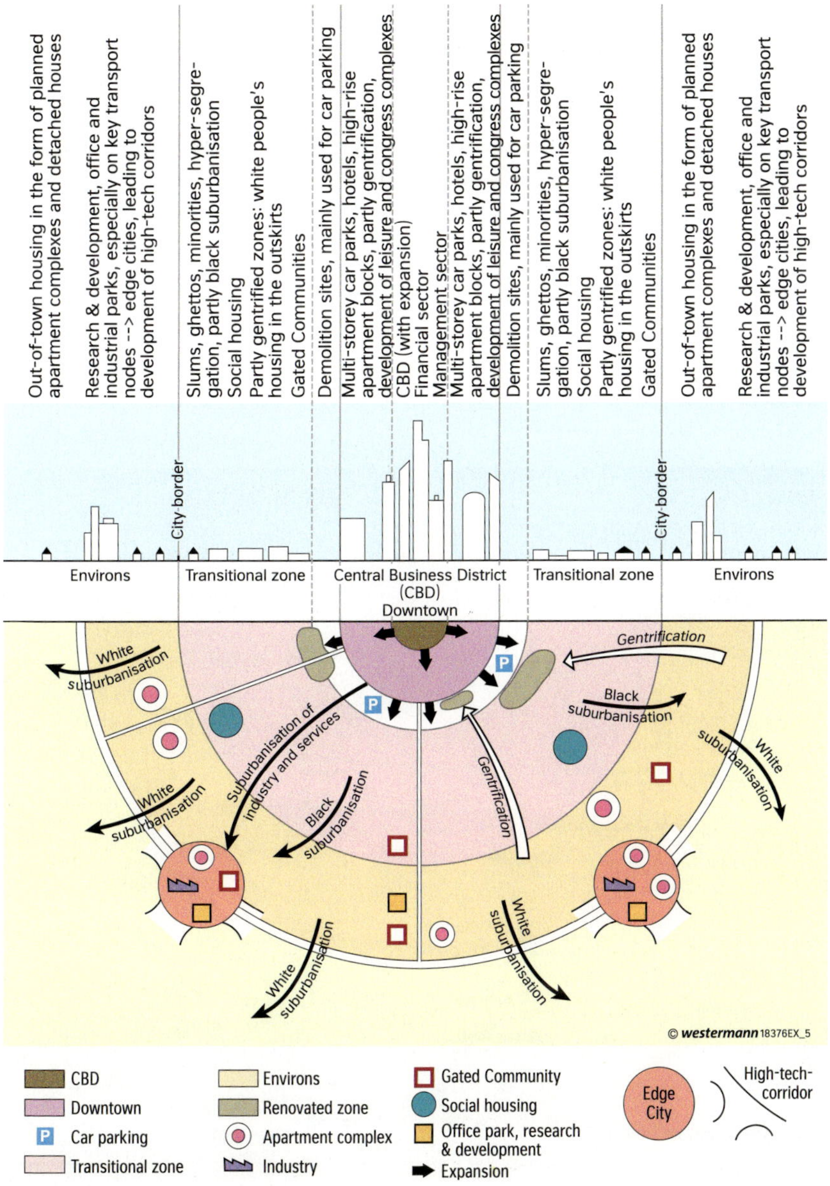

M5 Model of the North American city

→ Zones in transition

The development of ghettos [...] in the residential districts adjacent to the CBD or downtown ("zones in transition" according to the ring model of Burgess, [page 140 M2]) was and is another characteristic of the US city. [...] Because the proportion of social housing for rent [...] is small in the USA, the lower-income population has always had to move into the older building fabric in the inner parts of the city which had been vacated by the middle classes, [... which have thus become] catchment areas [...] for the so-called urban underclass.

→ Edge cities

[In the course of] suburbanisation, edge cities emerge in the proximity of the access or slip roads of orbital motorways. They are settlements in the periphery [...] with commercial and industrial estates possessing all the functions of a city [...]. Their favourable transport location makes them more accessible [...]. The commuting and shopping traffic that was formerly oriented radially towards the CBD is now supplemented by additional traffic flows in a tangential direction .

Source: Claaßen, K., Siedlungsräume, Braunschweig 2009

- More pollution
- Loss of wildlife habitats
- Traffic jams
- Farmland loss
- Increased taxes
- Increased school costs
- Degraded downtown areas
- Loss of community

M7 Why is sprawl bad?

Urban development in North America

Ethnic and social segregation – Los Angeles

The Americans are debating again about racism in their country. The divide between the groups in US society has become less, the US political scientist Jackson Janes said on Deutschlandfunk radio. Obama is the personification of this, he added; but many have been left behind.

Source: Müller, D., Deutschlandfunk: Interview with J. Janes, 20.08.2014

1. Draft a short talk about current events in connection with the debate about racism in the USA (newspapers, magazines, Internet).
2. Illustrate urban sprawl in Los Angeles and its accompanying physical geographical factors (M1).
3. Explain "white flight" using the example of Los Angeles (M2, M4, p. 139 → Segregation, Internet).
4. Ⓞ Characterise, in the form of a short talk, a district of Los Angeles:
   - A with a white majority population.
   - B with an Afro-American majority population.
   - C with a Hispanic majority population (M4, Internet).
5. Compare the nationwide ethnic distribution of the US population with the distribution in selected cities and in Los Angeles (Atlas, Internet: for source see M4).
6. Comment on ethnic segregation in the USA (M2 – M10, Atlas).
7. Ⓢ Explain the ethnic composition of the population in Los Angeles against the background of the history of immigration (M5, p. 146 M2).

→ Demographic development, Ghetto, Segregation

The "losers" of urban sprawl were the inner cities, because a social and ethnic thinning-out process took place there. Higher earners, and especially persons with white skins, turned their backs on the city core. This process is called "white flight". Conversely, black people began moving away from the southern states, where discrimination predominated, to the north of the USA as early as the 1920s. In search of jobs in so-called "blue collar" occupations, as well as in flight from the threat of violence, they moved into those parts of the city where housing was barely affordable. This in turn is the origin of the emergence of what are termed "ghettos", which have a fixed place in the model of the North American city.

M2 "White flight" and ghetto-building

[Barack Obama on 18.07.2013, speaking after the acquittal of a neighbourhood watchman who had shot dead a 17-year-old African American in his neighbourhood:] "There are very few African American men in this country who haven't had the experience of being followed when they were shopping in a department store. That includes me. There are very few African American men who haven't had the experience of walking across the street and hearing the locks click on the doors of cars. That happened to me — at least before I was a senator. There are very few African Americans who haven't had the experience of getting on an elevator and a woman clutching her purse nervously and holding her breath until she had a chance to get off. That happens often." [...] The New York Times wrote on its opinion page [on Obama's speech...]: "He addressed the racial fault lines in the country by laying bare his personal anguish and experience."

Source: M. Kolb, Der Präsident als Kellner, www.sueddeutsche.de, 20.07.2013

M3 Obama speaks about his experience with racism

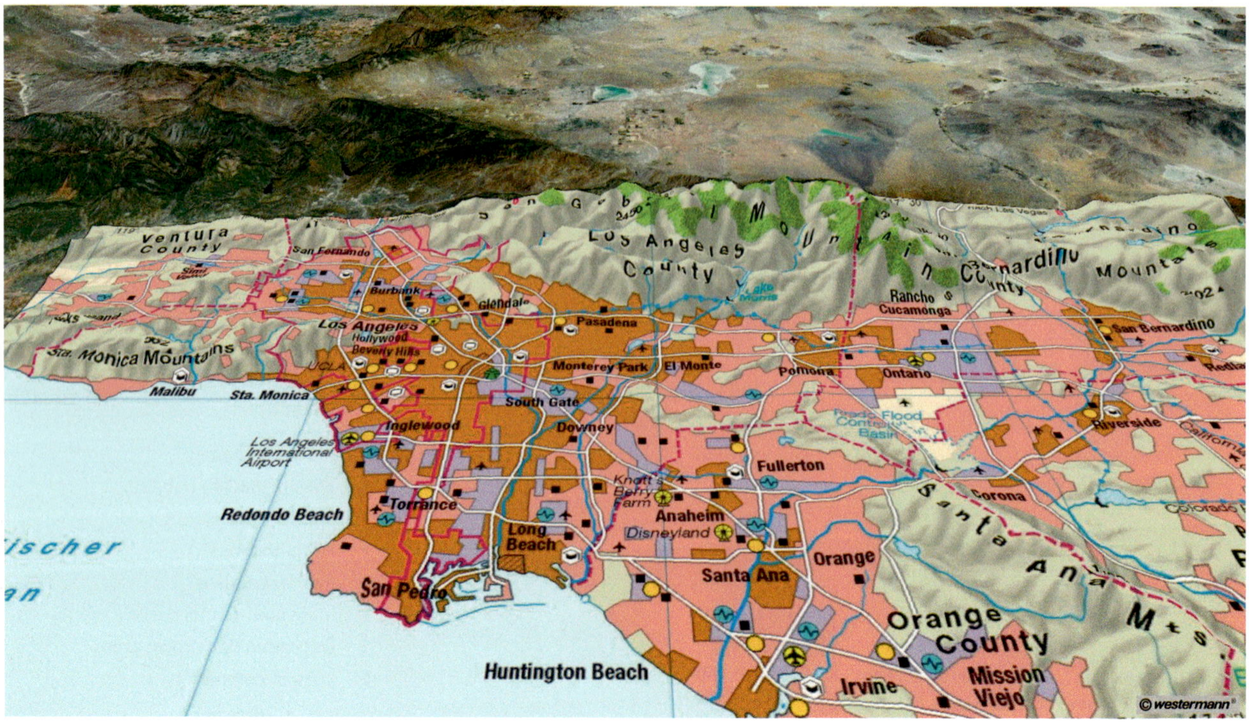

M1 Los Angeles – urban landscape (as shown in Diercke Globus Online)

M4 Ethnic distribution of the population in Los Angeles (2014) (Source: http://demographics.coopercenter.org/DotMap/index.html)

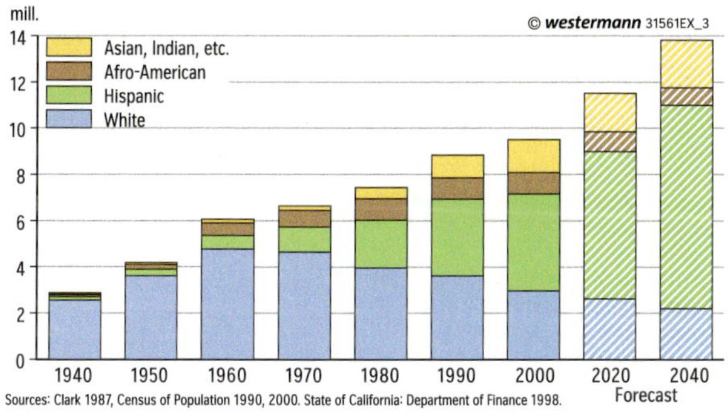

M5 Los Angeles County: demographic development and ethnic differentiation

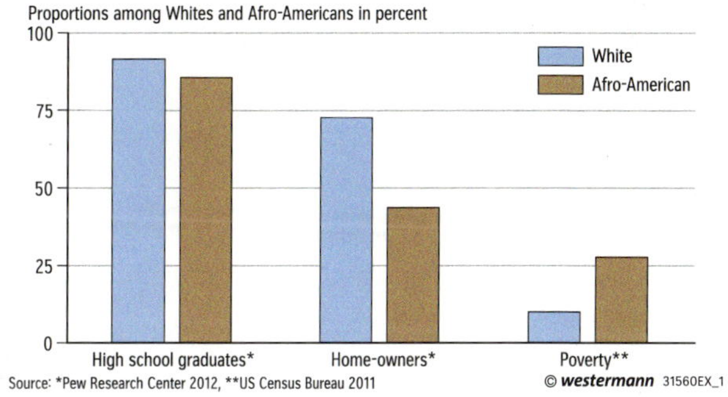

M8 Social inequality in the USA (2011/2012)

Race	General Population	Homeless Population
Hispanic	47%	33%
White	30%	14%
African American	9%	50%
Asian/Pacific Islander	12%	2%
Other	2%	less than 1%

M6 Ethnic distribution of the homeless in Los Angeles 2011 (total: c. 254,000)

Some 12 million illegal immigrants live in the USA. They live a shadowy existence on the fringe of society. [...] The majority [...] of them are Latinos [Hispanics]. They come from Mexico, Latin or Central America. At the same time, with a population of some 50 million, the Latinos who are legal immigrants represent the largest and most important minority in the USA.

Source: Klein, V., Deutsche Welle, 24.11.2012

M9 Living with fear: Illegal immigrants in the USA

M7 Malibu

M10 Border security between San Diego, USA (left) und Tijuana, Mexico (right)

The essentials in brief

Urban geography is concerned among other things with the historical-genetic, functional and social-spatial structure of urban agglomerations.
The historical-genetic structure takes as its subject the urban development phases of successive historical epochs, starting with the favourable locational factors of the towns and cities under consideration. In the epoch of industrialisation, a growth in urban areas took place in Central Europe. At that time the living conditions in the town cores that had developed in the Middle Ages and their adjacent working-class districts were mostly very poor. With the garden city model and the Athens Charter, urban planning in the first half of the 20th century adopted new ideas for improving the quality of life based on a separation of functions. The urban development principles of the post-war years continued along these lines. From the time of Germany's "economic miracle", urban development in Central Europe was marked by pronounced suburbanisation, which frequently resulted in a strict separation of the basic functions of working and living. With the increased environmental consciousness in the final decades of the 20th century, concepts of sustainability moved into the focus of planning. In areas marked by revitalisation, a functional change took place towards a mix of uses. In today's urban and spatial planning, ideally the participation of the citizens is desired.
A pronounced segregation is frequently a characteristic feature of the social-spatial structure of cities. In this context, Wilhelminian districts are often especially susceptible to massive gentrification.
The central business districts (CBD) of cities mainly house consumer and business-oriented services as employers. In the shopping zones, extensive chain store development often predominates. Cities today, in competition with other cities, do not only rely on a broad-based range of shopping opportunities. Today a process of public presentation and festivalisation of cities is taking place, among other things in order to promote urban tourism as a source of added value.
The ring model, sector model and multiple nuclei model of the Chicago School can be applied to cities in both Central Europe and North America.
In North America, in the course of inward migration in the era of colonialism but also in the later opening and settlement of the continent, large parts of the native Indian population were driven out and destroyed. In the north-east of the USA, the "Manufacturing Belt" developed during the era of trans-continental railway-building into what was then the largest industrial area in the world.
Today the USA is often described as a land of cities. The process of "urban sprawl" has created vast and connected urban regions, which are still continuing to expand. Characteristic of North American cities is the central business district (CBD), which is marked in physiognomic terms by a distinct skyline. In the past decades, "edge cities" have emerged on the periphery of the cities, which possess all city functions and which provide relief to the original CBD or have even taken on a role as competitors.
In the "zones in transition" bordering on the downtown area, ghettos of the urban underclass have developed in the past which have a far higher than average proportion of Afro-Americans. In the USA, ethnic segregation is unmistakeable. Characteristic features of this demographic trend are a declining white population accompanied above all by strong growth in the Hispanic population.

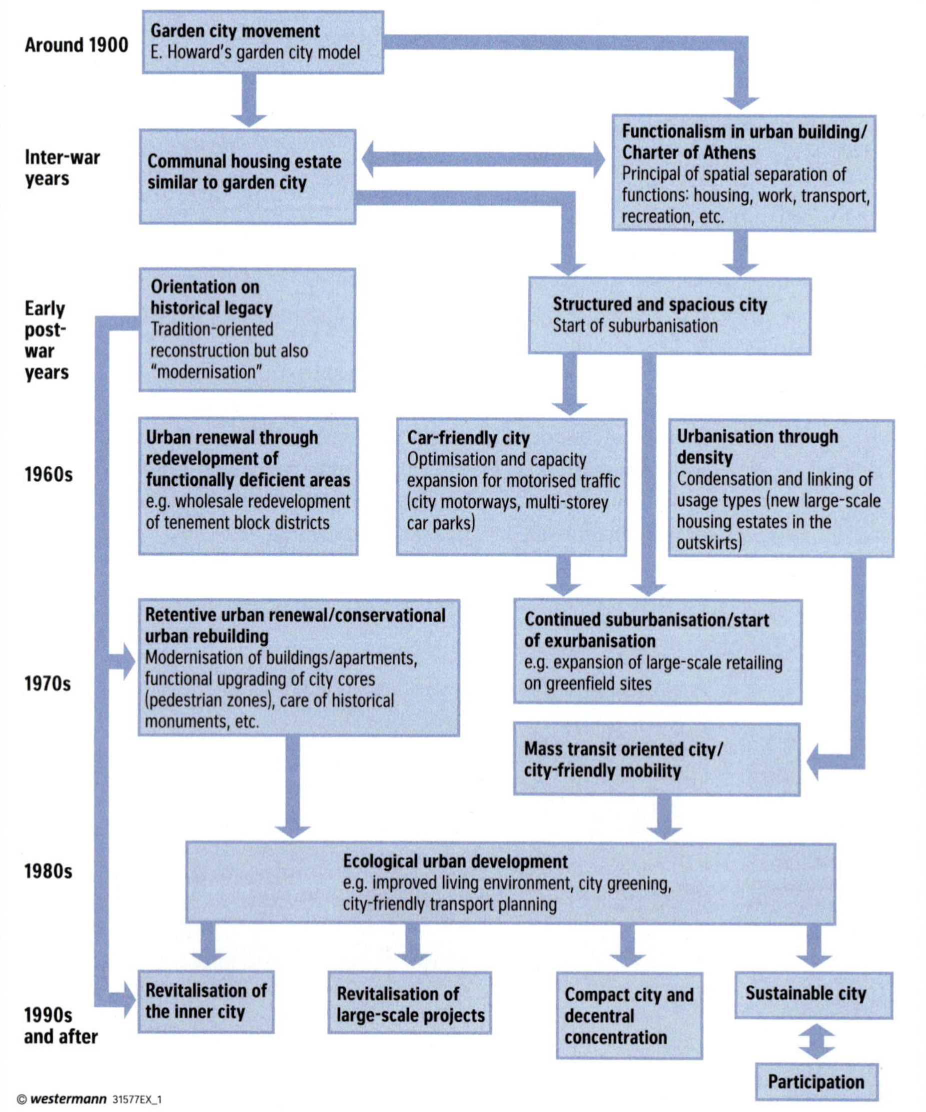

M1 Principles of urban development in West Germany (20th century)

Skill Check

All the skills that you were able to acquire in this chapter are listed here.
You can judge for yourself if you have mastered each skill: ***securely***, ***moderately*** or ***barely***.

Explanatory skills

Can I ...		Unsure? Look it up on these pages
1.	categorise urban regions according to genetic, functional and social features, using e.g. the examples of Cologne and Munich?	130–139
2.	describe the genesis of specific urban structures in different cultural regions with reference to different urban development models?	140/141, 148/149
3.	describe the influence of suburbanisation and segregation processes on present-day urban structures, e.g. with reference to the North American city?	148–151
4.	outline the variety of the tertiary sector using the examples of retailing as well as of consumer-oriented and business-oriented services?	142–145

Methodological skills

Can I ...		
5.	orient myself directly on the ground and indirectly with the aid of complex physical, thematic and digital mapping services?	136/137
6.	extract general geographical core statements from complex models and assess them with reference to concrete geographical examples?	140/141, 148/149
7.	independently research information in the Internet and in Internet-based geo-information services using appropriate search strategies, and analyse it in a manner relevant to the question?	150/151

Evaluation skills

Can I ...		
8.	evaluate the significance of urban development models with regard to their applicability to real geographical regions?	140/141, 148/149
9.	evaluate the consequences of suburbanisation and segregation processes in terms of ecological aspects and with regard to the coexistence of different social groups?	148–151

Activity skills

Can I ...		
10.	present possibilities for influencing spatially-related and spatial planning processes?	136/137

Examination training

Historical-genetic development and functional transformation of cities – the example of Regensburg

1. Locate Regensburg and characterise the historical-genetic development of the city.
2. Illustrate the importance, structure and functional transformation of Regensburg.
3. Critically evaluate the impact of the Regensburg Arcaden on the inner city.

These additional materials are required to complete the assignments:

M1 Atlas maps of your choice
M2 Regensburg – funktionale Gliederung/ historische Entwicklung, Diercke Weltatlas (2008), p. 69,5
M3 Regensburg – Altstadt, Diercke Weltatlas (2008), p. 69,6
M4 Regensburg – Einkaufszentrum, Diercke Weltatlas (2008), p. 69,7

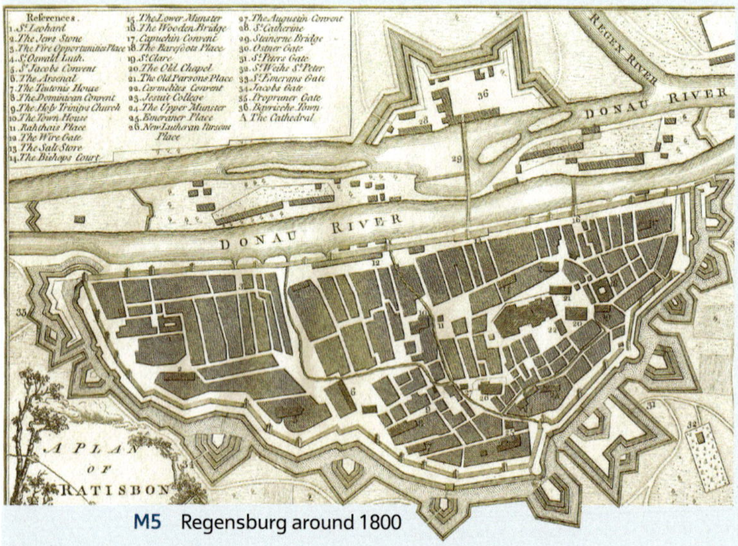

M5 Regensburg around 1800

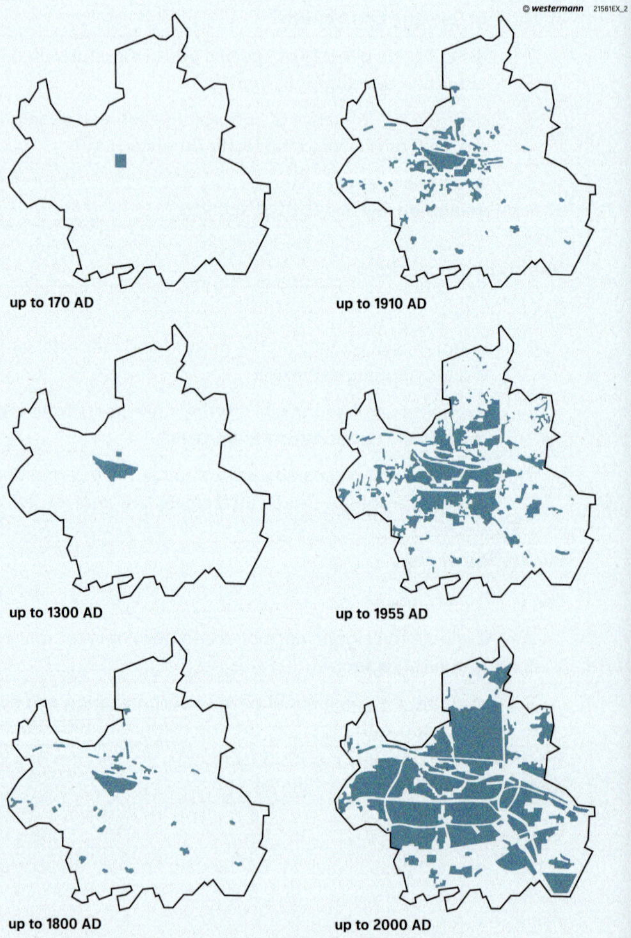

M7 Development of the area of settlement in Regensburg's urban area

An important instrument for the preservation of the "Old Town of Regensburg with Stadtamhof" is the carefully implemented and sustainable restoration of the Old Town.

Since 1945 the Old Town of Regensburg has been the only preserved large medieval city in Germany. In the post-war years this presented two challenges for conservationists. On the one hand it was deemed important to keep the core of the city attractive to business, while on the other hand it was equally important to improve the living conditions of residents in the Old Town. While in other towns the large-scale wartime destruction resulted in the construction of modern buildings, Regensburg was obliged to restore its existing, often centuries-old residential quarters.

General objectives of restoration:

It's not just about conserving Regensburg's historic ensemble. More importantly, it's about residents and visitors being able to live and interact with the building fabric from earlier epochs within a functioning city. As a result, in 1977 the city council set a number of objectives for restoration:

The restoration principles:

- Our uppermost goal is to conserve the historic old town in its macro-structural and micro-structural essence.
- We must conserve the land use structure of the old town.
- Existing residential use has priority over any other re-designation of land use.
- The micro-structural element of individual ownership must continue to thrive.
- We must ensure that shops and small businesses, whether services or trades, can flourish.

Almost half of all the buildings within the "Regensburg Old Town and Stadtamhof" ensemble have already been renovated. This process has primarily taken place in the western part of the Old Town.

Source: www.regensburg.de, accessed 11.10.2014

M6 Modern urban development and restoration

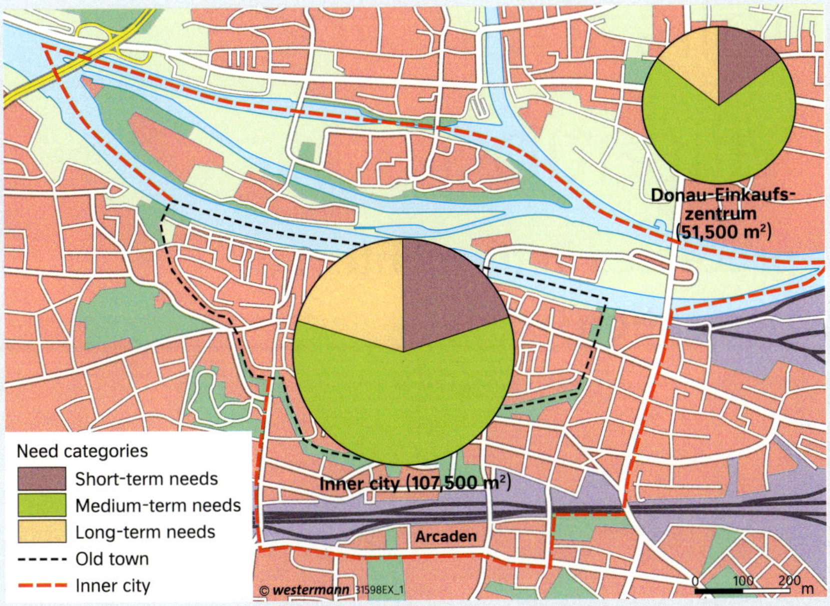

M8 Locations with a regional function – need categories of product assortments

Once a flourishing European trading metropolis and political centre of the Holy Roman Empire, today Regensburg is the best-preserved large medieval city in Germany and 2006 UNESCO World Heritage Site since 2006.
(Source: https://www.regensburg.de/welterbe)

Many expectations are associated with this nomination as a UNESCO World Heritage Site. Among other things, it is hoped to attract more attention to the city in a national and international environment, bring more visitors from near and far, and provide a soft locational factor for the economy, a component in a sustainable urban development strategy, and not least a contribution to the town's profile and sense of identity.
Source: Ripp, M. in: Informationen zur Raumentwicklung, 2011

M10 UNESCO World Heritage Site: Old Town of Regensburg with Stadtamhof

Shopping centres are regarded as a threat to the inner cities. A key reason for this is the market power of the chain store branches that are concentrated there and the centre managements that coordinate them, which comes into play especially when the sales floor area of the shopping centres is disproportionately large in relation to the rest of the inner city. But the discussion takes too little account of the fact that the decisive factor for the future chances of the historic inner city is not only the relation of the sales area or number of businesses, but also and very importantly the orientation of the offerings. [...]
Regensburg is an unusual special case. Initially, at the time of the "economic miracle", the city began to adapt the still-intact Old Town to the requirements of a modern major shopping district. But by the mid-1960s, more attention was paid to the value of its historical heritage. Consequently, the establishment of the Danube- Einkaufszentrum [DEZ] (opened in 1967) at a distance of 1.5 km from the Old Town north of the Danube and its step-by-step expansion from a retail sales area of 16,000 m^2 to some 52,000 m^2 (2010) were approved. [...] Since the Old Town could not offer the expanding retail chains the desired opportunities for opening new stores (especially with larger floor areas), after long discussions the city facilitated the establishment of an additional shopping centre 600 m south of the Old Town behind the railway station. Here, the company MFI (Management für Immobilien) opened the Regensburg Arcaden in 2002 with (in 2010) a retail sales area of 22,700 m^2 (a total commercial area of some 33,000 m^2 including catering and services). Thus the total sales area of the two centres together, when compared with approx. 78,500 m^2 in the Old Town itself (September 2010), is much larger than would normally be considered acceptable [...]. For many residents in the surrounding areas, the Danube-Einkaufszentrum has even replaced the inner city as their destination of choice when they "drive into the city to shop". [...] The 100 businesses in the DEZ and 73 businesses in the Arcaden compare [however] to some 600 businesses (in 2010) in the Old Town. Thus the inner city (excluding the Arcaden) accounts for only 24% of Regensburg's total sales area but 50% of the businesses. [...]
52% of the businesses located in the Old Town have no more than 50 m^2 [...]; 67% are businesses with only a single shop, 4% are chain store headquarters, and only 29% are branch stores or franchisees.
Source: Monheim, R., Die Regensburger Altstadt - Shopping-Spezialisierung im Schatten zweier Einkaufszentren. In: Berichte des Arbeitskreises Geographische Handelsforschung No. 28, 2010, p. 18-25.

M9 The structure of retailing in Regensburg

With some 133,000 inhabitants, Regensburg is the fifth-largest city in the Federal State of Bavaria. [...] As well as a clearly recognisable architectural connection to the south, it is above all on account of its extraordinary attitude to life that Regensburg is often described as "the most northerly Italian city". In recent years, Regensburg has ascended to one of the leading positions in Bavaria's economic ranking. The city profits from the outstanding scientific potential of its hospital, university, and university of applied sciences (with a combined total of 23,000 students), [...]. According to a study by the renowned PROGNOS institute, this city at the most northerly point on the River Danube holds tenth place among Germany's technology locations.
Source: www.regensburg.de

M11 COMFORT City Report, Regensburg 2010

VI Metropolisation and marginalisation

Unavoidable processes in the context of worldwide urbanisation?

Mumbai (India) – the metropolis contains a high proportion of people living in marginalised conditions.

The world of cities

Megacities – bigger, more important, more vulnerable

"Urbanisation is one of the megatrends of our times – and as such it bears a vast complexity. While the pull of the cities often creates problems for rural regions in the industrialised countries, massive urban population growth is posing great challenges for the metropolises in many developing countries. For often enough, the growth of cities exceeds the capacity of authorities to develop and maintain adequate social and physical infrastructure." (World Risk Report, 2014, p. 11)
2007 represented a turning-point in history, because since that date, for the first time ever, more people have been living in urban than in rural areas. In the year 2014 it was already 54%. In 1950 it was only 30%. What are the causes of urban growth? What impact does urbanisation have on the townscape?

Through increasing urbanisation, especially in the developing and fast-developing countries, centres of political and economic power are formed. But in precisely these cities, there are also many people who do not participate in this. This problem, which can be described with the terms metropolisation and marginalisation, is covered in this chapter. Are metropolisation and marginalisation two processes that are inextricably linked together? How do the people in marginal districts organise themselves? What effect does this have on the governability of cities?

M2 Lima: One city, ...

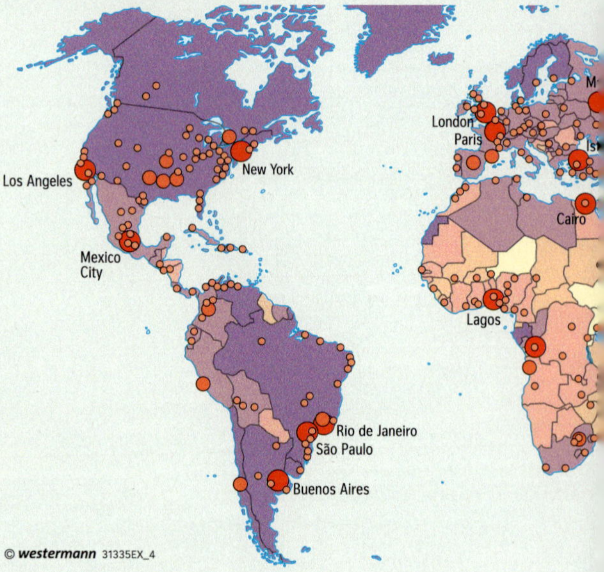

Source: World Urbanization Prospects 2014, p. 9

M3 Urban agglomerations (2014)

Urbanisation is understood as a spreading, increase and expansion of cities in a region in terms of numbers, surface area and population. **Megacities** are usually distinguished according to quantitative attributes, based on at least five, eight or ten million inhabitants according to various definitions. Some authors additionally determine a population density threshold (at least 2,000 inhabitants/km^2) and only include cities with a monocentric structure, while others also count polycentrically structured regions and speak of "mega-urban regions" (UN 2008). Cities with over 20 million inhabitants are referred to as **metacities**.
But there are problems in the collection of statistical data. Urbanisation causes many cities to grow beyond their actual administrative boundaries. This results in variations in the cities' population data. Some population figures only count the number of people within the city's boundaries, while other sources go further and take into account the population figures in the metropolitan region (agglomeration), also beyond the administrative boundary of the city itself (see M5, M6). Also, many cities are subject to a high development dynamic, so that the figures quickly go out of date or immigrants, especially in marginal settlements, are not counted at all.
Agglomerations are regional concentrations of housing and commercial buildings, inhabitants, workplaces and their associated infrastructure. As a rule, agglomerations consist of one larger city (monocentric agglomerations) or multiple cities (polycentric agglomerations).
The term **metropolis** refers to the capital city or the political, social and economic focal point of a country. One speaks of **metropolisation** when one city in a particular country predominates over the other cities in that country in terms of size and importance.
Marginalisation means the economic, political, social and spatial exclusion of a segment of the population.

M1 Definitions

M4 ... different faces

	Mega-/Metacity	State
Population	Pearl River Delta: 48 mill. Tokyo: 35.5 mill. Mexico City: 19.5 mill.	Spain/Portugal: 48 mill. Canada: 30.8 mill. Australia: 19.2 mill.
Volume of migration	Volume of inland labour migration into five megacities of China: c. 25 – 30 mill. people	Immigrants from Mexico into the USA: legal 7 mill., illegal 2 – 2.5 mill. people
CO_2 emissions (kg per head/year) with roughly equal populations	Beijing: 253 Mexico City: 101 Los Angeles: 166	Belgium: 101 Netherlands: 43 Hungary: 73

Source: Praxis Geographie 7-8/2009 p. 5

M6 Mega-/metacities and states: comparative dimensions

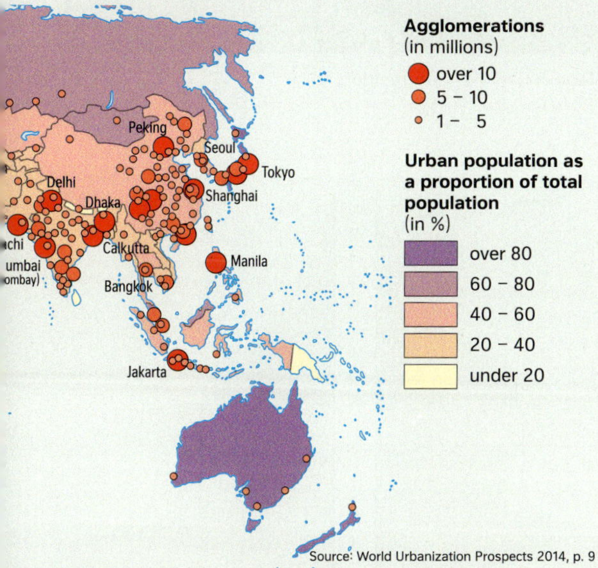

Source: World Urbanization Prospects 2014, p. 9

© westermann 18344EX_2

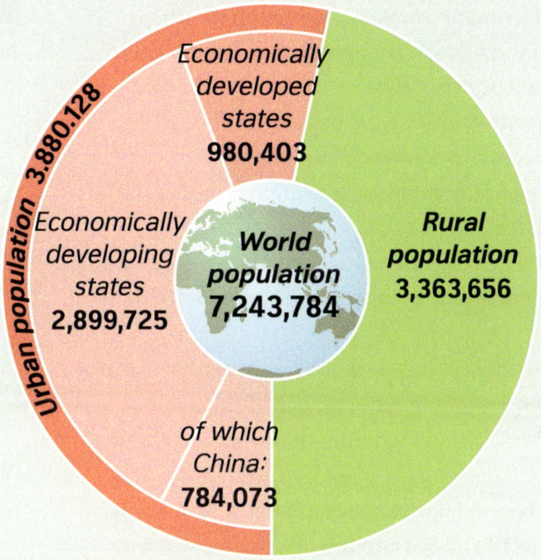

Source: United Nations: World Urbanization Prospects, 2014

M7 Worldwide urbanisation (2014) in thousands

Rank	1950		1990		2014		2030*	
	Agglomeration	Pop.	Agglomeration	Pop.	Agglomeration	Pop.	Agglomeration	Pop.
1	New York / Newark	12.34	Tokyo	32.53	Tokyo	37.83	Tokyo	37.19
2	Tokyo	11.27	Osaka-Kobe	18.39	Delhi	24.95	Delhi	36.06
3	London	8.36	New York/Newark	16.09	Shanghai	22.99	Shanghai	30.75
4	Paris	6.28	Mexico City	15.64	Mexico City	20.84	Mumbai	27.80
5	Moscow	5.36	São Paulo	14.78	São Paulo	20.83	Beijing	27.71
6	Buenos Aires	5.10	Mumbai	12.44	Mumbai	20.74	Dhaka	27.37
7	Chicago	5.00	Calcutta	10.89	Osaka-Kobe	20.12	Karachi	24.84
8	Calcutta	4.51	Los Angeles	10.88	Beijing	19.52	Cairo	24.50
9	Shanghai	4.30	Seoul	10.52	New York/Newark	18.59	Lagos	24.24
10	Osaka-Kobe	4.15	Buenos Aires	10.51	Cairo	18.42	Mexico City	23.87

M5 The ten largest agglomerations 1950–2030 (*projection) in millions.
Source: UN Population Division (2012), World Urbanization Prospects (2014)

1. Describe the distribution of urban agglomerations worldwide (M3).
Ⓞ 2. A Analyse M5.
   B Give reasons for the change in the list of the ten largest cities worldwide from 1950 to 2030.
3. Select two mega- or metacities. Research five different sources in which the number of inhabitants is stated. Give reasons for the differing figures (M3 or M5).
4. Illustrate the meaning of megacities (M6, M7).
5. For the cities with more than ten million inhabitants (M3), research the HDI of the country and the growth rate. Draw conclusions from the results.
Ⓢ 6. With the help of the Atlas, find all cities larger than five million inhabitants in M3.

Causes of the growth of megacities

The pull of cities – China

Worldwide urbanisation is ongoing. Especially the developing and fast-developing countries will experience a drastic increase in their urban populations in the coming decades. What is the cause of this immense growth in cities? For what motives do people migrate?

1. Analyse the development of urban populations (M5).
2. Research the growth of population in each of three industrial, fast-developing and developing countries. Then clarify for each country what influence these values could have:
   a) on rural-urban migration.
   b) on urban growth.
3. (O) A Interpret the cartoon by Luisa Beyer (M9).
   B Draw a cartoon about the push-pull problem.
4. With the help of the Atlas, characterise the demographic and economic structure of China.
5. Describe the age structure in rural regions of China (M3).
6. Illustrate the causes and consequences of migration in China.
7. Evaluate the influence of natural population growth on the growth of cities (M1).
8. Discuss the impact of China's official one-child policy, which has meanwhile been slightly relaxed, on the growth of cities.
9. (S) Go in search of evidence (real or digital) in your nearest large city. Find facilities that are of more than local importance and make a list of them. Discuss whether these facilities have a pull effect.
10. (S) A migrant who was in Europe and returned to Africa was asked why he did not go back to the place where he was born. His answer was: "Ha! I didn't want to show my face there again. They all knew about me. It is shameful when you don't make a success of it." Discuss what effect this might have on urban and rural inhabitants.

→ Migration, Pull factors, Push factors

M2 Village in China's countryside

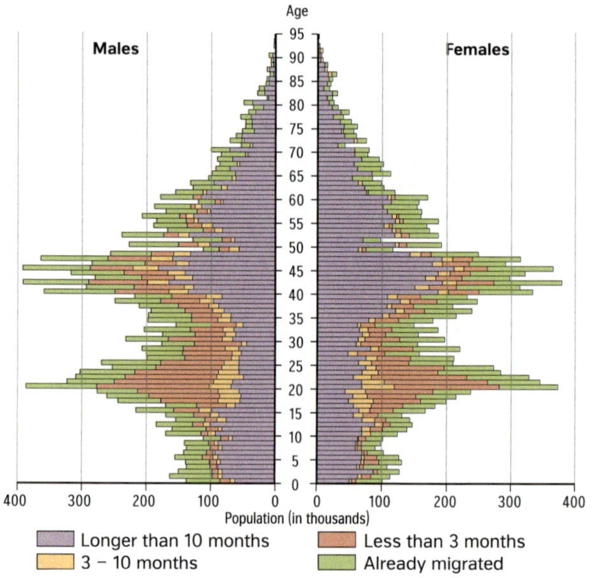

Source: ANU Press: Rebalancing and Sustaining Growth in China, 2012 © westermann 31337EX_1

M3 Age pyramid of rural regions in China showing the length of stay in the place of origin (2012)

→ Migration

Migration is the movement of individual people or groups of people resulting in a change in their place of residence that is not merely short-term. If this migration takes place from rural regions into urban areas, one speaks of rural-urban migration.

Rate of unemployment	
Urban regions	4.0%
Rural regions	30.0%

M4 Unemployment in China (2012)

	1995	2014	2025*
China	1.0	0.4	0.0
South Korea	0.8	0.2	-0.1
India	1.9	1.3	1.0
Argentina	1.2	1.0	0.7
Nigeria	2.5	2.5	2.3
Germany	0.3	-0.2	-0.3

Source: www.census.gov

M1 Natural population growth in percent (* projection)

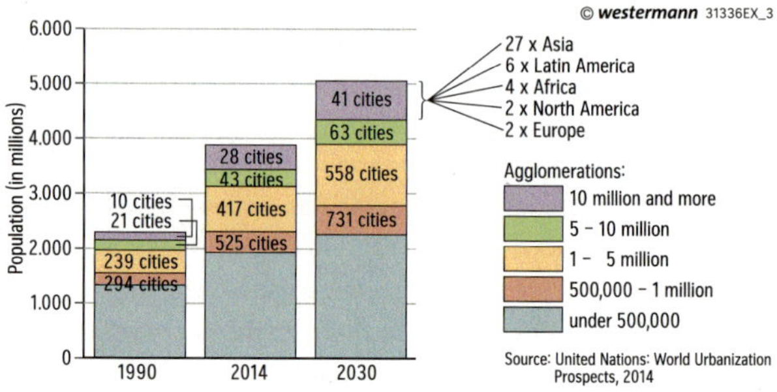

M5 Growth of urban population by size of city (2030 projection)

M6 Migrant workers in Shanghai

M9 Cartoon by schoolgirl Luisa Beyer, Q1

"My name is Quang Phong. I am 20 years old and come from the province of Qinghai, one of the poorest regions of China. Many people there are unemployed. I too have found no work in the last few years – and there is hardly enough money to live on. Many work as farmers, but there are too few jobs outside of agriculture. And not everybody can work as a farmer, because the families here are growing but the agricultural area is not. My parents cannot read or write, but I was able to go to school. Later I want to be an engineer. Therefore I decided – like many of my friends – to go to Shanghai. There I work on the building site of a new skyscraper. The work is really very hard and dangerous, but at least the pay is much better than where I come from. For the rice harvest I travel back home and help my parents. Then I take a large part of my earnings and give it to them, so that they can also afford meat or new clothes occasionally. In the city I am much better able to afford such things. At home it is nicer, not so noisy and dirty, but I do not regret my decision to start a new life."

M7 A migrant worker tells his story

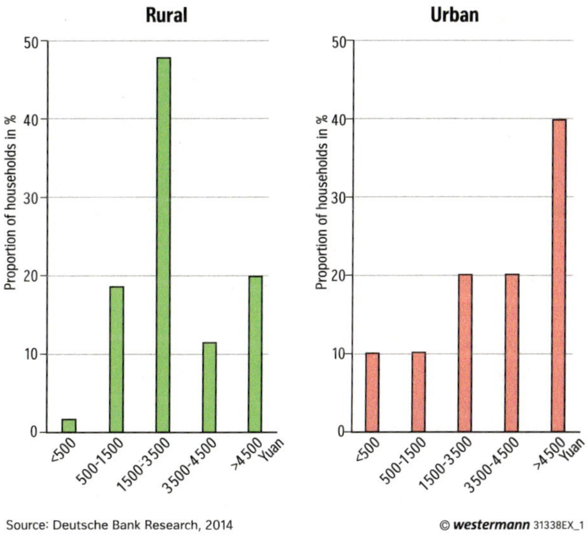

M10 Annual net income per capita in rural and urban areas in China (in Yuan; 1 Euro = 8.16 Yuan) (2013)

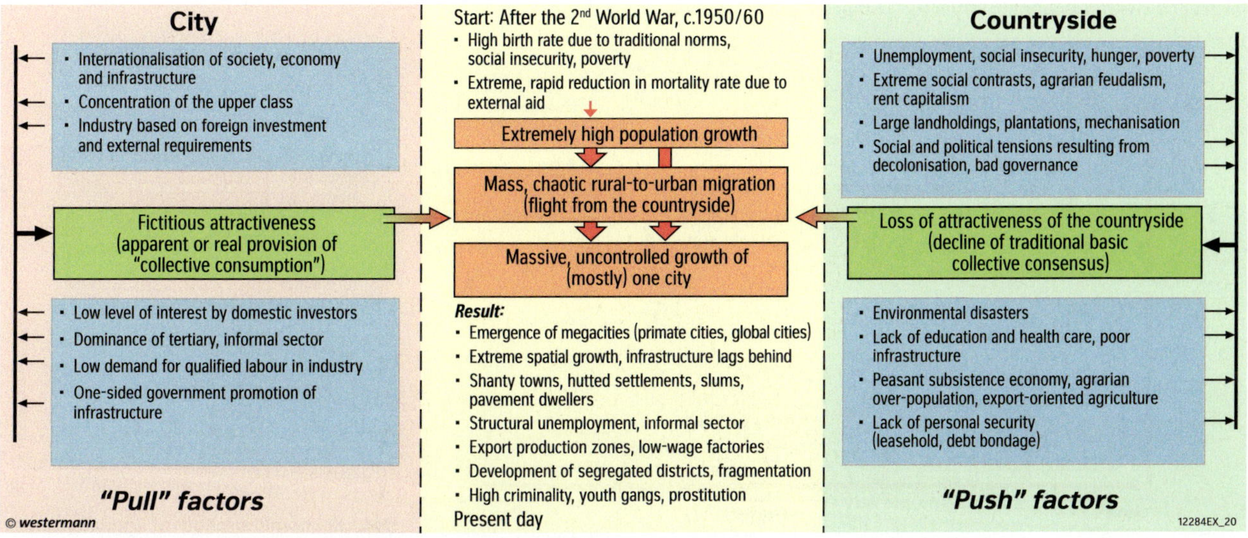

M8 Urbanisation and population growth in developing countries

Primate cities – predominance in all fields

Unipolar orientation in South Korea – the Seoul Metropolitan Area

Demographic and economic growth changes the urban structure in a country. Often this growth is oriented towards one central place. Why do such centres of gravity emerge? What is their significance?

1. Explain the terms demographic and functional primate city (M3).
2. Calculate the Primacy Index for Seoul and compare it to Germany (Fischer Weltalmanach 2014) (M3, M5, M7):
   Seoul 10,388,055 Berlin 3,375,222
   Busan 3,492,518 Hamburg 1,734,272
3. Explain the advantages and disadvantages of the primate city character.
4. Foreign direct investment is concentrated in the Seoul Metropolitan Area.
   a) Give reasons why this is the case.
   b) Outline the consequences for Seoul and South Korea.
5. Describe the polarisation process (M1).
6. Assess the applicability of the polarisation process model to Seoul (M1, M6, M8, M9).
7. ⓞ Illustrate the primate city character of Seoul. Also make use of the Atlas.
   A Write a text in examination style.
   B Produce a poster.
   C Prepare the material for a digital presentation.
8. Ⓢ Using the pictures (M2), work out what functions are recognisable that could lead to Seoul achieving a position of predominance.

→ Backwash effect, Polarisation, Primacy Index, Primate city, Spread effect

→ Primacy Index
(also called metropolisation quota or Index of Primacy).
The Primacy Index expresses the degree of demographic predominance. It is based on the relationship of the largest to the second-largest city within a country. When the Primacy Index is greater than two, one speaks of a position of predominance.

M2 Impressions of the Seoul Metropolitan Area ...

Many countries in the world are experiencing a powerful process of metropolisation. This means that one city, usually the country's capital city, grows into a demographic and economic centre. A primate city comes into being, which predominates over all other cities in the country in terms of population size, economic strength and political power.
If one city predominates over all others in terms of the size of its population, one speaks of a demographic primate city character. In the case of a functional primate city character, there is a predominance in all key areas of life. The functional primate city predominates over all other cities in the country in economic, cultural, political and infrastructural terms. Not only the quantity but also the quality of its facilities is better. Thus the functional primate city also offers the best locational factors for businesses. A polarisation develops, because the increasingly better locational factors in the primate city attract more and more businesses and people from the periphery, so that the hinterland, the periphery, increasingly declines in importance. A self-reinforcing process occurs. The development of the rural regions is thus hindered. An immense gulf develops between poor rural regions and rich urban regions. The increasing polarisation thus also fosters migration into the primate city. Functional primate cities emerge particularly frequently in developing and fast-developing countries.

M3 The meaning of primate cities

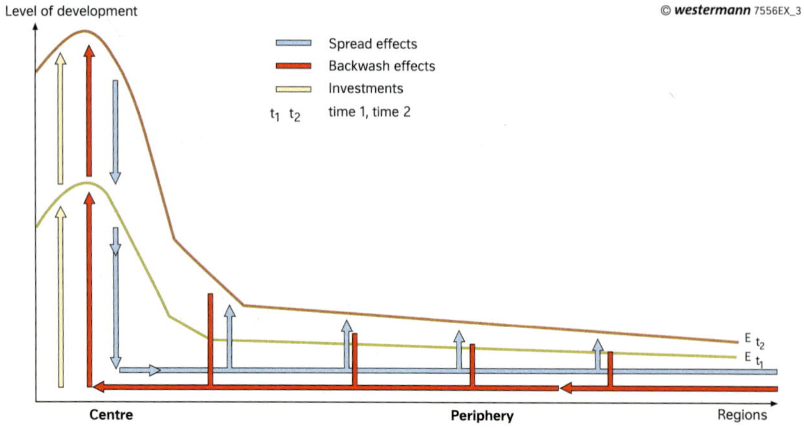

M1 The polarisation process (according to Myrdal)

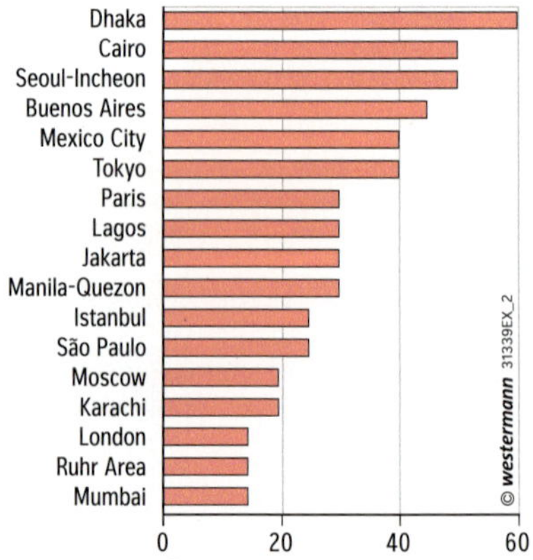

M4 Economic strength of agglomerations (in percent of national GDP) (2012)

The ongoing process of "unipolar" concentration is a matter of concern from an ecological and regional policy standpoint, but from a purely economic perspective it offers very great advantages as explained by the following "benefits of urbanisation":

- Close interaction of politics, administration and the economy
- Concentration of the headquarters of practically all large companies at the place where key decisions are taken
- Importance of personal communication ("face-to-face contact")
- Locational prestige
- Enhanced international competitiveness of the economy in respect of its ever higher level due to the concentration of top-ranking functions
- Availability of the greatest information density
- Site advantages in the heart of the largest and most differentiated labour and consumer market
- Transport hub with outstanding infrastructure
- Fascinating educational and cultural offerings
- Chances of economic and social advancement
- World city with its possibilities for encounters, pleasures of life and diversions

Source: Flüchter, W., Geographische Fragestellungen, Strukturen, Probleme. In: Länderbericht Japan. Bonn 1994, pp. 17 – 53

M5 Benefits of urbanisation

The metropolitan region around the South Korean capital city of Seoul (Seoul Metropolitan Area), comprising the cities of Seoul and Incheon as well as the province of Gyeonggi with its provincial capital of Suweon, has some 24 million inhabitants and forms the economic, political and cultural centre of the country. It is the home of the majority of large South Korean companies like Hyundai Corp, LG Group, Pantech Curitel and Samsung Group. Thanks to the international airport at Incheon, Seoul is an important hub for intercontinental transport to North America and Europe, and with the construction of an international cruise terminal the port of Incheon has developed into a centre for cruise ships in East Asia. In South Korea, as in Japan, this one-sided concentration on the capital city region has occurred at the cost of a lack of balanced development of the country.

Source: Feldhoff, T., Ostasien. Diercke Spezial, Braunschweig 2014, p. 89

M7 Unipolar concentration on Seoul

	1970	1990	2010
Seoul	5.5 (17.6%)	10.6 (24.4%)	10.1 (20.4%)
Gyeonggi Province	3.3 (10.7%)	8.0 (18.4%)	14.2 (28.7%)
SMA	8.9 (28.2%)	18.6 (42.8%)	24.3 (49.2%)
South Korea	31.4	43.4	49.4

Source: Diercke Spezial – Ostasien, Braunschweig 2014

M8 Population growth in the Seoul Metropolitan Area (SMA) in million (% = proportion of the national total)

	South Korea	City: Seoul	City: Busan	Province: Gyeonggi	Province: Gang-won	Province: Gyeong-buk
Population (in millions)	49.4	10.1	3.5	11.6	1.5	2.6
Area (in km²)	99,392	605 (0.6%)*	526 (0.5%)*	10,189 (10.3%)*	16,894 (17.0%)*	19,440 (19.6%)*
Population density (in inhabitants/km²)	497	16,613	6,589	1,136	88	135
GDP (in billion Won)	1,243	284 (22.8%)*	62,7 (5.0%)*	243 (19.6%)*	30,3 (2.4%)*	81 (6.5%)*
Disposable income/inhab. (in 1,000 Won)	14,472 (100.0)**	16,840 (116.4)**	14,844 (102.6)**	13,529 (93.5)**	11,122 (84.5)**	10,813 (82.2)**
Private consum/inhab. (in 1,000 Won)	13,160 (100.0)**	16,834 (127.9)**	13,064 (99.3)**	14,199 (107.9)**	12,525 (86.5)**	13,157 (90.9)**

(*proportion of national total; ** relative to country average); Source: Diercke Spezial – Ostasien, Braunschweig 2014

M6 Demographic and regional economic indicators in parts of South Korea and for South Korea in total (2011)

M9 Centres of economic activity

Marginalisation in megacities

Fragmentation – slum districts and gated communities in Buenos Aires

In megacities, rich and poor, integrated and excluded (disintegrated) populations often live in close proximity. This means that slums often arise immediately adjacent to economically active districts of the city. This occurs in many metropolises in the world. Here a special focus is placed on Latin American cities and in particular on Buenos Aires. What is the structure of the townscape? What socio-economic consequences are associated with it?

Ⓞ 1. Explain the causes and consequences of fragmentation in megacities against the background of globalisation (M3, M4, M7, M8).
A Produce a causal network.
B Write an essay in the style of an examination assignment.

2. Analyse the socio-economic structure of Buenos Aires (M2, M5, M6, M9).

3. Characterise the model of the Latin American city (M10).

4. Assess the applicability of the model of the Latin American city to Buenos Aires.

Ⓢ 5. Go on a virtual excursion (M1).

→ Fragmentation, Gated communities, Marginal settlement

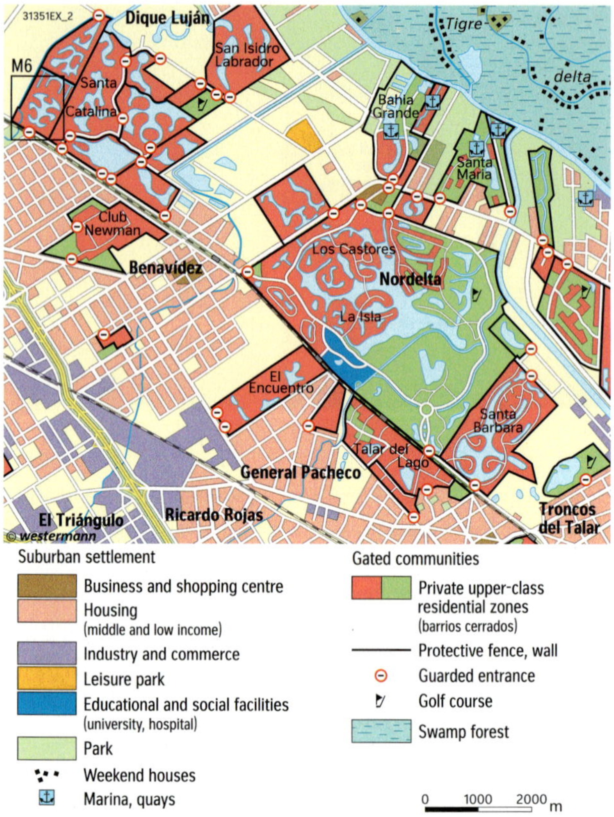

M2 Buenos Aires – segregation

Step 1: Select a Latin American megacity and search the city in the internet for gated communities and other features of a Latin American city.
Step 2: Use Diercke Globus, Google Earth or Google Maps and zoom in to the areas you are researching. Save the images of the areas.
Bonus: For many areas you can use Google Streetview.
Step 3: Produce a presentation. Tip: Introduce, as the first chart, an overview map of your selected city on which all your subsequent images can be located.

M1 Making a virtual excursion

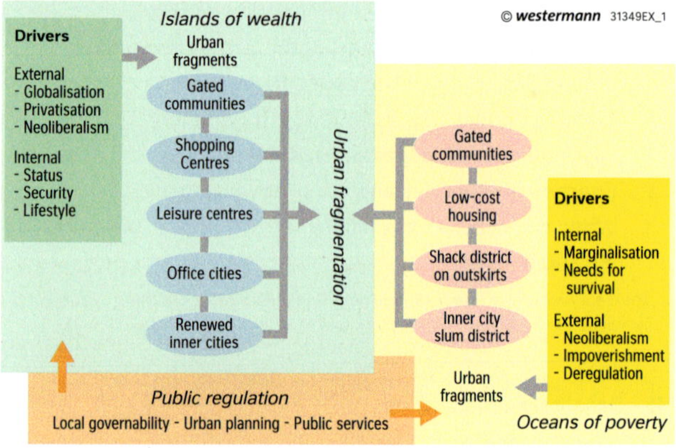

M3 Fragmented cities in developing countries (based on Scholz)

→ Fragmentation
occurs in urban quarters that are spatially segregated from one another with differing degrees of global integration. An indicator for fragmentation in many developing countries is the unequal provision of the population with public services (e.g. drinking water).

→ Gated communities
are closed residential facilities that are secured against unauthorised entry. They are marked by a combination of communal and individual ownership, self-administration and restricted access.

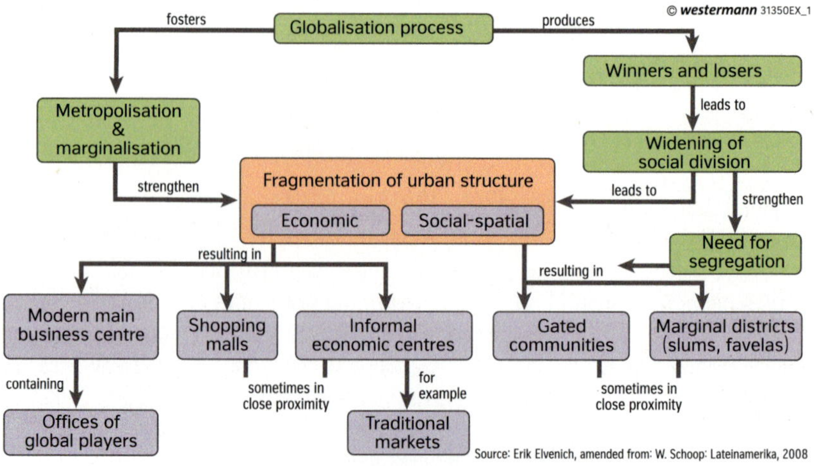

M4 Fragmentation of the urban structure depicted in a concept map

M5 Buenos Aires – social structure

M6 Upper-class residential area in Nordelta (from a height of 1 km)

M9 Lower-class district near the inner city (from a height of 1 km)

"[Megacities] not only have a high population but are also characterised by large-scale horizontal expansion, traffic chaos and infrastructural under-provision or non-provision. In social-spatial terms they are punctuated into fragmented districts. On the one hand there are islands of prosperity ("paradises"), isolated gated communities in the form of spatially closely confined, high-rise ("vertical paradises") and villa complexes ("no-entrance areas"), guarded and surrounded by walls or fences. And on the other side there are extensive oceans of poverty ("hells"), widespread shanty and slum districts ("no-go areas") which cannot be entered by outsiders on account of the dominating violence and criminality and which are not without dangers for the inhabitants themselves."

Source: Claaßen, K., Die Stadt. Diercke Spezial, Braunschweig 2012, p. 105.

M7 "Hells" and "paradises" (based on Scholz)

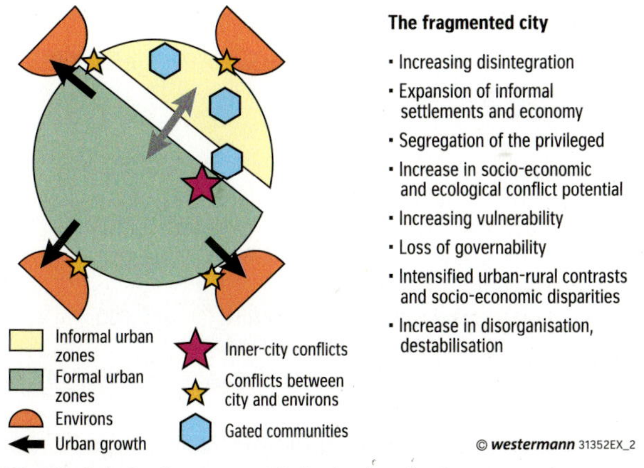

M8 Model of a fragmented city in developing countries

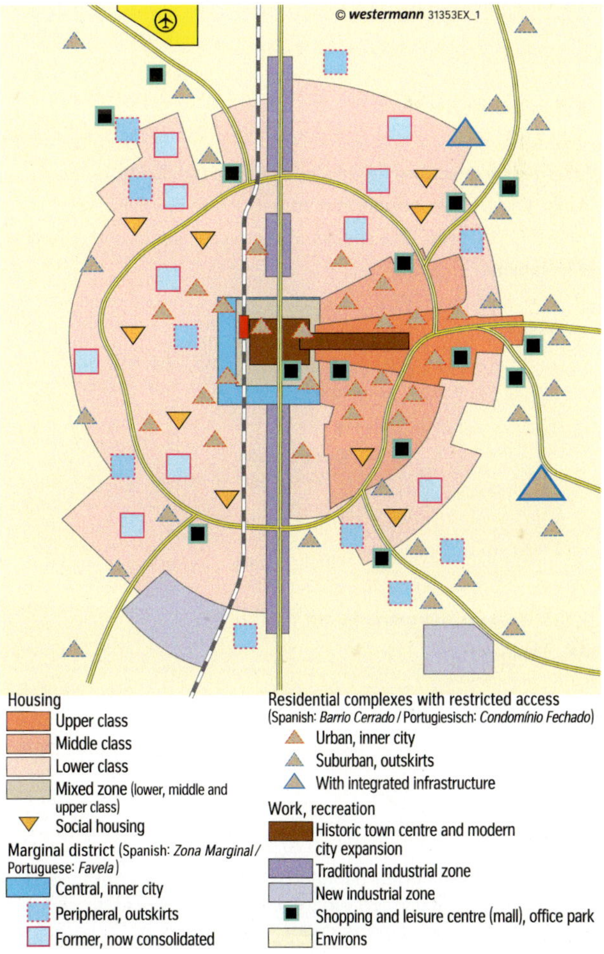

M10 Model of a Latin American city

Megacities – with high vulnerability

Threats from natural and anthropogenic dangers – Tokyo

Megacities worldwide have more in common with one another than with their own hinterlands. Through globalisation, a close interconnection has thus come about. This brings many advantages, but also dangers, because a catastrophic event in a megacity can also have an impact on the world economy.
But what are the specific dangers that threaten megacities? Why is it that megacities in particular are especially threatened? Are megacities in industrialised countries also endangered?

1. Produce a table of man-made hazards and environmental hazards that could threaten cities (M3, M4, M8).
2. Research in the Atlas and the internet whether other megacities are threatened by specific dangers.
3. The high degree of marginalisation also increases the vulnerability of megacities. Explain.
4. Explain the terms "natural event", "natural danger" and "natural disaster" (M1).
5. Illustrate Tokyo's vulnerability (M2, M3, M8, M10, M11).
6. "Megacities in developing countries – ticking social time bombs" was the title of a geographical article. Comment on this statement (M4).
7. Ⓢ It has frequently been planned to remove the capital city function from Tokyo and build a new capital with all ministries further in the country's interior. Evaluate this proposed idea (M3, M7, Atlas).

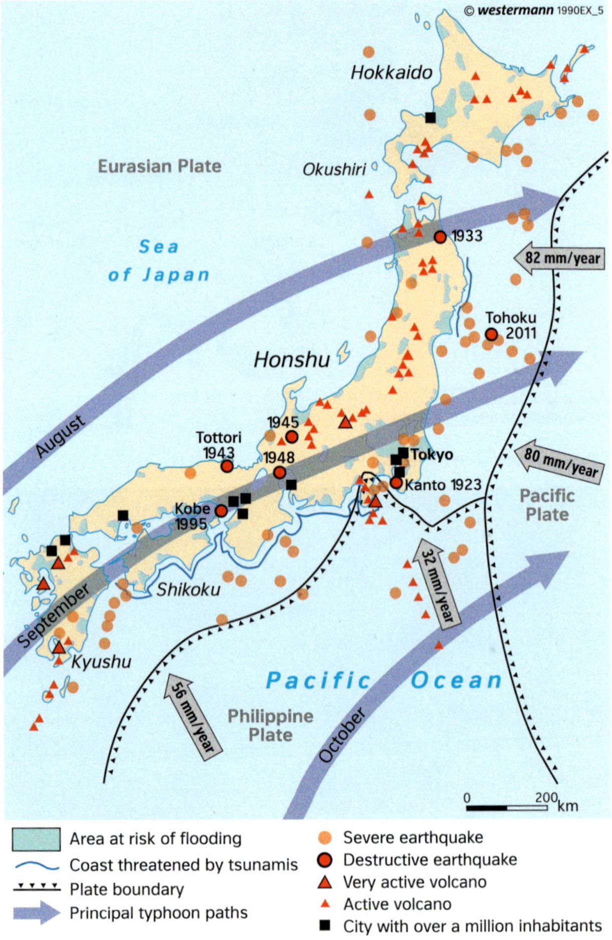

M3 Japan – natural risks

→ Vulnerability

→ Vulnerability
Vulnerability describes the susceptibility or sensitivity, or the risk of injury, of people, society and infrastructure in a living space and economic area. One speaks of ecological, social and technical vulnerability.

© westermann 31341EX_1

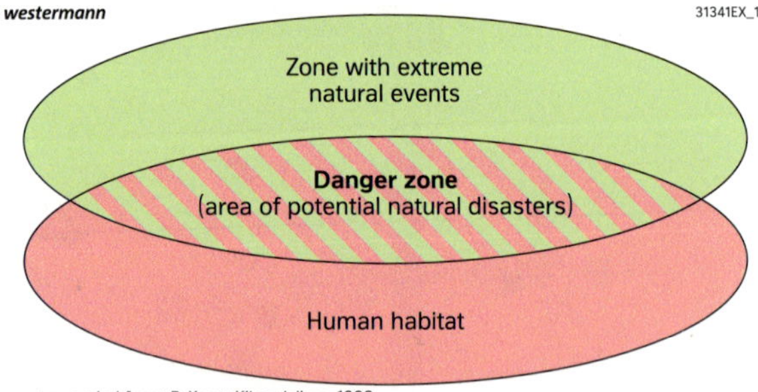

Source: amended from: P. Kunz: Klimarisiken, 1998

M1 Danger zone

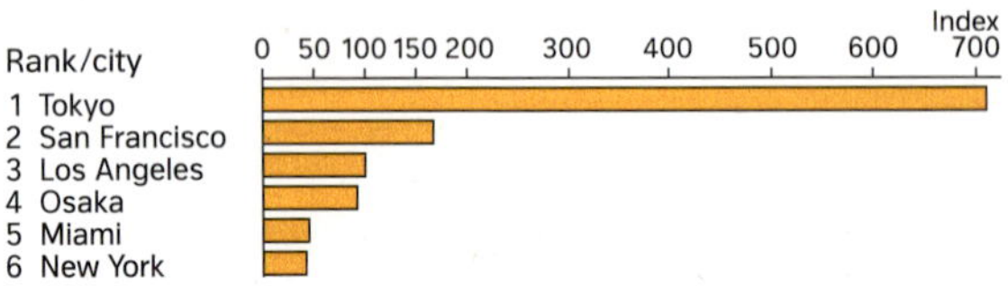

M2 Risk index of natural dangers by the Munich Reinsurance company. Natural dangers regarded as relevant are earthquakes (incl. tsunamis), storms, floods, volcanism, bush fires and frost.

Megacities are subject to global ecological, socio-economic and political change while at the same time decisively influencing it through their high development dynamic. Therefore they are mostly categorised as global risk areas, where natural dangers or a shortage of resources can have appalling consequences for large numbers of people. And risks from human causes, such as economic crises, emissions, industrial accidents, ethnic-religious conflicts or terrorism can also lead to global consequences reaching far beyond the affected megacity itself. [...]
But the fact is often neglected that, at the same time, profound transformation processes take place in megacities that can turn them into centres of innovation due to their high development dynamic as well as an often wide range of available human capital and globally-networked actors.
Source: Kraas, F., Megastädte. In: Gebhardt et al., Geographie, (2011), p. 881

M4 Vulnerability of megacities

Date	Event	Location	Damage (in million US$)	Deaths
11.03. 2011	Earthquake, tsunami	Japan, Fukushima	210,000	16,000
17.01. 1995	Earthquake	Hygogo Prefecture, Kobe, Osaka, Kyoto	100,000	6,430
01.09. 1923	Earthquake	Tokyo, Yokohama	2,800	143,800

M5 The three most costly earthquakes/tsunamis in Japan

M6 Tokyo with a view of Mount Fuji (Fujijama)

In Japan, one person in six lives in a coastal region that lies no more than five metres above sea level. Thus, 21.8 million out of 128 million Japanese people live in regions that would be more or less defenceless against a massive tsunami such as the one that occurred on 11 March 2011. [...] Complete resettlement is out of the question on account of Japan's mountainous topography. Only one-third of the country is habitable. The plains near the coasts offer themselves as ideal residential areas.

Source: Knüsel, J. In: Die Stadt. Diercke Spezial 2013, p. 104

M7 Tsunami risks in Japan

Because persons, values and infrastructure are concentrated into a confined space, megacities possess a very much higher potential for damages in comparison to rural areas. Even minor events can cause major damage. The breakdown of a vital commuter railway line in the morning rush hour in a metropolis such as Tokyo [...] can result in huge short-term chaos and massive losses in production. But the long-term risks are far more serious. Many megacities are literally predestined for major natural disasters. [...] Finally, megacities are also particularly vulnerable to one of the greatest dangers of our time – terrorism.

Source: Munich Re, in: Siedlungsräume. Diercke Spezial, 2005, p. 76

M8 Risk assessment by an insurance company

Date	Event	Location	Damage (in million US$)	Deaths
26-28. 09.1991	Typhoon Mireille (No. 19*)	Japan	10,000	62
06-08. 09.2004	Typhoon Songda (No. 18*)	Japan, Sth Korea	9,000	41
22-25. 09.1999	Typhoon Bart (No. 18*)	Japan, Sth Korea	5,000	29
17-22. 09.1998	Typhoons Viki and Waldo (Nr. 7/8*)	Japan	3,000	121

M9 The four most costly typhoons in Japan
(* Typhoon number within the given year)

Eight-lane urban motorways stacked one above the other, driving schools that have been forced to move up onto skyscraper roofs: for a European motorist the traffic in the Japanese metropolis of Tokyo seems positively absurd. Hours-long traffic jams are normal, and in order to be permitted to register a car it is required to show proof that one has a parking space.
Nowhere in the world does the European and American car industry motto, "bigger, faster, more powerful", seem so out of place as in Tokyo [...]. In this Asian conurbation the motorist can only drive at an average speed of 15 kilometres per hour. [...] Anyone who finds themselves caught up in the traffic of Japan's capital city can immediately understand why one cannot think in terms of size or speed records here. 36 million people live in an urban area where rental prices are dependent on closeness to the nearest railway station. In Tokyo, one in every four residents possesses a car. By comparison, in Hamburg it is one in two. But it is the difference in population density that reflects the special problem of Tokyo. The city has 20,500 inhabitants per square kilometre. In Hamburg it is only 2,300.

Source: www.welt.de, 14.11.2013

M10 Traffic in Tokyo

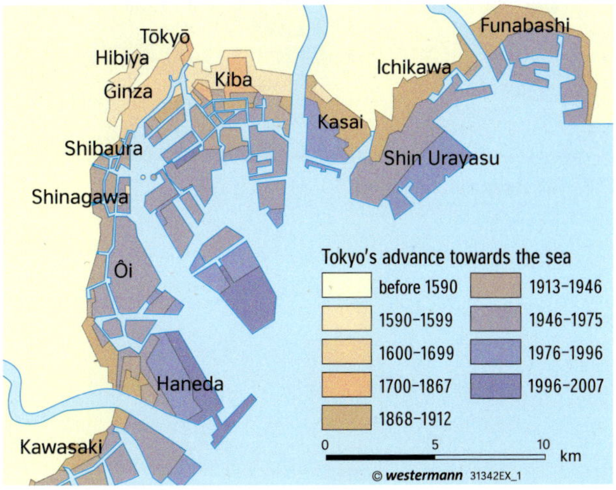

M11 Tokyo's advance towards the sea

Solution strategies in megacities and metropolises

The fields of action of traffic, emissions and marginalisation

"Social change and reform processes mostly begin in the big cities. In addition they are the bridgeheads to the globalised economy, and therefore also – at least in the ideal case – the points of connection for economic development." (Claaßen, K., 2013, p. 99)
What strategies are on offer?

Ⓞ **1. Analyse the different fields of action:**
A For the fields of action presented in this section, produce fact sheets describing the relevant fields of action in the form of keywords. Research further facts where necessary.
B Be an expert on a field of action and work collaboratively. Prepare the results in visual form (poster or presentation).
2. Research further facts on the presented fields of action in the internet. Note your results in the form of keywords.
3. Discuss the chances and risks of the presented fields of action.
Ⓢ **4. Formulate further possible fields of action which could be applied in future urban planning.**

→ Emission, Marginalisation, Megacity, Slum

M1 Toll station in Singapore

FIELD OF ACTION: TRAFFIC

Concept 1: Traffic minimisation in Ulaanbaatar / Mongolia

Today, the predominant mode of transport in the city is the individual car. Bus services are little used, and no other forms of public transport currently exist. [...] Already today, the road network is largely overloaded [...].
A particular problem in the future will be the traffic between the new residential areas [...]. Here, residential districts have come into existence for more than fifty thousand inhabitants with only two completely inadequate road links, which are already overloaded. There is currently a regulation in the city, according to which vehicles with certain numbers are not permitted to use the roads on certain specified days. The hope is that this will reduce traffic levels. (ulaanbaatar.de)

Thus, the first digit on the number plate determines the weekday on which the car may not be used (e.g. on Tuesdays, all plates beginning with a three must stay in their parking places). The consequence: rich Mongolians register a second car.

Source: http:// ulaanbaatar.de/12.html

M2 Traffic in Ulaanbaatar

Concept 2: Traffic minimisation in Singapore

For all those who venture onto the roads in Singapore, it beeps. Because nothing moves here without ERP, and certainly no traffic. The abbreviation stands for "Electronic Road Pricing", introduced in 1998, and the system costs the motorist money. Every car and every motorbike in this tropical city requires a chip card, the "Cash Card". And on all, absolutely all roads into the city centre and the majority of motorways, large gantries are installed with reading devices. When one drives underneath them, they automatically withdraw an amount of 50 cents, or sometimes more than one Singapore dollar (about half a euro), from the card. At that moment, a brief signal sounds in the car. When the inner city is full at peak periods, the cost goes up. "If you drive more you pay more" is the simple principle of the traffic authority. "But those who pay more can enjoy practically congestion-free roads", they say. At three in the morning, when nobody wants to go into town, entrance is free of charge. Every quarter of an hour, the authority measures traffic density and then calculates the price for entering the city. Signal boards in front of the gantries show the currently applicable charge. And one minute before the price falls, for example at ten in the morning, frugal Singaporean motorists are already awaiting their chance to drive into the city cheaper. When the amount remaining on the chip card falls below three dollars, a continuous beep starts to sound, reminding the driver to recharge his card. If he fails to do this, the number plate is photographed when he drives under the gantry, and a fine is levied. Thus, driving in Singapore becomes even more expensive than it already is on account of the high car registration fee which can double the purchase price of a car. But for all those who cannot afford a car, the city provides a cheap and very well developed public transport system.

Source: www.faz.net/aktuell/gesellschaft/singapur-gebuehren-werden-ueber-die-cash-card-abgebucht-1462845.htm, accessed 9.10.2014.

M3 Traffic in Singapore

FIELD OF ACTION: EMISSIONS

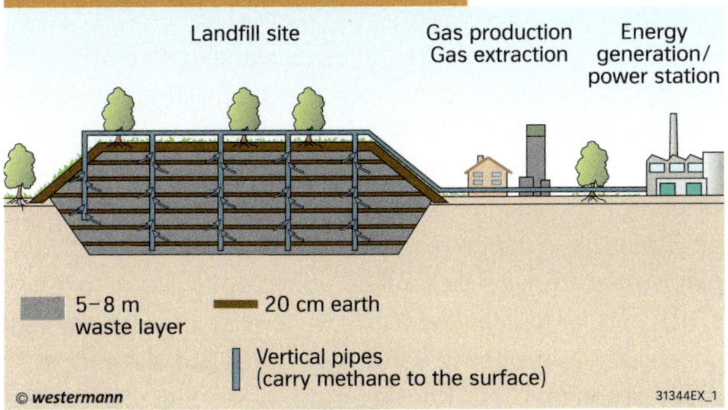

M4 Biogas extraction from landfill sites

Concept 1: Gas to Energy Project in São Paulo

The Bandeirantes Landfill Gas to Energy Project (BLFGE) aims to provide an environmental, social and financial solution to the release of landfill gas into the environment by utilizing this methane gas produced by the Bandeirantes landfill to generate electricity. The BLFGE is located in the metropolitan region of São Paulo. The people of São Paulo generate nearly 15,000 tons of waste daily. Half of this waste was disposed in the Bandeirantes landfill up until 2007, when the landfill was deactivated.

[...] In order to deal with the environmental dangers that resulted from methane emissions, Biogás proposed the "Bandeirantes Landfill Gas to Energy Project", which generates renewable energy through 24 engines with a capacity of 20 MW.

The Bandeirantes project is the largest landfill gas recuperation plant in the world with an annual generation of 170,000 MWh. Since the landfill stopped accepting waste in April 2007 the site has been remediated, covered over and planted with grass.

The current strategy is to extract methane gas until 2018. The collected biogas is sold as fuel to the Bandeirantes Thermoelectric power plant, a clean energy power plant that began its operations in 2003. The electricity generated through the project's biogas provides enough energy to supply 400,000 inhabitants per year.

Source: www.iclei.org, accessed 9.10.2014

M5 The BLBFGE project in São Paulo

Concept 2: Improved architecture

Urban areas are responsible for more than 70 percent of global energy consumption and CO_2 emissions, mostly from buildings, and over the next two decades an area roughly equal to 60 percent of the world's total building stock is projected to be built and rebuilt in urban areas. In light of this, the International Union of Architects (UIA) has made a significant move by pledging to phase out carbon emissions by buildings by 2050.

The pledge is captured in the 2050 Imperative which represents about 1.3 million architects in 124 countries worldwide.

The 2050 Imperative was initiated and drafted by Architecture 2030, a non-profit organisation whose mission is to rapidly transform the built environment from being a major contributor of greenhouse gas emissions to a central part of the solution to the climate and energy crises.

The action items in the 2050 Imperative are based in part on the recent "Roadmap to Zero Emissions" developed by Architecture 2030 and presented at the UN Climate Change Conference in Bonn in June 2014.

Source: www.newsroom.unfccc.int, 22.08.2014

M6 Architecture 2030

FIELD OF ACTION: MARGINALISATION

M7 The PSUP team

The Participatory Slum Upgrading Programme (PSUP)

Mrs Sommer, you are the head of the PSUP of UNHABITAT. What are the aims of this programme?

The PSUP has the aim of improving the living conditions of the marginalised population. The guiding principle of our programme is "halving the number of slum dwellers by 2020". This takes into account Millennium Development Goal 7 of the United Nations [editor's note: a significant improvement in the living conditions of at least 100 million slum dwellers by 2020]. The reason for the establishment of the programme was the rapid process of urbanisation which has led to increasing levels of urban poverty.

Who participates in the PSUP?

The programme is aimed at the African, Caribbean and Pacific countries. Since the establishment of the programme, 35 countries have developed over 50 development plans and strategies that include slum upgrading and prevention.

How does the PSUP work?

The PSUP is divided into three phases:

Phase 1 has the objective of creating motivation and a political will for slum upgrading. Coordination, cooperation and interchange are created between all the participating groups, politicians and residents, etc.

Phase 2 is aimed a setting a new political direction. This involves cooperation with non-governmental organisations (NGOs), community based organisations (CBOs), and directly with the slum population.

In Phase 3, pilot projects will be implemented that directly produce an improvement in the lives of the slum population. In addition, the responsibility for the slum upgrading process will be handed over more and more to the slum population so that they can implement the projects for themselves. [help for self-help]

What can one understand by "participatory"? Is it possible for the slum dwellers to participate in defining the aims and activities?

Yes, the PSUP fosters the 'bottom up' principle. Experience has shown that an important factor in the successful implementation of a project has been the participation of population groups from the slum dwellers or CBOs. These are brought into the planning and implementation. Therefore the projects in the various countries and regions are different and are aligned to the needs of the respective slum populations.

How long is it expected to take, or how long is it forecast that it will take to work through all the phases?

We normally aim to implement the programme in two to four years. This means that processes are initiated in such a way that they can continue on a sustainable basis.

M8 Interview with Kerstin Sommer (head of the PSUP project)

The essentials in brief

In the course of worldwide urbanisation a multiplicity of metropolises have emerged, especially in the developing and fast-developing countries. These metropolises become centres of gravity for both the economy and society. Often, primate cities develop that predominate over all other cities in the country in demographic and functional terms. Alongside an often high natural population growth, people are more and more drawn towards the cities owing to their growing importance. Push and pull factors interact with one another and lead to expansion of the cities through rural-urban migration.

Along with the process of metropolisation goes a process of marginalisation, because not every person can acquire a formal job and/or accommodation. Such people have no, or only very little, participation in the formal social, economic and political life of the metropolis. They are increasingly marginalised, and organise themselves on an informal basis. This leads to changes in the townscape. Marginal districts emerge in which infrastructural deficiencies exist. Conversely, the more affluent social groups sometimes cut themselves off and set up gated communities. Often, marginal districts and gated communities are in close proximity to each other and are scattered throughout the city area. A growing fragmentation occurs. Globalisation reinforces this fragmentation, because the disparities in the townscape between the main business districts of the global players and the marginalised districts become more extreme.

Frequently, marginal districts grow up in unsuitable areas where formal building permission would never have been granted. These danger zones could be for example in flood-plains near to rivers or on mountain slopes prone to land-slides. Settlements in these areas increase the vulnerability of the city. Metropolises and megacities are vulnerable in many respects. They often lie on the coasts, especially at the mouths of rivers. Due to their situation, many metropolises and megacities are subject to natural dangers which, on account of their high population density and the associated potential for damage, can have disastrous consequences. But the process of metropolisation also increases the dangers from human causes. Thus, megacities are today categorised as risk areas. Strategies are required for solutions to cushion this vulnerability. This chapter has shown that the problems and solutions are many-sided, and at the same time difficult. But the fact cannot be ignored that metropolises and megacities possess a great innovative and economic potential which will play an ever greater role, especially in the increasing process of globalisation.

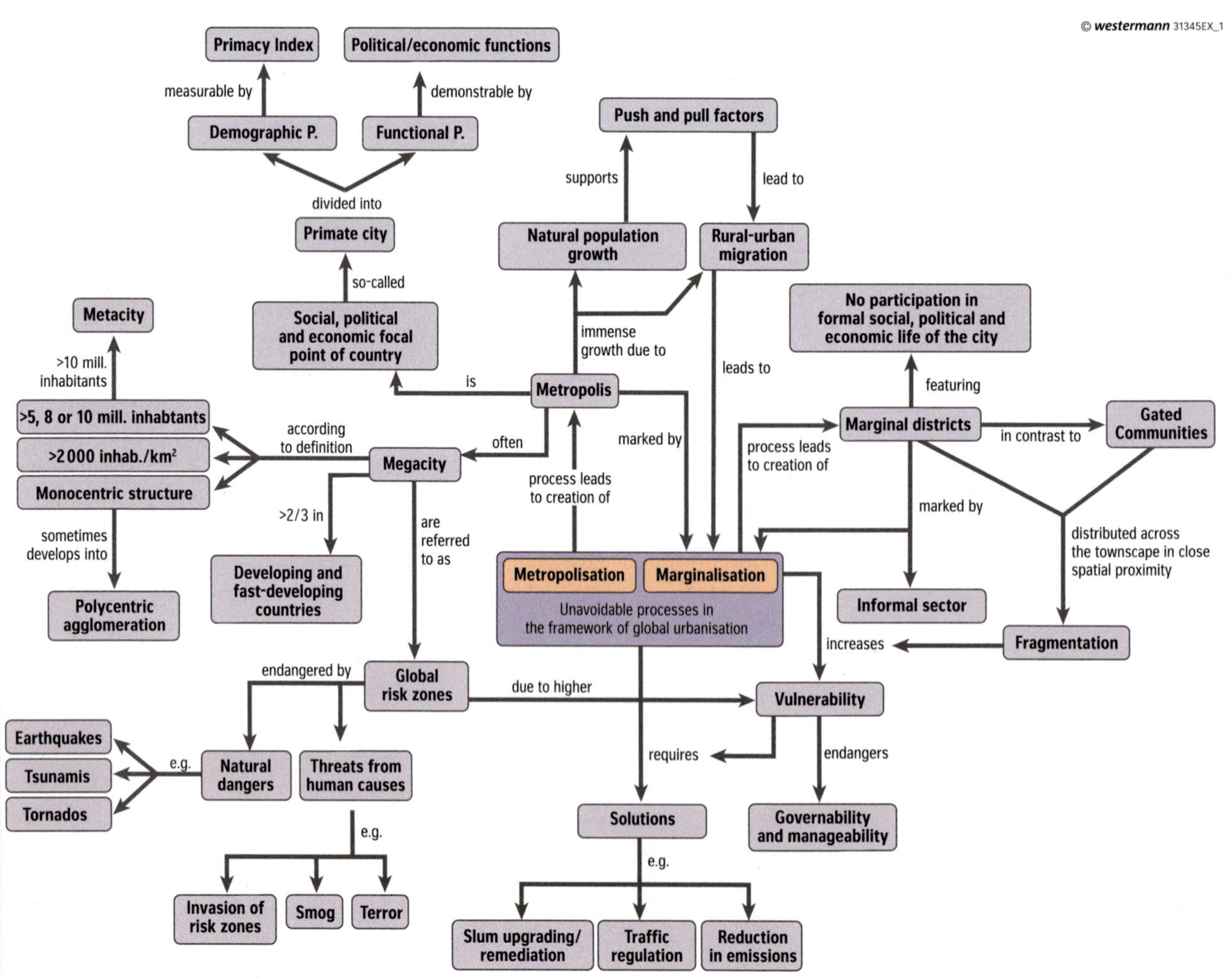

M1 Suggestion for a concept map summarising the topic

Skill Check

All the skills that you were able to acquire in this chapter are listed here.
You can judge for yourself if you have mastered each skill: ***securely***, ***moderately*** or ***barely***.

Explanatory skills

Can I ...		Unsure? Look it up on these pages
1.	illustrate the emergence of megacities as a result of rural-urban migration?	160/161
2.	illustrate rural-urban migration with reference to push and pull factors?	160/161
3.	illustrate metropolisation as a process of concentration of the population, economy and high-ranking functions?	162/163
4.	outline the increasing spatial and social marginalisation of cities in developing and fast-developing countries?	164/165
5.	explain local fragmentation as a process reinforced by globalisation?	164/165
6.	systematise geographical processes and structures by means of a content-related network of technical terms?	158–169, especially 169

Methodological skills

Can I ...		
7.	orient myself with the aid of physical and thematic maps and digital mapping services?	158–169
8.	identify problem-related geographical facts and independently develop corresponding questions and hypotheses about metropolisation and marginalisation processes?	158–169
9.	use complex presentation and working materials (maps, images, statistics, graphics and text) to assess hypotheses about metropolisation and marginalisation processes?	158–169
10.	use correct terminology to outline more complex geographical facts about marginalisation and metropolisation processes in a differentiated way, orally and in writing?	158–169
11.	substantiate written and oral statements with differentiated and correct references to materials and citations?	158–169
12.	outline complex geographical information in graphical form?	172

Evaluation skills

Can I ...		
13.	discuss the opportunities and risks posed by concrete measures for the development of urban areas, such as e.g. slum upgrading or combating emissions?	168/169
14.	discuss the problem of the increasing ecological and social vulnerability of urban agglomerations in connection with advancing metropolisation and marginalisation?	166/167
15.	evaluate measures for sustainable urban development, such as e.g. the problem of waste disposal or the reduction of emissions?	168/169

Activity skills

Can I ...		
16.	present the results of your work in a way that is factual, problem-oriented and appropriate to the target group using appropriate terminology?	158–169
17.	develop differentiated solutions for the problem of metropolisation and marginalisation?	168/169

Examination training

Problems of megacities – the example of Lagos (Nigeria)

1. Locate Lagos and characterise the importance of the city.
2. Analyse the causes and consequences of migration into Lagos.
3. Evaluate the opportunities and risks for the future development of Lagos.

These additional materials are required to complete the assignment:

M1 Atlas maps of your choice

Gross national income per capita	1,200 US-$
Population of Nigeria	162,471,000
Growth rate of Nigeria ****	2.5%
Largest cities	
Lagos (2011)	11.22 mill.
Ibadan (2010) *	5.18 mill.
Benin City (2010) *	2.41 mill.
Kano (2010) *	2.10 mill.
Population density in certain urban areas of Lagos (inhab./km²) ***	some 30,000
Population density of Berlin (inhab./km²) ***	3,800
HDI (2012)*	0.471 (rank 153)
Persons living in slum districts in Lagos ***	50-70%
Informal occupation in Lagos **	69%
Households in poverty in Lagos ***	53%

Source: Fischer Weltalmanach, *Wikipedia, **URBAN21; ***bpb.de; **** Census.gov

M2 Structural data of Lagos and Nigeria (2011)

The number of people who actually live in the city in the Gulf of Guinea is not known. Every day, people stream into Lagos from the surrounding areas in the hope of finding work and a better future for themselves and their families. But the constant growth in the population – a real hyper-growth – is bringing the city and its infrastructure to the point of collapse. [...] Life in Lagos – both private and public – positively spills out onto the streets. The life of the city is played out in the market places and along the roads: immediate, chaotic, exhausting.

[...] Following the privatisation of waste disposal and the drinking water supply, neither of these function properly, or even at all. The environmental and health problems are constantly increasing and hit the poorest first. And in Lagos, as in the whole of Nigeria, the brain drain prevails.

Source: www.bpb.de/internationales/weltweit/megastaedte/64606/lagos?p=all; accessed 09.10.2014

M4 Source text on Lagos

Year	Lagos	Nigeria	Degree of urbanisation
1950	9.74%	no data	no data
1980	6.61%	no data	no data
1990	5.82%	no data	no data
2000	5.13%	2.24%	43.9%
2010	3.26%	1.95%	52.2%
2020*	no data	1.58%	59.3%

Source: Federal Agency for Civic Education; * Forecast

M5 Population growth of Lagos and Nigeria

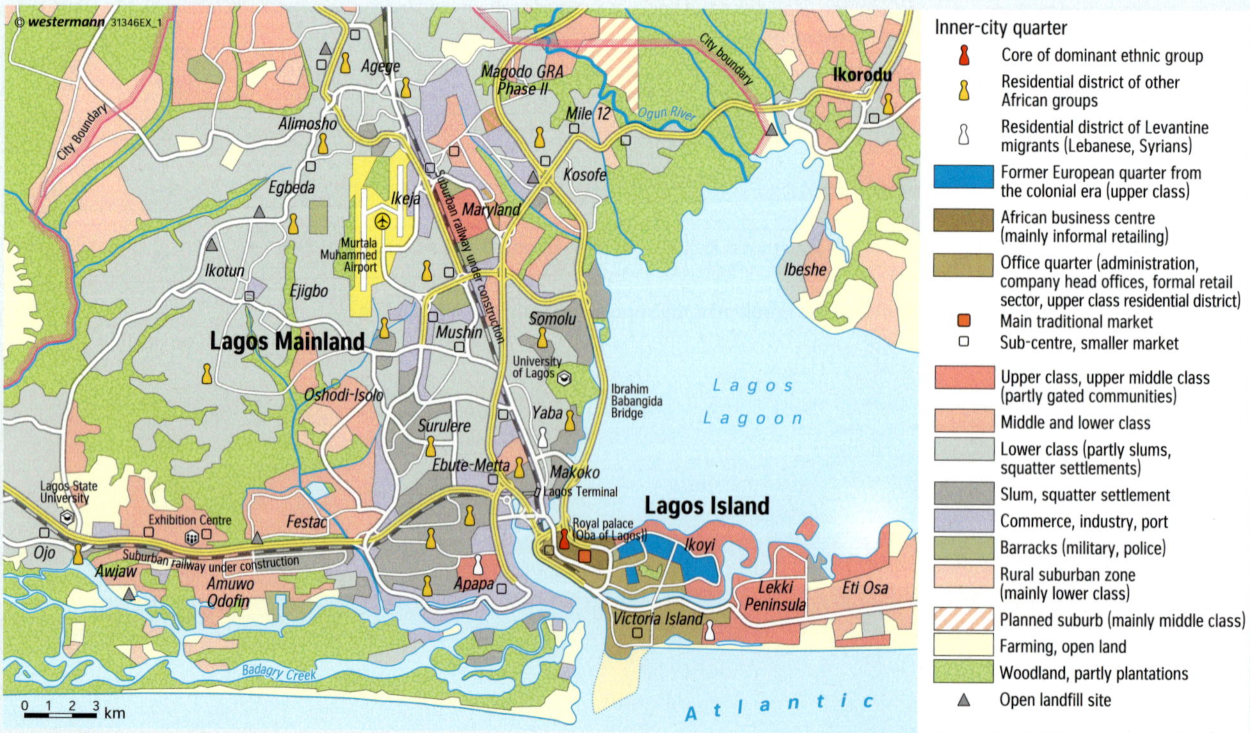

M3 Lagos – urban structure

M6 Impressions of Lagos

An explosion in a pipeline in the Nigerian metropolis of Lagos has killed at least 850 people. The site of the accident is covered with charred corpses and more and more victims are being counted, said a Red Cross spokesman. [...] According to eye-witness accounts, two bands of thieves triggered the explosion, when one after the other they both drilled into the same pipe in order to illegally siphon off the highly-inflammable fuel.

Source: www.stern.de/panorama/:Pipeline-Explosion--850-Tote-Flammeninferno/579328.html, 26.12.2006

M7 Pipeline explosion in Lagos

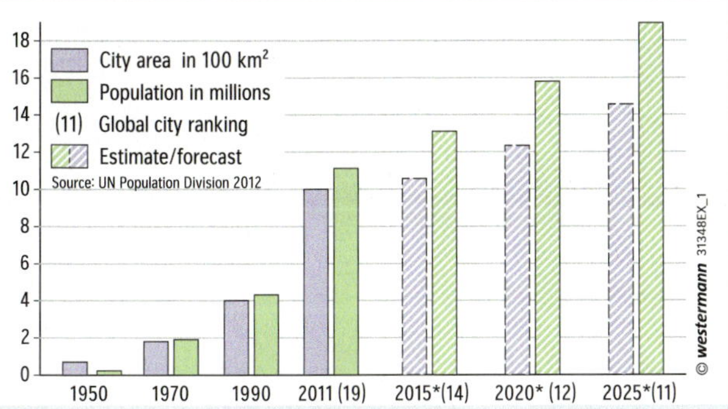

M8 Development of population and city area, Lagos

- Nigeria's financial and banking centre
- Possesses three ports: largest transshipment point for imports to Nigeria
- International airport at Ikeja
- Location for many industries (including Volkswagen)
- Location for universities and colleges as well as research institutes

M10 The importance of Lagos

The metropolitan region of Lagos has no overall city government. [...] The informal sector accounts for a large part of the economy. The people who stream into Lagos from the surrounding areas build more and more informal settlements. The building activity is spontaneous. In the same way, the people are forced out by the government, without warning and without alternatives. [...] And even life in the sheltered luxury settlements does not make the Moloch outside the door disappear.

Source: www.bpb.de/gesellschaft/staedte/megastaedte/64606/lagos?p=all; accessed 09.10.2014

M11 Megacity problems in Lagos

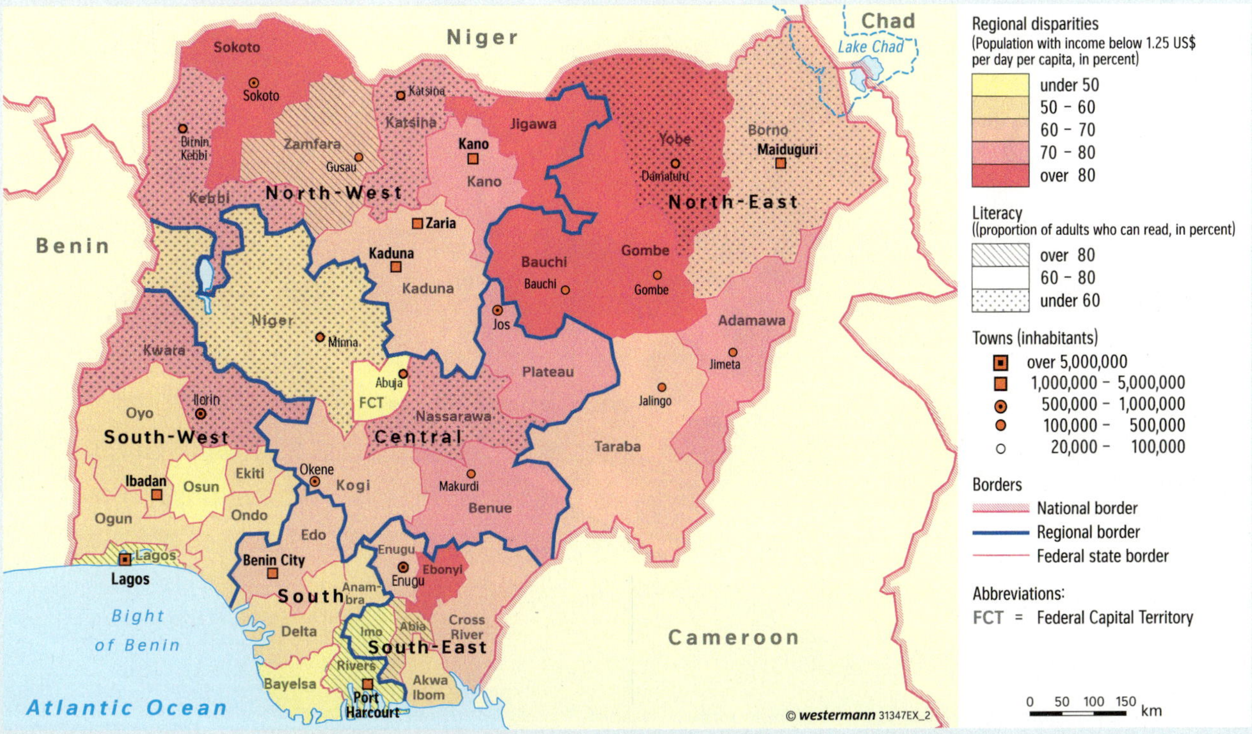

M9 Nigeria – differences in development

VII The city, a good place for all to live in?

Problems and strategies for future-oriented urban development

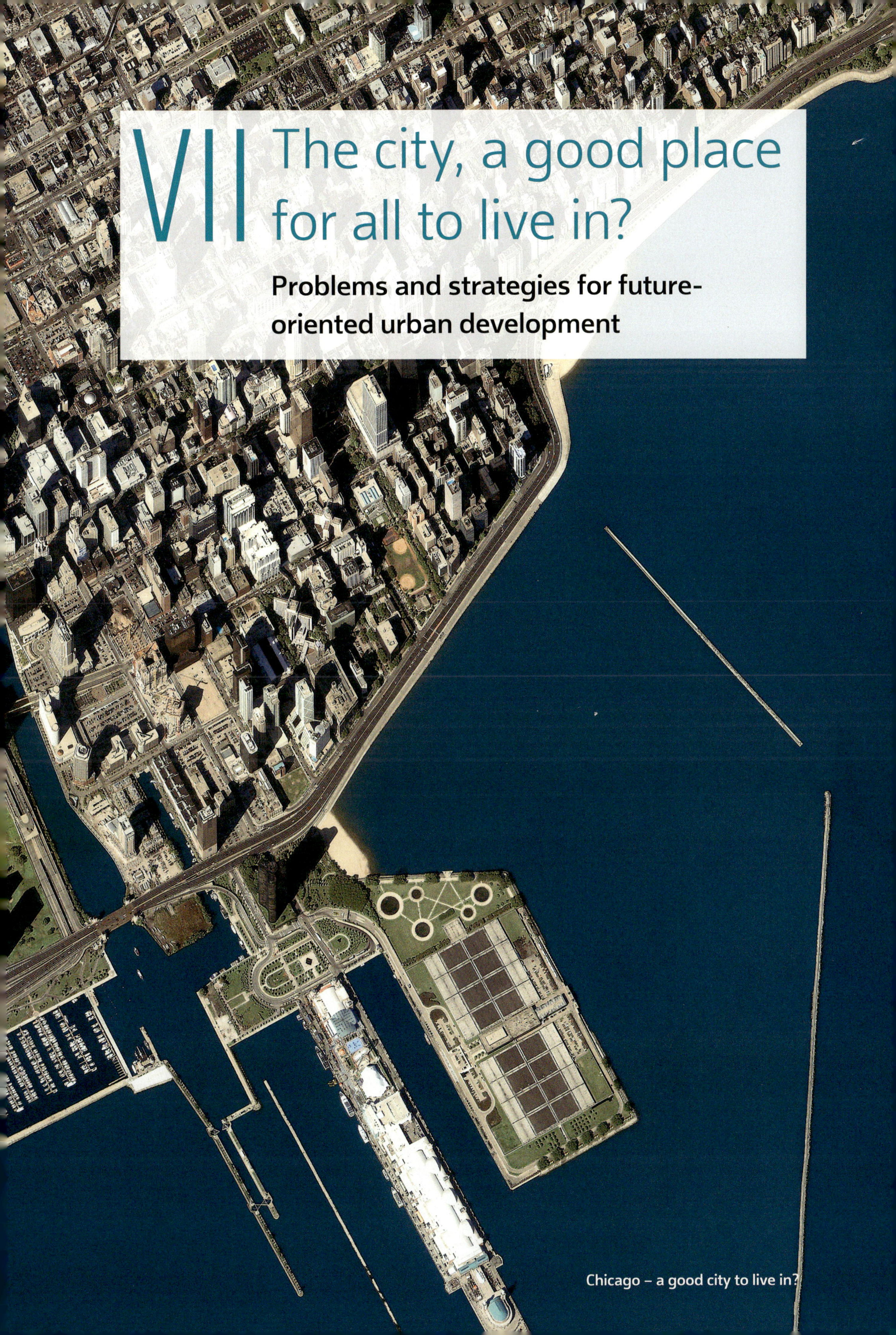

Chicago – a good city to live in?

The city as living space: different demands – different functions

weblink

- Denkwerk Zukunft lebenswerte Stadt

Cities provide a living space for many people, and must fulfil many functions in order to live up to the demands placed on that living space. Not all cities are equally successful in this. Two tendencies can be observed worldwide. There are cities that are experiencing inward migration, i.e. that are growing, and cities whose population is in decline because many inhabitants are moving away. In other words, the needs of the inhabitants are fulfilled or – at least for a part of the population – not fulfilled. Cities in China, for example, are recording extreme growth rates due to internal migration, while extreme decline is experienced by, for example, the city of Detroit in the USA.

Depending on the country and population group, the needs that a city must fulfil can be different. In studies on the quality of life in cities, the following criteria are often analysed: political stability, criminality, economic conditions (jobs), freedom of the individual and the press, health care provision, the education system, housing, environmental pollution, electricity and water supply, the telephone and transport network as well as the availability of food and also recreational facilities. However it must be said that a ranking of cities based on these criteria may not be of decisive relevance for the individual, because his or her personal living situation, for example unemployment, may result in poor quality of life in a city that is otherwise regarded as a good place to live.

How does the state seek to intervene to manage the situation? How can the needs of all the inhabitants of a city be taken into account? What problems must be solved and with what strategies can future-oriented urban development be achieved? That is what this chapter is about. But it is also about the evaluation of different strategies and the involvement of the inhabitants in the planning process. As the foundation "Denkwerk Zukunft" has formulated in its principles: "Cities in future [will be] even more strongly dependent than before on the involvement of their citizens, [and] those with political responsibility [must] bring these fully into the processes of shaping the city. Citizens must once again perceive their cities as what they really are: the living space that they must shape and for which they are responsible" (www.denkwerkzukunft. de). How can this be achieved?

Finally, the chapter will go into the question of how far one can inform oneself, with the aid of digital media, on whether or not a city or a district of a city can fulfil one's personal needs.

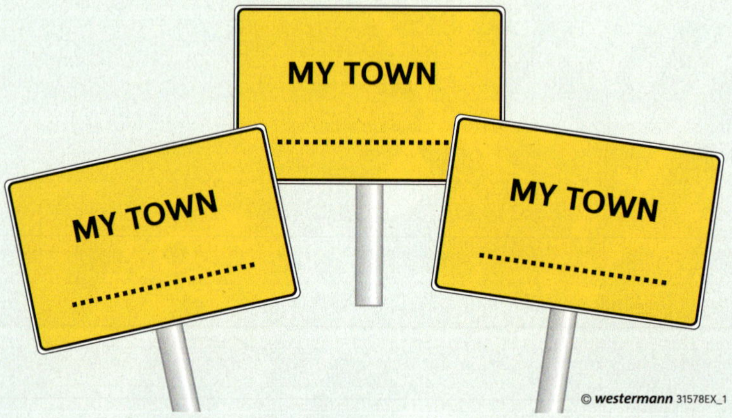

M1 Urban visions

M2 Detroit

M3 Freiburg

M4 Cartoon

M6 Cartoon

Lass uns gehen – Revolverheld (23.9.2014)

Hallo, hallo
Bist du auch so gelangweilt,
Genervt und gestresst von der Enge der Stadt
Bist du nicht auch längst schon müde
der Straßen, der Menschen, der Massen
Hast du das nicht satt?

Ich kann nicht mehr atmen
Seh kaum noch den Himmel
Die Hochhäuser haben meine Seele verbaut
Bin immer erreichbar und erreiche doch gar nichts
Ich halte es hier nicht mehr aus
[...]
Die Stadt frisst die Ruhe
Mit flackernden Lichtern
Schluckt Tage und Nächte in sich hinein
Gehetzte Gesichter in der drängelnden Masse
Jeder muss überall schnell sein
[...]
Lass uns hier raus
[...]
Lass uns gehen, lass uns gehen, lass uns gehen
[...]

M5 Song text by the German band Revolverheld

Towns and cities

The German language only has one word for an urban settlement: "Stadt". English has two words – "town" and "city" – whereby the distinction between them is a matter of debate. It may be a question of size: a city is usually larger than a town. Or it may be a question of function: in England a town with a cathedral is defined as a city, even when its population is small. The capital of a nation is normally a "city", not a "town". Or it may be a question of legal status: a town may become a city by obtaining a royal charter. In the USA, the definition of "city" is a matter of state law and varies widely from state to state.

In this chapter, the word "town" may be used in the context of historical town development and to distinguish urban settlements from "villages". The word "city" is mainly used for the discussion of particularly large cities like London (p. 178) or New York (p. 194), or in the context of modern global urbanisation trends and the growth of megacities.

1. Draft an urban vision for "your" town or city.

2. Give reasons why the town or city in which you live is good to live in or not good to live in for you personally.

3. According to statistics, Suhl and Greiz are towns with high outward migration rates while Munich and Potsdam are towns or cities with high inward migration rates.
   a) Locate the cities named (Atlas).
   b) To which town or city would you like to move or not like to move? Give reasons.

4. a) Compare the cartoons in terms of their statements and how these are presented (M4, M6).
   b) Comment on the way the problem is outlined in the cartoons.

Ⓢ **5.** Plan a district of a town or city that is "good to live in" for all population groups. Draw a plan of this district with explanatory legends.

Former port areas – problems and perspectives

The revitalisation of London's East End

What was formerly the largest port in the world finally lost its function in the 1980s due of the development of container ships, which were unable to sail up the Thames on account of their size. Already in the preceding decades, the textile industry had moved away and many port facilities had migrated down-river. In the adjoining East End, the working-class district in the boroughs of Tower Hamlets and Hackney, hundreds of thousands of workers lost their means of existence – 58,000 between 1971 and 1981 alone. The area was condemned to decline. At the same time, an area of 22 square kilometres of former port land became derelict. Can urban development cope with such a situation?

1. Locate London's Docklands and describe the history of Docklands up to the time of its decline.
2. Illustrate social segregation in London with reference to London's East End (Atlas, M3, M4).
3. Explain the revitalisation measures in London's Docklands (M2, M6–M9).
4. Analyse further strategies for the revitalisation of London's East End (M1, M5, M10–M12).
5. Ⓢ Comment on the social impact of the measures (M12).

→ Revitalisation, Segregation

M2 West India Docks (part of today's Docklands) in 1962

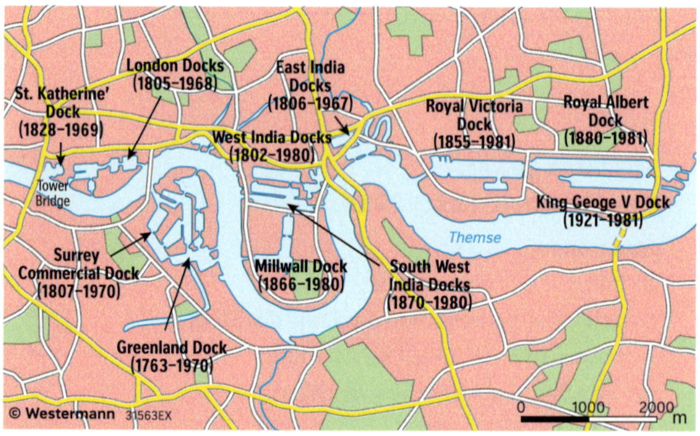

M3 London's historical Docklands

The East End of London: For many years it was a place of horror with undertones of damnation of the most extreme kind. And no wonder. Here, after all, was where Dorian Gray sinned at will and went unpunished, while the as yet unidentified Jack the Ripper was murdering prostitutes in the foggy nights [...]. For centuries, London exiled everything that was unwanted into that no man's land outside the eastern walls of the city. The wind blew towards the east, so please put everything there that is dirty and smells bad – whether industries or immigrants.

"When I arrived in the East End and opened my first restaurant, everybody shook their heads. Who lives here apart from immigrants and artists? None of them have any money," says master chef Nuno Mendes. His first restaurant went bankrupt, but the man from Portugal stayed on. His second restaurant, the Viajante at the Town Hall Hotel in Bethnal Green, which has been awarded a Michelin star, is fully booked every day [...]. "Here in those days was like New York in the 1980s. Firstly the artists were followed by money, and then came the tourists. People were curious about us. And now we are all profiting from it." [...] The East End is no longer only the part of London with the highest density of artists, [...] now it has also become the new culinary stronghold of Britain's capital city.

Source: Alpsten, E., Der lockende Stern des Jesus von Nazareth, www.faz.net, 01.03.2014, accessed 09.09.2014

M1 London's East End

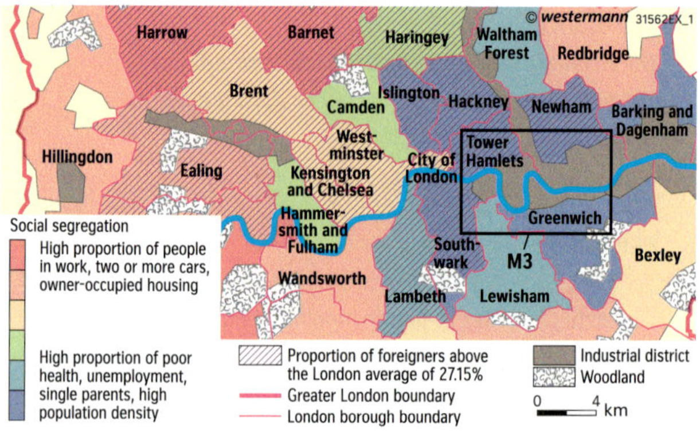

M4 Social segregation in London's boroughs (section)

"With the growth in the importance of the production-oriented and business-to-business service sector, and the decline in the importance of the industrial sector, a considerable social change takes place in the cities. On the one hand there are the well-paid jobs in globally operating companies. Yuppies ("Young Urban Professionals"), Dinks ("Double Income, no Kids") and Bobos ("Bourgeois Bohemians") are the abbreviated names for the new urban elites who are active in an international job market and can attain a high income. On the other side are the losers in this process, the old working class stratum, which has lost out in terms of political and economic influence. [...]

Source: Fassmann, H., Stadtgeographie I, Braunschweig 2009

M5 The city as a deindustrialised management centre

M6 London's Docklands today

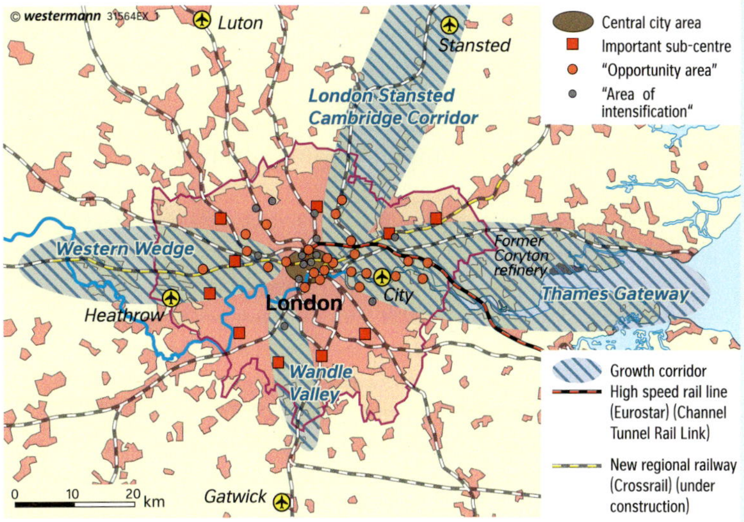

M11 The London Plan (Greater London Authority)

"Why not convert the warehouse into a back office for Credit Suisse First Boston [...]?"
"How about the Isle of Dogs as a front-office location, [...] a state-of-the-art solution to the bank's accomodation problem?"

Source: London – von der Hauptstadt des British Empire zur Alpha-Global-City

M7 He had an idea: Michael von Klemm, investment banker (1935–1997)

England is cleaning up its biggest ruin. The entire area of what was once the most powerful port in the world is being turned upside down and refurbished – an area of 22 square kilometres, eight-and-a-half times larger than the square mile of the City of London. [...] The port [...] is suddenly blossoming as an "urban development area". An incomparable urban district is emerging, with smart apartments in old warehouse buildings, skyscrapers for high finance, an airport, fast river boat connections and an underground rail link to the city [...].

Source: Krüger, K.-H., Der Spiegel, 04.08.1986

M8 Newspaper article: Wall Street on the river

Now the wider area of Canary Wharf is one of London's two main financial centres and is home to the likes of Barclays, HSBC and KPMG.
The 97-acre estate got its name from the fact that many of the imports which arrived there in the past when it was a dock were from the Canary Islands.
Around 15 million square feet of office and retail space now exist on the site, with the first tenants arriving in 1991. Now, more than 93,000 people work there.

Source: www.dailymail.co.uk

M9 Canary Wharf as a financial centre

London [is...] the most important financial centre in Europe and beside New York the most important financial centre in the world. In comparison to the financial centres of New York, Shanghai or Tokyo, whose importance is largely derived from their domestic economies, London profits from its global orientation and the European market. [...] With a share of 7.9 percent in value creation, the financial sector in Great Britain is of major economic importance in international comparison. The financial industry makes a disproportionate contribution to the country's tax income. [...]

Source: Federal Foreign Office

M10 The financial centre of London

taz: [...]***The former left-wing Mayor, Ken Livingstone, had sold [the 2012 Olympic Games in London] to the IOC as an opportunity to do something for the East End of London, the last great area of poverty in the inner city. One spoke again and again of the "legacy" of the Games. What remains of this now?***

Michael Edwards: Today a whole range of things are presented as results of the Games that actually have nothing to do with them, for example the improved public transport in the east of the city or the shopping centre in Stratford. These were all planned long before London was selected for the Games. The main actual result is the Olympic Park [...].

taz: ***Instead of an improvement in conditions, many people feared that the poor would be driven out of the East End, i.e. gentrification.***

The area is indeed facing strong pressure from gentrification. House prices and rents rose sharply before and after the Olympic Games. Added to this is the policy pursued by Newham, the borough in which the Olympic Park is situated. Although Labour is in charge there, the town hall has concentrated on attracting more and more people with higher incomes into the borough. [...] This is an extreme case, but the tendency is going in the same direction in other Labour-run boroughs, for example in neighbouring Hackney or in Greenwich. By contrast the Labour-run council of Tower Hamlets, also in the East End, is seeking to foster the construction of social housing. [...]

taz: ***Where do the poorer segments of the population go when they can no longer afford to live in the East End? Do they simply move out farther east, to Barking and Dagenham?***

In some cases. Some also move out of London completely. Others live in overcrowded apartments. There are even individual cases where residents share the beds: One sleeps at night, the other during the day ...

taz: ***... like the so-called "Schlafburschen" (sleeping lodgers) in Berlin at the time of industrialisation ...***

... yes, the horrors of the 19th century are coming back. [...]

Interview: Reeh, M., Alles ist außer Kontrolle, www.taz.de, accessed 09.09.2014

M12 Interview with London urban planner Michael Edwards

Population loss and solution concepts

Wittenberge – a shrinking town
Problem-solving through clearance

"Firstly we must recognise that we are shrinking. And then we must try to turn it into a culture," says an urban architect in Wittenberge. This is easier said than done, because Wittenberge is shrinking continually. Some 18,000 inhabitants still live here, but within five years there will be 2,000 to 3,000 fewer according to projections. There are more than enough places to live, but many dwellings stand empty. The vacancy rate gives rise to costs. Therefore an urban renewal concept was developed that won first prize in a nationwide competition in 2002. Since then the urban renewal has commenced. How far can the concept counteract the shrinkage process?

1. Analyse population development in Wittenberge and its effects (M4, M1).
2. Give reasons for the development of the age structure (M5).
3. Discuss the urban renewal concept using the example of the Allende Quarter (M2, M3, M6 – M8).
4. Ⓞ Formulate an opinion on the urban renewal concept in the form of a reader's letter:
   - A Express the standpoint of a young person from the Allende Quarter (M6, M7, M9).
   - B Adopt the perspective of a family (M6, M7, M9).
5. The former oil mill was converted into a high-class hotel. This is an example of the repurposing and renovation of old building fabric. Discuss the possibility of renovation of old towns as an urban renewal concept for reducing outward migration.
6. Ⓢ Produce a presentation on the concrete slab blocks in socialist urban construction in the former GDR (Internet).

→ Clearance, Demographic change, Shrinking city, Shrinking process

M2 Allendestraße in the Allende Quarter before clearance

M3 Clearance in the Allende Quarter. Every empty apartment costs an average of 633 € per year in upkeep.

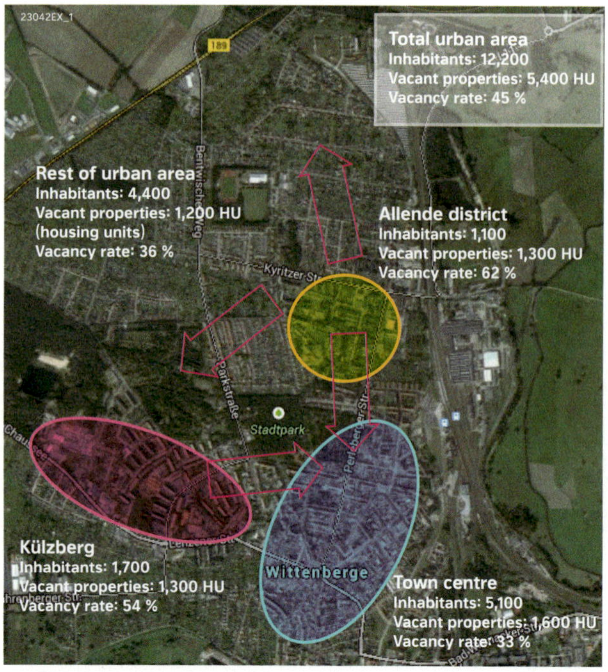

M1 Scenario without clearance, 2030 (HU = housing unit)

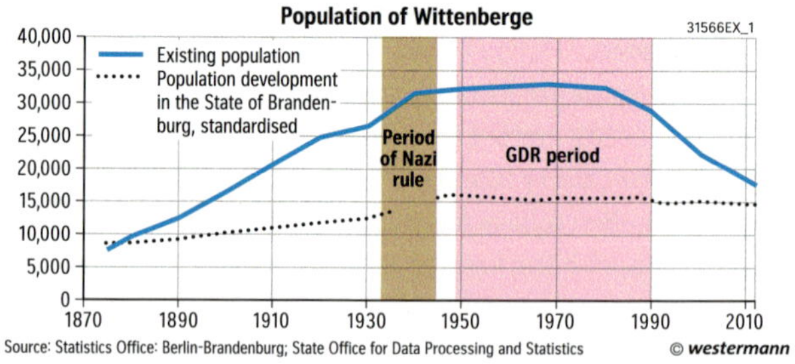

M4 Population development in Wittenberge

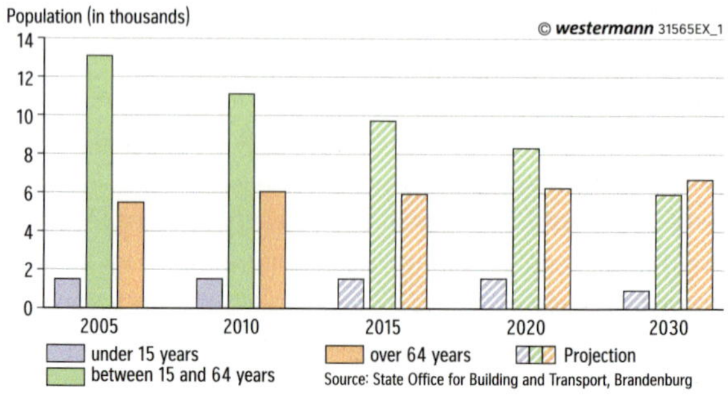

M5 Development of the age structure of Wittenberge

Description of the Allende Quarter

- Named after the socialist President of Chile
- Estate of concrete slab apartment blocks
- 2,000 inhabitants
- Average age 65 years
- High vacancy rate (2012: 364 housing units = 21%)

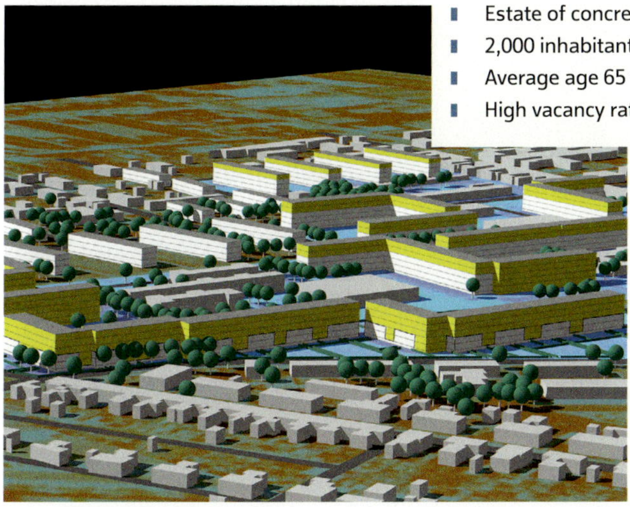

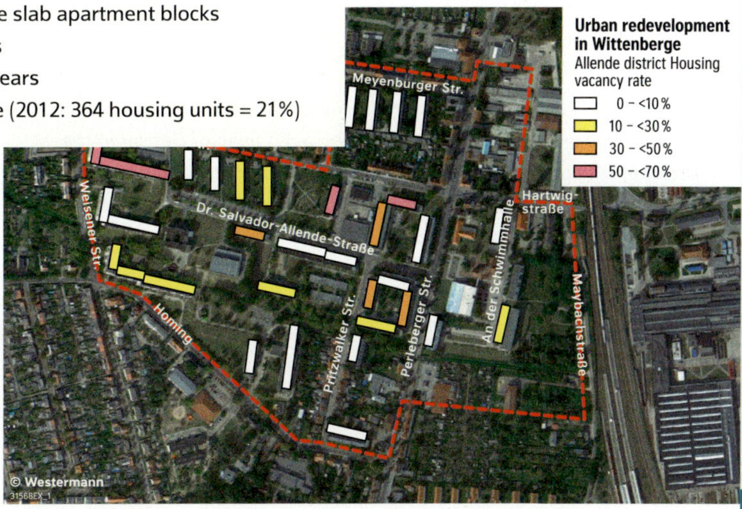

M6 The Allende Quarter in 2012

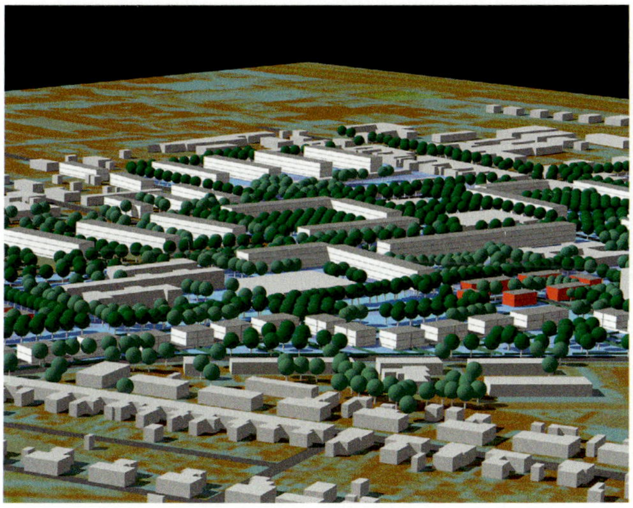

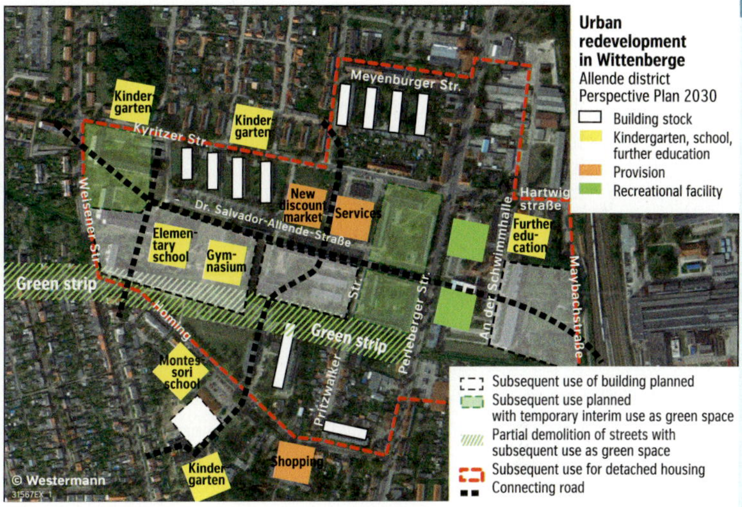

M7 The Allende Quarter after clearance

1823 Oil mill (now closed)
1835 Opening of the port on the Elbe river
1846 Connection to the Berlin–Hamburg railway line
1846 Soap factory (now closed)
1849 Chemical factory (now closed)
1875 Railway repair workshop (today maintenance works of Deutsche Bahn AG)
1903 Sewing machine factory (now closed)
1935 Norddeutsche Maschinenfabrik (now closed)
1937/38 Cellulose and rayon factory (now closed)

New industries after the political change in 1989:
Austrotherm: manufacturer of insulating materials
Francotyp-Postalia: manufacturer of franking machines
Schacht GmbH: manufacturer of transformers

M8 Wittenberge as an industrial location

- The concrete slab blocks should be completely demolished.
- I don't think clearance is good, many older people are living there who feel comfortable in their familiar surroundings.
- Urban renewal? Such hypocrisy. Firstly Wittenberge as an industrial location was deliberately destroyed, and now a part of the town that has the best infrastructure, when it comes to provision, in the whole of Wittenberge.
- It is a shame to destroy such a nice residential area. Lifts and renovation, that would be enough, then the people would want to go on living there.
- You can quickly reach the town centre. Good shopping possibilities. And it is comparatively quiet.
- Here you can live among greenery, and the infrastructure is good.

Online survey by the local newspaper "Prignitzer", non-representative www.svuz.de/lokales/prignitz/was-wird-aus-dem-allende-viertel-id6092541.html

M9 Opinions on the urban renewal concept

A large city in decline?

Detroit – a shrinking city

When Henry Ford developed assembly-line manufacture some hundred years ago, the growth of the then medium-sized town of Detroit in the State of Michigan began. It rapidly grew into a metropolis, was regarded as progressive, and embodied the American dream. But for many the dream has turned into a nightmare, and Detroit represents a classic example of a shrinking city. Almost every fifth house in the city is empty. It is also the most dangerous city in the USA.
How could a city lose its shine again in such a short time? How far has the decline altered the urban landscape? And what chances are seen by those who do not want to give up the hope of a city that is good to live in?

1. Detroit experienced a drastic rise and fall in the size of its population.
A Outline the development of Detroit's population and unemployment statistics in a diagram (M1).
B Discuss reasons for the development of the population and unemployment statistics since 1950 (M1, M3–M5, M7).
2. a) Illustrate the importance of the automobile industry for the economic and social situation of Detroit (M2, M3, M7, Atlas).
b) Compare the socio-economic data for Detroit with that of the USA as a whole (M4).
3. a) Describe the usage pattern and changes in downtown Detroit (M5, Atlas).
b) Describe the effects of the crisis using films, photos and press reports from the internet.
4. The economist Myrdal, in his theory of unequal economic growth, speaks of "cumulative growth and shrinking processes" (p. 122/123). Discuss how far this theory can be applied to Detroit.
5. Describe the efforts to revitalise the city and the actors involved in this (M6, M7).
6. Research other shrinking cities. Present the reasons for their shrinkage and contrast them with the available potential (Internet, p. 180/181).

→ Shrinking city

Year	Population	Year	Unemployment rate in %
1900	285,704	2000	7.3
1920	993,078	2002	12.0
1940	1,623,452	2004	14.0
1960	1,670,144	2006	16.3
1980	1,203,339	2008	15.9
2000	951,270	2010	23.0
2013	688,701	2013	19.9

M1 Population development and unemployment rates in Detroit

M2 General Motors - architectural contrast

The once flourishing US car metropolis of Detroit has filed for bankruptcy. [...] It is the first time in the history of the USA that a city of this size has filed for bankruptcy. [...] According to media reports the city is in debt to the tune of some 19 billion dollars.
Car makers like General Motors, Ford and Chrysler helped the city, with sometimes as many as two million inhabitants, to flourish. But strong competition from Japan, wrong decisions by companies and mismanagement in the city administration allowed Detroit to fall into "60 years of ongoing decline", as Snyder [the city's official receiver] described the city's fall from grace. The automobile industry moved to new locations, many factories closed, both unemployment and criminality shot up to new heights. Although the car makers General Motors and Ford, which are still based in the region, have experienced a recovery, the city is caught in a deep crisis. Since 2008 the operating expenses for the city's utilities have exceeded income by some 100 million dollars per year. [...] Today, 78,000 buildings in Detroit are standing empty; 40 percent of the street lights are not working. Because there is no money for repairs, only a third of the emergency vehicles are operable. As Snyder explained in his report, after an emergency call the citizens of Detroit must wait for the police for an average of 58 minutes. The average for the country as a whole is eleven minutes. At the same time, the murder rate is at its highest level for nearly 40 years.
Source: www.sueddeutsche.de, accessed 13.01.2015

M3 Detroit is bankrupt

	Detroit	USA
Population*	688,701	316 million
Afro-Americans**	82.7%	13.1%
Persons aged over 25 years with at least a Bachelor degree**	12.7%	28.8%
Average per capita income in US-$*	14,870	28,155
Poverty rate*	39.3%	14.5%
Unemployment rate*	19.9%	8.9%
without health insurance*	21.8%	15.3%
Rate of population growth*	-3.5%	2.4%

* 2013, **2010; Source: www.census.com

M4 Socio-economic data for Detroit and the USA

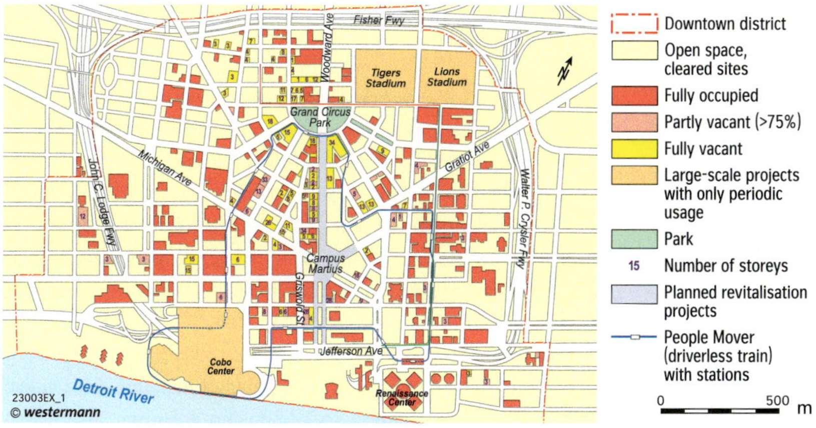

M5 Vacant properties in Detroit

M8 The Michigan Theater, built in the French Renaissance style, is part of a 13-storey office building in downtown Detroit. It already lost its function as a theatre in 1977 and has served since then as a car park.

Since the mid-1960s	Establishment of shopping malls, office centres and commercial parks along the traffic arteries
1977	Opening of the Renaissance Center on Detroit River (high-rise complex with General Motors headquarters, hotels, shops, restaurants and offices)
1999	Construction of three gaming casinos in the downtown district with 8,200 jobs and 38,000 visitors daily
2000	Opening of the Comerica Park baseball stadium for 42,000 spectators
2002	Opening of the Ford Field football stadium with 65,000 seats
2004	Revitalisation of central squares with broad pavements and pavilions

M6 Selected spatial changes in the Detroit agglomeration

weblinks
- www.shrinkingcities.com
- http://future.arte.tv/geisterstaedte

A cloudy day could not dampen the spirits of people gathered for the official opening of Downtown Detroit's newest garden, Lafayette Greens. The garden covers about three-quarters of an acre and grows fruits, vegetables and herbs.
The sponsor of the new garden, Compuware Corporation, turned a vacant lot on W. Lafayette and Shelby into this urban garden and relaxing green space in Downtown. Compuware has made arrangements with Gleaners Community Food Bank to give the food bank the fresh produce that is grown at the garden. For Peter Karmanos, Jr., the executive chairman and founder of Compuware, today's celebration was significant. Not only is he a master gardener, the volunteer effort made by Compuware employees shows they understand the culture of giving back to the community he has tried to build.
"A sense of community is embedded in Compuware's culture," he said. "We believe, as this place shows it is vital for our employees to be active and creative members of their communities. Lafayette Greens brings together this point through two great passions of mine, gardening and the City of Detroit."
Source: blog.thedetroithub.com, accessed 13.01.2015

[...] More positive is the construction of various office buildings in the inner city in recent times. At the beginning of the 1970s, three young people in the suburban area founded the company Compuserve. At the end of the 1990s, with tax breaks and the promise to only use software from Compuserve, the city of Detroit succeeded in convincing the company to settle in Detroit.
[...] Mayor Bing has recognised that Detroit cannot be saved by expensive construction measures. Instead, intelligent uses must be found for the vacant sites in future. Bing wants to concentrate the remaining population into selected locations in order to create lively neighbourhoods again. About a quarter of Detroit's land area is to be converted into parks and woodland. The implementation of this plan is difficult. It must firstly be decided which neighbourhoods are to be razed to the ground and which ones are to be revitalised. In any case the demolition of houses and the levelling of entire city districts will be expensive. [...]
Source: Hahn, B., Die US-amerikanische Stadt im Wandel, Berlin/Heidelberg 2014, pp. 145/146.

[...] Over the past several years at least seven bicycle makers have set up shop in the Detroit metro area, touting sleek, artisanal models. "Everybody in this town knows somebody who worked for the Big Three," says Steven Bock, a Ford Motor Co. clay sculptor who is now applying his car skills to bicycles. "It's kind of in the Detroit DNA to build things." Bock founded Detroit Bicycle Co. in 2011, where he makes custom handcrafted single-speed and fixed-gear bikes when he's not sculpting full-size clay models of cars for Ford. [...] The biggest Motor City bike maker, though, is Detroit Bikes. Founder Zak Pashak invested $2.5 million in a 50,000-square-foot factory [...] that mints about 10 bikes a day. Eventually he aims to produce as many as 50,000 a year. [...] Several factors seem to be driving the renaissance of the bike industry in Detroit. Beat-up by the Great Recession, Detroit's vacant factories and cheap rent have lured young entrepreneurs and artists to set up shop in the city. The vestiges of car manufacturing – leftover machinery, abundant powdercoat shops and of course, skilled auto industry veterans seeking work – have proven a treasure to bike makers and other craftspeople.
Source: www.fortune.com, accessed 13.01.2015

M7 Revitalisation efforts

New cities for the millions

Founding new cities in China

No other country in the world faces such comparatively great challenges with regard to its urban development as China. In a relatively short time, urban housing space must be created for millions of people. Where will new cities be built? Who will live in them? What are the concepts and models for founding these new cities?

1. a) Describe the extent of urbanisation in China (M1, M2, M3, M5).
   b) Explain the background for this development. Go particularly into the question of economic development and spatial disparities (M3, M4, Atlas).
2. Illustrate the two urban development strategies based on the examples of Shenzhen in Hong Kong and Meixi Lake near Changsha (M4, M6, Atlas).
3. Illustrate the concept of Meixi Lake City (M6, M7).
4. (O) Using media from the internet, analyse developments up to the present in one of the following cities:
   A Meixi Lake (near Changsha).
   B Dongtan (near Shanghai).
   C Tianducheng (near Hangzhou).
   D Ordos (province in Inner Mongolia).
5. (S) On the basis of the data in the master plan, draw a rough sketch of the city map of Meixi Lake (M7).

→ Ecological urban development, Urbanisation

In the next 15 years, some 221 cities [in China] will have more than one million inhabitants. In comparison, Europe currently has just 35 such cities. The two existing megacities of Beijing and Shanghai will be joined by a total of six other cities with more than ten million inhabitants and 15 cities with five to ten million inhabitants. The road network will be expanded by five billion square metres and the cities by five million new buildings. This could include up to 50,000 skyscrapers – corresponding to ten times the surface area of New York City.

Source: Hefele, P. , Bade, J., Die Stadt neu erfinden? In: Konrad Adenauer Foundation (KAS) Auslandsinformationen 9/10 2011 p. 13

M1 New cities in China

Development of population distribution, 1950 – 2030				
Indicator	1950	1990	2010	2030
Rural population (in thousands)	480,632	840,095	718,307	557,019
Proportion of total population (in %)	88.2	73.6	53.0	38.1
Urban population (in thousands)	64,319	301,995	635,839	905,449
Proportion of total population (in %)	11.8	26.4	47.0	61.9
Total population (in thousands)	544,951	1,142,090	1,354,146	1,462,468

Source: Hefele, P. and Bade, J., Die Stadt neu erfinden? In: Konrad Adenauer Foundation (KAS) Auslandsinformationen 9/10 2011, p. 13

M2 Development of population distribution

Already by 2020, 850 million Chinese people will be living in the urban centres of the Middle Kingdom. Ten years later it will be around a billion people. Only 400 to 500 million farmers will remain in the countryside. With a striking slogan, Premier Li described the planned [...] urbanisation up to the year 2020 as the "three times 100 million project". As the first step, Li aims for 100 million migrant workers, half of those living today in China's cities, to be entered in the population register and turned into regular city dwellers.
His second approach is aimed at a hundred million farmers who are living in slum-like dwellings on the edges of medium-sized cities. These are to be resettled in social housing. A further 100 million farmers will be encouraged to migrate from their villages to the medium-sized cities in the underdeveloped regions of western China.

Source: Erling, J., China startet sein riskantes Urbanisierungsprojekt. In: Die Welt 25.03.14 www.welt.de/126186975, accessed 13.01.2015

M3 The "three times 100 million project"

In the framework of the Go West Strategy (xibu dakaifa), cities will be intensively rebuilt and expanded in order to gain control over regional imbalances and steer migration flows from the overpopulated eastern provinces into the country's interior.
The latest considerations are aimed at creating conurbation areas instead of, as in the past, promoting a scattered pattern of urbanisation. Cities in conurbations can not only give one another mutual financial and economic support, but can also provide for a reduced level of environmental pollution.
The most important plans for the concentration into conurbations involve the Pearl River Delta in the south of China around Shenzhen, the region on the Yangtze Delta around Shanghai, and the Beijing-Tianjin- Hebei nexus.

Source: Hefele, P. & Bade, J., Die Stadt neu erfinden? In: Konrad Adenauer Foundation (KAS) Auslandsinformationen 9/10 2011, p. 21, 22

M4 Strategies for further urbanisation

Classification of cities		Population
Super-Megacity		over 10 million
Megacity		5 to 10 million
Large City	Large City I	3 to 5 million
	Large City II	1 to 3 million
Medium City		500,000 to 1 million
Small City	Small City I	200,000 to 500,000
	Small City II	under 200,000

Source: Super-Megastadt, Chinas neuer Stadttyp. In: German.people.cn, Friday, 21 November 2014

M5 New classification of cities by the Chinese government, 2014

M6 Meixi Lake – a newly-established city for c. 200,000 people (computer animation)

Meixi proposes to offer a new model for the future of the Chinese city. [...] This lake provides for boat transport linkages, [...] and makes places for cultural venues. Around the circular heart of this water body is wrapped the mixed use CBD. Here, high rise building districts are connected by a pedestrian tram street, reducing the need for car use in the city centre.

[...] a series of canals, allowing for boat transport from the city centre to any one of eight neighbourhood clusters. Each cluster houses about 10,000 people, and includes a village centre featuring a school, shopping area, and other public functions. These neighbourhoods are separated from one another by green buffers which accommodate exercise fields and natural landscape zones. The architecture of each "village" will be different. [...]

The radial geometry of the city plan allows for a highly efficient transport system, reducing potential pollution and energy use. Other environmental strategies include collective grey and black water systems, distributed energy plants, and urban agriculture. A river flood plain is turned into a linear park which includes recreational areas, micro farms, and residential rows.

[...] Meixi Lake will serve as the head of the West Changsha Pioneer Zone; as an urban model, we expect it to lead the way to a new way of thinking about the city of the future.

Source: www.kpf.com/project.asp?ID=135, accessed 13.01.2015

M7 Meixi Lake – the master plan: ecological urban development

M8 Meixi Lake under construction – already a tourist attraction

Spatial development and regional planning in Germany

The point-axial spatial concept

To live in a large city, or in a small town, or in the countryside – those who have the chance to choose can weigh up the advantages and disadvantages of the different possibilities for themselves. For Germany's inhabited space as a whole, however, problems can arise if the living conditions in different spatial areas are extremely unequal with the result of certain spaces becoming overloaded, or in conflicts of use. What measures can be used to "organise" and "plan" the space in order to make it possible to live together in a socially, ecologically and economically sustainable way?

1. a) Describe the interconnection of places with different levels of centrality in Christaller's model, also taking into account the functional amenities of the places (M1, M3).
   b) Note possible reasons why the ideal-typical pattern of central places as described in Christaller's model does not exist in reality.
2. Apply the model to the place where you live and its neighbourhood:
   a) Determine whether you live in a major, middle-order or minor centre (A, B or C place) (M1, p. 189 M5).
   b) Create a table of the amenities in the place where you live (M3, M4).
   c) Determine the distance to the next major or middle-order centre.
3. Using the example of regional infrastructure provision, assess whether the goals of spatial planning in Germany are fulfilled (M2, M4, M5).
4. ⓞ Discuss whether the creation of equal living conditions can be achieved by the point-axial system (M2, M3, Definition), by:
   A presenting the arguments for and against in a table.
   B drafting a text.
5. a) Explain the rethinking proposed by Hans-Peter Gatzweiler with regard to principles of spatial development (M5).
   b) Comment on it.
6. Ⓢ Show the opportunities and risks of spatial planning measures, also with reference to future developments (M2, M3, M5).

→ Development axis, Point-axial spatial planning concept, System of central places

→ System of central places

Spatial planning in Germany is founded on a theoretical concept that was developed by Walter Christaller in the 1930s, the system of central places. A central place performs provision functions for its surrounding areas. The ideal-typical distribution of central places with different levels of centrality produces a web pattern.

→ Development axis

Development axes connect individual conurbations; they are transport and communication corridors. Their function is to give development impulses for the adjacent areas. The system of central places and development axes is the basis for the point-axial spatial planning concept.

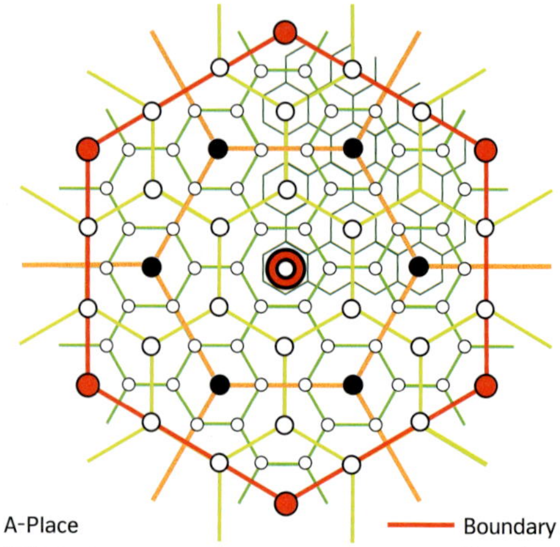

M1 Model of the concept of central places based on Christaller

- Creation of equivalent living conditions in all of Germany's spatial zones.
- Retention of a decentral settlement structure with its strong urban regions.
- Retention and development of the wide-scale structure of open spaces.
- Retention of established cultural landscapes.
- Protection, care and development of nature and the landscape.
- Development of rural areas as independent living and economic areas.
- Spatial concentration of settlement activity on a strong system of central places.
- In conurbations: orientation of settlement activity towards an integrated transport system and protection of open space.
- Reduction in traffic loads by producing a spatial usage mix.
- Prioritisation of internal development over requiring the development of open land areas.
- Strengthening of regional cooperation and thus the sustainability of regions in a united Europe.

Source: Priebs, A., Raumordnung und Raumentwicklung als Zukunftsaufgabe. In Geographische Rundschau, Vol. 3/2005, p. 4–9.

M2 Goals and areas of focus of spatial planning in Germany

	Number of inhabitants	Education provision	Health and social provision
Major centre	as a rule > 100,000	Technical college, university	Special clinics, Specialist doctors
Middle-order centre	as a rule > 20,000	Grammar school, secondary school, vocational school	General hospital, old people's home, counselling/ information centre
Minor centre	as a rule > 30,000	Primary school, secondary modern school	Family doctors

M3 Amenities in central places (selection)

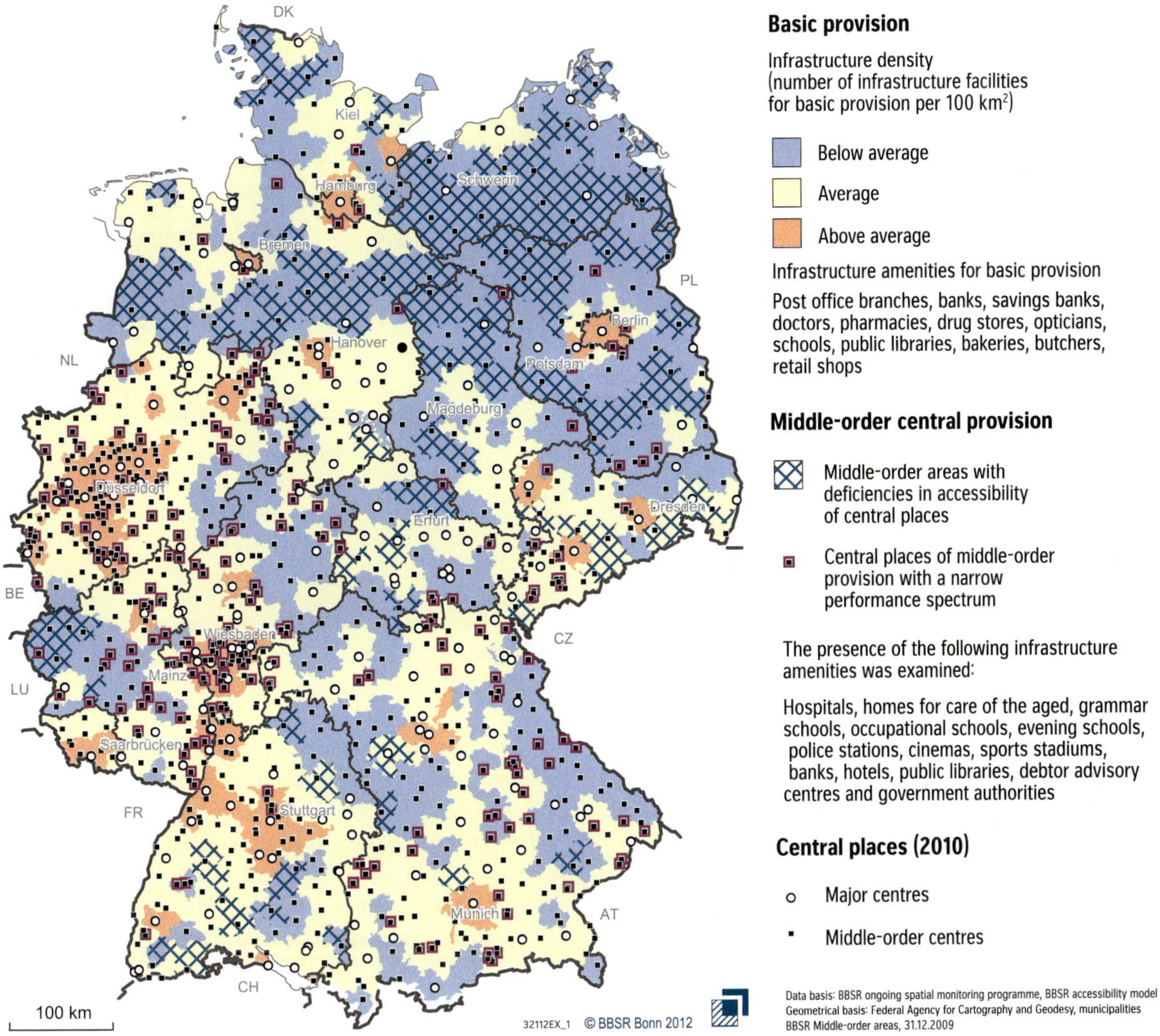

M4 Regional Infrastructure provision

In many rural areas, especially in the north and north-east of Germany, more than one-third of the population must drive for more than 15 minutes to reach their nearest middle-order centre. Disparities are also intensified by the fact that many of these places only have a limited provision of infrastructure or a narrow spectrum of amenities. Already today, and certainly in the medium term, demographic change will lead to problems for the viability of service facilities in central places. The need for action in the provision of infrastructure, triggered by population decline and ageing, makes clear that – with the exception of the East Bavarian border region – it is primarily the rural areas in the new federal states where an appropriate provision of infrastructure must be assured in the future. [...]

In the Federal Republic of Germany, government equalisation policy in pursuit of the constitutional requirement of "the establishment of equivalent living conditions" has a long tradition. With a multiplicity of national assistance programmes and the European Structural Funds, Germany possesses a highly differentiated variety of assistance measures. In addition, the financial equalisation policy and the social security systems are also of outstanding importance for spatial development policy aspects. Financial equalisation policy intervenes directly in the financial arrangements between the federal states (financial equalisation) and municipalities (communal financial equalisation) with the aim of putting the federal states and municipalities in a position to be able to provide public services without major regional differences (goal of equivalent living conditions). Here, the equalisation effect of the social security systems is expressed in the fact that regions that generate a higher contribution than they receive in payments are indirectly giving financial support to those regions that receive more in payments that they pay in contributions. [...]

Also in future, as the analyses show, an equalisation-oriented spatial development policy will face major challenges. It will require the creation of adequate employment possibilities as well as ensuring an appropriate provision of infrastructure in all spatial zones in Germany. However, spatial development policy cannot (and should not) impede shrinkage processes. Rather, it should seek to bring existing structures and systems into alignment with changed conditions. [The objective is to ensure a minimum of economic strength and infrastructure provision] in order to avoid a further self-reinforcing downward spiral. In principle this means a departure from the welfare-based principle of equivalent living conditions towards a principle of economic, social and territorial cohesion inspired by European law. Spatial development policy and spatial planning at federal and state level in Germany should also accept the need to look reality in the face.

Source: Gatzweiler, H.-P., Regionale Disparitäten in Deutschland – Herausforderung für die Raumentwicklungspolitik. In: Geographische Rundschau, Vol. 7–8/2012, pp. 59–60

M5 Spatial disparities in Germany and equalisation-oriented spatial development policy

Spatial development and regional planning in Germany

State development plan, North Rhine-Westphalia

On 25 June 2013, the federal state government of North Rhine-Westphalia decided to work out a new state development plan. The draft was presented to the public, and opinions could be submitted between August 2013 and February 2014. The new state development plan replaces the old one from 1995. What were the developments that made it necessary to work out a new state development plan? What objectives and principles, and what strategies for future-oriented urban development, are considered in the state development plan?

Ⓞ 1. Outline graphically the changed framework conditions for spatial development in North Rhine-Westphalia (M1):
   A by means of a mindmap.
   B by means of a causal network.
2. a) Describe the structure of central places in North Rhine-Westphalia (M5).
   b) Make concrete reference to your local area and provide a detailed description.
   c) Give reasons for the deviations from the structure of central places in the model (M5, p. 186 M1).
3. Evaluate the structure of central places in North Rhine-Westphalia with regard to the establishment of equivalent living conditions (M5).
   Substantiate your argumentation with examples.
4. Analyse the principles, goals and concepts of state development planning in North Rhine-Westphalia with regard to sustainable development (M4).
5. Future-oriented urban development also includes protection of open spaces. Comment on this statement.

Ⓢ 6. The city as a living space for all! Discuss how far the state development planning can reach this goal.

→ Decentral concentration, Gender mainstreaming, Open space planning, State development plan, Sustainability

M2 A place for all to live in – gender mainstreaming in spatial planning

Girls and boys, women and men, elderly people, singles, couples, families or groups – they all want to have an equal right to use the public space.
People place differing demands on free space. Different needs arise according to age, gender, education or family structure. An important aspect of landscape and open space planning is the ability to offer the appropriate "free" space for these manifold demands.
Gender mainstreaming (taking into account the different living situations and interests of women and men) is therefore an important basis for all landscape planning activities.
Source. www.wien.gv.at

M3 Gender mainstreaming

weblink

- www.landesplanung.nrw

In consequence of dense settlement and the associated competition between a wide variety of claims on a limited amount of space, spatial planning in North Rhine-Westphalia is of particular importance [...]. The state has become "over-planned", and therefore the present state development plan (LEP) can build on earlier state development plans and the comprehensive availability of regional plans. But since the production of the currently applicable LEP in the 1990s, the framework conditions for spatial development have changed and require the adjustment of spatial planning goals and principles. This applies especially to the foreseeable development of population in North Rhine-Westphalia ("demographic change"), the continuing globalisation of the economy and climate change, as well as developments in retailing. [...]
Throughout the state, the proportion of elderly people in the population as a whole will significantly increase. [...] Thus the orientation of the settlement structure to local provision, and the barrier-free accessibility of services, will become increasingly important. At the same time, this will improve the social inclusion of people with disabilities. [...]
Structural changes in the economy and the internationalisation of markets have led to an intensification of competition between cities and regions. [...] Municipalities find themselves increasingly facing international competition. [...] Parallel to this – due to demographic change – competition for qualified labour will intensify. In choosing where to live and work, employees not only consider purely occupational aspects but are also increasingly taking "soft locational factors" into account. Therefore the improvement of spatial quality and "development of the cultural landscape" as well as a family-friendly and barrier-free infrastructure are of increasing importance in competition between locations. [...]
Settlement and traffic planning mutually influence each other and are mutually dependent. Traffic planning leads on the one hand to an upgrading of areas of settlement by improving their accessibility, while on the other hand traffic also causes disruption within and outside of the areas of settlement. The improved coordination of settlement and traffic planning seeks to achieve reductions in the demand for space for building as well as in traffic loads [...].
Source: North Rhine-Westphalia state development plan, www.landesplanung.nrw

M1 Changed framework conditions for spatial development

- **Principle of "decentral concentration"**
  The settlement structure should be developed in accordance with the principle of "decentral concentration". This should be based on the structure of central places.
- **No ribbon developments and splinter settlements**
  Ribbon development along transport routes should be avoided. The emergence, consolidation or expansion of splinter settlements should be prevented.
- **Principle of the "sustainable European city"**
  Settlement development should be designed in a compact form, in line with the concept of the "sustainable European city", and the respective centres should be strengthened. [...] Large settlement zones should be structured and loosened in terms of settlement structure and with a graduated system of urban open space. This should also fulfil the requirement of adjusting to climate change.
- **Strengthening of retailing in the centres**
  Owing to demographic change, the centres are becoming even more important as locations for provision. Especially elderly people as well as families require local amenities that can be reached in a short distance without a car. For this reason too, the existing centres are to be consistently strengthened as locations for jobs, commerce and housing. This will ensure the effective future utilisation of capacity in public and private amenities for the provision of essential services, the reduction in the demands on open spaces to a minimum, and the avoidance of traffic.
- **Retention of open spaces**
  Open space performs important ecological, economic and social functions and services. It is a prerequisite for the retention of soils with their habitat, regulation and production functions, and it is also a habitat for wild animals and plants. The protection of unsurfaced areas of open space serves for the regulation of a balanced water balance, in particular for the regeneration of groundwater reserves and the harmless drainage of flood waters. Open spaces have equalisation effects in terms of climate and air cleanliness that extend into climatically burdened areas of settlement.

Source: North Rhine-Westphalia state development plan (LEP NRW), draft dated 25.06.2013, pp. 2, 29, 30, 53, 72
Originator / author: State chancellery of the Federal State of North Rhine-Westphalia, regional planning authority, Stadttor 1, 40219 Düsseldorf

M4 Principles, goals and concepts for regional development planning in NRW

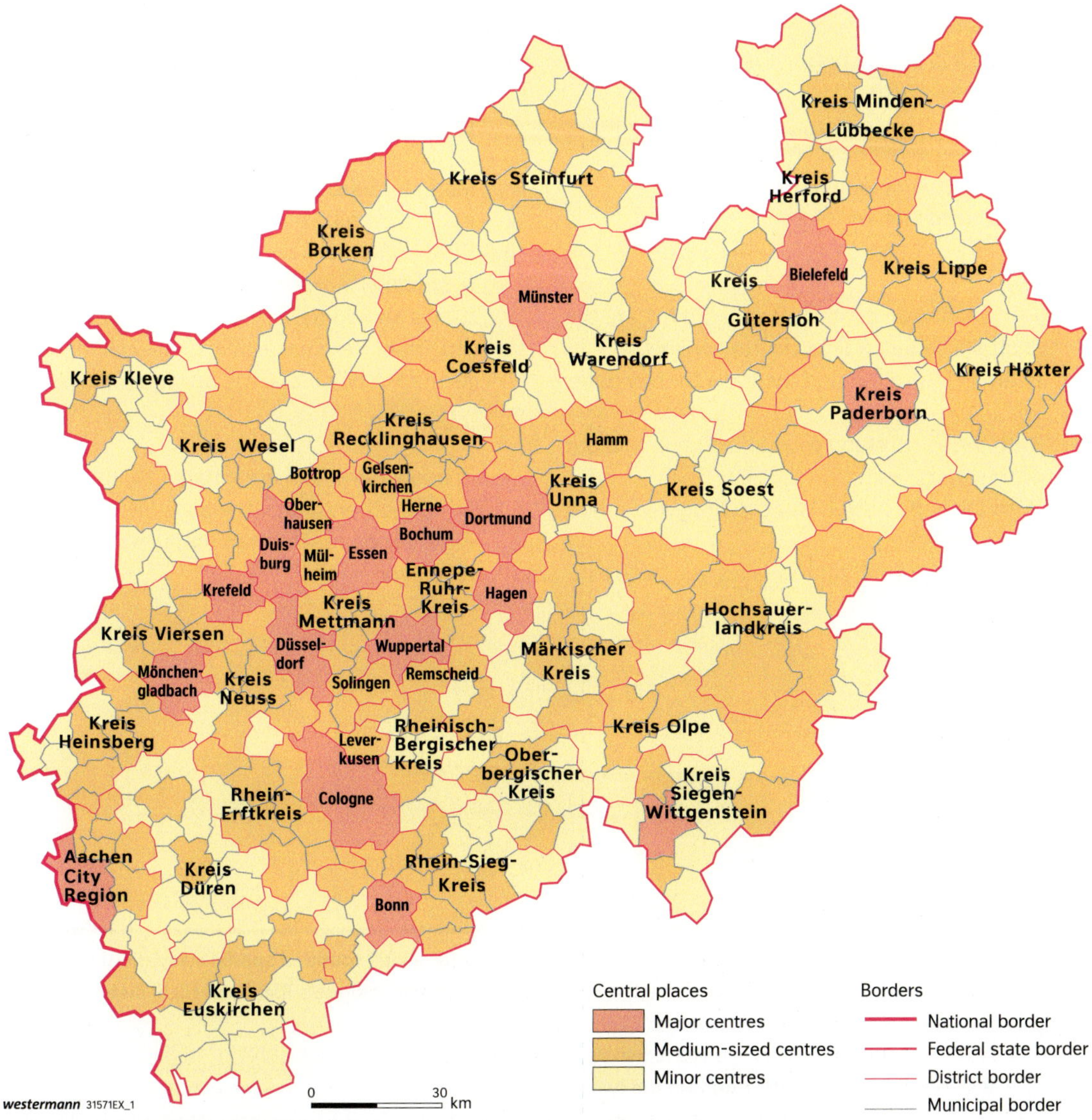

M5 Structure of central places in North Rhine-Westphalia, state development plan NRW

METHOD One spatial area – different evaluations

Multi-perspective spatial evaluation with the use of new media

Digital maps, satellite and aerial images can provide extensive information of the most varied kind about a spatial area.
Google Earth and Diercke Online Globus, for example, provide valuable information. In addition, internet-based geodata services from ministries and authorities make digital geodata available free of charge. TIM-online NRW is a service that makes digital geodata available and displays it in a viewer. TIM stands for Topographical Information Management. The viewers in various other services are built in a similar way.

Working and operating instructions for TIM-online NRW

STEP 1

→ Create a Word or Powerpoint document in advance for your spatial evaluation. This is where you should document your activities.
→ Prepare screenshots of the maps and photographic images that you use (the "Print" button takes a picture of your screen, then paste the screenshots into the document with the right-hand mouse button) and label them with explanatory texts.

STEP 2

→ Open ***www.tim-online.nrw.de*** and launch TIM-online.

STEP 3

→ The areas circled with 1, 2 and 3 In M1 are the central navigation fields in TIM-online:
→ In area "**1**" you will find the tools for navigation within the map.
→ With the +/- buttons you can zoom in and out of the maps.
→ With the hand button you can drag and move the map section.
→ The house (home) button takes you back to the overview map.
→ Depending on the subject, the 3D button for a three-dimensional display of the spatial area may be of interest.
→ All the buttons on the page are explained in the help function "?".

STEP 4

→ You will find the central navigation element of TIM-online in the left-hand frame marked with "**2**". Here you can load the individual maps into the map area (see also M2).
→ Underneath the *"Kartenwahl"* tab, you can load standard maps such as e.g. topographical maps, real estate maps or aerial photos.
→ By clicking the + button (*"Dienst hinzuladen"*) beside the *"Kartenwahl"* tab, you open the field that is shown to the right of this operating instruction. Here you can load special maps such as maps showing areas in danger of flooding.

STEP 5

→ The left-hand tool area marked with "**3**" offers, among other things, the possibility of loading legends for the map that is currently being displayed.

1. **Sketch the information that you consider to be important for a well-founded spatial evaluation.**
2. **Using Google Earth and Google Street View, give an overview of Cologne's Riehl and Niehl districts.**
Ⓞ **3.** **Document with the aid of TIM-online NRW:**
A **selected transport functions in the two districts.**
B **selected recreational functions in the two districts.**
Ⓢ **4.** **Analogous to assignments 2 and 3, outline what you consider to be the three most interesting pieces of information about the area where you live.**

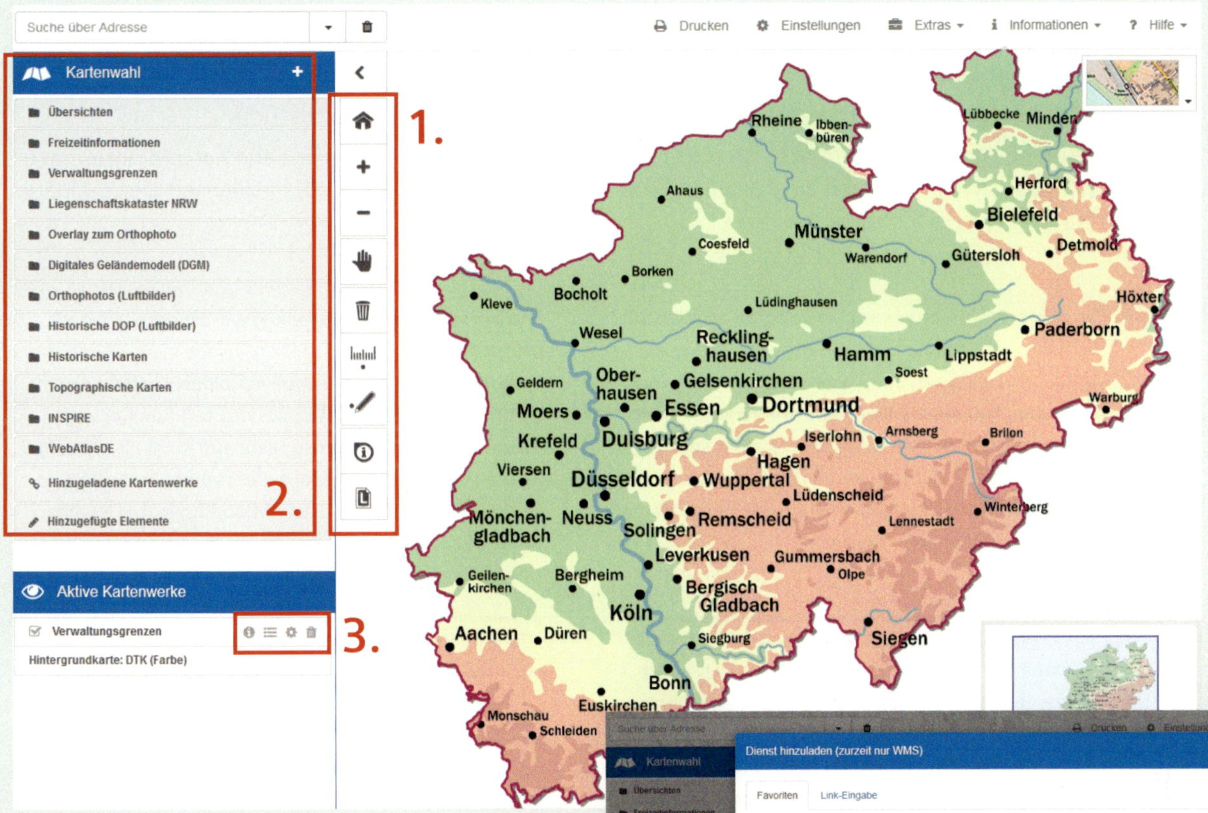

M1 Basic TIM-online map with navigation elements

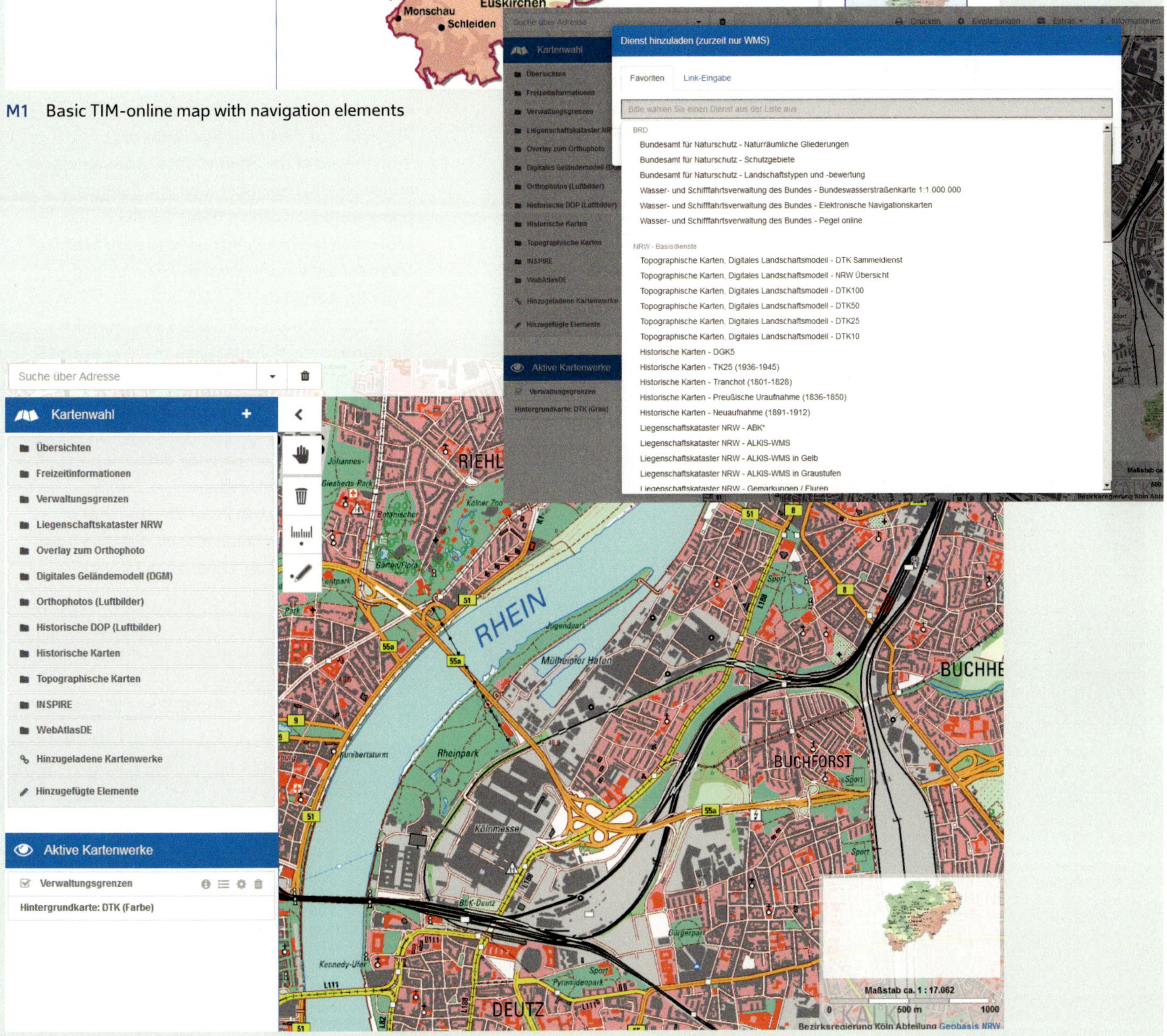

M2 Topographic map DTK25 with additionally loaded data from the NRW recreational register

METHOD One spatial area – different evaluations

Multi-perspective spatial evaluation of Cologne's Riehl and Niehl districts

The wishes and demands placed on a spatial area are very different, and so is the need for information with regard to specific spatial structures. Every spatial area can be explored, familiarised and evaluated from extremely different perspectives.

The perspective of a person seeking an apartment

You have just taken your university entrance exam (Abitur) and will soon start your studies or training in Cologne. You need a small apartment where you can move in by yourself or as part of a flat share. Your parents will pay the rent. But they have made it a requirement that the apartment must be located in Cologne's Niehl or Riehl districts.

1. Using keywords, sketch the aspects that are important and interesting for you as an apartment-seeking student or trainee in your choice of location.
2. Analyse and document Cologne's Niehl and Riehl districts from your adopted perspective with reference to the aspects you have listed. Use Google Earth, Google Street View and TIM-online.
3. Evaluate and document specific streets, or – in the case of longer streets – specific sections of the street, where you would prefer to look for an apartment in the future. Give reasons for your selection.

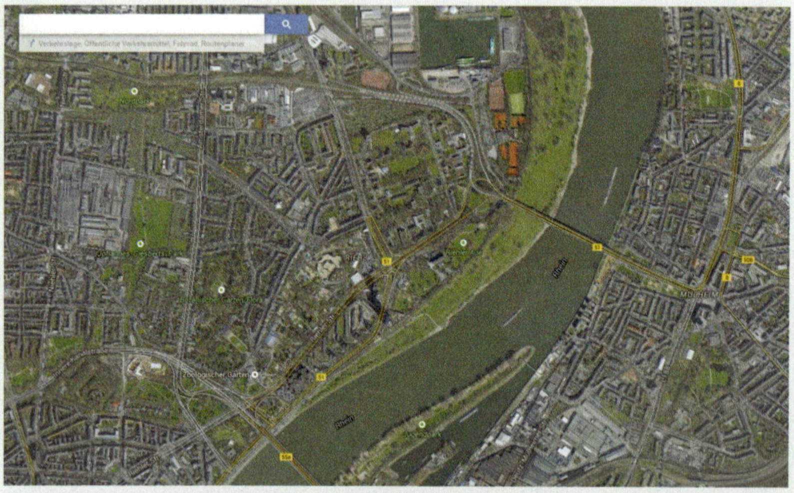

M1 Google Earth screenshot of the area under study

The perspective of an employee in Cologne's flood protection centre

You have accepted a new job in Cologne's flood protection centre and must make yourself familiar with the situations in Cologne's Niehl and Riehl districts. In future your supervisor will expect you to know how to estimate the differing risks of flooding in this locality. What flooding risks is the area under study subject to?

1. Analyse the catchment area of the Rhine. Then give consideration to what natural event would have to occur in order to present an acute risk of flooding in Cologne. Here you should make use of the knowledge you acquired in previous lessons. For this assignment, use the internet site of the International Commission for the Protection of the Rhine (www.iksr.org).
2. With the aid of the internet sites of Cologne's municipal drainage operation and Cologne's flood protection centre, name the flood protection measures that have already been taken for Cologne (www.steb-koeln.de and www.hw-karten.de).
3. Illustrate the maximum water levels at which the flood protection measures in the area under discussion are effective.
4. Illustrate the scenario that would occur in the event that the flood protection measures are no longer effective. Compare the different parts of the selected spatial area.
5. Place the flooding depths of the stretches of road analysed in relation to their distance from the Rhine and find an explanation for your discoveries!

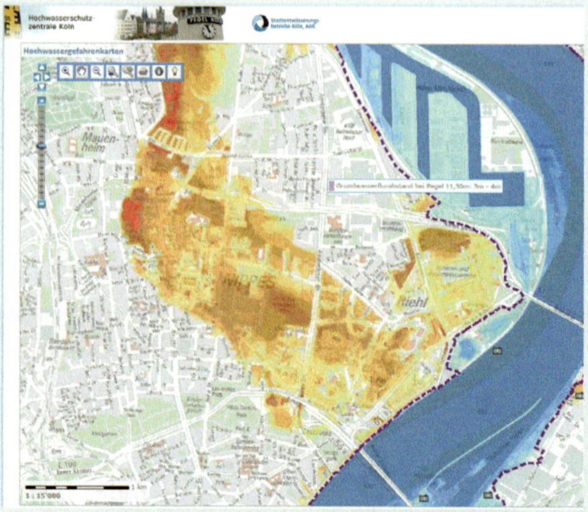

M2 Map of flooding risks in the area under study

The perspective of a home buyer

You plan to settle in Cologne with your family (two children of school age) on a long-term basis and invest in the purchase of a house or apartment in the area under discussion.
Since you are planning to be no longer only a tenant in future, but to become a property owner, the potential risk of flooding also represents a factor to be taken into account in the evaluation. You should therefore include your knowledge with regard to the flooding problem in Cologne in your analysis. Since you are wishing to make an investment "for life", you should try to integrate as many factors as possible in your spatial evaluation. Therefore you should use all the information possibilities that you are aware of.

1. Evaluate the spatial area from the adopted perspective of a home buyer.
2. Then, in your evaluation, narrow down the stretches of road in which you would want to search for a property in the form of a house or apartment or an empty piece of land for building.
3. Give as detailed reasons as possible for your choice of area in your written explanations and present them!

It is not only a possible risk of flooding of the house or apartment that represents a negative factor in your evaluation. Ambient noise, e.g. on a busy main road, can also have a negative effect on subjective feelings about quality of life. In M4, for example, street noise (24h noise level) is shown in the area under consideration.
The internet site of the Ministry for Environment, Agriculture, Conservation and Consumer Protection of the State of North Rhine-Westphalia provides information on this subject.
(www.umgebungslaerm-kartierung.nrw.de)

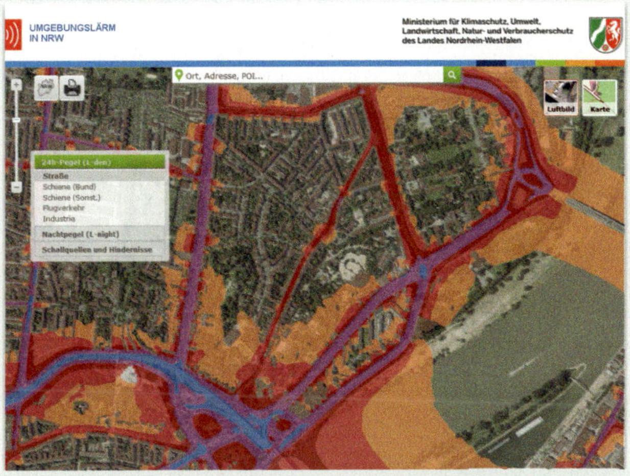

M4 24h level of street noise in Cologne's Riehl district

In addition to the information platforms that you are already familiar with, the internet sites named below are also available to you. Since you do not have an unlimited amount of money at your disposal, an analysis of benchmark land values in the area under consideration is of interest. In this context, the internet site of the Senior Expert Committee for Land Valuation of the State of North Rhine-Westphalia makes spatially-related information available which provides a benchmark value. In M3 these values are shown for a section of the map.
(www.boris.nrw.de)

The same ministry also operates a further internet site that provides very wide-ranging information on nature, water, forests, air, noise and sewage. Here too, you can find positive and negative locational factors for your choice. On this site you can superimpose different pieces of information one above the other. An example of this is shown in M5.
(www.uvo.nrw.de)

M3 Map of property values in Cologne's Riehl district (www.boris.nrw.de)

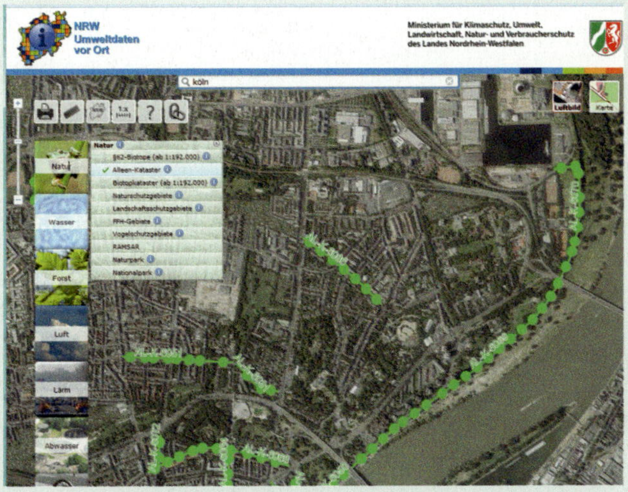

M5 Environmental data for Cologne's Riehl district (avenue register)

Global cities – modern centres of the world economy

New York – global city number one?

Manhattan, skyscrapers, Central Park, Broadway – these are what many people associate with New York. But the city is also a classic example of a global city. Like no other city, it is a central node of the world economy. What features characterise New York as a global city and modern world city?

Ⓞ 1. A Produce a list of features that characterise New York as a modern global city (M1–M7, Atlas).
   B Produce a mindmap of the features that characterise New York as a modern global city (M1–M7, Atlas).
2. All that glitters is not gold. Using various examples, discuss how far this applies to New York as a global city (M5, Atlas).
3. Illustrate the worldwide distribution of global cities according to Bronger (M6, M7).
4. Discuss consequences that could possibly occur on account of the worldwide distribution of global cities (M6, M7).

Ⓢ 5. Compare the spatial structure of Manhattan with that of the City of London and Canary Wharf (Atlas).

→ FIRE sector, Global city, Service-based society

M1 The UN building in New York City is the headquarters and most important location of the United Nations

With a population of some 18 million in its metropolitan area, New York is by far the largest city in the USA. Its population is constantly growing due to its global and national importance. More company headquarters, financial and media firms are concentrated here than in any other US city. In 2013, of the 500 companies with the largest turnover worldwide, 18 were headquartered in the New York metropolitan area (Beijing is in 1st place with 48 companies, Tokyo in 2nd place with 46 and Paris in 3rd place with 19). Of the 500 companies with the largest turnover in the USA, 47 are based in New York compared to 25 in the second-largest metropolitan area, Houston. New York is by far the most important stock exchange centre in the USA; all the major banks, brokers and insurance companies have their headquarters here. New York also has a leading position in the media industry. For historical reasons, companies in the advertising industry, the print media and the television industry have concentrated in Manhattan. The trend towards a globalised service-based society is also reflected in New York's occupational structure. Today, about a quarter of all employed persons are working in the so-called FIRE sector (Finance, Insurance, Real Estate).

The major significance of New York in the financial sector is also reflected in the turnover of the stock exchanges NYSE (New York Stock Exchange) and NASDAQ. These two stock exchanges have the highest trading volumes worldwide and are regarded as global reference stock exchanges. At the NYSE, 200 million shares in more than 2,000 firms are traded every day. The headquarters of the United Nations (UN) on East River also gives New York a key political importance.

With its many tourist attractions, 500 galleries, some 200 museums, more than 150 theatres and more than 18,000 restaurants, the city enjoys a world reputation and roughly 50 million visitors are recorded every year.

For decades, New York has been setting trends in fashion, cuisine and night life. New York is cult – over and over again, regardless of whether it is one's first visit or one's hundredth. This is also due to the fact that the city is constantly reinventing itself. What was hip yesterday, is out today. To be a trendsetter here, one must get up early and keep one's eyes and ears open.

M2 New York City – a modern world city

Stock exchange	Location	Trading volume in billion US dollars
NYSE Euronext US	New York City	13.7
NASDAQ QMX US	New York City	9.6
Japan Exchange Group	Tokio	6.5
Shenzhen Stock Exchange	Shenzhen	3.9
Shanghai Stock Exchange	Shanghai	3.8
London Stock Exchange Group	London	2.3
NYSE Euronext Europe	New York City	1.7
Deutsche Börse	Frankfurt	1.7
Korea Exchange	Busan	1.3

Source: Statista, http://de.statista.com

M3 The largest stock exchanges by trading volume, 2013

NYC rank	US rank	World rank	Company	Income in billion US dollars	No. of employees worldwide	Industry
1	16	48	Verizon Communication	115.8	183,400	Telecommunications
2	18	55	J.P. Morgan Chase & Co	108.2	258,965	Banking
3	26	79	Citigroup	90.8	259,000	Banking
4	38	125	American International Group	70.1	63,000	Insurance
5	39	128	INTL FC Stone	69.3	1,074	Div. financial services
6	40	129	MetLife	68.2	64,000	Health insurance
7	48	148	Pfizer	61.2	91,500	Pharmaceuticals
8	68	254	Goldman Sachs Group	41.7	32,400	Banking
9	75	279	Hess	38.4	14,775	Petroleum processing
10	89	324	New York Life Insurance	34.3	11,165	Health insurance

Quelle: fortune.com/global500

M4 The ten largest industrial and service companies in New York City (2013)

New York is the classic melting pot. For centuries, millions of people have migrated to here from all parts of the world and created a new American society with multicultural flair. While in the 1980s in particular the number of Chinese immigrants expanded, it is currently the number of immigrants from Latin America and Eastern Europe that is growing. With some 180 ethnic groups, the population of New York is very heterogeneous. The largest group are the non-Hispanic whites with 34.4 percent. The proportion of non-Hispanic blacks or Afro-Americans accounts for 24.3 percent. Against this, Hispanics now form the second-largest population group with a total of 28 percent. The Asians are the fastest-growing group and now make up 11.3 percent of the population of New York.

Within the city area, spatially separate areas of concentration of the different ethnic and immigrant groups have sometimes formed. Thus for example, Manhattan is principally a residential area for whites while the Bronx and Harlem are areas for the Afro-American and Hispanic populations. New York is thus also a city of contrasts – rich and poor often live directly adjacent to each other.

Summarised: http://projects.nytimes.com/census/2010/explorer?ref=us and M. Felsch, R. Köhler www.diercke.de/kartenansicht.xtp?artId=978-3-14-100700-8&seite=203&id=5190&kartennr=2

M5 New York City, a melting pot

There are numerous definitions of a global city (e.g. by Friedmann, Sassen, Kulke). The same applies to their features and rankings. Globalization and World Cities Research (GaWC) uses for example the following aspects for its ranking:

- Economic (such as banks or the number of law offices and chartered accounting firms)
- Cultural (e.g. media conglomerates, architectural and engineering offices)
- Political (embassies, UNO offices) and
- Social (NGOs, scientific publications)

Only New York and London are in the top category Alpha +++

The geographer Dirk Bronger chose eight purely economic indicators in order to make global cities comparable:

1. Headquarters of the 500 largest global players by number
2. ... and by turnover
3. Headquarters of the 500 largest banks by turnover
4. Location of the largest stock exchanges by turnover
5. Largest international airports by passenger numbers
6. ... and by freight volume
7. Largest seaports by freight volume
8. Location of important worldwide (international) institutions

M7 Features of a global city (based on D. Bronger)

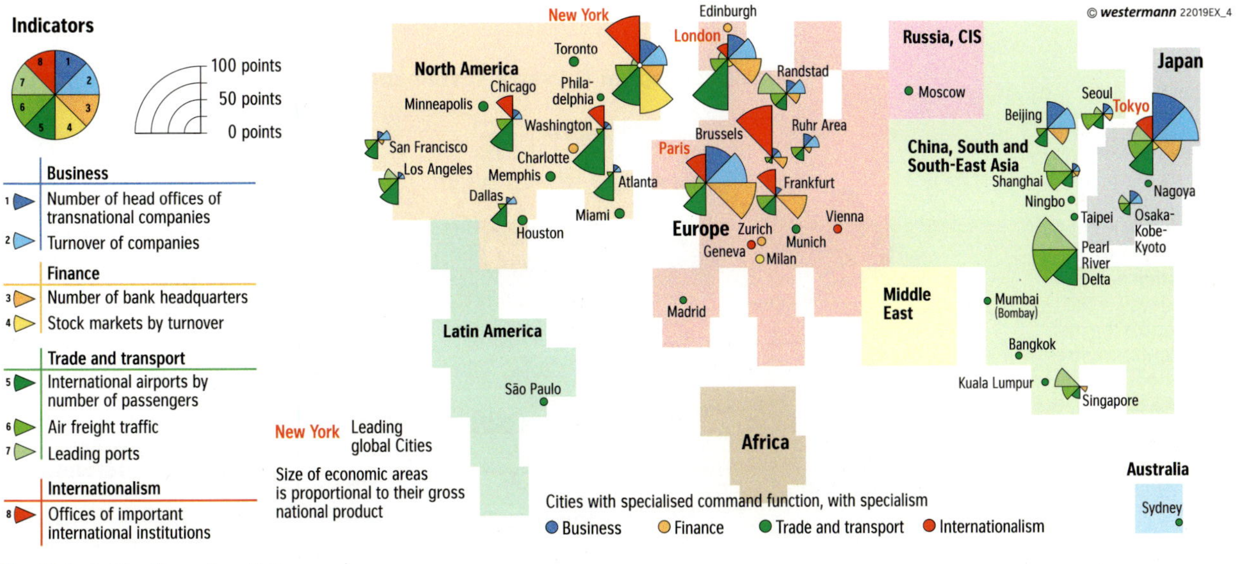

M6 Global cities (based on D. Bronger)

Modern cities – sustainable planning concepts?

Fujisawa – an "intelligent" town within a town

On a former industrial site in Fujisawa, a town south of Tokyo, a fully-electronic town of prefabricated houses with 1,000 housing units was created in a building phase of just two years: Fujisawa Sustainable Smart Town (Fujisawa SST). It was planned and built by the electronics company Panasonic. The town's energy provision is based on regenerative energies. A central computer regulates the efficient use of energy. But the lifestyle of the residents is also intended to reflect the slogan "Bringing Energy to Life". The aim is to express "vitality" in the community, in mobility, security, and in health provision. Can Fujisawa be a model for the city of the future?

1. Describe the physiognomic and functional urban structure of Fujisawa SST (M1, M4, M5).
2. Illustrate to what extent Fujisawa SST is a "smart town" (M1 – M5).
3. ⓞ "The 'Fujisawa model' is a revolutionary town-creation scheme that will bring energy to life, enhancing people's lives with solar power, security, mobility, community, and healthcare. Energy will be brought to life in a sustainable smart town that will open its doors to a new age of hope." (Source: http://panasonic.net)
   Discuss this thesis by:
   A Noting arguments that support the thesis (M1 – M6).
   B Formulating a critical comment opposing the thesis (M1 – M6).
4. Discuss the opportunities and risks of future-oriented urban planning that is financed by private investors such as Panasonic (M2, M4 – M6).
5. Evaluate how far Fujisawa can be seen as an opportunity for the use of derelict industrial land in urban areas (M2).
6. Give reasons for whether you would like to live in Fujisawa.
7. Ⓢ Analyse the urban planning with reference to the special threats to Japanese cities from natural disasters (M1, M5).

→ Smart city, Sustainable urban development

[Fujisawa Sustainable Smart Town (FSST) is a district of Fujisawa], a town within a town. [...] The aim of the project is not only to equip eco-houses with a lot of technology. The Fujisawa Smart Sustainable Town (FSST) is also intended to be a model for the future in social terms.

The idea, and the money for it, does not come from the government but from the conglomerate company Panasonic, which heads a consortium of a total of 18 private firms and which made a former factory site available. Homes will be equipped with the most modern technology available. With solar modules and fuel cells, they will largely generate the energy for their approximately 3,000 residents by themselves, as also happens in other green model estates [...]. Furthermore, in Fujisawa a whole network of services will contribute to fostering relationships between the residents and thus create a kind of ecological community in which, for example, elderly people can look after children and the residents can share electric cars. There is a choice of detached houses with a floor area of some 120 to 140 square metres and apartments for sheltered living for the elderly.

As well as their house keys, everyone who moves in from the spring of 2014 will be given access to the FSST Internet Community. Here, one can not only book a hairdresser, but also forge contacts with others in a social network – a kind of Facebook for the city of the future.

The residents can meet one another not only in the internet but also at the communal sports ground, in the planned cafés and shops, or for a chat in the main square, which the planners have sentimentally named Wellness Square [...].

The town will also have its own security personnel, cameras at all entrances, and lights that automatically switch on when somebody passes by at night [...].

The model homes also contain further security features. They will be equipped with a backup battery of lithium cells. [...] The whole thing will be managed by means of energy management systems for individual houses and for multi-family blocks as well as for the entire estate. [...]The model town will be fully completed in 2018 – the year in which the company will celebrate the 100th anniversary of its existence and seek to present itself as a pioneer of the sustainable economy.

Source: Martin-Jung, H., Süddeutsche Zeitung, 20.11.2013

M2 Fujisawa, a completely electronic town

Basic concept of Fujisawa sustainable smart town

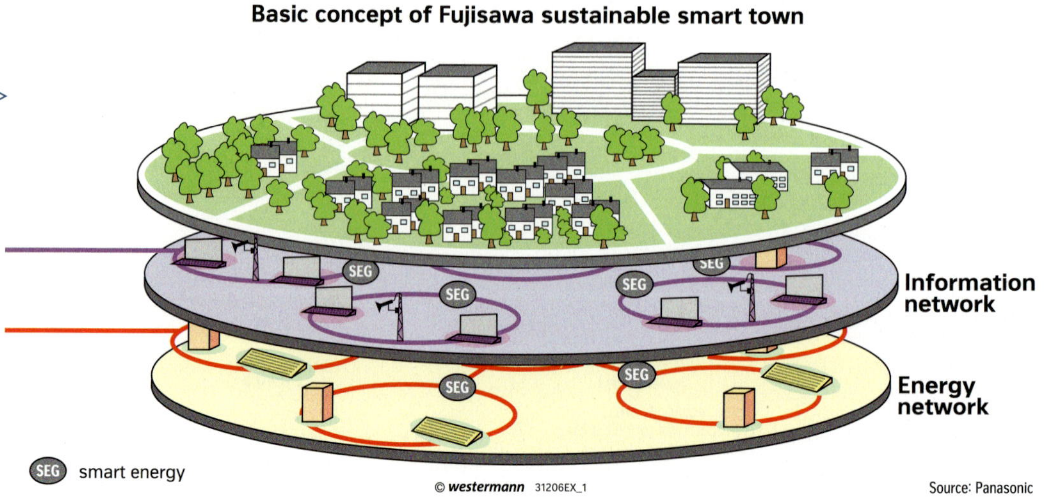

M1 Fujisawa SST has multiple functional levels. Central computers (bottom level) control the energy and information network (middle level), which in turn controls the individual control centres in each house. In the event of a disaster, the town can provide for itself for a period of three days.

◁ **M3** Fujisawa: Planning and status of construction, 2014. Fujisawa, the first town in the world to be planned with energy-saving prefabricated houses, could become a model of mass production for towns and cities. The estate has been planned around a central square where it is intended for the residents to meet one another (see M1 and M2).
▽

→ Smart City

Smart means intelligent, clever. Smart cities are cities where technology-based innovations are put into practice in order to make the use of resources more efficient.

In Fujisawa SST, everything is networked with everything else. The central computers control a multiplicity of computers in the individual houses which can in turn control the full range of household devices via an internet TV as control centre. To save electricity, refrigerators or air conditioning systems can adjust their cooling performance to the environment. Thus the latest refrigerators from Panasonic monitor the surrounding light, the temperature inside and outside the refrigerator and learn the rhythm of life of the families that own them. The refrigerator uses the data to predict usage behaviour and control the cooling in a targeted way. According to the company, this alone reduces electricity consumption by 12 percent in summer and 15 percent in winter in comparison to models without sensors.

Source: Koelling, M, www.welt.de accessed 09.10.2014

M4 The "smart" world of Fujisawa

Experts predict a huge market for fully-networked eco-cities. [...] The keywords of the coming lifestyle revolution do not begin with abstention, but with "smart" (intelligent): Smart City, Smart Grid and "smart" products. Equipped with sensors, they will be able to sense their environment, communicate with one another and use resources more efficiently. [...]
This week the Smart City Week was held in Yokohama, where experts from all round the world explored the potential of the new world. Not only Panasonic, but also the other electronics firms such as Hitachi, Fujitsu and Toshiba are preparing for life in intelligent, environmentally-friendly cities.

Source: Koelling, M., http://www.welt.de/print/die_welt/wissen/article13687020/In-zwei-Jahren-schluesselfertig.html 29.10.2011, accessed 09.10.2014

M6 Smart – the magic word for a sustainable future?

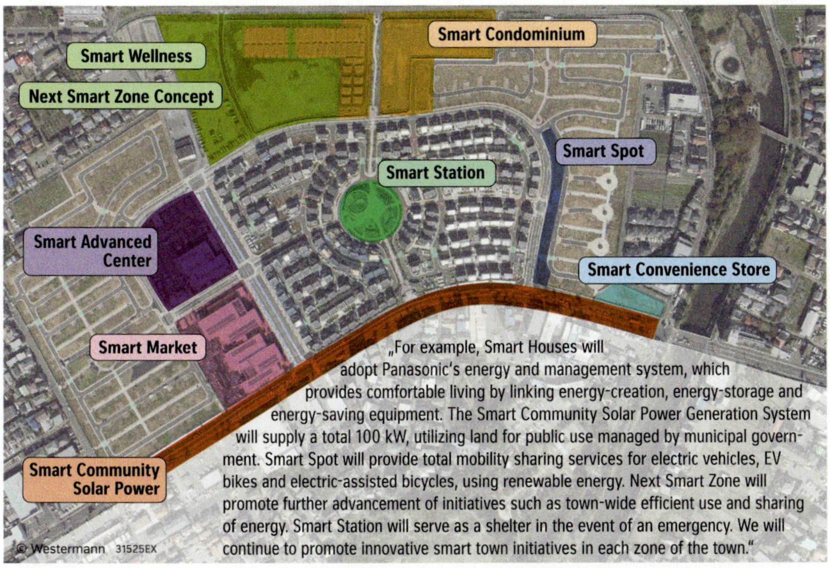

M5 The urban amenities of Fujisawa SST

weblink
http://panasonic.net/es/fujisawasst (Film)

Modern cities – sustainable planning concepts?

Lavasa – a multifunctional city

The city of Lavasa, some 200 km south of Mumbai, consists of five "towns". Two are already complete, while the others are still under construction. The basis for the "towns" is the neighbourhood principle. The aim of this is for the city – planned for over 200,000 people – to remain clearly comprehensible and with short travel distances. The city stretches over several hills and beside a lake. From the city centre, a series of zones with different kinds of buildings run up the hills. The city was planned according to the principles of New Urbanism. The "Transect Model" is also implemented. What do these planning principles in Lavasa look like?

1. a) Illustrate the Transect model (M1).
   b) Evaluate its implementation in Lavasa with consideration of the natural geographical conditions (M4).
2. Outline in a table how far all three sectors of the economy have been taken into account in Lavasa (M2, M5).
3. ⓞ "Live, work, learn, play" are named on its website as functions of the city. Using examples, show how these functions are realised (M2, M5, Internet).
   A Formulate an explanatory text.
   B Outline the examples in a diagram.
4. Evaluate the concept of New Urbanism as a basis for future urban development, also using concrete examples of its implementation in Lavasa (M5).
5. Modern cities – exclusively centres of the service sector? Comment on this question with reference to the examples of Seoul, Fujisawa and Lavasa.
6. Ⓢ Compare the urban planning concepts for Seoul, Fujisawa and Lavasa in terms of the respective needs of men, women and children.

→ Neighbourhood principle, New Urbanism, Smart Mobility

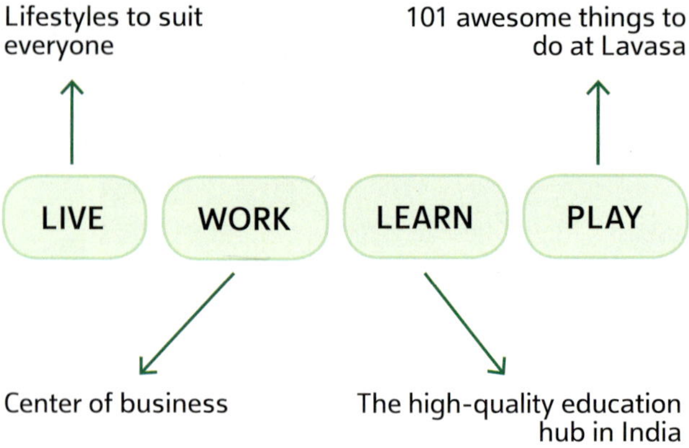

M2 Functions of the city

- Planned city consisting of 5 "towns" on 7 hills
- **Location:** 200 km south-east of Mumbai in the Pune District on the Warasgaon Dam Reservoir Lake
- 60 km shoreline
- **Surface area:** 100 km²
- **Size:** 200,000 to 250,000 inhabitants (planned), with 30,000 to 50,000 inhabitants per "town"
- **Builder (private construction project):** Hindustan Construction Company (HCC) (a global company)
- **Start of building:** 2002, currently 2 "towns" completed
- **Planned completion:** 2020
- **Functional mix:** Housing estates, industry (non-emitting; sectors: high-tech, biotechnology, medical equipment, bamboo furniture factory) and commerce, services (administration, provision, education/training, leisure, tourism)

M3 Description of Lavasa

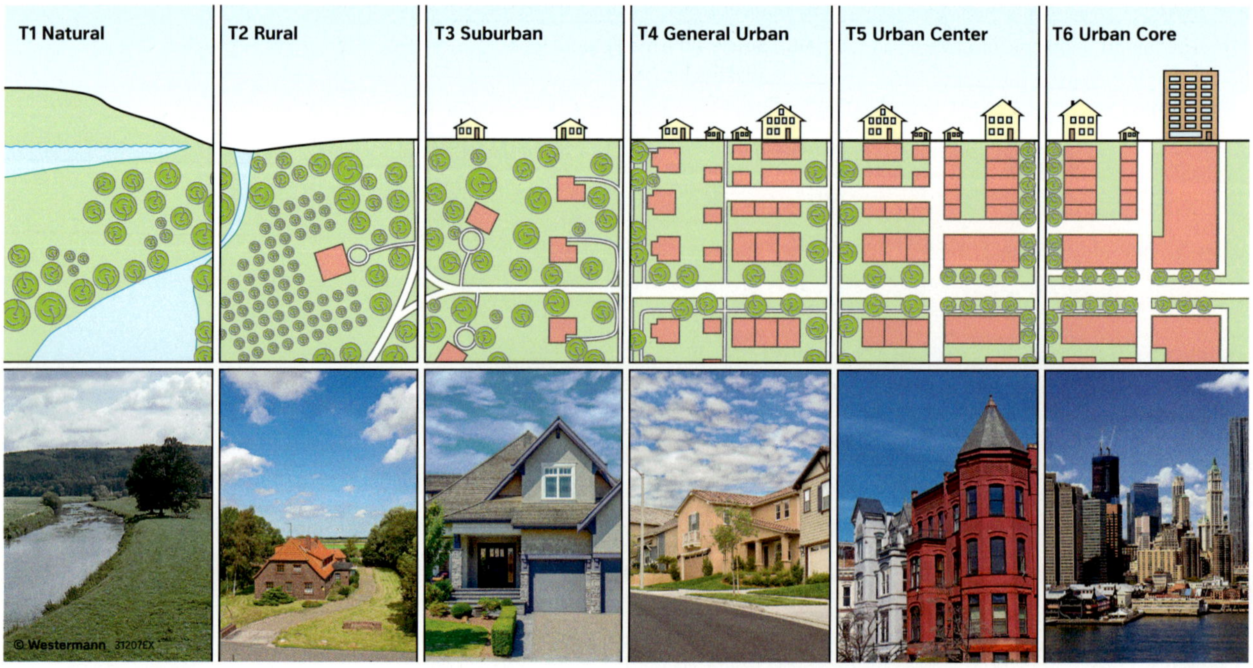

M1 The Transect model, developed by Andrés Duany on the basis of New Urbanism. Urban planning based on this model is also aimed at counteracting urban sprawl (see page 206).

M4 Lavasa in 2014

→ Neighbourhood principle

The complete plan for a large settlement is structured in the form of a series of smaller construction units which are easy for residents to comprehend, offer amenities for the supply of basic needs, and in which personal contacts between residents can lead to the formation of a community.

weblink

www.lavasa.com

	Principles of New Urbanism	Translated into the Master Plan
Commuting, accessibility	Walkability with everything within a 10 minute radius from work or home	A well-connected system of roads and pathways to make most facilities within walking distance
Connectivity	A network of streets, boulevards and alleys to easily disperse traffic	An interconnected combination of roads, streets and walkways to ensure unhindered movement of traffic
Mixed use and diversity	A mix of commercial and residential premises within neighbourhoods* and blocks	The Town Hall is at the centre of the town with residential apartments and commercial complexes dispersing in varied zones from the centre
Mixed housing	A range of living spaces based on a variety of factors, size, proximity to the town centre, pricing, etc.	Housing for people across the socio-economic spectrum, studio apartments, 1/2/3 bedroom apartments and villas in varying sizes
Quality architecture and urban design	Detailed attention to aesthetics and human comfort	Contemporary design combined with timeless elements and architectural themes (e.g. the Italian town of Portofino)
Traditional neighbourhood structuring	A discernable city centre and more open public spaces that encompass a range of uses and densities	People-friendly pedestrian walkways and meeting places, plus arcades, galleries, street-side cafes and a variety of gardens and semi-covered spaces
Planned increased density	Transect planning, so that population density decreases progressively as it moves away from the town centre	Residential apartments are densest around the centre of town and decrease at a pre-determined pace farther from the centre. The hillside villas are laid out in planned neighbourhoods
Smarter transportation	An advanced commuting network for enhanced efficiency. Smart mobility	An integrated transport system with varied modes of transport, walkways, bus lanes and automobile channels; Geographische Information Systems (GIS) and GPS
Sustainability	Minimal impact on the environment	Optimal utilisation and minimal exploitation of available natural resources; measures to prevent erosion on the slopes with continuous contour trenching. plantations and greening (70% of the surface area is green); use of bionics as a scientific basis for urban planning (bionics = copying of nature)
Quality of life	A better life and soulspace	An exhaustive range of organisations, services and information for education, recreation, employment and business

*Neighbourhood = smaller, compact building unit within a residential district

Source: http://www.corruptioninmaharashtra.com/uploads/2011/03/Lavasa_EBrochure.pdf

M5 The principles of New Urbanism (an urban development movement that emerged in the USA at the end of the 1980s) and their implementation in Lavasa

The essentials in brief

M1 Cartoon

The development of cities worldwide shows two tendencies. Many cities are growing, in some cases extremely, as shown by examples in China, while in others the population is falling. This leads to vacancy levels that can reach extreme proportions, as the example of Detroit shows. Both developments cause problems which national governments, federal states or the respective city administrations seek to counteract.

In China it is planned to meet the growing flows of migrants into the cities from the countryside by constructing new cities. Here, the large number of newly-planned cities can act as a test-bed for the sustainability of urban development concepts.

In other Asian countries too, new cities are coming into being that pursue concepts of sustainability. The use of "intelligent" technology provides the basis for many sustainable urban development and urban planning concepts. The networking of housing, mobility, energy provision, health care, administration and services is designed to lead to increased efficiency in the use of resources. "New Urbanism" follows another approach. In this concept, the city fulfils the function of a service centre but also serves as a living environment for the urban population. The concept is based on the neighbourhood principle, which it implements in a targeted way.

In Germany, efforts are made to relieve the burden on larger towns and cities with the aid of the point-axial concept, i.e. to achieve deconcentration. The urban functions are distributed to different categories of central places, ideally resulting in the equalisation of living conditions in a city and its environs. In reality this ambitious goal can only be achieved to a limited extent.

Measures and strategies against the loss of importance of the town or city as a living space are dependent on the specific situation. In Wittenberge, high vacancy levels in the estates of concrete slab apartment blocks are counteracted by clearance measures, while in Detroit whole districts are demolished. It is aimed to revitalise the fragmented city by means of new concepts such as urban greening. In London's East End, decline has been counteracted by a change in economic use. On the site of what was once the largest port in the world, new office blocks have arisen, former docks are used as yacht marinas, and old warehouses have been repurposed as apartment blocks.

But for all such measures, it is important to involve the public in the planning, because it is only in this way that the needs can be understood and coordinated. Thus the production of a new state development plan in North Rhine-Westphalia makes provision for a consultation period with the public.

Skill Check

All the skills that you were able to acquire in this chapter are listed here.
You can judge for yourself if you have mastered each skill: ***securely***, ***moderately*** or ***barely***.

Explanatory skills

Can I ...		Unsure? Look it up on these pages
1.	outline urban renewal measures and the transformation of towns and cities as a necessary adjustment to changing social, economic and ecological framework conditions?	178–181, 194–199
2.	outline development axes and development poles as control elements in spatial development?	186–189
3.	explain the interconnection of places at differing levels of centrality with their different functional amenities?	186/187

Methodological skills

Can I ...		
4.	analyse different presentation and working materials for answering questions relating to the city as a good place to live in?	176–185
5.	analyse cartoons in a way that is relevant to the question and topic?	177, 200
6.	carry out a multiperspective spatial analysis with the aid of new media?	190–193
7.	substantiate written and oral statements (e.g. on urban renewal measures) with appropriate and concrete references to materials and citations?	178–185
8.	outline, orally and in writing, the opportunities and risks posed by concrete measures for the development of urban spatial areas, using correct terminology in a way that is factually logical, structured and relevant to the problem?	178/179 182/183
9.	using appropriate search strategies, independently research information in libraries, the internet and internet-based geoinformation services and analyse it in a way that is relevant to the question and hypothesis?	196
10.	outline geographical facts, orally and in writing, using correct terminology in a way that is differentiated, problem-related, factually logical, structured and relevant to the tasks, operators and materials?	194–199

Evaluation skills

Can I ...		
11.	discuss the opportunities and risks of concrete measures for the development of urban spatial areas?	180/181
12.	evaluate measures für sustainable urban development in the field of tension between mobility and quality of life?	194–197
13.	evaluate the impact of revitalisation measures in the context of sustainable urban development?	178/179
14.	discuss the opportunities and risks of measures of deconcentration with regard to economic, ecological and social aspects?	188/189
15.	discuss changes in urban development principles as an expression of changing economic, demographic, political and ecological framework conditions?	188/189
16.	discuss the extent and limits of large-scale projects as impulses for the revitalisation of inner cities?	178/179
17.	evaluate processes of urban change as a challenge and opportunity for future urban planning, also taking into account the needs of men, women and children?	198/199

Activity skills

Can I ...		
18.	outline the results of my work on the subject in a school publication using correct terminology, in a way that is factual, problem-oriented and appropriate to the target group?	194–199
19.	present the results of my work on spatially-related facts in class using correct terminology, in a way that is factual, problem-oriented and appropriate to the target group?	194–199

Night-time activity at the Leipzig hub airport

VIII Goods and services – always available?

The importance of logistics and freight transport

Goods and services in a global world economy

World trade and communication – the world is getting smaller

With the click of a mouse, a logistics and freight transport apparatus is set in motion. Individual processes in the preparation and shipment of products have become fully automatic; people have become superfluous. Information can be obtained at any time by telephone, and modern communication technology is not tied down to locations and time zones. Transactions can be carried out in seconds, and often an office-based workplace is no longer necessary because the "home office", a desk at the worker's home, is globally networked. Agreements can be reached via video conferencing. The innovations in information and communication technology have changed our everyday lives, and relationships between people have also changed. Everyone can be reached at any time; friendships are managed in social networks.

While in the past the market place in a town or city was the centre for the handling of goods, today it is container ports, airports and freight centres that supply our supermarkets and internet stores. With increasing transport capacity and modern transport logistics, transport costs now only make up a small proportion of the total price of goods. This is also necessary in order to benefit from the cost advantages of outsourcing parts of the production process to low-wage countries, for example. The just-in-time delivery of components needed for production is a further service that modern logistics must be able to perform. But not all countries can participate in global world trade to the same extent.

Conquering space and time – how far have we already achieved this utopia? And what "price" must we pay for it? More space is required for roads, truck parking spaces, airfields and port facilities, and more energy is consumed in the transport of goods. Costs arise from the maintenance of roads and bridges, and also for the scrapping of older means of transport. The environment is increasingly burdened. Services are available at all times and in all areas of life, but the impact on the individual living space is severe.

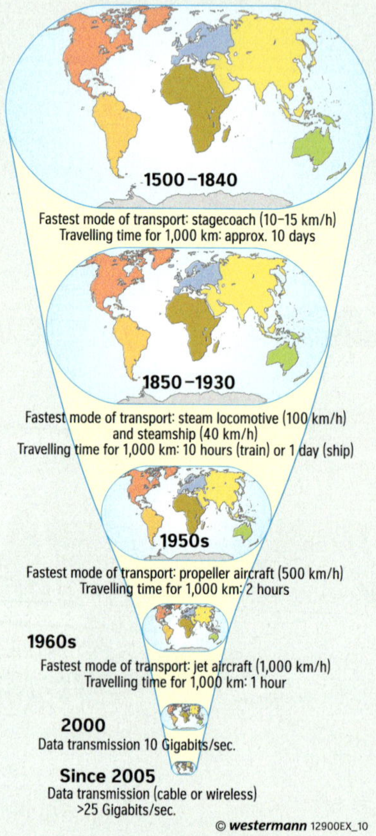

M2 The world is "shrinking"

M1 Global trade flows ▷

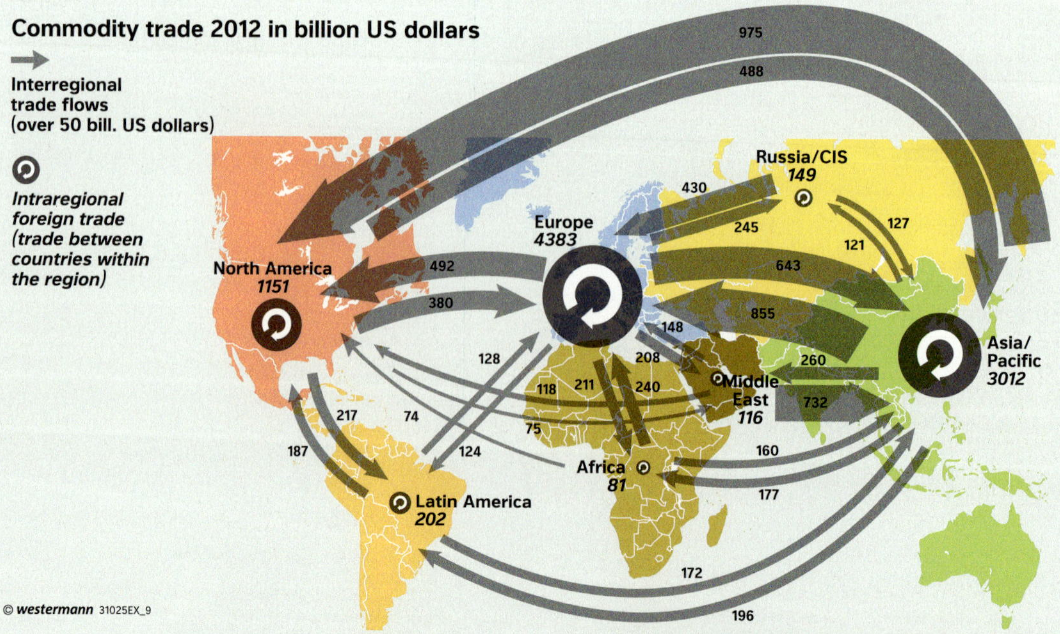

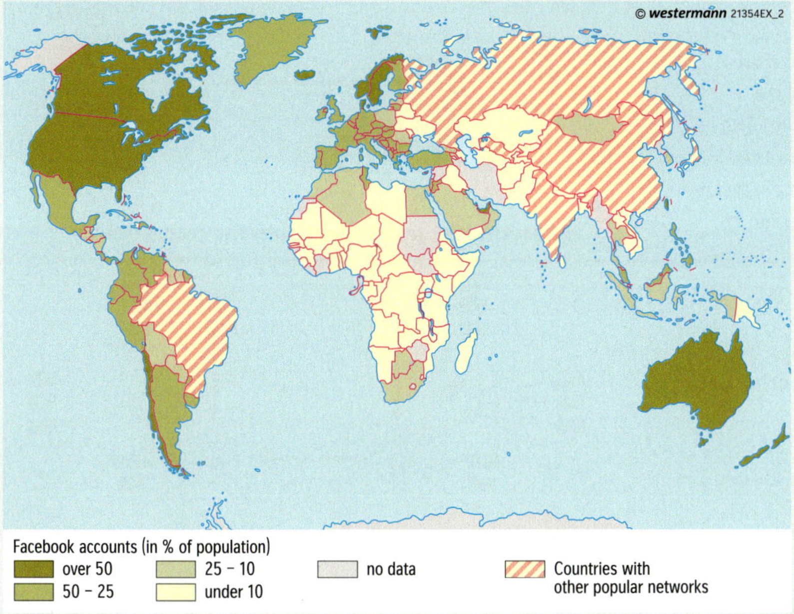

M3 Facebook accounts, 2012

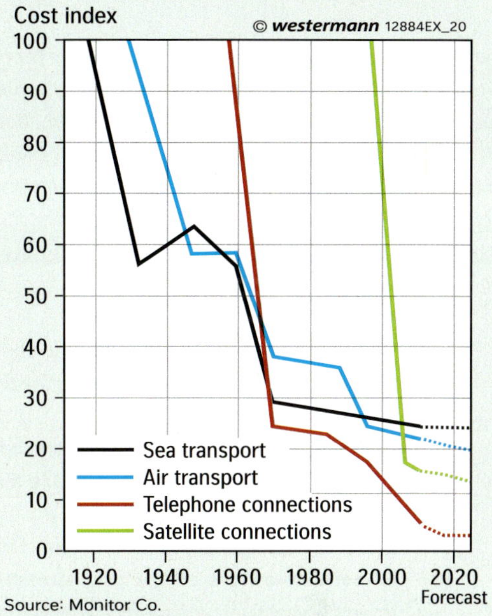

M5 Development of the costs of world trade

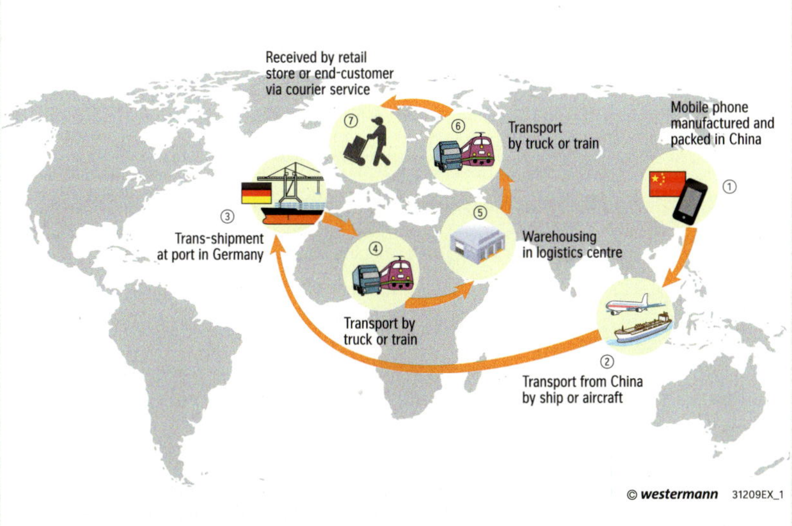

M4 Transport chain for a smartphone from China

M6 Cartoon: Delivery services of the future

1. The world is becoming ever smaller. Illustrate this statement (M2).
2. Characterise the most important world trade flows (M1).
3. a) Summarise the core statement of the cartoon in M6.
   b) Give your opinion of the cartoon.
4. Give reasons for the development of the costs of world trade (M5, M4).
Ⓞ 5. Outline your personal "network" by:
   A designing a cartoon.
   B drawing a diagram.
   C formulating a text.
Ⓢ 6. Outline the importance of modern information and communication technology in a mindmap.

Global sourcing – a challenge for logistics and freight transport

Transport chains in global freight traffic

Bridge closures, traffic jams and delays are barriers for freight transport. However, the success of the German economy would not be possible without a well functioning transport system. But the volume of goods traffic, which will continue to grow in future, should also take into consideration the requirements of climate and environmental protection as well as social needs. To achieve this, the efficiency of all modes of transport must be increased. How can this be made to work with modern transport management systems?

1. The invention of the container has revolutionised freight transport. Explain what advantages the transport of goods in containers brings (M3).
2. Illustrate the changes in the transport chain (M2).
3. Explain how service providers adapt to the changes in freight transport (M1, M4, M6).
4. (O) Evaluate the significance of a well functioning infrastructure in a synergetically networked economy from three perspectives: consumers, a global company, a logistics provider.
   - A Produce a chart.
   - B Formulate the assessment in a text.
5. a) Describe the development of goods transport in Germany for different modes of transport (M5).
   b) Comment on the discussion about the approval of long trucks (M7).
6. (S) Discuss the employment of drones in freight transport.

→ Direct shipment, Logistics, Roll-on-roll-off, Supply Chain Management, Transport chain

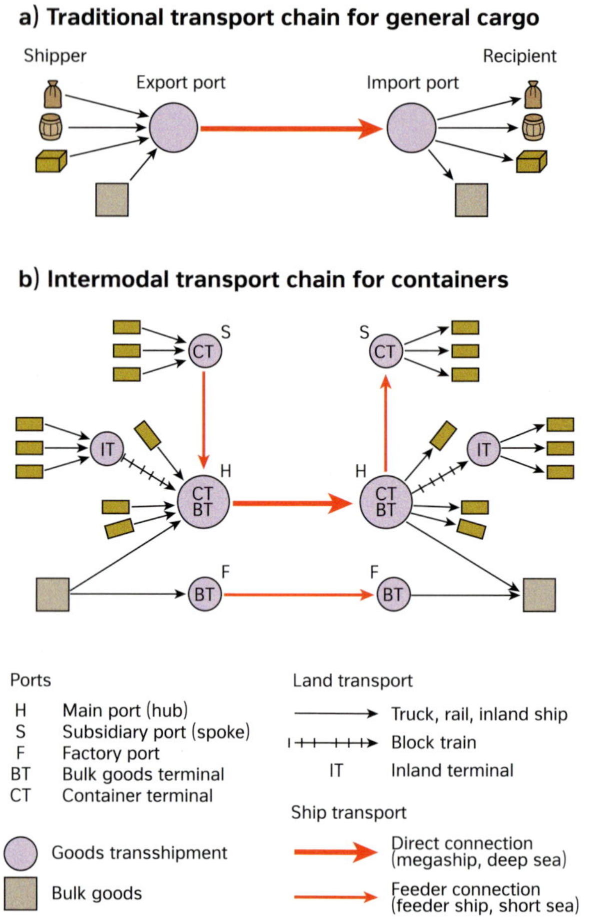

Source: Nuhn, H.: Strukturwandelungen im Seeverkehr und ihre Auswirkungen auf die Häfen, Geographische Rundschau 46 (1994) Vol. 5, p. 285 (amended) © westermann 31211EX_2

M2 The changing transport chain

→ Transport chain

The connection between the places of origin and destination through one or more means of transport produces the so-called transport chain. Goods transport takes place in different transport chains. Monomodal transport chains, which do not involve any transshipment of the goods, are also referred to as direct shipment. A change from one means of transport or transport carrier to another takes place within the framework of transshipment processes.

→ Supply Chain Management

Supply Chain Management refers to the organisation of complex and dynamic supplier and customer networks.

© Westermann 23002EX

M1 RoRo ship for roll-on-roll-off transport

M3 Cologne's Eifeltor freight centre, Germany's largest container handling station for combined road/rail freight transport. The former goods station in Cologne has now become a media park. There was not enough space available on the old site to build a modern station for container handling.

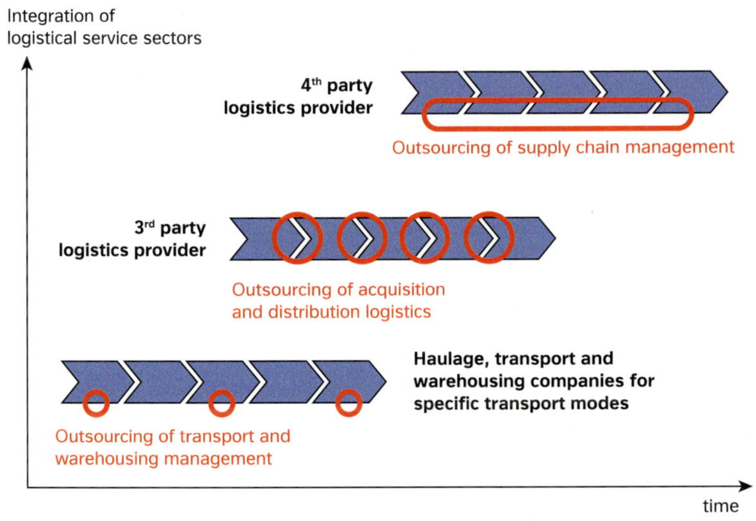

Source: Geographische Rundschau, 5/2007 © westermann 31212EX_1

M4 Development of logistics from freight forwarding companies to Supply Chain Management

4th party logistics providers (4LP):

External service providers who coordinate the logistical processes of a company, without providing their own vehicles, warehouses or other kinds of logistical facilities. They use and coordinate service offerings from different logistical service providers.

3rd party logistics providers (3LP):

External providers of logistical services who undertake transport, storage and other services for their customers.

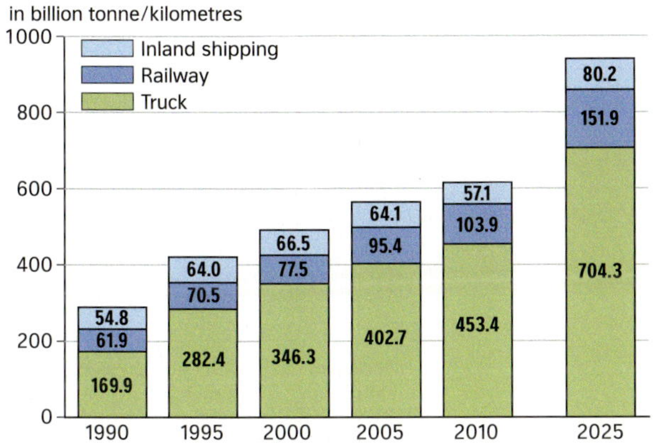

Source: German Association of the Automotive Industry © westermann 31213EX_1

M5 Goods transport in Germany by means of transport

The Swiss company Kühne + Nagel AG, founded in Bremen in 1890 as a transport company for cotton, quickly moved into import and export freight forwarding.
In **1903** the first branch office was opened in Hamburg. After the difficult years of the world wars, in which civilian maritime shipping collapsed, the company also moved into air freight forwarding in **1950**. Since the 1950s, branches were set up in Canada, Baghdad and Beirut, and representative offices in the Far East.
In **1974** the company moved its headquarters to Switzerland. From the middle of the 1980s, a Europe-wide transport, storage and distribution network was built up in anticipation of the European Internal Market.
Since 1993 the company intensified its global activities. Since then, 70 companies have been acquired in the road transport, rail transport, maritime freight, air freight and contract logistics sectors [...] and integrated into the existing business. Today the company is active in all sectors of the logistics industry.

Souce: Neiberger, C., Logistikunternehmen im Globalisierungsprozess. In: Geographische Rundschau, Vol 5/2007, p. 25

M6 The company history of a logistics service provider

The length of goods vehicles in Germany is currently restricted to a maximum of 18.75 metres. In a field trial designed to run for five years, the Federal Ministry of Transport now wishes to test trucks with a length of up to 25.25 metres and a total permitted weight of up to 44 tonnes. These trucks [are] also called "Eurocombis" or "Gigaliners". In thinly-populated regions of Sweden and Finland, such trucks (with a weight of up to 60 tonnes) have been in use for 40 years. An EU regulation from 1996 permits their use in the countries of the European Union, but there is no general approval for their use. The critics include some regional governments, trade unions, municipal associations, motoring clubs, pro-rail organisations and environmentalists. They perceive a range of disadvantages. They fear that the excessively long vehicles could become a safety risk. The huge trucks could block railway level crossings or intersections, get stuck on roundabouts, or make overtaking more dangerous.

Source: Lilienthal, B., Öko- oder Monstertruck? www.web.ard.de/themenwoche_2011/?p=898, accessed 05.09.2014

Long trucks place less strain on the infrastructure than existing goods vehicles, because the total weight is distributed across more axles. With existing combinations the weight is carried on a maximum of five axles, but on a long truck there are seven or eight axles. This results in a more favourable axle-load distribution. The Federal Highway Research Institute estimates that road damage (road surface fatigue, rutting) is reduced by 30 percent per truck. And when, in addition, fewer trucks are on the move, roads can be kept in use for longer. This saves some 5 percent of the costs of maintenance. There is also no danger to bridges. With an unchanged total weight of a maximum of 44 tonnes, the load-bearing capacity and long-term stability of the structures are assured.

Source: VDA Verband der Automobilindustrie

M7 Discussion about the use of long trucks

Markets must be accessible

Ports adapt themselves – Singapore

"In 1819, the English agent Thomas Stamford Raffles founded in Singapore an office of the East India Company, which at that time handled the entire trade between Great Britain and South-East Asia. The island, which at that time was very thinly populated, grew into one of the largest commercial centres in South-East Asia. Today the city-state is home to one of the biggest ports in the world." (www.wasistwas.de) The development of the port of Singapore is a classic example of how ports are adapting to the needs of global container transport.

1. a) Explain the structural and functional transformation of ports (M2, M6).
   b) Outline the impact of this transformation on the port facilities (M2, M5, M6).
   c) Illustrate how sea ports like Singapore are responding to changes in maritime transport (M3, M5).
2. a) The largest ships are not necessarily the cheapest to operate. Comment on this statement (M4).
   b) Give reasons why the long-distance route (calling at as few ports as possible) is advantageous (M4).
3. a) Compare the positions of the largest container ports with the worldwide container routes (M1, M9).
   b) Characterise the position of Singapore as a port location (M1, M10, Atlas).
   c) Illustrate the importance of Singapore as a port location (M3, M9, M10).
4. Put together the advantages and disadvantages of the container ship in comparison to aircraft and trucks (M7, M8).
5. Ⓢ Hamburg has built a new container port further downriver. Give reasons for this decision. Research how the old port is used today.

→ TEU, Transport chain

→ TEU = Twenty-foot Equivalent Unit (German term: "Standardcontainer"), is an internationally standardised unit of measurement in container transport (20 foot container = 6.10 m x 2.44 m x 2.59 m).

weblink
www.singapur.net/singapur-hafen.php (Film)

Since the middle of the 1960s, ports have been subject to a transition in their structure and function. [...] With the introduction of the container, [...] the interim storage, sea transport packing, appropriate stowage or preparation and care of the goods while in port have become unnecessary. Workers have lost their jobs, and general cargo centres, storage facilities and warehouses have lost their function. [...] At the same time, with the focus on the rapid throughput of containers, the ports have also lost their formerly important control function in the logistics chain.

Source: Nuhn, H. & Pfister, S., Seehäfen in der globalen Transportkette. In: Praxis Geographie, Vol 2/2012, p. 30

M2 Ports in transition

According to data from the Singaporean-German Chamber of Industry and Commerce (AHK), a total of 5,000 logistics and distribution chain providers are represented in Singapore, including the global giants Schenker, NYK, Keppel Logistics and YCH. According to data from the Maritime Port Authority (MPA), 4,200 foreign multinational companies and 26,000 international companies are located in Singapore – often on account of the country's strategic location and the excellent logistics infrastructure that permits them to use Singapore as a distribution centre for the South-East Asian region.

Source: Wälterlin, U., Handelsblatt 22.11.2011. © Handelsblatt GmbH. All rights reserved.

M3 Locational advantages of the Port of Singapore

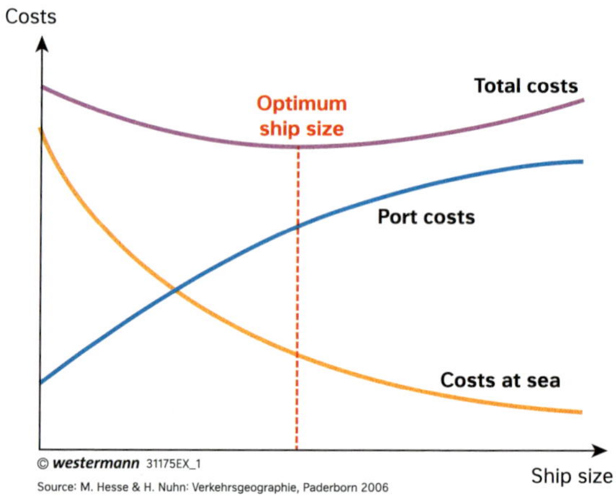

M4 Operating costs and optimum ship size

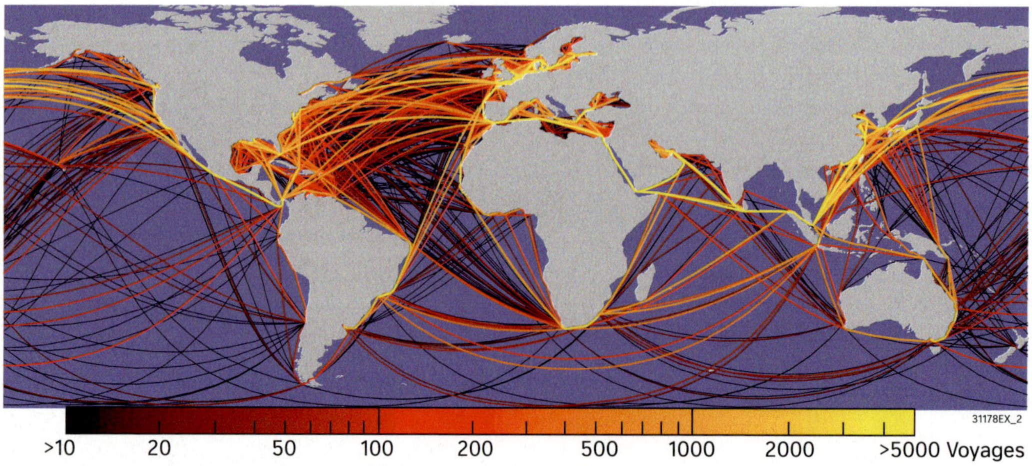

M1 Worldwide container routes (voyages per year)

M5 The container port of Singapore is regarded as a paragon of efficiency.

Volume of freight handled, 2013 in million TEU	
Shanghai (China)	33.6
Singapore (Singapore)	32.6
Shenzhen (China)	23.3
Hong Kong (China)	22.3
Busan (South Korea)	17.7
Ningbo (China)	17.3
Tsingtau (China)	15.5
Canton (China)	15.3
Los Angeles (USA)	14.6
Dubai (UAE)	13.6

Source: www.statista.com

M9 Ranking list of the ten largest container ports

Year	Capacity (TEU)	Length (m)	Width (m)	Depth (m)
1956 – 1970	500 1,000	135 200	< 25.0	< 9.0
1970 – 1980	1,000 – 3,000	200 – 215	< 28.0	10.8
1980 – 1988 Panamax*	3,000 4,500	250 294	32.2 32.2	11.0 12.0
1988 – 1995				
Post-Panamax	4,500 – 5,000	280 – 305	41.1	11.4 – 12.7
1995 – 2005 Super-Post-Panamax	5,000 – 10,000	300 – 350	40 – 43	13 – 14.5
2006				
Suezmax**	10,000 – 15,000	350 – 400	50 – 60	15 – 17
Since 2013 Triple E	18,000	400	59	15.5

*maximum size of ship for passage through the Panama Canal before its enlargement
**maximum size of ship for passage through the Suez Canal
Source: Rodrigue, J.-P. et al., Geography of Transport Systems. New York.

M6 Growth in the size of container ships

Singapore is bursting at the seams. Although the nation is among the most urbanised countries in the world, more than half of the city-state is covered by vegetation – including rain forest and park land. And that is how it should stay. Therefore, Singapore is expanding by land reclamation, i.e. landfill in coastal areas. In this way, Singapore has expanded from 581.5 to 704 square kilometres since the 1960s.

An important reason for the heavy demand for more land is the expanding logistics industry. Due to its unique geographical location in the heart of South-East Asia in terms of defence and economic policy, Singapore has for centuries been a centre for trade, exchange and the presence of businesses.

Source: Wälterlin, U., Handelsblatt, 22.11.2011

M10 Singapore's tradition of logistics

[A Suezmax container ship] at full power [has a] fuel consumption [of] 0.171 kg/kWh, which corresponds to some 14,380 litres of fuel per hour. This amounts to 2.1 litres of heavy oil per 14 t container and 100 km transport distance. The diesel engine's relatively low fuel consumption is due to its high efficiency of 49.0 percent (modern car engines today can only attain 35 to 45 percent). A full tank of fuel costs 5.3 million €.

M7 Fuel consumption of a container ship (Suezmax)

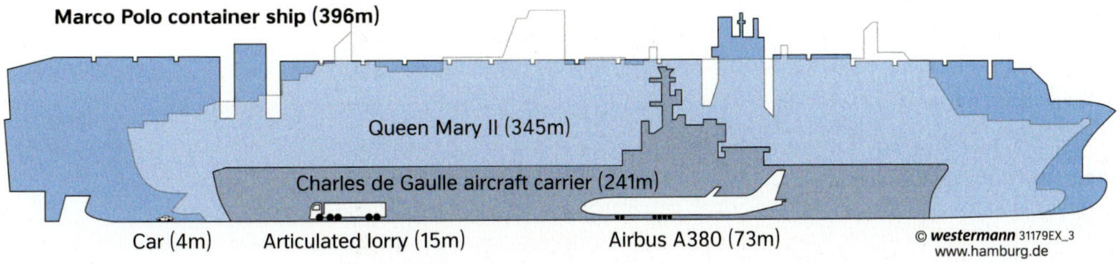

M8 Size comparison: car/truck/aircraft/ship/container ship

Markets must be accessible

The transformation of the international air transport network

Dubai World Central International Airport is not an exceptional case. All over the world, the construction and enlargement of hub airports is seen as a development strategy.
Where are new hub airports being built? How are they changing global air traffic flows? And what impact could this have on air transport in Germany?

1. Describe the projected changes in the volume of air traffic up to 2032 (M1).
2. What influence could the development of hub airports have:
   a) on global air traffic flows (M2, M4, M6)?
   b) on the German hub airports of Frankfurt and Munich (M2, M4, M6)?
3. ⓞ "In many places, airports are seen as well suited for the establishment of a centre for growth." Explain this with reference to:
   A an example of your own choice (M2, M3, M5, M6, M7).
   B Aerotropolis Dubai.
4. ⓞ Describe the development of a hub airport of your choice based on internet sources:
   A Dubai.
   B Doha.
   C Mexico City.
   D Istanbul.
5. Ⓢ Draw a world map, in which you:
   a) enter the most important hub airports corresponding to their passenger numbers (M6).
   b) clearly show the growth of the most important hub airports (M7).

→ Aerotropolis, Hub airport

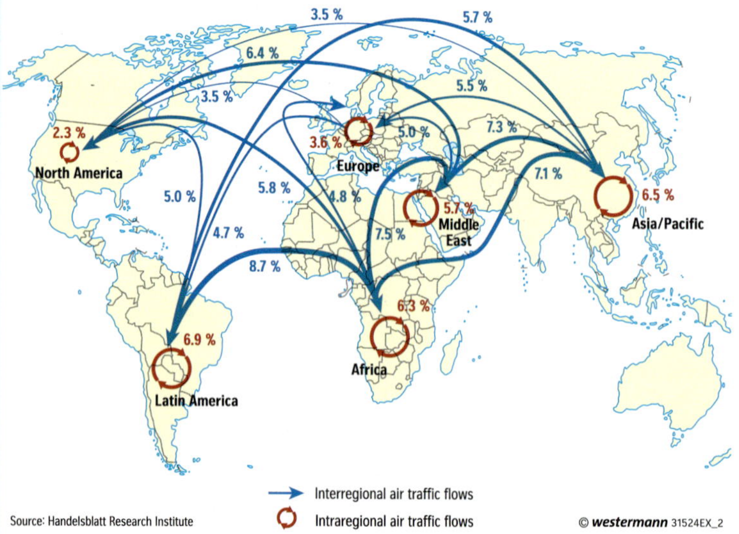

M1 Growth rates of passenger flows 2012–2032

Mexico's President [...] presented the plans for a gigantic new airport in Mexico City. [...] The new airport is just one of at least six large-scale projects that have the potential to massively change the traffic flows in air transport. Four of these – Doha, Dubai, Abu Dhabi and Istanbul – are so favourably located that, together with their locally-based airlines Qatar Airways, Emirates, Etihad and Turkish Airlines, they can become a serious threat to the old hubs in Europe such as Frankfurt, Paris or London, not to mention smaller locations like Zürich, Vienna or Milan. [...]
Airports have long ago taken over the function that was previously performed by sea ports – at least for passengers and high-value cargo. Countries like UAE or Turkey are pumping billions into the projects because they anticipate that the rest of their economies will also profit from them. It is also striking how much the economic policy goals of Mexico and Turkey resemble each other. They both aim to become important trading centres and attract new industries with the aid of structural reforms and investments.
In China, too, dozens of new airports have been built in a period of just a few years. Last year, Beijing Capital International Airport (BCIA) was ... the second-largest in the world with 83 million passengers. But in a few years' time, a new facility will be built to the south of the city – supposedly for up to 200 million passengers per year – that is more than five times the current passenger traffic in Munich. [...]
Thus the new airport at Dubai [...] will not be the largest in the world, because it is only designed to handle 160 million passengers. But it is much more of a threat to Frankfurt or Munich and the airlines based here. Dubai (and Abu Dhabi, Doha and Istanbul) are in such favourable geographical locations that with modern long-haul aircraft they can reach practically any destination in the world non-stop. [...] Emirates can thus divert passengers on long-distance flights, who previously transferred in Frankfurt, to its own hub. [...] Just a few years ago the international airport of Abu Dhabi was just a quiet backwater. The emirate mainly focused its attention on the petroleum business and showed less interest in general trading. But this changed. In 2003 the government founded Etihad Airways. [...] To gain access to more passengers for the Abu Dhabi hub, the airline even acquired shares in European airlines like Air Berlin or Alitalia.
But Istanbul could soon become even more of a threat than Dubai, Doha and Abu Dhabi. Here too, a new airport for up to 150 million passengers is due to open in October 2017. [...] Istanbul and Turkish Airlines have the advantage that the hub is at least three hours of flying time closer to Europe than the Gulf airports. Turkish Airlines can thus easily reach Germany and all the other markets in the European Union with short-haul aircraft like the Airbus A 320. This is cheaper, and cities with less traffic volume can also be reached. In future these transfer passengers will be lost to Frankfurt or Munich.
Source: Flottau, J., Landung in der Zukunft. In: Süddeutsche Zeitung, 5.9.2014, p. 18

M2 Landing in the future

M3 Mexico City Airport – a new hub in America (designed by Norman Foster)

Airport	Passengers in millions	Change from 2008 in %
Beijing PEK	81.9	+ 81.9
London Heathrow (LHR)	70.0	+4.6
Chicago O´Hare (ORD)	66.8	-5.7
Paris Charles de Gaulle (CDG))	61.6	+1.2
Dubai (DXB)	57.7	+54.1
Frankfurt Main (FRA)	57.5	+ 7.6
Amsterdam Schiphol (AMS)	51.0	+ 7.6
Madrid Barajas (MAD)	45.2	- 11.1
Istanbul Atatürk (IST)	45.1	+ 57.9
Munich (MUC)	38.4	+ 11.1
Doha (DOH)	21.2	+72.4
Abu Dhabi (AUH)	14.7	+ 63.1

Source: Handelsblatt Research Institute, Determinanten der Wettbewerbsfähigkeit im Internationalen Luftverkehr 2014, p. 52

M6 Passenger numbers at the largest international hub airports, 2012

Airport	Passengers in mill.		Rank	
	2000	2013	2000	2013
Atlanta	80	94	1	1
Beijing	no data	84	no data	2
London Heathrow	64	72	4	3
Tokyo	56	72	6	4
Chicago	67	69	2	5
Los Angeles	66	67	3	6
Dubai	no data	66	no data	7
Paris	48	62	8	8
Dallas	61	60	5	9
Jakarta	no data	60	no data	10
Hong Kong	33	60	22	11
Frankfurt	49	58	7	12
Singapore	29	53	28	13
Amsterdam	40	53	10	14
Denver	39	53	11	15
Guangzhou	no data	52	no data	16
Bangkok	30	51	26	17
Istanbul	no data	51	no data	18
New York	33	50	21	19
Kuala Lumpur	no data	47	no data	20
Shanghai	no data	47	no data	21

M4 Airports with the highest passenger numbers

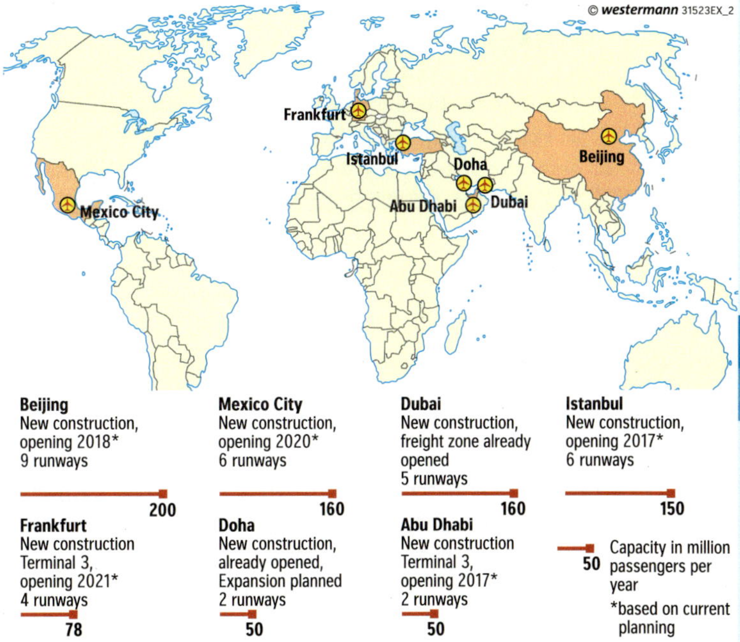

M7 The largest airport building projects in the world (in 2014)

Cathedrals of our time

Gigantic halls reaching to a breathtaking height [...]. The architecture aims to make passengers gaze in wonder. In this sense, these airports are the new cathedrals of our time. At the end of last year, a 500,000 square metre terminal opened in Shenzhen, China, completely in white. [...] The main terminal of Istanbul Airport will be one million square metres [...]. Here, slender white columns will carry a cross vault that would make any Gothic church builder green with envy.
The days when an airport was only for flying are definitely over. Already today, airports earn more from retailing outlets on the group than from the handling of air passengers. Since it is hardly possible for large companies today to succeed without international business connections, this trend is likely to continue.
For the American economist John D. Kassarda, the urban future will be called "Aerotropolis": cities docking on to their airports, offering the arriving business people not only perfect working conditions for their meetings, but also sufficient recreational possibilities for afterwards. [...] It is no wonder that airports are so much in demand. The new airport for Mexico City has been designed by the British architect Norman Foster. [...] In the early 1980s he designed Stansted Airport, and in 2008 the then largest airport in the world in Peking. [...] In Mexico he aims to go one better. Foster reckons with a building period of 50 years. After all, a cathedral needs time.

Source: Weissmüller, L., Landung in der Zukunft. In: Süddeutsche Zeitung, 5.9.2014, p. 18

M5 Are large airports merely prestige objects?

Shopping worldwide, day and night – the World Wide Web

Leipzig, a goods mail order centre

Shopping in the internet is becoming more and more popular. According to a study, 60 percent of consumers with access to the internet use this method of shopping – and only four out of ten web-savvy consumers prefer to buy everything in a physical store. According to the experts, the future will belong to online trading, and buying via smartphone, with shopping all round the clock. The logistics industry is responding to this trend. The Leipzig-Halle location has become a goods hub for mail order business. Leipzig-Halle Airport has no ban on night-time flying, so that a 24-hour service can be offered (www.logistik-heute.de).

1. Summarise the locational factors that have led to the development of the logistics cluster at Leipzig-Halle (M2, M4, M5, M7).
2. The logistics cluster offers business-to-consumer and business-to-business services. Explain with the aid of examples (M1, M5, M6, M7, M8).
3. ⓞ All three sectors of the economy are connected in Leipzig. Illustrate this (M7):
   A in a text.
   B with the aid of a diagram.
4. Give reasons showing how far the Leipzig-Halle location is an example of synergy effects (M7).
5. Assess the statements in the promotion of the new Airport Park with respect to the advantages of the site (M8, Atlas).
6. Ⓢ Produce a digital presentation about Leipzig as a business location.

→ Cluster, End of Runway concept, Freight hub, Hub, Logistics centre, Synergy effect

M3 Logistics centre in Leipzig

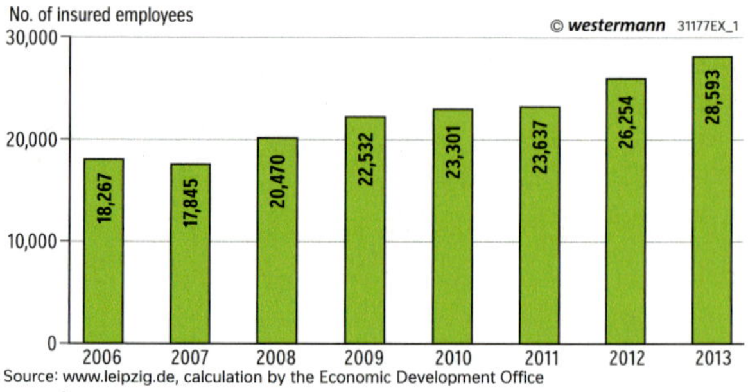

M4 Trend in the number of employees in the Leipzig logistics cluster

According to the bevh [the German E-Commerce and Distance Selling Trade Association] every second package now comes from the B2C [B2C = business-to-consumer and refers to trade between companies (mostly retailers) and consumers] segment and no longer from the B2B (business to business) segment.
The growth of e-commerce sets new challenges for interactive trading and the package market.
[...] With 54 percent, the four highest turnover product groups – apparel, books, CDs and DVDs, and household electronics – cover somewhat over half of the total volume of packages in the B2C segment.

Source: EXTRA "E-Commerce und Versand", LOGISTIK HEUTE, Issue 9/2014, 5.9.2014

M1 Internet shopping

- 413 m-long warehouse (total size corresponds to 5 football pitches)
- Germany's largest distribution and sorting facility for packages and documents
- High-tech sorting facility (cost: some 70 million €)
- Hourly throughput: 100,000 shipments
- In operation 24 hours, 365 days in the year
- Handling of 60 aircraft per night from all round the world
- 3,600 m long runway
- Aircraft hangar for maintenance work

M5 The DHL hub in figures

M2 Location of Leipzig as a cargo hub

Our End of Runway concept combines the following features:

- Latest acceptance times for time-sensitive goods shipments
- Integrated return and repair services for fastest turnaround times and maximum product availability
- Flexibility through connections to the entire breadth of DHL transport networks

Source: www.dhl.de

M6 Advertising for DHL's End of Runway concept

Rewe opens its first main warehouse in Leipzig

In April 2014 the Cologne-based Rewe supermarket chain commissioned its first main warehouse nationwide for fruit and vegetables in Leipzig's freight transport centre (GVZ). [...] The new building has a logistics area of 10,000 square metres. The fruit and vegetables are delivered fresh every day and stored in two cool zones before their onward transport. The first zone can be regulated to a temperature of 4 to 5°C, while the second covers a temperature range of 10 to 12°C. The loading ramps, exterior walls and roof are specially insulated. A total of 38 delivery and despatch gates make rapid handling of the goods possible.
In future the main warehouse in Leipzig will supply Rewe's regional warehouses in the conurbations of Berlin, Dresden and Leipzig/Halle. The aim is to reduce the volume of fruit and vegetables stored in the respective warehouses. Previously, a large part of the entire fruit and vegetable assortment had to be kept in stock in each of the regional warehouses. In future this will only be necessary in the main warehouse.
Source: Anja Kiewitt (akw), in: Logistik heute, 4.4.2014

DB Schenker Logistics increases capacity in its Leipzig logistics centre

Since the summer of 2013, a total of some 1,500 employees have been supplying components to BMW automobile factories in China and South Africa. More than 100 containers are packed every day. Since the summer of 2011, some 8,000 different components for BMW automobile models have been received, packed and securely stowed in containers in the 63,000 square metre facility. Conservation for the ocean voyage through various climatic zones, for example for metal parts, is also carried out here in Leipzig. Currently up to 50 containers leave the logistics centre every day. They travel to Rosslyn in South Africa by sea. The containers are transported to Shenyang in China by rail. For more than a year, the transport over the nearly 11,000 kilometre route has been carried out by DB Schenker Rail with its partners.
Source: www.dbschenker.com4

Leipzig/Halle – base for DHL/Lufthansa Cargo air freight company

Since 2007, Leipzig/Halle Airport has been the home base for the first air freight company in central Germany. With the establishment of the new, globally-operating freight line by DHL and Lufthansa Cargo, Leipzig/Halle has become the most important logistics location in the region. Cargo transport will be handled via Halle-Leipzig Airport. Logistics and storage will be controlled from the logistics centre. The distribution centre has been given the promotionally effective title of "goods hotel".
Source: nach: www.lifepr.de

weblink

- www.dpdhl.com/de/logistik_populaer/aus_den_unternehmensbereichen/hub_leipzig.html (Film DHL)

M7 Synergy effects at the Leipzig location: press releases and promotional materials from leading companies at the Leipzig-Halle site

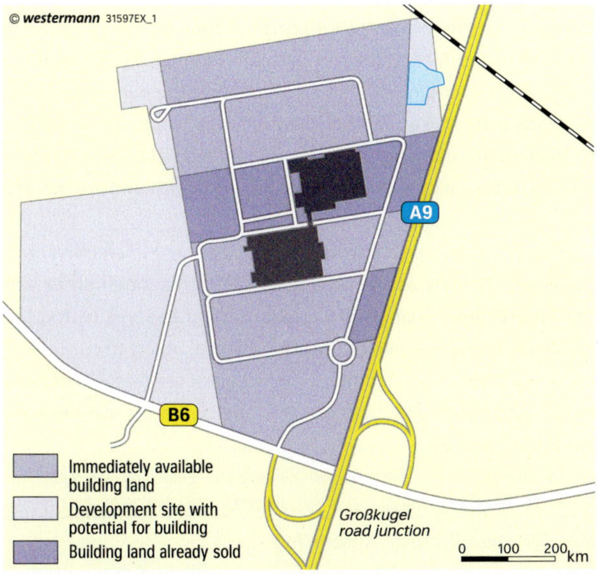

M8 The new Leipzig-Halle Airport Park

Leipzig-Halle Airport Park

- Sites for production & logistics in the heart of Germany [sites marketed from July 2013]
- 317,000-m² site available for building
- Properties for immediate use
- Fully developed
- Individualisation possible
- All approvals in place
- Government assistance still possible
- Many large companies (BMW, Porsche, Amazon, DHL) located within 30-minute truck radius
- Areas for expansion already planned
- Large and interconnected sites
- Directly on the A9 (Großkugel exit) and B6
- Directly facing Leipzig Airport
- On the Magdeburg–Leipzig railway line

Call centres – networking of global services

Calling Manila – services around the clock

Just this evening, your electrical device decides to go on strike. You quickly call the manufacturer's phone number and ask for servicing. A lady with a slight accent answers the telephone and makes a note of the necessary details. The repair will be carried out in the next few days. But the call centre where the lady works is not located in Germany, but in Dublin, Istanbul or even Manila, the "Call Centre Capital of the World" (Manila Bulletin), where the time is already after midnight. But the service is provided nevertheless. How far do customers and businesses profit from the outsourcing of customer services to countries like the Philippines?

1. Sketch in a sketch map the position of Manila as well as the positions of Europe and the USA (Atlas).
2. a) Work out the local time in Manila when a customer from Germany calls at 17:00 hrs German local time (Atlas).
   b) North American firms in particular use the call centres in Manila. Calculate the time differences between Los Angeles and New York and Manila (Atlas).
3. (O) Outsourcing as a motor for jobs? Comment on this question, by:
   A writing a reader's letter from the standpoint of a call centre agent;
   B drafting your opinion in the form of an argument.
4. (S) Call centres provide a service in the context of logistics and goods transport. Show the relationships (M3, M6).

→ Call centre, Outsourcing

M2 Friendliness and patience are prerequisites for working in a call centre

- **Number of call centres in the Philippines:** approx. 800
- **Employees in call centres**: approx. 350,000
- **Turnover in 2010:** 6 billion US-$
- **Growth rate in recent years**: 15–20%
- **Companies represented (selected)**:
  IBM, Shell, HSBC, Procter & Gamble, Bosch, Henkel, Ericsson, Nestlé
- **Qualifications of a call centre agent:**
  Linguistic adaptability
  Cultural adaptability
  Friendliness
  Respect for the customer
  Patience
  Anger tolerance
- Staff fluctuation rate: 60–80% per year

Source: Bethge, W., Callcenter auf den Philippinen – Eine „Sonnenschein" Branche? http://bethge.freepage.de/callcenters.htm2011, accessed 05.09.2014

M1 Data on call centres in the Philippines

With Business Process Outsourcing (BPO), a company outsources certain business activities that can be provided more cheaply elsewhere in order to focus on its own core business. Business areas that can be outsourced may include, among others, finance and accounting (bookkeeping), logistics, payment systems and web design as well as computer analyses in general. Customer care is a major aspect of this, and here the call centre plays a key role. In the Philippines it generates some two-thirds of total BPO turnover.

In the activities of a call centre, a distinction is made between inbound and outbound calls. Inbound calls are calls made by the customer, perhaps to enquire about a product, or make a booking or place an order. With outbound calls, a call centre agent telephones the (potential) customer. As a rule, this is for the purpose of selling products and services. Further objectives of telephone marketing are to investigate customer satisfaction or for market research surveys. Successful sales calls are generally more difficult and are therefore also generally higher paid.

[...] The call centre industry wants only "the best". Selection procedures, which often last for two weeks, are correspondingly exacting and demanding. Using simulations, candidates are tested for – among other things – voice quality, patience, ability to concentrate, and strength of argumentation. There is evidence that, out of twenty applicants, often only between two and five are accepted for an initial trial period.

Source: Bethge, W.: Callcenter auf den Philippinen – Eine „Sonnenschein" Branche? bethge.freepage.de/callcenters.htm2011, accessed 05.09.2014

M3 Business Process Outsourcing

In Eastwood Cyberpark in Manila, night is turned into day. It is 2:30 in the morning, and the streets are as busy as in broad daylight. All around, multi-storey office blocks rear up into the night sky, their floors brightly lit. Here, the clocks tick differently, in harmony with the USA and Canada, situated more than 10,000 kilometres and numerous time zones away from Manila. Thousands of telephone agents sit in Eastwood, speaking with customers at the other end of the world. This mini-city is one of the many outsourcing centres that have sprung up in the Philippines. [...]
Christopher Boughton developed the technical department of the publishing house Cambridge University Press in the Philippines. "For the money that we would pay for five people in Great Britain, here we get 35," he says. The manager is enthusiastic about the training of the IT specialists and the flexibility with which they respond to customers' wishes. "We like the way they work. They do exactly what we ask them to," he says.
Source: Outsourcing als Jobmotor, www.focus.de, accessed 05.09.2014

M4 A call centre in Manila

Call centres are one of the fastest-growing industries in the Philippines. There are two reasons for this. On the one hand, there are too few other jobs in the country offering a comparable income. And on the other hand, companies in the industrialised countries are seeking to save on wage costs. [...]
The working conditions are similar to those in a factory. Thus, customer care agents must take 80 calls per day (i.e. 10 calls per hour) and they are constantly supervised. [...] Since the call centre agents have to work at the times when the callers are awake [...], above all the job involves night work. [...]
For the agents, night work, sometimes also associated with changing shift patterns, means that they live in a different time rhythm to that of their families and friends. [...] Their everyday life starts to revolve around the call centre. Thus, new circles of friends become established, mainly consisting of colleagues in the call centre industry.
In these circumstances, working in call centres is de facto another form of labour migration, but one that manifests itself not in spatial but in socio-cultural and temporal terms.
Source: Reese, N., Wir leben in einer anderen Zeitzone. Praxis Geographie, Vol. 3/2011, p. 36

M5 Working in a call centre

Earnings of a call centre agent

USA: 12–15 US dollars/hour
Philippines: 2–3 US dollars/hour

Earnings in the Philippines

Teacher:
10,000 – max. 13,000 pesos/month
(220–300 US dollars/month)

Call centre agent*:
10,000–25,000 pesos/month
(220–570 US dollars/month)

*Promotion to Team Leader or Manager with a higher salary is possible

Source: Reese, N., Wir leben in einer anderen Zeitzone. Praxis Geographie, Vol. 3/2011, p. 36

M7 Comparative earnings

As a rule, customer service requires spatial and temporal closeness. When, as is the case with telephone services, one cannot see the person one is speaking to, the service provider must create this feeling of closeness. Customers must be given the feeling that the conversation is taking place "at home". Therefore the agents are taught by special trainers to speak English with an American accent (see photo). They are also expected to watch American television and keep up to date on what is happening in the USA (or, depending on the client, in Australia or Canada), in order to be able to engage in a little small-talk about it and thus generate a good atmosphere. Some agents are even still expected to pretend that they are working somewhere in the USA and that one is calling to them there. Until a few years ago, that was even the rule. Some agents even have to use a new name if their Philippine name sounds too foreign to western ears. And all agents must go through a kind of "mentality training". For example they must get used to the direct, demanding style that is adopted by many western customers. They are more accustomed to a non-confrontational mode of interaction, which is called "smooth interpersonal relationships" in the Philippines. But when a customer gets angry about this kind of pretence, it is also the agent's job to absorb this anger.

Source: Reese, N., Wir leben in einer anderen Zeitzone. In: Praxis Geographie, Vol. 3/2011, p. 37

M6 Working in different time zones and with different identities. The call centres in the Philippines are used especially by companies in North America.

The ecological rucksack in goods transport

Where are we going?

Without realising it, with every product that we buy, we also buy an ecological rucksack. We cannot see the weight of the product's ecological rucksack by looking at it. For example, a gold ring weighing 5g has an ecological rucksack of 2,000 kg. The larger a product's ecological rucksack is, the more harmful it is to the environment.
How can this tension between economics and ecology be regulated in the future?

Ⓞ **1. Illustrate how far goods transport contributes to the ecological rucksack of a product (M2–M5, p. 205 M4).**
   A Visualise it in the form of a diagram.
   B Formulate a text.
2. Smartphones are employed for the intelligent use of energy and products (p. 196). The ecological rucksack of a smartphone weighs 73 kg. Discuss this dilemma.
3. Comment on the global responsibility of the consumer in Germany (M1, M3).
4. Explain the Cradle-to-Cradle concept with reference to goods transport (M6, M7, M8).
5. Comment on the statement: Cradle-to-Cradle is the next industrial revolution (M7).
Ⓢ **6. Outline the model of the ecological rucksack by means of a cartoon.**

→ Cradle-to-Cradle concept (C2C), Ecological rucksack, Material Input Per Service Unit (MIPS)

→ Ecological rucksack

The ecological rucksack (model of Friedrich Schmidt-Bleek 1994) of a product contains all the primary materials that are taken from nature for its manufacture and use. It shows the quantity of wastes and emissions that are associated with this product from the production of the raw materials until its final disposal.

→ MIPS

"Material Input Per Service Unit" (MIPS) is used as a way of measuring the ecological rucksack.
The consumption of materials from nature is divided by the number of service units (uses of the product).

How to make the ecological rucksack lighter:

- Lend, share or swap instead of buying
- Buy second-hand products
- The less transport the better
- Consume sparingly
- Care, repair, clean, and use products for as long as possible
- Avoid waste, pass on or re-use products

Source: http://wupperinst.org/uploads/tx_wupperinst/MIPS_fuer_Kids_Brosch.pdf, p. 25

M1 MIPS tips for everyday life

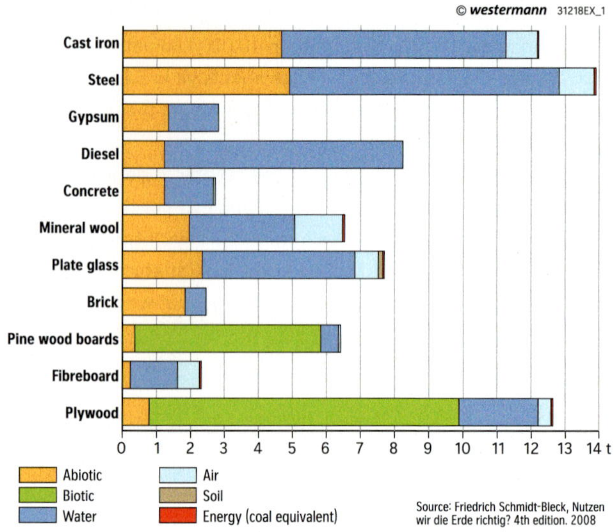

M2 The ecological rucksacks of selected products in comparison

Traded goods have different-sized ecological rucksacks. In very simplified form, it can be said that in general metals have a larger rucksack than biomass. Biomass, in turn, has a larger ecological rucksack than fossil fuels, and fossil fuels are larger than minerals. This means that a more severe intervention in the environment is required to obtain a kilogramme of copper ore than to obtain a kilogramme of wheat. Naturally there are considerable differences within the four categories of materials, and also between individual products. [...]
A calculation of the balance of the ecological rucksacks of imports and exports indicates those countries where the environmental burden remains at home and those countries which transfer it away from their territory. [...] If the ecological rucksacks of all imported and exported goods are offset against one another and grouped by large regions, it can be seen [which continents have picked up the environmental burden]. Their exports carry larger ecological rucksacks than their imports. [...] [Other continents shift the environmental burden to other regions of the world.] [...] Within the continents there are [however] large differences.

Source: Dittrich, M., Verlagert der Norden Umweltbelastungen in den Süden? In: Geographische Rundschau, Vol. 4/2010, p. 19

M3 Unequal global distribution of the environmental burden

Germany is among those countries that, to a large extent, shift the environmental burden to other countries and regions of the world. [...] Particularly affected are resource-rich countries like Brazil, Chile, Russia and Indonesia, from which Germany obtains a large part of its industrial raw materials. It is often possible to identify individual raw material resources that are responsible for a significant part of the environmental burden. Thus, for example, Germany's imports of copper are [responsible] for 92% of the environmental burdens transferred to Chile. Almost half of all the ecological rucksacks that are carried by Indonesia can be ascribed to the export of palm oil and coconut oil.

Source: Dittrich, M., Verlagert der Norden Umweltbelastungen in den Süden? In: Geographische Rundschau, Vol. 4/2010, p. 21

M4 Germany's environmental burden

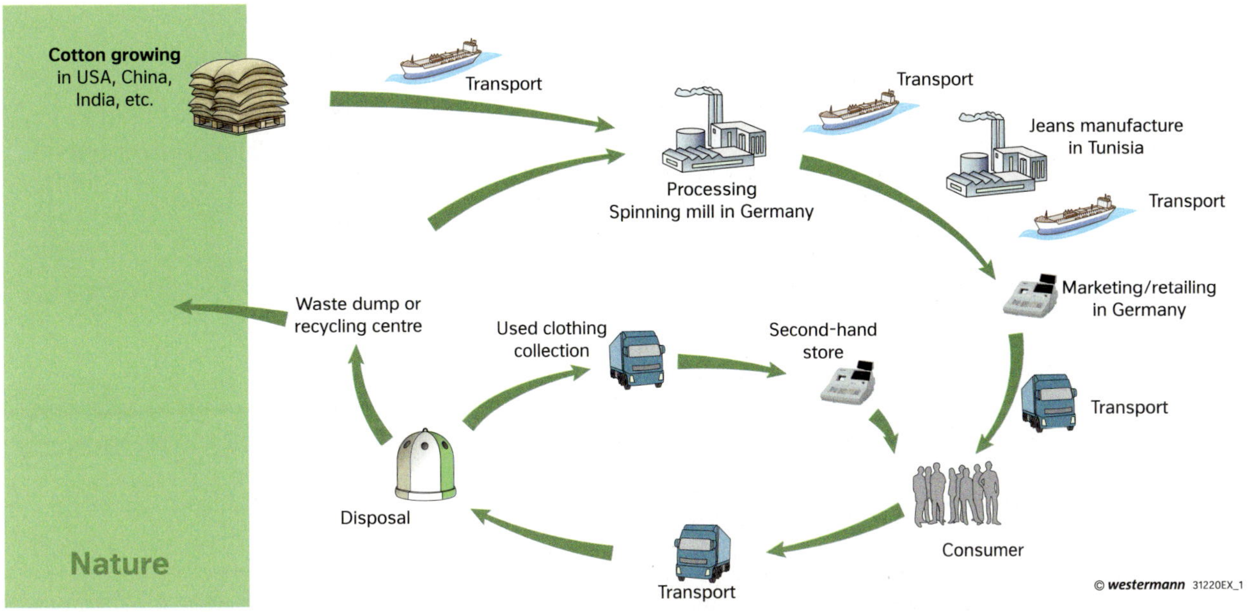

M5 The lifecycle of a pair of jeans, weight 600 g, ecological rucksack 32 kg. Major contributors to the ecological rucksack of the jeans are water consumption and use of pesticides and fertilisers for growing cotton, water and energy consumption in processing the cotton, the use of chemicals for dyeing, energy consumption in transport, energy, water and detergent consumption during use by the wearer, consumption of energy, materials and land in final disposal.

[In the 1990s the researcher Michael Braungart in Hamburg developed] a concept by which the product lifecycle does not move from "cradle" to "grave" (rubbish tip) but from "cradle to cradle". [...]

The product either returns to nature as compost if it is natural and free of pollutants, or it becomes an industrial raw material again. That was the vision of a fully waste-free economy following nature's example. Braungart: "Nature produces no waste, therefore it has no need to avoid it."

Now Braungart, the former Greenpeace activist, is standing in a hall at the Frankfurt exhibition centre and has something to celebrate. The "Cradle-to-Cradle" idea, C2C for short, has caught on. Sneakers, t-shirts, women's underwear, office chairs, furnishing materials, carpets and lamps that were manufactured according to Braungart's principle are on display. [...] Trigema is present with a "compostable wellness shirt". Instead of landing in the trash bin after use, it can go on the compost heap or in the organic waste bin. Tests showed that the textile fibre is degraded by fungi and bacteria with no residue. After six months it is practically all gone. [...]

A similar approach, says Braungart, could also be used in the electronics industry for example. His suggestion is simply to borrow devices like televisions, computers or MP3 players from the manufacturers, so that they give more consideration to their products and design them for maximum reusability. At their end of their working life, such novel products do not become waste but raw materials for the next products.

Source: Wille, J., Frankfurter Rundschau, 14.11.2008

M6 The Cradle-to-Cradle concept

While currently the term "sustainability" is mainly equated with abstinence, economy and efficiency, the credo of Cradle-to-Cradle says: Less bad is still not good. It is a question of designing quality in all areas of everyday life in such a way that humans and nature profit from it.

Cradle-to-Cradle is not an environmental concept in the traditional sense. Rather, it is a new form of economy, in which all materials and processes are designed in such a way that they are not only not harmful, but are actually useful. In short: Cradle-to-Cradle is is the next industrial revolution.

Source: https://www.c2c-ev.de

M7 Sustainability vs. Cradle-to-Cradle

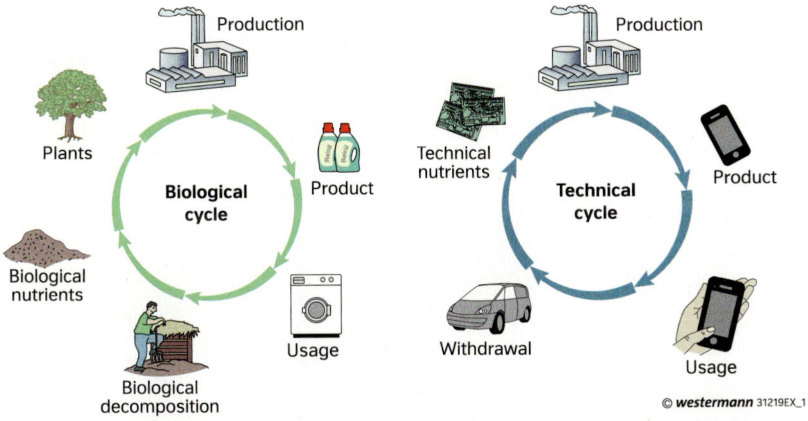

◁ **M8** Recycling economy

The world in process of globalisation

Networked thinking – globalisation

The word "globalisation" evokes widely differing associations in people. They range from unlimited IT communication and the worldwide distribution of certain branded products, through to exploitation, unemployment and hunger. The use of the term "globalisation" is correspondingly varied and contradictory. Globalisation is often understood as a world-embracing process of permeation. Scientists speak of an increasing process of networking throughout the world in economic, cultural and political terms.
It is also not easy to determine when globalisation began, because it cannot be linked to any specific event. Is globalisation a continuation of historical processes, or something completely new?
In many topics in the qualification phase, features and consequences of globalisation have already been directly or indirectly discussed. After a general introduction to the subject, Precisely these topics will be picked up again on this double page in the form of a search for clues in the context of globalisation.

1. Describe what you understand by globalisation.
2. With the aid of materials M1–M8, describe the preconditions, features and consequences of globalisation by producing a mind map.
3. ⓞ "The world in the process of globalisation". Search for clues on this subject. From topic areas A – F, select at least one concrete example with which you can illustrate specific features and consequences of globalisation. Produce a mindmap or causal network on the topic.
   A Economic regions in transition (p. 40–57, 66–69).
   B Promotion of economic zones (p. 58–67).
   C Population development and migration (p. 70 –92).
   D Services and their importance for peripheral and underdeveloped regions (p. 116–119).
   E Goods and services – always available (p. 202 –223).
   F Any other example from the qualification phase.
4. "Globalisation – blessing or curse?" Comment critically on on this.
5. The global world in 2050: Discuss possible perspectives.

→ Globalisation, Neoliberalism, Transnational companies

"You drive a Japanese car, drink French wine, eat Chinese food, own an American computer, buy Canadian lumber and vacation in Mexico. How can you be AGAINST free trade?!"

M1 Thoughts about globalisation

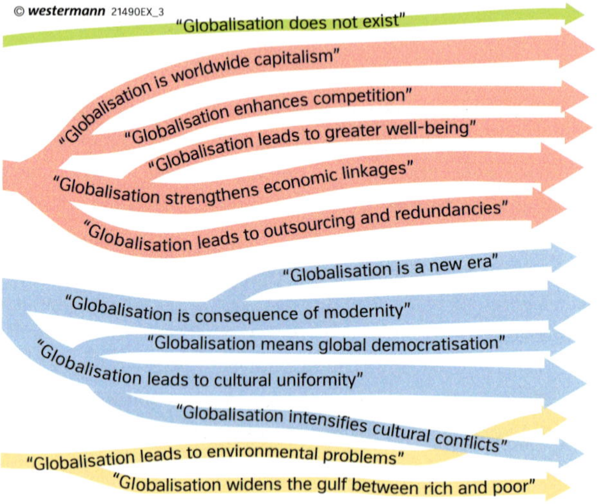

M2 Attitudes to globalisation

→ Globalisation

The phenomenon of globalisation is based on a series of factors. These determinants include technical advances, innovations in the organisation of production, global political changes, economic events and scientific concepts. Between these determinants there exist many-sided links and interconnections that characterise globalisation.

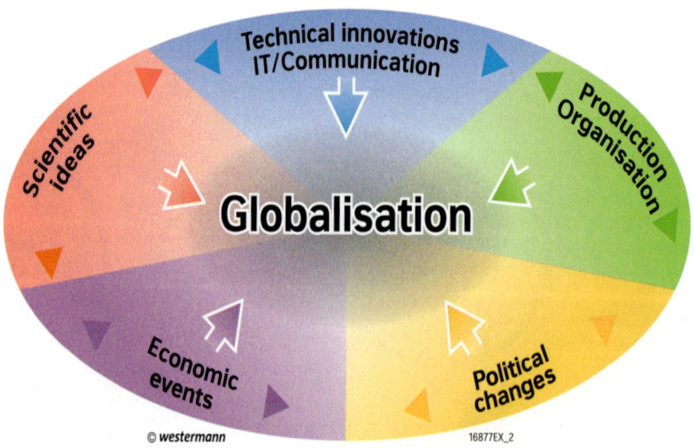

M3 Determinants of globalisation

Phases	Europeanisation		(Atlanticisation)			Globalisation
Time	c. 1500	c. 1750-1770	c. 1850	1945	c. 1990	
Economic regime	Oriental trade	Colonial trade	Free trade Industrialisation	Imperialistic trade	"Bloc" trade	Global trade
Idea/motives	Scholasticism	Discoveries, colonialism	Free trade	Imperialism	Cold War	Development cooperation / Neo-liberalism
Sci./tech. innovations	Collar harness (horse) Yoke (oxen)	Globe	Steam engine	Steamship, automobile, aircraft	Electronics	IT, internet, containers
Actors	Merchants	Seafarers, trading companies		States, governments, international firms	Transnational	companies, virtual firms
Place of origin	Southern Europe	SW Europe	W Europe (England)	Europe, USA, Japan	USA, USSR	Triads
Spatial distribution	Old world	Colonies – mother countries / periphery – centre		Mother country – colonies (empires)	First, Second & Third World	World: global/globalised places – regions
Form of production	Exchange capitalism	Trade capitalism	Industrial capitalism		(market/planned economy)	Information capitalism

M4 Schema of globalisation

Cross-border trade in goods and services has increased significantly in recent decades, and considerably more strongly than worldwide gross domestic product (GDP). The liberalisation of capital markets was introduced later than cross-border trade in goods and services. It was only the technical revolutions of the 1980s and 1990s (computers, internet, e-mail) that made possible the emergence of a global capital market. At the same time, the risk of global financial crises also increases. Overseas investments by companies have risen substantially in recent decades. This dynamic has been driven above all by multinational companies. The revolution in communication technology, in connection with drastically reduced transport costs, made widely-spread manufacturing and service companies, distributed across many countries, technically and economically possible. Today some 80,000 multinational companies determine international trade in goods. [And] the mobility of people has also increased in recent decades – albeit much more slowly.

Source: www.bpb.de/veranstaltungen/netzwerke/teamglobal/67281/oekonomie, www.teamglobal.de, accessed 11.12.2014

M5 The economic dimension of globalisation – "A global domestic market"

Without technical progress in the fields of communication and transport the spurt of globalisation that has been apparent since 1970s would not have been possible.
For years, an important application of modern technology has been telecommunication. New digital transmission technologies have been developed and the price of telephone calls has fallen on account of technical innovations, market liberalisation and the emergence of a mass market. [...]
A new dimension in worldwide data transmission was reached when the internet made it possible for a computer to exchange data with practically every other computer in the world. [...]
Technical advances and developments also laid the basis for the expansion of transport capacities, without which global trade in today's dimensions would not have been possible. Thus, since the 1980s the building of ever more powerful tankers and freight ships, cargo systems, passenger and freight aircraft has been possible, and new, cheap airlines and highly modern airports have come into being worldwide.

Source: Scholz, F., Globalisierung, Braunschweig 2010, p. 27–29

M7 Communication as a dimension of globalisation – "Networked worlds"

Population growth, vast mountains of waste, the daily extinction of species, excessive consumption of energy and raw materials, and the increasing pollution of the air, soil and water, are expressions of the increasing balancing act when Planet Earth's ecosystem is nearing its breaking point. At least since the Brundlandt Report of 1987, and Agenda 21, which was adopted in Rio in 1992, the awareness has taken hold in the public consciousness and among politicians that ecologically sustainable patterns of production and consumption represent a prerequisite for future human development. But there is still a lack of real action to implement it.

Source:www.bpb.de/veranstaltungen/netzwerke/teamglobal/67332/oekologie, www.teamglobal.de, accessed 11.12.2014

M6 The environment as a dimension of globalisation – "The world as a community of risk"

[The significance of the system of national states changes in the process of globalisation. The national state as a territorially delimited "container" with a homogeneous population and a national economy becomes less significant.]
With globalisation, cultural exchange – represented by the global dissemination of formerly local values, norms and symbols – has sharply increased. Through this exchange, people are confronted by other value systems and other lifestyles. This can be seen as an enrichment, for example when the culinary variety of restaurants in the neighbourhood is increased. But there are also fears of a loss of culture, for example through the Americanisation of lifestyles.

Source: Backhaus, N., Globalisierung, Braunschweig 2009, p. 42

M8 The social dimension of globalisation – "The world as a global village"

The essentials in brief

M1 Goods and services, available around the clock

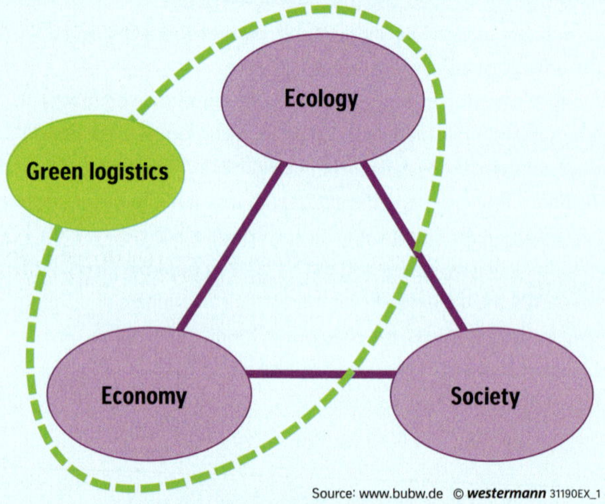

M2 Green and sustainable logistics

Mobility as well as worldwide financial and data flows have become the engines of globalisation. According to a study by the management consulting firm McKinsey, 6.4 trillion euros were spent on the transport of people and goods worldwide in 2010 alone. With increasing mobility, the global CO_2 emissions of the transport sector also increase. According to this study they will rise by some 80 percent by 2050 in comparison to today.
Goods must often travel a long way to reach their final destination. For maritime transport, ever larger container ships are employed, ports have developed into freight transport hubs, and canals such as the Panama Canal have adapted to technical developments in order to avoid being cut off from global traffic flows. Air freight transport has also adapted. Global centres fulfil the function of hubs and achieve synergy effects. The logistics companies that have settled at the airport locations are no longer simply freight forwarders, they have become "logistics providers".
Goods and services are available around the clock. This is ensured by a global network of communication. Ordered in Manila and delivered via Leipzig – and it all happens in the shortest possible time. For the selection of locations for mail order commerce, the transport situation and a large site area have become decisive locational factors. If the location does not operate any ban on night-time flights, this is also considered to be an advantage.
The increasing importance of logistics and goods transport stands in contradiction to sustainable development, because the economic dimension determines what happens in the economy. A "green logistics", which for example used technical innovations to reduce the burden on the environment, would be a first step in the direction of sustainability. But sustainable development cannot be achieved without the cooperation of the consumer. The willingness of consumers to inform themselves actively about sustainable products is comparatively low in Germany. Ideas such as the Cradle-to-Cradle concept presuppose that the consumer is also willing to pay higher prices for a product. In this concept, the recycling economy would even go beyond the principle of sustainable development, because products are no longer "consumed" but "used".

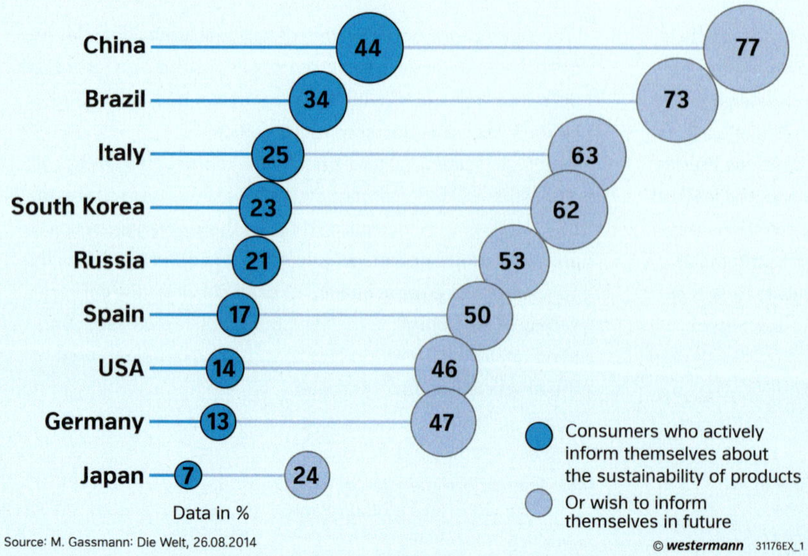

M3 Survey on sustainable consumption among 30,000 consumers worldwide

Skill Check

All the skills that you were able to acquire in this chapter are listed here.
You can judge for yourself if you have mastered each skill: ***securely***, ***moderately*** or ***barely***.

Explanatory skills

Can I ...		Unsure? Look it up on these pages
1.	outline the variety of the tertiary sector using the example of the retailing and transport sectors as well as consumer-oriented and business-oriented services?	204 – 219
2.	outline the interactions of the tertiary sector with the secondary sector using the example of the retailing and transport sectors?	212/ 213
3.	explain the importance of logistics and freight transport for consumer-oriented and business-oriented services?	204 – 219
4.	explain the continuing process of tertiarisation in terms of changing socio-economic and technical factors?	214/ 215
5.	describe the spatial development processes due to freight transport?	204/ 205, 208 – 211
6.	describe spatial usage demands and conflicts in connection with logistics and freight transport?	216/ 217
7.	systematically outline the geographical processes and structures resulting from global world trade by means of a content-related network of technical terms?	218/ 219

Methodological skills

Can I ...		
8.	outline geographical facts on the importance of logistics and freight transport orally and in writing, using correct terminology, in a way that is factually logical, structured and relevant to the materials?	204 – 219
9.	outline geographical Information on the subject graphically (sketch maps, diagrams, flow charts, causal networks)?	204 – 207, 212 – 215
10.	substantiate written and oral statements with differentiated and correct references to materials and citations?	204 – 219

Evaluation skills

Can I ...		
11.	evaluate the importance of a strong Infrastructure for companies in the tertiary sector?	206 – 209
12.	evaluate the importance of logistics and goods transport for the development of spatial areas?	208 – 215
13.	evaluate the development of global freight transport and its effects?	204/ 205, 210 – 213
14.	evaluate different courses of action as well as my own behaviour with regard to the goods and communication flows they cause?	216/ 217
15.	discuss the problem of evaluating spatially-related facts arising from contradictions (e.g. smartphone usage)?	204/ 205
16.	evaluate the importance of a strong Infrastructure for the development of a synergetically networked economy?	208 – 211

Activity skills

Can I ...		
17.	present the results of my work on the subject in class in a way that is factual, problem-oriented and appropriate to the target group as well as using correct terminology?	204 – 219
18.	adopt differing perspectives and positions with regard to spatial usage conflicts and evaluate them in a differentiated way?	216

Examination training

Ports as hubs for goods transport – the example of Duisburg

1. Describe the situation of Duisburg and the structural change that has take place there since 1985.
2. Characterise the current importance of Duisburg as a location for logistics and goods transport.
3. Evaluate the structural change with regard to sustainable economic development.

These additional materials are required to complete the assignments:

M1 Atlas maps of your choice

M2 Duisburg – Binnenhafen, Diercke Weltatlas (2008), p. 63,5
Duisburg – Binnenhafen, Diercke Weltatlas (2015), p. 65,5

City of Duisburg

Population: 495,668 (2007)
488,005 (2012)

Number of persons in employment (2012): 158,486

Share of employment in transport and warehousing: 8.1%

Share of employment in commerce, repair/maintenance of vehicles and consumer goods: 13.8%

Unemployment rate: 12.4% (2014)

Inbound commuters: 95,178

Outbound commuters: 87,681

Sources: IT NRW, Landesdatenbank NRW, Agentur für Arbeit Duisburg, GFW Duisburg; www.gfw-duisburg.de/standort_duisburg/daten/arbeitsmarkt.php

M5 Population and employment in Duisburg

Duisport

- The largest inland port in Europe
- Logistics location of international importance
- Inland hub for the ports of Amsterdam, Rotterdam, Zeebrügge, Antwerp
- Some 36,000 jobs (direct and indirect)
- 21 harbour basins
- 5 intermodal container terminals
- 2 roll-on-roll-off facilities
- Location of about 300 logistics-oriented companies
- Annual value creation: some 3 billion euros

Logistics centre: logport

- Part of the Port of Duisburg, Duisport
- Trimodal logistics location (water, rail, road)
- Logport I on the site of the former Rheinhausen steelworks (closed in 1993)
- Logport II on the site of a former metal works
- Logport I: 2 trimodal container terminals
- Roll-on-roll-off facility for inland and ocean vessels
- Regular rail connections in combined transport
- Rail and inland shipping shuttles to Rotterdam, Antwerp, Amsterdam und Zeebrügge
- Handling of 18,000 trains, 2,000 sea-going river vessels and more than 20,000 ocean vessels per year
- Logport I and II: 50 firms, including 25 leading national and international logistics companies
- Logport III: bimodal terminal at Uerdingen
- Logport IV: bimodal logistics centre at Kamp-Lintfort

Sources: http://www.duisport.de; Prossek, A. et al. (editors), Atlas der Metropole Ruhr.2009, p. 122/123.

M3 Information about Duisport

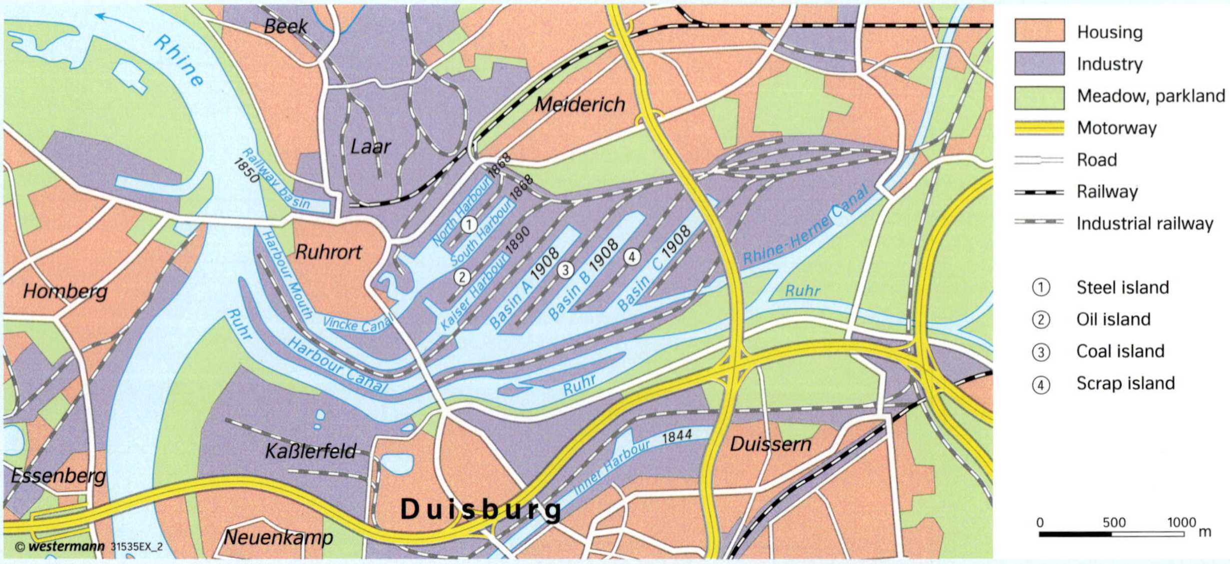

M4 Duisburg's inner harbour in 1985: handling of bulk cargoes (coal, ore, oil)

Duisburg celebrates rail link to China

[...] The train, which takes only 16 days for the journey from China [Chongqing] to the Rhine/Ruhr area, has been running on the Trans-Eurasian link for the last two years. [...] "The train is twice as fast as transport by sea, but at only half the cost of air freight. On the Chinese side it is already referred to as a new silk road," says Erich Staake, Chairman of Duisburger Hafen AG [...].
The link has expanded the international network [in terms of global delivery chains] of Duisport. [...] Many companies in the electronics, computer and high-tech industries, such as for example the US manufacturer Hewlett Packard (HP), the Taiwanese supplier of components for electronic devices, Foxconn, or the Taiwanese computer manufacturer Acer, but also automobile manufacturers and component suppliers as well as machinery manufacturing companies, have their production facilities in [Chongqing]. [...]
The 10,300 km Trans-Eurasian route through China, Kazakhstan, Russia, Belarus, Poland and Germany was developed by DB Schenker Rail and Trans Eurasia Logistics, a joint venture of DB AG and the Russian railway enterprise RZD, established in 2008, as an alternative to the heavily used and 2,000 km longer northern route via the Trans-Siberian railway.
10.9.2013 Verkehrs Rundschau

Audi distribution hub is a successful model for Duisport

The latest success story for Duisport is the establishment of the Audi distribution centre for automobile components on the Logport II site in Wanheim. Here, halls with a floor area of 53,000 m^2 are currently under construction. In future, Audi will bring more than 800,000 m^3 of automobile components through a logistics partner company from its manufacturing sites to Duisburg where they will be stowed in containers in the Duisport halls and shipped to China, India and Mexico where they are assembled into A 4, A 6 or Q 7 models. Duisport has invested 25 million euros in its logistical "full assortment" and is pleased about Audi's largest distribution location worldwide.
10.4.2013 WAZ (Westdeutsche Allgemeine Zeitung)

Duisport increases container handling by 16 percent

At Duisburg's port, significantly more containers were handled this year in combined transport than in 2012. According to current projections, the result for the year will be some three million TEU, representing a growth of around 16 percent compared to the previous year, as reported by the Duisport Group. With this new record result, Duisburg is counted among the 50 largest container ports in the world. Thus the port also remains the largest inland container transshipment point.
13.12.2014 Verkehrs Rundschau

M6 Duisport – a successful model? Reports about Duisport

M7 Connections of the Port of Duisburg in combined transport

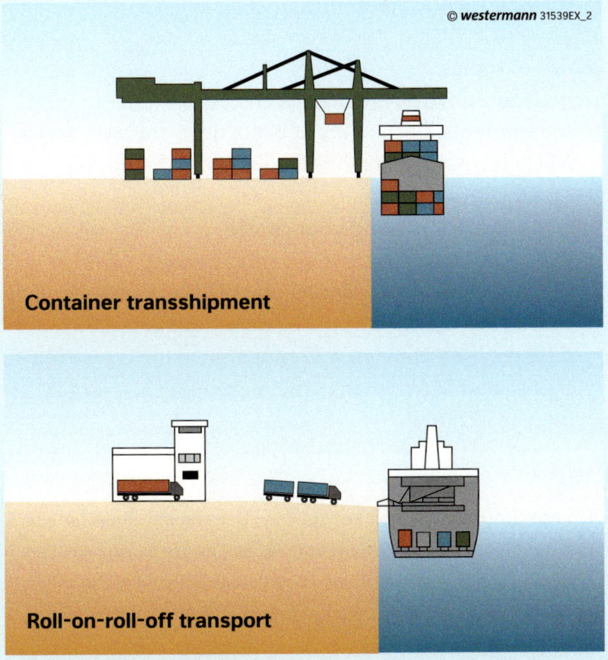

M8 Combined transport

The written university entrance diploma exam (schriftliches Abitur)

In all subjects, the basis for the centrally-set written assignments in the university entrance diploma (Abitur) examination are the core syllabuses for the upper school (core syllabus for the Secondary Level II – upper school/ comprehensive school in North Rhine-Westphalia, Frechen 2013).

In the geography lessons in the qualification phase, you have acquired explanatory, methodological, evaluation and activity skills and are thus fully prepared for the central exam. And in case you are still unsure, at the end of each chapter of the book you will find a Skill Check where you can test whether you are sufficiently prepared and, if necessary, go back and read the specified pages again. Because in the exam you will call upon the skills that you have acquired in the course of the entire qualification phase.

The written university entrance diploma exam

In its structure, the university entrance diploma (Abitur) exam does not differ from the exams that you have already taken in the qualification phase. Every written exam thus also represents a practice exercise. It underlines the importance of intensive follow-up after the exam and your teacher's comments on the strengths and weaknesses of your own essays. The final exam in Q2, the preparatory university entrance diploma exam, is written under Abitur conditions. Here you can again practise your time management and choice of assignments.

The special features of the exam:

Centrally set examination

→ In contrast to the exams in the qualification phase, the exam is not set by your teacher but is set centrally for your federal state.

Choice of topics

→ In geography you are given a choice of three different assignments. Each of these has a different topic focus, which is made clear in the formulation of the topic.

Time allowed for making your choice

→ In addition to the writing time you are also given a selection time of 30 minutes to make your choice, so that the duration of the exam amounts to 285 minutes (255 minutes + 30 minutes) in the advanced course and 210 minutes (180 minutes + 30 minutes) in the basic course.

Tip:

Do not choose your topic too quickly. Use the selection time to thoroughly consider which of the three assignments you can best answer. Do not decide until you have carefully read the working instructions for the individual assignments and also inspected their associated materials.

Preparation for the exam

Continuous participation

→ The best preparation is of course your continuous active participation in geography lessons during the entire qualification phase. This includes preparation and follow-up for the topics covered in the lessons, consistent participation and note-taking in the lessons, preparation and follow-up of the exams (see above), but also and above all your interest in the subject!
The modern media make it possible for you to find information about, and thus access to, practically all spatial areas in the world, You can inform yourself about natural, economic, social or ecological developments worldwide. A multiplicity of sometimes excellent documentary sources and reports give you the possibility to deepen your knowledge of spatial areas and their developments. This continuous extension of your spatial knowledge will certainly also be of benefit to you in the university entrance diploma (Abitur) exam. A wide-ranging knowledge of spatial areas and spatial interconnections is in any case an advantage.

Methodological skills

→ As in the exams in the qualification phase, the university entrance diploma (Abitur) exam is supported by materials. This means that, here too, it is necessary to analyse different kinds of material (maps, statistics, diagrams, etc.) in a way that is relevant to the assignment and make links between the individual statements.
In the course of the qualification phase you are confronted with a wide range of different materials that must be analysed. Make sure that you are able to analyse different kinds of material in a differentiated way. The method pages in the book, and the methodological skill checks at the end of each chapter, give you further opportunities to test your abilities.

Practice

→ To practise, make use of the written exams in the qualification phase, the questions on specific topic areas that are set in this book, and also the university entrance diploma exams from previous years that are available in the internet (see below). Time yourself by making use of the time allowed for the exam and practise writing the exam in one sitting. Then, using the solution key, check to make sure that you have identified all the essential content, considered all aspects and made important links.

weblinks

- **www. www.standardsicherung.schulministerium.nrw.de/abitur-gost/fach.php?fach=9....**

Writing the exam

Having passed through the qualification phase, you are really an exam professional already! But here is another reminder of the most important aspects to be considered when writing a geography exam.

→ ***Read the exam topic carefully!***
From the problem-oriented formulation of the topic you can already recognise the direction in which you should work in the exam. In the same way, the spatial example that you should work on when answering the questions will also be specified.

→ ***The – generally three – parts of the assignment represent an aid for structuring the solution of the assignment (rough outline).*** The working instructions contain operators to guide you. The operators also help you to recognise the requirement area to which each part of the assignment is allocated.

→ ***Start with a topographical classification of the spatial example*** (M1: Atlas maps of your choice; if necessary information from further materials).

→ ***Now analyse the working materials in relation to the assignment!*** Highlight important statements. Use the calculator if necessary to illustrate developments or comparisons based on statistical data. Look out for possible comments (footnotes), explanations and source references. At this stage, make a note of important specialist terms that describe the situation or development meaningfully.

→ ***Now structure your results in a logical way*** ("common thread"). To answer the questions it is generally necessary to show links between the individual statements in the working materials.

→ ***Do not start writing the final essay until you have carefully worked through all the questions for the assignment and thoroughly analysed the working materials.***
Formulate an introduction to the assignment as a whole. As a rule, an assignment-related localisation is required, which can be placed at the beginning as an introduction along with the problems to be solved. Do not forget to include brief connecting bridges or introductions to the parts of the assignment.

→ ***Support your argument with the materials.*** In other words, your answers must contain concrete references to the material. Always state to which materials your statements refer (e.g. M1) at the end of the sentence or section.

→ ***Also make concrete reference to the spatial example in the last part of the assignment, where you are required to make assessments, evaluations and comments***. Refer back to the results that you worked out in the previous parts of the assignment.

→ ***Formulate final conclusions.***

Don't forget that one-fifth of the obtainable points in the evaluation are allocated for the standard of presentation. Therefore plan sufficient time for final checking.
Carefully check your essays again for correct language, i.e. accurate spelling, punctuation and grammar.

You will find the core syllabus for the upper school, the list of obligatory operators, the concrete annual specifications for the written university entrance diploma (Abitur) exam for your year, and examples of assignments from previous years, in the internet at:
www.standardsicherung.schulministerium.nrw.de

Operators

Below is a list of the operators that are obligatory for the central university entrance diploma (Abitur) exams in geography in NRW. You must be familiar with the explanations in the list of operators in order to know exactly what is expected of you in the individual parts of the assignment.

Operator	Definition	RA *
Analyse *(analysieren)*	Bring together complex materials or facts in their individual aspects with the aim of pointing out developments or relationships between them	II – III
Apply *(anwenden)*	Place theories/ models/ rules in relation to concrete facts, case studies or spatial examples	II – III
Assess *(überprüfen)*	Investigate hypotheses/ theories/ arguments/ forms of presentation for their appropriateness/ cogency/ efficiency	III
Characterise *(kennzeichnen)*	Describe spatial areas or facts on the basis of specific criteria with reasons	II
Classify *(ein-/ zuordnen)*	Allocate spatial areas or facts to a specific position in a systematic framework on the basis of pre-set features	II
Comment (critically) on *[(kritisch) Stellung nehmen]*	Arrive at a reasoned opinion about facts or assertions by weighing up different arguments	III
Compare *(vergleichen)*	Bring together and illustrate similarities and differences between (comparable) structures/ processes based on criteria	II – III
Describe *(beschreiben)*	Reproduce material statements or facts in a structured way in your own words using correct terminology	I – II
Discuss *(erörtern)*	Clarify facts by weighing up different pro and contra arguments, and then develop a conclusive opinion	III
Evaluate *(beurteilen/ bewerten)*	Arrive at a factually based, qualifying estimation/ develop your own well-founded and differentiated opinion on the basis of knowledge of the subject or information in the materials or your own conclusions, making clear/ reflecting on the criteria used	III
Explain *(erklären)*	Show the rationales, preconditions and consequences of specific structures and processes	II
Illustrate *(erläutern)*	Clearly show factual connections with the aid of supplementary information	II
Locate *(lokalisieren)*	Place a case study or spatial example within a known topographical orientation framework	I – II
Name *(nennen)*	Present information/ facts without commenting on them	I
Outline/ point out *(darstellen)*	Present (graphical/ textual) information and factual connections known from lessons or taken from the material in a structured way	I – II

* Scope of the requirement area

The oral university entrance diploma exam (mündliches Abitur)

Export-oriented agricultural production as a chance for developing countries? The example of cultivation of cut flowers in Naivasha/Kenya

1. Describe the natural spatial preconditions for the cultivation of cut flowers in Naivasha.
2. Characterise the cultivation of cut flowers in Naivasha and the economic importance of cut flower cultivation for Kenya.
3. Discuss how far the cultivation of cut flowers in Naivasha offers a chance for sustainable development.

These additional materials are required to complete the assignment:
M1 Atlas maps of your choice

For geography, in North Rhine-Westphalia you can take the university entrance diploma (Abitur) exam in the 4th examination subject orally, naturally presupposing that you took the subject of geography in the qualification phase in the basic course.
An oral exam in the 1st – 3rd subject is also possible as a deviation exam in the event that your marks in the exam deviate by more than 4 points from the previous marks, or as a voluntary exam if you wish to improve your average marks for the university entrance diploma.

The oral exam procedure

The procedure for oral exams for the university entrance diploma (Abitur) is identical in all subjects. The exam, which takes a minimum of 20 minutes and a maximum of 30 minutes, consists of two parts.

In the first part of the exam, you present a prepared assignment. As in a written exam, you are given an assignment that you work through in a preparation time of 30 minutes. You then present your solution in an oral presentation lasting at least 10 minutes.
The second part of the exam consists of a 10 to 15 minute exam interview. In this, your subject teacher will ask you questions on further topic areas from the qualification phase, which you should answer in as complete and differentiated way as possible.

The first part of the exam

For the first part of the exam, you receive an assignment set by your subject teacher in the form that you are already familiar with from the set exams. Here too, it takes the form of a multi-part assignment using material, but designed in such a way that the assignment can be completed within the preparation time of 30 minutes. Compared to a written exam, the questions are more limited, the sections of the assignment are less complex and the scope of the material is considerably smaller. On this double page you will find an example that you can use for a practice exercise.

In the ***preparation phase*** you work through the questions in the same way that you are accustomed to working in a written exam. The advice for the written university entrance diploma (Abitur) exam (p. 224 – 225) applies equally here. But in contrast to the written exam, you present your results orally. For preparation, this means that you must carefully examine important information in the material, note specialist terms and keywords for your presentation, and above all also work out a structure. As in the written exam, the multi-part assignment also represents a structuring aid. A practical tip is also to number the important aspects and allocate them to the different parts of the assignment. This preparatory work is particularly important because you will be expected to present the solution to the assignment in a way that is as factually logical as possible. It is a very bad idea to append "forgotten" aspects at the end after you have already presented the reasoning for your arguments.
As a rule, the examiners will not interrupt you during your presentation. You will also not receive any direct feedback about your presentation.

The second part of the exam

In the ***second part of the exam,*** your knowledge of further topic areas from the entire qualification phase will now be tested.

In the ***exam interview,*** you will respond to questions and stimuli from the examiner, and prove your specialist and interdisciplinary knowledge and your understanding of the problem.
The same advice applies for the preparation for the exam interview as for preparation for the written exam (p. 224 – 225). The more intensively you have studied the geographical topics in the qualification phase, the easier you will find it to respond to the questions that are asked, and not only to recount individual aspects that you have learned, but – and this is decisive – categorise your answers in overarching factual contexts and develop them further.

M2 Lake Naivasha: a freshwater lake in the East African Rift, approx. 180 km² in size with no visible outlet, fed from a catchment area of some 3,400 km²; lake water also feeds groundwater

M3 Development of cut flower exports from Kenya (KSh = Kenya Shilling)
(Note: 46.3 billion Ksh corresponded to c. 545 million US-$ in 2013)

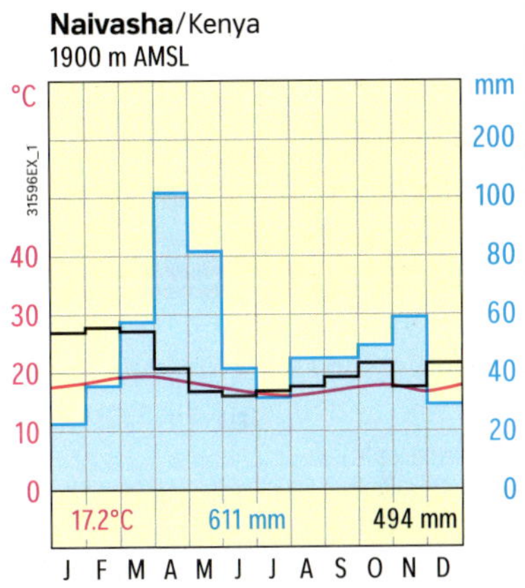

M5 Climate diagram for Naivasha

Cut flowers	– Roses, lilies, asters and others – Cut flowers require constant warmth and – a continuous supply of fresh water – No overhead irrigation of buds and blossoms – Water requirement: 60 m³ water per ha/day (rose farm) (in the Naivasha Region: water extracted from Lake Naivasha, Fair-trade farms partly use groundwater)
Employment	2013: 90,000 directly employed and a total of 500,000 (direct and indirect) employed in the flower industry
Cultivation in the Naivasha Region	– Naivasha: Centre of the Kenyan cut flowers industry – c. 70% of cut flower production, c. 60 flower farms, with up to 1,500 employees depending on size – c. 1,900 ha cultivated area, of which 1,200 ha in greenhouses, – Flower farming in the region: c. 9% of Kenyan foreign currency earnings
Kenya's foreign trade in 2012	Imports: 16.3 billion US-$, Exports: 6.1 billion US-$

Fischer Weltalmanach 2015 The Dutch Ministry of Economic Affairs, Agriculture und Innovation (2012): A Study on the Kenyan-Dutch Horticultural Supply Chain. The Hague
WWF (2011): Hintergrundinformation: Rosen, Wasser und der Naivashasee. Berlin.

M4 Data on the flower industry in Kenya

In: Diercke Weltatlas (2015), p. 269, 3
Note: 1969: c. 7,000 inhabitants in Naivasha, 2009: 91,933 inhabitants (FW 2015)

M6 Naivasha – Rose cultivation for the EU market

Long essay (Facharbeit)

An independent research assignment

In the qualification phase, the school may decide to replace a written exam with a long essay (§14 Abs.(3) APO-GOSt (Abiturprüfung in der Gymnasialen Oberstufe, NRW)).
You can also write this essay in the subject of geography. The long essay has the same value as a written exam in terms of marks.

Assignment and goals of the long essay

The long essay (Facharbeit) is an extensive piece of written homework, to be produced independently. It is considered to be particularly suitable for introducing pupils to the principles and forms of independent, preparatory scientific learning.
In producing a long essay you will learn in practice how to compose scientific research. But the comprehensive scientific development of a topic is not the purpose of the long essay. This distinguishes it from e.g. the special assignment (besondere Lernleistung) according to § 17 APO-GOSt (see page 229).

By preparing a long essay you will learn to:
→ select, define and structure topics,
→ plan a complex research project and execute it while observing the parameters (thematic, formal and terminological) set by your school,
→ obtain and analyse the required information and materials,
→ assess different solution possibilities and, if required, make necessary revisions,
→ apply the conventions used for presenting scientific work (e.g. for citations and literature references),
→ produce a terminologically appropriate written presentation.

The long essay (Facharbeit) in geography

The subject of geography offers a wide range of topics on spatially-related developments or problems. You can select topics that relate to the region where your school is located and which offer the possibility of carrying out your own investigations and mapping, or topics that you can cover by researching the materials. It could be that you discover an interesting topic by making observations during your holidays or in the framework of a school exchange visit. Perhaps you can get ideas from a current discussion about spatially-relevant changes at the place where your school is located, or ideas may come up during lessons.
Since both the working time (6 weeks) and the parameters for the length of the long essay are laid down, it is important to choose a topic that is manageable within the framework of the parameters. As a rule, suitable topics are those relating to a limited spatial area (e.g. part of a city or a region).
The questions that you will have to deal with should already be recognisable from the way the topic is formulated. Thus for example, a long essay on the topic of "Skiing tourism in the Alps – secure for the future despite climate change?" is not about skiing tourism in the Alps generally, but instead it should investigate whether winter tourism will need to change in the long-term due to climatic developments. The scope of the topic can be further refined by choosing a limited spatial example. Here, one could take e.g. Oberstdorf as an example.

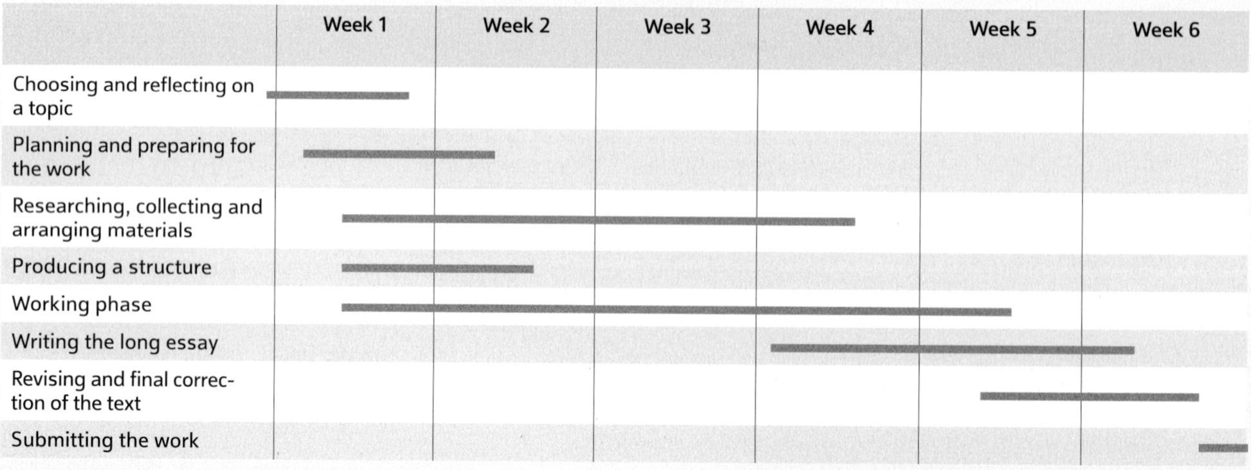

M1 Timetable for producing a long essay

Producing a long essay – working steps

The production of a long essay (Facharbeit) is divided into numerous phases, some of which may overlap (see M1). Make sure that you observe the concrete parameters for the production of long essays at your school. The following overview can provide an orientation.

STEP 1
Choosing and reflecting on a topic

→ Think about the topic
(What subject interests me? What questions do I associate with the subject? Can I find accessible materials? Can the topic be meaningfully defined – see above)?
→ Discuss and agree on the topic with your subject teacher
→ Formulate the topic

STEP 2
Planning and preparing for the work

→ Produce a timetable
→ Set up a working protocol

STEP 3
Researching, collecting and organising materials

→ Research in libraries
(perhaps a university library) in books, magazines, etc.
→ Research in the internet
(save relevant web pages)
→ Perhaps approach experts, contact persons in authorities, etc.

STEP 4
Producing a structure

→ Work through the topic in a factually logical way
→ Draft a structure
(rough and detailed outlines)
→ Discuss the structure with your subject teacher

STEP 5
Working phase: analysis of materials, own empirical research if necessary

→ Analysis and structuring of the information in the material
→ Research for additional information if necessary to answer the question
→ Work on location if necessary: enquiries, mapping, measurements, etc.
→ Modify the structure if necessary

STEP 6
Writing the long essay

→ Present the content clearly
→ Avoid mental jumps, repetitions, etc.
→ Make appropriate use of specialist geographic terminology
→ Integrate suitable images, maps, charts, tables, etc. (if necessary produce your own tables, charts, etc.)
→ Produce a table of contents and indexes of illustrations, literature and sources

STEP 7
Revision and final correction of the text

→ Avoid linguistic or stylistic irregularities (empty phrases, colloquialisms, filler words, etc.)
→ Pay attention to formal aspects (correct language, correct citation style, footnotes, etc.)

Tip:
A print-out of the text is easier to correct than an on-screen text. As a rule, a computer spell-checking programme is not sufficient!

STEP 8
Submitting the long essay

Examples of topics for a long essay (Facharbeit) in geography

- **Skiing tourism in the Alps – secure for the future despite climate change?** The example of x in y.
- **Desertec – power supply from the desert?!**
- **The Football World Cup in Qatar 2022** – a large-scale sporting event at all costs?
- **Living in slums – a hopeless situation?** The example of the Kibera slum (Nairobi).
- **Success or disappointment in urban district x?** The process of gentrification in district x in y.
- **Regenerative energies – a contribution ot regional power supply?** The example of wind farm x in y.

Special Assignment (Besondere Lernleistung)

You can also bring into the overall qualification a special assignment (besondere Lernleistung) that has been produced in the framework or scope of a course lasting at least two terms. Projects qualifying as a special assignment could be a comprehensive essay from a competition sponsored by a federal state, the results of the project course or of a comprehensive disciplinary or interdisciplinary project. The work must be submitted by the time of admission to the Abitur exam at the latest. In a 30-minute colloquium, you present the results of the special assignment before a board of examiners. You can obtain more detailed information about this from your subject teacher and the upper school coordinators.

Source: Kernlehrplan für die Sekundarstufe II. Geographie. www. standardsicherung,nrw.de

Index

Image Sources

|123RF.com, Hong Kong: Jan Kranendonk 31. |Aerophoto-Schiphol b.v., Schiphol: 30. |afronline.org, I-Mailand: GLEZ 19. |akg-images GmbH, Berlin: arkivi UG 43. |alamy images, Abingdon/Oxfordshire: chuck 161; Dinodia Photos Titel o.li., 156; Edward Parker 10; John Warburgon-Lee Titel m.; Mira 106; robertharding 104; Tim Graham 173. |Beyer, Luisa: 161. |Bezirksregierung Köln / www.tim-online.nrw.de, Köln: 191. |BMW Group, München: 69. |Brinkmann-Brock, Ursula, Paderborn: 32. |Brot für die Welt, Stuttgart: Florian Kopp 16. |Canary Wharf Group, London: 179. |CartoonStock.com, Bath: David Brown 218. |Colourbox.com, Odense: 194. |Creative Commons License - All content is licensed by Paul Rogé under a CC Attribution 4.0 International License unless specified otherwise: 13. |Daimler AG, Stuttgart: Titel u.m.. |Der Obere Gutachterausschuss für Grundstückswerte im Land Nordrhein-Westfalen, Düsseldorf: © Daten der Gutachterausschüsse für Grundstückswerte NRW 2018, dl-de/by-2-0 (www.govdata.de/dl-de/by-2-0) https://www.boris.nrw.de 193. |Dessel, Jochen, Sprockhövel: T. Gaupp 111. |Diercke Globus online: 150; NASA 227. |dreamstime.com, Brentwood: JoeRavi 63; Samrat35 111. |Elvenich, Erik, Hennef: 168. |eoVision, Salzburg: GeoEye, 2010, distributed by e-GEOS 174. |Fechner & TOM GmbH, Halle (Saale): 48. |fotolia.com, New York: 158; Kaarsten 10; lofik 45; stefan welz 56; think4photop 117; vichie81 220. |Fritz, Martin, Tokyo: 197. |Geobasis NRW, Köln: 131, 135. |Gerber, Wolfgang, Leipzig: 198.|Getty Images, München: AFP/Issouf Sanogo 98; Bill Pugliano 183; Cloyd Teter/The Denver Post 22; Dado Galdieri/Bloomberg 97; Jeff Kowalsky/Bloomberg 182; Karim Sahib/AFP Titel o.re., 77; Lonely Planet Images/Johnny Haglund 106; Mario Tama 97; Phillip Lissac 112; Timothy Fadek Titel u.li.. |Google Earth: 165, 192. |Google Maps: 181. |Greenpeace Deutschland e.V., Hamburg: Bernd Arnold/visum 20; Paul Hilton 19. |Günther, Holger, Berlin: 10. |HafenCity Hamburg GmbH: Herzog & DeMeuron 145. |Helvetas, Zürich: Swiss Intercooperation/Tanja Demarmels 102. |Historic-Maps, Hamburg: 154. |HOK and Arvind Photography, St. Louis, MO: Arvind Photography 199. |i.m.a - Information.Medien.Agrar e.V., Berlin: 85. |Interfoto, München: Friedrich 42; Simmons Aerofilms/SSPL 178. |Island Press, Washington, D.C.: From: Agriculture at a Crossroads: Global Report, by the IAASTD. Copyright © 2009 IAASTD. Reproduced by permission of Island Press 34. |iStockphoto.com, Calgary: generacionx 15; gionixxx Titel u.re.; gionnixx 117; grahamnorris 209; guenterguni 10; holgs 109; horstgerlach 145; imagixian 176; jameslee999 160; JESPG2 58; justhavealook 176; pawel.gaul 198; ranplett 100; rest 120; SeanPavonePhoto 162, 163, 163; TanjalaGica 163; Tarzan9280 120; vinhdav 94; xxz114 Titel o.m.; zxvisual 159. |Klohn, Werner Prof. Dr., Vechta: 38. |Kohn Pedersen Fox Associates, Courtesy of, New York, NY: 185. |Kowalke, Hartmut Prof. Dr. habil., Dresden: 180. |Krauze, Andrzej, London: 177. |Liebermann, Erik, Steingaden: 177. |Magistrat der Stadt Eschborn, Eschborn: Fotos 57. |Matzel, Markus, Essen: 173. |mauritius images GmbH, Mittenwald: Alamy 173; IPS 167. |Mester, Gerhard, Wiesbaden: 21. |Mette, Til, Hamburg: 200. |Ministerium für Klimaschutz, Umwelt, Landwirtschaft, Natur- und Verbraucherschutz des Landes NRW, Düsseldorf: 2018 192, 193. |NASA, Washington: 25. |NASA/JPL: NASA/METI/AIST/Japan Space Systems, and U.S./Japan ASTER Science Team 30. |National Geographic Creative, USA-Washington, DC: John Stanmeyer Llc 72; Robin Hammond 8. |Panasonic, Hamburg: 197. |Pelican Vertriebsgesellschaft, Hannover: 10.|Picture-Alliance GmbH, Frankfurt/M.: 108, 144; AP/Rebecca Blackwell 103; Chromorange/TipsImages/Guido Alberto Rossi Titel m.re.; dpa-ZB/euroluftbild.de/Ulli Müller 143; dpa/Andreas Gebert 138; dpa/Henning Kaiser 206; dpa/Peter Brenneken 46; dpa/Stephan Scheuer 60; EFE/Jarbas Oliveira 101; EPA/Presidency of Mexico / HANDOUT 211; euroluftbild.de/Hans Blossey 43; Heinrich Bäsemann Titel m.li.; Imaginechina/Gao yuwen 42; Marc Müller 138; Philippe Lissac /GODONG 113; Ralph Goldmann 133; ROPI/Alessandro Puglia 70; ROPI/An Ming/Featurechina 61; ZB/Peter Endig 212. |Plaßmann, Thomas, Essen: 84, 87, 90. |PSUP - Participatory Slum Upgrading Programme / mirror.unhabitat.org: 169. |Reese, Niklas: aus: Praxis Geographie 3/2001 215. |Römisch-Germanisches Museum, Köln: Roderic Stokes 132. |Sander, Nikola - Institut für Demographie (ÖAW), Wien: „The Global Flow of People“ von Nikola Sander, Guy Abel, Ramon Bauer, Inst. für Demographie der Österreichischen Akademie der Wissenschaften, publiziert online auf www.global-migration.info und in „Science“ am 28. März 2014 / Vol: 343: 1520-1522 73. |Schaper, Oliver, Dortmund: 40. |Schopf, Oliver, Wien: 205. |Schoßig, Uwe, Leipzig: 202. |Schray, Björn, Köln: 134, 147, 148, 149. |Shepard, Wade, www.VagabondJourney.com, Farmington, NY: 185. |Shutterstock.com, New York: Andrei Medvedev 198; Gemenacom 31; Ionia 85; Johnny Habell 198; joyfull 188; Kilschner 198; Madlen 11; Marchan 94; romakoma 198; Steve Heap 151; Tracing Tea 111; trekandshoot 23; Tupungato 133; Volosina 11. |siliconangle.com: 54. |Stadt Wittenberge - Bauamt: nach: Teilräumliches Konzept Innenstadt der Stadt Wittenberge, 2011 180. |Stark, Friedrich, Dortmund: 75. |Thomson Reuters (Markets) Deutschland GmbH, Berlin: Ascui 118; Carlos Barria 92; ERIK DE CASTRO 214; Parivatran Sharma 62; STRINGER 81. |ThyssenKrupp Steel AG, Duisburg: 47. |U.S. Department of Defense, Arlington County, Virginia: 151. |UN World Food Programme (WFP) - Welternährungsprogramm der Vereinten Nationen, Berlin: Franco Mattioli 111. |United Nations Publications, New York, NY: From „Trade and Environment Review 2013“, © 2013 United Nations. Reprinted with the permission of the United Nations 34. |Volkswagen AG, Wolfsburg: 53. |W&R IMMOCOM / fm, Leipzig: 213. |Werkladen Conzen Kunst Service GmbH, Köln: 132, 133, 137; Frank Warda 128, 134, 136, 137; Picasa 135; Reinald Witsch 135. |Wiktorin, Dorothea, Köln: aus: Wiktorin, D. et al.: Köln. Der historisch-topographische Atlas, Köln 2001, ISBN 3-89705-229-6, Seite 85, verändert 134. |www.umbaustadt.de: Studien für eine Umstrukturierung des Allendeviertels im Rahmen des Stadtumbaukonzeptes für die Stadt Wittenberge im Jahr 2002, Büro Eichstädt/Emge, seit 2006 Büro UmbauStadt 181. |Zeitungsverlag Schwerin: Redaktion Prignitzer 180. |Zentralverband der Deutschen Geflügelwirtschaft, Vechta: 27.

Das Buch entstand unter Mitwirkung von Urs Piazolo und Wolfgang Stark.

Buv